Mauritius, Réunion & Seychelles

Seychelles
p284

Madagascar

Mauritius
p46

Rodrigues
p166

Réunion
p180

THIS EDITION WRITTEN AND RESEARCHED BY
Anthony Ham, Jean-Bernard Carillet

Contents

MAHÉ'S WEST COAST,
SEYCHELLES P286

PORT LOUIS, MAURITIUS
P48

LONELY PLANET ©

FLORENCE GUILLEMAIN / GETTY IMAGES ©

Contents

SPECIAL FEATURES

Welcome to Mauritius Réunion & Seychelles

Blessed with superlative landscapes and idyllic beaches, Mauritius, Réunion and the Seychelles offer the best cure for winter blues.

From Beach to Adventure

Believe it or not, a day will come during your stay when you decide you've had enough of the beach lounging. Mauritius, Rodrigues, Réunion and the Seychelles aren't just about pampering and relaxation; when it comes to recharging adrenaline levels, they have big surprises up their sleeves. Hike the footpaths that criss-cross the islands, ranging from meandering trails to trudges up mountains; scuba dive in enticing warm waters, marvelling at more than 300 species of fish (and the odd shipwreck or two); catch the wind and waves on a kiteboard; take a boat tour; explore magnetic canyons; or discover the countryside on horseback.

Life's a Beach

The Seychelles (and, to a lesser extent, Mauritius) is home to perhaps the sexiest beaches in the world. From intimate, hard-to-reach coves to mile-long crescents of white sand, the choice is endless. They're so consistently perfect that it's hard not to become blasé about them. There's nothing better to do than spend days under the bright tropical sun on the beach, swinging in hammocks, splashing in the sea and sipping a cocktail. Even Réunion, which doesn't fit the cliché of a sun-soaked Edenic paradise, has a few good stretches of sand.

To Luxe or Not to Luxe

It's hardly surprising that the Seychelles and Mauritius are choice destinations for honeymooners: here the world's most exclusive hotels compete with each other to attain ever-greater heights of luxury, from personal butlers and private lap pools to in-room massages and pillow menus – not to mention sensuous spas. But if this is not in your budget, don't let that dissuade you from buying a ticket to these destinations. Small, family-run hotels, bed and breakfasts and self-catering establishments offer a closer-to-the-culture experience at prices that won't require you to remortgage the house.

Cultural Gems

The biggest mistake anyone could make would be to assume that these islands are for beach holidays, nature and adrenaline only – there's so much more to each destination that any trip will be an unforgettable and exciting experience. Try exploring Mauritius' fascinating colonial past in its myriad mansions or museums, attending a music festival or a fire-walking ceremony, visiting an old sugar factory or a restored Creole villa, or simply soaking up the atmosphere of a picturesque village. One thing's for sure, culture buffs won't be disappointed.

Why I Love Mauritius, Réunion & Seychelles

By Jean-Bernard Carillet, Writer

On my first trip to Mauritius, I was blown away by the wealth of religious buildings and the rich Indian cultural heritage. On Rodrigues, I'll never forget the sensational dives in La Passe St François. On subsequent trips, I did plenty of hiking in Réunion, including a memorable week across Cirque de Mafate. The Seychelles? After six trips there, I confess I have a soft spot for La Digue, because life is so unhurried on this tiny island, it's affordable and the beaches are just incredible. My favourite is Anse Cocos. See you there!

For more about our writers, see page 360

Above: Rivière Noire (p91) and Le Morne Brabant (p103), Mauritius

Mauritius, Réunion & Seychelles

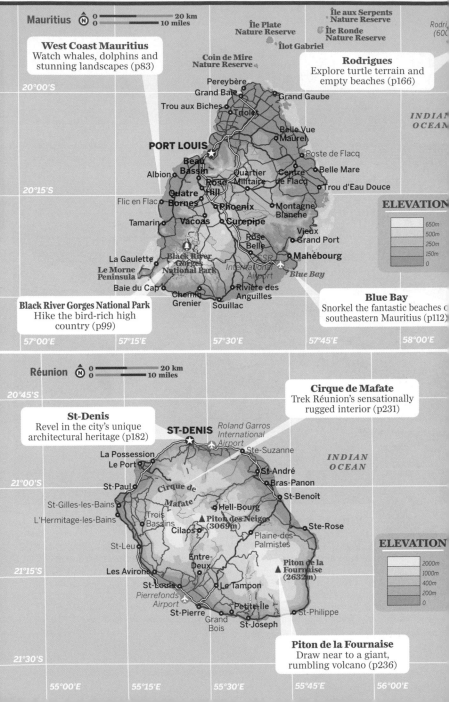

Mauritius ⊙ ⊹ 0 ⊢⊢⊢⊢⊢ 20 km / 10 miles

Île Plate Nature Reserve
Île aux Serpents Nature Reserve
Île Ronde Nature Reserve
Îlot Gabriel
Rodri (600

West Coast Mauritius
Watch whales, dolphins and stunning landscapes (p83)

Rodrigues
Explore turtle terrain and empty beaches (p166)

Coin de Mire Nature Reserve

Pereybère
Grand Baie
Trou aux Biches ○ Triolet
Grand Gaube

INDIAN OCEAN

20°00'S

Belle Vue Maurel

PORT LOUIS ★
Poste de Flacq

Beau Bassin
Albion ○
Quartier Militaire
Centre de Flacq
Belle Mare

Rose Hill
Trou d'Eau Douce

20°15'S

Quatre Bornes
Flic en Flac ○
Phoenix
Montagne Blanche

ELEVATION

Tamarin ○
Vacoas ○ Curepipe

Vieux
Rose Belle ○ Grand Port

650m
500m
250m
150m
0

La Gaulette ○
Black River Gorges National Park
SSR

Mahébourg

Le Morne Peninsula
International Airport
Blue Bay

Baie du Cap ○
Chemin Grenier
Rivière des Anguilles
Souillac

Black River Gorges National Park
Hike the bird-rich high country (p99)

Blue Bay
Snorkel the fantastic beaches o southeastern Mauritius (p112)

57°00'E 57°15'E 57°30'E 57°45'E 58°00'E

Réunion ⊙ ⊹ 0 ⊢⊢⊢⊢⊢ 20 km / 10 miles

20°45'S

Cirque de Mafate
Trek Réunion's sensationally rugged interior (p231)

St-Denis
Revel in the city's unique architectural heritage (p182)

ST-DENIS ★
Roland Garros International Airport

La Possession ○
Le Port ○
Ste-Suzanne

INDIAN OCEAN

St-André
Bras-Panon

21°00'S

St-Paul ○
Cirque de Mafate
St-Benoît

St-Gilles-les-Bains ○
Hell-Bourg

L'Hermitage-les-Bains ○
Trois Bassins ○
Piton des Neiges (3069m)

Cilaos ○
Ste-Rose

St-Leu ○
Plaine-des-Palmistes

ELEVATION

Entre-Deux ○

21°15'S

Les Avirons ○
Piton de la Fournaise (2632m)

2000m
1000m
400m
200m
0

St-Louis ○
Pierrefonds Airport
Le Tampon
Petite-Île

St-Pierre ○
Grand Bois
St-Joseph
St-Philippe

Piton de la Fournaise
Draw near to a giant, rumbling volcano (p236)

21°30'S

55°00'E 55°15'E 55°30'E 55°45'E 56°00'E

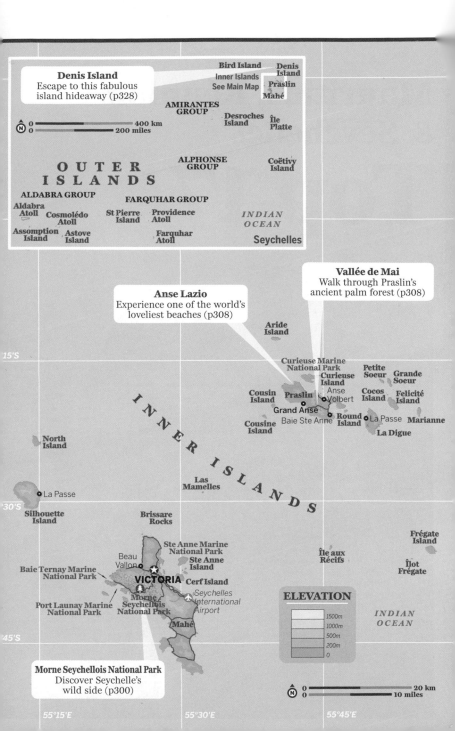

Denis Island
Escape to this fabulous island hideaway (p328)

Bird Island · Denis Island
Inner Islands See Main Map · Praslin · Mahé

AMIRANTES GROUP · Desroches Island · Île Platte

0 ————— 400 km
0 ————— 200 miles

OUTER ISLANDS

ALPHONSE GROUP · Coëtivy Island

ALDABRA GROUP · FARQUHAR GROUP

Aldabra Atoll · Cosmolédo Atoll · St Pierre Island · Providence Atoll · INDIAN OCEAN

Assomption Island · Astove Island · Farquhar Atoll · **Seychelles**

Vallée de Mai
Walk through Praslin's ancient palm forest (p308)

Anse Lazio
Experience one of the world's loveliest beaches (p308)

Aride Island

Curieuse Marine National Park · Petite Soeur · Grande Soeur
Curieuse Island
Cousin Island · Praslin · Anse Volbert · Cocos Island · Felicité Island
Grand Anse
Cousine Island · Baie Ste Anne · Round Island · La Passe · Marianne
La Digue

North Island

INNER ISLANDS

Las Mamelles

La Passe

Silhouette Island · Brissare Rocks

Frégate Island

Ste Anne Marine National Park
Beau Vallon · Ste Anne Island · Île aux Récifs · Îlot Frégate

Baie Ternay Marine National Park · **VICTORIA** · Cerf Island

Port Launay Marine National Park · Morne Seychellois National Park · Seychelles International Airport

ELEVATION
1500m
1000m
500m
200m
0

INDIAN OCEAN

Mahé

Morne Seychellois National Park
Discover Seychelle's wild side (p300)

0 ————— 20 km
0 ————— 10 miles

15'S · 30'S · 45'S

55°15'E · 55°30'E · 55°45'E

Mauritius, Réunion & Seychelles' Top 17

Hiking Through the Cirque de Mafate (Réunion)

1 Perhaps the finest set of multiday hikes anywhere in the Indian Ocean, Cirque de Mafate (p231) feels like you're traversing the end of the earth. Wild and remote, watched over by fortress-like ridges and riven with deep valleys, this is an extraordinary experience. A four-day hike through the Haut Mafate can be combined with the four-day, even-more-secluded Bas Mafate. Best of all, these hikes take you through quiet mountain hamlets where you'll find *gîtes* (self-catering accommodation) where the welcome is warm and genuine.

Denis Island (Seychelles)

2 Welcome to paradise. It may be a much-abused cliché but the coral island of Denis Island (p328) comes as close to living up to this claim as anywhere on the planet. This is a place where warm tropical waters lap quietly upon a beach of white sand, while the lagoon offshore dazzles in magical shades of blue. The island's luxury lodge combines romance with seclusion to perfectly capture the idyll of barefoot luxury (no TV, no mobile phones), and you'll share the island with giant tortoises and gorgeous bird species.

SIMEON / GETTY IMAGES ©

PITAMITZ SERGIO / HEMIS.FR / GETTY IMAGES ©

ARCO IMAGES GMBH / ALAMY STOCK PHOTO ©

Diving & Dolphins (Mauritius)

3 Some of the Indian Ocean's best dives are found off the west coast of Mauritius (p83). The architecture of the underwater rock formations and the substantial schools of fish make the waters off Flic en Flac in particular a world-class dive destination. The best sites are the walls and drop-offs on the edge of the turquoise lagoon and La Cathédrale, near Flic en Flac, is simply marvellous. A little to the south, off Tamarin, whales and dolphins swim in the open water.

The Land Time Forgot (Rodrigues)

4 Marooned out in the Indian Ocean, Creole Rodrigues (p166) is the sort of place where life moves to a different beat. There's so much to do here – Port Mathurin's busy Saturday market, a boat trip out to Île aux Cocos, the coastal walk from Graviers to St François past some of the loveliest beaches we know, snorkelling off the south coast or diving La Passe St François. But come here first and foremost to leave the world and its noise behind. Saturday Market, Port Mathurin (p167)

The Mighty Volcano (Réunion)

5 Piton de la Fournaise (p236) is Réunion's crowning glory. Seen from the viewpoint at Pas de Bellecombe, *le volcan* (as it's known to locals) broods black and beautiful, its shapely form towering over the island. But even though this is an active volcano, it's still possible to climb up to the crater rim and stare down into the abyss – one seriously memorable sight. Hiking and horse trails lead to the summit, while a scenic helicopter flight offers the ultimate bird's-eye view down into the caldera.

Anse Lazio (Seychelles)

6 On the northwest tip of Praslin Island, Anse Lazio (p308) is a reminder of just why the Seychelles has become one of the most alluring destinations in the Indian Ocean. The beach here is near perfect, a stereotype come to life with golden sands, granite boulders at either end, palm trees and unbearably beautiful waters somewhere between turquoise and lapis lazuli. Ideal for hours spent lying on the beach, snorkelling or eating in the beachfront restaurant, Anse Lazio is the sort of place you'll never want to leave.

Southeastern Mauritius

7 Choosing your favourite beach in Mauritius is like trying to pick a flavour of ice cream – they're all so good! The eastern and southeastern shores are quieter than those elsewhere, particularly the beaches at Pointe d'Esny, near Blue Bay, and Belle Mare, and they're close to the native forests of Vallée de Ferney and the offshore Île aux Aigrettes (p112). The last, with its highly endangered bird species, giant tortoises and low-slung ebony forests, is like stepping ashore on Mauritius before human beings came and tamed the landscape.

Pink pigeon, Île aux Aigrettes (p113)

PLAN YOUR TRIP MAURITIUS, RÉUNION & SEYCHELLES' TOP 17

Morne Seychellois National Park (Seychelles)

8 In their quest for the perfect beach, many travellers are oblivious to the fact that there are fantastic experiences to be had in this lush and splendid national park (p300). Take a guided hike through dense forest, coastal mangroves and rugged mountains and you'll soon believe that the world and its clamour belong to another planet. While exploring, you'll come across rare species of birds, reptiles and plants, not to mention some breathtaking viewpoints.

Paragliding in St-Leu (Réunion)

9 Fabulous views and reliably uplifting thermals year-round make St-Leu (p208) a brilliant place to go paragliding. Launch off and soar high above the earth surrounded by silence and an overwhelming sense of freedom. At every turn, there is some utterly dramatic natural feature – the towering volcanoes of the interior, the turquoise waters of the lagoon – and the experience will appeal as much to beginners as to those with more experience. Touching down on a white-sand beach is the perfect finale.

Chambres & Tables d'Hôtes (Mauritius)

10 Whether along the west coast of Mauritius or in the quiet highlands of Rodrigues, staying in a *chambre d'hôte* (family-run guesthouse; p145) is a wonderful way to learn about local life. Rooms are often simple, but the warmth and personal nature of the welcome you'll receive and the nightly *table d'hôte* (meal served at a *chambre d'hôte*), where the guests and hosts gather together for a traditional meal, make for the kind of experience that you'll remember long after the luxury resorts have faded in your memory.

Seafood by the Beach

11 The day's catch fresh to your table, with your toes buried in the sand. It's not just a dream but a very real possibility on the islands of Mauritius, Réunion and the Seychelles. Lobster, octopus, grilled fish, calamari – they're all staples of the Indian Ocean table. If you can't decide, all are regular inhabitants of your standard seafood platter; try Cabanne du Pecheur (p69) in Trou aux Biches. Best of all, the rich stew of sauces and cultural influences adds flavour, from Indian curries to red Creole sauces.

Architectural Gems in St-Denis (Réunion)

12 The advantage of St-Denis (p182) not having a beach is that it forces you to turn your gaze inland and admire the city's architectural portfolio. The 19th-century town hall, prefecture and a host of 'minor' palaces and mansions adorn the city with neoclassical columns, elaborate verandas and exquisite *lambrequins* (ornamental window and door borders). Throw in Creole mansions and a coexistence of mosque, cathedral, Chinese pagoda and Hindu temple, and the effect is at once international and quintessentially Réunionnais.
Conseil Général de la Réunion – Direction de la Culture (p182)

ALES-A / GETTY IMAGES ©

Black River Gorges & Chamarel (Mauritius)

13 Some of the most dramatic scenery in Mauritius is found in the southwest. The thick forests of Black River Gorges National Park (p99) shelter fantastic and endangered birdlife that has been saved from the fate of the dodo, quite apart from the exceptional views from along the myriad hiking trails. After a morning's hiking, lunch just has to be in Chamarel, home to a series of superb restaurants and a well-regarded rum distillery nestled in the hills. Chamarel Waterfall (p96)

Shark-Spotting in the Seychelles

14 Discerning divers have long known of the Seychelles' claims to being one of the Indian Ocean's most rewarding dive destinations. We like it especially for its variety of sea life, and the unmistakable cachet of swimming with whale sharks and massive rays off Mahé (p286). There are wreck dives and mind-blowing fish varieties off Brissare Rocks, but nothing beats the frisson of getting up close and personal with the whale sharks who frequent the area. Whale shark (p297)

Vallée de Mai (Seychelles)

15 If you can tear yourself away from the beach, Vallée de Mai (p308), on Praslin Island, is a paradise of a different kind. Inscribed by Unesco on its World Heritage List, and home to endangered birdlife and the rare and singularly beautiful coco de mer palms and a host of other endemic plants, Vallée de Mai is all about immersion in the lush tropical forest, being serenaded by birdsong and losing yourself along quiet hiking trails that meander agreeably through this verdant mini wilderness.

Gardens & Great Houses (Mauritius)

16 Mauritius' interior is, for the most part, steep and rugged, and it shelters some exceptional sites. First on many travellers' lists are the vast and soothing botanical gardens at Pamplemousses (p81); the giant lily pads have to be seen to be believed. Not far away are two of the finest remnants of colonial plantation architecture in existence – the Chateau Labourdonnais just north of the gardens, and Eureka, further south in the Central Plateau town of Moka. Giant lily pads, Pamplemousses

Hindu & Creole Festivals

17 Hindu festivals are a wonderful way to liven up your visit to Mauritius or Réunion. The biggest festival of all, in February or March, is the 500,000-strong Hindu pilgrimage to the sacred lake of Grand Bassin (p98) in Mauritius. March is also the month of colourful Holi festivities, October means Divali, and Teemeedee in December or January is all about fire-walking wherever Hindus are found. For celebrations of Creole culture, October is particularly exuberant in Rodrigues, the Seychelles and Réunion. Cavadee festival (p262)

PLAN YOUR TRIP MAURITIUS, RÉUNION & SEYCHELLES' TOP 17

Need to Know

For more information, see p145 (Mauritius), p278 (Réunion), p336 (Seychelles).

Currency
Mauritian rupee (Rs) in Mauritius, euro (€) in Réunion, Seychellois rupee (Rs) and euro (€) in the Seychelles

Language
French (Mauritius, Réunion, Seychelles), English (Mauritius, Seychelles), Creole (Mauritius, Réunion, Seychelles)

Visas
Visas are not required for most Western nationals for stays of up to three months.

Money
ATMs are widely available in major towns. Credit cards widely accepted.

Mobile Phones
GSM mobile phones can be set to roaming; local prepaid SIM cards are available.

Time
GMT/UTC plus four hours; no daylight saving time

When to Go

• **Victoria (Seychelles)**
GO Apr–Dec

Madagascar

Port-Louis (Mauritius)
GO Mar–Dec

Port Mathurin (Rodrigues)
GO Mar–Dec

St-Denis (Réunion)
GO Apr–Nov

High Season (Dec–Jan & Jul–Aug)
➡ Hindu festivals and cultural events are usually held in December and January.

➡ Whale sharks and whales visit in July and August.

➡ Hotels raise prices during Christmas and New Year and often require minimum stays of one week.

Shoulder (Apr–May & Sep–Nov)
➡ The best time to travel – less rain, lower humidity and bluer skies.

➡ Easter is busy.

➡ Perfect for outdoor activities, especially hiking and whale watching.

➡ Pleasant temperatures, calmer seas and fewer visitors.

Low Season (Feb–Mar & Jun)
➡ Some resorts offer discounted packages.

➡ Cheaper airfares.

➡ Rain and cyclones (February and March) in Mauritius and Réunion can disturb travel plans.

Useful Websites

Lonely Planet (www.lonely planet.com/mauritius, www. lonelyplanet.com/reunion, www. lonelyplanet.com/seychelles) Destination information, hotel bookings, traveller forum and more.

Île de la Réunion Tourisme (www.reunion.fr) The official tourist-board website; information on attractions, restaurants, accommodation, activities and lots more.

Seychelles Travel (www. seychelles.travel) The official tourist-board website; information on attractions, accommodation, activities and much more.

Mauritius Tourism Promotion Authority (www.tourism-mauritius.mu) The country's main tourism portal; generally excellent but some sections a little thin.

Important Numbers

There are no area codes in Mauritius, Réunion or the Seychelles. To dial a phone number from abroad, dial your international access code, the country code, then the number (without the '0').

Mauritius country code	230
Réunion country code	262
Seychelles country code	248
Police (Mauritius & Seychelles)	999
Police (Réunion)	17

Exchange Rates

For exchange rates, see p150 (Mauritius), p280 (Réunion) and p338 (Seychelles).

Daily Costs

Budget: Less than €150

➡ Bed in a *gîte* (lodge) in Réunion: €17

➡ Double room in a guesthouse: €60

➡ Takeaway meal: €4–8

➡ Bus ticket: €0.40–4

Midrange: €150–300

➡ Double room in a hotel or B&B: €90–150

➡ Lunch and dinner in local restaurants: €20–50

➡ Ferry ride in the Seychelles: €60

➡ Short taxi trip: €8–20

Top End: More than €300

➡ Room in a resort (promotional deal): from €200

➡ Top restaurant dinner: €40–80

➡ Helicopter tour: from €150

Opening Hours

Banks 8am or 9am to 2pm, 3pm or 4pm Monday to Friday, sometimes on Saturday morning

Government offices 8.30am–noon and 2pm–5pm Monday to Thursday, to 3pm Friday

Restaurants 11.30am or noon to 2pm and 6.30pm or 7pm to 9pm (later in tourist hubs)

Shops and businesses 8am or 9am to 5pm or 6pm Monday to Saturday; some shops closed at lunchtime and on Monday in Réunion

Arriving in Mauritius, Réunion & the Seychelles

Sir Seewoosagur Ramgoolam International Airport (Mauritius; p57) Semiregular buses between Port Louis or Curepipe and Mahébourg go via the airport and pick up passengers from outside the arrivals hall. Most travellers get where they're going by hiring a taxi – there's a taxi desk with set prices in the arrivals hall.

Roland Garros International Airport (Réunion; p283) Between 6.30am and 6pm there's a regular shuttle bus service from the airport to central St-Denis (€4, 12 daily). Taxis from just outside the airport cost from €20 to central St-Denis (20 minutes).

Seychelles International Airport (p339) The Seychelles' only international airport is located on Mahé, about 8km south of Victoria. Big hotels provide transport to and from the airport. Taxis from just outside the airport.

Getting Around

Car Outside cities, renting a car gives unmatched flexibility and convenience. Cars can be hired in major towns and at the airports. Drive on the left in the Seychelles and Mauritius; on the right in Réunion.

Air Most convenient services are between Mauritius and Rodrigues and between Mahé and Praslin.

Boat The preferred mode of interisland transport in the Seychelles. Fast and reliable but quite expensive.

Bus Very cheap. In all three countries getting around by public transport is possible but sometimes complicated and rather slow.

Taxi In some cases hiring a taxi is a great way to explore an area, especially if you can share costs with other travellers.

For much more on **getting around**, see p153 (Mauritius), p283 (Réunion), and p339 (Seychelles).

If You Like...

Beaches

Anse Lazio, Seychelles On the island of Praslin and simply as gorgeous as you'll find in the Indian Ocean. (p308)

Anse Soleil, Seychelles On the west coast of Mahé and somewhere close to heaven. (p304)

Grand Anse, Seychelles Quieter than other Seychelles stunners and every bit as beautiful. (p321)

Anse Source d'Argent, Seychelles La Digue's most popular slice of paradise and with very good reason. (p320)

Trou d'Argent, Rodrigues Pick any beach on Rodrigues' east coast, but this is our favourite. (p175)

South Coast, Mauritius There's a reason that five-star resorts love this area. (p117)

Le Morne & Tamarin, Mauritius Pretty beaches with dramatic mountainous backdrops in western Mauritius. (p83)

Plage de Grande Anse, Réunion Cliffs and white sand in the wild south of the island. (p247)

L'Hermitage-les-Bains, Réunion The longest and most appealing white-sand beach in Réunion. (p202)

Hiking

Piton de la Fournaise, Réunion Climb to the rim of an active volcano – a classic hike. (p239)

Tour des Cirques, Réunion Five days of mountain bliss and quite simply one of the most beautiful hikes on the planet. (p41)

Haut Mafate, Réunion Four-day hike that takes you through some of Réunion's wildest Cirques. (p39)

Bas Mafate, Réunion Four-day trek across the roof of Réunion. (p41)

Black River Gorges National Park, Mauritius Hiking trails through bird-rich wilderness and the island's last great forest. (p99)

Lion Mountain, Mauritius Underrated hike that scales the heights with great views and good birdwatching. (p116)

Graviers to St François, Rodrigues Lovely coastal walk past Rodrigues' best beaches. (p175)

Morne Seychellois National Park, Seychelles The country's best hiking. (p300)

Vallée de Mai, Seychelles Easy short hikes through a fabulous ancient palm forest. (p308)

Wildlife

Curieuse Island, Seychelles A veritable Galápagos of giant Aldabra tortoises, the last surviving Indian Ocean species. (p316)

Bird Island, Seychelles Nesting seabirds, giant tortoises and hawksbill turtles. (p329)

Île aux Aigrettes, Mauritius An island Noah's ark where tortoises and pink pigeons live free as they once did everywhere in Mauritius. (p113)

Black River Gorges National Park, Mauritius Rare bird species and old-growth forest add up to Mauritius' premier wilderness experience. (p99)

Vallée de Ferney, Mauritius Go looking for the Mauritius kestrel, once the world's most endangered bird. (p116)

Le Grand Brûlé, Réunion The island's best birdwatching in the wild and beautiful south. (p258)

Spectacular Landscapes

Piton de la Fournaise, Réunion The single most dramatic landform in the Indian Ocean, bar none. (p236)

Cirque de Cilaos, Réunion Perfect hiking country amid a landscape that reaches magnificently for the sky. (p217)

Plaine des Sables, Réunion
Otherworldly atmosphere atop
this lava-formed plain. (p236)

Cirque de Salazie, Réunion
Another beguiling mountain
kingdom. (p226)

Le Morne Peninsula, Mauritius
Unesco site with stunning beauty
and a tragic story to match.
(p103)

**Black River Gorges National
Park, Mauritius** Waterfalls off
the high plateau, dense forest
and a deep river canyon. (p99)

Silhouette, Seychelles The most
dramatic island in the Seychelles
archipelago. (p327)

Denis Island, Seychelles The
coral idyll that evokes the desert
island of childhood imaginings.
(p328)

Romantic Getaways

North Island, Seychelles A mix
of heavenly paradise, James
Bond glamour and the last word
in luxury. (p328)

Alphonse, Seychelles Remote
island with a low-key resort and
phenomenal fishing and diving.
(p329)

Le Saint Géran, Mauritius
Beach butlers, indulgent beauty
treatments and glorious
accommodation. (p128)

Le Prince Maurice, Mauritius
There's something in the air
at Belle Mare and this sublime
complex is close to heavenly.
(p128)

Le Touessrok, Mauritius More
east-coast luxury with its very
own islands to enhance the paradise credentials. (p125)

Lux Le Morne, Mauritius Luxury
at every turn in the shadow of
the most beautiful mountain in
Mauritius. (p104)

PLAN YOUR TRIP IF YOU LIKE...

Top: Giant tortoise (p335), Cousin Island, Seychelles
Bottom: Le Touessrok (p125), Trou d'Eau Douce, Mauritius

Month by Month

January

January is high season for all of the islands, with warm temperatures, but rain and even cyclones are possibilities, the latter primarily in Mauritius and Réunion. Hotel prices soar over the Christmas and New Year period.

Chinese New Year

Chinese New Year in Mauritius and Réunion falls in late January or early February. On New Year's Eve, homes are spring cleaned and decked in red, the colour of happiness, and firecrackers are let off to protect against evil spirits.

February

Weather-wise, February is fairly similar to January with humid conditions and the chance of rain. However, because most of Europe and elsewhere is now back at school, crowds are generally smaller.

Maha Shivaratri

This massive pilgrimage in February or March sees up to 500,000 Hindus make their way by all means possible to the holy lake of Grand Bassin in Mauritius, close to Black River Gorges National Park; the lake's waters are said to come from the sacred Ganges River. (p98)

March

March continues the trend of warm temperatures with possible rain. The chance of cyclones remains, but is diminished. Festivals across all islands add plenty of local colour.

Holi Hindu

Holi, the festival of colours that is celebrated in Mauritius and Réunion, is known for the exuberant throwing of coloured powder and water. The festival symbolises the victory of divine power over demonic strength. On the night before Holi, bonfires are built to symbolise the destruction of the evil demon Holika.

Fish Festival

Rodrigues lives and breathes fish, and the Fête du Poisson, held in the first week of March, marks the opening of the fishing season. It is celebrated with all sorts of festivities, including fishing expeditions – and lots more eating.

April

The weather starts to turn around April – this is usually the last month when cyclones affect weather patterns across the region and from now on temperatures drop slightly and rains generally ease.

Tamil New Year

Wherever there are large Indian communities (Mauritius and Réunion), the Tamil New Year is marked with great gusto, with dance displays often forming the centrepiece of the celebrations. The New Year can ensure that things grind to a halt in predominantly Tamil areas.

May

Although this can change depending on the timing of French school holidays, May is generally a great time to visit – fewer tourists, milder temperatures and rain or wind is rarely a problem.

☆ FetAfrik

With the possible exception of the Mauritian island of Rodrigues, the Seychelles is the most African of the Indian Ocean islands, and it celebrates its African origins with FetAfrik, a weekend of music and dance in late May. It's one of the more exuberant festivals in the region.

June

June is generally considered low season and some hotels across the region drop their prices. The Indian Ocean winter has arrived, but not so you'd notice if you've flown in from Europe.

July

A fairly quiet month with relatively mild temperatures, little rain to speak of and lower hotel prices (unless French school holidays fall during the month).

☆ Rodrigues Kitesurfing

Some of the world's best kitesurfers descend on Rodrigues in late June or early July for the Rodrigues International Kitesurfing Festival, which has been running since 2013.

August

August is one of the driest months in the Indian Ocean, and neither temperatures nor humidity reach the heights of later in the year. European holidays often push prices upwards.

September

An extension of the Indian Ocean winter, September remains cooler and generally dry, although in the Seychelles, where temperatures are getting warmer, the rains are just around the corner and can arrive early.

🎎 Christian Holy Day

The most important date for many Mauritian Christians is 9 September, Père Laval Feast Day, which marks the anniversary of the priest's death. Pilgrims from around the world come to his shrine at Ste-Croix, on the outskirts of Port Louis, to pray for miracle cures.

October

October is an excellent month to visit the Seychelles, with generally dry and calm weather conditions. Elsewhere, this is the month when high-season crowds arrive, although you may find bargains early in the month.

🎎 Festival Kreol

Late October is when Creole culture comes to the fore. On predominantly Creole Rodrigues, there's the three-day Festival Kréol, while the Seychelles dedicates a week to the outpouring of Creole cuisine, theatre, art, music and dance for its own Festival Kreol. Réunion also gets into the spirit with its Semaine Créole.

🎎 Divali

Both Réunion and Mauritius mark the Tamil festival of light Divali (Dipavali), in late October or early November. It celebrates the victory of Rama over the evil deity Ravana, and to mark this joyous event countless candles and lamps are lit to show Rama the way home from his period of exile.

November

November is a good time to visit the islands, but it's especially good for Mauritius and Réunion. The weather's warming up, the rains usually don't arrive until later in the year and the crowds of December have yet to arrive.

December

The first half of December is much like November, although the rains can make an appearance to dampen things a little. As Christmas approaches, prices soar to their highest all year.

🎎 Teemeedee

Teemeedee is a Hindu and Tamil fire-walking ceremony held to honour various gods. Held throughout the year, most celebrations are in December and January when participants walk over red-hot embers scattered along the ground.

Itineraries

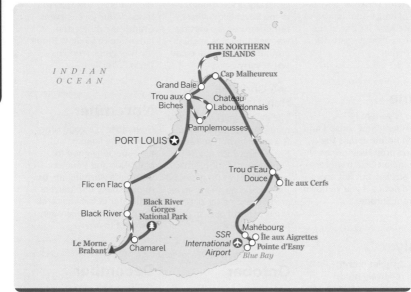

 **Essential Mauritius**

This itinerary takes you from the stunning coast of Mauritius southeast to the dramatic mountain landscapes of the interior and far southwest. En route, you'll visit some of the country's prettiest offshore islands, explore the stunning botanical gardens of Pample-mousses and go canyoning in Black River Gorges National Park.

Start along the stunning sands of **Pointe d'Esny**. Snorkel the sparkling azure lagoon at **Blue Bay**, eco-explore **Île aux Aigrettes**, then slip up to sleepy **Mahébourg** for the Monday market.

Drive north along the coast. Embrace the fisherfolk lifestyle in **Trou d'Eau Douce**, then glide through the crystal lagoon to **Île aux Cerfs**. Pass through the sky-reaching sugar cane before emerging at gorgeous **Cap Malheureux**. In **Grand Baie**, hop on a catamaran bound for the scenic **northern islands**, then treat yourself to a meal in lively **Trou aux Biches**. A day-trip loop could then take in the botanical gardens and sugar factory at **Pamplemousses** and lovely **Chateau Labourdonnais**.

Emerge on the west coast for a spot of diving in **Flic en Flac**, then base yourself around **Black River**. From here, you could try canyoning in **Black River Gorges National Park**, biking in **Chamarel** or climbing the iconic **Le Morne Brabant**.

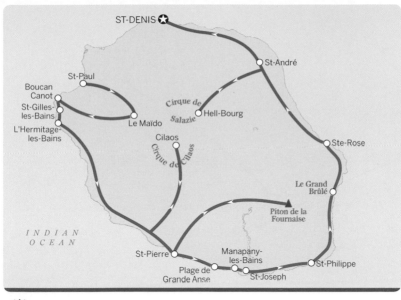

 **Tour of Réunion**

From sophisticated beach resorts to mountain villages, art galleries to volcanoes, two weeks is a minimum to sample the variety Réunion has to offer. Get hooked on the hiking and you could easily fill a month. This tour covers around 400km.

Kick things off in **St-Paul**, which is a good transit point before heading inland to **Le Maïdo** for a bird's-eye view of the Cirque de Mafate. Then drive down to the coast for some beach action in **Boucan Canot**, one of Réunion's trendiest towns. A five-minute drive south takes you to **St-Gilles-les-Bains**, a classic Indian Ocean resort with fine beaches and some pretty rowdy nightlife. The best beach to recover from it all is **L'Hermitage-les-Bains**. Allow three days to make the most of the area's botanical gardens, museums and watersports.

Next detour to **Cilaos**, where you should allow at least two days to soak up the rugged mountain scenery and the laid-back atmosphere. Hiking and canyoning opportunities will immerse you in some of the best scenery you'll see anywhere, while there are also thermal springs, wine to taste and ecotourism possibilities thrown in for good measure.

Next make for the bright lights of **St-Pierre** – if possible, get here for the huge Saturday market. From St-Pierre, it's a long but scenic drive up to Bourg-Murat, which is the obvious launch pad for the **Piton de la Fournaise**, one of the most accessible volcanoes on earth.

Return to St-Pierre and follow the RN2 that hugs along the scenic south coast. You may want to enjoy a picnic lunch at **Plage de Grande Anse** or unwind in **Manapany-les-Bains** before spending the night near **St-Joseph**. Proceeding east, you'll pass through charmingly rural **St-Philippe** and the lunar landscapes of **Le Grand Brûlé** before reaching **Ste-Rose**, where lava laps at the door of a church and narrowly misses the Virgin Mary.

As you head to the north of the island, go inland and stay at least two nights in **Hell-Bourg**, exploring the Cirque de Salazie. Finally, set off towards the north via the Indian-influenced **St-André**. End your trip sampling cafe culture and Creole architecture in the capital, **St-Denis**, which can also serve as a return to civilisation (without the clamour of a big city) if you've been climbing volcanoes and hiking the Cirques.

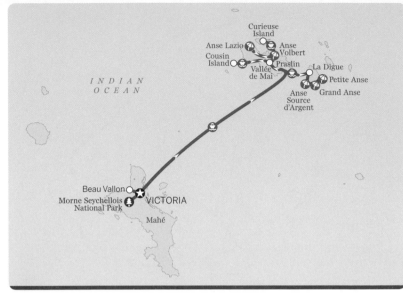

2 WEEKS Essential Seychelles

Two weeks is fine for a taster of the Seychelles' islands – allowing plenty of time for enjoying the very best of the country's superb beaches.

On the first day, tune into island life in the capital, **Victoria**, checking out the market and strolling among the palm trees in the botanical gardens. Move on to **Beau Vallon**, where three days can easily be spent messing around in and on the water. Devote the next two days to the beaches and byways of Mahé, and visiting the **Morne Seychellois National Park**, which has a little bit of everything: a colonial-era ruin, a tea factory and some fabulous hiking.

Next, cruise over to Praslin, which closely resembles paradise. Ogle curvaceous coco de mer nuts in the Unesco World Heritage-listed **Vallée de Mai**, hike amid massive palm fronds and then flake out on the perfect, sugar-white sands at **Anse Lazio**, which is one of the prettiest beaches we know. Fill the next four days with snorkelling, diving and swimming off **Anse Volbert**, getting up close and personal with giant tortoises on **Curieuse Island**, home to a large breeding farm of giant Aldabra tortoises, and walking among cacophonous clouds of seabirds on **Cousin Island** with more than 300,000 birds and numerous endemic species – even amateur bird-watchers will want to spend more time here than most tours allow.

From Praslin, make sail for La Digue – if you thought Praslin was paradise, just wait until you lose yourself on La Digue. Three days is the perfect amount of time to lapse into La Digue's slow vibe. Visit **Anse Source d'Argent** – the archetypal idyllic beach, although it's by no means the only one on La Digue. Get there late afternoon for the best atmosphere and try to avoid high tide, when the beach all but disappears. Take a snorkelling trip around nearby islands, then find solitude on the beaches of **Grand Anse** and **Petite Anse**. Grand Anse is incredibly scenic and has a great restaurant, **Loutier Coco**, where you can enjoy a superb lunch buffet. Petite Anse, which is accessible on foot only, feels wilder and more secluded. All too soon, it will be time to tear yourself away for the trip back to Victoria.

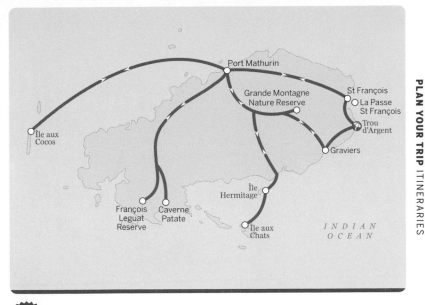

Rodrigues – The Other Mauritius

1 WEEK

A week is ample time to discover the delights of this small, mountainous island. You can divide the days walking, diving and taking boat trips to nearby islands, as well as kicking back on the beach and indulging in seafood feasts at one of Rodrigues' great family run restaurants.

First, spend half a day strolling the streets of **Port Mathurin** – and make sure you come on a Saturday, when the island's endearingly sleepy 'capital' springs into life and it seems the entire population descends for the weekly market. Devote another day to two of the island's not-to-be-missed sights: the giant tortoises at **François Leguat Reserve** and the caves at **Caverne Patate**. Another day could be taken up by the classic coastal hike from **Graviers to St François**, passing en route a gem of a beach at **Trou d'Argent** – this is perhaps our favourite coastal walk anywhere in Mauritius. From St François linger over lunch at one of the village's excellent restaurants, walk back the way you came or take a bus to Port Mathurin. Another day should be dedicated to the boat excursion to **Île aux Cocos**, with its quiet beaches and lively seabird colonies; set aside a couple of hours on the same day for a hike in search of endangered species in the **Grande Montagne Nature Reserve**.

You're spoilt for choice when it comes to diving. Start your Rodrigues diving experience by exploring the channel off St François, **La Passe St François**, on the edge of the lagoon, with more options beyond the reefs. For something a bit less exciting but a marvellous day trip nonetheless, follow up the diving with the good snorkelling around the little-visited **Île aux Chats and Île Hermitage** off the south coast.

And of course, along the way you'll want to dedicate as much time as you can to simply kicking back on the beach for hours at a stretch and indulging in seafood feasts at one of the great family-run restaurants scattered around the island. Perhaps reserve your spot at **Graviers'** La Belle Rodriguaise for lunch on your final day – it's an excellent choice to round off your week on Rodrigues.

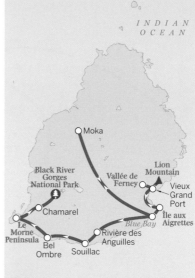

Réunion's Sud Sauvage & Hautes Plaines
1 WEEK

Réunion's 'Wild South' and central plains offer volcanic landscapes, massive ravines, wave-lashed cliffs and sensational hiking trails. You can discover the best of the region in a reasonably leisurely week.

Start at **Ste-Rose** and head south to find the first tongues of lava tumbling down to the sea. Cross the threatening lava fields of **Le Grand Brûlé** to spend a night or two near **St-Joseph**; stay in the hills for a real taste of rural life. From here you can explore the picturesque **Rivière Langevin** valley – bring a picnic.

Continuing west, take a dip in **Plage de Grande Anse** before spending the night in **St-Pierre** and partying up at its buzzing nightlife. The next morning, head to the high plateau of **Plaine-des-Cafres** to visit the Cité du Volcan. Take the magnificent forest road up to **Piton de la Fournaise**, Réunion's restless volcano. Now drop back down to Plaine-des-Cafres, where you could spend a couple of days hiking to **Grand Bassin**, a village at the end of the world. Finally, head for **Plaine-des-Palmistes**, where the hikes through the Forêt de Bébour-Bélouve provide unforgettable experiences.

Southern Mauritius
1 WEEK

The south of Mauritius offers the perfect combination of outstanding beaches and glorious natural scenery.

Blue Bay is everything its name suggests, and its proximity to a host of postcard-pretty landscapes makes it the perfect base for the island's southeast. Don't miss the excursion to **Île aux Aigrettes**, where you can spy pink pigeons and giant tortoises. Just north, **Vieux Grand Port** is where Mauritius' human story began centuries ago. There's an untouched feel to the nearby forests of **Vallée de Ferney**, home to the iconic Mauritius kestrel, which you can see being fed most mornings. **Lion Mountain** is a challenging but extremely rewarding hike. From your Blue Bay base, consider a day trip inland to Eureka in **Moka**, high on the Central Plateau.

Now head west, pausing at La Vanille in **Rivière des Anguilles**, then in **Souillac** and **Bel Ombre** to enjoy the pretty coast. Continue on to World Heritage-listed **Le Morne**, where dramatic hiking trails await. Climb into the hills to **Chamarel**, with its terrific eating scene and rum distillery – it's the perfect base for scenic drives and hikes through **Black River Gorges National Park**.

Plan Your Trip
Diving

Though largely overshadowed by the iconic Maldives, scuba diving in Mauritius, Réunion and the Seychelles is increasingly popular. Beneath the clear turquoise waters is a trove of unbelievable riches: rainbow-coloured fish and large pelagic species (and yes, sharks are part of the package), a dramatic seascape and a host of drop-offs and reefs. It's not the cheapest place on earth to dive (Thailand or the Red Sea it ain't), but it's a great place to learn, and in turn love, scuba diving. Good news: bar a few areas, the dive sites are never crowded.

Mauritius

So, you want variety? Abundant marine life, dramatic seascapes, atmospheric wrecks – Mauritius has it all, not to mention well-established, high-quality dive operators. Mauritius is almost entirely surrounded by a barrier reef, within which turquoise lagoons provide great possibilities for snorkellers, swimmers and novice divers. And then there's the pièce de résistance: Rodrigues, which has virgin sites and outstanding fish life.

Where to Dive

North

The north coast is a magnet for divers of all levels, and it's no wonder: there's a good combination of thrilling dives, wrecks, drop-offs and easy dives.

The islands off the coast (Île Plate, Coin de Mire) are the main highlights, with splendid sites and diverse undersea life – not to mention a sense of wilderness. To the northwest, Trou aux Biches is the main jumping-off point for a variety of superb dives.

Best Dives For...

Wrecks
Stella Maru (Mauritius)
Kei Sei 113 (Mauritius)
Antonio Lorenzo (Réunion)
Aldebaran (Seychelles)

Beginner Divers
Tug II (Mauritius)
Le Jardin des Kiosques (Réunion)
Anse Sévère (Seychelles)

Experienced Divers
Manioc (Mauritius)
Shark Bank (Seychelles)
Haï Siang (Réunion)
Tombant de la Pointe aux Canonniers (Mauritius)

➡ **La Fosse aux Requins** (Map p64) Iconic site famous for its congregations of blacktip reef sharks.

➡ **The Wall** (Map p64) Dramatic underwater cliff.

➡ **Djabeda** (Map p64) Atmospheric wreck dive.

➡ **Holt's Rock** (Map p67) Domes and boulders in 25m.

➡ **Tombant de la Pointe aux Canonniers** (Map p67) Has an exhilirating drop-off to about 60m.

➡ **Kingfish** (Map p67) Drift diving down to 28m.

➡ **Waterlily & Emily** (Map p67) Good wreck diving for beginners.

➡ **Stella Maru** (Map p67) A not-to-be-missed wreck in 25m.

West

The Flic en Flac area ranks among the best in Mauritius when it comes to diving. Conditions are optimal year-round – it's protected from the prevailing winds – and visibility is usually excellent.

And the southwest coast? The area between Le Morne Peninsula and Black River (Rivière Noire) has a few diving hotspots, but they lack the 'wow' factor. The weak points are the average visibility and the fairly dull topography.

➡ **Rempart Serpent** (Snake Rampart; Map p86) Sinuous rock in 25m attracting a huge number of fish.

➡ **La Cathédrale** (The Cathedral; Map p86) A scenic, memorable seascape.

➡ **Couline Bambou** (Map p86) Less crowded than La Cathédrale; a kaleidoscope of changing scenery.

➡ **Manioc** (Map p86) A deep, atmospheric dive beloved by seasoned divers.

➡ **Kei Sei 113** (Map p86) Good wreck diving for experienced divers.

➡ **Tug II** (Map p84) Good wreck diving with brilliant fish life.

➡ **Passe St Jacques** (Map p84) One of Mauritius' best drift-dive sites, with depths of 3m to 30m.

Southeast

Off the southeast coast it's the dramatic underwater terrain that impresses more than anything, making for unique profiles. You'll be rewarded with a profusion of caves, tunnels and giant arches – it's very scenic – as well as large numbers of pelagics thrown in for good measure. The hitch? From June to August most sites are exposed to the prevailing winds – expect choppy seas in rough weather.

➡ **Colorado** (Map p106) A 400m-long canyon pocked with chasms and crevices.

➡ **Roches Zozo** (Map p106) Like Colorado, which it's close to, this is another must-dive site.

➡ **Grotte Langouste** (Map p106) A cave brimming with lobsters.

➡ **Sirius** (Map p106) Great for wreck buffs.

➡ **Blue Bay** (p112) A safe, lovely spot to learn to dive, with a parade of reef fish to be observed.

East

The east is not known for its diving, but there are two standout sites if you don't fancy a trip elsewhere on the island.

➡ **Belmar Pass** (Map p122) Stunning seascapes, and a good chance to see grey reef or bull sharks because of the strong currents.

➡ **Passe de Trou d'Eau Douce** (Map p122) Worth visiting, though less spectacular than Belmar.

MARINE CONSERVATION

The main pressures on the marine environment are pollution, over-exploitation and inappropriate activities such as the use of drag anchors and explosives for fishing. In recent years Mauritius, Réunion and the Seychelles have introduced laws banning destructive practices, such as shell and coral collection, shark finning and spearfishing. Each has also established marine reserves to protect at least some of their coral reefs. If you're interested in helping, there are good volunteering opportunities, especially in Mauritius and the Seychelles.

THE FIRST TIME

You've always fancied venturing underwater on scuba? Now's your chance. Mauritius, Réunion and the Seychelles are perfect starting points for new divers, as the warm waters and shallow reefs are a forgiving training environment. Most dive centres offer courses for beginners and employ experienced instructors.

Just about anyone in reasonably good health can sign up for an introductory dive (from €50), including children aged eight and over. It typically takes place in shallow (3m to 5m) water and lasts about 30 minutes, escorted by a divemaster.

If you choose to enrol in an Open Water course, count on it taking about four days, including a few classroom lectures and Open Water training. Once you're certified, your C-card is valid permanently and recognised all over the world.

Rodrigues

This is the Indian Ocean at its best. A true gem, Rodrigues boasts numerous untouched sites for those willing to experience something different. There's a profusion of coral that you won't see anywhere else in Mauritius and the density of fish life is astounding. The underwater scenery is another pull, with a smorgasbord of canyons, arches and caves.

➜ **La Passe St François** (Map p168) A kilometre-long channel down to 30m, offering the full gamut of reef species.

➜ **Le Canyon** (Map p168) A truly atmospheric site: a canyon that runs under the reef.

➜ **La Basilique** (The Basilica; Map p168) Tunnels, caves and some fabulous underwater topography.

➜ **Karlanne** (Map p168) Dense marine life and healthy coral formations.

➜ **La Grande Passe** (Map p168) Considered by many dive instructors to be among the best medium-depth reefs in the area.

Practicalities

Diving Conditions

Although Mauritius is diveable year-round, the most favourable periods are October to December, March and April (January and February are peak months for cyclone activity). During July and August, when the southeastern trade winds are at their strongest, the seas are too rough and murky for diving all along the south and east coasts and around Rodrigues. Visibility is heavily dependent on weather and thus varies a lot – from a low of 10m at certain sites at certain periods to 40m at others.

Current conditions vary greatly, from imperceptible to powerful. Water temperatures range from a low of 22°C in August to a high of 28°C between December and February.

Dive Operators

There are at least 40 professional dive centres in Mauritius. Most belong to the **Mauritius Scuba Diving Association** (MSDA; ☎454 0011; www.msda.mu), which is affiliated with the Confédération Mondiale des Activités Subaquatiques (CMAS) and makes regular and rigorous checks. Most dive centres are also affiliated with one or more of the internationally recognised certifying agencies, usually Professional Association of Diving Instructors (PADI) or CMAS.

Many dive centres in Mauritius are hotel-based, but all welcome walk-in clients. In general, you can expect well-maintained equipment, good facilities and professional staff, but standards may vary from one centre to another, so it pays to shop around.

Réunion

Who said that diving in Réunion wasn't interesting? OK, the island is mostly famous for its trekking options, but it shouldn't be sneezed at. You'll be positively surprised: there's a wide choice of shallow dives inside the lagoon for novices and deeper dives (mostly 25m to 40m) just outside for more experienced divers, as well as a few purpose-sunk wrecks thrown in for good measure.

Where to Dive

Most dive sites are located off the west coast between Boucan Canot and St-Pierre.

St-Gilles-les-Bains

If you want relaxed diving, St-Gilles will appeal to you. Diving here is focused on the reefs, which slope gently away in a series of valleys to a sandy bottom in about 25m – very reassuring. Pelagics are rare, but small reef species are prolific.

➡ **Tour de Boucan** (Map p192) A fantastic site suitable for all levels. Super underwater terrain, with a massive boulder that provides shelter to numerous species.

➡ **Le Pain de Sucre** (Map p192) The setting is the strong point, with a contoured terrain and lots of small critters in the recesses (damselfish, parrotfish, triggerfish, lobsters), as well as a few seafans. Great for beginners.

➡ **Petites Gorgones** (Map p192) Also known as Saliba, this is an easy site suitable for all levels. Keep an eye out for leaf scorpion fish and turtles.

➡ **La Passe de L'Hermitage** (Map p192) An exciting dive. The terrain is nicely sculpted, with little canyons and large boulders that act as magnets for a wealth of species. Sadly, visibility is often reduced.

➡ **Haï Siang** (Map p192) With a maximum depth of 55m, this atmospheric wreck is accessible to very experienced divers only. Fish life is scarce.

➡ **Navarra** (Map p192) This wreck is not in good shape but it acts as a magnet for lots of reef species. The catch? It lies in 55m of water and is accessible to experienced divers only.

➡ **La Barge** (Map p192) Off St-Paul, a relaxing wreck dive in less than 22m. The wreck is not in good shape but it's home to plenty of small fish. Beginners will love it!

St-Leu

St-Leu features splendid wall diving and good coral fields, but fish life is said to be less abundant than off St-Gilles-les-Bains. Here walls tumble steeply to several dozen metres.

➡ **Tombant de la Pointe au Sel** (South of St-Leu, this is widely regarded as Réunion's best all-round dive site. In addition to great scenery, this stunning drop-off offers a fabulous array of fish life and seldom fails to produce good sightings of pelagics, especially tuna, barracudas and jacks. Suitable for experienced divers.

➡ **Le Jardin des Kiosques** With a depth ranging from 3m to 18m, it's very secure yet atmospheric for beginners. It's all about little canyons and grooves.

➡ **La Maison Verte** A relaxing site, blessed with good coral formations in less than 6m.

➡ **Antonio Lorenzo** Wreck enthusiasts will make a beeline for this well-preserved vessel that rests in about 38m on a sandy bottom off Pointe des Chateaux. Fish life is dynamic, and penetration in the hull is possible.

St-Pierre

Savvy divers, this area is for you. This area is unhyped and that's why we enjoy it so much. There are a host of untouched sites between St-Pierre and Grand Bois. The main drawcard is the topography, with numerous ridges, canyons and drop-offs.

➡ **Les Ancres & Le Tombant aux Ancres** A sloping reef festooned by healthy coral formations. You'll also see some old anchors dotted around the reef.

➡ **Demhotel** A lovely dive off Grand Bois along a contoured plateau with plenty of protruding basaltic formations and arches. Fish life is usually dense.

Practicalities

Diving Conditions

While it is possible to dive all year, the best time is October to April, when the water is at its warmest (about 28°C). However, you might want to avoid February and March, which is cyclone season. Water temperatures can drop to about 21°C in August.

Dive Operators

The dive centres are concentrated around St-Gilles-les-Bains, St-Leu and St-Pierre. The standard of diving facilities is high. You'll find professional dive centres staffed with qualified instructors catering to divers of all levels. Staff members usually speak English. Most dive centres are affiliated with PADI, Scuba Schools International (SSI) or CMAS – all internationally recognised dive organisations.

Take note that a simple medical certificate stating you are fit enough to dive is compulsory for diving in France. You can get one from your doctor in your home country or have it faxed or emailed to the dive centre. Otherwise, you can get one from any doctor in Réunion.

WHAT YOU'LL SEE

Let's be honest: the western Indian Ocean is not the richest marine realm in the world – some parts of the Caribbean, the South Pacific and the Red Sea boast more prolific fish life. But it's far from being poor – in fact, it has everything from tiny nudibranchs (sea slugs) to huge whale sharks. It's just a matter of quantities, not diversity.

Reef Fishes

Like technicolour critters? You'll encounter a dizzying array of species darting around the reef, including clownfish, parrotfish, angelfish, emperor-fish, butterfly-fish and various types of grouper. Moray eels are also frequently encountered.

Pelagics

Pelagic fish – larger beasts that live in the open sea, such as tuna and barracuda – sometimes cruise quite close to the reef in search of prey. Of the shark species inhabiting these waters, the most common are the whitetip reef shark, the hammerhead shark and the reasonably docile nurse shark. Whale sharks are also regularly encountered.

Rays

The most common species of ray found around the Seychelles and Mauritius is the manta ray. One of the larger stingray species, often encountered at Shark Bank off Mahé, is the brissant (or round ribbon-tailed) ray. It can grow up to 2m across. The blue-spotted stingray is quite common in the sandy areas between the granite boulders of the Seychelles.

Turtles

The best place to see turtles in the wild is the Seychelles, where there are a number of important breeding grounds for hawksbill and green turtles.

Coral

Coral is not the strongest point. The Indian Ocean's shallow-water reefs were badly hit by 'coral bleaching' in 1997 and 1998. In parts of the Seychelles, up to 90% of hard corals (the reef-building corals) were wiped out. They are still struggling, but there are encouraging signs of new growth.

Seychelles

Billed as one of the Indian Ocean's great diving destinations, the Seychelles almost rivals the Maldives, though it's much less hyped – all the better for you. You don't need to be a strong diver – there are sites for all levels.

There's excellent diving off Mahé, Praslin and La Digue, the three main islands, as well as off the other inner and outer islands. The strong point is the underwater scenery, complete with big granite boulders and seamounts – it's as atmospheric as on land.

Where to Dive

Mahé

➡ **Shark Bank** Mahé's signature dive, for experienced divers only. The name is misleading, because there are very few sharks around this 30m-tall granite plateau 9km off Beau Vallon (Mahé). Instead, you'll encounter brissant rays the size of a small car, eagle rays, barracuda, batfish, and teeming yellow snapper and bigeyes. There is nearly always a strong current at this site.

➡ **Îlot** This granite outcrop, just off north Mahé, consists of several large boulders topped by a tuft of palm trees. The current in the channel can be quite strong, but the cluster of boulders yields one of the highest densities of fish life in the Seychelles. Golden-cup coral festoons the

Top: Diving in Brissare Rocks (p300), Mahé, Seychelles

Bottom: Snorkelling off Île Cocos (p321), La Digue, Seychelles

canyons and gullies, and gorgonians and other soft corals abound. Îlot is about a 15-minute boat ride from Beau Vallon.

➡ **Brissare Rocks** About 5km north of Mahé, this granite pinnacle is accessed from Beau Vallon. The site features abundant fire coral and great concentrations of yellow snapper, wrasse, parrotfish and fusiliers, as well as groupers and eagle rays. It's covered with bright orange sponges and white gorgonians.

➡ **Twin Barges** If you need a break from offshore dives, these two adjoining shipwrecks will keep you happy. They sit upright on the seabed in about 20m in Beau Vallon bay.

➡ **Aldebaran** This boat was scuttled in 2010 off Anse Major, the maximum depth is 40m. It shelters moray eels, groupers and rays.

➡ **Alice in Wonderland** Famous for its healthy coral formations. Off Anse à la Mouche.

➡ **Jailhouse Rock** A high-voltage drift dive for experienced divers with prolific fish life. Off Pointe Lazare.

➡ **Shark Point** Whitetip reef sharks, nurse sharks and grey reef sharks are commonly sighted here. Off Pointe Lazare.

Praslin & La Digue

➡ **Aride Bank** Off Aride Island, this pristine site can be accessed from Praslin if you don't mind the tedious 30-minute boat trip to get to the site. A hot fave among local divemasters, it features rays, snappers, nurse sharks, jacks, barracudas and Napoleon wrasses as well as magnificent seafans.

➡ **Booby Islet** Approximately halfway between Aride Island and Praslin, this exposed seamount consistently sizzles with fish action. In less than 20m of water, you'll come across parrotfish, Napoleon wrasses, moray eels, turtles, eagle rays and nurse sharks.

➡ **Anse Sévère** An easy site, close to the shore of La Digue.

➡ **Cousin** An easy site in the waters off Cousin Island.

➡ **Marianne Island** An islet east of La Digue, famous for its dense fish life (including grey sharks, stingrays, barracudas, eagle rays and nurse sharks) and contoured seascape.

➡ **White Bank** Stunning seascape (tunnels, arches) and prolific fish life, including shoals of jacks and the occasional guitar shark.

➡ **Ave Maria Rocks** A seamount northwest of La Digue. Noted for its shark sightings and prolific marine life.

Other Inner Islands & Outer Islands

For wealthy divers, the private islands of Frégate, North, Silhouette and Denis offer fantastic diving options, with absolutely pristine sites and only one dive boat: yours. One step beyond, you'll find Aldabra, Cosmoledo and Astove, the stuff of legend. They feature the best sites in the eastern Indian Ocean, with electric fish action in a totally virgin territory and high-voltage drift dives. The catch? They are not accessible because of piracy in the area.

➡ **Napoleon** (Alphonse Island) One of Alphonse's iconic dives, Napoleon is always full of action. You're sure to see Napoleon wrasses, giant sweetlips, snappers, skipjack tuna, huge turtles, bluefin trevallies, barracudas and triggerfish in less than 20m. The seascape is incredibly scenic, with a clutch of massive coral pinnacles dotted on a vast plateau.

➡ **The Abyss** (Alphonse Island) This scenic stretch of reef is peppered with ledges and overhangs that are coated with photogenic coral formations and seafans. You'll come across oriental sweetlips, spotted eagle rays, turtles, giant groupers and dogtooth tuna.

➡ **The Arcade** (Alphonse Island) One of Alphonse's most magical dives, the Arcade is known for its sheer abundance of underwater life and healthy coral gardens. Divers are bedazzled by the incredible variety of fish, including shoals of giant sweetlips and fusiliers, bigeye and bluefin trevallies, batfish, snappers, triggerfish and pufferfish. Huge sea turtles are also frequently seen in the area.

➡ **The Pinnacles** (Alphonse Island) This site consistently sizzles with fish action. Here the reef plunges into an incredible abyss along a steep slope decorated with large seafans, but you don't need to go deep – anthias, blue-striped and two-spotted snappers, honeycombed moray eels, groupers, bluefin trevallies and even silvertip sharks are frequently observed in less than 25m.

➡ **Morane** A 50-minute boat ride from Silhouette, Morane features an array of boulders dotted around a sandy floor in about 20m. It's an oasis of life, with huge stingrays, eagle rays, manta rays, scorpionfish, trevallies and lionfish, among others. Because of strong currents, this site is suitable for experienced divers only. Well worth the lengthy boat ride.

SNORKELLING

If the idea of total immersion doesn't appeal to you, snorkelling is possible in the three countries. It's a great way to explore the underwater world with minimal equipment and without the costs associated with diving. Even the shallowest reefs are home to many colourful critters. In all three destinations, rental gear is widely available from dive centres.

Mauritius

Top snorkelling spots include the marine park at Blue Bay and along the west coast off Flic en Flac and Trou aux Biches, not forgetting the lagoon around Rodrigues.

Réunion

The lagoon along the west coast between St-Gilles-les-Bains and La Saline-les-Bains offers great snorkelling, with particularly good marine life off L'Hermitage-les-Bains. Take advice before leaping in as the currents can be dangerous and stick to supervised areas.

Seychelles

The sheltered lagoons provide safe havens for swimming and snorkelling. The Ste Anne and Port Launay Marine National Parks are firm favourites in the waters around Mahé. In September and October divers have a chance to snorkel alongside whale sharks. Around Praslin, try just off Anse Lazio and Anse Volbert beaches, or take a boat trip from Anse Volbert to St Pierre Islet. Close to La Digue, the submerged granite boulders around Cocos, Grande Soeur and Marianne islands teem with fish life.

➡ **Sprat City** (Silhouette) This atmospheric dive site centres on a large reef north of Silhouette. It acts as a magnet for all sorts of fish life, including barracudas, wahoos, fusiliers and batfish, and is overgrown with various species of coral. During the southeast monsoon, it's famous for its incredible concentration of sprats.

➡ **Turtle Rock** Just off the northeastern tip of Silhouette, Turtle Rocks features a series of atmospheric coral formations at around 10m. Keep your eyes peeled for eagle rays, barracudas, trevallies, fusiliers and green turtles.

➡ **Barracuda Rock** The underwater scenery is the main draw here, with a profusion of small caves, arches and fissures. They shelter hosts of small colourful fish that provide photographers with great opportunities in clear water. Eagle rays, tuna, giant trevallies, nurse sharks and stingrays can also be spotted.

➡ **Lion Rock** Frégate's signature dive, Lion Rock is a tiny islet visible from the main island. The varied underwater terrain acts as a magnet for a host of species, including nurse sharks, eagle rays, lionfish and lobsters. Bull sharks and tiger sharks also regularly patrol the area.

➡ **Little Fregate** Famous for its astoundingly dense fish life and its varied underwater terrain.

Practicalities

Diving Conditions

Diving in the Seychelles heavily hinges on the weather conditions, currents and direction of the wind. However, diving can be sampled during all seasons as there are always sheltered conditions. The seas are calmest from April to May and October to November. Due to currents and wind, visibility is temperamental and can drop to 5m. But in normal conditions you can expect 25m visibility.

Dive Operators

The Seychelles' 15-odd diving centres have first-rate personnel and facilities. You'll find dive centres in Mahé, Praslin, La Digue, Ste Anne, Silhouette, Frégate, Denis, North and Alphonse. Most centres are affiliated with PADI.

Le Maïdo viewpoint (p194) on the rim of Cirque de Mafate (p231)

Plan Your Trip
Hiking in Réunion

Hiking is the very best of what Réunion has to offer. Formed from one mighty dead volcano (Piton des Neiges) and one active volcano (Piton de la Fournaise), the island is a paradise for hikers, adventure-sports enthusiasts or indeed anyone who is receptive to the untamed beauty of a wilderness environment.

Hiking Tips

Safety is basically a matter of common sense and being prepared. Remember:

Before You Leave

➡ Get a detailed and up-to-date map.

➡ Double-check the state of the paths before setting out.

➡ Check the weather report.

➡ Tell people where you're going if you are hiking alone.

➡ Leave early enough to reach your destination before dark.

Take Along

➡ Comfortable hiking boots.

➡ Wet-weather gear.

➡ Plenty of water and energy-rich snacks.

➡ A basic medical kit.

When to Hike

The best time to hike is during the dry season, from around late April to the end of October. May and June, as well as September and October, are probably the best months of all. July and August are a bit chilly, and during the rainy months a number of paths are not accessible. The weather is extremely changeable from one part of this small island to the other.

The weather in Réunion has a tendency to become worse as the day goes on. As the hours pass, the island's uplands seem to delight in 'trapping' any cloud that happens to come their way. An early start is therefore one of the best defences against the vagaries of the elements.

The next day's weather forecast is shown on the two main TV channels after the evening news. You can also get the forecast by telephoning the Météo France voice service on ☎0892 68 02 00 (per min €0.35). Cyclone bulletins are available on ☎0897 65 01 01 (€0.60 per call). Both these services are in French. Also check out the website www.meteofrance.re.

What to Bring

Good shoes are essential for hiking the trails of Réunion, which are made of gravel and stone and are often very steep, muddy or slippery.

Be sure to carry water (at least 2L for a day's hiking), wet-weather gear, a warm top, a hat, sunscreen, sunglasses, insect repellent, a whistle, a torch and a basic medical kit including plasters (Band-Aids), elastic bandages and muscle balm for blisters and minor muscle injuries. The *gîtes* (lodges) provide sheets and blankets, but if you intend sleeping out at altitude, you'll need a decent sleeping bag, as temperatures in the Cirques can fall rapidly at night.

In most places to stay and places to eat, payment will be expected in cash, so bring a stash of euros with you. The only places to get euros in the Cirques are the ATMs at the post offices in Salazie, Hell-Bourg and Cilaos, and these can't be depended on.

You will be able to buy most last-minute supplies at a sporting-goods store or one of the big supermarkets in Réunion or Cilaos.

Hiking Trails

There are two major hiking trails, known as Grande Randonnée® Route 1 (GR® R1) and Grande Randonnée® Route 2 (GR® R2), with numerous offshoots. The GR® R1 does a tour of Piton des Neiges, passing through Cilaos, the Forêt de Bébour-Bélouve, Hell-Bourg and the Cirque de Mafate. The GR® R2 makes an epic traverse of the island all the way from St-Denis to St-Philippe via the three Cirques, the Plaine-des-Cafres and Piton de la Fournaise. A third trail, the Grande Randonnée® Route 3 (GR® R3), does a tour of Cirque de Mafate and overlaps with some sections of the GR® R1 and GR® R2.

The trails are well maintained, but the tropical rainfall can eat through footpaths and wash away steps and handrails. Even experienced hikers should be prepared for tortuous ascents, slippery mud chutes and narrow paths beside sheer precipices. The routes are well signposted on the whole, but it's essential to carry a good map and you should check locally on the current situation; trails are occasionally closed for maintenance, especially following severe storms.

Hiker in Cirque de Cilaos (p217)

Information

Hiking information is provided by the Centrale d'Information et de Réservation Régionale – Île de la Réunion Tourisme (p190) and by associated tourist offices, including those in Cilaos, Salazie, Hell-Bourg, Ste-Suzanne, St-Gilles-les-Bains, St-Pierre, St-Leu, Plaine-des-Palmistes, Ste-Anne, St-Joseph and Bourg-Murat. All these offices organise bookings for *gîtes d'étape et de randonnée* (walkers' lodges) and can give advice on which paths are currently closed.

The agency's website (www.reunion.fr) is by far the most useful website for hikers. It allows you to book your accommodation on-line. The websites www.randopitons.re and www.gites-refuges.com are also helpful.

For information on *état des sentiers* (closed trails), check the website www.onf.fr/la-reunion/sommaire/loisirs_en_foret/randonner/organiser.

The **Fédération Française de la Randonnée Pédestre** (FFRandonnée; www.ffrandonnee.fr) is responsible for the development and upkeep of the GR® walking tracks.

The definitive guide to the GR® R1, GR® R2 and GR® R3 is the TopoGuides GR® Grande Randonnée *L'Île de la Réunion* (2014), published by the FFRandonnée. It uses 1:25,000 scale IGN maps and details the itineraries. The GR® R1 is described in six *étapes* (stages), the GR® R2 in 12 stages and the GR® R3 in five stages.

The FFRandonnée also publishes the TopoGuide PR® *Sentiers forestiers de L'Île de la Réunion* (2011), which covers 25 walks varying from one-hour jaunts to six-hour hikes.

Published locally by Orphie, *52 Balades et Randonnées Faciles* is designed with children in mind and describes outings that can be covered in less than four hours. A broader range of walks is covered by *62 Randonnées Réunionnaises* (also by Orphie).

EMERGENCIES

In a real emergency out on the trail, lifting both arms to form a 'V' is a signal to helicopter pilots who fly over the island that you need help. If you have a mobile phone, call the emergency services on ☏112.

Hiker enjoying a break

Maps

Réunion is covered by the six 1:25,000 scale maps published by the Institut Géographique National (www.ign.fr). These maps are reasonably up to date and show trails and *gîtes*. Map number 4402 RT is one of the most useful for hikers, since it covers Cirque de Mafate and Cirque de Salazie as well as the northern part of the Cirque de Cilaos.

Tours & Guides

Réunion's hiking trails are well established and reasonably well signposted, but you may get more information about the environment you are walking through if you go with a local guide.

Fully qualified mountain guides can be contacted through the Centrale d'Information et de Réservation Régionale – Île de la Réunion Tourisme (p190) and local tourist offices. Rates are negotiable and vary according to the length and degree of dif-

ficulty of the hike; an undemanding one-day outing should start at around €50 per person (minimum four people).

Aparksa Montagne (p219)

Austral Aventure (p228)

Kokapat Rando (☑0262 33 30 14, 0692 69 94 14; www.kokapatrando-reunion.com)

Réunion Mer et Montagne (☑0692 83 38 68; www.reunionmeretmontagne.com)

Run Evasion (p219)

Sleeping & Eating

Most of the accommodation for hikers consists of *gîtes de montagne* (mostly found in isolated locations on the trails themselves) or of privately run *gîtes d'étape* along the walking trails. Both offer dorm beds and meals. There's often very little to separate the two types of *gîte* in terms of comfort or facilities. Almost all *gîtes* provide hot showers (they're solar heated). A third option consists of small, family-run *chambres d'hôtes* (mostly found in the villages at the

Hell-Bourg (p227), Cirque de Salazie

a camping stove. Bear in mind that you are not allowed to light fires anywhere in the forest areas. Some villages in the Cirques have shops where you can purchase a very limited variety of food.

Bookings

Book your accommodation before arriving in Réunion, especially during the busiest months (July, August and around Christmas). At other times it's best to book at least a couple of months in advance, particularly for popular places such as the *gîtes* at Caverne Dufour (for Piton des Neiges) and Piton de la Fournaise.

The *gîtes de montagne* are managed by the Centrale de Réservation – Île de la Réunion (p190) and must be booked and paid for in advance. This can be done through its website and at tourist offices. When you pay, you will receive a voucher to be given to the manager of the *gîte* where you will be staying. You must call the *gîte* to book your meals at least one day in advance; this can be done at the same time as the original booking if you'd rather, but meals still have to be paid for on the spot.

For the privately owned *gîtes* things are less restrictive in terms of logistics; you can book directly through the *gîte*.

ends of the hiking trails). Your choice of where to stay will most likely be based on where you can find a room. There are also a few hotels in Hell-Bourg and Cilaos for that last night of luxury (and central heating) before you set out on your hike.

One night's accommodation without food costs between €16 and €18. For half board, budget around €45 per person.

You can also camp for free in some areas in the Cirques, but only for one night at a time. Setting up camp on Piton de la Fournaise (the volcano) is forbidden for obvious reasons.

Most *gîtes* offer Creole meals, which are normally hearty, though a little rustic for some palates. The standard fare is *carri poulet* (chicken curry), *boucané* (smoked pork) or *rougail saucisses* (sausage with spices and rice), often with local wine or *rhum arrangé* (rum punch) thrown in. Breakfast usually consists of just a cup of coffee with *biscottes* (rusks) – or, if you're lucky, bread – and jam.

If you plan to self-cater, you will need to bring plenty of carbohydrate-rich food. Note that only a few *gîtes* are equipped with cooking facilities; you are best off bringing

Best Multiday Hikes
The Haut Mafate

What's not to love in the Haut Mafate? Highlights include the forested Plaine des Tamarins, the deep valley of the Rivière des Galets, the waterfall at Trois Roches and the ruins of Maison Laclos, which is said to be the oldest dwelling in the Cirque. Of course, you'll also enjoy phenomenal views wherever you look.

The most scenic areas of the Haut Mafate can be completed in a four-day loop that takes in the hamlets of La Nouvelle, Roche-Plate and Marla. This hike can easily be combined with the Bas Mafate (add another four days).

There are various access points into the Haut Mafate, but the most convenient option is the Col des Bœufs car park, in the Cirque de Salazie. From the car park to La

AZAM JEAN-PAUL / GETTY IMAGES ©

Top: Trois Bassins
waterfall

Bottom: Hiking to Piton
de la Fournaise (p236)

ECOWALKING

To help preserve the ecology and beauty of Réunion, consider these tips when hiking.

Rubbish

➡ Carry out all your rubbish. Don't overlook easily forgotten items, such as silver paper, orange peel, cigarette butts and plastic wrappers. Empty packaging should be stored in a dedicated rubbish bag.

➡ Never bury your rubbish: digging disturbs soil and ground cover and encourages erosion. Buried rubbish will likely be dug up by animals, who may be injured or poisoned by it.

➡ Minimise waste by taking minimal packaging and no more food than you will need. Take reusable containers or stuff sacks.

➡ Sanitary products, condoms and toilet paper should be carried out despite the inconvenience. They burn and decompose poorly.

Human Waste Disposal

➡ Contamination of water sources by human faeces can lead to the transmission of all sorts of nasties. Where there is a toilet, use it. Where there is none, bury your waste.

Erosion

➡ Hillsides and mountain slopes, especially at high altitudes, are prone to erosion. Stick to existing tracks and avoid shortcuts.

➡ If a well-used track passes through a mud patch, walk through the mud so as not to increase the size of the patch.

➡ Avoid removing any plant life – it keeps the topsoil in place.

Nouvelle in the Haut Mafate, it takes about two hours.

IGN's 1:25,000 topographic map 4402 RT covers the area.

The Haut Mafate Hike at a Glance

Duration 4 days

Distance 20.4km

Difficulty moderate

Start/finish Col des Bœufs car park

Nearest town Grand Îlet

The Bas Mafate

The most popular circuit starts from the Rivière des Galets valley and takes in all the *îlets* (hamlets) of Bas Mafate, including Aurère, Îlet à Malheur, La Plaque, Îlet à Bourse, Grand Place Les Hauts, Grand Place, Cayenne, Les Lataniers and Îlet des Orangers. It's a four-day hike, but you can

design a longer or shorter itinerary depending on how pressed and how energetic you are.

If time allows, you can rejoin the Haut Mafate itinerary (another four days). A path connects Îlet des Orangers and Roche-Plate. From Les Lataniers, you can also get to Roche-Plate via the Sentier Dacerle.

IGN's 1:25,000 topographic map 4402 RT covers the area.

The Bas Mafate Hike at a Glance

Duration 4 days

Distance 30km

Difficulty moderate

Start Deux Bras

Finish Sans Souci

Nearest towns Rivière des Galets and Sans Souci

Grand Étang lake (p264), St-Benoît

Tour des Cirques

The Tour des Cirques (Round the Cirques) is a Réunion classic that is sure to leave you with indelible memories. Combining the best of the three Cirques, it offers three distinct atmospheres and varied landscapes. As a bonus, you'll cross a few towns that are well equipped with cosy accommodation facilities.

The walk is best started in Cilaos, which has excellent facilities for walkers and the added advantage of a health spa where you can unwind after your hike. It covers 51.5km and is usually completed in five days, taking in the Piton des Neiges, Hell-Bourg, Grand Îlet, La Nouvelle (via Col des Bœufs) and Col du Taïbit.

Tour des Cirques Hike at a Glance

Duration 5 days

Distance 51.5km

Difficulty demanding

Start/finish Cilaos

Day Hikes

If you don't have time for a multiday trek, there are also plenty of great day hikes that will give you a taste of life in rural Réunion. A not-to-be-missed day hike is the climb up the Piton de la Fournaise (the volcano) from Pas de Bellecombe. Réunion's highest point, Piton des Neiges, can also be done in a day if you're super fit, but most people choose to stay overnight at Gîte de la Caverne Dufour (p221).

Another popular activity related to hiking is exploring lava tubes on the southeast coast. You'll walk (make it scramble) over slippery wet rocks through tunnels and caves that were formed by the volcanic eruptions.

Tourist offices have plenty of recommendations for short, easy walks.

Islands at a Glance

Four unique island destinations cast adrift in the warm azure waters of the Indian Ocean; Mauritius, Rodrigues, Réunion and the Seychelles can all stake a convincing claim to being a piece of paradise. But there are plenty of characteristics that set each island apart from the next – you can zero in on the islands that best suit you. Mauritius achieves perfect balance with its blend of culture and coast, while Réunion, with its surreal mountainous landscapes, is heaven on earth for activities enthusiasts. Beach bums will be better off in the Seychelles, which is blessed with some of the most alluring beaches in the world. Rodrigues is a rural gem that time forgot. It will delight those in search of something a little different.

Mauritius

Culture
Beaches
Watersports

Past & Present

Visitors are often overwhelmed by the sense of devotion that emanates from the incredibly colourful festivals – whether Hindu, Christian, Chinese or Muslim – held throughout the island. Architecture buffs will make a point of visiting the country's historic buildings, especially the colonial plantation houses.

Mind-Blowing Beaches

When it comes to beaches, you'll be spoilt for choice. Most resorts and guesthouses here have access to perfect white sand and amazing sapphire water. Good news: despite the crowds, it's easy to find your own slice of paradise.

Aquatic Delights

Mauritius is the place to be if you want to get your feet (and the rest) wet. Pretty much everything's on offer here, from kitesurfing and kayaking to windsurfing to excellent snorkelling and diving. Oh, and beachcombing counts too.

p46

Rodrigues

Diving
Village Life
Walking

Pristine Underwater World

The lack of resorts and a remarkably well-preserved marine environment make Rodrigues one of the best places to dive in the Indian Ocean. Sharks, giant trevallies and barracudas galore!

Lost in Time

Slip into island time in Port Mathurin, the somniferous capital of Rodrigues, and savour the unhurried pace of life. Accessible homestays, small markets, stuck-in-time villages and welcoming smiles – you'll be hard-pressed to find a mellower destination to maroon yourself for a languid holiday.

Coast Walks

The coastline between Graviers and St François in the island's east is extremely alluring: a string of hard-to-reach inlets and coves lapped by azure waters, with the mandatory idyllic beach fringing the shore, and vast expanses of rocks. Who knows, you may find a pirate's hidden booty!

p166

Réunion

Outdoors
Scenery
Food

Adrenaline Fix

With its extraordinarily varied terrain, Réunion is an incredible stage for the action seeker in search of anything from canyoning and paragliding to white-water rafting and horse riding. And when it comes to hiking, Réunion is in a league of its own.

Scenic Mountains

Soaring peaks, lush valleys, majestic summits, sensational lookouts, waterfalls taller than skyscrapers, stunning forests and one of the world's most active volcanoes: Réunion's rugged topography will take your breath away.

Bon Appétit

Foodies of the world, rejoice. In Réunion, even the simplest meal has a flavour you're unlikely to forget. Imagine French gastronomy, prepared with the freshest ingredients, add a dash of Creole, a smidgen of Indian and *voilà*!

p180

Seychelles

Beaches
Wildlife
Fabulous Resorts

Perfect White Sand

Many think the eye-catching brochure images of turquoise seas and shimmering white sands are digitally enhanced but, once here, they realise the pictures barely do them justice. The Seychelles is the tropical paradise you've always dreamed about.

Wildlife Spotting

The country is a nature-lover's dream. A variety of charismatic species can easily be approached and photographed. Scratch the neck of a giant tortoise, swim alongside a massive whale shark, observe thousands of nesting sooty terns or look for the smallest frog on earth. Don't forget your camera!

Lap of Luxury

Few islands have the concentration of world-class resorts that can be found in the Seychelles. Whether it's small and romantic, superglamorous or back-to-nature luxury, you'll find the right resort here.

p284

On the Road

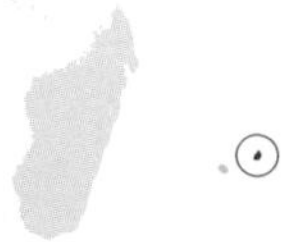

Mauritius

POP 1.34 MILLION / 📞 230

Best Places to Eat

➡ Eureka Table d'Hôte (p60)

➡ Le Château Restaurant (p119)

➡ Chez Tante Athalie (p83)

➡ Palais de Barbizon (p98)

➡ Cabanne du Pêcheur (p69)

➡ Lambic (p54)

Best Places to Sleep

➡ Le Saint Géran (p128)

➡ Le Prince Maurice (p128)

➡ Lux Le Morne (p104)

➡ La Maison d'Été (p129)

➡ Le Preskîl (p114)

Why Go?

Mark Twain once wrote that 'Mauritius was made first and then heaven, heaven being copied after Mauritius'. For the most part, it's true: Mauritius is rightly famed for its sapphire waters, powder-white beaches and luxury resorts. But there's so much more to Mauritius than the beach when it comes to attractions. There's bird watching and hiking in the forested and mountainous interior or world-class diving and snorkelling. Or there are boat trips to near-perfect islets and excursions to fabulous botanical gardens and colonial plantation houses. Either way, the possibilities can seem endless. And the real Mauritius – a hot curry of different cultures, traffic and quiet fishing villages – is never far away.

Ultimately, Mauritius is the kind of place that rewards even the smallest attempts at exploration. So, if your biggest discovery is the beach butler service at your hotel, then you'll need to plan a second visit!

When to Go

➡ Mauritius enjoys a typically tropical climate with year-round heat. The summer months are December to April, when it can be extremely humid, and the cooler winter, such as it is, runs from May to November. Coastal temperatures range between 25°C and 33°C in summer and between 18°C and 24°C in winter. On the plateau it will be some 5°C cooler.

➡ Peak cyclone months are January and February, with cyclones possible until April.

➡ High season roughly runs from November to April, with a Christmas–New Year peak, although other factors (French school holidays; for example) can also cause spikes in prices and visitor numbers.

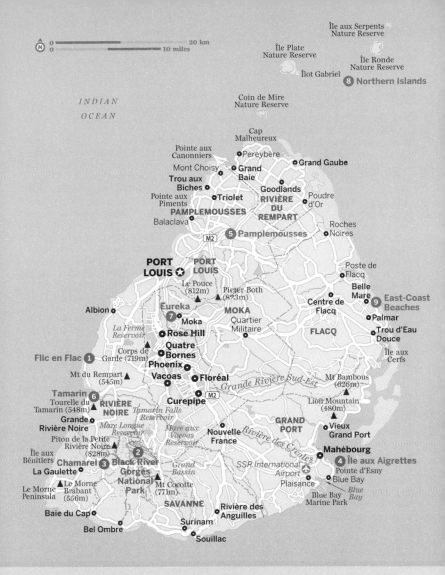

Mauritius Highlights

1 **Flic en Flac** (p83) Diving and snorkelling the best underwater sites of Mauritius.

2 **Black River Gorges National Park** (p99) Hiking through forested gorges, past waterfalls and looking for endangered birds.

3 **Chamarel** (p96) Pausing for lunch in this emerging foodie and mountain village.

4 **Île aux Aigrettes** (p112) Discovering how Mauritius once looked with a boat trip to this beautiful island.

5 **Pamplemousses** (p81) Exploring a botanical garden, a sugar museum and a fine architectural relic.

6 **Tamarin** (p91) Searching for whales and dolphins off the west coast.

7 **Eureka** (p59) Enjoying the best in colonial plantation architecture.

8 **Northern Islands** (p74) Cruising in a catamaran to beautiful offshore peaks.

9 **East-Coast Beaches** (p121) Finding your perfect patch of sand along the east coast.

PORT LOUIS

POP 140,430

Port Louis (*por* loo-ee), the island's capital and largest city, can feel like a kaleidoscope of countries and cultures, with flashes of India, Africa, Europe, China and the Middle East. Unless you've essential business to transact here, though, or you're in the country for a prolonged visit, there aren't that many reasons to come – there are numerous other day excursions that we'd rank above Port Louis.

But if you are here, it can be a good place to take the pulse of the country and get an alternative slant on the island's rarefied world of resorts and private beaches. Most interest lies amid the bustle of the downtown streets, the tangle of ethnic quarters and some wonderfully preserved colonial buildings. Apart from at Le Caudan Waterfront, it all shuts down after dark, when countless commuters rumble out of town en route to their homes on the Central Plateau.

History

Port Louis was first settled in the 17th century by the Dutch, who called it Noordt Wester Haven. It was the French governor Bertrand François Mahé de Labourdonnais, however, who took the initiative and developed it into a busy capital and port after 1736. He was rewarded with a much-photographed statue in Place d'Armes.

Few cities have bounced back from as many natural disasters as Port Louis, or Port Napoleon as it was briefly known in the early 19th century before the British took the island. Between 1773 and 1892 a series of fires, plagues and tropical storms all tried, and failed, to level the town. In 1819 cholera arrived from Manila on the frigate *Topaz,* killing an estimated 700 Port Louis residents. Things quietened down until 1866, when malaria suddenly appeared on the scene, causing a further 3700 fatalities. Around this time people started heading for the cooler (and healthier) Central Plateau, so the town's population was mercifully small when the 1892 cyclone whipped through and destroyed 3000 homes.

The 20th century saw Port Louis become one of Africa's most important financial centres and ports – to which the ever-growing number of high-rise glass-fronted banks in the city centre attests.

◉ Sights

Port Louis has a scattering of excellent museums, impressive architectural highlights and a roiling central market – more than enough reason to spend a half- or full day away from the beach. Most of the attractions can be reached on foot, but consider a taxi or bus to reach Père Laval's shrine.

★ Central Market   MARKET

(Map p50; ☉ 5.30am-5.30pm Mon-Sat, to 11.30pm Sun) Port Louis' rightly famous Central Market, the centre of the local economy since Victorian times, was cleaned up considerably in a 2004 renovation. Many comment that it's lost much of its dirty charm (you're far less likely to see rats, although it is possible), but it's still a good place to get a feel for local life, watch the hawkers at work and buy some souvenirs. Most authentic are the fruit and vegetable sections (including Chinese herbal medicines and aphrodisiacs).

★ Blue Penny Museum   MUSEUM

(Map p50; ☑ 210 8176; www.bluepennymuseum. com; Le Caudan Waterfront; adult/child Rs 245/120; ☉ 10am-5pm Mon-Sat) Although dedicated to the world-famous Mauritian one-penny and two-pence stamps of 1847, the Blue Penny Museum is far more wide-ranging than its name suggests, taking in the history of the island's exploration, settlement and colonial period, and even detouring into the Paul and Virginie legend. It's Port Louis' best museum, one that give visitors a then-and-now look at the city, although travellers with mobility issues should know that the stamps are on the 1st floor and there's no lift.

Central to the museum's collection are two of the world's rarest stamps: the red one-penny and blue two-pence 'Post Office' stamps issued in 1847. To preserve the colours, they are only lit up for 10 minutes at a time: every hour, at 25 minutes past the hour. The stamps are considered a national treasure and are probably the most valuable objects on the entire island.

On the ground floor you'll see a fantastic selection of antique maps, engravings from different periods in history, and photographs, as well as the country's most famous work of art: a superbly lifelike statue by Mauritian sculptor Prosper d'Épinay, carved in 1884. Based on Bernardin de St-Pierre's novel *Paul et Virginie*, the sculpture depicts the young hero carrying his sweetheart across a raging torrent.

MILLION-DOLLAR STAMPS

Philatelists (that's 'stamp collectors' to the rest of us) go weak at the knees at the mention of the Mauritian 'Post Office' one-penny and two-pence stamps. Issued in 1847, these stamps were incorrectly printed with the words 'Post Office' rather than 'Post Paid'. They were recalled upon discovery of the error, but not before the wife of the British governor had mailed out a few dozen on invitations to one of her famous balls.

These stamps now rank among the most valuable in the world. The 'Bordeaux cover', a letter bearing both stamps that was mailed to France, was last sold for a staggering US$3.8 million. In 1993 a consortium of Mauritian companies paid US$2.2 million for the pair of unused one-penny and two-pence stamps now on display in Port Louis' Blue Penny Museum. This is the only place in the world where the two can be seen together on public view.

Aapravasi Ghat   HISTORIC BUILDING

(Map p50; ☑ 217 7770; www.aapravasighat.org; 1 Quay St; ⊙ 9am-4pm Mon-Fri, to noon Sat) FREE Aapravasi Ghat, a small complex of buildings located on the seafront, served as the island's main immigration depot for indentured labourers from India. The highlight of a visit is the Beekrumsing Ramlallah Interpretation Centre, which hosts kids' activities. You'll get the most out of your visit if you ring ahead to book a (free) guided tour. Otherwise, some of the original stone buildings remain and there are strategically placed life-size models of the immigrants.

The ghat was listed as a World Heritage Site by Unesco in 2006 for its important role in the island's social history. And while it may not look like much at first glance, this site resonates with Mauritians across the island. Britain pioneered its indentured-servant scheme in Mauritius and from 1849 to 1923 over half a million immigrants were processed here before being shipped to various plantations or other colonial islands. Today, almost 70% of Mauritius' citizens can trace their roots back to Aapravasi Ghat.

Mauritius Postal Museum   MUSEUM

(Map p50; ☑ 213 4812; www.mauritiuspost.mu; Place du Quai; adult/child Rs 150/90; ⊙ 9.30am-4.30pm Mon-Fri, to 3.30pm Sat) This interesting museum beside the central post office houses a mishmash of commemorative stamps and other postal paraphernalia from around the world. A relatively new exhibit details the history of the Mauritius post using a rich assortment of photographs and artefacts. Of particular interest is the display about mail delivery to the remote dependencies of Agaléga and St Bandon.

Place d'Armes   SQUARE

(Map p50) The city's most imposing boulevard, Place d'Armes' is lined with royal palms and leads up to **Government House**, a beautiful French-colonial structure dating from 1738. Outside there's a typically solemn **statue of Queen Victoria** in full 'we are not amused' mode. The **statue of Mahé de Labourdonnais** at the quayside end of the avenue has become Port Louis' emblem throughout Mauritius.

Natural History Museum & Mauritius Institute   MUSEUM

(Map p50; ☑ 212 0639; La Chaussée St; ⊙ 9am-4pm Mon, Tue, Thu & Fri, to noon Sat) FREE The major attraction at this small but proud museum is the famous (though somewhat grubby) reconstruction of a dodo. Scottish scientists assembled the curious-looking bird in the late 19th century, using the only complete dodo skeleton in existence, although experts with whom we spoke suggested that the scale might be slightly larger than life.

Jardins de la Compagnie   GARDENS

(Company Gardens; Map p50; ⊙ 6am-8pm Oct-Mar, to 7pm Apr-Sep) Jardins de la Compagnie is by far the city's most attractive garden, with its vast banyan trees, huge number of statues, quiet benches and fountains. During the day it's perfectly safe, but avoid it at night, when it becomes a favoured hang-out for prostitutes and drug addicts. In early colonial times, the garden was the vegetable patch of the French East India Company. Today, it's best known for its statues of local sculptor Prosper d'Épinay and much-loved musician Ti Frère.

Chapel and Shrine of Marie Reine de la Paix   CHURCH

(Map p50; Monseigneur Leen Ave) The modern chapel and shrine of Marie Reine de la Paix is a popular spot for prayers, and the ornamental gardens offer views over the city. Pope John Paul II officiated his first Mass here during his visit to the island. Opening hours vary.

Port Louis

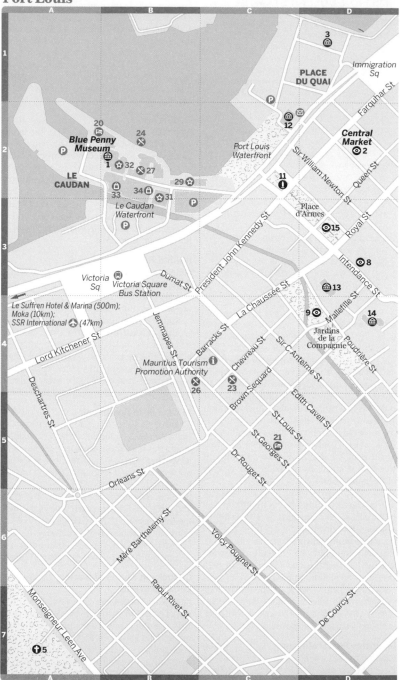

PLACE DU QUAI

Immigration Sq

3

Farquhar St

12

Central Market 2

Port Louis Waterfront

Sir William Newton St

Queen St

20

24

Blue Penny Museum

1

32

27

29

11

Place d'Armes

15

Royal St

LE CAUDAN

33

34

31

Le Caudan Waterfront

Intendance St

8

13

Malléfille St

9

14

Jardins de la Compagnie

Poudrière St

Victoria Sq

Victoria Square Bus Station

Durnat St

President John Kennedy St

La Chaussée St

Le Suffren Hotel & Marina (500m);
Moka (10km);
SSR International ✈ (47km)

Lord Kitchener St

Jemmapes St

Barracks St

Chevreau St

Sir C Antelme St

Mauritius Tourism Promotion Authority

26

23

Brown Sequard

Edith Cavell St

Deschartres St

St Louis St

St Georges St

21

Dr-Rouget St

Orleans St

Mère Barthelemy St

Volcy Pougnet St

De Courcy St

Raoul Rivet St

Monseigneur Leen Ave

5

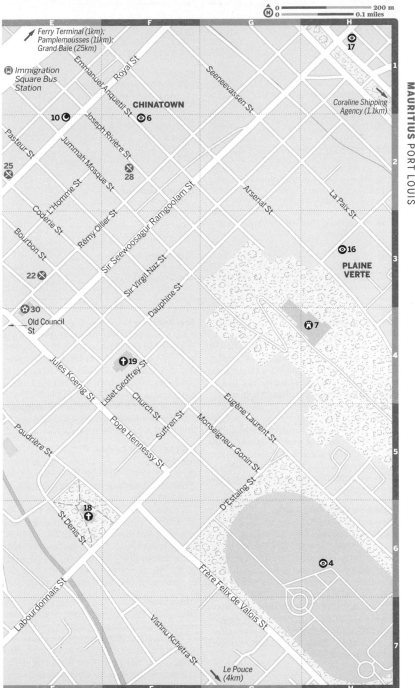

0 — 200 m
0 — 0.1 miles

Ferry Terminal (1km);
Pamplemousses (11km);
Grand Baie (25km)

Immigration
Square Bus
Station

CHINATOWN

10

6

Coraline Shipping
Agency (1.1km)

17

Emmanuel Anquetil St

Royal St

Seeneevassen St

Pasteur St

Joseph Rivière St

25

Jummah Mosque St

28

L'Homme St

Coderie St

Rémy Ollier St

Arsenal St

La Paix St

Bourbon St

Sir Seewoosagur Ramgoolam St

16

PLAINE
VERTE

22

Sir Virgil Naz St

30

Old Council
St

Dauphine St

7

Jules Koenig St

19

Lislet Geoffrey St

Church St

Suffren St

Pope Hennessy St

Monseigneur Gonin St

Eugène Laurent St

Poudrière St

D'Estaing St

18

St Denis St

4

Labourdonnais St

Frère Félix de Valois St

Vishnu Kchetra St

Le Pouce
(4km)

Port Louis

Photography Museum MUSEUM
(Map p50; ☑211 1705; www.voyaz.com/
musee-photo; Old Council St; admission Rs 150;
☺9am-3pm Mon-Fri) This small but engaging museum, down a cobbled lane opposite the Municipal Theatre, is the labour of love of local photographer Tristan Bréville. He's amassed a treasure trove of old cameras and prints, including several daguerreotypes (the forerunner of photographs) produced in Mauritius in 1840, just a few months after the technique was discovered in France. The museum also contains a vast archive of historical photos of the island, although only a fraction are on display.

Champ de Mars Racecourse RACECOURSE
(Hippodrome; Map p50; ☑212 2212; www.
mauritiusturfclub.com) This racecourse was a military training ground until the Mauritius Turf Club was founded in 1812, making it the second-oldest racecourse in the world. Mauritian independence was proclaimed here in 1968. The racing season lasts from around April to late November, with meetings usually held on a Saturday or Sunday. The biggest race of all is the **Maiden Cup** in September. For race dates, contact the Mauritius Turf Club or check local media.

Fort Adelaide FORTRESS
(Citadel; Map p50) Fort Adelaide resembles a Moorish fortress. Built by the British, the fort sits high on the crown of a hill, offering splendid views over the city and its harbour. The old barracks have been restored and transformed into a row of intriguing boutiques – good for a few minutes of window shopping. The quickest route up is via Suffren St. Allow around 10 minutes for the climb.

**SSR Memorial Centre
for Culture** CULTURAL CENTRE
(Map p50; ☑242 0053; Sir Seewoosagur Ramgoolam St, Plaine Verte; ☺9am-4pm Mon-Fri, to noon Sat) FREE This simple house museum near the Jardin Plaine Verte was home to Mauritius' father of independence, Sir Seewoosagur Ramgoolam, from 1935 until 1968. It's an interesting exhibit on his life, with some fascinating photographs, a collection of his belongings and even films about the great man, beloved by all Mauritians.

Chinatown AREA
(Map p50) The Chinese have traditionally occupied an important position in the life of Port Louis, and the area between the two 'friendship gates' on Royal St forms the centre of the city's Chinatown. Here you'll take in the rich mercantile life of the Chinese community,

busy Chinese restaurants and grocery stores, and streets echoing with the unmistakable clatter of mah-jong tiles.

Jummah Mosque
MOSQUE

(Map p50; Royal St; ⊗8am-noon & 2-4pm Mon-Thu, Sat & Sun) The Jummah Mosque, the most important mosque in Mauritius, was built in the 1850s and is a striking blend of Indian, Creole and Islamic architecture – it would look equally at home in Istanbul, Delhi or New Orleans! Visitors are welcome in the peaceful inner courtyard, except on Friday and during the month of Ramadan.

Plaine Verte
AREA

(Map p50) Located on the far side of the citadel, Plaine Verte is the Muslim quarter of the city and strongly contrasts with the glass towers in central Port Louis. Very little care is given to the area's facades – construction materials (usually concrete) are always left exposed – which gives the neighbourhood a certain dilapidated feel despite the lively bustle. After snooping around some of the alleyways for tucked-away bakeries, make your way to the vibrant fabric shops lining **Papillon Street**.

St James Cathedral
CATHEDRAL

(Map p50; Poudrière St) Inaugurated in 1850, St James is the oldest Anglican church in Mauritius, and has a peaceful, wood-panelled interior with plaques commemorating local worthies.

St Louis Cathedral
CATHEDRAL

(Map p50; Sir William Newton St) The slightly austere St Louis Cathedral dates from 1932 and is popular with the Chinese community.

🛏 Sleeping

We generally don't recommend staying in Port Louis – the selection of quality sleeps is minimal and the city is practically a ghost town after sunset. Even so, there is a handful of options, including two excellent choices at Le Caudan Waterfront.

Le St Georges Hotel
HOTEL €€

(Map p50; ☏211 2581; www.saintgeorgeshotel-mu.com; 19 St Georges St; s/d from Rs 2500/3550; ※@⍥☀) Towering above the surrounding residential neighbourhood in the AAA Tower, Le St Georges is excellent value for money. The rooms are fairly unexciting, but they are clean and equipped with all the necessary comforts. The location is also good, just a five-minute walk from the centre of town.

WORTH A TRIP

PÈRE LAVAL'S SHRINE

Père Laval's Shrine (Map p58; ☏242 2129; ⊗8.30am-noon & 1-4.45pm Mon-Sat, 10am-noon & 1-4pm Sun) The shrine of French Catholic priest and missionary Père Jacques-Désiré Laval is something of a Lourdes of the Indian Ocean, with many miracles attributed to pilgrimages here. The padre died in 1864 and was beatified in 1979 during a visit by Pope John Paul II. Père Laval is credited with converting 67,000 people to Christianity during his 23 years in Mauritius. To get here, take a bus signed 'Cité La Cure' or 'Père Laval' from the Immigration Sq bus station.

Père Laval is a popular figure with Mauritians of all religions. Pilgrims come from as far afield as South Africa, Britain and France to commemorate the anniversary of his death on 9 September. Notice the coloured plaster effigy of the priest on top of the tomb – it's been rubbed smooth by miracle-seeking pilgrims.

At other times of year the shrine is fairly quiet, though the services held on Friday at 1pm and 5pm attract a reasonable crowd. In the same complex is a large, modern church and a shop with a permanent exhibition of Père Laval's robe, mitre, letters and photographs.

★ Le Suffren Hotel & Marina
HOTEL €€€

(Map p58; ☏202 4900; www.lesuffrenhotel.com; Le Caudan Waterfront; r from €225; P※@⍥☀) Le Suffren is the trendier but quieter sister to the Labourdonnais, and just a short complimentary boat ride away. For better or worse, you feel as though you're out of the city, despite being just a hop from the waterfront. The hotel has a very pleasant, convivial feel, with an über-cool lounge bar, a good restaurant and stylish, contemporary rooms.

Labourdonnais Waterfront Hotel
HOTEL €€€

(Map p50; ☏202 4000; www.labourdonnais.com; Le Caudan Waterfront; r from €265; ※@⍥☀) An ultrasmart business hotel on the Caudan Waterfront, the Labourdonnais has excellent, light-filled rooms – even the standard ones are huge – and a recent refurbishment has seen an understated, slightly old-world elegance take centre stage. All rooms have cavernous bathrooms, and most have excellent views of the city and harbour, particularly the 'turret rooms' at each top corner.

Facilities include gym, pool and business centre, and there are a number of eateries.

Eating

Port Louis has a great eating scene in which the ethnic diversity of the city comes up trumps. As the middle classes tend to live outside the city, many places are only open for lunch – head to Le Caudan Waterfront in the evenings and on weekends.

City Centre

The Central Market, Chinatown and the bus stations provide happy hunting grounds for street-side nibbles, but you'll find stalls all over town selling *samousas* (samosas), *gâteaux piments* (chilli cakes) and *dhal puri* (lentil pancakes). The general rule is to queue behind the longest line – word travels fast and everyone seems to simultaneously know who's serving up the best stall grub.

Bombay Sweets Mart   SWEETS €
(Map p50; ☏ 212 1628; www.bombaysweetsmart. com; 7 Rémy Ollier St; ⊙ 9.30am-5pm Mon-Fri, to 12.30pm Sat) Bombay Sweets Mart is famous for the Indian nibbles colourfully known as *caca pigeon* (literally, 'pigeon droppings').

First Restaurant   CHINESE €
(Map p50; ☏ 212 0685; cnr Royal & Coderie Sts; mains from Rs 175; ⊙ 11.30am-2.30pm & 6.30-9.30pm Tue-Sun) If the age-old rule that a good Chinese restaurant is full of Chinese diners applies, then First is a winner. Packed with large family groups enjoying vast feasts of delicious Cantonese cooking, this is one of Chinatown's finest, and prices are extremely reasonable for the quality of the fare.

Ru Yi   CHINESE €
(Map p50; ☏ 217 9888; 32 Joseph Rivière St; mains from Rs 175; ⊙ 11am-2pm & 6-10pm) You can't go wrong with any of the restaurants in Chinatown, but this one is a favourite for no-nonsense, reliably good cooking. The atmosphere is a bit lacking, but when has an inner-city Chinese restaurant ever featured in a design magazine? It does set menus for groups upon request; á la carte choices are wide-ranging and cover most Chinese staples.

★Lambic   MAURITIAN, INTERNATIONAL €€
(Map p50; ☏ 212 6011; www.lambic.mu; 4 St Georges St; mains Rs 275-650; ⊙ 8am-10pm Mon-Thu, 8am-late Fri, 11am-10pm Sat) Set in a refurbished

colonial home in the heart of the capital's chaos, Lambic is a beer buff's paradise, with dozens upon dozens of local and imported beers, including a particularly rich selection from Belgium. The food spans all the usual fish and meat offerings, with some unusual local dishes such as Creole wild hare.

Waiters are well versed in the high art of matching platters to pints (yes, that's right – you match your meal to your beer here). And if the dark-wood bar, antique timber beams and fanned napkins don't win you over, then you'll surely be impressed by the glass-faced pantries covering all the interior walls – they reveal hundreds of alcoholic imports.

Courtyard   EUROPEAN €€
(Map p50; ☏ 210 0810; cnr St Louis & Chevreau Sts; mains Rs 500-1200; ⊙ noon-4pm Mon-Fri) Set around an attractive courtyard, this European-style restaurant also features a stylish indoor dining space in a restored stone structure. The impressive menu focuses on a memorable assortment of fusion tastes and fresh cuisine, such as a selection of carpaccio and seafood.

Le Caudan Waterfront

There's a wide variety of restaurants and cafes in the Le Caudan complex, from bustling food courts to upscale seaside dining.

Deck   SEAFOOD €€
(Map p50; ☏ 5759 2344; Le Caudan Waterfront; mains Rs 550-890; ⊙ noon-3pm & 6.30-10.30pm Mon-Sat) Inhabiting its own pontoon on the harbour, the Deck wins plaudits for its setting, which is slightly removed from the clamour of the riverside bars and has good views (if you ignore the floating rubbish that seems to gather nearby). The food is good without being really interesting – the calamari vindaloo caught our eye, but the grilled fish is also appealing.

Yuzu   ASIAN, FUSION €€
(Map p50; ☏ 202 4000; www.labourdonnais. com; Le Caudan Waterfront; set menu Rs 1600, mains Rs 550-1300; ⊙ noon-3pm & 7-10.30pm Mon-Fri, 7-10.30pm Sat) Thai, Vietnamese, Chinese and Japanese cooking fuse seamlessly at this swish and sophisticated restaurant at Labourdonnais Waterfront Hotel. You could order slow-cooked duck Thai red curry refreshed with coconut milk, snow peas and fried eggplant, and follow it up with pineapple and peanut dim sum for dessert.

Brasserie Chic INTERNATIONAL €€
(Map p50; 202 4017; www.labourdonnais.
com; Le Caudan Waterfront; mains from Rs 450;
6.30am-10.30pm) The Labourdonnais Waterfront Hotel (p53) boasts this cool and classy brasserie serving up salads, bagels, pasta, casseroles and prime cuts of steak. There's even a curry bar with six curries to choose from.

Namaste INDIAN €€
(Map p50; 211 6710; Le Caudan Waterfront; mains Rs 375-675, set menu Rs 1175-1800; 11.30am-3pm & 6.30-10.30pm) Atmospheric Namaste serves up excellent North Indian specialities such as tandooris, tikkas and butter chicken. Try for a balcony table. The place gets lively on Saturday evening, when meals start at Rs 450 and are followed by Bollywood tunes.

🍷 Drinking & Nightlife

With the exception of Le Caudan Waterfront, where there's always something going on, Port Louis is not exactly a happening place at night: come sunset the city is virtually silent as commuters retire to the Central Plateau towns.

☆ Entertainment

Municipal Theatre THEATRE
(Map p50; Jules Koenig St; tickets from Rs 100) The appealing Municipal Theatre has changed little since it was built in 1822, making it the oldest theatre in the Indian Ocean region. Decorated in the style of the classic London theatres, it seats about 600 over three levels and has an exquisitely painted dome ceiling with cherubs and chandeliers. Performances are in the evenings – usually at 8pm.

Look for announcements in the local press or call the tourist office to find out what's on. Tickets can be purchased at the box office in the theatre itself.

Keg & Marlin LIVE MUSIC
(Map p50; 210 2050; Le Caudan Waterfront; noon-midnight Mon-Thu, noon-3am Fri, noon-1am Sat & Sun) At the weekends the Keg & Marlin bar transforms into Port Louis' only live-music venue. Standards vary enormously from rock outfits to *séga* (traditional African music and dance), which is when the place really gets going.

Port Louis Casino CASINO
(Map p50; 210 4203; www.casinosofmauritius.
mu; Le Caudan Waterfront; 9.30am-2am, gaming tables 8pm-4am Mon-Sat, 2pm-4am Sun) The mighty popular city casino is about the liveliest place in town after midnight – its salient (some would say tackiest) feature externally is its ship-shaped design, crowned at its prow by the campest lion imaginable. Miaow. There are slot machines downstairs and blackjack and American roulette on the 1st floor. Smart-casual dress is required.

Star Cinema CINEMA
(Map p50; 211 5361; Le Caudan Waterfront; tickets from Rs 150) This is Port Louis' biggest and best cinema, with three screens offering mainstream international releases. Films are generally dubbed in French and there are usually four or five screenings a day.

🛍 Shopping

Most of the city centre's main streets have clusters of merchants selling similar items. Bourbon St has swarms of flower sellers, Coderie St (also spelt Corderie St) has silk and fabric vendors, and La Chaussée St is where locals go to buy electronics.

Le Caudan Waterfront is the place to go for trendy knick-knacks, upmarket designer boutiques, books, handicrafts and souvenirs. For a more earthy experience, there's always the Central Market (p48).

★ MAST HANDICRAFTS
(Map p50; 5423 8959, 211 7170, www.voiliers
ocean.intnet.mu; Le Caudan Waterfront; 9.30am-5pm Mon-Sat, to noon Sun) The model-ship manufacturer Voiliers de l'Océan (p62) has an outlet just outside the Craft Market.

Bookcourt BOOKS
(Map p50; 211 9146; Le Caudan Waterfront; 10am-6pm Mon-Sat, to 12.30pm Sun) The country's best bookshop sells a broad range of English, French and Creole books, including guidebooks, maps and an excellent range of books about Mauritius.

Craft Market MARKET
(Map p50; 210 0139; Le Caudan Waterfront; 9.30am-5.30pm) The Craft Market is less fun but also less hassle than the Central Market (p48). You'll find better-quality souvenirs, such as Mauritius glass, artworks and essential oils from the stalls arrayed over two floors inside the shopping mall.

SHOPPING IN MAURITIUS

Mauritius is increasingly promoting itself as a shopping destination. While clothing is a mainstay of any shopping experience here, other possibilities include the island's signature model ships, glasswork, artwork and basketware. Port Louis generally has the widest range of souvenirs and handicrafts, and there's a daily market in Port Louis, and weekly markets in Mahébourg and Port Mathurin (Rodrigues).

Clothing

Although the textile industry has been eclipsed by that of China, it remains one of Mauritius' biggest earners, to the extent that many of the brand-name clothes on sale in Europe, Australia and the USA are produced in the factories around Curepipe, Floréal and Vacoas. Shoppers can save by buying at the source, and many of the bigger suppliers have outlet stores where you can snap up items at a fraction of their usual retail price.

Floreal Knitwear in Floréal is renowned for its stylish sweaters and other knitted garments. The company supplies Gap, Next and other international outfitters, but you can buy the same items before the branded labels have been added for a fraction of the final cost at the Floréal emporium.

Handicrafts

Locally produced basketry, essential oils, sugar, spices, rums, teas and T-shirts all make very portable souvenirs. The Craft Market (p55) in Port Louis' Caudan Waterfront complex offers perhaps the widest choice. Most of the crafts and souvenirs sold at Port Louis' Central Market (p48) and the Grand Baie Bazaar (p76), like leather belts and bags, masks, embroidery and semiprecious-stone solitaire sets, are from Madagascar.

Model Ships

It's difficult not to be impressed by the skill that goes into producing Mauritius' famous model ships. Small-scale shipbuilding has become a huge business and you'll see intricate replicas of famous vessels, such as the *Bounty, Victory, Endeavour, Golden Hind* and even *Titanic*, for sale all over the island. Model shipbuilding dates back to only 1968, when an unknown Mauritian carved a model ship for fun and launched a whole new industry.

The models are made out of teak or mahogany (cheaper camphor wood is liable to crack), and larger ships take up to 400 hours to complete. Men usually work on the structure and women do the rigging and sails, which are dipped in tea to give them a weathered look.

One of the best model-ship builders is Voiliers de l'Océan (p62), in Curepipe. The company also has an outlet, MAST (p55), in Port Louis' Caudan Waterfront complex.

To get your goods home safely, shops will pack the models for carry-on luggage or in sturdy boxes to go in the hold, and deliver them to your hotel or the airport at no extra charge.

ℹ️ Information

DANGERS & ANNOYANCES

Port Louis is not safe at night just about anywhere south of the motorway; most of the streets empty as the workday ends. After dark all travellers should stick to well-lit main streets and avoid the Jardins de la Compagnie (p49), a favoured hang-out for all manner of unsavoury types. If you don't know your exact route, take a taxi. Le Caudan is generally fine as long as there are lots of people around.

By day, Port Louis is a very safe city, but beware of pickpockets anywhere, particularly in the market and around the bus stations.

EMERGENCY

Police (☑ emergency 999, headquarters 203 1212; Line Barracks, Lord Kitchener St)
Ambulance (☑ 114)
Fire Brigade (☑ 995)

MEDICAL SERVICES

Dr Jeetoo Hospital (☑ 212 3201; Volcy Pougnet St) Provides 24-hour medical and dental treatment and has a 24-hour pharmacy. Staff speak English and French.
Medical Training Pharmacy (☑ 210 4146; La Chaussée St) One of the best pharmacies in the city. Close to Jardins de la Compagnie.

TOURIST INFORMATION
Mauritius Tourism Promotion Authority
(MTPA; Map p50; ☑ 210 1545; www.tourism-mauritius.mu; 4th & 5th fl, Victoria House, St Louis St; ⊙ 9am-4pm Mon-Fri, to noon Sat) Distributes maps of Port Louis and Mauritius, and can advise on car hire, excursions and hotels throughout the country.

ℹ Transport

GETTING THERE & AWAY
Bus

Port Louis' two bus stations are both located in the city centre. Buses for northern and eastern destinations, such as Trou aux Biches, Grand Baie and Pamplemousses, leave from Immigration Sq (Map p50), northeast of the Central Market. Buses for southern and western destinations, such as Mahébourg, Curepipe and Flic en Flac, use the Victoria Sq terminus (Map p50) just southwest of the city centre.

The first departure on most routes is at about 6am; the last leaves at around 6pm.

DESTINA-TION	FARE (RS)	DURA-TION (HR)	BUS STATION
Centre de Flacq	38	2	Immigration Sq
Curepipe	38	1	Victoria Sq
Grand Baie	38	1	Immigration Sq
Mahé-bourg	38	1½	Victoria Sq
Pample-mousses	33	½	Immigration Sq

Ferry
Ferries to Rodrigues and Réunion dock beside the passenger terminal on Quai D of Port Louis harbour, 1km northwest of town.
Coraline Shipping Agency (☑ 217 2285; www.mauritiusshipping.net; Nova Bldg, 1 Military Rd, Port Louis)

Taxi
Taxis from Port Louis to Grand Baie cost Rs 1000. To Flic en Flac it's Rs 1000, to Mahébourg it's Rs 1600 and to Belle Mare it's Rs 1800. If you'd prefer a private vehicle, contact any of the island's rental agencies – they'll deliver the car to your hotel.

GETTING AROUND
To/From the Airport
There are no special airport buses, but regular services between Port Louis and Mahébourg call at **Sir Seewoosagur Ramgoolam International Airport** (SSR; Map p106; ☑ 603 6000; aml.

mru.aero); the stop is roughly 300m from the terminal buildings, near the large roundabout. Heading to the airport from Port Louis, allow two hours to be on the safe side and make sure the conductor knows where you're going, as drivers occasionally skip the detour down to the airport.

Expect to pay Rs 1200 for a taxi from Port Louis to the airport – the ride takes at least one hour.

Car
Given the number of traffic snarls, it's not worth trying to drive around Port Louis. Day trippers are advised to leave their car in one of the car parks at Le Caudan Waterfront. These are open from 7am to 11pm and cost Rs 50 for the first four hours plus Rs 50 for each additional hour. The turn-off to Le Caudan is located at a marked roundabout south of the city centre. Thus, if you are coming from the northern part of the island, you must drive all the way through the city, past the waterfront complex, then make a U-turn back towards the city on a signposted side road.

Cars can be parked on the street for a maximum of two hours at a time; a marked parking coupon, available at any filling station and some smaller Chinese stores, must be displayed on the dashboard.

Taxi
As a general rule, do not take a taxi around the gridlocked city centre during daylight hours – you'll quickly notice that the pedestrians are moving faster than the cars. After dark, expect to pay Rs 100 to Rs 150 for a short taxi ride across town. Always agree on a price beforehand.

CENTRAL PLATEAU

Home to a large majority of Mauritians, the cool and rainy centre of the island feels, for the most part, like a continuation of the urban chaos in Port Louis. There's very little to see in the corridor of towns that runs almost unbroken from the capital to Curepipe; in fact, it's pretty much the opposite of that postcard your friends sent you from their trip here last year.

Even so, for tourists interested in learning about life on the island beyond the sand and sun, there are a few worthwhile attractions hidden among the gridiron, among them a dormant volcano; Eureka, a charming plantation home and museum in Moka; the shopping possibilities in Curepipe and Floréal; and what could be the world's only sugar-estate theme park, in Pailles.

Central Plateau

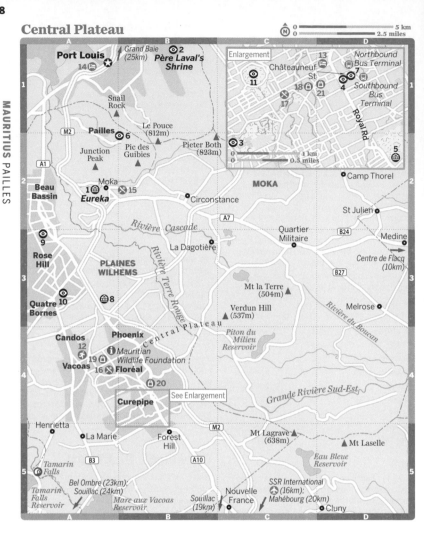

ℹ️ Getting There & Away

The Central Plateau towns are serviced by frequent bus connections with Port Louis. Other useful routes include the direct services between Quatre Bornes and Flic en Flac, on the west coast, and between Curepipe and Mahébourg, to the southeast; the latter service passes via the airport.

Pailles

POP 11,618

Just a few kilometres outside Port Louis, Domaine Les Pailles has transformed Pailles into a worthy destination for an enjoyable half-day excursion.

⊙ Sights & Activities

Domaine Les Pailles   AMUSEMENT PARK
(Map p58; ☑ 286 4225; www.domainelespailles. net; Rs 105; ⊙ 10am-4.30pm) The strange sugar-estate theme park of Domaine Les Pailles has been transformed into a cultural and heritage centre. Attractions include rides in horse-drawn carriages, a miniature railway, a working replica of a traditional ox-driven sugar mill, a rum distillery producing the es-tate's own brew, a spice garden, a quad-biking

Central Plateau

circuit and a playground. There is also a selection of upmarket restaurants. You pay for most of the attractions on top of the admission fee.

Les Écuries du Domaine HORSE RIDING
(☑286 4240; ☺8am-5.30pm Mon-Fri, to noon Sat) On weekdays it's possible to horseback ride around the Domaine Les Pailles estate. Call Les Écuries du Domaine to make a reservation.

❶ Getting There & Away

To get to the Domaine, take any bus running between Port Louis' Victoria Sq terminus and Curepipe and ask to be let off at the turn-off for Domaine Les Pailles (it's clearly signposted). From the main road it takes less than half an hour on foot to get to the reception centre. Alternatively, it's a 10-minute taxi ride from Port Louis or Moka.

Moka & Around

POP 8846

The most interesting of the Central Plateau towns, the country's academic centre and the official home of the president of Mauritius, Moka is a great place to visit for a taste of national history. The scenery is dramatic here, too, with waterfalls, valleys and the towering Le Pouce in the background. Moka's main attraction, though, is the captivating colonial mansion of Eureka. Almost perfectly preserved from the mid-19th century, it provides a window onto the island's plantation past.

◉ Sights

★**Eureka** HISTORIC BUILDING
(Map p58; ☑433 8477; www.maisoneureka. com; Moka; house Rs 300, house & waterfall Rs 400; ☺9am-5pm Mon-Sat, to 3.30pm Sun) If you're only going to visit one attraction related to Mauritius' rich colonial history, choose Eureka. This perfectly preserved Creole mansion was built in the 1830s and today it's a museum and veritable time machine providing incredible insight into the island's vibrant plantation past. The main manor house is a masterpiece of tropical construction, which apparently kept the interior deliciously cool during the unbearably hot summers, and boasts 109 doors and more rooms than a Cluedo board.

Rooms are adorned with an impeccably preserved collection of period furniture imported by the French East India Company – take special note of the antique maps, a strange shower contraption that was quite the luxury some 150 years ago and the mildewed piano with keys like rotting teeth.

The courtyard behind the main mansion contains beautifully manicured grounds surrounded by a set of stone cottages – the former servants quarters and kitchen. Follow the trail out the back for 15 minutes and you'll reach the lovely **Ravin waterfall**.

The estate's unusual name is believed to have been the reaction of Eugène Le Clézio when he successfully bid to purchase the house at auction in 1856.

HIKING THE CENTRAL PLATEAU

The mountain ranges fringing the Central Plateau offer some memorable rambles and hikes. Two of the best introductions to hiking in Mauritius are **Le Pouce** (812m), a thumb-shaped peak on the plateau's northern edge, and **Corps de Garde** (719m), a wedge-like ridge to the southwest that makes for a slightly more challenging endeavour.

Both hikes offer resplendent views down to the coastal plains but are best appreciated when tackled with a local guide, who can annotate the hike with detailed information about the flora and history. If you decide to go it alone, check out **Fitsy** (www.fitsy.com), a brilliant website that has mapped out the walks with extensive GPS and satellite detail. For planning purposes, allow about two hours for each hike if you're starting at the trailhead.

🛏 Sleeping & Eating

★ **Eureka Maison d'Hôte** GUESTHOUSE €€
(Map p58; ☑ 433 8477; www.maisoneureka.com; r incl breakfast Rs 3500) If you wish to spend the night at Eureka, a pair of authentic cottages on the property have been converted into lovely accommodation with ensuite facilities and kitchenettes. Both rooms at this *maison d'hôte* (guesthouse) have period furnishings from the French East India Company. The St George cabin, the smaller of the two units, was once the cell for the estate's priest.

★ **Escale Créole** MAURITIAN €€
(Map p58; ☑ 5422 2332; www.escalecreole.net; mains Rs 250-600; ☉ noon-3pm) Around 1km from Eureka, off Rte Bois Cheri, and well signposted all along the main road through Moka, this charming garden *table d'hôte* (privately hosted meal) serves up Mauritian specialities such as homemade Creole sausages and octopus bouillon with coconut chutney. Your hosts are the charming mother-daughter team of Majo and Marie-Christine. Bookings must be made at least a day in advance. Highly recommended.

★ **Eureka Table d'Hôte** MAURITIAN €€
(Map p58; ☑ 433 8477; www.maisoneureka. com; meals Rs 800; ☉ noon-3pm) Even if you don't stay overnight, to deepen your Eureka experience we recommend planning your visit around noon to enjoy a relaxing repast at the in-house *table d'hôte*. Sample an assortment of Mauritian classics like *marlin fumée* (smoked fish), lentils and curried fish while enjoying the delightful historical atmosphere. Call ahead, as sometimes the restaurant is closed for tour groups.

🛈 Getting There & Away

To get to Eureka, take a bus from Curepipe, or Victoria Sq in Port Louis, and get off at Moka. Eureka is signposted about 1km north of the bus stop. Otherwise, many hotels and most tour operators can organise half-day excursions here from anywhere on the island, and all taxi drivers know it.

Curepipe

POP 85,049

Effectively Mauritius' second city, Curepipe is a bustling highland commercial centre famous for its rainy weather, volcanic crater and retail shopping. Its strange name reputedly stems from the malaria epidemic of 1867, when people fleeing lowland Port Louis would 'cure' their pipes of malarial bacteria by smoking them here (although it's more likely that the area was named after a fondly remembered town in France).

Curepipe is the highest of the plateau towns. At 550m above sea level, it has refreshingly cool summer temperatures, but according to lowlanders, Curepipe has two seasons: the little season of big rains and the big season of little rains. The damp climate gives the buildings an ageing, mildewed quality. Bring an umbrella.

◉ Sights

Trou aux Cerfs VOLCANO
(Map p58) About 1km west of central Curepipe, the Trou aux Cerfs is a dormant-volcanic crater some 100m deep and 1km in circumference. The bowl is heavily wooded and from the road around the rim – a favourite spot for joggers and walkers – you get lovely views of the plateau. There are benches for rest and reflection, and a radar station for keeping an electronic eye on cyclone activity.

Botanical Gardens GARDENS
(Map p58; ☉ 6am-6pm May-Sep, 7am-7pm Oct-Apr) FREE The well-kept gardens of Curepipe were created in 1870 to foster foliage that thrived in cooler weather – the grounds in

Pamplemousses proved far too sweltering for certain species. It's not as spectacular as Pamplemousses, but it is much, much quieter.

Domaine des Aubineaux HISTORIC BUILDING
(Map p58; ☎676 3089; www.saintaubin.mu/larouteduthe; Royal Rd; adult/child Rs 350/175; ⊙9am-5pm Mon-Sat) The manor house of the Domaine des Aubineaux was built in 1872 in a classic colonial style; in 1889 it was the first residence on the island to be outfitted with electricity. The plantation was transformed into a museum in 2000, and today it marks the first stop on the historical Route du Thé (p121). Exotic plants fill the garden under the shade of camphor trees, and you can sip savoury teas in the converted billiard parlour.

Hôtel de Ville ARCHITECTURE
(Town Hall; Map p58; Châteauneuf St) Overlooking a small park in the centre of Curepipe, the Hôtel de Ville is one of Mauritius' best surviving structures from its colonial era. Notice the gable windows, veranda and decorative wooden friezes known as *dentelles* – all are signature traits of the island's early plantation architecture.

Carnegie Library LIBRARY, ARCHITECTURE
(Map p58; ☎674 2278; ⊙9.30am-6pm Mon-Fri, to 3pm Sat) FREE The stone building with the distinctive neoclassical porch houses the municipal Carnegie Library. Its collection includes rare books on Mauritius dating back to the 18th century.

MAURITIUS CUREPIPE

A TOUR OF THE CENTRAL PLATEAU

The area southeast of and inland from Port Louis can seem like one great conurbation, and in a sense it is. While most travellers pass right on by en route from coast to coast, there are enough sights to warrant a day or half-day excursion by taxi – we suggest you don't drive yourself or you'll waste valuable time trying to find each place. In addition to the following, consider adding the highlights of Moka, Pailles and Curepipe to your tour.

The town of **Rose Hill** (pronounced row-zeel by locals), wedged between Beau Bassin and Quatre Bornes in the heart of the Central Plateau's urban sprawl, is virtually a suburb of Port Louis. Here, architecture buffs will appreciate the unusual Creole structure housing the **Municipality of Beau Bassin-Rose Hill** (Map p58; St Jean Rd). The building was constructed in 1933 as a municipal theatre. The attractive Creole manse next door – **Maison Le Carne** (Map p58; St Jean Rd) – houses the Mauritius Research Council.

Another satellite of Port Louis, **Quatre Bornes** has little to detain you, other than on Thursday and Sunday, when scores of locals flock to the city to rummage through stall upon stall at the bustling produce and textile **market** (Map p58); there's also a popular vegie market on Saturday.

In **Phoenix**, the **Mauritius Glass Gallery** (Map p58; ☎696 3360; mgg@pbg.mu; Pont Fer, Phoenix; admission Rs 50; ⊙8am-5pm Mon-Fri, to noon Sat) produces unusual souvenirs made from recycled glass. You can see pieces being made using traditional methods in the workshop, which doubles as a small museum.

The neighbouring town of **Vacoas** is home to the oldest golf course in the Indian Ocean, **Mauritius Gymkhana Club** (Map p58; ☎696 1404; www.mgc.mu; Suffolk Close, Vacoas; green fees per person Rs 1500). It's the fourth-oldest fairway in the world (the three older courses are in Britain and India).

Another possibility is **Floréal**, the 'Beverly Hills' of Mauritius and a rather posh suburb northwest of Curepipe. The area has become synonymous with the high-quality knitwear produced by the Floreal Knitwear company. Fill your suitcase with clothes at **Floréal Square** (Map p58; ☎698 8011; Swami Sivananda Ave; ⊙9.30am-5.30pm Mon-Fri, to 4pm Sat), on the main road from Curepipe.

If you're in the neighbourhood, we highly recommend seeking out **La Clef des Champs** (Map p58; ☎686 3458; www.laclefdeschamps.mu; Queen Mary Ave; set menu per person from Rs 1250; ⊙noon-2pm & 7-11pm Mon-Fri), the *table d'hôte* – and pet project – of Jacqueline Dalais, chef to the stars. Known for her impressive library of self-created recipes, Jacqueline has earned quite the reputation on the island for her unparalleled cuisine: she is regularly called upon to cater for government functions, especially when foreign dignitaries are in town. Dishes served in her quaint dining room lean towards Provençal flavours; the presentation is exquisite.

🛏 Sleeping & Eating

Unless you're visiting family, it's hard to imagine why you'd want to stay in Curepipe – nowhere else on the island is more than an hour away by road, so the town is easily reached on a day trip.

Believe it or not, the cafeteria at the local hospital (Clinique de Lorette) serves a mean quiche at lunchtime – it's a local secret.

Auberge de la Madelon GUESTHOUSE €
(Map p58; ☑ 670 1885; www.auberge-madelon. com; 10 Sir John Pope Hennessy St; r €25-45; ✴@🛜) Excellent value and centrally located, this well-run place is simple, small and surprisingly stylish, boasting comfy ensuite rooms and a very helpful management.

La Potinière MAURITIAN €€
(Map p58; ☑ 670 2648; Bernardin de St-Pierre St; crêpes & mains from Rs 225; ⊘ 10am-3pm & 6.30-10pm Tue-Sat) Curepipe's most obviously upmarket restaurant hides in an unassuming concrete block, but inside all is starched linen and gleaming tableware. The menu features a selection of quintessential Mauritian eats: hearts of palm, wild boar and seafood.

🛍 Shopping

Curepipe is where the locals go to shop; you can find an incredible assortment of discounted items just by walking from the Royal College to the Arcade Currimjee.

Voiliers de l'Océan HANDICRAFTS
(Map p58; ☑ 674 6764, 676 6986; www.voiliers ocean.intnet.mu; Winston Churchill St; ⊘ 9am-6pm Mon-Sat) Travellers looking for model-ship showrooms and workshops should join the circuit and stop by Voiliers de l'Océan. Roughly 200 models are produced per month and visitors can watch the artisans at work.

Beauté de Chine ANTIQUES
(Map p58; ☑ 676 3270; Les Arcades, Rue du Jardin; ⊘ 9.30am-5.30pm Mon-Fri, to 1pm Sat) Beauté de Chine, one of the longest-running stores on the island, sells an assortment of old-world relics like copper, jade, silk and antique porcelain.

Galerie des Îles MALL
(Map p58; ☑ 670 7516; Arcade Currimjee; ⊘ 9.30am-5.30pm Mon-Sat) Galerie des Îles has a generous selection of local designs and artisans across more than a dozen shops.

ℹ Getting There & Away

Curepipe is an important transport hub, with frequent bus services to Port Louis (Victoria Sq), Mahébourg, Centre de Flacq, Moka and just about anywhere else on the island. There are two terminals: the northbound (Map p58) and the southbound (Map p58). Most services go from the northbound (Port Louis, Rose Hill, Quatre Bornes); southbound is served from the southbound. The terminals lie on either side of Châteauneuf St, at the junction with Victoria Ave.

From Curepipe, expect to pay Rs 1000 for a taxi ride to the airport, Rs 1700 to Grand Baie, Rs 1600 to Belle Mare, Rs 1000 to Port Louis, Rs 1000 to Flic en Flac and Rs 650 to Black River (Rivière Noire).

THE NORTH

Northern Mauritius puts on show the best and worst (such as it is) of the country's tourism. Grand Baie, the eye of the storm, has a somewhat over-hyped atmosphere, but it's the sort of place where you can take what you want – Mauritius' best nightlife, some excellent restaurants and numerous excursions, for example – and then head elsewhere.

As places to stay go, we prefer the smaller beachside villages around Grand Baie: Trou aux Biches, Mont Choisy, Cap Malheureux and Pereybère. They're quickly developing, but they generally retain the uncrowded beaches and village feel that first drew travellers to Mauritius.

The inland plain of sugar-cane fields – pocked with volcanic boulders stacked by indentured servants – is known as Pamplemousses and gently slopes towards the sea. Here you'll find a triptych of wonderful sites: Sir Seewoosagur Ramgoolam Botanical Gardens, Château Labourdonnais and L'Aventure du Sucre – a museum dedicated to Mauritius' traditional colonial export.

ℹ Getting There & Around

The most useful bus routes in and around this area are those running from Port Louis' Immigration Sq bus station along the coast road to Trou aux Biches, Grand Baie, Pereybère and Cap Malheureux. There are also express services direct from Port Louis to Grand Baie. Port Louis is the starting point for buses via Pamplemousses to Grand Gaube.

To reach this area from the airport, change buses in Port Louis. Alternatively, a taxi costs

Rs 800 from Port Louis to Balaclava, Rs 1000 to Grand Baie and Rs 1100 to Grand Gaube. Add Rs 1000 to/from the airport.

Most hotels and guesthouses have bikes for hire and can help organise car hire. Otherwise, you can approach the rental agencies directly. The largest concentration is in Grand Baie, and there is a smattering of outlets in and around Trou aux Biches and Pereybère.

Balaclava to Pointe aux Piments

Between sprawling Port Louis and busy Grand Baie, this stretch of coast from Balaclava (around 10km north of Port Louis) to Pointe aux Piments is quiet and pretty, with some good beaches, excellent hotels and a more tranquil air than those towns to the north and south.

◉ Sights

Rivulet Terre Rouge
Bird Sanctuary   WILDLIFE RESERVE
(Map p64; ☑217 2886; ⊙9am-2pm) FREE Just north of Port Louis, bird-watchers will want to take the signposted turn-off to the east that leads to the Rivulet Terre Rouge Bird Sanctuary. Sited on one of the largest estuary habitats in Mauritius, this Ramsar-recognised site draws countless migratory bird species, with large populations present from October to March in particular.

Baie de l'Arsenal Ruins   RUIN
(Map p64) You can still see the ruins of the French arsenal – along with a flour mill and a lime kiln – within the grounds of the Maritim Hotel at Baie de l'Arsenal, just south of Pointe aux Piments. Nonguests can obtain permission to visit the ruins from the security guard at the hotel entrance; the track begins about 30m inside the gate to the right.

Mauritius Aquarium   AQUARIUM
(Map p64; ☑261 4561; www.mauritiusaquarium. com; Coastal Rd, Pointe aux Piments; adult/child/ family Rs 250/125/650; ⊙9.30am-5pm Mon-Sat, 10am-4pm Sun) This small aquarium has a decent collection of tropical fish (including clownfish), but the real stars are the white-tip reef sharks and hawksbill turtles. There's daily shark feeding at 11am and fish feeding three times daily.

🛏 Sleeping

Accommodation along this stretch of coastline tends towards the upmarket and exclusive – at the southern end of things, there's very little passing traffic and few settlements, lending the hotels a true sense of blissful isolation.

★ **Le Récif Attitude**   HOTEL €€
(Map p64; ☑204 3820; www.recif-hotel-mauritius. com; Royal Rd, Pointe aux Piments; incl breakfast s/d garden view from €85/120, sea view €98/145; ✳@🛜🌊) Le Récif is a stylish three-star-superior beachfront resort with attractively turned-out rooms and a surprisingly reasonable price tag. The soothing public areas are riddled with pillow-strewn nooks, and there's a beachside bar, spa centre, plunge pool and plenty of the island's trademark thatch umbrellas.

★ **Oberoi**   HOTEL €€€
(Map p64; ☑204 3600; www.oberoihotels.com; Pointe aux Piments; r incl breakfast from €410, with private pool from €660; ✳@🛜🌊) Set in expansive gardens, the Oberoi boasts a gorgeous beach and stunning grounds, including a high-flowing waterfall that dominates the landscape. The select villas have their own pools and gardens; they enjoy total privacy, which makes them perfect for honeymooners. Inside it's all understated luxury, an inventive mix of African and Asian design.

Maritim Hotel   HOTEL €€€
(Map p64; ☑204 1000; www.maritim.mu; Royal Rd, Balaclava; s/d incl breakfast from €215/300; ✳@🛜🌊) German-owned Maritim Hotel has an enviable position out of the wind on Turtle Bay and attractive, luxury rooms. Its main plus is a 25-hectare park, complete with nine-hole golf course, tennis courts and riding stables. There's a great beach, with everything from snorkelling to waterskiing, and a choice of three restaurants, including a fantastic venue in a refurbished colonial manse.

❶ Getting There & Away

There are no bus services to Balaclava or Baie de l'Arsenal. A taxi from Port Louis will cost Rs 400 to 500, depending on your bargaining skills.

Trou aux Biches and Mont Choisy are served by buses running between Port Louis' Immigration Sq bus station and Cap Malheureux via Grand Baie. There are bus stops about every 500m along the coastal highway. A taxi from Port Louis to Grand Baie costs around Rs 600.

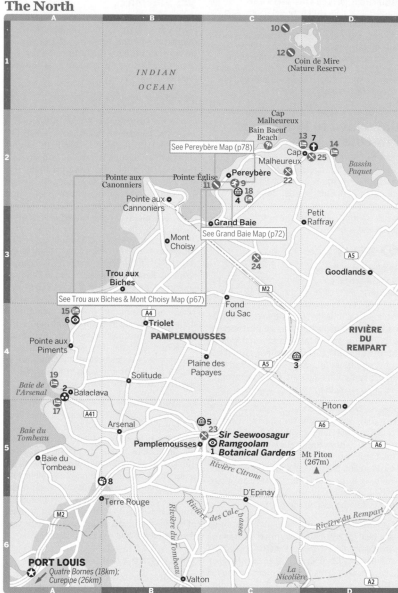

Trou aux Biches & Mont Choisy

Relaxed Trou aux Biches and neighbouring Mont Choisy (also spelt Mon Choisy) are fast-developing tourist destinations full of people seeking better (and quieter) beaches than those of Grand Baie. Trou aux Biches (Does' Watering Hole) enjoys gorgeous stretches of casuarina-lined sand that continue almost unbroken all the way to sleepy

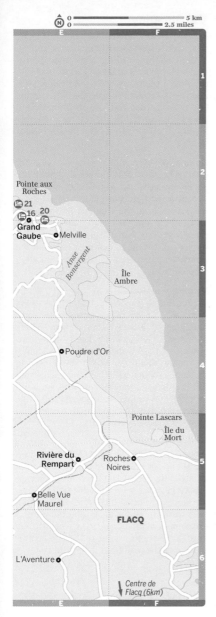

antly uncrowded during the week, although there's fierce competition for picnic spots on weekends.

🕴 Activities

Mont Choisy and Trou aux Biches are both important watersports centres. Activities on offer range from touring the lagoon in a glass-bottomed boat to parasailing, waterskiing, deep-sea fishing and diving.

Blue Safari Submarine   SUBMARINE
(Map p67; ☏ 265 7272; www.blue-safari.com; Royal Rd, Mont Choisy; adult/child Rs 4400/2700; ⊗9am-4pm) If you fancy diving but don't want to get wet, Blue Safari Submarine is a great option, taking you down among the coral to a depth

Mont Choisy. Trou aux Biches in particular has excellent places to stay and eat.

There's no doubt that development has begun to rob the area of its quiet, unspoilt feel, but it's still cheaper and far less hectic than Grand Baie. Even the beaches are pleas-

of 35m. The ride lasts roughly two hours, of which 40 minutes are spent underwater. Reservations recommended at least a day ahead. Hourly departures according to demand; no departures when seas are rough.

Boat House WATERSPORTS
(Map p67; ☑ 5727 0821; ☺ 9am-5pm) The boat house on Trou aux Biches' public beach rents out pedalos/kayaks/stand-up paddle boards (from Rs 700/400/1000 per hour) and offers a variety of other activities, including glass-bottomed boat tours (from Rs 600 per hour per person), inflatable-tube riding (Rs 600 per person) and parasailing (Rs 1600 per 10 minutes).

Diving

There are numerous Mont Choisy dive centres, charging around Rs 1500/2000 per day/night dive. They can arrange PADI-accreditation courses.

Dive Dream Divers DIVING
(Map p67; ☑ 265 5552; www.divedreamdivers. com; Mont Choisy; individual dive per person Rs 1500, pool training plus 1/2 sea dives per person Rs 2500/3500; ☺ 8.30am-4.30pm Tue-Sun) A PADI-accredited centre and excellent outfit offering some terrific packages for beginners. Off Trou aux Biches Rd.

Divers' Ocean DIVING
(Map p67; ☑ 265 5889; www.diversocean.com; Royal Rd, Mont Choisy; day/night dive Rs 1500/2000, pool training plus 1/2 sea dives Rs 2500/4000; ☺ 9am-4.30pm) French-run centre offering diving and undersea walks (Rs 1000 per person).

Blue Water Diving DIVING
(Map p67; ☑ 265 6700; www.bluewaterdiving center.com; Royal Rd, Mont Choisy; day/night dive Rs 1400/2200; ☺ 8am-4pm) A good option, Blue Water Diving caters to beginners and more experienced divers.

Horse Riding

The Maritim Hotel in Balaclava has an equestrian centre, while **Horse Riding Delights** (Map p67; ☑ 265 6159; www.horse ridingdelights.com; Mont Choisy Sugar Estate; adult/child Rs 2100/1900; ☺ 8.30am & 3pm Mon-Fri), an excellent riding school on the northern edge of Mont Choisy, offers 90-minute rides in over 200 hectares of land amid deer and giant tortoises.

🛏 Sleeping

It can seem as if almost every building along this stretch of coast is available for rent in some form. Much of the accommodation is in the midrange bracket and consists of self-catering apartments, villas and bungalows, often with terraces or balconies for viewing the sunset. What you lose in facilities and restaurants offered by the resorts and larger hotels you gain in privacy and the size of your rooms.

Be Cosy Apart Hotel APARTMENT €€
(Map p67; ☑ 204 5454; www.beapart.com; Trou aux Biches; studios/apt from €73/98; P ✴ ☞ ☀) The attractive new apartments here, off Royal Rd a block from the Trou aux Biches beach, all overlook the pool and there's a stylish cafe. Everything from the garden areas to the service needs time to mature a little, but the prices can be excellent value and the location is good.

Veranda Pointe aux Biches Hotel HOTEL, RESORT €€
(Map p67; ☑ 265 5901; www.veranda-resorts. com; Royal Rd, Trou aux Biches; r/f from €68/80; P ✴ ☞ ☀) Outrageously good value, this outpost of the Veranda chain mixes simplicity in the rooms (think pine bunk beds in the family rooms) with the reassuringly tropical surrounds of an upmarket resort: infinity pool, spa centre, watersports, kids club, more palm trees than we cared to count and hanging wicker swing-chairs.

Le Grand Bleu Hotel HOTEL €€
(Map p67; ☑ 265 5812; lgbtab@intnet.mu; Royal Rd; s/d incl half board €60/80; P ✴ ☞ ☀) Simplicity is the key at Le Grand Bleu, a lower-midrange hotel with friendly staff. Rooms are large but unexciting, the wi-fi is free but only works in public areas, and the value is excellent even though the food won't win any awards. The hotel is close to the dive centres but across the road from the beach.

★**Trou aux Biches Resort & Spa** HOTEL €€€
(Map p67; ☑ 204 6565; www.beachcomber-hotels.com/hotel/trou-aux-biches-resort-spa; Royal Rd, Trou aux Biches; r incl half board €118-762; ✴ @ ☞ ☀) Über-luxury is the name of the game at five-star Trou aux Biches Resort & Spa, with its clutch of traditionally inspired beachside suites and villas. The design

Trou aux Biches & Mont Choisy

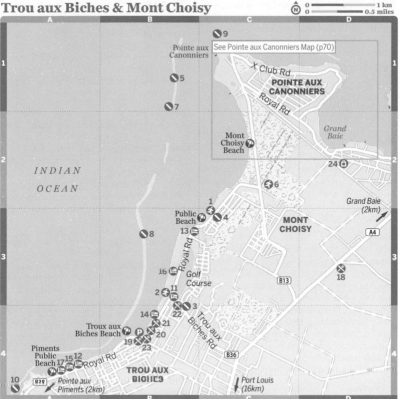

Trou aux Biches & Mont Choisy

scheme incorporates such rustic elements as thatch, wicker and hand-cut boulders into the unquestionably modern surrounds. Spas, pools and 2km of sand make this the most desirable address in Trou aux Biches.

★ **Le Sakoa** HOTEL €€€
(Map p67; ☑ 265 5244; www.lesakoa.com; Royal Rd, Trou aux Biches; d incl breakfast/half board from €195/250; ✳@🤝🏊) Easily the most stylish option in Trou aux Biches, Le Sakoa is instantly recognisable by its high-pitched roofs that match the neighbouring palms in both height and grandeur. Spacious accommodation is in wonderful two-storey thatched blocks radiating out from the fantastic beach. A charming dark-marble infinity pool anchors the hotel's centre, providing a luxurious setting for couples and families.

Bon Azur APARTMENT €€€
(Map p67; ☑ 204 6565; www.innlov.com/bon-azur-trou-aux-biches-mauritius/; Royal Rd, Trou aux Biches; apt from €250; P✳🤝🏊) Stylish, modern apartments, each with an expansive balcony overlooking the pool and small beach, make this a fine choice. The beach isn't really for swimming, but the whole set-up is excellent: numbers are kept to a minimum, families are welcome and it's a short drive (or longish walk) to the town's restaurant strip; you'll need a car for the supermarket.

Plage Bleu APARTMENT €€€
(Map p67; ☑ 265 6507; www.plage-bleue-appartements.com; Royal Rd, Trou aux Biches; 3-bedroom apt from €250; P✳🤝🏊) Large and luxurious serviced apartments on a quiet stretch of beach are what Plage Bleu is all about. Each has Weber gas barbecues, iPod docking stations and Nespresso coffee machines, and all face the sea. The beach is not really for swimming (it's lagoon mud underfoot), but that's the only fault we can find with this place.

Casuarina Hotel HOTEL €€€
(Map p67; ☑ 204 5000; www.hotel-casuarina.com; Royal Rd, Trou aux Biches; s/d incl breakfast from €150/225; ✳🤝🏊) Definitely one of the more interesting midrange places, Casuarina is decked out in a Moorish style that's matched by inventive apartment layouts. It's also pleasantly small and feels very relaxed. You have to cross the road to get to the beach and the cheaper rooms are a little overpriced, but otherwise this place is great.

✕ Eating

The competitive nature of Grand Baie's dining scene has begun to trickle down the coast. The increasingly broad selection of outlets caters for most tastes, with Trou aux Biches especially notable for its cluster of fine midrange options. It also has a supermarket (p69).

Kafé La Zétée CAFE €
(Map p67; ☑ 5767 4300; Trou aux Biches; Rs 250-350; ⊙9am-4pm Mon-Sat) A fresh and breezy alternative to its sister restaurant, La Pescatore, next door, Kafé La Zétée does breakfast, paninis, sandwiches, smoked-marlin salads and daily specials that might include *ceviche* (raw fish marinated in lemon and garlic) or tandoori chicken. Great coffee, too. It's off Royal Rd.

Bollywood Curry INDIAN €
(Map p67; ☑ 5758 2404; A4, Triolet; mains Rs 150-275; ⊙10.30am-2.30pm & 5.30-10.30pm; 🖍) Bollywood Curry serves out-of-this-world curries in über-basic surrounds (think buzzing neon bulbs and cracked tiles) – it doesn't get more authentic than this! Kormas, biryanis and masalas are all here, plus a few surprises. Coming from Grand Baie along the M2 and A4, it's around 500m on the left after the Mont Choisy turn-off.

La Marmite Mauricienne MAURITIAN €
(Map p67; ☑ 265 7604; Trou aux Biches Rd, Trou aux Biches; mains Rs 100-215; ⊙noon-2.30pm & 6-10pm) This basic but sweet place has a pleasant outdoor feel, with lots of tables on the terrace (although, sadly, it's on the rather busy Trou aux Biches Rd). The menu is Mauritian, featuring mostly seafood, noodles and curries.

Snack Kwan Peng CHINESE €
(Map p67; Royal Rd, Trou aux Biches; meals Rs 95; ⊙9am-4pm) Queues form here at lunchtime for some of the simplest and best Chinese food on the island. You basically put your own meal together by pointing to the pots you wish to try – beef, *boulettes* (small steamed dumplings in a variety of flavours), noodles, soup. Costs rarely jump above Rs 95 for a filling meal; drinks are extra.

L'Assiette du Nord INTERNATIONAL €
(Map p67; ☑ 265 7040; Trou aux Biches Rd, Trou aux Biches; mains Rs 100-650; ⊙noon-2.30pm & 6-10pm) At this popular place you can opt for the terrace or a slightly smarter dining area behind the fish-tank partition. Seafood

features strongly, served Chinese, Indian and Creole style. Try fish cooked in a banana leaf with Madras sauce or perhaps prawns in garlic butter.

Chez Popo SUPERMARKET €
(Map p67; ☑ 265 5463; Royal Rd, Trou aux Biches; ⊙ 9am-7pm Mon-Tue & Thu, 9am-8pm Fri & Sat, 10am-12.30pm Sun) In an area where self-catering apartments rule, a supermarket really matters. Chez Popo is well stocked, although parking is at a premium and opening hours can vary.

★Cabanne du Pêcheur MAURITIAN €€
(Map p67; ☑ 5711 2729; Royal Rd, Trou aux Biches; mains from Rs 450; ⊙ noon-10pm) You just don't get experiences like this if you never leave your resort. Run by Nathalie and her all-female crew, this seaside kiosk serves fabulous local specialities, among them prawns or fish in red Creole sauce and fish curry with eggplant. Servings are large and the ramshackle tables by the water could be our favourites along this stretch of coast.

★Café International INTERNATIONAL €€
(Flame Grill Cafe; Map p67; ☑ 5765 8735; Royal Rd, Trou aux Biches; mains Rs 300-850; ⊙ 3-10pm Tue-Fri, noon-10pm Sat & Sun) This popular South African–run spot serves up an excellent assortment of dishes from around the world. Burgers, curries, fresh fish and sandwiches are mainstays, but the highlights are the ribs and South African steaks that are so good we would (and, on at least one occasion, did) cross the island just to have them.

It's all watched over by friendly Deon (a former bodyguard for Nelson Mandela), and there's a secondhand bookshop as well.

★1974 ITALIAN, SEAFOOD €€
(Map p67; ☑ 265 7400; Royal Rd, Trou aux Biches; mains Rs 350-600; ⊙ 6.30-11pm Tue-Thu, noon-2.30pm & 6.30-11pm Fri & Sat, noon-5pm Sun) This fabulous place in warm terracotta hues is the work of Italians Antonio and Giulia. The food includes pasta and seafood with an emphasis on fresh local produce – the menu changes regularly.

Restaurant Souvenir MAURITIAN, INTERNATIONAL €€
(Map p67; ☑ 5291 1440; cnr Royal Rd & Trou aux Biches Rd, Trou aux Biches; mains Rs 150-540; ⊙ 9am-11pm) A wildly popular addition to the Trou aux Biches eating scene, Souvenir does everything from bog-standard Mauritian fried

noodles to steaks. The food is generally excellent, although service does go missing when things are busy (which is often); reservations are recommended at peak lunch and dinner times. There's also a well-stocked bar.

Le Pescatore SEAFOOD €€€
(Map p67; ☑ 265 6337; Mont Choisy; set menus Rs 1500-4000, mains Rs 850-1470; ⊙ noon-2pm & 7-9pm Mon-Sat) Wonderfully light decor and a great terrace overlooking the fishing boats set the scene for a truly superior eating experience. Dishes such as lobster in ginger and sake sauce should give you an idea of what to expect, but the fine set menus are all worth considering. It's off Royal Rd.

ⓘ Information

Shibani Foreign Exchange (☑ 265 5306; www.shibanifinance.com; Royal Rd, Mont Choisy; ⊙ 8am-5.30pm Mon-Sat, 8-11.30am Sun)

ⓘ Getting There & Away

Trou aux Biches and Mont Choisy are served by nonexpress bus services running between Port Louis' Immigration Sq bus station and Cap Malheureux via Grand Baie. There are bus stops about every 500m along the coastal highway.

A taxi to Grand Baie starts at around Rs 500, but fares depend on where your journey begins. It's Rs 600 to Pereybère.

ⓘ Getting Around

Figure on Rs 200 for a taxi ride in the Trou aux Biches/Mont Choisy area.

Grand Baie

POP 10,000

In the 17th century the Dutch used to call Grand Baie 'De Bogt Zonder Eynt', which meant the 'Bay Without End'. Today, it appears as though it's the development – not the bay – that's without end. Grand Baie has all the vices and virtues of beach resorts the world over. The virtues include good accommodation, bars and restaurants, while the vices can be found in water frontages consumed by concrete and touts, although the latter, in true Mauritian style, nudge rather than push. To escape the downtown scene, head for charming and quiet Pointe aux Canonniers.

⊙ Sights

Grand Baie's only specific sights are a couple of vividly colourful Tamil temples.

Pointe aux Canonniers

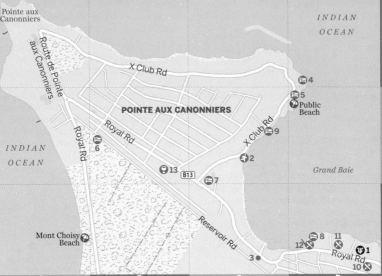

Pointe aux Canonniers

◎ Sights
1 Surya Oudaya Sangam D3

◎ Activities, Courses & Tours
2 Grand Baie Gym & Hydro Spa C2
3 Yacht Charters C3

◎ Sleeping
4 20° Sud D1
5 Baystone Hotel & Spa D2
6 Esprit Libre B2
7 Ocean Villas C2
8 Résidence Peramal D3
9 Sous Le Badamier C2

◎ Eating
10 Café Müller D3
11 Coolen – Chez Ram D3
12 Le Capitaine D3

◎ Drinking & Nightlife
13 Les Enfants Terribles B2

Surya Oudaya Sangam HINDU

(Map p70; Royal Rd; ⊗8am-5pm Mon-Sat) Surya Oudaya Sangam, located at the western end of town, is dedicated to Shiva. Visitors are welcome, but remove your shoes before entering.

Shiv Kalyan Vath Mandir HINDU

(Map p72; Royal Rd; ⊗8am-5pm Mon-Sat) Shiv Kalyan Vath Mandir is a vividly coloured Tamil temple that's older than Surya Oudaya Sangam. Remove your shoes before entering.

🏃 Activities

Grand Baie's prime attraction is the range of water-based activities on offer.

Croisières Australes BOAT TOUR

(☎263 1669; www.croisieres-australes.mu; adult €27-90, child €14-40) Arguably the most professional outfit in town, with a range of full- and half-day catamaran cruises.

Grand Bay Travel & Tours BOAT TOUR

(Map p72; ☎5757 8754, 263 8771; www.gbtt. com; Royal Rd) One of the more reliable operators in Grand Baie, this place offers full-day catamaran cruises to the northern islands from Rs 1600 per person, plus a range of other excursions.

Yacht Charters BOAT TOUR

(Map p70; ☎263 8395; www.isla-mauritia.com) Magnificent sailing ship the *Isla Mauritia* was built in 1852 and is claimed to be the world's oldest active schooner. Rates vary depending on season, itinerary and number of people.

Solar Sea Walk
ADVENTURE SPORTS

(Map p72; ☑263 7819; www.solarunderseawalk. com; Royal Rd; per person Rs 1700; ☺9am-4.30pm) For nondivers, Solar Sea Walk provides the unique experience of walking underwater while wearing a diver's helmet and weight belt. Solar-powered pumps on the boat above feed oxygen to you during the 25-minute 'walk on the wet side'. Walks are available to everyone over seven. In peak season it's advisable to book a day ahead. Last walk at 3pm.

Grand Baie Gym & Hydro Spa
GYM, SPA

(Map p70; ☑263 9290; 3 X Club Rd; day membership Rs 690; ☺7.30am-7.30pm) The Grand Baie Gym & Hydro Spa has a fabulous pool and gym, and you can indulge in a huge range of spa treatments, steam yourself in the *hammam* (Turkish bath) or enjoy lowfat dishes at the cafe across the street.

Skydive Mauritius
ADVENTURE SPORTS

(☑499 5551; www.skydivemauritius.com; sky dives Rs 13,000) 'Wanna get high?' asks Skydive Mauritius with a wink. This new outfit offers travellers a whole other way to check out the island – from 3000m in the air as you zoom towards the earth after jumping from a plane. It's based in a clearing towards Roches Noires in the east, but touts and transfers make Grand Baie a good departure point.

Sportfisher
FISHING

(Map p72; ☑263 8358; www.sportfisher. com; Royal Rd; half/full day per boat from Rs 23,000/26,450; ☺7am-6pm) Based beside the Sunset Blvd jetty, Sportfisher has four boats, each taking up to six people (three anglers and three companions). Remember its policy: 'All fish belong to the boat. However, should you wish to sample your fish we will gladly oblige'.

🛏 Sleeping

Grand Baie has two distinct classes of hotels: the grandiose resorts and the budget studios and apartments set back from the main drag. There are fewer luxury resorts in the area than one might think, although a clutch of smart hotels occupies the east side of the bay. Those for whom Grand Baie is just a little too busy might want to consider Pereybère nearby.

★ Sous Le Badamier
GUESTHOUSE €

(Map p70; ☑263 4391; www.souslebadamier. com; X Club Rd, Pointe aux Canonniers; incl breakfast s €51-66, d €60-78; ▣@◉) Once known as Chez Vaco for the artist's enchanting paintings

---

---

adorning almost every wall, this wonderful guesthouse now takes its name from the *badamier* trees that shade the charming entrance cloister. The delightful rooms are sponge painted in soothing tones and furnishings are accented with rattan – there's a warm minimalism here that feels stylish yet homely. This place is a real find.

Résidence Peramal
APARTMENT €

(Map p70; ☑263 8109; www.residence-peramal. com; Royal Rd; studios Rs 1200-1400, apt from Rs 2000; ▣) Excellent-value self-catering accommodation on a little promontory at the western entrance to Grand Baie.

Pépère Guest House
GUESTHOUSE, APARTMENT €

(Map p72; ☑263 5790; www.pepere-appartement. com; Royal Rd; s €20-30, d €30-40, 4-bed apt €50-60; ▣◉) Right in the heart of town, these simple, no-frills rooms are well priced and well maintained by the friendly owners. The property was for sale at the time of writing, so much could change by the time of your visit.

Trendzone Apartments
APARTMENT €€

(Map p72; ☑263 8277; www.trendzonemauritius. com; La Salette Rd; 1-/2-bedroom apt €55/80; ▣◉) Modern, if increasingly careworn, apartment units above the Trendzone boutique in the heart of town between Super U and the sea.

Grand Baie

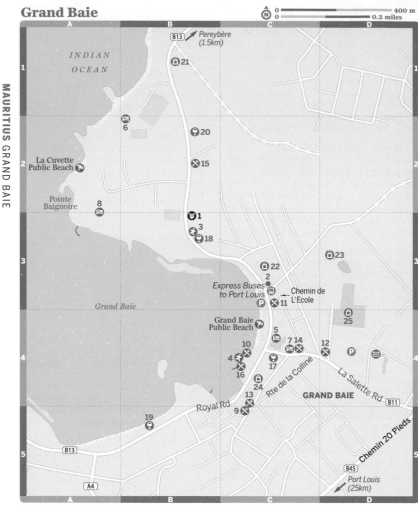

★ **Esprit Libre**   GUESTHOUSE €€
(Map p70; ☑ 269 1159; www.espritlibremaurice.
com; Rue Bourdet, Pointe aux Canonniers; incl
breakfast r €60-110, ste €90-140; ❋ ☎ ☲) Easily
among the best-value options on the island,
this charming guesthouse is run by two
friendly Québécois, Stéphane and André,
who manage their enclave of 'free spirits'
with one mantra in mind: customer service.
Rooms are simple and tastefully decorated
and the restaurant offers up an inventive
menu that has lured in a faithful crowd of
locals. It's well signposted off Royal Rd.

Ocean Villas   HOTEL €€
(Map p70; ☑ 263 6788; www.ocean-villas.com;
Royal Rd, Pointe aux Canonniers; r incl breakfast from
€40; ❋ @ ☎ ☲) Ocean Villas is recommended
for its broad range of accommodation, from
straightforward hotel rooms to self-catering
units for up to eight people and sleek honeymoon suites with sunken baths. Facilities include an excellent pool plus a small strip of
beach (with limited watersports on offer), a
restaurant and the love nest – a private house
on the beach.

Grand Baie

◎ Sights
1 Shiv Kalyan Vath Mandir........................ B3

◈ Activities, Courses & Tours
2 Grand Bay Travel & Tours C3
3 Solar Sea Walk B3
4 Sportfisher.. C4

⊜ Sleeping
Grand Bay Travel & Tours ....(see 2)
5 Pépère Guest House C4
6 Royal Palm... B2
7 Trendzone Apartments.......................... C4
8 Veranda Hotel A2

⊗ Eating
9 Boulette Ti Kouloir.................................. C5
10 Café de Grand Baie Plage...................... C4
11 Cocoloko C3
12 Happy Rajah D4

13 La Rougaille Créole C4
14 Lazy Dodo... C4
15 Luigi's... B2
Sauterelle ....(see 24)
16 Sunset Cafe... C4

⊜ Drinking & Nightlife
17 B52 .... C4
18 Banana Bar... B3
19 Beach House.. B5
20 Stardance... B2
Zanzibar...(see 18)

⊜ Shopping
21 Del Sol B1
22 Galerie Vaco... C3
23 Grand Baie Bazaar D3
24 Sunset Boulevard.................................... C4
25 Super U Hypermarket.............................. D4

★ 20° Sud
HOTEL €€€

(Map p70; ☑ 263 5000; www.20degressud.com; X Club Rd, Pointe aux Canonniers; d incl half board from €225; ❄@🕿🌊) Perhaps the boutiquiest resort on the island, 20° Sud has a cache of chic, plantation-inspired rooms. Walls are lavished with prim white paint, accented by draped linen and elegant dark-wood mouldings. Palatial oak doors initiate guests into the vine-draped public area, a lush palm grove with an inviting swimming pool and a cosy lodge-style library. Children under 12 not allowed.

Baystone Hotel & Spa
BOUTIQUE HOTEL €€€

(Map p70; ☑ 209 1900; www.baystone.mu; X Club Rd; incl half board r with sea view/direct beach access €350/390; 🅿❄@🕿🌊) On a lovely quiet stretch of beach that looks across the bay at the town, this classy boutique hotel is one of our favourite upmarket places in Grand Baie. Intimate where so many high-end hotels sprawl impersonally, this is luxury with a personal, discreet touch. The rooms are flooded with natural light and are supremely comfortable.

Royal Palm
HOTEL €€€

(Map p72; ☑ 209 8300; www.beachcomber-hotels.com/hotel/royal-palm; r per person from €375; ❄@🕿🌊) The flagship of the Beachcomber group, the Royal Palm is the pinnacle of luxury and a veritable playground for the rich and famous. Staff don safari-butler uniforms (stylish pith helmets!), and meticu-lously arranged bouquets are the centrepiece of every room. The hotel is off Royal Rd.

Veranda Hotel
HOTEL €€€

(Map p72; ☑ 209 8000; www.veranda-resorts.com; s/d incl breakfast from €110/160; ❄@🕿🌊) The rather elegant public areas here give the Veranda a sense of exclusivity unusual for the price bracket. The two pools, good facilities and relatively recent refit of the rooms also help. The beach is fine, but no great shakes, although the location is handy for town and there's a full-service spa to help with relaxation. It's off Royal Rd.

✖ Eating

While the centre of town is packed with eateries, the very best tend to be slightly outside the heart of Grand Baie, particularly towards Pointe aux Canonniers and Pereybère. Street vendors and vegetable stands can be found all along Royal Rd. They tend to be concentrated near the public beaches.

★ Domaine
MAURITIAN €

(Map p64; ☑ 263 5286; Narainen St, Upper Vale, The Vale; mains Rs 75-150; ⏱4-11pm Mon, 11am-11pm Tue-Sun) 'Domaine' is the answer every local offers when travellers ask where to go to savour some Mauritian home cookin'. The best dishes are those starred on the menu as local specialities – offerings such as *ourite safrané* (octopus cooked in ginger, garlic and turmeric) and chilli lamb. It can be hard to find and you'll need a private vehicle or taxi.

BOAT TRIPS TO THE NORTHERN ISLANDS

Coin de Mire, Île Plate & Îlot Gabriel

The distinctive Coin de Mire (Gunner's Quoin), 4km off the coast, was so named because it resembles the *quoin* (wedge) used to steady the aim of a cannon. The island is now a nature reserve and home to a number of rare species, such as the red-tailed tropicbird and Bojer's skink. None of the major catamarans stop here, as landing is often difficult. Despite the island's striking shape there's not much to see here anyway – it's the kind of place that looks much better from far away.

Most operators take you to the lagoon between Île Plate and Îlot Gabriel, 7km further north, which offers good snorkelling. Barbecue lunches are served on a sandy patch of Îlot Gabriel.

Boats to the islands depart from Grand Baie. You can book online at www.catamaran cruisesmauritius.com, through any local tour agent or directly with the cruise companies. Prices are Rs 1000 to Rs 1500 per person, including lunch. If you travel by speedboat, the price increases to around Rs 2000.

Île Ronde & Île aux Serpents

Île Ronde (Round Island) and Île aux Serpents (Snake Island) are two significant nature reserves about 20km and 24km, respectively, from Mauritius. It is not possible to land on them. Ironically, Île Ronde is not round and has snakes, while Île aux Serpents is round and has no snakes; the theory is that an early cartographer simply made a mistake.

Île Ronde covers roughly 170 hectares and scientists believe it has more endangered species per square kilometre than anywhere else in the world. Many of the plants, such as the hurricane palm (of which one lonely tree remains) and the bottle palm, are unique to the island. The endemic fauna includes the keel-scaled boa and the burrowing boa (possibly extinct), three types of skink and three types of gecko. Among the seabirds that breed on the island are the wedge-tailed shearwater, the red-tailed tropicbird and the gadfly (or Round Island) petrel. Naturalist Gerald Durrell gives a very graphic description of the island in his book *Golden Bats and Pink Pigeons*.

The smaller Île aux Serpents (42 hectares) is a renowned bird sanctuary. The birds residing on the island include the sooty tern, the lesser noddy, the common noddy and the masked (blue-footed) booby. Nactus geckos and Bojer's skinks are also found here.

Local recommendations mean that this inland haunt is starting to fill up with tourists. Go quick before someone else lets the cat out of the bag or tells the owner that his prices are remarkably low!

Take the M2 towards Port Louis, then turn left off the motorway at the first roundabout and follow the signs to The Vale. Once in the village, look for the 'Snack Mustapha' sign where the main road doglegs left – turn hard right and then take the second paved road on the left, around 250m down the hill.

★ **Boulette Ti Kouloir**　　MAURITIAN €
(Map p72; boulettes Rs 7, noodles Rs 80-90; ⊙11.30am-4pm & 6-9.30pm Mon-Sat, 5.30-9.30pm Sun) Off Royal Rd, this is one of Grand Baie's best snack joints. As the name suggests, this microscopic place really is just a *ti couloir* (li'l hallway), where Yvonne and friends cook up *boulettes* and piled-high bowls of fried noodles to lines of locals. For the *boulettes*, choose among chicken, pork, fish, calamari and lamb.

To get here, follow the low-slung billboard for La Rougaille Créole, pass the car park for the Sunset Boulevard shopping centre, then turn right – it's around 50m further along on the right, next to La Rougaille Créole.

Lazy Dodo　　MAURITIAN, EUROPEAN €
(Map p72; ☑263 6926; La Salette Rd; mains Rs 250-395; ⊙8am-9pm Mon-Sat) This cool roadside place has a handful of special deals (salad and curry from Rs 540, lunch main with chips, salad or rice for Rs 295) and does assured Mauritian and French cooking in a casual setting with smooth lounge music on the sound system. It's one of the best all-round deals for food and atmosphere in town.

Luigi's ITALIAN €
(Map p72; ✆269 1125; luigis.restaurant.mu; Royal Rd; pizza Rs 170-300, mains Rs 230-550; ☺6-10.30pm Tue-Thu, 6-11pm Fri, noon-2.30pm & 6-11pm Sat) There are no frilly adornments at this place, just good wood-fired pizzas, excellent pasta dishes and a breezy dining area. No wonder it's full most of the time.

★**Sauterelle** MAURITIAN, FRENCH €€
(Map p72; ✆263 8836; www.sauterellerestaurant. mu; Royal Rd; mains Rs 390-890; ☺noon-2.30pm & 7-10pm Tue-Sat, 7-10pm Mon) Rising above the Sunset Boulevard shopping precinct, this oasis of sophistication is a fine choice. Dishes range far and wide, and include roasted red-snapper fillet with grapefruit-and-rosemary sauce and prawn curry with green tea–infused noodles. Service is attentive and the food rarely misses a beat.

La Rougaille Créole MAURITIAN €€
(Map p72; ✆263 8449; mains Rs 350-800; ☺12.30-2.30pm & 7.30-10.30pm) Tucked away off Royal Rd behind the Sunset Boulevard shopping centre, but well signposted, this friendly place does local dishes extremely well without asking you to pay over the odds. The crab stir-fry and red fish in Creole sauce both caught our eye.

Café de Grand Baie Plage INTERNATIONAL €€
(Map p72; ✆263 7041; Royal Rd; mains Rs 490-850; ☺10am-10pm) The food here's a good, if unexceptional, selection of grilled meats, seafood dishes and other local and international staples, but you come for the views of the bay from a perch right above the water. Reservations are essential for lunch and dinner, especially if you'd like a front-row seat.

Sunset Cafe CAFE €€
(Map p72; ✆263 4172; Royal Rd; mains Rs 250-690; ☺8am-10.30pm) Pastas (including a few gluten-free options), grills and sandwiches make up a fairly generic international menu here, but the waterfront location makes it great for a meal or a milkshake at any time.

Happy Rajah INDIAN €€
(Map p72; ✆263 2241; www.happyrajah.com; La Salette Rd; Rs 290-650, lunch specials from Rs 230; ☺11.30am-2.30pm & 6-10.30pm) Right next to the entrance of the Super U Hypermarket, on the 1st floor, this well-regarded Indian restaurant serves all the usual suspects. If you're going to splurge, do it with the lobster masala. Otherwise, curries, tikkas and tandooris dominate, while the lunchtime thalis are similarly excellent.

Cocoloko INTERNATIONAL €€
(Map p72; ✆263 1241; Royal Rd; tapas Rs 175, mains Rs 295-725; ☺9am-11pm; ☎) Arranged around an inviting pebble-strewn courtyard across the street from the beach, Cocoloko brings a slice of cool and wannabe sophistication to downtown Grand Baie. Familiar international fare won't inspire devotion, but the atmosphere is very conducive to coffee, cocktails and outdoor dining. There are salads, steaks, tapas, sandwiches and pizza (or 'Pizzaloko', as it's known).

Throw in free wi-fi, live music most nights and a happy hour that runs from 4pm to 8pm, and there's a lot to be said for letting a long, lazy afternoon here segue effortlessly into the evening.

Coolen – Chez Ram MAURITIAN, SEAFOOD €€
(Map p70; ✆263 8569; Royal Rd; mains Rs 260-480; ☺11.30am-2pm & 6.30-10pm Thu-Tue) The clear favourite among Royal Rd's parade of restaurants, Coolen is often filled with locals. Customers are welcomed with a splash of rum while they thumb through the menu of Creole, North Indian and seafood staples. The octopus curry with papaya is terrific, and save room for the banana flambé.

Café Müller CAFE €€
(Map p70; ✆263 5230; Royal Rd; breakfast/ brunch buffet Rs 310/450, Fri buffet & grill adult/ child Rs 450/225; ☺8am-5pm Mon-Fri, to 4pm Sat) This charming German-run option is a great place for cakes, crêpes, coffee and juices; it also offers an excellent Saturday brunch in its lovely grassy garden and a daily breakfast buffet. On Friday it does a buffet and grill from noon to 2pm.

Le Capitaine SEAFOOD €€€
(Map p70; ✆263 6867; www.lecapitaine.mu; Royal Rd; mains Rs 590-1950; ☺noon-3pm & 6.30-10.30pm) This popular place serves good, seafood dishes in a convivial space that combines style with informality and partial bay views. Fresh lobster is the pick of a menu that ranges across island specialities, while other delicious mains include whole crab cooked in white wine, and lobster ravioli with fresh mushroom and cucumber quenelles. Reservations are essential in the evening.

🍷 Drinking & Nightlife

If you're looking for a party in Mauritius, you'll find it in Grand Baie. Many of the area's restaurants – including Cocoloko – have buzzing nightlife as well. Out near Luigi's (p75) just north of the town centre, nightclubs wax and wane with the seasons, but it's always worth checking what's happening.

★ Les Enfants Terribles   CLUB
(Ferrari Club; Map p70; ☑ 5263 1076; Royal Rd, Pointe aux Canonniers; ⊙ 7pm-3am Fri & Sat) The top pick for a night out on the town, the 'little terrors' has a roaring dance floor, a chilled-out lounge and a special VIP section that overflows with champagne. Walls bedecked with hundreds of crinkled photos of partiers confirm the sociable local vibe.

Beach House   BAR
(Map p72; ☑ 263 2599; www.thebeachhouse. mu; Royal Rd; ⊙ 11.30am-late Tue-Sun) Owned by Kabous Van der Westhuisen, a South African former rugby player, this lively joint bustles with about as much energy as a sports match in overtime. The owner is sometimes seen roaming around shirtless signing autographs. The unbeatable location is a major draw: the bar is smack-dab along the lapping waves of Grand Baie's emerald lagoon.

B52   COCKTAIL BAR
(Map p72; ☑ 263 0214; cnr La Salette & Royal Rds; ⊙ 10am-midnight Mon-Sat) This large, popular spot serves up great cocktails all day long in its open-air setting in the heart of town.

Stardance   CLUB
(Map p72; ☑ 5977 5566; Royal Rd; admission Rs 250; ⊙ 10pm-4am Fri & Sat) Nightclubs come and go in this corner of town, so whether it's called Stardance or something else, there's almost guaranteed to be a nightclub here. Stardance, if it lasts, does big themed nights, with some of the island's best DJs.

Zanzibar   CLUB
(Map p72; ☑ 263 0521; Royal Rd; ⊙ 11.30pm-late) Next to Banana Bar and the petrol station, this club has changed names numerous times over recent years, but there's always plenty going on. The dance floor is usually packed and the music is ideal for waving your hands in the air like you just don't care. A good in-town option.

Banana Bar   BAR
(Map p72; ☑ 263 0326; www.bananabeachclub. com; Royal Rd; admission Rs 150; ⊙ 10am-3am Mon-Sat, noon-3am Sun) In a petrol-station parking lot, this is one of the best spots for a drink and a chat. There's also live music at 8.30pm Wednesday to Saturday.

🛍 Shopping

Sunset Boulevard   SHOPPING CENTRE
(Map p72; Royal Rd) Sunset Boulevard, which sits either side of Royal Rd in the heart of town, is home to chic boutiques, including knitwear specialists Floreal, Maille St and Shibani; Harris Wilson for menswear; and Hémisphère Sud for fabulous leather goods.

Françoise Vrot   ARTS
(Map p67; ☑ 263 5118; Reservoir Rd; ⊙ 10am-1pm & 3-6.30pm) To purchase some original art, visit the studio of Françoise Vrot to see her expressive portraits of women fieldworkers.

Grand Baie Bazaar   HANDICRAFTS
(Map p72; ⊙ 9.30am-4.30pm Mon-Sat, to noon Sun) Hidden down an inland street away from Royal Rd, this market has a broad range of touristy Mauritian and Malagasy crafts. Prices aren't fixed, but wares aren't expensive and there's minimal hassling from vendors.

Galerie Vaco   ARTS
(Map p72; ☑ 263 6862; Dodo Sq; ⊙ 10am-5pm Mon-Sat) Head to Galerie Vaco, off Royal Rd behind Galito's Restaurant, to buy one of Vaco Baissac's instantly recognisable works.

Del Sol   ACCESSORIES
(Map p72; ☑ 757 4917; www.delsol.com; Royal Rd; ⊙ 10am-6pm Mon-Sat) Intriguing light-sensitive Del Sol products, from T-shirts to nail polish, are sold at a friendly boutique in Ventura Plaza.

Super U Hypermarket   SUPERMARKET, BOOKS
(Map p72; La Salette Rd; ⊙ 9am-8.30pm Mon-Thu, to 9.30pm Fri & Sat, to 4.30pm Sun) Around 250m inland from Grand Baie's main drag, the vast Super U Hypermarket is by far the best supermarket on the island and sells almost everything, including the north's best range of books and magazines.

ℹ Information

Cybercafes come and go in Grand Baie, with very few lasting longer than a season or two. Wander along the main street in the town centre and you're bound to find one.

Mauritius Commercial Bank (MCB; Royal Rd; ⊙ bureau de change 8am-6pm Mon-Sat, 9am-noon Sun) Has an ATM.

Thomas Cook (Royal Rd; ⊘8.30am-4.45pm Mon-Sat, to 12.30pm Sun) The best of the nonbank moneychangers.

ⓘ Getting There & Away

There are no direct buses to Grand Baie from the airport, so it's necessary to change in Port Louis and transfer between two bus stations to do so. Almost all people will have a transfer provided by their hotel; for others arriving after a 12-hour flight, we definitely suggest taking a taxi – or, better still, order one in advance via your hotel if your hotel is not one of the big players.

Express buses (Map p72) run directly between Immigration Sq in Port Louis and Grand Baie every half-hour. The terminus for express buses to/from Port Louis (Rs 38) is on Royal Rd about 100m north of the intersection of Royal and La Salette Rds. Nonexpress buses en route to Cap Malheureux will also drop you in Grand Baie. Buses between Pamplemousses and Grand Baie leave roughly every hour. Nonexpress services via Trou aux Biches stop every few hundred metres along the coast road.

Expect to pay Rs 2000 for a taxi to/from the airport. A return trip to Pamplemousses, including waiting time, should set you back Rs 600 or so.

ⓘ Getting Around

BICYCLE

Many hotels and guesthouses can arrange bicycle hire, and some even do so for free. Otherwise, rates vary, but expect to pay between Rs 150 and Rs 250 per day, less if you hire for several days. Most of the local tour operators have bikes for rent; just walk down Royal Rd and see what's on offer.

CAR

There are numerous car-hire companies in Grand Baie, and there's ABC (p80) in nearby Pereybère, so you should be able to bargain, especially if you're renting for several days. Prices generally start at around Rs 1000 per day for a small hatchback. Find out whether the management of your hotel or guesthouse has a special discount agreement with a local company. Motorbikes of 50cc and 100cc are widely available in Grand Baie; rental charges hover at around Rs 500 per day, less if you rent for several days.

Pereybère

POP 8450

As development continues to boom along the north coast, it's becoming rather difficult to tell where Grand Baie ends and Pereybère (peu-ray-bear) begins. This area is very

PEREYBÈRE'S SAND SCULPTOR

There are many reasons to visit Pereybère's main beach, but one of the more unusual is to witness the extraordinarily skilful sand sculptures of local resident Sanjay Jhowry. Twice a week for the past 10 years, the friendly Sanjay has sculpted sand into the finest of forms, from above-average sand castles to 6m-high masterpieces that take two days to complete; on the day we visited he had produced a wonderful rendition of the Eiffel Tower. On most days, the tide washes away his handiwork, but ask to see his photo album, which contains the more-than-400 sculptures he has created over the years.

much the second development on the north coast after Grand Baie and has found the sweet spot between being a bustling tourist hub and a quiet holiday hideaway, although it leans more towards the former with each passing year.

◉ Sights

Galerie du Moulin Cassé GALLERY
(Map p64; ☑263 0672; Old Mill Rd (Chemin de Vieux Moulin Cassé); ⊘10am-6pm Fri) Housed in a charmingly restored sugar mill, the Galerie du Moulin Cassé features the vibrant floral scenes of painter Malcolm de Chazal (1902-82) and a collection of photographs by Diane Henry. The most impressive display, however, is the collection of over 20,000 terracotta pots lining the vaulted arcs of the ceiling.

Lookout VIEWPOINT
(Map p78) Good views of the coast and northern islands.

🏃 Activities

Ocean Spirit Diving DIVING
(Map p78; ☑263 4428; www.osdiving.com; Royal Rd; 1/3 dives Rs 1200/3360; ⊘8am-4.30pm) French-run and with an office on the main road in town, this recommended outfit is the pick of the dive centres in Pereybère itself.

Orca Dive Club DIVING
(Map p64; ☑5940 2016; www.orca-diveclub-merville.com) This professional German-run dive centre is based at the Merville Hotel, between Pereybère and Grand Baie.

Pereybère

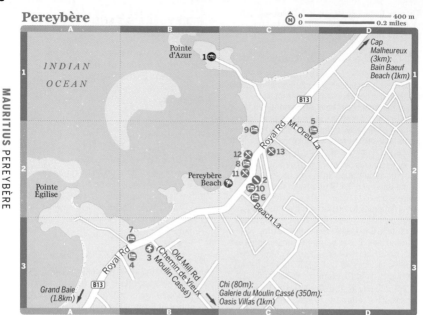

Pereybère

⦿ Sights
1 Lookout...B1

➕ Activities, Courses & Tours
2 Ocean Spirit Diving...............................C2
3 Surya Ayurvedic Spa............................B3

🛏 Sleeping
4 Bleu de Toi...B3
5 Casa Florida Hotel & Spa....................C2
6 Flowers of Paradise Hotel...................C2
7 Hibiscus Hotel..B3
8 Le Beach Club...C2
9 Ocean Beauty..C2
10 Pereybère Hotel & Apartments..........C2

✖ Eating
11 Caféteria Pereybère..............................C2
12 Sea Lovers Restaurant.........................C2
13 Wang Thai...C2

Surya Ayurvedic Spa SPA

(Map p78; ☎263 1637; www.suryaspa.com; Royal Rd; ☺9am-8pm) For some indulgent relaxation, head to the very smart Surya Ayurvedic Spa and treat yourself to an Indian massage or a steam in the *hammam*.

Chi SPA

(The Spa; Map p64; ☎263 9621; Old Mill Rd (Chemin de Vieux Moulin Cassé); ☺9am-7pm) The 90-minute 'Chi Balance' (a foot bath with five essential-element oils) costs Rs 1375 – quite reasonable when compared to the prices of the in-house spas at the surrounding hotels.

🛏 Sleeping

While there are a few larger hotels on the beach side of the main road, most accommodation here consists of charming guesthouses and little hotels in the backstreets, a short walk from the town centre and public beach.

⭐ **Bleu de Toi** GUESTHOUSE €€

(Map p78; ☎269 1761; www.bleudetoi.mu; Coastal Rd; r from €92; ❋@🛜⛱) Owned by friendly Belgians, this lovely B&B is the area's only worthy contender in the guesthouse category. Rooms feature simple yet tasteful furnishings, and adorable arched doorways abound. Don't miss the charming *table d'hôte* (€12 to €18) in the evenings. Things also get cheaper the longer you stay. No children are allowed.

Flowers of Paradise Hotel HOTEL €€

(Map p78; ☎5934 5320; www.hotel-paradise-mauritius.mu; Beach Lane; incl breakfast s €75-90, d €90-110; ❋🛜⛱) Set back from the main road, but a short walk from the beach, this gorgeous hotel has a vaguely boutique feel, with beautifully appointed rooms and good service. Highly recommended.

Hibiscus Hotel
HOTEL €€

(Map p78; ☑ 263 8554; www.hibiscushotel.com; Royal Rd; incl half board s €90-125, d €125-180; ❊ 🛜 ☲) Hibiscus boasts a stone path that wends past thick jungle-like gardens, a super pool and a private beach of sorts (although there's quite a bit of rock to negotiate). Accommodation is in clean, comfortable rooms in three-storey blocks. The wooden furniture is somewhat heavy.

Le Beach Club
HOTEL €€

(Map p78; ☑ 263 5104; www.le-beach-club.com; Royal Rd; r with sea/garden view from €95/75, 4-bed apt from €125; ❊ 🛜) This complex of studios and two-bedroom apartments is one of the few places on the seafront and has a great little beach perfect for swimming. Rooms have festive tropical colours and the location's brilliant. Complaints? We're nitpicking, but rooms are starting to look a little dated and the common areas are so tiny they feel like storage spaces for stacked furniture.

Plan your check-in time before arriving – the reception has limited hours.

Ocean Beauty
HOTEL €€

(Map p78; ☑ 263 6039; www.ocean-beauty.com; Pointe d'Azur; r incl breakfast €60-225; ❊ @ 🛜 ☲) Aimed squarely at honeymooners, this hotel is boutique in the sense of having an intimate feel, but it's also basic: the rooms are stylish and atmospheric, but there's very little else to the hotel. Despite this, it's a great spot for romance – breakfast is served on your balcony and there's direct access to the lovely town beach.

Casa Florida Hotel & Spa
HOTEL €€

(Map p78; ☑ 262 6208; web.casaflorida.net; Mt Oreb Lane; s/d incl breakfast Rs 1750/2140; ❊ 🛜 ☲) Friendly staff and attractive rooms swathed in earth tones make this place a well-priced Pereybère option. It's a five-minute walk to the beach.

Pereybère Hotel & Apartments
HOTEL €€

(Map p78; ☑ 263 8320; www.pereyberehotel.com; Royal Rd; d/apt/ste €56/70/75; ❊ @ 🛜 ☲) Right in the thick of things and across the road from the public beach, this old-timer looks dated from the front, but the rooms are surprisingly neat. The promised sea views are more like

peer-hopefully-through-the-trees-in-search-of-the-sea views. And the Jacuzzis promised in some rooms are actually just showers with fancy nozzles and buttons.

Oasis Villas
VILLA €€€

(Map p64; ☑ 422 8435; www.oasis-villas-mauritius.com; Old Mill Rd (Chemin de Vieux Moulin Cassé); villas from €222; ❊ 🛜 ☲) Trendy Asian-inspired decor enhances the lavish open-air floor plans. Security is tight, privacy is sacred and there's a real sense of being a VIP. The only downside is that you'll need a private vehicle to get to the beach. The villas are a steal if you're travelling with family or friends.

🍴 Eating

Pereybère has a handful of good places to eat, although the choice is much larger in Grand Baie.

Cafétéria Pereybère
CAFE €

(Map p78; ☑ 263 8539; Royal Rd; mains Rs 250-620; ⊙ 10.30am-10pm) This friendly all-day, no-frills cafe-restaurant behind the public beach offers uninspired grilled fish, curries, and steak and chips from an extensive menu. Portions are on the small side and it's cash only. Come for the proximity to the beach and the low prices, rather than the quality of the cooking.

⭐ Wang Thai
THAI €€

(Map p78; ☑ 263 4050; www.thai.mu; Royal Rd; mains Rs 290-490, set menus Rs 250-500; ⊙ noon-2.30pm Tue & Wed, noon-2.30pm & 6-10pm Thu-Sun) Long the best restaurant in town and a pioneer of authentic Thai food in Mauritius, Wang Thai is a sophisticated, airy place with Buddha statues and raw silks setting the scene for surprisingly affordable cuisine. Treat your taste buds to such classics as *tom yum thalay* (lemongrass-laced seafood soup), green curry, fish in tamarind sauce or *phad thai* (mixed fried noodles).

Sea Lovers Restaurant
SEAFOOD €€

(Map p78; ☑ 263 6299; Royal Rd; mains Rs 350-750; ⊙ noon-2.30pm & 6-9pm Wed-Mon) This is undoubtedly the area's smartest restaurant setting, with a gorgeous terrace built right into the sand and unquestionably stylish furniture. The service, however, can be a bit lacking and the food doesn't live up to the locale. It's worth stopping by to take in the atmosphere, and the fish fillet wrapped in a banana leaf is reasonable.

ℹ Getting There & Away

Buses between Port Louis and Cap Malheureux stop in Pereybère as well as Grand Baie. Services run roughly every 30 minutes.

ℹ Getting Around

You can rent cars, motorbikes and bicycles through the local tour agencies. Cars start at Rs 1000 per day and motorbikes at Rs 500 for a 50cc or 100cc bike. Pedal bikes cost upwards of Rs 150 per day. Most of Grand Baie's car-hire companies will also drop off and pick up cars in Pereybère.

ABC Car Rental (☑263 1888; www.abc-car-rental.com) Northern outpost of this reliable chain.

Ara Tour (☑262 7158; www.aratoursmauritius.com) Local car-rental agency.

Cap Malheureux

POP 5070

The northern edge of Mauritius has stunning views out to the islands off the coast, most obviously the dramatic headland of Coin de Mire. Although it feels like rather a backwater today, Cap Malheureux (Cape Misfortune, named for the number of ships that foundered on its rocks) is a place of great historical importance for Mauritius: it was here that the British invasion force finally defeated the French in 1810 and took over the island. A little past the cape lies the minuscule, picturesque fishing village also known as Cap Malheureux.

◎ Sights

Notre Dame Auxiliatrice   CHURCH
(Map p64; Royal Rd) Cap Malheureux's much-photographed church, the red-roofed Notre Dame Auxiliatrice, is worth a quick peek inside for its intricate woodwork and a holy-water basin fashioned out of a giant clamshell. A sign strictly prohibits newlyweds 'faking' a church wedding for the photographers here, but newlyweds, genuine or otherwise, photographers in tow, are a common sight in the church grounds. You can attend Mass here at 6pm on Saturday and 9am on Sunday.

🛏 Sleeping

While there isn't the choice that you'll find in nearby Grand Baie or Pereybère, Cap Malheureux does have some excellent hotels that appeal to those who value a quieter stay one step removed from the clamour of tourist Mauritius.

Kuxville   APARTMENT €€
(Map p64; ☑262 8836; www.kuxville.com; Royal Rd; studios/apt/villas from €70/110/190; ❋🖤) There's a huge choice of accommodation at this perennially popular complex about 1.5km west of Cap Malheureux village. Accommodation is in impeccably clean studios or apartments sleeping up to four; 'garden-side' units are in a newer compound across the road. There's a fine little beach and a small kiteboarding and dive school headed by affable owner Nico Kux – see www.sindbad.mu.

⭐**Le Paradise Cove**   RESORT €€€
(Map p64; ☑204 4000; www.paradisecovehotel.com; Anse la Raie; s/d/ste incl half board from €380/520/850; ❋@🖤🏊) A five-star boutique resort aimed at honeymooners, understated Paradise Cove is as luxurious as its name suggests. It inhabits an attractive small cove; the beach is at the end of an inlet, which gives it remarkable privacy. Other great touches include golf course, tennis courts, free watersports, a dive centre and 'love nests' on the promontory overlooking the northern islands.

🍴 Eating

Apart from the hotel restaurants there are just a few eating options in the area. Otherwise, Pereybère and Grand Baie aren't far away at all.

Helena's Cafe   CAFE €
(Map p64; ☑5978 1909; Royal Rd; mains Rs 225-490; ☺7.30am-4pm) Across the road from the church car park near the island's northernmost tip, this appealing little cafe is all decked out in marine blue and white, and serves up sandwiches, paninis and a few mains such as grilled chicken or fish, noodles or rice.

⭐**Amigo**   SEAFOOD €€
(Map p64; ☑5251 9264; amigo.restaurant.mu; Le Pavillon, Royal Rd; mains Rs 225-950; ☺noon-3pm & 6-10pm Mon-Sat) Everyone adores this friendly joint tucked behind Cape Malheureux township near the sugar-cane farms. The writing's on the wall (literally): contented customers have left myriad messages of love and affection on every flat surface in the restaurant. The tables, however, are graffiti-free – they're reserved for the excellent seafood specialities.

Side note: the letters in the restaurant's name are the first initials of the owner (sadly now deceased) and his four sons. Ironically, the owner didn't speak a lick of Spanish. Delivery available.

ⓘ Getting There & Away

Buses run roughly every half-hour between Port Louis' Immigration Sq bus station (Rs 42) and Cap Malheureux, via Grand Baie. A taxi to Port Louis will cost Rs 1000, to Grand Baie Rs 400 and to the airport Rs 2000.

Grand Gaube

Grand Gaube, about 6km east of Cap Malheureux, is where the development of northern Mauritius currently ends, and the town remains a tiny fishing village with a good beach. Beyond the small rocky bays of Grande Gaube there are almost no beaches until a long way down the east coast, making any trip beyond here an illuminating glimpse into traditional Mauritian life without the tourists. In 1744 the *St Géran* foundered off Grand Gaube in a storm, inspiring the famous love story *Paul et Virginie* by Bernardin de St-Pierre.

🏃 Activities

Yemaya KAYAKING
(www.yemayaadventures.com; half-/full-day from Rs 1500/2000) It's possible to explore Île Ambre offshore on a sea-kayaking trip with Yemaya. It also does longer expeditions and can organise mountain biking.

🛏 Sleeping

Exclusive private resorts dominate here, but they're well concealed from the roadside – so well in fact that only those who stay there know of their existence.

★Veranda Paul & Virginie HOTEL €€€
(Map p64; ☑266 9700; www.veranda-resorts.com; s/d incl breakfast from €125/175; ❄@ 🕸 ⛱) The longest-established hotel in Grande Gaube is a pleasant surprise. It's small enough not to be overwhelming yet offers all the amenities required for luxury: two pools, a couple of restaurants, a Seven Colours spa, plenty of activities, and a kids club. The spacious rooms, all with sea views, are stylishly fitted out, and there's a small but attractive beach.

Zilwa Attitude RESORT €€€
(Map p64; ☑204 9800; www.zilwa-hotel-mauritius.com; Royal Rd, Calodyne; r from €362) Zilwa Attitude is a lovely four-star place with all the features you'd expect from this excellent chain. These include an infinity pool with fabulous views, good restaurants, rooms

with rustic wooden furnishings, and plenty of watersports, from kitesurfing and stand up paddling to boat excursions to the offshore islands.

Lux* Grand Gaube HOTEL €€€
(Map p64; ☑698 9800; www.luxresorts.com; r €175-2200; ❄@ 🕸 ⛱) This very large, stylish establishment enjoys an idyllic location miles from the mass tourism found further down the coast. Guests have the run of the pretty bay and the hotel's well-appointed surroundings. The hotel is feng shui themed, and romance is what this place is all about.

ⓘ Getting There & Away

Buses run roughly every 15 minutes between Port Louis' Immigration Sq bus station and Grand Gaube (Rs 44). A taxi to Port Louis will cost Rs 1000, to Grand Baie Rs 500 and to the airport Rs 2100.

Pamplemousses

POP 8850

One of the island's main attractions, the botanical gardens at Pamplemousses (roughly halfway between Grand Baie and Port Louis) are soothing, tranquil and brimful of endemic and foreign plant species. Also of interest is the decommissioned Beau Plan sugar factory nearby, which has been converted into a fascinating museum.

Pamplemousses itself was named for the grapefruit-like citrus trees that the Dutch introduced to Mauritius from Java. The town is typically Mauritian in a quiet, untouristy and slightly decaying kind of way, and feels a million miles from Grand Baie or Trou aux Biches.

⊙ Sights

★Sir Seewoosagur Ramgoolam Botanical Gardens GARDENS
(Jardins de Pamplemousses, Royal Botanical Gardens; Map p64; adult Rs200, guide per person Rs 50; ⊙8.30am-5.30pm) After London's Kew Gardens the SSR Gardens is one of the world's best botanical gardens. It's also one of the most popular tourist attractions in Mauritius and easily reached from almost anywhere on the island. Labelling of the plants is a work in progress and we strongly recommend that you hire one of the knowledgeable guides who wait just inside the entrance; golf-buggy tours are available upon request for those with limited mobility.

WORTH A TRIP

CHÂTEAU LABOURDONNAIS

If you've come to explore the botanical gardens and sugar museum at Pamplemousses, there's one more stop in the area that we highly recommend.

One of the loveliest examples of colonial architecture on the island, recently restored **Château Labourdonnais** (Map p64; ☑ 266 9533; www.chateaulabourdonnais.com; adult/child Rs 375/200; ☉9am-5pm) was completed in 1859. Built in teak and sporting an Italian neoclassical style, the chateau is perfectly proportioned and filled with sober Victorian furnishings interspersed with some exceptionally lovely design flourishes. Compulsory guided tours last for 45 minutes. After the tour, wander through the lush gardens, taste the rum from the on-site distillery and stay for a meal at the restaurant, where the menu changes daily. There's also a classy gift shop.

To get here, head north along the M2 motorway for around 3km, then take the exit for Mapou and follow the signs.

The centrepiece of the gardens is a pond filled with giant *Victoria amazonica* water lilies, native to South America. Young leaves emerge as wrinkled balls and unfold into the classic tea-tray shape up to 2m across in a matter of hours. The flowers in the centre of the huge leaves open white one day and close red the next. The lilies are at their biggest and best in the warm summer months, notably January.

Palms constitute the most important part of the horticultural display, and they come in an astonishing variety of shapes and forms. Some of the more prominent are the stubby bottle palms, the tall royal palms and the talipot palms, which flower once after about 40 years and then die. Other varieties include the raffia, sugar, toddy, fever, fan and even sealing-wax palms. There are many other curious tree species on display, including the marmalade box tree, the fish poison tree and the sausage tree.

Another highlight is the abundant birdlife – watch for the crimson hues of the Madagascar fody – while there are captive populations of deer and around a dozen giant Aldabra tortoises near the park's northern exit.

The gardens were named after Sir Seewoosagur Ramgoolam, the first prime minister of independent Mauritius, and were started by Mahé de Labourdonnais in 1735 as a vegetable plot for his Mon Plaisir Château (which now contains a small exhibition of photographs). Close to the chateau is the funerary platform where Sir Seewoosagur Ramgoolam was cremated (his ashes were scattered on the Ganges in India). Various international dignitaries have planted trees in the surrounding gardens, including Nelson Mandela, Indira Gandhi and a host of British royals.

The landscape came into its own in 1768 under the auspices of French horticulturalist Pierre Poivre. Like Kew Gardens, the gardens played a significant role in the horticultural espionage of the day. Poivre imported seeds from around the world in a bid to end France's dependence on Asian spices. The gardens were neglected between 1810 and 1849 until British horticulturalist James Duncan transformed them into an arboretum for palms and other tropical trees.

L'Aventure du Sucre   MUSEUM
(Map p64; ☑ 243 0660; www.aventuredusucre.com; adult/child Rs 380/190; ☉9am-5pm) The former Beau Plan sugar factory houses one of the best museums in Mauritius. It not only tells the story of sugar in great detail but also covers the history of Mauritius, slavery, the rum trade and much, much more. Allow a couple of hours to do it justice.

The original factory was founded in 1797 and only ceased working in 1999. Most of the machinery is still in place, and former workers are on hand to answer questions about the factory and the complicated process of turning sugar cane into crystals. There are also videos and interactive displays as well as quizzes for children. At the end of the visit you can taste some of the 15 varieties of unrefined sugar, two of which were invented in Mauritius.

✖ Eating

There are a couple of excellent lunch options in Pamplemousses, while the cheaper restaurants that lie scattered along the western perimeter of the gardens are your best bet if you're here for dinner. Otherwise, head to Grand Baie or Port Louis.

★**Chez Tante Athalie**   MAURITIAN €€
(Map p64; ☑243 9266; Centre de Flacq Rd,
Mont Gout; menu Rs 500; ⊙noon-2.30pm Mon-
Sat) The best-known *table d'hôte* in the area,
open-sided Chez Tante Athalie offers fresh,
simple Creole tastes overlooking a garden
filled with vintage cars. There's an oasis-like
feel to the place. From the entrance to the
botanical gardens follow the signs around
500m to the T-junction, turn left and then
watch for a signposted driveway 2km further
on your left.

Le Fangourin   MAURITIAN €€
(Map p64; ☑243 7900; www.aventuredusucre.
com; mains Rs 295-860; ⊙9am-5pm) If all the
sugar in L'Aventure du Sucre museum has
set your taste buds working, you could sup
a glass of sugar-cane juice at Le Fangourin,
a stylish cafe-restaurant in the museum
grounds. It specialises in sophisticated Creole
cuisine and all sorts of sugary delights. It also
does a fine vegetarian platter.

🛍 Shopping

Le Village Boutik   FOOD & DRINK
(Map p64; ⊙9am-5pm) Right next to the
sugar museum, this impressive shop has sugar in all manner of gift packs, as well as rum
made from local sugar cane. Staff members
encourage you to try before you buy.

❶ Getting There & Away

Pamplemousses can be reached by bus from
Grand Baie, Trou aux Biches, Grand Gaube and
Port Louis. Services from Grand Baie and Trou
aux Biches run approximately every hour and
stop near the sugar museum on the way to the
botanical gardens.

Buses from Port Louis' Immigration Sq bus
station and Grand Gaube operate every 10 to 15
minutes. These buses only stop at the botanical
gardens, from where it takes about 15 minutes
to walk to the museum.

THE WEST

Mauritius' western wonderland is the nation's most diverse coast. The bustling tourist
hub of Flic en Flac may not be to everyone's
taste, but treasures lie just beyond. Along
the coast are the sandy bays and mountainous backdrops of Black River (Rivière Noire)
and Tamarin, and dramatic beauty Le Morne
Brabant, an awesomely photogenic crag, caps
the coastline's southern tip. Nor far inland,

---

❶ DIVING IN THE WEST

Western Mauritius is the pick of the
places to dive in Mauritius, with a couple
of excellent dive centres in Flic en Flac
and good year-round diving. The following, all accessible from Flic en Flac or Le
Morne, are our favourites.

Rempart Serpent (Map p86)

La Cathédrale (Map p86)

Couline Bambou (Map p86)

Passe St Jacques (Map p84)

Manioc (Map p86)

Mauritius rises steeply; this part of the island
encompasses fauna-filled Black River Gorges
National Park and beguiling Chamarel, one of
the loveliest towns anywhere on the island.

❶ Getting There & Away

The main bus routes in western Mauritius are
those from Port Louis down to the southern end
of Rivière Noire (Black River). There is also a
regular service between Quatre Bornes, on the
Central Plateau, and Chamarel.

Your hotel or guesthouse should be able to
arrange bike and car hire.

Note that there are only two petrol stations in
the west: one at Flic en Flac and one in Rivière
Noire.

Flic en Flac
POP 2378

As wonderful and whimsical as the name
sounds, Flic en Flac isn't quite the picture of
paradise you saw on your travel agent's website. The area's moniker is thought to be a cor-
ruption of the old Dutch name Fried Landt
Flaak (Free and Flat Land); the endless acreage of shoreline was undoubtedly striking
when explorers arrived in the 18th century.
Today the area is exploding with apartment
complexes, souvenir shops, moneychangers
and pinchpenny holiday rentals. Although
development in Flic en Flac has gone the way
of Grand Baie, the town's still about a dozen
clubs and restaurants short of attracting a
party crowd.

All is not lost, however; the beach is still
one of the best in Mauritius, and if you stay
at any of the high-end resorts in the Wolmar
area outside the town, you'll uncover some
stellar stretches of sand, glorious diving and
a handful of palate-pleasing restaurants.

The West

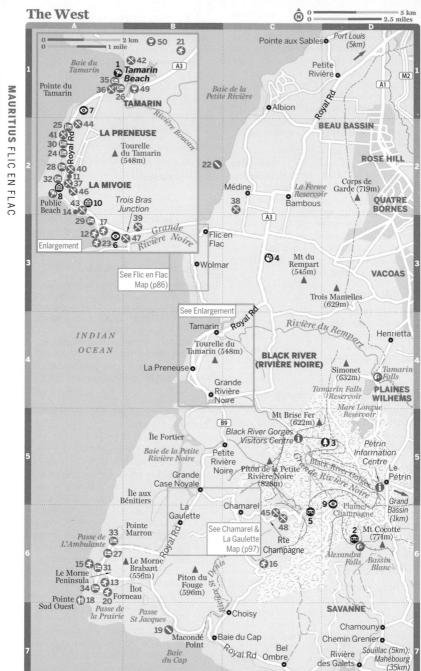

The West

◎ Sights

Casela World of Adventures ZOO

(Map p84; ☎401 6500, 452 2828; www.casela park.com; adult/child Rs 740/475; ⊙9am-5pm May-Sep, to 6pm Oct-Apr) When you arrive at this 14-hectare nature park, you're greeted with a bewildering range of options – in addition to being a zoo (with big cats, rhinos, giraffes and other African mammals), the beautifully landscaped reserve offers a giant slide, animal interactions, and a variety of heart-pumping activities like ziplines, canyoning and quad-bike 'safaris' around a neighbouring home to zebras, impalas, waterbucks, rhinos and monkeys. Casela is on the main road 1km south of the turn-off to Flic en Flac.

Children are well catered for with a pet-ting zoo, a playground, giant tortoises, fish-ing and minigolf. Check out the website for a full list of prices or spend some time at the information desk before the main entrance to get a handle on how to spend your day.

If you simply pay the admission fee, you'll be free to wander the grounds, where you'll see tortoises, a huge range of exotic birds and a few primate species in cages. And make sure you pass by the Mirador restaurant, which has fabulous sweeping views of the coastal plain. Also included in the price is a trip in a safari vehicle, during which you get out and look at lions, cheetahs and hyenas from view-points overlooking large, grassy enclosures, and another driving through a much larger area roamed by zebras, ostriches etc.

The park is famous for offering 15-minute 'interactions' (Rs 750) with the big cats, which means you're actually in the enclosure

Flic en Flac

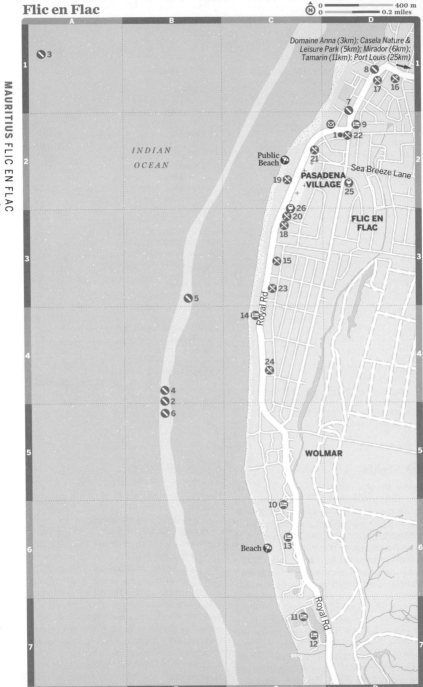

Domaine Anna (3km); Casela Nature &
Leisure Park (5km); Mirador (6km);
Tamarin (11km); Port Louis (25km)

INDIAN
OCEAN

Public
Beach

PASADENA
VILLAGE

Sea Breeze Lane

FLIC EN
FLAC

Royal Rd

WOLMAR

Beach

Royal Rd

Flic en Flac

with them armed with nothing more than a large stick, and the hour-long 'walking with lions' experience (Rs 3750). We don't recommend either of these two options. These are wild animals, despite having been bred in captivity. Incidents in which visitors have been mauled by big cats in similar places in Africa aren't common, but they do occur; participants here are asked to sign an indemnity form before they draw near to the animals. Questions have also been raised by animal rights groups about the quality of life for big cats in such establishments, as well as about the animals' future when they are too old to take part in activities.

🏃 Activities

Some of Mauritius' best dive sites can be found just beyond the emerald lagoon near Flic en Flac, where the shallow waters suddenly give way to the deep. The most popular site in the area is La Cathédrale, with its signature stone arches and tucked-away cavern.

In addition to the dive shops, most of the upmarket hotels in Wolmar have their own diving operators, all of which are open to nonguests. Check out www.msda.mu for a list of licensed and insured dive operators.

Sea Urchin Diving Centre   DIVING
(Map p86; ☑ 453 8825; www.sea-urchin-diving. com; Royal Rd; dive for beginners/experienced divers Rs 2000/1200; ⊙ 8am-4pm Mon-Sat, dives 9am, 11.30am & 1.30pm Sat) This German-run centre is professionally run and, conveniently, you'll find it along the main road.

Sun Divers   DIVING
(Map p86; ☑ 5972 1504; www.sundiversmauritius. com; 1/3 dives Rs 1700/4400; ⊙ 8am-4pm Mon-Sat, to noon Sun, dives 9am, noon and 2.30pm daily) Based at La Pirogue hotel (p89), Sun Divers is one of the top dive operators in the area and among the oldest outfits on the island. It also runs PADI courses and sessions on underwater photography. Dives have a minimum of three participants. There are discounts for those who have their own equipment.

Ticabo Diving Centre   DIVING
(Map p86; ☑ 5973 6316, 453 5209; www.dive-ticabo.com; Royal Rd; day/night dive Rs 1200/1700, 5-dive package Rs 5500; ⊙ 8.30am-4pm Mon-Sat) One of a number of recommended professional dive centres along the main road through town.

Blue Coral Tour   BOAT TOUR
(Italy Tour; Map p86; ☑ 257 7202; Pasadena Village, Royal Rd; ⊙ 8.30am-6.30pm Mon-Sat, 9am-1pm Sun) This professional, Italian-run operator runs half-day dolphin-watching and snorkelling trips as well as full-day excursions to Île aux Cerfs and Îlot Gabriel, and fishing excursions.

La Pirogue Big Game Fishing   FISHING
(Map p86; ☑ 483 8054; www.lapiroguebiggame. com) Fishing outings and other boat excursions can be arranged with La Pirogue Big Game Fishing, based at La Pirogue hotel.

DOLPHIN-WATCHING

Swimming with dolphins is one of the most popular activities anywhere along the west coast of Mauritius, with bottlenose and spinner dolphins frolicking in the sea off Flic en Flac and Tamarin. They can be found most mornings in the bay – most boat operators head out by 8am to spend an hour or two dolphin-watching and sending their paying guests into the water with snorkels when the creatures draw alongside.

Watching the dolphins is one thing, but we have travelled on these boats and observed them in action and we have serious (and increasing) concerns about the impact of these excursions.

The boats – sometimes more than 20, all with outboard motors – mount a lookout and then race in the direction of a pod whenever one is sighted. The aim is clearly to get in as near as possible and then offload their clients into the water so that they can get as close as they can to the dolphins. But in our experience, the practice of most operators amounts to nothing less than harassment and carries the possibility of causing significant stress to these gentle creatures.

Guidelines from scientists for interacting with wild dolphins suggest that it is very difficult to ensure that it is not an intrusive or stressful experience for the animals. When done badly, such interactions can disrupt dolphins' feeding, resting, nursing and other behaviour. Pursuing dolphins in this way may also have long-term impacts on the health and well-being of individual dolphins and whole populations. There are also the risks of injury to dolphins by boat propellers and of dolphins becoming dependent on humans for food – some operators try to lure the animals towards their boat by throwing scraps into the water.

If you do decide to swim with dolphins, please keep your distance from them, do not touch them if they come near, and encourage your operator to keep an appropriate distance from the pods. One local operator we recommend for its sustainable approach is Dolswim (p92).

Sleeping

Central Flic en Flac is decidedly *not* upmarket, with condos and apartment complexes lining every street. South of Flic en Flac, in the Wolmar area, you'll find several charming luxury options directly on the sand.

As always, if you're considering one of the pricier choices, it is best to book through a travel agent, which should get significant discounts. Rack rates are quoted in listings.

Easy World Hotel HOTEL €

(Map p86; ☎453 8571; easy-world-beach-apartments.holiday-rentals.mu/; Royal Rd; r/studios Rs 890/1200; P ❄ @ ≈) Basic, cheap, though rather threadbare, the Easy World Hotel is conveniently set along the main road through town. Ask for a room on one of the upper floors – it's quite a climb, but the sea breezes should compensate once you get there. Ask the owner about his other, slightly pricier property nearby.

Aanari HOTEL €€

(Map p86; ☎453 9000; www.aanari.com; Royal Rd; s/d from €92/121; ❄ @ ≈ ≋) Perched atop Pasadena Village, Aanari attempts boutique sophistication with a clutch of oriental statues and it does a pretty good job of removing itself from the slightly tacky downtown milieu. Rooms feel distinctly Asian, with lacquered furnishings, errant flower petals and silk bed runners. The hotel's biggest drawcard is the window-filled spa and fitness centre on the roof.

Its proximity to everything is either a plus or a major drawback, depending on your perspective.

Villas Caroline HOTEL €€

(Map p86; ☎453 8580; www.villa-caroline-hotel-mauritius.mu; Royal Rd; s/d from €120/130) Less pretentious than other places around here and popular with families, Villas Caroline has attractive rooms, many of which front right onto the beach. It also has a dive centre and a more-than-adequate portfolio of swimming pools.

★ **Maradiva** HOTEL €€€

(Map p86; ☎403 1500; www.maradiva.com; Wolmar; villas €560-4565; ❄ @ ≈ ≋) Perfectly manicured grounds sprinkled with luxurious villas lie off Royal Rd at Maradiva. The place oozes charm, serenity and impeccable service, from the entry gate to the sleek seaside resto-lounge. Rooms are large and beautifully presented and come with private pools.

★ La Pirogue
HOTEL €€€

(Map p86; ☑ 403 3900; www.lapirogue.com; r incl half board from €250; ❄ @ 🛜 ⛱) Mauritius' oldest resort shares the same management as Sugar Beach next door, but there's a completely different feel here. Rather than a colonial-manse theme, La Pirogue opts for a charming fishing-village vibe, with semicircular clusters of adorable hut-villas arranged along the 500m of spectacular sandy beach.

To some, it may feel like the resort is starting to show its age, but to most visitors, La Pirogue represents a classic paradigm of Mauritius' beachside hospitality.

Sugar Beach Resort
RESORT €€€

(Map p86; ☑ 403 3300; www.sugarbeachresort. com; Royal Rd, Wolmar; s/d incl half board from €166/235; ❄ @ 🛜) With its mock plantation mansion look and wonderfully colonial lawns, Sugar Bay is a well-run resort catering to a huge number of people coming to enjoy the smart setting and great beach. It's a very family-friendly resort (think lots of kids in the pool and live entertainment at dinner) and shares facilities with La Pirogue next door.

Sands Suites Resort & Spa
RESORT €€€

(Map p86; ☑ 403 1200; www.sands.mu; Wolmar; d incl half board from €239; ❄ @ 🛜 ⛱) With gorgeous views from the beachside pool onto Tamarin Bay and towards Le Morne, this sophisticated yet unpretentious option has an airy, tropical elegance that permeates the open, timber-framed lobby. The rooms sport subtle tones, generous bathrooms and seaview balconies. There are two restaurants, a spa and plenty of activities, including a dive centre. The resort is off Royal Rd.

HOLIDAY RENTALS

Flic en Flac trumps all of the island's other beach towns when it comes to cheap holiday rentals. None of the options are located directly on the beach, as the coastal road lies between developments and the sandy shore, but there are still plenty of beach views to be had.

The most popular rental operator in the area, **Jet-7** (☑ 453 9600, 467 7735; www.jet-7.com), manages a handful of properties.

✖ Eating

Wealthier vacationers tend to take advantage of their upmarket hotels' 'half board' holiday packages, while budgetarians usually self-cater or go for cheap street fare. Thus there's a noticeable lack of out-of-this-world establishments in central Flic en Flac.

Foodies should book a table at a restaurant on the grounds of one of the top-end hotels, or drive down to Black River for a more memorable and eclectic assortment of eats.

Jeanno Burger
BURGERS €

(Map p86; ☑ 5202 4500; Royal Rd; mains Rs 60-175; ⊙ 11am-9pm Tue-Sun) The pick of the food vans between the road and the beach (although the places selling fresh pineapple do give it a run for its money), Jeanno's serves up good burgers to a long line of devotees. It's a one-man show, so things can take a while when it's busy, but no one seems to mind – there are worse places to wait.

Ah-Youn
CHINESE, MAURITIAN €

(Map p86; ☑ 453 9099; Royal Rd; mains Rs 150-350; ⊙ noon-3.30pm & 6-10pm) We're not sure how great a compliment it is to say that Ah-Youn's best features are its swift service and generous portions, but it's true. Don't worry, though: the food is perfectly palatable and it's a much better choice than many other restaurants in town. The focus is Chinese fare, but Mauritian flavours have crept onto the menu, too.

Spar Supermarket
SUPERMARKET €

(Map p86; Pasadena Village, Royal Rd; ⊙ 8am-8pm Mon-Sat, to 1pm Sun) Well-stocked supermarket for self-caterers.

★ Zub Express
INDIAN, CHINESE €€

(Map p86; ☑ 453 8867; www.zub-express. com; 286 Coastal Rd; mains Rs 125-950; ⊙ 10am-9.30pm Fri-Wed, 5-10pm Thu) Indian-Chinese fusion cooking sounds rather fancy, but the reality is far simpler, featuring dishes like excellent biryanis, expertly grilled fish and lobster, and fine ideas like fish butter masala. Throw in friendly service and it's no wonder this place gets rave reviews from travellers and locals alike.

★ Canne à Sucre
MAURITIAN €€

(Chez May; Map p86; ☑ 917 8282; Royal Rd; meals from Rs 800; ⊙ 8am-noon & 4pm-late) Now here's something special: an authentic slice of Mauritian life in the midst of touristy Flic en Flac. May has converted her roadside bar-restaurant into a cosy space that captures the essence of coastal Mauritius. She offers multicourse Creole dinner feasts – rice, chicken, octopus, Creole sausages and 'some vegetables you've never heard of' – with dessert and rum thrown in.

You'll need to order the day before you plan to visit, but *don't* let that put you off and *don't* miss it.

★ **Domaine Anna** CHINESE, SEAFOOD €€
(Map p84; ☑ 453 9650; Médine; mains from Rs 350; ⊙ 11.30am-2.30pm & 6.30-10.30pm Tue-Sun) You'll need a taxi or rental car to get here, but you'll be glad you made the trip: this is Flic en Flac's most refined dining experience, set in colonial-style pavilions. The predominantly Chinese menu is the brainchild of chef Hang Leung Pah Hang, and the food is excellent – locals come from all over for their fix of crab, calamari and lobster.

Paul & Virginie MAURITIAN €€
(Map p86; ☑ 403 3900; www.lapirogue.com; La Pirogue; mains from Rs 600; ⊙ 12.30-2.30pm & 7.30-10pm Mon-Sat, 12.30-2.30pm Sun) With lovely thatched platforms extending over swimming pools and towards the ocean, Paul & Virginie makes for a romantic meal. The food matches the setting – grilled fish, palm-heart salads, curries and seafood in many guises – and the service rarely misses a beat. You don't need to be staying at La Pirogue hotel to eat here, but you will need to reserve.

Le Bougainville MAURITIAN €€
(Map p86; ☑ 453 5959; Royal Rd; mains Rs 260-550; ⊙ 10am-10.30pm Thu-Tue) Mauritian dishes, seafood, Chinese, the occasional Indian inflection – Le Bougainville is your typical roadside Flic en Flac restaurant, with unimaginative but solid cooking. It's handy if you don't want to stray too far from the beach.

Twin's Garden MAURITIAN, INTERNATIONAL €€
(Map p86; ☑ 453 5250; Royal Rd; mains Rs 350-680, Fri buffet Rs 600; ⊙ noon-3pm & 7pm-late) A sprawling collection of agreeable outdoor tables just across the road from the beach, Twin's does dishes like grilled lobster flamed with local rum and garlic butter, and lamb shanks in Rodrigues honey. Friday night there's a buffet, a live *séga* floor show and bands playing music from the '60s through to the '80s. We prefer the other nights, but each to their own.

FOOD TRUCKS

For something a little more earthy, you'll find fast-food trucks parked under the weeping *filao* trees along the sand at the northern end of the public beach. Vendors serve fruit, chips, drinks, kebabs and all manner of baguettes, all for no more than Rs 60. You can't see Le Morne from this part of the beach, but it's a scenic spot to enjoy a bite nonetheless.

Ocean Restaurant SEAFOOD, CHINESE €€
(Map p86; ☑ 453 8549; Royal Rd; mains Rs 150-475; ⊙ 10am-3pm & 6.30-9pm; ☑) Set in slightly classier surrounds than we're accustomed to in Flic en Flac, this elegant place serves decent seafood dishes.

Chez Pepe ITALIAN €€
(Map p86; ☑ 453 9383; Royal Rd; mains Rs 220-400; ⊙ 11.30am-late) Chez Pepe is a lively spot serving up Italian favourites like pizza, seafood spaghetti and rustic Tuscan meats, as well as local specialities like smoked-marlin salad. It won't be a particularly memorable meal, but it's one of the best places for a bite along Flic en Flac's beachside road.

Mirador MAURITIAN, INTERNATIONAL €€
(Map p84; ☑ 452 0845; Casela World of Adventure; mains Rs 300-475; ⊙ 10.30am-4pm) It's well worth planning your visit to Casela around lunchtime to grab a bite at the on-site restaurant. This charming open-air cafe has photogenic views of the sea and western plains, and serves a variety of international and local dishes, including snacks, salads, paninis and pizzas.

Banane Créole MAURITIAN €€
(Le Papayou; Map p86; ☑ 453 9826; Royal Rd; mains Rs 200-500; ⊙ 9.30am-3pm & 6-10pm Mon-Sat) Service can come with a smile or a scowl at this tiny local joint, but that's all part of the charm. The cheap, eclectic menu mixes international staples (such as pizza) and local dishes such as curries; try the signature dessert *papayou* (cooked papaya sweetened with sugar and ice cream) with a cup of fresh-brewed coffee – Flic en Flac's finest.

♟ Drinking & Nightlife

You'll find plenty of bars around the Pasadena Village complex (you'll hear them before you see them) and across the road from the beach further south. There's nothing much of any real quality, but things can get lively during high season.

KenziBar   BAR

(Map p86; ☑453 5259; ⊗6.30pm-midnight Tue-Sat) KenziBar, a block or two back from the waterfront, is your best bet for nightlife in Flic en Flac, and one of few places where it's about more than just noise. There's tongue-tingling *rhum arrangés* (rum punch), fire-spurting torches, live music (Friday and Saturday) and a mangy, pat-hungry dog that calls the bar home – welcome to Mauritius!

Shotz   BAR, CLUB

(Map p86; ☑453 5626; www.shotz.mu/the-club/; Royal Rd; ⊗11pm-4am Fri & Sat) Both lounge bar and nightclub, Shotz is about as glamorous as things get beyond the high walls of the upmarket resorts.

ℹ Information

Post Office (Map p86; ⊗8.15-11.15am & noon-4pm Mon-Fri, to 11.45am Sat) In a light-blue *case*-style house across the street from the Pasadena Village complex.

ℹ Getting There & Away

There is a bus from Port Louis to Flic en Flac and Wolmar every 15 to 20 minutes. Public buses constantly ply the coastal route in Flic en Flac and many tourists use them as a cheap and quick hop-on, hop-off service. A taxi from Port Louis to Flic en Flac will cost Rs 1000. Figure on Rs 2000 for a taxi to the airport, Rs 1500 to Le Morne and Rs 1800 to Belle Mare. A ride to Black River costs Rs 500.

ℹ Getting Around

All accommodation and travel agencies in the area can help arrange bicycle and car hire. Count on Rs 250 for a bike. Cars start at Rs 900 for a manual and Rs 1200 for an automatic. Numerous such agencies line the main road through town and most offer the exact same products and swipe identical commission.

Tamarin & Rivière Noire

POP 11,725

The beach-fringed land between Flic en Flac and Le Morne is known to most Mauritians as Rivière Noire (Black River). One of the island's last coastal areas to witness development, this constellation of townships has grown by leaps and bounds over the last few years. Despite the sudden appearance of modern structures, Black River offers a more active yet quieter experience – resorts are few and far between and you've a choice of sea and mountains when it comes to getting out and exploring. Sensational hiking, scenic shorelines, top-notch fishing and interesting historical relics are all within arm's reach.

◎ Sights

★Tamarin Beach   BEACH

(Map p84) Locals like to wax nostalgic about Tamarin Beach and its surfing heyday, and in many ways this sandy cove still feels like a throwback to earlier times – especially since the centrally located Tamarin Hotel looks as though it hasn't been renovated since *Jaws* was in cinemas. But Tamarin – unmarred by high-walled resort compounds – remains a popular place and its beach has one of the most spectacular backdrops (looking north) in the country.

Once upon a time the area was known as Santosha Bay and offered wave hunters some of the best surfing on the planet. In fact, before the bay earned the name Santosha, locals refused to give the beach a moniker because they didn't want outsiders to discover their cache of surfable seas! Today, the waves and currents have changed and the surfing diehards have moved down the coast to Le Morne.

The walk between Tamarin Beach and southern Wolmar is very scenic and not accessible by car (women are advised not to do it alone).

World of Seashells   MUSEUM

(Map p84; ☑5259 0197, 483 1938; Coastal Rd; adult/child Rs 250/125; ⊗9.30am-6pm Mon-Sat) This oddly beguiling collection of over 8000 seashells in nearly 70 display cabinets is to be found in the Ruisseau Créole shopping complex. It's all the lifelong passion of Eric Le Court and most of the shells come from Mauritius. There's a small shop attached.

La Balise Marina   HARBOUR

(Map p84; ☑483 7272; www.labalisemarina.
com) The billboards are everywhere – La
Balise Marina promises to revolutionise the
tourism industry in Mauritius by creating the
island's first port welcoming luxury yachts.
Construction of the marina and its adjoining
complex of shops and apartments is well under way, but once it's complete, Black River
is expected to overflow with some seriously
upmarket tourist traffic.

Martello Tower   MUSEUM, FORT

(Map p84; ☑471 0178; ⊗9.30am-5pm Tue-Sat, to
1pm Sun) FREE In the 1830s the British built
five 'Martello' towers – copies of the tower at
Mortella Point in Corsica (vowel order was
apparently not a priority for the British) – to
protect their young colony from predators
(namely the French, who were suspected of
supporting a slave rebellion). The one at La
Preneuse is now a small museum where captions explain the tower's ingenious design
– 3m-thick walls are crowned by a copper
cannon that could apparently destroy a target
2km away.

La Route du Sel   HISTORIC SITE

(Map p84; ☑483 8764; Royal Rd) Not quite a
route like the Route du Thé, the 18th-century
salt flats along the main road in Tamarin are
a popular stopping point for camera-happy
travellers. Sadly, the whole thing has closed
temporarily, ostensibly due to a lack of funding, but as this was until recently the last place
in Mauritius where salt was still produced, it's
worth checking in to see if it has reopened.

🏃 Activities

Although hiking in Black River itself is next
to impossible, it serves as an ideal base for
the ample hiking opportunities at Black River Gorges National Park further inland and
Le Morne Peninsula to the south.

★ Chez Philippe   COOKING COURSE

(Map p84; ☑5250 8528, 483 7920; www.
facebook.com/chez.philippe.75; Coastal Rd; adult/
child Rs 1500/900) Philippe runs this fantastic
cooking school with small classes (five
people max) covering a range of cuisines:
local, Asian, Italian, seafood etc. Follow him
on Facebook, then check in for the upcoming
program. Classes take place on Thursday and
Friday (and sometimes Saturday) and cover
three dishes over three hours. Then you get
to eat what you prepare.

DEEP-SEA FISHING

The fisheries around Mauritius support
large maritime predators such as marlin, wahoo and tuna, luring big-game
anglers from around the world. Annual
fishing competitions are held in Black
River in November and February.

Game fishing has far less environmental impact than commercial fishing,
but fish weights and the number of fish
caught have shown a marked decline
since game fishing's heyday in the
1970s. It's now rare to catch anything
over 400kg. Practising 'tag and release'
is an option for those who want the thrill
without depriving the ocean of these
magnificent creatures.

Anglers get to take home a trophy
such as the marlin's nose spike, or a
couple of fillets, but the day's catch
belongs to the operator, who sells it to
be served up at local restaurants.

Most of the big hotels run boats,
and there are several private operators
based at Black River, Trou aux Biches
and Grand Baie. Most outfits have a
minimum hire time of around six hours,
and each boat can normally take three
anglers and three guests. Expect to pay
upwards of Rs 20,000 per day per boat.

Philippe also runs two-hour children's
classes on Wednesday at 3.30pm.

Dolswim   WILDLIFE WATCHING

(Map p84; ☑5422 9281; www.dolswim.com;
La Jetée Rd, Black River; adult/child whale-
watching Rs 3000/1800, dolphin-watching from Rs
1700/1000) ✐ Dolswim bucks the trend of
dolphin-watching operators along the west
coast by taking a more sustainable approach
to excursions – its staff has been trained by
local marine and conservation authorities.
Unusually, it also runs whale-watching excursions from July to October or November,
when humpback whales migrate north along
the west coast.

Tamarina Golf, Spa & Beach Club   GOLF

(Map p84; ☑401 3006; www.tamarinagolf.
mu; Tamarin Bay; ⊗9-/18-hole green fees Rs
3000/5000) The magnificent Tamarina Golf,
Spa & Beach Club is an 18-hole course designed by Rodney Wright. It sprawls across
206 hectares along an old hunting estate situated between the coastal townships and the

looming spine of the inland hills. The property also features restaurants and over 100 rentable villas (p94).

Zazou Fishing FISHING

(Map p84; ☑ 5729 9222, 5788 3804; www.zazoufishing.com; Ave des Rougets, Tamarin) Zazou Fishing is a reputable operator offering an excellent deal, with a six-person maximum on its boats.

Le Morne Anglers' Club FISHING

(Map p84; ☑ 483 5801; www.morneanglers.com; Colonel Dean Ave; ⊙ 6.30am-8.30pm) Le Morne Anglers' Club, signposted beside the crumbling police station in Black River, offers deep-sea fishing outings, as well as sightseeing boat charters.

JP Henry Charters Ltd BOAT TOUR

(Map p84; ☑ 5729 0901; www.blackriver-mauritius.com) JP Henry Charters Ltd offers deep-sea fishing. It's signposted along the main road through Black River.

🛏 Sleeping

Noticeably devoid of monstrous upmarket resorts, Black River prefers old-school inns, quiet villas and welcoming *chambres d'hôtes* tucked down narrow, tree-lined lanes.

The residential vibe in Black River means that there's a wide selection of private apartments and villas for rent.

Chez Jacques HOTEL €

(Map p84; ☑ 5741 3017, 483 6445; www.guesthouse chezjacques.com; Lagane's Place, Tamarin Beach; s/d with fan Rs 1200/1800, with air-con Rs 1400/2200; ✳ @ ⑦) Squeeze down a side road on the way to Tamarin Beach and you'll uncover the famous Chez Jacques. Forty years ago Jacques' parents opened their home to visiting surfers and, although the number of wave hunters has dwindled, there's still a laid-back vibe here – this is as close as you'll get on the island to a backpacker's hostel.

Jacques can help watersports enthusiasts get kitted up; he also hosts regular guitar jam sessions.

Tamarin Hotel HOTEL €€

(Map p84; ☑ 483 6927; www.hotel-tamarin.com; Tamarin Beach; s/d from €90/115; ✳ @ ⑦ ☒) This one-time throwback to the '70s has had a makeover, although the public areas carry nostalgic echoes. The rooms now sport bright colours, contemporary art and fresh flowers. Even if you don't stay here, it's worth swinging by for the chilled-out atmosphere

and night-time concerts. There's a pool, a sociable stretch of sand and a welcoming restaurant.

Watersports enthusiasts should ask at the front desk about surfing lessons.

La Mariposa APARTMENT €€

(Map p84; ☑ 483 5048, 5728 0506; www.lamariposa.mu; Allée des Pêcheurs, La Preneuse; apt incl breakfast €100-180; ✳ ⑦ ☒) Set directly along the sea and surrounded by a wild tropical garden, this quiet option features an L-shaped row of double-decker apartments. Rooms are breezy and simple, with cream-coloured walls, scarlet drapes and rounded balconies promising memorable sunset views. This is one of few hotels in Mauritius that openly advertises its gay-friendly credentials.

Marlin Creek Residence GUESTHOUSE €€

(Map p84; ☑ 483 7628; www.ilemauricelocation.fr; 10 Colonel Dean Ave; d/bungalows incl breakfast €89/155; ✳ ⑦ ☒) This relatively new addition to Black River's sleeping scene sits along the cerulean bay just a stone's throw from the jetty. The buzzing fisherfolk next door give the property a wonderfully local feel. Rooms are attractive, if a little wood-heavy, and it has an unusually long and narrow pool.

★ Bay Hotel BOUTIQUE HOTEL €€€

(Map p84; ☑ 483 6525; www.thebay.mu; Ave des Cocotiers, La Preneuse; s/d from €120/205; ✳ @ ⑦ ☒) What a find! The Bay comes pretty darn close to boutique chic while still keeping prices relatively low. The thoughtfully decorated rooms (bright pillows, fresh tropical flowers, pristine white linen and arty wall hangings) are arranged on two floors around a white-walled courtyard. Don't miss the seaside restaurant and pool out the back. Half board is available for €20 per person. There's also yoga on the beach and a pampering spa.

★ Les Lataniers Bleus GUESTHOUSE €€€

(Map p84; ☑ 483 6541; www.leslataniersbleus.com; d from €165; ✳ @ ⑦ ☒) If you're hoping to partake of the Mauritian *chambre d'hôte* experience, look no further – Les Lataniers Bleus offers local hospitality at its finest. Josette Marchal-Vexlard is the head of the household, and she dotes upon her guests with effortless charm and an infectious smile. The darling rooms are spread across three houses situated on an ample, beachside orchard.

Every comfort has been considered – there's even a power point hidden in a tree trunk so that you can update your blog while sitting in the sand! The evening *table d'hôte* on the veranda is a great way to meet other guests and learn about life on the island from the affable hostess.

Latitude Seafront Apartments
APARTMENT €€€

(Map p84; www.homefromhome.mu/accommo-dation/latitude/; Royal Rd; 2-bedroom apt €165-200, 3-bedroom apt €176-357; P ✴ 🛜 🐾) Opened in late 2015, this fine South African–run complex has stunning, spacious contemporary apartments, many with their own splash pool, and a real sense of minimalist style. There's a lovely infinity pool, barbecues and coffee machines in each apartment, and a boat jetty, but no beach. Avoid the row of apartments at the back that overlook the car park.

West Island Resort
RESORT €€€

(Map p84; ✒ 483 1714; www.westislandresort.com; 2-bedroom apt from €352; P ✴ 🛜 🐾) Is this a vision of the future? The luxury apartments at La Balise Marina may be the first signs of an upmarket-tourism surge in the area. You've all the facilities of a resort, plus there's the chance to rub shoulders with the country's great and good.

Belle Crique
APARTMENT €€€

(Map p84; ✒ 403 5304; www.belle-crique-mauritius.com; Coastal Rd; apt from €235; P ✴ 🛜 🐾) Beautiful modern apartments with understated flair make this place one of the best complexes along this stretch of road. Contemporary art, designer furnishings, Nespresso coffee machines and Weber barbecues all make this feel like home. There's usually a three-night minimum stay.

Tamarina Golf, Spa & Beach Club
RESORT €€€

(Map p84; ✒ 404 0150, 404 8502; www.tamarina.mu; Tamarin; villas €300-700) Golf enthusiasts should consider leasing a luxurious villa here – rental packages include golfing privileges. As the resort is protected from the main road by tall trees and has no passing traffic, you might just feel as if you've found your Mauritian idyll.

✗ Eating

The townships have a terrific selection of dining choices. In general, prices are high relative to the rest of the island, as the target customers are expat South Africans and wealthy Franco-Mauritians.

Those in search of street eats will usually find *boulette* vendors at Tamarin Beach (across from the eponymous hotel) on weekends between noon and 7.30pm. Locals say that these are among the best on the island.

Crêperie Bretonne
CRÊPERIE €

(Mam Gouz; Map p84; ✒ 5732 8440; Coastal Rd; salads from Rs 300, crêpes Rs 80-275) It's hard to know if this appealing roadside place will last the distance – it was never full when we passed or visited – but its sweet and savoury crêpes are a welcome alternative from curries and seafood platters.

Cosa Nostra
ITALIAN €

(Map p84; ✒ 483 6169; cnr Anthurium Lane & Royal Rd, Tamarin; pizzas from Rs 250; ⊙ 10am-3pm & 6-10pm Sat-Sun) Two things make this popular pizza joint famous: the whisper-thin crust (you'll swear that you're just eating toppings) and the turtle-speed service (you'll think the servers went back to Italy to fetch your slice).

Le Cabanon Créole
MAURITIAN €

(Map p84; ✒ 483 5783; Royal Rd, La Preneuse; mains from Rs 200; ⊙ 11am-9.30pm) Friendly service and spicy spins on Creole home cooking make this family-run place a perennial favourite. There's a limited range of daily dishes, such as *rougaille saucisses* (spicy sausages) and chicken curry; specials, like lobster or whole fresh fish, can be ordered ahead. It's best to reserve in the evenings as there is only a handful of tables. Delivery available.

Pavillon de Jade
CHINESE €

(Map p84; ✒ 483 6151; Trois Bras Junction, Royal Rd, Grande Rivière Noire; dishes Rs 100-350; ⊙ noon-3pm & 6.30-9.30pm) The proud owner of this no-frills Chinese joint above a faded supermarket refuses to sell his land to the hungry developers of the Balise Marina project. It's all about simple Chinese cooking here.

London Way
SUPERMARKET €

(Map p84; ✒ 696 0088; Royal Rd, Grande Rivière Noire; ⊙ 8.30am-7pm Mon-Tue & Thu, to 8pm Fri & Sat, to 12.30pm Sun) London Way looks a bit worn out, but it has the widest selection of items in Black River – ideal if you're in a self-catering apartment.

★ Frenchie Café
CAFE €€

(Map p84; ✒ 463 6125; www.frenchiecafe.mu; mains Rs 350, brunch per person Rs 600; ⊙ 8am-midnight) One of the coolest places on the island, French-run Frenchie does carpaccios, quick bites and more substantial (but reasonably priced) mains, as well as breakfasts and a Sunday brunch. It's also a stylish cocktail bar with Saturday-night DJs. On the road to the Black River Gorges Visitor Centre (p100); the turn-off is almost opposite La Balise Marina (p92).

★ **La Bonne Chute** MAURITIAN, SEAFOOD €€
(Map p84; ☑483 6552; Royal Rd, La Preneuse; mains Rs 350-700; ☺11am-3pm & 6.30-10.30pm Mon-Sat) Don't be dissuaded by the petrol-station-adjacent location; La Bonne Chute has built its reputation on its flavourful dishes and attractive garden setting. From duck confit to prawn cassoulette to the best palm-heart salads we tasted, the kitchen always seems to get it right. Save room for a home-made dessert. Mario, Juliette and the rest of the family are welcoming hosts.

Kozy Garden TAPAS, INTERNATIONAL €€
(Map p84; Coastal Rd; mains Rs 350-600, tapas from Rs 200; ☺9.30am-midnight Mon-Sat) This very cool designer spot with a funky cocktail bar and poolside seating makes for one of the trendier eating experiences in the west. Dishes include half-cooked tuna in sesame seeds or four spices and honey duck breast. The tapas bar is open all day, but the restaurant mains are only available at lunch and dinner.

Chez Philippe DELI €€
(Map p84; ☑483 7920; chez.philippe@orange.mu; Coastal Rd; mains from Rs 350; ☺9.30am-6.30pm Tue-Sat, 9am-noon Sun) Best known as a cooking school, Chez Philippe also has a fabulous little deli serving up prepared takeaway meals, such as salads, lasagne and creative interpretations of local dishes. There's also foie gras, cheeses and exceptional desserts – the tiramisu is a local institution.

Lazy Lizard INTERNATIONAL €€
(Map p84; ☑483 7700; Nautica Commercial Centre, Royal Rd; mains Rs 200-500; ☺8am-3pm Mon & Tue, to 10pm Wed-Sat) This slick cafe has just undergone a major refurbishment and it's aiming for a sophisticated market with light meals (sandwiches, pasta, omelettes); Friday night is sushi night, and the burger-and-beer night on Saturday loosens things up a little. If you'd like something more substantial, try the evenings-only grilled calamari or the grilled dorado (fish).

Al Dente ITALIAN €€
(Map p84; ☑483 7919; Ruisseau Créole Shopping Complex, Grande Rivière Noire; pasta Rs 250-500, pizza Rs 180-460; ☺10.30am-2.30pm & 5.30-11pm) High-quality Italian dishes like beef carpaccio, homemade pasta and osso bucco are a

virtual trip to the mother country. The restaurant's down some steps at the back of the hip Ruisseau Créole shopping complex.

La Madrague INTERNATIONAL €€
(Beach Club; Map p84; ☑483 0260; www.tamarinahotel.com; Tamarina Golf, Spa & Beach Club, Tamarin Bay; mains Rs 350-750, Sun brunch Rs 800-1200; ☺noon-10pm) This place feels like a poolside restaurant at a posh resort, yet there's no hotel in sight – it's hidden down a dirt track that begins near the entrance gate to the Tamarina golf grounds. The menu features standard international dishes (club sandwiches and lamb chops), but the real draw is the inviting infinity-edge swimming pool bedecked with shimmering dark marble.

While away a sunny day under the shade of a coconut palm and, when you're ready for some sand, simply scamper down the stairs to the semiprivate beach below.

🍷 Drinking & Nightlife

Noticeably quieter than the scene in Grand Baie or Flic en Flac, the communities of Black River prefer house parties to loud club nights. Still, there are a couple of places to go in the evening, and many of the area's restaurants have a great after-hours vibe. Do keep in mind, though, that Flic en Flac is only a 15- to 25-minute taxi ride up the coast.

Le Dix-Neuf BAR
(Map p84; ☑483 0300; Tamarina Golf, Spa & Beach Club, Tamarin Bay; ☺noon-7.30pm) Hidden behind the walls of Tamarina's exclusive golfing grounds, this classy lodge-like venue, situated at the clubhouse, is a great place for a sundown snifter. Notice how the pentagonal window behind the dark-wood bar perfectly frames the sharp, roof-like ridges of the nearby hills.

Big Willy's BAR, CLUB
(Map p84; ☑483 7400; www.bigwillys.mu; Royal Rd, Tamarin; ☺3pm-2am Tue-Fri, 9am-2am Sat, 11am-2am Sun) Owned by a South African and perennially popular with the expat crowd, Big Willy's is *the* it spot for DJ-ed dance beats and rugby on the tube. It's all good, clean fun.

☆ Entertainment

★ **Tamarin Hotel** JAZZ
(Map p84; www.hotel-tamarin.com; ☺8.30pm) Concerts indulge the passion for jazz of the hotel's owner (he's the one on sax) – the result is one of the best live-music venues on the island. On Tuesday jazz takes a break for

some local *séga* rhythms, before normalcy is restored the rest of the week with everything from swing, bebop, bossa nova and soul to go with modern jazz staples.

🛍 Shopping

Tutti Frutti   HOMEWARES
(Map p84; ☑ 483 6866; www.tuttifrutti.mu; Coastal Rd; ⊙ 9.30am-8pm Mon-Sat) Designer homewares and furnishings that capture the refinement of Mauritian coastal living are arrayed around a number of showrooms next to the lovely Kozy Garden tapas bar.

❶ Getting There & Away

Buses headed for Tamarin leave Port Louis roughly every hour and Quatre Bornes every 20 minutes. These buses also stop in La Preneuse. A taxi from Port Louis costs Rs 1000. Expect to pay Rs 1800 for the airport, Rs 600 for Flic en Flac, Rs 700 for Le Morne and Rs 1800 to reach Belle Mare.

Chamarel

POP 790

Known throughout the island for its hushed, bucolic vibe, cool breezes and world-class rum, Chamarel is a wonderful mountain hamlet and an alternative to coastal Mauritius and all those beaches. The town has an excellent eating scene, it's home to the famous Terres de 7 Couleurs and Rhumerie de Chamarel, and it's the western gateway to Black River Gorges National Park.

◉ Sights

★ **Curious Corner of Chamarel**   MUSEUM
(Map p97; ☑ 483 4200; www.curiouscorner ofchamarel.com; Baie du Cap Rd; adult/child Rs 50/25, incl all exhibits Rs 275/150; ⊙ 9.30am-5pm) This eclectic place is utterly unlike anywhere else on the island. Essentially an interactive gallery of illusions and art, it has a 200-mirror maze, a laser room and plenty of other attractions that play on your curiosity (and wreak havoc with your sense of perspective!). There's a cafe, the Puzzles & Things Shop and an overarching sense of playful originality. It's opposite the turn-off to Terres de 7 Couleurs.

★ **Rhumerie de Chamarel**   MUSEUM
(Map p97; ☑ 483 4980; www.rhumeriede chamarel.com; Royal Rd; adult incl tasting Rs 350, child Rs 175; ⊙ 9.30am-4.30pm Mon-Sat) Set among the vast hillside plantations of Chamarel, the *rhumerie* is a working distillery that doubles as a museum showcasing the

rum-making process. The pet project of the Beachcomber hotel tycoon, the factory opened in 2008 and uses a special 'ecofriendly' production method ensuring that all materials are recycled. The rum is quite tasty and makes for a pleasant coda to a guided tour of the plant. Time your visit so you can enjoy lunch at the museum's restaurant, L'Alchimiste (p98).

Chamarel Waterfall   WATERFALL
(Map p97) About halfway (1.5km) between the Terres de 7 Couleur's entrance gate and the colourful sands is a scenic viewpoint over the Chamarel waterfall, which plunges more than 95m in a single drop. With a reservation, you can abseil with Vertical World (p100) from the top of Chamarel Waterfall all the way into the pool at its base.

Terres de 7 Couleurs   LANDMARK
(Chamarel Coloured Earths; Map p97; ☑ 483 8298; adult/child Rs 200/100; ⊙ 7am-6pm) For reasons that remain something of a mystery to us, the Chamarel Coloured Earths have become one of the sights on the island's usual tourist circuit. Most travellers find them quite underwhelming after a long journey, but if you temper your expectations and approach an excursion here as a quirky side trip, then there's a greater chance of enjoying the variations of colourful sand – a result of the uneven cooling of molten rock. The site is 4km southwest of Chamarel.

Tortoises are kept in an enclosure just below the coloured earths, which lie 3km inside the Terres de 7 Couleurs property.

The entire property was once the private estate of Charles de Chazal de Chamarel, who hosted Matthew Flinders during Flinders' captivity in Mauritius during the Napoleonic Wars.

🏇 Activities

La Vieille Cheminée   HORSE RIDING
(Map p84; ☑ 483 5249; www.lavieillecheminee. com; 1/2hr trail ride Rs 1300/1600) La Vieille Cheminée, a farm and rustic lodge, offers guided trots on horseback through the hilly countryside and along shady ravines.

Yemaya   MOUNTAIN BIKING
(☑ 283 8187, 5752 0046; www.yemayaadventures. com) Full- and half-day adventures can be arranged with professional 'cycle-path' Patrick Haberland at his outfit, Yemaya. It also arranges hikes through Black River Gorges National Park.

Chamarel & La Gaulette

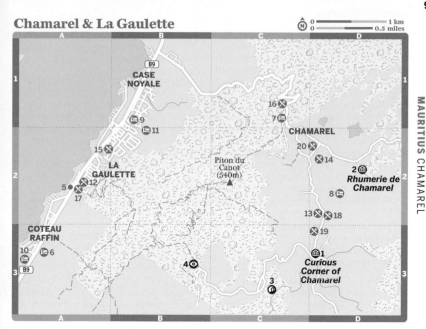

Chamarel & La Gaulette

🛏 Sleeping

Chamarel's sleeping options are far outweighed by restaurants, which may be why many visitors come here on day trips. There are, however, a couple of excellent choices.

★ **Le Coteau Fleurie**   GUESTHOUSE **€€**
(Map p97; ☎ 5733 3963; www.coteaufleurie.com; Royal Rd, Chamarel; r per person incl breakfast €50; @) Plucked from the sky-scraping ridges of Réunion, this lovely *chambre d'hôte* feels miles away from anything else in Mauritius.

A quaint Creole-style option, it embraces its traditional roots, and owners Geneviève and Gérard offer travellers a welcome retreat among fruit and coffee trees and thick jungle trunks.

Chalets en Champagne   CABIN **€€**
(Map p84; ☎ 5988 7418; www.leschaletsen champagne.mu; 110 Rte Champagne, Chamarel; per person Rs 2000; ❄) These beautiful log cabins sleep between four and eight people and are tucked into the mountainside amid gnarled tropical trees. The decor stays true

WORTH A TRIP

GRAND BASSIN

According to legend, Shiva and his wife Parvati were circling the earth on a contraption made from flowers when they were dazzled by an island set in an emerald sea. Shiva, who was carrying the Ganges River on his head to protect the world from floods, decided to land. As he did so a few drops of water dripped from his head and landed in a crater to form a lake. The Ganges expressed unhappiness about its water being left on an uninhabited island, but Shiva replied that dwellers from the banks of the Ganges would one day settle there and perform an annual pilgrimage, during which water from the lake would be presented as an offering.

The dazzling island is, of course, Mauritius; the legendary crater lake is known as Grand Bassin (Ganga Talao). It is a renowned pilgrimage site, to which up to 500,000 of the island's Hindu community come each year to pay homage to Shiva during the Maha Shivaratri celebrations. This vast festival takes place over three days in February or March (depending on the lunar cycle) and is the largest Hindu celebration outside India.

The most devoted pilgrims walk from their village to the sacred lake carrying a *kanvar* (a light wooden frame or arch decorated with paper flowers). This is no easy feat – February is Mauritius' hottest month and it almost always rains during the festivities. Once the pilgrims arrive they perform a *puja* (act of reverence), burning incense and camphor at the lakeshore and offering food and flowers.

to the wooded theme (think thatch roofs and stone-lined bathtubs) while gently incorporating modern touches (air-con, DVD players etc). Hikers will appreciate the surrounding network of marked trails that weaves across the tree-lined terrain.

★**Lakaz Chamarel**　　　　　　LODGE €€€
(Map p97; ☑483 5240; www.lakazchamarel. com; Piton Canot; incl half board s €145-340, d €195-490; P❋⟨⟩❄) This 'exclusive lodge' in the countryside around Chamarel is a wonderfully conceived collection of rustic (yet oh-so-elegant) cabins offering a blissful getaway amid gorgeous forests, gardens and streams. Rooms are tastefully decorated, with chic safari-style trimmings. Not to be missed are the serene spa and the charming swimming pool adorned with stone goddess statues.

✕ Eating

Chamarel has gained an island-wide reputation for the charming *tables d'hôtes* sprinkled around its hilltops. Lately (although rarely), unscrupulous taxi drivers have been capitalising on the area's newfound popularity with foodies by overcharging tourists and demanding hefty commissions from local restaurants. We recommend navigating the area with a private vehicle and choosing a dining option at your leisure.

Note that most places open only for lunch.

★**Palais de Barbizon**　　　　MAURITIAN €
(Map p97; ☑495 1690; lebarbizon@yahoo.fr; Ste-Anne Rd; meals Rs 450; ⟨⟩noon-4pm) Barbizon may not look like much, but it's a fabulous place. Marie-Ange helms the kitchen, whipping up traditional Mauritian flavours from her family's cookbook while Rico L'Intelligent (what a name!) entertains at the tables. He doesn't give you a menu. Instead, he offers a feast of rum punch, rice, five vegetables, and fish or chicken.

★**L'Alchimiste**　　　　　　MAURITIAN €€
(Map p97; ☑483 7980; www.rhumeriedechamarel. com; Rhumerie de Chamarel, Royal Rd; mains Rs 500-750, set menus Rs 1000-1500; ⟨⟩noon-3pm Mon-Sat) The Rhumerie de Chamarel's chic restaurant boasts an impressive menu that promises to satisfy, with game meats and palm heart from the surrounding hills the highlights. The chef's philosophy is definitely gourmet; flavourful Mauritian favourites are whipped into eye-pleasing concoctions such as braised wild boar cooked in Chamarel rum.

Mich Resto　　　MAURITIAN, INTERNATIONAL €€
(Map p97; ☑438 4158; www.michresto.mu; Royal Rd; ⟨⟩11am-4pm) Consistently glowing reviews from travellers, a classier setting than most in the area, friendly waiters, one of the best palm-heart salads we've tasted, excellent seafood... Mich Resto, which opened in 2015, is a fine place for lunch.

Le Domaine de Saint-Denis   MAURITIAN €€
(Map p84; ✆ 5728 5562; www.domainedesaint
denis.com; Chamarel; mains from Rs 600, set menu
from Rs 1500; ☺ by reservation only) Le Domaine
features recipes from the kitchen of Jacqueline Dalais, the unofficial First Lady of Mauritian cuisine, who oversees this gem of a
restaurant. Order the scallop carpaccio with
olive oil and lime if it's on the menu. It's signposted off the road from Chamarel to Black
River Gorges National Park.

Varangue sur Morne   MAURITIAN €€
(Map p84; ✆ 483 6610, 483 5710; Plaine Champagne Rd; mains from Rs 650; ☺ noon-4.30pm) This
former hunting lodge is an institution, and
it's not hard to see why. Its stunning location
offers great views over the forested hillsides
towards the ocean, and the superb menu is
pricey (some say overpriced) but excellent:
braised wild boar, prawns flambéed in Île de
France rum, palm-heart salad with smoked
marlin and a laundry list of clever cocktails.
Reservations are advised.

Chez Pierre Paul   MAURITIAN €€
(Map p97; ✆ 483 5079; Rte Champagne; mains
from Rs 450, set menu Rs 750; ☺ noon-4pm) No de-
lusions of grandeur here, just simple Creole
cuisine that hits the spot every time. Don't be
put off by the empty tables – this place is a
match for most others in town.

Domaine du Cachet   MAURITIAN, SEAFOOD €€
(Map p97; ✆ 483 5259; La Montagne; mains
from Rs 600, set menus Rs 1500-2300; ☺ 11.30am-
4pm) This restaurant with a honey-tinged
facade is not what it was, but the Mauritian
cooking is excellent, featuring palm-heart
salad, octopus curry, smoked marlin and the
like. Domaine du Cachet is along the Baie du
Cap–Chamarel Rd beyond the post office but
before the Terres de 7 Couleurs.

Les Palmiers   INDIAN, MAURITIAN €€
(Map p97; ✆ 483 8364; Royal Rd; mains from Rs
500; ☺ noon-4pm) This popular place does a
roaring trade with curries and *faratas* (pan-
fried flat breads) served in a pleasant dining
area.

**Le Chamarel
Restaurant**   MAURITIAN, INTERNATIONAL €€
(Map p97; ✆ 483 4421; le-chamarel.restaurant.
mu; La Crête; ☺ noon-3pm) Perched on a hillside 1km west of Chamarel along the descending road to Black River, this local
mainstay was undergoing major renovations
when we visited. While we can't comment on

the food in the interim, you can be sure of a
postcard-perfect panorama of the west coast
when the new restaurant finally takes shape.

ℹ Getting There & Away

Although there's a bus service from Quatre
Bornes to Chamarel, we highly recommend
using private transport. Do not visit Chamarel by
taxi – drivers are given exorbitant commissions
for bringing tourists to the various attractions
and *tables d'hôtes*.

Black River Gorges National Park

Mauritius' biggest and best national park is a
wild expanse of rolling hills and thick forest
covering roughly 2% of the island's surface.
It's difficult to overstate the importance of
this park – it's the last stand for Mauritian
forests and many native species. It's also the
most spectacular corner of the island, so if
you make only one day trip from the coast,
make it here.

Once prime hunting grounds, the area became a protected reserve in 1994 after scientists identified over 300 species of flowering
plant, nine endemic species of bird and a population of giant fruit bats that numbered more
than 4000. This is also an important habitat
for three of the island's most endangered bird

ℹ PREPARING TO HIKE

If you decide to attempt a trip under
your own steam, you'll need a private
vehicle as getting to the trailheads can
be near impossible with public transport. The best option is to get a taxi to
drop you off at a trailhead and then pick
you up at the lower end of the park.

We suggest checking **Fitsy** (www.fitsy.
com) before you head out into the wild.
This handy website features detailed
trail information using GPS and satellite
coordinates.

Note that there is nowhere to buy
food or drinks in the park. Make sure you
bring plenty of water and energy-boost-
ing snacks. You'll also need insect
repellent, wet-weather gear and shoes
with good grip – no matter how hot and
sunny the coast may be, it is usually wet
and humid within the park. Consider
binoculars for wildlife-watching.

HIKING THE BLACK RIVER GORGES

Numerous trails crisscross Black River Gorges National Park like unravelling shoestrings. While all of the trailheads are clearly marked along one of the two roads running through the park, many of the paths can quickly get obscured in the brush, leaving hikers confused. It's well worth stopping at one of the visitors centres to grab a crude map and check in about the current state of the trails. We recommend hiring a guide if you're serious about exploring the park and uncovering the better viewpoints. You can also contact the visitors centres ahead of time to enquire about hiring a ranger.

If you choose one of the one-way trails that ends at the Black River Gorges Visitor Centre, you may need to pre-arrange a time with a taxi to pick you up, as it's a long, one- to two-hour walk to the coast road where buses pass by.

The best time to visit the park is during the flowering season between September and January. Look for the rare *tambalacoque* (dodo tree), the black ebony trees and the wild guavas. Bird-watchers should keep an eye out for Mauritius kestrels (best seen from September to February), pink pigeons, echo parakeets and Mauritius cuckoo-shrikes.

Trails

The main trails are as follows. If you only have time to make one trek, choose between the Macchabée Trail, the Macchabée Loop and the Parakeet Trail.

Macchabée Trail (10km one way, strenuous, four hours) Begin at the Pétrin Information Centre, hiking along the plateau to the stunning Macchabée Viewpoint, then down to the Black River Gorges Visitor Centre.

Macchabée Forest Trail (14km return, moderate, three hours) Begin at the Pétrin Information Centre, but remain on the plateau with a loop through some lovely tropical forest.

Macchabée Loop (8km return, moderate, three hours) Hike along the plateau to the Macchabée Viewpoint, then return along the same path to the Pétrin Information Centre.

Parakeet Trail (8km one way, strenuous, three hours) Begin at the Plaine Champagne Police Post (halfway between the Gorges Viewpoint and Alexandra Falls along the tarred road from Chamarel), following a ridge down into the gorge and then along the river to the Black River Gorges Visitor Centre.

Mare Longue Reservoir (12km return, moderate, four hours) Begin and end at the Pétrin Information Centre, taking in a dwarf native forest and a large reservoir at the little-visited northern tip of the park.

species: the Mauritius kestrel, the echo parakeet and the pink pigeon. Introduced wild boar, macaque monkeys and deer also wander through the vast swaths of old-growth ebony, and sightings are not uncommon.

🏃 Activities

Otélair   ADVENTURE SPORTS
(☑251 6680; www.otelair.com) Otélair organises hiking, climbing, abseiling and canyoning trips, many of which take place inside Black River Gorges National Park.

Vertical World   ADVENTURE SPORTS
(☑697 5430, 251 1107; www.verticalworldltd.com) For a truly unique and unforgettable experience, adventurers can abseil from chute to chute on a half- or full-day canyoning excursion with Vertical World.

ℹ Information

Staff at both of the visitors centres can offer advice on the trails, brief you about the area's wildlife through captioned displays and hand out (fairly sketchy) maps.

Black River Gorges Visitors Centre (Map p84; ☑258 0057; ☺7am-5pm Mon-Fri, 9am-5pm Sat & Sun) At the park's western entrance, about 7.5km southeast of Black River's Trois Bras Junction.

Pétrin Information Centre (Map p84; ☑5507 0128, 471 1128; ☺8am-3.15pm Mon-Fri) At the eastern entrance to the park.

❶ Getting There & Away

There is little public transport through the park. Semi-regular buses pass the Pétrin Information Centre en route between Souillac and Vacoas or Curepipe, with similarly infrequent services from Curepipe or Quatre Bornes to Chamarel. You're much better visiting with your own wheels or hiring a taxi to get you to the trailheads. Buses run along the Coastal Rd, a one- to two-hour walk from the Black River Gorges Visitors Centre.

La Gaulette

POP 2375

South of Black River, the mountains draw ever closer to the coast. You'll find pinewoods and mangroves mingling with the lapping waves but little in the way of habitation besides the ramshackle settlements along the road. Then, a small township emerges under the shade of the nearby hills – it's a quiet place where the laid-back fisherfolk lifestyle effortlessly mixes with the carefree surfer vibe. Welcome to La Gaulette.

🏃 Activities

Ropsen   TOUR
(Map p97; ☑451 5763, 255 5546; www.ropsen. net; Royal Rd) La Gaulette's top tour operator, Ropsen organises catamaran excursions, dolphin-watching tours and island tours, as well as car rental and accommodation.

🛏 Sleeping

Gaining popularity among the kitesurfing crowd, La Gaulette represents excellent value for money. There is currently a handful of notable options in the village.

★ Maison Papaye   GUESTHOUSE €
(Map p97; ☑451 5976, 5752 0918; www.maison papaye.com; r incl breakfast €50-80; ✴@🛜🏊) Set among imposing homes on a residential street away from the sea, this stately *chambre d'hôte* is a real find. Although the whitewashed facade, gabled roof and periwinkle shutters may hint at a colonial past, the building is only a few years old – the owners designed their retirement getaway to invoke the island's plantation past. The owners keep tradition alive every evening with their Creole-inspired *table d'hôte* dinners (€15), served on the shaded veranda. There's a four-night minimum stay.

TAMARIN FALLS

Positioned on the outskirts of the Black River Gorges roughly 8km southwest of Curepipe in central Mauritius, this set of seven scenic cascades (some say 11) is a wonderful reward for those willing to take on a challenging hike.

Attempts to access the falls should not be made without a guide. Local guides (charging Rs 500 to 1000) usually wait around the bus station at Henrietta, a township near Curepipe, although we prefer linking up with Yana-ture (p103).

For a truly unique and unforgettable experience, adventurers can abseil from chute to chute on a half- or full-day canyoning excursion with Vertical World or Otélair. Both operators start their trips from Henrietta as well.

Pingo Studios   APARTMENT €
(Map p97; ☑5755 9773; Royal Rd; r from €45; P✴🛜) Around halfway between La Gaulette and Le Morne, these self-catering apartments get the thumbs up from travellers – midrange prices within sight of Le Morne are, after all, difficult to come by. Rooms are large and unpretentious but extremely comfortable.

Rusty Pelican   GUESTHOUSE €
(Map p97; ☑5978 9140; rusty-pelican.com; apt from €60; ✴@🛜🏊) This fabulous place at the northern end of town is a fine addition to La Gaulette's array of sleeping options. The rooms are flooded with natural light and have excellent bathrooms. The owners give you a mobile to use for the duration of your visit (you just pay for calls) and they love helping you plan your stay.

Ropsen   ACCOMMODATION SERVICES €
(☑451 5763, 5255 5546; www.ropsen.net; Royal Rd; studios & apt €30-60, 4-bed villas €100-125; ✴@🛜) From modern studios to large multi-bedroom apartments, friendly Ropsen proffers such a vast array of high-quality options that you'll start to think every building in La Gaulette is a rentable villa under his name! Almost all of Ropsen's properties have wi-fi, and guests without a laptop can check their email at the computer terminal in Ropsen's office. Insist on a sea view.

BLACK RIVER GORGES SCENIC DRIVE

Although we strongly recommend that you explore the Black River Gorges National Park on foot, if that's not possible you can still get a taste for this beautiful region. Before we get started, a word of advice: avoid making this trip on weekends if you can, as the otherwise quiet roads are flooded with locals driving slowly and stopping by the roadside while they hunt for wild berries.

Begin along the coast road on Mauritius' western coast at Grand Case Noyale (around 1.5km north of La Gaulette and around 7km south of Black River), where a signpost points inland towards Chamarel; if you're looking for a landmark, there's a cream church set back from the corner. After crossing the coastal plain, the road begins to climb steeply through increasingly dense forest. Around 4km after leaving the coast road, close to the top of the first ridgeline, a lookout on your right offers fine, sweeping views of the coastal plain and out to sea.

Passing through Chamarel, ignore the signs to Terres de 7 Couleurs (p96), which is not a patch on the scenery in the national park up ahead, and bear left through Chamarel. After passing the entrance to the Rhumerie de Chamarel (p96), continue climbing through the forest for around 6km to the **Gorges Viewpoint** (Map p84). On a clear day the views from here across the gorge rank among the best on the island. Look for the **Piton de la Petite Rivière Noire** (Black River Mountain peak; 828m) on your left, and keep an eye out for the Mauritius kestrel, tropicbirds and fruit bats.

A further 2km along the paved road, you pass the **Plaine Champagne Police Post** (Map p84) (trailhead for the Parakeet Trail), with the turn-off for **Alexandra Falls** a further 2km on. Turn right off the main road, passing beneath a pretty honour guard of trees, then follow the short path out to the falls' **viewpoint** (Map p84). While there, you can admire the cloud forest of **Mt Cocotte** (771m) and the view down to the south coast.

Back on the main road, turn right towards Chamouny at the roundabout 2.5km beyond the Alexandra Falls turn-off and follow the road down the hill through the thinning forest. After around 3km, pull into the unpaved parking area on the right (west) side of the road – from the low ridge of dirt and rock there are good views down into the crater lake called **Bassin Blanc**. If you wait here long enough, you might just see some of the region's rare birds passing through, although none breed here.

Return up the hill and continue straight ahead at the roundabout. After just over 2km, turn right and follow the signs to Grand Bassin (p98), an important pilgrimage site for the island's Hindus 2.5km from the turn-off. Long before you arrive, you'll see the massive and curiously hypnotic Shiva statue that watches over this sacred spot.

Return the 2.5km to the main road and at the T-Junction you'll see the Pétrin Information Centre (p100). Even if you're not planning to hike, park your car and wander around the back to an enclosure where pink pigeons are being prepared for release into the wild.

La Reine Créole B&B €

(Map p97; ☑ 451 5558; www.mauritius-lrc.com; 103 Rue des Manguiers; s €29-59, d €41-75) This charming B&B run by Marc and Corinne has large rooms, a welcoming feel and a quiet location; some of the rooms have fine views.

✗ Eating

The small *superettes* (small self-service grocery stores) that line the main street through town serve the legions of self-caterers; there are only a few restaurants in the area. For more options, consider driving up to Chamarel or Black River.

Chez Meilee MAURITIAN €

(Map p97; ☑ 451 6218; Coastal Rd; mains from Rs 250; ☺ noon-3pm & 6-9.30pm) A simple roadside cafe, Chez Meilee has friendly service and a mix of local and Chinese dishes. Try the battered prawns to begin; the curries are no frills but expertly cooked. If you order the day before, they'll fish for, and then cook, fresh fish or lobster from the lagoon.

Le Prestige MAURITIAN €

(Map p97; ☑ 451 6107; Coastal Rd; mains from Rs 175; ☺ noon-3pm & 6-9pm) Simple, down-home Mauritian cooking – curries and seafood, not surprisingly, feature prominently – make this an excellent choice.

Enso
MEDITERRANEAN €€

(Map p97; ☑451 5907; 1st fl, Village Walk Supermarket Centre; mains Rs 290-790; ☺6pm-late Tue-Sat; 🖘) Styling itself as a lounge bar and restaurant, this place does cool very well, with its laid-back pool table and Saturday-night DJs. The food itself is generally good without being spectacular – think pizzas, pasta and seafood – but it's better when they keep it simple, as with the mixed grill or seafood platter.

Ocean Vagabond
PIZZA €€

(Map p97; ☑451 5910; Royal Rd; pizza Rs 360-790; ☺5-10pm Wed-Mon) Ocean Vagabond has good pizzas and something of a surfer's vibe, with DVDs and a Saturday-evening happy hour. It all falls a bit flat when things are quiet, but that changes when a crowd's in. Good orders include the seafood salad and the chicken curry.

❶ Getting There & Away

Buses (every 20 minutes) between Quatre Bornes and Baie du Cap stop in La Gaulette. There are no direct buses from Port Louis; instead, you have to go via Quatre Bornes or take the bus from Port Louis to Black River and change.

A taxi between Port Louis and La Gaulette will cost around Rs 1200; it's Rs 1800 to the airport. Do not take a taxi to Chamarel – rent a vehicle (p155) instead.

Le Morne Peninsula

Visible from much of southwestern Mauritius, the iconic **Le Morne Brabant** (556m) is a stunning rocky crag from which this beautiful peninsula takes its name. Shaped like a hammerhead shark, the peninsula itself has some of the island's best beaches, now home to a number of upmarket hotels.

The coastline from the peninsula along to Baie du Cap is some of the most beautiful in the country, and it's blissfully free of development.

🏃 Activities

Although the area's upmarket hotels have gobbled up most of the peninsula's beachfront property, the beaches themselves are still open to the public. Travellers not staying at one of the local resorts can find several access points along the public roads, and there's easily accessible sand at the southern tip of the peninsula.

> ### LE MORNE: THE MOURNFUL ONE
>
> Although almost totally uninhabited by locals, Le Morne has deep resonance in Mauritian culture. According to legend, a group of escaped slaves fled to the peninsula in the early 19th century, hiding out on top of the mountain to remain free. The story goes that the slaves, ignorant of the fact that slavery had been abolished just before their escape, panicked when they saw a troop of soldiers making their way up the cliffs. Believing they were to be recaptured, the slaves flung themselves from the clifftops to their deaths in huge numbers. And thus the crag earned its name – Le Morne means Mournful One. Although there are no historical records to substantiate the story, it's an important tale for Mauritians and was critical in Le Morne being granted Unesco World Heritage status in 2008.

Hiking

Added to the Unesco World Heritage list in 2008, Le Morne is the star of many postcards, as it slopes through the sky and then plunges back into the blue. Few tourists, however, realise that the view from the top is even more spectacular. As you ascend the crag you'll pass through an indigenous forest that's the only place on the island where you'll find Mauritius' national flower, the *boucle d'oreille* ('earring'). When you reach 500m, you'll be treated to unobstructed vistas of the colourful reefs to the west and south. The trail increases in difficulty the higher up you go – those with limited mobility can still take in the views from a midway point (around 260m).

★ Yanature
HIKING

(Trekking Île Maurice; ☑5428 1909, 5731 4955; www.trekkingmauritius.com; 3-4hr hike per person Rs 1500; ☺7am Mon-Sat Apr-Oct, 6am Mon-Sat Nov-Mar) The best way to explore Le Morne Brabant is on a hike with Yanature. Yan, the founder, is a nature enthusiast and eighth-generation Mauritian who grew up at the base of Le Morne and wandered the snaking trails well into his teenage years. He and his fellow guides Henri and Nicolas have exclusive permission from the Gambier family (the landowners of Le Morne) to bring tourists through.

WORTH A TRIP

ÎLE AUX BÉNITIERS

The area's most notable attraction is the lovely Île aux Bénitiers, which floats just above sea level in the reef offshore. The islet is considerably larger than many of the other outcrops in the lagoon (keep an eye out for the interesting rocky projection that looks like the top half of an hourglass) and sports a beautiful picnic-worthy beach, a small coconut farm and a colony of migratory birds.

The island's keeper is quite the local character – he travels around with an ever-growing pack of chipper dogs. Note that, while the beach is publicly accessible, the island's interior is largely off-limits.

Most of the fishers docked at La Gaulette offer small excursions to the island. The number of boat operators that visit the island continues to grow each year and most of the products are identical: crowded catamarans and a picnic lunch on the sand. Check out www.catamarancruisesmauritius.com and expect to pay €60 per person for a full day's outing. Note that many cruise operators combine a trip to Île aux Bénitiers with dolphin-watching (p88).

After Le Morne, consider joining one of Yanature's other hiking excursions through Black River Gorges National Park, or perhaps to Tamarin Falls and the Corps de Garde. Discounts are offered to those who participate in multiple outings.

Horse Riding

Haras du Morne　　　　　　　HORSE RIDING
(Map p84; ☎450 4142; www.harasdumorne. com; Le Morne; 60/90/120min ride Rs 3000/ 3500/4500) Expensive horse rides are on offer at this upmarket equestrian centre, but the landscape through which they go (the forest and beaches around Le Morne) is among the prettiest on the island. The centre is off Royal Rd.

Surfing

The area is home to the ultimate surfing spot in all of Mauritius: **One Eye** (p148).

Windsurfing & Kitesurfing

The combination of Indian Ocean winds (the claim is 300 days of ideal winds a year, a claim we were unable to verify...), sheltered western waters and a fine backdrop make Le Morne ideal for windsurfing and kitesurfing. For the latter, beginners should start at 'Kite Lagoon'; the southern winds are much more severe and unpredictable.

Son of Kite　　　　　　　　KITESURFING
(Map p84; ☎451 6155, 5972 9019; www. sonofkite.com; classes per person per hr €32.50-75, rental per hr €25) Kiteboarders of every ilk (from newbies to pros) can sign up for a class with the recommended professionals at Son of Kite.

Yoaneye Kite Centre　　　　　　KITESURFING
(Map p84; ☎5737 8296; www.yoaneye.com; 114 Villa Mona, Le Petit Morne; classes per person from €40) Yoaneye Kite Centre, an IKO-affiliated centre, offers kitesurfing classes for beginners and more experienced kitesurfers, as well as stand-up paddle boarding.

Kite Lagoon　　　　　　　　KITESURFING
(Map p84) Kitesurfing beginners should start here on the western side of the peninsula in the 'Kite Lagoon'; the southern winds are much more severe and unpredictable.

ION Club　　　　　KITESURFING, WINDSURFING
(Map p84; ☎450 4112; www.ionclubmauritius. com/en) The worldwide surfing organisation ION Club operates intensive kitesurfing and windsurfing courses from its school at Le Morne; equipment rental is also possible for those who know what they're doing. Figure on around €75 for a one-hour private course.

🛏 Sleeping

Largely the domain of five-star properties, the fan-shaped swath of sand below the looming Le Morne Brabant is a wonderful place to spend your days on Mauritius if you're looking for a lazy beach holiday. You will need to rent a private vehicle (or pay taxis for day excursions) to get around.

★Lux Le Morne　　　　　　　RESORT €€€
(Map p84; ☎401 4000; www.luxresorts.com; Coastal Rd; r from €385) When you dream of a Mauritian idyll, this might be the place you're thinking of. This resort does everything and does it well: über-luxurious rooms, top-notch restaurants, dreamy swimming pools, a high-class spa, watersports.

Dinarobin HOTEL €€€

(Map p84; ☑ 401 4900; www.dinarobin-hotel.com; Coastal Rd; d incl half board from €310; ✱ @ ☎ ⊠) A ravishing Beachcomber beauty, with a sprawling campus of 172 suites, this property is named after the first moniker given to the island by Arab merchants in the 10th century. Rated 'five star plus', it lives up to expectations, with five swimming pools, four restaurants, a golf course and a pampering spa.

Paradis HOTEL €€€

(Map p84; ☑ 401 5050; www.beachcomber-hotels.com; d incl half board from €260; ✱ @ ☎ ⊠) Stunning sea views, luxurious accommodation, a golf course and endless activities. What more could you ask for? Not to be missed is the fresh seafood at Blue Marlin, one of the in-house restaurants.

Riu Le Morne RESORT €€€

(Map p84; ☑ 650 4203; www.riu.com; d incl half board from €210; ✱ @ ☎ ⊠) Besides the remote stretch of gorgeous beach, Riu Le Morne's strong suit is the wide range of activities, including kitesurfing. It's for adults only, which gives a vaguely honeymoon air to the experience, and there's an on-site disco, as well as an artistic workshop to indulge your inner creative.

THE SOUTHEAST

With many charms, the sultry southeast of Mauritius is a seductress. This dramatic stretch of coast, watched over by landforms like Lion Mountain, has lovely turquoise bays (such as Blue Bay), long stretches of sand (Pointe d'Esny) and some of Mauritius' best wildlife-watching at Île aux Aigrettes and Vallée de Ferney. The main settlement, Mahébourg, combines grit with a somnambulent seaside appeal and a fabulous Monday market, while Vieux Grand Port is where Mauritius' human story began some 400 years ago.

ⓘ Getting There & Away

Mahébourg is the main transport hub in this region, with buses departing for destinations along the east and south coasts. The Mahébourg–Blue Bay area is an excellent place to arrange car and bike hire.

SSR International Airport (p57) is just 15 minutes by taxi from Mahébourg, Pointe d'Esny and Blue Bay.

Mahébourg

POP 17,042

There is something relentlessly charming about bite-size Mahébourg (my-boor), where it's all about simple pleasures: an interesting museum, a buzzing market, spicy street food, good budget lodgings, a pretty backdrop and beautiful beaches to the north and south. You still hear talk of ambitious plans to transform Mahébourg's waterfront into a mammoth complex like Le Caudan in Port Louis, but it will be years before this takes shape.

Founded in 1805, the town was named after French governor Mahé de Labourdonnais. The town was once a busy port, but these days it's something of a backwater, with a small fleet of fishers and a grid of dilapidated buildings.

◉ Sights

You can cover Mahébourg's smattering of sights in a couple of hours, leaving plenty of time to wander the backstreets and stroll along the seafront. Everything can be tackled on foot, though you might want to hire a bike to get out to the biscuit factory.

★**Monday Market** MARKET

(Map p110; ☺ 8am-5pm) Don't miss the central *foire de Mahébourg*, near the waterfront. The initial focus was silks and other textiles, but these days you'll find a busy produce section, tacky bric-a-brac and steaming food stalls. It's the perfect place to try some local snacks – *gâteaux piments* (chilli cakes), *dhal puri* (lentil pancakes) and *samousas* (samosas) – usually dispensed from boxes on the backs of motorcycles. The market is open every day but doubles in size on Monday.

It doesn't take long to navigate the snaking rows of vendors, but it's well worth taking your time to explore every last corner.

★**National History Museum** MUSEUM

(Map p106; ☑ 631 9329; Royal Rd; ☺ 9am-4pm Wed-Sat & Mon, to noon Sun) **FREE** This museum contains some fascinating artefacts, including early maps of the island and paintings of Mauritius' original fauna – including, of course, the dodo. There are also a few dodo bones in a glass case, along with those of other disappeared species such as the red rail and Rodrigues solitaire. One real curio is an engraving of Dutch gentlemen riding in pairs on the back of a giant tortoise, a species that also went the way of the dodo.

The South & Southeast

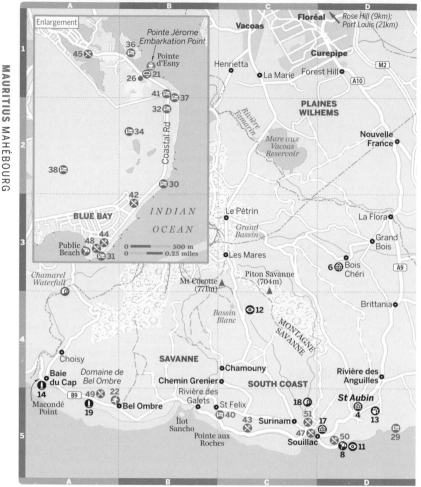

The colonial mansion housing this museum used to belong to the Robillard family and played an important part in the island's history. It was here in 1810 that the injured commanders of the French and English fleets were taken for treatment after the Battle of Vieux Grand Port (the only naval battle in which the French got the upper hand over their British foes). The story of the victory is retold in the museum, along with salvaged items – cannons, grapeshot and the all-important wine bottles – from the British frigate *Magicienne*, which sank in the battle.

The bell and a cache of Spanish coins from the wreck of the *St Géran* are also on display. The ship's demise in 1744, off the northeast coast of Mauritius, inspired the famous love story *Paul et Virginie* by Bernardin de St-Pierre.

Recent additions to the museum include a retrofitted train carriage out the back and a replica of Napoleon's boat used in the infamous battle defeating the English.

Rault Biscuit Factory   MUSEUM
(Map p106; ☑ 631 9559; www.biscuitmanioc.com; adult/child Rs 140/100, incl tasting Rs 175/125;

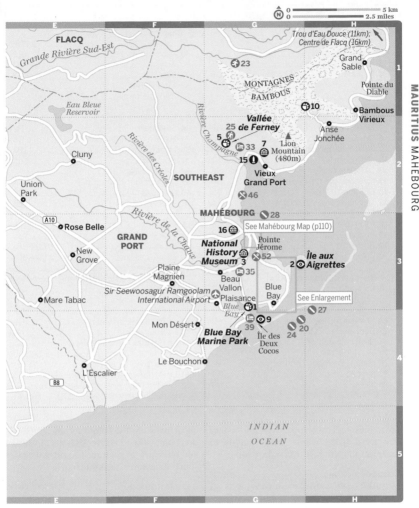

9am-3pm Mon-Fri) In 1870 the Rault family started producing manioc biscuits at its little biscuit factory on the northern outskirts of Mahébourg, and the factory has changed hardly a jot since. The crispy square cookies are made almost entirely by hand using a secret recipe passed down from generation to generation and baked on hotplates over stoves fuelled with dried sugar-cane leaves. The 20-minute tour ends with a chance to sample the finished product – with a nice cup of tea, of course.

The factory is on the far side of the Cavendish Bridge; when you cross the bridge,

turn left at the brown-and-white factory sign and then follow the further signs. Packets of the biscuits (we recommend butter flavour; reaching this decision involved pleasurable research...) are on sale for Rs 65.

Notre Dame des Anges   CHURCH

(Map p110) The butter-coloured tower of Notre Dame des Anges church dominates the Mahébourg skyline. The original church was built in 1849, but it has been restored several times over the years, most recently in 1938. Take a quick peek inside at the baronial roof timbers. Local people visit throughout the

The South & Southeast

day to make offerings to beloved missionary Père Laval (p53), whose statue stands to your right immediately inside the door.

Mosque　　　　　　　　　　　　MOSQUE
(Map p110) Mahébourg's main mosque is an important local landmark.

🏃 Activities

The most popular activity in the area is an excursion by boat to the offshore islands (Île aux Aigrettes, Île de la Passe, Île aux Vacoas and Île au Phare) or the über-popular Île aux Cerfs further north. Most of the trips involve snorkelling and include lunch. Scores of boatswains park along the shores of Mahébourg and Blue Bay awaiting customers and all offer relatively similar experiences.

Croisières Turquoise　　　　SNORKELLING
(Map p106; ☑631 1640; www.croisieres-turquoise. com; Coast Rd; per person Rs 2000) This outfit runs day-long boat trips to Île aux Cerfs,

departing from the Pointe Jerome embarkation point close to Le Preskîl hotel at 9.30am and returning at 4.30pm. The price includes snorkelling and a barbecue lunch.

Case Nautique　　　　DIVING, KAYAKING
(Map p110; ☑631 5613; casenautique@gmail. com; cnr Rue Shivananda & Rue de Labourdonnais; kayak hire per day Rs 500, snorkelling per 2hr Rs 750) Good for equipment rental if your hotel can't help, as well as snorkelling excursions to Île aux Cerfs and other islands.

Jean-Claude Farla　　　　BOAT TOUR
(☑423 1322, 631 7090) Our operator of choice is local legend Jean-Claude Farla, a six-time national swimming champion who competed in the Indian Ocean games. He is the only person to offer outings on a traditional 22ft pirogue (others have souped-up boats with motors). Figure on €20 for a half-day trip, gliding through the blue and stopping periodically to snorkel and free dive.

It's €50 for a full-day excursion to Île aux Cerfs, with a stop at Île de Flamant and a BBQ lunch on Île aux Mangénie. It's best to call at least two days ahead to ensure that he's available (there's a six-person minimum).

🛏 Sleeping

You won't come across any grand hotels in quaint Mahébourg, but you will find a proliferation of good, simple guesthouses, making the town an ideal base for budget travellers. Staying in Pointe d'Esny further down the coast is a good, quieter alternative.

Chill Pill   B&B €
(Map p110; 🕿 5787 4000; www.chillpillmauritius. com; Rue Shivananda 6; d incl breakfast from €56; ❄ 🛜 ≋) Simple but bright rooms with tiled floors and sea views make this a good choice. The location, where Mahébourg begins to peter out and the wide horizons of the ocean take hold, is ideal for those who like the best of both worlds.

Tyvabro   GUESTHOUSE €
(Map p110; 🕿 631 9674; www.tyvabro.com; Rue Marianne; d incl breakfast €27; ❄ 🛜) This family-run operation earns high marks for friendly and eager service. Little perks like in-room DVD players and a welcoming roof deck with a hammock more than make up for the past-their-prime furnishings in the rooms.

Hotel les Aigrettes   HOTEL €
(Map p110; 🕿 631 9094; www.hotellesaigrettes. com; cnr Rue du Chaland & Rue des Hollandais; incl breakfast s/d small Rs 800/1000, large Rs 1100/1400; ❄ 🛜 ≋) Seemingly always under construction, this hotel resembles a Jenga tower with its stack of bedrooms and protruding balconies winding several storeys high. The rooms are clean and some even have sea views. Our pick is No 32: the bathroom's across the hall (although it's not shared), but the combination of views and comfort is splendid. The owner has a big smile.

Coco Villa   GUESTHOUSE €
(Map p110; 🕿 631 2346; www.mahecocovilla.net; Rue Shivananda; s/d incl breakfast Rs 1000/1500; ❄ 🛜 ≋) Simple, light-filled spaces right by the water are what this place is all about. Most of the rooms have unobstructed sea views, and the location on Mahébourg's southern outskirts combines the best in proximity to the town and all it offers and a quiet coastal atmosphere.

DIVING IN THE EAST & SOUTHEAST
....

Off the southeast coast the main highlight is the dramatic underwater topography – expect various drop-offs, tunnels, boulders and caves and, if you're lucky, a few marauding pelagic species, such as sharks, tuna and barracudas.

Further north there are excellent, strong-current sites off Belle Mare and Trou d'Eau Douce.

There are very few dive centres in the island's east and south, but most major resorts can put you in touch with one. Otherwise, check online at www.msda. mu for a list of licensed and insured dive operators. The following are fabulous places to dive.

Sirius (Map p106), off Mahébourg: 18th-century wreck at 20m to 25m.

Colorado (Map p106), off Pointe d'Esny and Blue Bay: dive down 35m in shark-rich waters.

Roches Zozo (Map p106), off Pointe d'Esny and Blue Bay: dive down 40m where reef meets open ocean.

Belmar Pass (Map p123), off Belle Mare: strong currents; good for sharks and barracudas.

Nice Place Guesthouse   GUESTHOUSE €
(Map p110; 🕿 631 9419; www.niceplace.orange. mu; Rue de Labourdonnais; s/d from Rs 600/700, with shared bathroom Rs 400/500; ❄ 🛜) As the name suggests, this simple guesthouse has nice rooms – if simple and a bit faded – tended by a lovely Indian couple. For this price, it's the best in town.

ONS Motel   HOTEL €
(Map p110; 🕿 5918 0811; www.onsmotel.com; Royal Rd; r €30-55; ❄ 🛜) If you had a Mauritian grandmother, this might be the sort of guesthouse she'd run, with its slightly flowery decor and homey sense of welcome. The rooms are simple but a good size, and the hotel gets consistently positive reviews from travellers.

🍴 Eating

Mahébourg has dozens of back alleys riddled with hidden eateries known only to locals. If you're planning to swing by for a visit, make sure you come on Monday, when

MAURITIUS MAHÉBOURG

Mahébourg

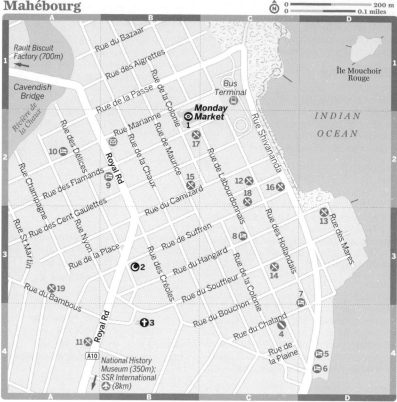

Mahébourg

the local market is in full force – you'll be treated to the colourful clanging of street stalls as vendors hawk savoury snacks to lines of shoppers.

★ **La Vielle Rouge**   SEAFOOD €
(Map p110; ☎ 631 3980; cnr Rue de Hangard & Rue des Mares; mains Rs 180-350; ⊙10am-11pm) Fish and seafood cooked fresh or with a few Asian inflections make Le Vielle Rouge one

of the standout options in town. Service is friendly and signature dishes include the calamari with ginger sauce or fresh lobster with garlic sauce. The outdoor setting in the back garden is lovely, too.

★ Pyramide
MAURITIAN €

(Map p110; ✆631 9731; Rue de Labourdonnais; kebabs Rs 55, small/large biryani Rs 85/115; ☺9.30am-4pm or 5pm Mon-Sat) This hero of the street-food scene is beside the petrol station just across from the market. Delicious biryani (rice cooked in a steel pot with various eastern spices and meat or fish) and 'kebabs' (salad, meat and sauce in a baguette) seem to emerge from the kitchen in factory proportions as fishers and hawkers queue for a midday meal.

Whether eating in or taking away, order at the small counter on the right as you enter. Kebabs come with or without chilli and are spectacularly good whichever way you have them.

Shyam
MAURITIAN €

(✆5764 2960; rotis & dhal puris Rs 12; ☺11am-4pm) For the best *dhal puri* in town, look no further than Shyam (you can call him 'Sam'). He scoots around scooping out flavourful snacks from an empty aquarium tank on the back of his motorbike. On Monday he's at the market (p105), but if you're desperate for *dhal puri* at other times, give him a ring and he'll come find you.

Shyam also makes an appearance at the public schools when the students are set free from class in the afternoon.

Le Bazilic
MAURITIAN, INTERNATIONAL €

(Map p110; ✆5788 9534; Rue de Maurice; mains Rs 150-300; ☺10am-8pm) The ubiquitous fried noodles, grilled seafood and octopus curry all appear here, on a menu that owes less to creative combinations than to simple dishes done well.

Saveurs de Shin
CHINESE, MAURITIAN €

(Map p110; ✆5751 5932, 631 3668; Rue de Suffren; mains Rs 150-395; ☺10am-2pm & 6-10pm Wed-Mon) This place a block back from the water may not look like much, but the quality is high, the prices are low and the servings are large – a winning combination in anyone's language. The half/full Peking duck is outrageously good value at Rs 450/800, but you could choose anything from this extensive menu and not be disappointed.

L'Ajoupa
MAURITIAN, INTERNATIONAL €

(Map p110; ✆5290 1268; Rue du Souffleur; snacks & mains Rs 50-250; ☺10.30am-3pm & 6.30-10pm Thu-Tue) L'Ajoupa is worth an honourable mention for its homely tree-lined garden hidden behind a scratched picket fence. It's the perfect place to catch up with friends for a drink and some *poisson frit* (fried fish), rice or a burger.

Tabagi Bambous
MAURITIAN €

(Map p110; ✆5796 0070; Rue du Bambous; rotis Rs 10; ☺7.30am-9.30pm) Dark and dimly lit, *tabagis* (convenience stores) line the streets of every town in Mauritius. If you've yet to visit one, the unusually popular Bambous is the perfect place to lose your *tabagi* virginity. Proprietor Amrita dishes out her signature *rotis* while Bollywood heroines clink their bejewelled costumes on the TV screen.

Amrita herself is quite the anomaly – it's very rare for a woman to run her own business in the less-developed parts of the country.

La Colombe
MAURITIAN €

(Map p110; ✆631 8594; Rue des Hollandais; mains Rs 175-350; ☺11am-3pm & 6-9.30pm) Disco lights, kitsch decor and smiling staff await you at this lively venue located on a side street set back from the promenade. House specials include venison and a smattering of seafood. Things liven up a bit on Saturday, which is occasionally *séga* night.

Chez Patrick
MAURITIAN, CHINESE €

(Map p110; ✆631 9298; Royal Rd; mains Rs 225-350; ☺11.30am-3pm & 6-10pm) Patrick's is popular with locals and tourists for its unpretentious atmosphere and authentic Creole cooking. There's everything from octopus curry to Creole clams, and the seven-course seafood feast (Rs 675) is one of the south's best bargains, even if three of those courses are taken up by French fries, salad and vegetables.

London Way
SUPERMARKET €

(Map p106; ✆696 0088; ☺8.30am-7pm Mon-Tue & Thu, to 8pm Fri & Sat, to 12.30pm Sun) The modern London Way supermarket is on the main road heading towards Pointe d'Esny.

Les Copains d'Abord
MAURITIAN, SEAFOOD €€

(Map p110; ✆631 9728; Rue Shivananda; mains Rs 375-1000, snacks Rs 90-225; ☺10am-3pm & 6-9pm) Les Copains d'Abord occupies an enviable position along the seafront promenade on the south side of town. Tasty Mauritian dishes (fresh seafood curry, prawn croquettes, palm-heart salad, flavourful *rougaille saucisses* (spicy sausages) and wild-boar ribs in Rodrigues honey), smart decor and frequent fits of live music will quickly help you forget that the menu is at times overpriced.

❶ Information

HSBC (☑ 631 9633; Royal Rd)

Mauritius Commercial Bank (MCB; ☑ 631 2879; Rue des Délices)

Thomas Cook (Rue Marianne; ⊘ 8.30am-4.30pm Mon-Wed, Fri & Sat, to 3.30pm Thu) Handy for the market and with good exchange rates.

❶ Getting There & Away

Mahébourg's bus station (Map p110) is an important transport hub. There are express buses every half-hour to/from Port Louis (Rs 38, two hours), from where there are connections to Grand Baie and other destinations. Most but not all of these buses stop at the airport en route; check before boarding. A shuttle from Mahébourg to Blue Bay runs roughly every 30 minutes.

Buses running north from Mahébourg go to Centre de Flacq via Vieux Grand Port every 20 minutes or so. Heading south, there are less frequent services to Souillac via Rivière des Anguilles.

A taxi for the 15-minute hop from SSR international airport to Mahébourg costs Rs 500. From Mahébourg, you'll pay Rs 1600 to reach Port Louis, Rs 1600 to reach Flic en Flac and Rs 1300 to reach Belle Mare.

❶ Getting Around

You'll find a variety of local car renters who also offer rides to the airport. Your accommodation can hook you up with a vehicle.

Pointe d'Esny & Blue Bay

Pointe d'Esny and Blue Bay have some of the most beautiful stretches of beach on the entire island and they're many travellers' favourite corners of the country. Pointe d'Esny is also the jumping-off point for those interested in visiting the nature reserve on Île aux Aigrettes.

◎ Sights

★ Île aux Aigrettes   ISLAND
(Map p106) This popular ecotourism destination is a 26-hectare nature reserve on an island roughly 800m off the coast. It preserves very rare remnants of the coastal

forests of Mauritius and provides a sanctuary for a range of endemic and endangered wildlife species. Visits are only possible as part of a guided tour, and these leave from Pointe Jérome, close to Le Preskîl. Highlights include Aldabra giant tortoises, ebony trees, wild orchids, and the endangered pink pigeon and other rare bird species.

As the guides to Île aux Aigrettes rightly point out, this is the last place in Mauritius where you can see it as the first explorers did almost five centuries ago – everywhere else, the land has been tamed. The Mauritian Wildlife Foundation manages the reserve and conducts tours.

★ Blue Bay Marine Park   WILDLIFE RESERVE
(Map p106) In an effort to protect the area's rich underwater forest of rare corals from encroaching development, the government has given Blue Bay 'marine park' status. Besides a mandate barring high-speed watercraft, though, it seems that conservation plans are a bit laissez-faire. Local environmentalists fear that irreversible coral bleaching is inevitable, which is a shame as this is the best snorkelling spot on the island.

There are no 'official' tours of the marine park like those on Île aux Aigrettes, but the protected patches of coral can be easily explored on a snorkelling outing or during an excursion aboard a glass-bottomed boat (figure on around Rs 200 per person for one hour).

Île des Deux Cocos   ISLAND
(Map p106; www.iledesdeuxcocos.com) Île des Deux Cocos sits at the edge of the azure lagoon and was once used by flamboyant British governor Sir Hesketh Bell to entertain guests. Today, the Lux hotel group has maintained this hospitable tradition by offering tourists a relaxing day of swimming, beach lazing and snorkelling. Welcome drinks, an immense buffet lunch and rum tasting are also included. Transport to the island can be arranged by any of the Lux hotels or via the website.

Travellers with serious cash to burn can rent out the island's sole villa (constructed by Bell over a century ago) for an eye-popping €2000 per night, give or take a few hundred depending on the season.

🏃 Activities
Boat Trips
Like Mahébourg to the north, Blue Bay is home to numerous operators offering journeys on glass-bottomed boats and excursions to the nearby islands. Travellers should be careful, however, when choosing a boatswain here – the area has seen an increased number of drug dealers and addicts in recent years; always seek a recommendation from a local or your hotel before handing over any money. Also, the tides vary greatly in this part of the island; only a knowledgeable tour leader will know the optimal times for going to sea. Recommended operators:
➡ Jean-Claude Farla (p108)
➡ Le Preskîl (p114)
➡ Case Nautique (p108)
➡ Croisières Turquoise (p108)

Diving
There are several dive sites of note off the southeastern coast of Mauritius. These scuba hot spots – mostly wall dives and dropoffs – have interesting rock formations that plunge to 40m and attract a good number of

---

THE WILDLIFE OF ÎLE AUX AIGRETTES

In 1985, the Mauritian Wildlife Foundation (p112) took out a lease on Île aux Aigrettes and began the difficult task of ridding it of introduced plants and animals, including rats and feral cats. It also began a massive planting program, removing introduced species and reintroducing native plants. Until the foundation began its work, the island was a popular place for day trips and most native plant species had been cut down for firewood. One exception was a small but significant stand of ebony forest. The forest survives, including some trees that may be 400 years old, and most guided tours pass through it.

The foundation was able to bring some of the most endangered species in Mauritius to the island in the hope that they would find refuge and breed in a suitable natural habitat free from predators. Along with other sites, such as Round Island (off the north coast) and Black River Gorges National Park (in the southwest), the island has become a bulwark against extinction, not to mention a stunning conservation success story. Île aux Aigrettes is now home to around 50 pink pigeons (out of just 470 left in the wild today), 25 olive white-eye pairs (out of 100 to 150 pairs) and 150 Mauritian fodies (out of 400). On most guided visits there's a good chance of seeing the pink pigeon, but you'll need luck to see the other species.

Interestingly, not all endangered species made it here – the Mauritian kestrel was introduced but didn't find the habitat to be suitable (the canopy was too low and there was not enough prey), and so the birds crossed the water and found more suitable habitats on the main island, including nearby Kestrel Valley (p116) and Vallée de Ferney (p116).

Other stars of the show include around 20 adult Aldabra or Seychelles tortoises (as well as a number of young), the last of the giant Indian Ocean tortoise species. This is one of very few places in Mauritius to see these soulful creatures in the wild. Note also the five or so caged (and endangered) Mauritian fruit bats and around 450 Telfair's skinks (important competitors for the introduced – and undesirable – Indian shrews, the only remaining mammal species on Île aux Aigrettes).

colourful fish. The most noteworthy sites are Colorado (p28) and Roches Zozo (p28).

Coral Diving
DIVING

(Map p106; ☑604 1084; www.coraldiving.com; lagoon/sea dive Rs 1800/2000; ☺8.30am-4.30pm) Friendly Tony, one of the most knowledgeable divers in Mauritius, runs Coral Diving, the southeast's main scuba operator. It is primarily located on the sandy grounds of Le Preskîl but is open to those not staying at the hotel. The sea dive includes pool training for beginners.

🛏 Sleeping

Pointe d'Esny and Blue Bay are among the epicentres of tourism in the south and there's a lot to be said for staying here. Close to the airport and to the charms of Mahébourg, the area also has a good mix of upmarket resorts, private villas, apartment complexes and charming *chambres d'hôtes*.

Chez Henri
GUESTHOUSE €

(Map p106; ☑631 9806; www.henri-vacances.com; Coastal Rd; r incl breakfast Rs 1800; ❄@) Staying at Henri and Majo's welcoming *chambre d'hôte* feels like a trip to the countryside to visit your long-lost uncle and aunt. Rooms are lovingly filled with loads of wood and wicker, and each one sports a useful kitchenette. Don't miss the excellent three-course dinners (Rs 500 to Rs 600), served on the patio. Staying or eating here is a great opportunity to meet other guests and listen to Henri recount his various adventures while rattling off an endless stream of double entendres (it helps if you speak French, though).

Le Blazon
GUESTHOUSE €

(Map p106; ☑5771 7917, 631 1699; www.residence-leblason.com; r incl half board from €60; ❄⏚) Set a block inland from the main coastal road, Le Blazon has a decidedly residential vibe since traffic rarely ever zooms by. There are four rooms spread across two floors, a guest kitchen and an inviting Japanese sauna.

Blue Beryl
GUESTHOUSE €€

(Map p106; ☑631 9862; www.blueberyl.com; Coastal Rd; r incl breakfast €60-80) Despite what you might expect, many – perhaps even most – of the lodgings in Pointe d'Esny and Blue Bay are divided from the beach by a road. Blue Beryl bucks that trend with simply furnished studios, most of which face right onto the beach. Air-con costs €5 extra; you can upgrade to half board for an additional €10 per person.

Noix de Coco
GUESTHOUSE €€

(Map p106; ☑5772 9303; www.noixdecocoguesthouse.com; Coastal Rd; r incl breakfast €64-81; ❄) Dorette has opened her charming home to travellers. Several rooms have sea views, though you'll spend most of your time lounging on the sand-swept terrace.

Villa Vakoa
VILLA €€

(Map p106; ☑431 1099, 5727 3216; www.pointedesny.com; Pointe Jérome; villas €150-300; ❄❄) Large two-storey property located 300m south of Le Preskîl, with travertine floors, an American-style kitchen and spacious bedrooms. Sleeps six.

Pingouinvilla
APARTMENT €€

(Map p106; ☑637 3051; www.pingouinvillas.com; Rue Daurades, Blue Bay; studios per day/week €50/325, apt €60/420; ❄⏳) This charming complex of fully equipped apartments is a few blocks back from the beach. There's maid service twice a week.

★ Le Preskîl
RESORT €€€

(Map p106; ☑604 1000; www.lepreskil.com; Pointe Jérome; s/d incl half board from €130/201; ❄@⏳⏚) An unparalleled position on a secluded spit of sand? Check! Romantic views of the turquoise lagoon and rolling jungle mountains? Check! This four-star resort is a slice of paradise and we can't find a reason not to stay here. Attractive rooms, expansive grounds and plans for a major refurbishment add up to one of the island's best deals.

In addition to the usual bevy of watersports and activities, Le Preskîl boasts a kids club, expert scuba diving and a private catamaran shuttling vacationers to the nearby marine park and Île aux Cerfs.

Astroea Beach
BOUTIQUE HOTEL €€€

(Map p106; ☑631 4282; www.southerncrosshotels.mu; Coastal Rd; s/d incl half board from €200/300; P❄@⏳⏚) Fronting onto the beach in Pointe d'Esny, this fine spot styles itself as a luxury boutique hotel. Rooms, all decked in white and aquamarine blue, are large and lovely, and many have ocean views. There's the Ylang Spa, an excellent restaurant with sea views and a full suite of watersports activities and excursions.

Shandrani
RESORT €€€

(Map p106; ☑601 9000; www.beachcomber-hotels.com; s/d from €89/178; ❄@⏳⏚) On the southern side of Blue Bay, this relaxed, family-friendly resort rambles across a private peninsula with luscious jungle foliage. It has three beaches and boasts all the facilities you'd expect from a heavy hitter in the top-end category, but with a far more reasonable price tag than you might think.

The resort also has four restaurants, a golf course, tennis courts, a dive centre and more.

Le Jardin de Beau Vallon HISTORIC HOTEL €€€
(Map p106; ☑631 2850; www.lejardindebeauvallon.com; Rue de Beau Vallon; s/d Rs 2300/3200; ✴☎) Beau Vallon is primarily known for its charming restaurant, set on the ground floor of an 18th-century colonial manor house. There are, however, several suites and bungalows on the property that make for a memorable vacation experience, as long as you don't mind being a 10-minute drive to the beach.

Several newer bungalows are arranged in a row just beyond the main building and are adorned with plantation-style incarnations of wood and wicker.

✖ Eating

Despite the palpable residential vibe, Pointe d'Esny and Blue Bay have a few noteworthy options spread along the coastal road – Blue Bay in particular has some fine choices. And if you're here for a while and in need of a little variety, Mahébourg is rarely more than a 10-minute drive away.

Jonquille Maryse MAURITIAN €
(Chez Maryse; Map p106; ☑978 8211; Coastal Rd; mains from Rs 250; ☺11.30am-3pm & 6-9pm) After winning a 'women's empowerment' grant from the Mauritian government, friendly Maryse and her family opened a small restaurant in her backyard. Savoury Creole eats are stewed under the yellow tin roof and served to contented customers gathered around the haphazard collection of tables.

★**Le Jardin de Beau Vallon** MAURITIAN €€
(Map p106; ☑631 2850; www.lejardindebeauvallon.com; Rue de Beau Vallon; mains Rs 200-600; ☺noon-3pm & 7-10pm) Emerging from an inland thicket of trees and sky-scraping cane leaves, Beau Vallon is an enchanting colonial estate that has been lovingly refurbished over the last few decades. Romantic dark-wood panelling, flavourful island spices and the lazy spin of frond-shaped ceiling fans make for an atmospheric setting. If only the staff could be as charming as the surrounds...

★**Blue Bamboo** ITALIAN, MAURITIAN €€
(Map p106; ☑631 5801; Coastal Rd; pizza Rs 240-390, mains Rs 380-480; ☺11.30am-3pm &

6-11pm) Blue Bamboo has many charms: a cosy plant-filled cloister, delicious pan pizza, friendly owners and an inviting lounge on the 2nd floor. The upstairs bar is open 6pm to midnight every day except Monday. In high season it's best to call ahead if you'd like a table in the bamboo-lined courtyard.

La Belle Créole MAURITIAN €€
(Assiette du Pêcheur; Map p106; ☑631 1069; Royal Rd; mains Rs 450-900) Excellent Creole cooking – such as venison curry or *rougaille saucisses* (spicy sausages) – combined with an attractive lagoon-side, open-air setting (bring the mosquito repellent) make this one of our favourite choices in the area. It's around halfway between Mahébourg and Pointe d'Esny.

Charka Steakhouse STEAK €€
(Map p106; ☑604 1000; Le Preskîl, Pointe Jérome; mains Rs 590-880; ☺7-10.30pm) Set deep within the grounds of Le Preskîl resort, but billed as its own separate restaurant, Charka is a must for meat lovers. Fresh South African steaks of the highest quality are grilled to perfection in modern surrounds accented by the odd African mask or hunting spear. Reservations are essential, especially if you aren't staying at the hotel.

Le Bougainville MAURITIAN €€
(Map p106; ☑631 8299; Coastal Rd; mains Rs 250-450; ☺10am-10pm) Worth a mention for its breezy terrace, friendly atmosphere and convenient location across from Blue Bay beach, Le Bougainville is a popular hang-out for locals and tourists alike. The menu is vast, with salads, pizza, fish, curries etc.

ⓘ Getting There & Away

Buses to and from Mahébourg run every 30 minutes. A taxi there will cost Rs 350, and it's Rs 500 to Rs 600 to the airport.

Pointe Jérome Embarkation Point (Île aux Aigrettes Departure Point; Map p106) Ferries leave from here to go to Île aux Aigrettes.

JH Arnulphy (Chez Henri; ☑631 9806; www.henri-vacances.com) Henri at JH Arnulphy is a reliable choice for car rental. Prices start at Rs 1450 per day for a small car with unlimited kilometres.

ⓘ Getting Around

All of the area's guesthouses can arrange car hire. Try Henri at JH Arnulphy (p115), who offers cars from Rs 1450 per day. Arnulphy can also help with bicycle hire; rates start at Rs 150 per day.

Vieux Grand Port

POP 3150

'Old Grand Port', north of Mahébourg, is the cradle of Mauritian history: the place where the first human inhabitants of the island landed on 9 September 1598 under the command of Wybrandt Van Warwyck. The Dutch later built a fort 3km further north in what is now the town of Vieux Grand Port. It was the local headquarters of the Dutch East India Company until 1710, when the Dutch abandoned the island. The site was then taken over by the French.

Most travellers stop here as they travel along the east coast. You won't need more than an hour or two to take in all the sights.

◉ Sights

★ **Vallée de Ferney**   WILDLIFE RESERVE
(Ferney Valley; Map p106; ☑ 5729 1080, 634 0440; www.valleedeferney.com; tours per person Rs 750, kestrel feeding Rs 200 (with tour free); ⊙ 10am-3pm)
Protecting a 400-year-old forest, this reserve is an important habitat for the Mauritius kestrel, one of the world's most endangered raptors, and a visit here is far and away your best chance of seeing one. Guides take you along a 3km trail, pointing out fascinating flora and fauna. At noon (arrive no later than 11.30pm), staff feed otherwise wild kestrels at the trailhead. Bookings (which can be made by phone, online or at La Falaise Rouge) for the tour are essential.

As an important habitat for endemic species, Vallée de Ferney promises to be an important conservation and ecotourism area in the coming years. The Mauritius Wildlife Foundation, which helps to train the reserve's guides and provides important input into its policies, has ambitious plans to reintroduce a number of endangered species, including the pink pigeon and echo parakeet.

The Vallée de Ferney is also well known as the site of a conservation demonstration that ignited when a Chinese paving company recently sought to construct a highway directly through the protected hinterland. Attempts at development were unsuccessful, but scars remain: trees daubed with red paint alongside the walking trail were to be chopped down to make way for the road.

The turn-off to the 200-hectare reserve is clearly marked along the coastal road, around 2km south of Vieux Grand Port.

A FAMOUS BATTLE

The sleepy Mauritian town of Vieux Grand Port may seem a long way from Paris, but this place has history. Vieux Grand Port is where the story of human settlement on Mauritius began, but it is even more famous as the site of the only French naval victory to be inscribed on Paris' Arc de Triomphe. Relics of the 1810 battle with the English are on display at the National History Museum (p105) in Mahébourg.

Kestrel Valley   WILDLIFE RESERVE
(Domaine d'Anse Jonchée; Map p106; ☑ 634 5011)
Primarily a hunting reserve for Javanese deer, scenic Kestrel Valley covers 950 hectares of forested mountain terrain that also acts as a reserve for numerous endemic bird species, including the Mauritius kestrel – one of the world's rarest birds of prey. Four marked trails (from 2km to 6km long) wind through the park. At the time of writing, Kestrel Valley was closed, officially for restoration works, but its future is uncertain.

Monument to Dutch Landing   MONUMENT
(Map p106) A monument marks the site where the Dutch first landed on the island on 9 September 1598.

Frederik Hendrik Museum   MUSEUM
(Map p106; ☑ 634 4319; ⊙ 9am-4pm Mon-Sat)
FREE A few clay pipes, wine bottles and other items left behind by the town's Dutch and French occupants are on display in the Frederik Hendrik Museum. The museum also outlines the history of the Dutch in Mauritius.

🏃 Activities

★ **Lion Mountain**   HIKING
(Map p106) Immediately recognisable by its sphinx-like profile, Lion Mountain offers a challenging but rewarding half-day hike with stunning coastal views. The walk climbs the lion's 'back' to finish on the 'head'. We recommend hiring a local guide, though if you decide to go it alone you'll find the trailhead beside the police station at the north of Vieux Grand Port.

Check out www.fitsy.com for detailed GPS information about the hike, though the main trail is fairly obvious and runs straight along the ridge and up over a rocky area to the peak. There are a few hairy scrambles over the rocks before you reach the flat area on the lion's head. From here you can see right across the interior of the island. Return the same way you came up. Allow three to four hours for the return trip.

🛏 Sleeping & Eating

★**La Hacienda** VILLA €€
(Map p106; ☑ 263 0914; www.lahaciendamauritius. com; Lion Mountain; r from €70; P❄@🛜🏊) On the slopes of Lion Mountain, La Hacienda has four stunning villas with some of the best views on this side of the island. The self-contained villas have kitchens, decks with fine views and plenty of space, not to mention a real sense of blissful isolation from all the clamour.

La Falaise Rouge MAURITIAN €€
(Map p106; ☑ 471 2017; mains Rs 450-800; ☺ 11am-3pm) The restaurant affiliated with the Vallée de Ferney reserve is actually a few kilometres away, signposted off the main coastal road. The menu includes locally sourced venison vindaloo and roast venison, and the waterside setting is a huge plus. The restaurant also serves as a booking office for the reserve.

ℹ Getting There & Away

The best way to explore around Vieux Grand Port is by private vehicle; most tour operators can hook you up with a half- or full-day visit to any part of the southeast region. Public transport is also available, though it's significantly less convenient. Buses between Mahébourg and Centre de Flacq ply the coast road, passing through Vieux Grand Port, Anse Jonchée and Bambous Virieux. There are departures every 20 minutes or so.

SOUTH COAST

Mauritius' southern coast, known as Savanne, features some of the country's wildest and most attractive scenery. Here you'll find basalt cliffs, sheltered sandy coves, hidden falls and traditional fishing villages. Beyond the shoreline lie endless sugar-cane fields and dense forests that clothe the hillsides in a patchwork of vibrant greens. Long considered too harsh to develop due to its rugged topography, the region staved off developers until quite recently.

The region is devoid of any prominent towns save Rivière des Anguilles and Souillac. Both can be used as bases from which to explore the nearby parks and preserves, though

---

WORTH A TRIP

DOMAINE DE L'ÉTOILE
....
Teetering between the east and southeast realms of the island, this popular **forest reserve** (TerrOcean; Map p106; ☑ 448 4444, 729 1050; www.terrocean. mu) is set on over 2000 hectares of unspoilt hinterland – the perfect terrain to explore by horse, on foot or by quad bike. Mountain biking, guided hikes and archery are also on offer. Enjoy a bite at the restaurant while you're here.

If you're lucky, you'll spot Javanese stags hiding in the forest – there are over 1000 living in the reserve.

---

we recommend staying elsewhere and visiting during a day trip in a private vehicle.

ℹ Getting There & Away

Most people rent a car to explore the south coast or charter a taxi for the day. It can be slow going if you're driving down here – consisting of back roads with the usual Mauritius traffic that slows to a crawl as it passes through the many little towns – but the rewards are worth it.

Regular buses connect Souillac with Mahébourg, Port Louis and Curepipe; most go via Rivière des Anguilles. From Souillac, buses travel along the coast almost hourly.

Souillac
POP 4392
The largest settlement along the south coast is Souillac, 7km from Rivière des Anguilles. Most travellers come here on a day trip along the south coast or as an add-on to a visit to La Vanille zoo (p120). The town itself has little to offer, but the clutch of (somewhat) interesting sights close by and some decent restaurants just about make it worth the detour.

◉ Sights

Gris Gris Beach BEACH
(Map p106) East of central Souillac, a grassy clifftop affords fine views of the black-rock coastline. A path leads down to the wild Gris Gris beach; a wooden sign warns of the dangers of swimming here. The term *gris gris* traditionally refers to 'black magic' and, looking at the tortuous coastline, you can see how the area got its name. Then again, another story suggests that the beach was named after the puppy (!) of a French cartographer who visited in 1753.

LE SOUFFLEUR

Le Souffleur, a hidden attraction known only to locals, requires a bit of gumption (and a 4WD) to tackle. But if you ask anyone in the know, they'll say that it's well worth the adventure.

Situated on the coast about halfway between Souillac and Blue Bay, this geological anomaly is a half-formed grotto on the side of a cliff that spouts a geyser-like fountain of water (up to 20m high!) when the seas are rough. As the waves crash against the cliff the seawater pushes through a crack in the bluffs like a blowhole on a whale. If the seas aren't particularly rough during your visit, there's a natural land bridge nearby that's worth a camera click or two. It was formed when the roof collapsed on another naturally formed grotto.

To reach the super-secret *souffleur* (grotto), head for the Savannah sugar estate near the village of L'Escalier, cross the estate, then follow the snaking track once you reach the sea. Even if you don't seek permission to cross the sugar estate, which you probably should, we highly recommend bringing a local with you – otherwise you may never find the place.

La Roche Qui Pleure   LANDMARK
(The Crying Rock; Map p106) Right at the end of the headland after Gris Gris beach, 600m further on and well signposted, La Roche Qui Pleure resembles a crying man – you'll have to stand there puzzling it out for quite some time, and the waves really have to crash for the 'tears' to come out, but it's oddly satisfying when you finally get it.

Rochester Falls   WATERFALL
(Map p106) Rochester Falls are by no means the country's most spectacular falls, but they're worth a detour if you're in the area. Follow the makeshift signs from the main road through Souillac – the route is rather circuitous but is reliable nonetheless, although it's a rough ride along the stone-strewn track. Prepare yourself for hawkers who'll want a tip for telling you where to park. The gushing cascade emerges from the cane fields after a five-minute walk from your car.

Robert Edward Hart Museum   MUSEUM
(Map p106; 625 6101; 9am-4pm Mon & Wed-Fri, to noon Sat) FREE Robert Edward Hart (1891–1954) was a renowned Mauritian poet, apparently appreciated by both the French and the English, although we've yet to meet anyone who's heard of him. His house, La Nef, is an attractive coral-stone cottage that was opened to the public as the Robert Edward Hart Museum in 1967. On display are some originals and copies of Hart's letters, plays, speeches and poetry, as well as his fiddle, spectacles and trusty Britannic toilet.

Hart's award from the National Institute of Sciences for services to 'telepathy, hypnotism and personal magnetism' could do with some explanation. Sadly, the captions are only in French. This is definitely rainy-day tourism.

🛏 Sleeping

The best sleeping option in the area is nearby Andréa (p121). The other choices, which we find it difficult to recommend, are rather lacklustre and attached to popular eating establishments.

🍴 Eating

Eating choices are best east and west of the town centre, with especially good options out in the Gris Gris district. If you're eating by the sea, opt for something with seafood – it was probably caught within sight of your table.

⭐ Le Gris Gris   MAURITIAN, SEAFOOD €
(Chez Rosy; Map p106; 625 4179; Gris Gris Beach; mains Rs 285-400; 11am-4pm) Rosy's place is a simple affair with a motley assortment of wicker and plastic furniture. The food, however, never misses the mark – locals and tourists rave about the home-cooked Mauritian and Chinese dishes.

Le Rochester Restaurant   MAURITIAN €
(Map p106; 625 4180; mains Rs 275-400; noon-3pm & 6-9pm Wed-Mon, noon-3pm Tue) The charming Madame Appadu runs her restaurant in an old colonial building by the bridge to Surinam. A delightful mix of Creole, Indian and Chinese staples is served on a shady terrace situated atop a gushing ravine. Upstairs you'll find three small guest rooms, but they're nothing to write home about.

Le Batelage   MAURITIAN €€
(Map p106; 625 6083; www.lebatelage.com; Village des Touristes, Royal Rd, Port Souillac; mains Rs 600-1250; noon-3pm & 6-9pm) Drop down off

the main road at the western end of Souillac for a lovely waterside eating experience. The food (the usual mix of Mauritian staples and seafood) is a touch overpriced, but it's still worth it for the setting. Service can be a bit hit or miss, especially when there are big groups in attendance.

Escale des Îles MAURITIAN, SEAFOOD €€
(Map p106; ☑ 625 7014; Gris Gris; mains Rs 250-925; ⊙ 9.30am-9pm) Just across from the car park overlooking Gris Gris beach, Escale des Îles is set within a brightly coloured building and is popular with large groups. It lists its specialities as seafood, Mauritian, Chinese, European and Indian – quite a list that sums up its catch-all approach to cooking. Expect to leave more full than inspired.

❶ Getting There & Away

There are buses roughly every half-hour from Mahébourg to Souillac via the airport and Rivière des Anguilles. From Port Louis, buses run hourly, calling at Rivière des Anguilles en route. There are also frequent services to/from Curepipe, with three buses a day taking the coast road via Pointe aux Roches. Buses heading along the coast to Baie du Cap (from where you can pick up onward transport to the west coast) depart hourly.

Bel Ombre

POP 2417

Despite being miles from the bucket-and-spade atmosphere of Flic en Flac or Grand Baie, Bel Ombre has quickly developed into a cosy tourist bubble along the wild southern shores. It's very much an upmarket crowd, but the public beaches still get popular with locals.

◉ Sights & Activities

Trevassa Monument MONUMENT
(Map p106) About 1km west of Bel Ombre village, this monument commemorates the sinking of the British steamer *Trevassa* in 1923. She went down 2600km off Mauritius. Sixteen survivors were eventually washed ashore at Bel Ombre after surviving 25 days in an open lifeboat.

Domaine de Bel Ombre OUTDOORS
(Map p106; ☑ 623 5522; www.domainede belombre.mu; Bel Ombre) The main attraction in Bel Ombre is the Domaine de Bel Ombre, an open nature reserve set on a sugar plantation developed by Charles Telfair between 1816 and 1833. Today, it's a multifaceted venture with a brilliant golf course, the ruins of a colonial mill and the Valriche Nature Reserve – a haven for quad biking, hiking and touring on 4WDs. Out on the lagoon, you can go windsurfing, diving or snorkelling, or simply float around in a glass-bottomed boat.

⌑ Sleeping & Eating

The sumptuous Domaine de Bel Ombre features two five-star hotels, both run by Verandah Resorts. Budget and midrange travellers will need to look elsewhere.

Heritage Awali HOTEL €€€
(Map p106; ☑ 601 1500; www.heritageresorts.mu; Domaine de Bel Ombre; r from €227; P ✳ @ 🛜 🛋) The Awali celebrates an African heritage, with abounding masks, drums and tribal art. There's also a golf course and a spa complex for the ultimate indulgence.

Heritage Le Telfair HERITAGE HOTEL €€€
(Map p106; ☑ 601 5500; www.heritageresorts.mu; Domaine de Bel Ombre; s/d from €277/355; P ✳ @ 🛜 🛋) The Heritage Le Telfair has perfectly captured the luxury and grandeur of the island's colonial yesteryear, with stately rooms, expansive grounds, exceptional service and unrelenting attention to detail. Natural fibres, soothing earth tones and a classic style of wood and whitewash make this a sophisticated choice.

★ Le Château Restaurant FUSION, MAURITIAN €€€
(Map p106; ☑ 623 5522; mains from Rs 1200; ⊙ noon-3pm Mon-Thu, noon-3pm & 6.30-9pm Fri & Sat) The Domaine de Bel Ombre reserve has 12 (!) restaurants. Our pick of this rather large bunch is Le Château, set in a stunning conversion of the old Bel Ombre plantation house. This is the place for an exceptional meal of traditional Franco-Mauritian cuisine with contemporary flourishes.

❶ Getting There & Away

To range beyond Bel Ombre, most travellers rent a car or taxi from their hotel. A regular bus service runs from Curepipe to Bel Ombre via Nouvelle France and Chemin Grenier.

Around the South Coast

The south coast's hinterland has enough fascinating attractions to fill at least a day, with a wildlife park, some fine examples of colonial architecture and a take on the coloured-earth phenomenon, not to mention some fine hotels.

◉ Sights & Activities

★ St Aubin   HISTORIC BUILDING
(Map p106; ☏ 626 1513; www.saintaubin.mu; without/with restaurant set menu Rs 450/1100; ☻9am-5pm Mon-Sat) St Aubin is an elegant plantation house that dates back to 1819; it originally sat alongside the factory but was moved in the 1970s so that its owner could get a quieter night's sleep. The estate no longer produces sugar, but in the gardens of the house there is a traditional rum distillery and a nursery growing anthurium flowers and vanilla – you'll learn all about the fascinating history of vanilla production on the tour.

The height of the St Aubin experience is a meal at the wonderfully charming **table d'hôte** (Map p106; ☏ 626 1513; mains Rs 395-1375; ☻noon-3pm) in the main manor house. The dining room is one of best throwbacks to colonial times: dainty chandeliers cast ambient light over the white tablecloths and antique wooden furniture. The set menu showcases the fruits of the plantation: hearts of palm, pineapple, mango and chilli, to name a few. Reservations are recommended.

If you wish to stay the night, the **Auberge de St Aubin** (Map p106; ☏ 626 1513; www.saintaubin.mu/larouteduthe/fr/auberge_st_aubin.aspx; per person incl half board Rs 2200-3400; ☀) has three rooms in the plantation manse across from the estate's main building. The bedroom at the front of the house perfectly captures the charming colonial ambience, with creaky wooden floors and cotton gauze over the four-poster bed. The two rooms at the back are noticeably more modern and have a bit less character.

La Vanille   ZOO
(Réserve des Mascareignes; Map p106; ☏ 626 2503; www.lavanille-reserve.com; Rivière des Anguilles; adult/child Mon-Fri Rs 425/235, Sat & Sun Rs 250/115; ☻8.30am-5pm) This exciting zoo and reserve makes for a fantastic field trip with kids. The park has the greatest number of giant tortoises in captivity in the world (over 1000). It's worth coming to La Vanille just to check out the immense collection of mounted insects (over 23,000 species!). There's also a farm of Nile crocodiles (population 2000), which can grow up to 7m. Allow at least one hour for a complete visit.

The tortoises are the undoubted highlight, the result of a wildly successful breeding program for the Aldabra and *radiata* species. Chances are that you'll see the former breeding in front of your eyes.

The on-site **Hungry Crocodile Restaurant** (La Crocodile Affamé; Map p106; mains Rs 150-650; ☻11am-5pm) specialises in all things crocodilian – croc curry, croc burger, croc fritters in a salad, croc cooked in a vanilla sauce... (It also does more conventional dishes such as spaghetti bolognaise and beef burgers.) Don't forget your mozzie repellent - you won't be the only one feasting at the lunch table.

La Vanille is a few kilometres northwest of Souillac or 2km south of Rivière des Anguilles.

La Vallée des Couleurs   LANDMARK
(Map p106; ☏ 251 8666; www.lavalleedescouleurs.com; Mare Anguilles; adult/child Rs 250/125; ☻9am-5pm) Despite having 23 colours, as opposed to seven at Chamarel (p96), La Vallée des

---

BAIE DU CAP

Baie du Cap marks the eastern end of one of the island's most stunning coastlines (running west to Le Morne Peninsula). It's more a place to admire as you drive along the coast than somewhere to visit as a destination in its own right, but there is a low-key sight here – the **Matthew Flinders Monument** (Map p106).

The monument stands on the shore 500m west of Baie du Cap and was erected in 2003 to honour the 200th anniversary of the arrival of English navigator and cartographer Matthew Flinders. He was less warmly received at the time; the poor bloke didn't know that England and France were at war and he was swiftly imprisoned for six years. For an interesting read on the subject, take a look at Huguette Ly-Tio-Fane Pineo's book *In the Grips of the Eagle: Matthew Flinders at the Île de France, 1803–1810*.

Bus services along here are limited. Baie du Cap is the terminus for buses from Souillac and Quatre Bornes (via Tamarin). Buses run approximately every 20 minutes.

Couleurs is the less impressive of the island's two 'coloured earths'. The reserve does, however, have a scenic nature trail that passes trickling waterfalls, memorable vistas, crawling tortoises and blossoming tropical flowers. It takes about an hour to complete the reserve's circuit.

Bois Chéri Tea Plantation   MUSEUM

(Map p106; ☑ 617 9109, restaurant 471 1216; www.saintaubin.mu; Grand Bassin; without/with restaurant set menu Rs 400/700; ⊙ 9am-5pm Mon-Sat, restaurant 10.30am-3.30pm) This 250-hectare tea factory and museum is located about 12km north of Rivière des Anguilles amid a vast acreage of cane. Hour-long tours of the tea-processing facility end with a stop at a small exhibition space detailing the island's tea history by means of machines and photos. The best part of the visit is undoubtedly the sampling session at the end. It's advisable to visit in the morning, as most of the action takes place before noon.

After your tour, stick around for lunch – the in-house restaurant takes a formidable stab at gourmet cuisine and uses locally sourced ingredients. The commanding views over the riverine plains are also quite captivating.

🛏 Sleeping & Eating

High-end luxury retreats are the main options along the southern coast, save for two excellent and highly original midrange choices. Most visitors come here on a day trip.

Beyond the luxury-resort compounds, there are some lovely choices for a special meal – notably at the St Aubin sugar plantation and the Domaine de Bel Ombre – while Souillac has good midrange restaurants.

Andréa   CABIN €€

(Relais des Lodges; Map p106; ☑ 471 0555; www.relaisdeslodges.com; s/d incl half board Rs 2800/4600; ❋ ⊛) Andréa's 10 lovely cottages, along the sea, have gabled roofs and glass-panelled walls facing the rugged Ireland-esque coast. There's also a swimming pool and a reputable restaurant. Rates include a guided hike through the forest beyond the sugar cane. Guests can arrange 4WD excursions and quad biking; tours of the neighbouring sugar estate are possible between December and June.

★ Shanti Maurice   HOTEL €€€

(Map p106; ☑ 603 7200; www.shantimaurice.com; St Felix; r incl breakfast from €419; 🅿 ❋ 🛜 ⊛) One of the loveliest places to stay along the

---

LA ROUTE DU THÉ

La Route du Thé (www.saintaubin.mu/larouteduthe) offers tourists a window onto the island's plantation past by linking three of the island's remaining colonial estates. The first stop is the Creole manse turned museum at the Domaine des Aubineaux (p61) near Curepipe. Then the route veers south to the vast Bois Chéri Tea Plantation. The final stop is the stately St Aubin, with its lush gardens and rum distillery. Despite the itinerary's name, the focus of the trip extends far beyond tea – each stop has a charming *table d'hôte* and a museum, and the St Aubin even offers period-style accommodation.

True architecture buffs and historians should consider doing the route backwards and tacking on the resplendent Eureka (p59) estate at the end of the journey.

---

south coast, and among the island's signature resorts, the Shanti Maurice oozes luxury. All of the expansive rooms face the sea, the beach is superb, and the tropical, 14-hectare grounds are gorgeous. There's also yoga, a kids club, watersports, gym, spa, and attentive staff to make possible your every whim.

Green Palm Restaurant   INDIAN €€

(Map p106; ☑ 625 8100; Coastal Rd, Riambel; mains Rs 225-495; ⊙ 11am-3.30pm & 6.30-10.30pm) Roadside Green Palm serves well-regarded Indian cuisine west of Souillac in the sleepy hamlet of Riambel. It's especially proud of its range of *naan* breads, but everything's good. The beach – across the road and through the trees – is lovely, so eating here means you can make a day of it.

THE EAST

Known by the rather romantic sobriquet La Côte Sauvage (The Wild Coast), the island's east coast is a world away from the touts, nightclubs and souvenir shacks of Flic en Flac in the west and Grand Baie in the north. It does have its resorts, but the eastern face of Mauritius feels blissfully untouched by mass tourism. Best of all, some of the island's very best beaches line this quiet coast. Not surprisingly, this most exclusive side of the

The East

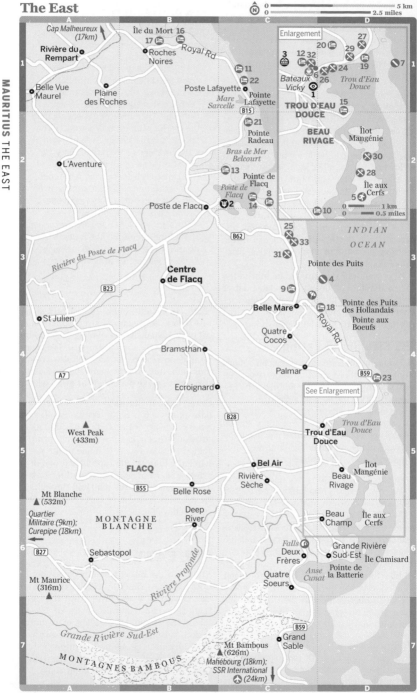

The East

island attracts the kind of visitor likely to take a helicopter transfer from the airport when they arrive.

The closest the east comes to a resort town is Trou d'Eau Douce, which has retained the feel of a sleepy fishing village despite rubbing shoulders with the grand hotels next door. It's the jumping-off point for the wildly popular Île aux Cerfs.

🛈 Getting There & Away

The main transport hub for eastern Mauritius is the inland town of Centre de Flacq. You'll have to change here if you're arriving by bus from Port Louis, the Central Plateau towns or Mahébourg in the south.

There are onward connections from Centre de Flacq to villages along the east coast, although some services are pretty infrequent. You can bank on bus transport from Centre de Flacq to Palmar and Poste Lafayette (with continuing service to Rivière du Rempart), but there are no buses to Belle Mare. Figure on at least Rs 500 for a taxi between the coastal towns and Centre de Flacq.

Trou d'Eau Douce

POP 5672

'Sweet water hole' sits at a set of major crossroads, making it the tourism hub on this side of the island. From some perspectives, it's a lovely little place, if a bit melancholy, where

fishers unravel their nets after a morning at sea and women walk around with baskets of vegies balanced on their heads.

But the place is a real draw for other reasons: the sea is a stunning shade of blue here and Trou d'Eau Douce boasts easy access to the massively popular Île aux Cerfs, a favoured destination for day-tripping tourists.

As a result, this seaside township can be a little overwhelming with its touts, but they don't persist for long and it makes a great base for exploring the east coast – especially for those on a tighter budget.

⊙ Sights & Activities

Two of the island's best golf courses are located in the area – the Bernhard Langer-designed fairway masterpiece on Île aux Cerfs and the Ernie Els–designed dreamscape in the Anahita resort complex.

Victoria 1840 GALLERY
(Map p122; ☑ 480 0220; www.maniglier.com; Victoria Rd; ⊘ 7.30-10pm Mon-Fri) Worth a look, Victoria 1840 is an old sugar mill that has been lovingly refurbished to house some of the works of Yvette Maniglier, a bewitching French painter who spent a year under the wing of Henri Matisse. The juxtaposition of industrial brick and splashy modern art works surprisingly well. The gallery can only be visited while dining at the in-house restaurant, Le Café des Arts (p126).

WORTH A TRIP

SCENIC DRIVE: THE HEART OF THE ISLAND

The divide between coastal Mauritius and the island's interior can be stark, but the small scale of everything here means that it's easy enough to experience both on a rather short drive.

Begin anywhere in the east and make your way to the regional centre of **Rivière du Rempart**. From there, head southwest, passing through small towns (some barely discernible) such as **Belle Vue Maurel** and **Barlow**; the signage can be a little confusing, but until you pass Barlow, follow the signs to Port Louis along the B21. After Barlow, the views open up, with some decent views of the inland mountains where you're headed. At the crossroads around 11km after leaving Rivière du Rempart, turn left towards 'La Nicolière'. A lovely honour guard of trees arcs over you for around 2km, whereupon you make a right turn, again following the signs for **La Nicolière**.

The traffic thins as you pass through more sugar-cane fields (no Ashok Leyland buses at last!), before crossing the dam wall. After the wall, the road climbs, alternating between lovely thick forest and some fine views out over the coastal plains to the east. After around 4.5km of climbing, the road crosses a plateau haired with agriculture. At the T-junction around 2km further on (look for the 'Selazi Forest Service' sign), turn left, following signs for St Pierre. You're largely back in civilisation with all the attendant construction, sugar cane and traffic, but it's worth it for the views away to the west from **Ripailles** and its approach – **Calebasses** (632m), **Pieter Both** (823m), **Grand Peak** (326m) and **Le Pouce** (812m) are all stunning.

From Ripailles it's downhill all the way – literally. In St Pierre, you could turn left (east) and return to the east of the island via Quartier Militaire. An alternative is to pause in Moka to visit the tranquil tropical mansion of Eureka (p59).

Natural Spring   SPRING
(Map p122) The actual *trou d'eau douce* for which the town is named can be found in a human-made stone hole next to the national coastguard's office. To find the natural spring, follow the fork in the main road away from the Gothic church as it slopes down the hill to the docks – the well is on the right. Locals visit the stash of fresh water when the government supply gets corrupted after a strong storm.

Johaness Entertainment   BOAT TOUR
(Map p122; ☑ 480 0872; www.johaness.com; Royal Rd; excursions to Île aux Cerfs per person Rs 1500-1800) One of more professional operators, Johaness runs speedboat or catamaran trips to Île aux Cerfs that leave Trou d'Eau Douce at 9.30am and return at 3.30pm, including a barbecue lunch and time for snorkelling and exploring the island.

🛏 Sleeping

There's more choice in and around Trou d'Eau Douce than anywhere else on the east coast, and you'll find a decent range of budget and midrange accommodation. The area's upmarket sleeps are, for the most part, a little way out of town and you'll need a taxi or private vehicle to reach them.

An endless parade of luxury hotels marches along the east coast from here, all the way up to the northern part of the island.

Le Dodo   APARTMENT €
(Map p122; ☑ 480 0034; christa0307@hotmail.com; Royal Rd; apt €25-35; ❄ 🛜) Le Dodo is like an orphanage for outdated furniture. The decor is horribly mismatched, but somehow it all seems to work. The owner is kind and the apartments come fully outfitted with retro fixtures. Ask for one of the apartments higher up – although there's no elevator, the views over the cluttered village and azure sea are memorable.

Villa La Fourche   APARTMENT €
(Map p122; ☑ 5745 6888; www.villalafourche.com; 2-bedroom apt from €50; ❄ 🛜) Tucked down a backstreet away from the coastal buzz, this quiet option is a good deal for large families, but the furnishings need updating, as with so many places in this price bracket.

⭐ **Tropical Hotel Attitude**   HOTEL €€
(Map p122; ☑ 480 1300; tropical-hotel-mauritius.com; Royal Rd; s/d from €70/83; ❄ @ 🛜 🏊) Part of the smart but reasonably priced Attitude chain, this place on Trou d'Eau Douce's northern outskirts is a refreshingly accessible

slice of semi-luxury right on the waterfront. The rooms have a white-linen look and most face the sea. Highly recommended.

★ Le Touessrok   HOTEL €€€

(Map p122; ☑ 402 7400; www.shangri-la.com/mauritius/shangrila/; r from €275; P ❋ @ ☎ ≋) Le Touessrok has one of the best reputations on the island, and the accolades are well deserved. Rambling across a sandy peninsula, the hotel blends Moorish architecture and thick patches of jungle. The resort distinguishes itself from the rest of the five-stars with its two offshore islands: the famous Île aux Cerfs and the exclusive Robinson Crusoe–style hideaway Îlot Mangénie.

★ Four Seasons Resort at Anahita   HOTEL €€€

(Map p122; ☑ 402 3100; www.fourseasons.com/mauritius; Beau Champ; villas incl breakfast €750-5000; P ❋ @ ☎ ≋) Located in Beau Champ, slightly south of Trou d'Eau Douce, the Four Seasons Resort is part of a vast luxury complex known as Anahita and features a beautiful assortment of holiday villas. The design scheme plays with local materials like tropical timber and volcanic rock while seamlessly integrating every modern convenience.

Four stone-cut pools, a spa and the stunning Ernie Els–designed golf course are also big draws, while most rooms have private plunge pools.

Villa Mahé   VILLA €€€

(Map p122; ☑ 452 1010; Royal Rd; villas from €180; ❋ ☎) For a spot of luxury at a very reasonable price, go for this endearing holiday home owned by the Montocchio family. There's a certain beachy charm about the place with its weathered white-wood exterior and slap-shut colonial shutters. The semidetached house (three-night minimum stay) sleeps 10 and has stunning sea views from the balconies.

✕ Eating

Trou d'Eau Douce is the kind of place where you'll do perfectly fine just grabbing a chair and table at the first joint you stumble upon. It's a town of fishers, after all, so stick with the seafood. If you're looking for a more upmarket experience, you can't go wrong with any of the restaurants at Le Touessrok.

Snack Pelouse   SEAFOOD €

(Map p122; ☑ 5702 8604; Royal Rd; mains Rs 150-400; ⊙9am-9pm) You could easily walk past this small eatery, a few steps down off the main road, but it's an appealing choice for its informal surrounds and some of the freshest fish in town. Most people stop in to buy from the small selection of groceries but end up staying for lunch.

Gilda's Restaurant   ITALIAN, MAURITIAN €

(Map p122; ☑ 428 0498; mains Rs 100-500; ⊙8am-10pm Wed-Mon) Pasta, South Indian curries and *ceviche* (raw fish marinated in

---

WORTH A TRIP

EXCURSIONS TO ÎLE AUX CERFS

Île aux Cerfs, encircled by gin-clear waters, is many people's idea of a postcard-perfect tropical island. It's overrun by tourists and touts during peak season, when it becomes a victim of its own popularity, yet it remains one of the most picturesque island excursions for visitors to Mauritius. There's a world-class golf course, 4km of sandy bliss and a real sense of paradise beneath the palm trees.

Guests of Le Touessrok (p125), including those who have reserved a round of golf, get whisked over to the island for free on the hotel launch. For everyone else, every boat owner in Trou d'Eau Douce seems ready to take you out to the island at a moment's notice. Ask at your accommodation to be set up with a reliable option, or try **Bateaux Vicky** (Map p122; ☑ 480 0775, 5755 1483; m_dardenne@outlook.com; Île aux Cerfs return per person Rs 450), a ferry or water-taxi service that runs from Trou d'Eau Douce to Île aux Cerfs every half-hour, with the first boat at 9am and the last returning at 4.30pm.

The other way to reach the island is on a popular catamaran or speedboat day trip, which usually includes snorkelling, sunbathing and an expansive barbecue lunch (Rs 1000 to Rs 1800 per person depending on your choice of food). The day trip usually begins around 9.30am and runs until 3.30pm (if you're leaving from Trou d'Eau Douce).

Most coastal hotels across the island also offer day trips to Île aux Cerfs, or check out www.catamarancruisesmauritius.com for a list of possibilities. In Trou d'Eau Douce, try Johaness Entertainment (p124).

lemon and garlic) all appear on this varied menu, which can be enjoyed with fine views on the elevated terrace out the back.

★ Chez Tino   MAURITIAN €€

(Map p122; ☑480 2769; Royal Rd; mains from Rs 450; ☺8.30am-10pm Mon-Sat, to 4pm Sun) Head for the wonderful terrace on the 1st floor for the best views here. Chez Tino keeps it simple, dishing up superb meals of Mauritian cooking with an emphasis on seafood (*langouste* – lobster – in particular). Standout dishes include octopus curry with green pawpaw and grilled fish with lemon.

Green Island Beach Restaurant   INTERNATIONAL, MAURITIAN €€

(Map p122; ☑251 7152; Royal Rd; mains Rs 200-525; ☺1.30-9.30pm Tue-Sun) The friendly staff here serves a delicious assortment of international and local favourites, often in surprising juxtaposition. Have some *rougaille saucisses* (spicy sausages) with a slice of pizza – the menu is extensive and everything's well priced.

Le Four à Chaud   SEAFOOD €€

(Map p122; ☑427 4117; Royal Rd; mains Rs 525-1650; ☺noon-3pm & 7.30pm-midnight Sun-Fri, 7.30pm-midnight Sat) Head to the smartest place in central Trou d'Eau Douce to feast on *fruits de mer* and enjoy a fantastic list of matched wines. Reserve to get one of the few balcony tables with sea views, and note that the menu is exclusively seafood. The name is a play on words: it's opposite the old *four à chaux* (lime kiln).

★ Le Café des Arts   MAURITIAN €€€

(Map p122; ☑480 0220; www.maniglier.com; Victoria Rd; set menu Rs 2900-3600; ☺7.30-10pm Mon-Sat) This intriguing dining option is located within an old mill that has been transformed into Victoria 1840 (p123), an oddly charming gallery space, with canvases of wicked brushstrokes adorning the cracked brick walls. The food, a modern nod to traditional island flavours, mirrors the old-meets-new surrounds. Lunch can be reserved for as few as two diners with 24 hours' notice.

❶ Information

Thomas Cook Foreign Exchange (Royal Rd; ☺8.30am-4.30pm Mon-Sat)

❶ Getting There & Away

There are no direct buses between Port Louis and Trou d'Eau Douce. You'll need to change at Centre de Flacq, from where onward services to Trou d'Eau Douce run roughly every half-hour. Taxis cost Rs 500 to Rs 600 from Centre de Flacq, Rs 1800 to the airport and Rs 1700 to Port Louis.

Île aux Cerfs

Like Marilyn Monroe and Cleopatra, Île aux Cerfs' killer looks have triggered its demise. Once sparsely populated by *cerfs* (stags; imported for hunting from Java), this picturesque island is now overrun with touts and replete with tourists baking under the tropical sun or lazing in the perfect, gin-clear waters. The obtrusive crowds and general summer-camp vibe may be off-putting at first, but few people realise that the island boasts over 4km of sandy bliss. Hike a mere kilometre down the beach and you'll uncover an idyllic ocean vista that you can have all to yourself.

☆ Activities

Île aux Cerfs Golf Club   GOLF

(Map p122; www.ileauxcerfsgolfclub.com; Île aux Cerfs) Much of the island's interior belongs to the stunningly manicured, 18-hole Île aux Cerfs Golf Club. Designed by Bernhard Langer, the course is perhaps one of the world's most scenic spots to tee off. Green fees are free for guests of certain hotels (check the website) and €89 for everyone else for 18 holes – nonguests are welcome with advance bookings.

⌨ Sleeping

There's nowhere to stay on the island, but a full portfolio of hotels lies just across the water in Trou d'Eau Douce. It's also possible to get here from almost anywhere on the island by means of a catamaran day trip.

✕ Eating

All of the boat operators to Île aux Cerfs can arrange (pricey) barbecue lunches as part of their excursions. If you've just paid for the boat and no extras, either take food or consider the island's limited eating options.

Paul & Virginie   SEAFOOD €€

(Map p122; ☑402 7426; mains Rs 250-500; ☺noon-3.30pm) A sociable spot at the watersports centre serving a scrumptious assortment of fresh fish and seafood. Popular with tour groups, it's a microcosm of Île aux Cerfs: a lovely setting that gets overrun to the point of spoiling it.

> **SATURDAY NIGHTS ON ÎLE
> AUX CERFS**
>
> Taking a cue from Ibiza and Nikki Beach,
> the management of Le Touessrok
> (p125) turns the sands of Île aux Cerfs
> into a raging dance floor every Saturday
> night between October and March. The
> all-night romp starts at 11pm and DJed
> beats continue until 5am. Admission is
> Rs 500 and includes boat service and
> a drink.

La Chaumière Masala   INDIAN €€
(Map p122; ☑ 402 7400; www.masala-ile-aux-
cerfs.restaurant.mu; Île aux Cerfs; mains Rs 325-750,
thalis from Rs 375; ⊙ noon-4pm) This memorable dining experience offers Indian dishes
adjusted to suit the European palate. Tables
are perched atop stilts amid the trees.

🛈 Getting There & Away

Guests of Le Touessrok (p125), including
those who have reserved a round of golf, get
whisked over to the island for free on the hotel
launch. Lesser mortals must choose from a variety of dizzying transport options; despite what
the signs say, there is no public ferry to Île aux
Cerfs – all services are run by private operators.

Dozens of boats owned by former fishers in
Trou d'Eau Douce offer a water-taxi service to
the island for Rs 450 return. Ask at your accommodation to be set up with a reliable option or
try Bateaux Vicky. The taxi boats run every 20 to
30 minutes between 9am and 4pm, with the last
boat back at 4.30pm or 5pm (the island 'closes'
to visitors at 5pm sharp). The trip takes between
15 and 30 minutes depending on your point of
departure. It's not necessary to book ahead.

Many of these local operators also offer a side
trip to the waterfalls at Grande Rivière Sud-Est
(Rs 650).

Another, popular way to reach the island is
on a catamaran or speedboat day trip, which
usually includes snorkelling, sunbathing and an
expansive barbecue lunch (Rs 1000 to Rs 1800
per person depending on your choice of food).
The day trip usually begins around 9.30am and
runs until 3.30pm if you're leaving from Trou
d'Eau Douce. Most coastal hotels across the
island offer day trips to Île aux Cerfs, or check
out www.catamarancruisesmauritius.com for
a list of possibilities. In Trou d'Eau Douce, try
Johaness Entertainment (p124).

Belle Mare & Palmar

North of Trou d'Eau Douce as far as Pointe
de Flacq, a 10km-long beach includes some
of the best white sand and azure ocean in
Mauritius. The towns of Belle Mare and Palmar may pass in the blink of an eye, but the
area is also home to an impregnable string of
luxury resorts. There are stretches of public
beach, including around 4km and 8km north
of Trou d'Eau Douce.

◉ Sights

Sagar Shiv Mandir   HINDU TEMPLE
(Map p122; ⊙ dawn-dusk) This white Hindu
temple sits on a teeny islet tenuously teth-
ered to the mainland by a thin land bridge.
The views of the dazzling bastion are best appreciated from Indian Pavilion (p129), the
restaurant at Le Saint Géran.

🏃 Activities

Watersports

Mauritius' east coast has a few notable dive
sites, including **Belmar Pass** (Map p122),
close to where the reef meets the ocean
northeast of Belle Mare.

The area's five-star hotels – including Le
Saint Géran (p128) and Belle Mare Plage
(p128) – all have reputable scuba outfits.
Visit www.msda.mu for a complete list of
registered operators.

Golf

The proliferation of top-end sleeps means
that there are plenty of places to tee off in
the area. In addition to the golf courses
further south at Anahita and Le Touessrok
(p125), you'll find greens at Belle Mare
Plage (p128) and Le Saint Géran (p128).

Spas

Most of Mauritius' top-end resorts have a
spa, but if you're looking for a unique pampering experience, try the Pedi:Mani:Cure
Studio.

Pedi:Mani:Cure Studio   SPA
(Map p122; ☑ 401 1688; www.bastiengonzalez.
com; Le Saint Géran, Pointe de Flacq; ⊙ 10am-7pm)
This spa at Le Saint Géran was developed by
renowned French podiatrist Bastien Gon-
zalez. The not-to-be-missed signature treatment (Rs 5500) invigorates and revives tired
hands and feet, giving them a radiant glow.

🛏 Sleeping

The sandy beaches of Belle Mare and Palmar provide sea frontage for a long string of upmarket hotels, each one an opulent attempt to outdo the next. There's also a cache of stately seaside villas.

Most resorts should be booked well in advance through a travel agent – the advertised rates are eye-watering.

★ Émeraude Beach Attitude   HOTEL €€

(Map p122; ☑ 415 1107; emeraudebeach-hotel-mauritius.com; Belle Mare; s/d incl breakfast from €90/104; ❄ @ 🛜 🌊) Set in a breezy garden facing the public beach in Belle Mare, Émeraude is a breath of fresh air compared to the sky-high walls of the neighbouring five-star compounds. Some 20 semidetached and extremely comfortable cottage units with gabled roofs frame a sociable pool area, an open-air restaurant and a bar.

★ Le Prince Maurice   HOTEL €€€

(Map p122; ☑ 413 9130; www.constancehotels.com; Pointe de Flacq; s/d incl half board €440/550; ⓟ ❄ @ 🛜 🌊) The sense of perfect tranquillity is immediately striking as you pass through the entryway – this is a world unto itself that knows no limit to luxury. The lobby's marble architecture and flowing infinity pools can only be described as sublime, and the opulent suites, hidden just beyond, continue the timeless elegance. This is one of the most beautiful hotels in Mauritius.

The abundance of open-air pavilions and trim thatch is meant to elicit the ancient days of the spice trade – modern amenities are cleverly hidden and butlers are dressed in muted tones as they move across the grounds catering to every whim. Swimming pools, spas, access to Belle Mare Plage's golf courses and a floating restaurant (you'll see) round out the amenities list.

★ Le Saint Géran   HOTEL €€€

(Map p122; ☑ 401 1688; www.oneandonlyresorts.com; Pointe de Flacq; ste incl half board from €350; ❄ @ 🛜 🌊) Le Saint Géran is classic Mauritian luxury at its finest. And the clientele seems to agree. The resort sees more repeat customers than any other top-end hotel on the island (the guest list is a veritable who's who of movie stars and celebrities). Spacious rooms, under the signature bright-blue roofs, are arranged along the seemingly endless oceanfront – everyone has a to-die-for view.

Watersports are plenty, there's a charming kids club, and the top-notch butler service caters to every request. Le Saint Géran has set the bar unmatchably high in the dining category as well. Of its numerous restaurants, world-class Indian Pavilion is the pick.

Residence   HOTEL €€€

(Map p122; ☑ 401 8888; www.cenizaro.com/theresidence/mauritius; Belle Mare; s/d incl breakfast from €203/271; ❄ @ 🛜 🌊) Evoking the forgotten grandeur of colonial India, the Residence's vast complex of hotel rooms occupies an enviable stretch of sand. Rooms are simply decorated – with white drapery everywhere and framed Darwin-esque animal sketches on the walls – and perfectly capture the idea of this being a home away from home rather than a hotel.

Belle Mare Plage   HOTEL €€€

(Map p122; ☑ 402 2600; www.constance hotels.com; Pointe de Flacq; s/d from €200/275; ❄ @ 🛜 🌊) One of Mauritius' most delightful hotels, the Belle Mare Plage ticks every box. Pass through the inviting lobby – scented with vanilla and ylang-ylang, no less – before uncovering an enviable beach and a cache of top-notch amenities. Golfers relish the two championship-level courses and well-respected academy, while you can also enjoy expert massage therapy and then dine at the superb restaurants.

🍴 Eating

As the hotels are so all-encompassing, there is little incentive for guests to dine elsewhere. All the hotels, however, welcome nonguests at their à la carte restaurants, and the choice is superb. Prices are high, but the quality is almost always unimpeachable and it's well worth stopping by for a special occasion.

Elsewhere, roadside eateries serve up Mauritian and Chinese cuisine, with seafood a recurring theme. Belle Mare township has several *superettes* (small self-service grocery stores).

Seasons

Restaurant & Bar　　SEAFOOD, MAURITIAN €€
(Map p122; www.orchidvillas.mu; Royal Rd, Belle Mare; mains Rs 280-1250; ⊘noon-2.30pm & 6-9pm Tue-Sat, noon-2.30pm Sun) Part of the Orchid Villas complex, this roadside restaurant doesn't have sea views, but the food and service are both surprisingly good. Try the grilled lobster in Creole sauce and lemongrass emulsion.

Symon's Restaurant　　SEAFOOD, MAURITIAN €€
(Map p122; ☑415 1135; Belle Mare; mains Rs 350-780; ⊘11am-10pm) One of the better options in Belle Mare beyond the all-star line-up of hotel restaurants, Symon's serves up a variety of Indian, Mauritian and Chinese dishes. The views are ho-hum, but at least you won't break the bank, and some dishes – such as octopus curry with coconut milk, and the grilled catch of the day – stand out.

East Side　　MAURITIAN, CHINESE €€
(Map p122; ☑415 1254; Royal Rd, Belle Mare; mains Rs 350-450; ⊘11am-10pm) This roadside restaurant does OK seafood dishes, local fare such as octopus in saffron and a range of Chinese dishes. It's nothing to write home about, but it's easy on the wallet and handy if you're driving down the east coast.

Indian Pavilion　　INDIAN €€€
(Map p122, ☑401 1888; Le Saint Géran, Pointe de Flacq; mains Rs 1000-1450; set menu Rs 2900; ⊘12.30-3.30pm & 7-10pm) Indian Pavilion occupies an open-air veranda made of slatted jungle trunks tucked under a generous awning of thatch. While appreciating the views of the lagoon, cane-draped hills and a Taj Mahal–like temple, diners savour a dynamic assortment of contemporary North Indian–inspired dishes such as tandoori lobster or herb-marinated prawns served with cumin pulao and cashew-nut sauce.

❶ Getting There & Away

Buses connect Palmar with Centre de Flacq and Poste Lafayette, but there are no buses to Belle Mare. Count on Rs 500 for a taxi to the bus station in Centre de Flacq, or Rs 1800 for a taxi all the way to Port Louis.

Poste de Flacq & Roches Noires

POP 8500

Even quieter and more rugged than the sandy shores of Belle Mare, this calm area bordering the island's north still has a distinctive Creole vibe and is generally untouched by up-market developers. Holidaymakers seeking tranquillity should look no further than the lovely selection of private villas dotting the stone-strewn coast.

🛏 Sleeping & Eating

With a noticeable lack of resorts, Poste de Flacq is a haven for upscale villa rentals that work out to be a much better deal than many of the luxury-hotel packages (especially if you're travelling with friends and/or family). Contact **CG Villas** (☑262 5777; www.villas-maurice.com) or **EasyRent** (☑452 1010; www.easyrent.mu) to organise your stay – they manage a sizeable collection of beach houses in the area.

⭐**La Maison d'Été**　　BOUTIQUE HOTEL €€€
(Map p122; ☑410 5039; www.lamaisondete.com; Poste Lafayette; r incl breakfast €150-205; ❋@🛜≋) We're yet to hear a bad word about La Maison d'Été, one of Mauritius' top B&Bs, and we can understand why. The Franco-Mauritian owners have hit the nail on the head: an effortless charm pervades the collection of poolside rooms, each decorated with tasteful tributes to island life. The property also has an inviting restaurant (p130), two pools and a private beach.

Recent renovations added a touch more class with very little increase in price.

⭐**L'Ilot**　　VILLA €€€
(Map p122; ☑452 1010; www.lilot.biz; Royal Rd, Roches Noires; villas for 2 people €300-1500; ❋🛜) Go one better than staying at a five-star resort and rent your own private island! This four-bedroom masterpiece sits on its own islet attached to the mainland by a concreted bridge made from boulders. The villa is faultlessly decorated and you'll never have to fight for a sun lounge.

Radisson Blu Azuri Resort & Spa　　HOTEL €€€
(Map p122; ☑402 3700, 402 6200; www.radissonblu.com/en/hotel-mauritius-azuri; Rivière du Rempart; r from €200; P❋@🛜≋) With everything you'd expect from this reliably luxurious chain, the Radisson combines large-hotel facilities with a sense of quiet intimacy. The

pretty white rooms look onto the garden or the beach, and there are enough bars and restaurants here that you'll never have to leave, if that's the kind of holiday you're after.

Villa La Mauricienne   VILLA €€€

(Map p122; ☑ 262 5777; www.villas-maurice.com; Royal Rd, Poste Lafayette; villas from €656; ❋ 🛜 ☒) Sheltered by a massive roof of thatch and bamboo, this opulent retreat feels decidedly Asian in theme with abounding bursts of fuchsia and orange. The master suite is lofted above the open-air terrace, which looks out over the enormous swimming pool and giant strip of private sand.

Villa Lafayette   VILLA €€€

(Map p122; ☑ 262 5777; www.villas-maurice.com; Royal Rd, Poste Lafayette; villas from €305; ❋ ☒) This traditional Mauritian beach house feels slightly Mediterranean with its white-and-blue colour scheme. The pool is tucked within an interior courtyard and the backyard faces a wild stretch of sand and sea. The decor is more homely than luxurious, but it's still supremely comfortable.

★ La Maison d'Été   MAURITIAN €€

(Map p122; ☑ 410 5039; Poste Lafayette; pizzas Rs 250, mains Rs 290-1600; ⊙ noon-3pm & 7-9.30pm Mon-Sat, 7-9.30pm Sun) The restaurant at La Maison d'Été (p129) is run like a stand-alone establishment, serving an enticing assortment of Mauritian and fusion food of the highest quality. The inn's owner often moonlights as the chef and takes special care when preparing locally sourced dishes matched with international wines. There's also a Sunday lunch buffet menu. Ring for a reservation if you're not staying here.

❶ Getting There & Away

Most bus services along the east coast pass through Roches Noires.

UNDERSTAND MAURITIUS

Mauritius Today

Mauritius flies under the radar when it comes to its international profile, and that's just how locals like it. A stable political scene, a steady economy that weathered the global financial crisis relatively unscathed, and a general lack of social unrest may not make for great headlines, but put them together and you'll find a country largely at peace with itself. It is, of course, more complicated than that, but not by much.

Economic Progress

Mauritius gets little credit for its remarkable economic success story. When it became independent in 1968, the country had few resources beyond sugar cane. Five decades later, the country's inhabitants enjoy living standards the envy of just about every other nation in this part of the world. For most of those decades, the catch cry for economic policymakers in Mauritius has been diversification – away from sugar cane, then away from textile manufacturing in the face of competition from China, and so on. And it's a challenge that the country has largely met. Moves towards what former prime minister Paul Bérenger described as a 'quantum leap' to transform Mauritius into a 'knowledge island', canny forays into the world of international banking and establishing Mauritius as call-centre hub all helped. From 2010 until 2015, at a time when developed economies across the world were foundering, Mauritius maintained growth at a highly respectable 3% to 4%. With unemployment below 8% and GDP per capita rising to nearly US$20,000 in 2015, these are no abstract economic numbers but the outward signs of an economy that continues to bring significant benefits to its people.

Political Stagnation?

Politics in Mauritius tends to work pretty well – government transitions have always taken place by means of the ballot box and political debate rarely strays into dangerous territory. But talk politics with many Mauritians and you'll quickly find that there are two overriding problems with Mauritius' political scene. First, politics here has long been the preserve of career politicians and their families, with three names recurring across the history of independent Mauritius: Aneerood Jugnauth (the current prime minister, who has served six times as prime minister since 1982), Paul Bérenger (political leader of the Franco-Mauritian community and six-time leader of the opposition since the early 1980s), and two-time prime minister Navin Ramgoolam (the son of independence leader Sir Seewoosagur). With the same faces in power for almost four decades, many Mauritians argue, real change becomes more difficult. The second problem with an unchanging political landscape is the fear that ethnic tensions, which flared briefly but powerfully in 1999, have never been addressed in any meaningful way and continue to simmer beneath the surface.

Climate Extremes

Mauritius may not be one of those ocean islands that will disappear beneath the water when global warming causes sea levels to rise. But that doesn't mean it will be immune from the effects of climate change. Mauritius (and Rodrigues) inhabit a tough neighbourhood when it comes to climate – the cyclone season begins in January, and the sometimes-devastating cyclones that come with it have been a hazard of Mauritian life for as long as anyone can remember. Even so, the country was ill-prepared for the torrential rains that battered it in late March 2013, causing flash flooding, particularly in Port Louis, and the deaths of 11 people. Then prime minister Navin Ramgoolam blamed climate change for the devastation. While many saw his claim as an attempt to detract attention from the failure of successive governments to maintain basic infrastructure – most of the flooding was caused by blocked drains – everyone feared that there might just be a little truth in what he said.

Tourism's Impact

It would be a brave Mauritian who would question the benefits that tourism has brought to the country. The industry has, after all, played a major role in Mauritius' economic prosperity for decades and the clever positioning of the country as a luxury destination has protected the industry from the vagaries of falling tourist numbers that affect the midrange travel market during tough economic times. But that's not to say that there aren't some important issues in play here. Serious water shortages in Rodrigues already trouble hotels (not to mention ordinary Rodriguans), with fears about the long-term impact of tourism on the island's resources. And while tourism is playing an important role in boosting programs to restore habitats and assist in the recovery of endangered species along the east coast (as in Île aux Aigrettes and Vallée de Ferney), there are growing concerns over the sustainability of a number of popular activities such as diving and dolphin-watching over in the west and their impact on the environment.

History

Mauritius had no indigenous population predating the European colonisers, and so – unlike many other small islands, for which colonisation resulted in the savage destruction of the original inhabitants a short time later – its history is pleasantly free of episodes of brutality, at least until the advent of slavery. This historical point is key to understanding the country's culture of tolerance and easy acceptance of all people: there's nobody in the ethnic melting pot able to claim precedence over the others.

The First Colonisers

Although Arab traders knew of Mauritius – which they rather unfairly called Dina Arobi (Isle of Desolation) – as early as the 10th century, the first Europeans to discover these uninhabited islands were the Portuguese, around 1507. They, too, were more interested in trade and never attempted to settle.

In 1598 a group of Dutch sailors landed on the southeast coast of the island at what is now called Vieux Grand Port, and claimed the island for the Netherlands. For the next 40 years the Dutch used Mauritius as a supply base for Batavia (Java), before deciding to settle near their original landing spot. Settlement ruins and a museum can still be seen at Vieux Grand Port, near Mahébourg.

The colony never really flourished, however, and the Dutch abandoned it in 1710. Nevertheless, they left their mark: the Dutch were responsible for the extinction of the dodo and for introducing slaves from Africa, deer from Java, wild boar, tobacco and, above all, sugar cane.

Île de France

Five years after the Dutch abandoned Mauritius, it was the turn of the French, when Captain Guillaume Dufresne d'Arsel sailed across from what is now Réunion and claimed Mauritius for France in 1715. The island was rechristened Île de France, but nothing much happened until the arrival in 1735 of dynamic governor Bertrand François Mahé de Labourdonnais, Mauritius' first colonial hero. He not only transformed Port Louis into a thriving seaport but also built the first sugar mill and established a road network.

DIEGO GARCIA & THE CHAGOSSIAN BETRAYAL

One of the most prolonged betrayals in British colonial history is that surrounding the secret exile of the Chagos Islanders from their homeland in the 1960s and 1970s, in order to lease the main island, Diego Garcia, to the USA for use as a military base.

The Chagos Islands were excised from Mauritian territory by the British prior to independence in 1965, and Mauritius and the UK continue to dispute the sovereignty of the islands. The islanders were 'resettled' in Mauritius and the Seychelles between 1965 and 1973. Some 5000 now live in abject poverty in the slums of Port Louis, where they continue to fight for their right to return home. The islanders won derisory compensation of £4 million from the British in 1982, which was paid out to the poverty-stricken islanders in return for them signing away their rights – many did not realise what the legal documents they were signing meant.

In 2000, the UK High Court ruled that the Chagossians had been evicted illegally and upheld their right to be repatriated. Nothing happened, so the Chagossians went back to court. In October 2003, the judge rejected their claim for further compensation, though he acknowledged that the British government had treated the islanders 'shamefully' and that the compensation had been inadequate. In May 2007, the Chagossians won a further case at the Court of Appeal in London, in which the government's behaviour was condemned as unlawful and an abuse of power. The judges in the case also refused to place a stay on the ruling, meaning the Chagossians were free to return to all islands (with the exception of Diego Garcia itself) with immediate effect. In 2008, the case was overturned. The Chagos Archipelago has now been ceded to the US military until 2016, while the islanders continue to pursue their rights through the European Court of Human Rights.

John Pilger gives his angle on the story in his documentary *Stealing a Nation* (2004). You can watch it online. Further information and ways to help the Chagossians can be found at www.chagossupport.org.uk. For additional information on the Chagos Islanders, check out David Vine's book *Island of Shame*.

It was around this time that Mauritius' best-known historic event occurred: the *St Géran* went down during a storm off the northeast coast in 1744. The shipwreck inspired Bernardin de St-Pierre's romantic novel *Paul et Virginie,* an early bestseller.

As the English gained the upper hand in the Indian Ocean in the late 18th century, Port Louis became a haven for pirates and corsairs – mercenary marines paid by a country to prey on enemy ships. The most famous Franco-Mauritian corsair was Robert Surcouf, who wrought havoc on British shipping.

In 1789, French settlers in Mauritius recognised the revolution in France and got rid of their governor. But some policies were a bridge too far: they refused to free their slaves when the abolition of slavery was decreed in Paris in 1794.

British Rule

In 1810, during the Napoleonic Wars, the British moved in on Mauritius as part of their grand plan to control the Indian Ocean. Things started badly when they were defeated at the Battle of Vieux Grand Port. Just a few months later, however, British forces landed at Cap Malheureux on the north coast and took over the island.

The new British rulers renamed the island Mauritius but allowed the Franco-Mauritians to retain their language, religion and legal system, and the all-important sugar-cane plantations on which the economy depended. The slaves were finally freed in 1835, by which time there were over 70,000 on the island. They were replaced or supplemented by labour imported from India and China. As many as 500,000 Indians took up the promise of a better life in Mauritius, often to find themselves living and working in appalling conditions on minimum pay.

By sheer weight of numbers, the Indian workforce gradually achieved a greater say in the running of the country. Their struggle was given extra impetus when Indian political and spiritual leader Mahatma Gandhi visited Mauritius in 1901 to push for civil rights. However, the key event was the introduction of universal suffrage in 1958, and the key personality was Dr (later Sir) Seewoosagur Ramgoolam.

Founder of the Labour Party in 1936, Seewoosagur Ramgoolam led the fight for independence, which was finally granted in 1968.

Independence

The prime minister of newly independent Mauritius was, not surprisingly, Sir Seewoosagur Ramgoolam. He remained in office for the next 13 years and continued to command great reverence until his death in 1985. A host of public buildings have been named in his honour.

The political landscape since Sir Seewoosagur's death has largely been dominated by the trio of Anerood Jugnauth, the Indian leader of the Mouvement Socialiste Militant (MSM); the Franco-Mauritian Paul Bérenger, with his leftist Mouvement Militant Mauricien (MMM); and Navin Ramgoolam, son of Sir Seewoosagur and leader of the Mauritian Labour Party. The former two parties formed their first coalition government in 1982, with Jugnauth as prime minister and Bérenger as finance minister. In the years that followed, the two men were in and out of government, sometimes power sharing, at other times in opposition to each other, according to the complex and shifting web of allegiances that enlivens Mauritian politics. In 1995 and again in 2005, Navin Ramgoolam beat the MSM-MMM coalition with his Alliance Sociale coalition.

On the economic front, meanwhile, Mauritius was undergoing a minor miracle. Up until the 1970s the Mauritian economy could be summed up in one word: sugar. Sugar represented more than 90% of the country's exports, covered most of its fertile land and was its largest employer by far. Every so often, a cyclone would devastate the cane crop, or a world drop in sugar prices would have bitter consequences.

From the 1970s the government went all out to promote textiles, tourism and financial services, much of it based on foreign investment. Soon Mauritius was one of the world's largest exporters of textiles, with clothes by Ralph Lauren, Pierre Cardin, Lacoste and other famous brands all manufactured on the island. Income from tourism also grew in leaps and bounds as the government targeted the luxury end of the market.

The strategy paid off. The 1980s and 1990s saw the Mauritian economy grow by an extremely healthy 5% a year. Unemployment fell from a whopping 42% in 1980 to less than 6% by 2000 and overall standards of living improved. Even so, rates of unemployment and poverty remained high among the Creole population (people of mixed Afro-European origin), many of whom also felt frustrated at their lack of political power in the face of the Indian majority. These tensions spilled out onto the streets of Port Louis in 1999, triggered by the death in police custody of the singer Kaya, an ardent campaigner for the rights of the disadvantaged Creole population. The riots brought the country to a standstill for four days and forced the government to make political concessions.

Culture

Mauritius is often cited as an example of racial and religious harmony, and compared with most countries it is, as on the surface there are few signs of conflict. However, racial divisions are still apparent between the Hindu majority and Muslim and Creole minorities, and these tensions constitute one of the few potential political flashpoints. Such issues usually only surface during elections, when parties aren't averse to playing the race card.

ETIQUETTE IN MAURITIUS

The people of Mauritius have a well-deserved reputation for tolerance. That said, there are a few 'rules' of behaviour that you should try to abide by.

Clothing Although beachwear is fine for the beaches, you will cause offence and may invite pestering if you dress skimpily elsewhere. Nude bathing is forbidden; women going topless is tolerated around some hotel pools but rarely on the beaches.

Temples and Mosques Miniskirts and singlet tops are no-nos, and it is normal to remove your shoes. Many temples and mosques also ask you not to take photos, while some Hindu temples request that you remove all leather items, such as belts. At mosques, you may be required to cover your head in certain areas, so remember to take along a scarf. Never touch a carving or statue of a deity.

Living Standards

As a result of the ongoing economic boom and political stability, overall living standards have improved in recent years and the majority of houses now have mains water and electricity. However, the gap between rich and poor is widening. It is estimated that the top 20% of the population earns 45% of the total income and that around 10% lives below the poverty line. A labourer's wage is just Rs 6000 per month, while a teacher might earn Rs 12,000. You'll see a few people begging around the markets and mosques, but the visible presence of poverty on the streets is relatively discreet.

Mauritians place great importance on education – not just to get a better job but as a goal in its own right. Lawyers, doctors and teachers are regarded with tremendous respect. The pinnacle of success for many is to work in the civil service, though this is beginning to change as salaries rise among business people.

A National Identity?

Despite being a relatively young country with a diverse population, and although ethnicity is often a primary touchstone of identity for many Mauritians, a strong sense of national identity continues to transcend racial and cultural ties.

Of the various forces binding Mauritians together, the most important is language – not the official language of English, but Creole, which is the first language of 70% to 80% of the population and understood by virtually all Mauritians. Another common bond is that everyone is an immigrant or descended from immigrants. Food and music are other unifiers, as is the importance placed on family life.

Mauritius is also a small, tight-knit community. Living in such close proximity breaks down barriers and increases understanding between different groups. Respect for others and tolerance are deeply ingrained in all sectors of society, despite the occasional flare-up of racial tension.

Family Life & the Role of Women

In general, each ethnic group maintains a way of life similar to that found in their countries of origin, even if they are second- or third-generation Mauritian.

WOMEN IN MAURITIUS

➡ Maternal mortality rate per 100,000 live births: 53

➡ Life expectancy for men/women: 71.94/79.03 years

➡ Adult literacy for men/women: 92.9/88.5%

➡ Fertility rate: 1.76 children per woman

Often, several generations live together under one roof and the main social unit is the extended family – as evidenced by the size of family parties on a Sunday picnic. There is minimal social-security provision in Mauritius; people rely on their family in times of need. Mauritians are usually married by the age of 25 and the majority of wives stay home to raise the family, while husbands earn the daily bread. Arranged marriages are still the norm among Indian families, while the Hindu caste system has also been replicated to some degree. Among all groups, religion and religious institutions continue to play a central role in community life.

As with elsewhere, this very traditional pattern is starting to break down as the younger generation grows more individualistic and more Westernised. Young people are far more likely to socialise with people from other communities, and intermarriage is on the rise.

Other forces for change are the growth of consumerism and the emergence of a largely Indian and Chinese middle class. Middle-class couples are more likely to set up their own home and to have fewer children, while the wife may even go out to work. Statistics also show a slight decline in the number of marriages, while the divorce rate has doubled over the last 20 years.

Women's equality still has a long way to go in Mauritius. Many women have to accept low-paid, unskilled jobs, typically in a textile factory or as cleaners. Even highly qualified women can find it hard to get promotions in the private sector, though they do better in the public service. In 2003 the government passed a Sex Discrimination Act and set up an independent unit to investigate sex-discrimination cases, including sexual harassment at work. The unit is also charged with raising awareness levels and educating employers about equal opportunity.

People of Mauritius

Mauritius is made up of five ethnic groups: Indo-Mauritian (68%), Creole (27%), Sino-Mauritian (3%), Franco-Mauritian (1%) and the new kids on the block – South African expats (1%). Another small group you might come across are the Chagos Islanders.

INDO-MAURITIANS

The Indian population (the majority of which is Hindu) is descended from the labourers who came to the island to work the cane fields. Nowadays, Indians form the backbone of the labouring and agricultural community and own many of the island's small- and medium-sized businesses, typically in manufacturing and the retail trade. Central Plateau towns such as Rose Hill have a definite Indian character.

Indians also tend to be prominent in civic life. Local elections are often racially aligned, and since Indo-Mauritians are in the majority, they tend to win at the polls. The prime minister between 2003 and 2005, Franco-Mauritian Paul Bérenger, was the first non-Indian at the helm in the country's history.

CREOLES

After the Indo-Mauritians, the next largest group is the Creoles, descendants of African slaves, with varying amounts of European ancestry. Creoles as a whole form the most disadvantaged sector of society. Despite the fact that all forms of discrimination are illegal under the Mauritian constitution, it is widely recognised that the Creole minority has been socially, economically and politically marginalised.

PEOPLE STATS

➡ Population: 1.34 million

➡ Growth rate: 0.64%

➡ Proportion under 15 years old: 20.74%

➡ Average age: 34.4

➡ Proportion living in urban areas: 39.7%

➡ Population density: 651.7 people per sq km (higher than the Netherlands and one of the world's highest)

The majority work in low-paid jobs or eke out a living from fishing or subsistence farming, and it's a vicious circle. Creoles find it harder to get work, partly because of low levels of literacy, but few Creole children complete secondary school because they're needed to help support the family. Expectations are also lower – and so it goes on.

Rodrigues is the epicentre of Mauritian Creole culture, with Creoles making up 98% of the population.

SINO-MAURITIANS

Mauritius' 30,000 Sino-Mauritians are involved mostly in commerce. Despite their small numbers, the Chinese community plays a disproportionate role in the country's economy, though they tend to avoid politics. Most came to the country as self-employed entrepreneurs and settled in the towns (particularly Port Louis), though most villages have at least one Chinese-run store.

KAYA

It was a black day for Mauritius, and a blacker one still for the Creole community. On 21 February 1999, singer Joseph Topize (aka Kaya) was found dead in his police cell, seemingly a victim of police brutality, after being arrested for smoking cannabis after a pro-legalisation rally.

As the pioneer of *seggae*, a unique combination of reggae and traditional *séga* beats, Kaya provided a voice for disadvantaged Creoles across the country. His death in the custody of Indian police split Mauritian society along racial lines, triggering four days of violent riots that left several people dead and brought the country to a standstill.

An autopsy cleared the police of wrongdoing, but the events forced the Indian-dominated government to acknowledge *le malaise Créole*: Creoles' anger at their impoverished status in a country that has been dominated by Indians since independence. It is an anger that still simmers almost 18 years after the singer's death.

In contrast to these violent scenes, Kaya's music is full of positive energy. The classic album *Seggae Experience* is a tribute to the singer's unique vision.

FRANCO-MAURITIANS & SOUTH AFRICAN EXPATS

Franco-Mauritians are the descendants of the *grands blancs* (rich whites), who were the first European settlers on Mauritius and who quickly parcelled the best arable land out among themselves in the 18th century. Franco-Mauritians own most of the sugar mills, banks and other big businesses, and tend to live in palatial private residences in the hills around Curepipe. They also own almost all the luxurious holiday houses along the coast. Many have decamped completely to live in South Africa, Australia and France. In fact, there are now more South African expats living on the island (congregated on the west coast) than there are Franco-Mauritians.

Religion

There is a close link between religion and race in Mauritius and a remarkable degree of religious tolerance. Mosques, churches and Hindu temples can be found within a stone's throw of each other in many parts of the country and we know of one case in Floréal where they are separated only by a shared wall.

Official figures put the number of Hindus at 48.5% of the population, and all are Indian in origin or ethnicity. Festivals play a central role in the Hindu faith and the calendar's packed with colourful celebrations.

There's a certain amount of resentment towards Hindus in Mauritius, not for religious reasons but because the Hindu majority dominates the country's political life and its administration. Up until now, with the economy in full swing, this has merely resulted in grumbling about discrimination and 'jobs for the boys', but there's a fear this might change if the economy really begins to falter.

Around one-quarter of the population is Roman Catholic. Catholicism is practised by most Creoles, and it has picked up a few voodoo overtones over the years. Most Franco-Mauritians are also Catholic and a few Chinese and Indians have converted, largely through marriage.

Muslims make up roughly one-fifth of the population. Like the Hindus, Mauritian Muslims originally came from India. In Mauritius, where Islam exists in close proximity to other religions, it tends to be fairly liberal. Attendance at mosque is high and many Muslim women wear the hijab.

Sino-Mauritians are the least conspicuous in their worship. The one big exception is

MALCOLM DE CHAZAL

Few figures loom as large over the arts in 20th-century Mauritius as Malcolm de Chazal. Aside from being the father of modern Mauritian literature, the surrealist de Chazal produced paintings full of light and energy – the most famous is *Blue Dodo*. Pereybère's Galerie du Moulin Cassé features his work.

Chinese New Year, which is celebrated in Port Louis with great gusto. There are also a few Chinese temples scattered around the capital.

Arts

Mauritian literature and fine arts are firmly based in the French tradition. The country's music, however, is African in origin and is very much alive and kicking.

Literature

Mauritius has provided the backdrop for a number of historical novels, but it's the growing profile of local writers that makes Mauritians most proud.

BOOKS BY MAURITIAN WRITERS

Those who want to read a 20th-century Mauritian novel should try something by Malcolm de Chazal, whose most famous works are *Sens-Plastique*, available in translation, and *Petrusmok*. Chazal was an eccentric recluse, but he inspired a whole generation of local writers. His works are a highly original blend of poetry and philosophy, and are peppered with pithy statements, such as 'Avoid clean people who have a dirty stare'.

Of living writers, perhaps the best known internationally is Carl de Souza. In his novel *Le Sang de l'Anglais* he looks at the often ambivalent relationship between Mauritians and their countries of origin, while *La Maison qui Marchait Vers le Large*, set in Port Louis, takes inter-community conflict as its theme. *Les Jours Kaya* is a coming-of-age book set against the violence following Kaya's death.

Other contemporary novelists to look out for include Ananda Devi, Shenaz Patel and Nathacha Appanah-Mouriquand. Unfortunately, their works as yet are only available in French, which is regarded as the language of culture.

BOOKS SET IN MAURITIUS

Mauritius' most famous contribution to world literature – one that has become entangled in the island's history – is the romantic novel *Paul et Virginie* by Bernardin de St-Pierre, which was first published in 1788. An English translation of the novel is widely available in Mauritius. The author captures the landscapes beautifully, though his ultra-moralistic tear-jerker is less likely to appeal to modern tastes.

Joseph Conrad's oblique love story *A Smile of Fortune*, collected in *'Twixt Land and Sea* (1912), is set in Mauritius, although it's hardly very flattering about the place. Set in the late 19th century, it does, however, give a taste of the mercantile activity of the time and the curious mix of 'negroes', Creoles, 'coolies' and marooned Frenchmen who populated the island then. Visitors to the island will certainly identify with Conrad's description of Mauritius as the 'Pearl of the Ocean…a pearl distilling much sweetness on the world' but will undoubtedly find the current inhabitants far more pleasant to deal with than the characters described in the story.

Music & Dance

You'll hear *séga*, the music of Creole culture, everywhere nowadays, but in the early 20th century it fell seriously out of fashion. Its revival in the early 1950s is credited to the Creole singer Ti Frère, whose song 'Anita' has become a classic. Though he died in 1992, Ti Frère is still the country's most popular *séga* star. More recent Creole groups and singers

JMG LE CLÉZIO

Mauritius can lay claim (sort of) to a winner of the Nobel Prize for Literature. French author JMG Le Clézio, the 2008 Nobel laureate, has a Mauritian father and set a number of his novels in Mauritius, of which *Le Chercheur d'Or* (The Prospector) has been translated into English.

with a wide following include Cassiya, Fanfan and the prolific Jean-Claude Gaspard.

Séga evolved slightly differently in Rodrigues. Here the drum plays a more prominent role in what's known as *séga tambour*. The island's accordion bands are also famous for their surprising repertoire, which includes waltzes, polkas, quadrilles and Scottish reels. Over the years these were learned from passing European sailors and gradually absorbed into the local folk music. They're now an essential part of any Rodriguan knees-up.

A newer Mauritian musical form was invented by Creole musician Kaya in *seggae*, which blends elements of *séga* and reggae. With his band Racine Tatane, Kaya gave a voice to dissatisfied Creoles around the island. Tragically, the singer died in police custody in February 1999. Following in Kaya's footsteps, Ras Natty Baby and his Natty Rebels are one of the most popular *seggae* groups; sales gained an extra boost when Ras Natty Baby was imprisoned for heroin trafficking in 2003…

SÉGA!

Séga is the powerful combination of music and dance originally conceived by African slaves as a diversion from the injustice of their daily existence. At the end of a hard day in the cane fields, couples danced the *séga* around campfires on the beach to the accompaniment of drums.

Because of the sand (some say because of the shackles), there could be no fancy footwork. So today, when dancing the *séga*, the feet never leave the ground. The rest of the body makes up for it and the result, when the fire is hot, can be extremely erotic. In the rhythm and beat of *séga*, you can see or hear connections with the Latin American salsa, the Caribbean calypso and the African origins of the people. It's a personal, visceral dance where the dancers let the music take over and abandon themselves to the beat.

The dance is traditionally accompanied by the beat of the *ravanne*, a goatskin drum. The beat starts slowly and builds into a pulsating rhythm, which normally carries away performers and onlookers alike. You may be lucky enough to see the dance being performed spontaneously at beach parties or family barbecues. Otherwise, you'll have to make do with the less authentic *séga* soirées offered by some bars and restaurants and most of the big hotels, often in combination with a Mauritian buffet.

Recently, *ragga*, a blend of house music, traditional Indian music and reggae, has been gaining a following. Mauritian *ragga* groups include Black Ayou and the Authentic Steel Brothers.

Visual Arts

Historically, Mauritian artists took their lead from what was happening in Europe, particularly France. Bizarrely, some of the 18th- and 19th-century engravings and oils of Mauritian landscapes you see could almost be mistaken for European scenes. The classical statue of Paul and Virginie in Port Louis' Blue Penny Museum and the one of King Edward VII at the city's Champ de Mars Racecourse were both created by Mauritius' best-known sculptor, Prosper d'Épinay.

Contemporary Mauritian art tends to be driven by the tourist market. One artist you'll find reproduced everywhere is Vaco Baissac; his work instantly recognisable by the blocks of colour outlined in black, like a stained-glass window. His Galerie Vaco is in Grand Baie.

Other commercially successful artists include Danielle Hitié, who produces minutely detailed renderings of markets as well as rural scenes, and Françoise Vrot, known for her very expressive portraits of women fieldworkers. Both artists are exhibited in galleries in Grand Baie, where Vrot also has her studio.

Keep an eye out for exhibitions by more innovative contemporary artists, such as Hervé Masson, Serge Constantin, Henry Koombes and Khalid Nazroo. All have had some success on the international scene, though they're less visible locally.

Architecture

Much of Mauritius' architectural heritage has become buried under a sea of concrete, but thankfully a handful of colonial-era mansions survived, and it's these that provide the architectural highlights for visitors to the country.

COLONIAL ARCHITECTURE

In 2003 the government set up a National Heritage Fund charged with preserving the country's historic buildings. The plantation houses dating from the 18th and 19th centuries have fared best, and you'll still see them standing in glorious isolation amid the cane fields. Many are privately owned and closed

---

BEST COLONIAL ARCHITECTURE

The following colonial-era mansions are all open to the public and well worth visiting. Apart from the buildings' innate historical and aesthetic values, visiting them makes a statement that these are places of beauty *and* value, which may just lead to more of them being preserved.

➡ Eureka (p59), Moka

➡ Government House (p49), Port Louis

➡ Château Labourdonnais (p82), Mapou

➡ National History Museum (p105), Mahébourg

➡ Hôtel de Ville (p61), Curepipe

➡ Le Jardin de Beau Vallon (p115), near Mahébourg

➡ Domaine des Aubineaux (p61), Curepipe

➡ St Aubin (p120), Rivière des Anguilles

➡ Le Château Restaurant (p119), Bel Ombre

---

to the public. One such is Le Réduit, near Moka, which is now the president's official residence. Others have been converted into museums and restaurants.

The first French settlers naturally brought with them building styles from home. Over the years the architecture evolved until it became supremely well suited to the hot, humid tropics. It's for this reason that so many of the grand plantation houses have survived the ravages of time.

In many of these buildings, flourishes that appear to be ornamental – vaulted roofs and decorative pierced screens, for example – all serve to keep the occupants cool and dry. The most distinctive feature is the shingled roof with ornamental turrets and rows of attic windows. These wedding-cake touches conceal a vaulted roof, which allows the air to circulate. Another characteristic element is the wide, airy *varangue* (veranda), where raffia blinds, fans and pot plants create a cooling humidity.

The roofs, windows and overhangs are usually lined with delicate, lace-like *lambrequins* (decorative wooden borders), which are purely ornamental. They vary from simple, repetitive floral patterns to elaborate pierced friezes; in all cases a botanical theme predominates.

Lambrequins, shingled roofs and verandas or wrought-iron balconies are also found in colonial-era town houses. The more prestigious buildings were constructed in brick, or even stone, and so are better able to withstand cyclones and termites. In Port Louis, Government House and other buildings lining Place d'Armes are all fine examples.

CONTEMPORARY ARCHITECTURE

A few attempts at daring contemporary structures have been made, but the most prestigious in recent times has been Port Louis' Le Caudan Waterfront development. Given its location at the very heart of the capital, the architects decided to incorporate elements of the traditional architecture found around the city's Place d'Armes. Further inspiration came from the nearby stone-and-steel dockyard buildings.

Plans are under way, although they have stalled in recent years, to build a Caudan-like complex in sleepy Mahébourg. Close to completion, the country's first luxury-yacht port, La Balise Marina, is taking shape in Black River.

Food & Drink

Mauritian cuisine is very similar across the island – a rich and delicious mix of Indian spices and fresh local ingredients prepared with strong influences from Chinese, French and African cuisine. The food of Rodrigues is quite different – less spicy but with more fresh fruit and beans used as ingredients.

Staples & Specialities

Rice and noodles are two of the staples of everyday life, although to a great extent what people eat depends on their ethnic background. A Sino-Mauritian may well start the day with tea and noodles, a Franco-Mauritian with a *café au lait* and croissant, and an Indo-Mauritian with a *chapatti* (thin pancake). However, come lunchtime nearly everyone enjoys a hot meal, whether it be a spicy seafood *carri* (curry) or *mines* (noodles), and a cooling beer. Dinner is the main meal of the day and is usually eaten *en famille* (with family).

While meat is widely eaten (especially in Chinese and French cuisine) – venison and wild boar are mainstays around Mahébourg, and the distinctive Creole sausages are ever-popular – the mainstays of Mauritian cuisine (regardless of culture) are fish and seafood. Marlin, often smoked, is a big favourite, as are mussels, prawns, lobster and calamari. Octopus (*ourite*) is a special highlight, and appears in all manner of guises – salads, cooked in saffron, or in a curry (sometimes with green papaya). The fish of the day is nearly always a good order.

When it comes to street food, *dhal puri* (lentil dhal served in a *chapatti*) and *boulettes* (tiny steamed Chinese dumplings) are fantastic.

Drinks

Mauritians love their cocktail hour, and so you'll nearly always have access to an *apéro* (aperitif) or a *ti punch* (small punch) – usually a rum-based fruit cocktail.

Unsurprisingly, the national drink is rum. Although most experts agree that Mauritian rum isn't up to the standard of the Caribbean equivalent, there are still some excellent brands, particularly Green Island, the dark variety of which is superb. An excellent way to gain an insight into local rums is the Rhumerie de Chamarel (p96), where you can see how it's made, have a wonderful meal and try the product. Despite a long history of rum production in Mauritius, the socially preferred spirit tends to be whisky – a hangover from the 150-year British rule.

The national beer is Phoenix, an excellent pilsner produced since the 1960s and a regular prizewinner at festivals around the world. The other premium brand of the brewery, Blue Marlin, is also very good.

Mauritians are also great tea drinkers – you shouldn't miss trying the range of Bois Chéri teas on sale throughout the country. The vanilla tea is the most famous and is quite delicious and refreshing even in the heat of the day. You'll have a chance to see it being made and can taste it at the Bois Chéri tea plantation (p121) in southern Mauritius.

During Hindu and Muslim festivals, deliciously flavoured drinks such as *lassi* (Indian yogurt drink) and almond milk (almond- and cardamom-flavoured milk) are prepared.

Where to Eat & Drink

There tends to be quite a bit of segregation between 'tourist' restaurants and 'local' ones, particularly around bigger resort areas. In places such as Port Louis and the central highlands this is a lot less pronounced, and most places have a mixed clientele.

Nearly all restaurants have menus in English, or at least staff who speak English, so communication difficulties are at a minimum.

Most restaurants have several cuisines served up cheek by jowl, although they're nearly always separated from each other on the menu. While in better restaurants this will mean each cuisine is prepared by a different expert chef, on the whole most chefs are decent at cooking one cuisine and prepare the remaining dishes with something approaching indifference. The rule is a fairly obvious one – don't go to a Chinese restaurant for a good curry.

The best places to eat throughout the country tend to be *tables d'hôtes* (privately hosted meals); these are often given by people who run guesthouses as well, but they're just as often offered alone. These give you a unique insight into local life, as you'll usually dine with the host couple and often their children, plus any other travellers who've arranged to come by (or people staying in the guesthouse) and you'll enjoy traditional dishes spread over a number of courses. It's nearly always necessary to book a *table d'hôte*, preferably a day in advance, although it's always worth asking – bigger operations will sometimes be able to accommodate last-minute additions.

It's the Creole element that shines through most strongly at the *tables d'hôtes*. If you don't eat at a *table d'hôte* at least once in Mauritius, you've missed an essential part of its gastronomic culture.

QUICK EATS

Places to enjoy eats on the run are in plentiful supply in Mauritius. Street vendors are at every bus station and town square, and takeaway shops can be found in numerous shopping centres and markets; both offer inexpensive local treats, including Indian, French and Chinese delicacies. Almost all restaurants, except the most upmarket, will do takeaway.

In Mauritius, roadside stalls serving dinner dishes such as biryani (curried rice), Indian rotis and *farattas* (unleavened flaky flour pancakes) are popular. Street eats cost around Rs 5 to Rs 10 for snacks like rotis, *dhal puris* (lentil pancakes) and *boulettes* (tiny steamed Chinese dumplings) served at markets, along public beaches and in the capital.

The atmospheric markets are worth visiting for the popular *gâteaux piments* (chilli cakes), which are cooked on the spot. You should also try the delicious *dhal puris* (lentil pancakes), rotis, samosas and *bhajas* (fried balls of besan dough with herbs or onion).

Indian and Chinese restaurants offer quick and inexpensive meals and snacks. Remember to buy some Indian savouries such as *caca pigeon* (an Indian nibble) or the famous Chinese *char siu* (barbecued pork).

Vegetarians & Vegans

Vegetarians will fare well in Mauritius, although they may be disappointed by the lack of variety. Indian restaurants tend to offer the best choice, but often this is limited to a variation on the theme of *carri de légumes* (vegetable curry). Chinese restaurants are also good for vegetarians, while Creole and French places are much more limiting. That said, almost everywhere has a vegetable curry on the menu. Pescatarians will be spoilt for choice, as almost every eatery in the country offers fresh seafood and freshly caught fish cooked to perfection.

Vegans will find things harder, but not unassailably so – most resorts will be able to offer vegan options with notice, and again Indian restaurants will offer the most choice.

Habits & Customs

Eating habits vary across ethnic groups. Some groups eat with their fingers, others don't eat meat on Fridays and some abstain from eating pork – it's hard to generalise across the community.

Other than in hotels and *chambres d'hôtes* where buffets are the norm, breakfasts are normally very quick and informal. Lunch is also a fairly casual affair, although at the weekend it tends to be more formal, when family and friends gather to share the pleasures of the table. In restaurants, special menus are offered for weekend lunches. Before dinner, which is a very formal occasion, *gajacks* (predinner snacks) and an *apéro* (aperitif) or a *ti punch* (small punch) is commonly served; during the meal, wine or beer is usually available.

As eating and drinking are important social activities, behaviour at the table should be respectful. Locals can be strict about table manners, and it's considered rude to pick at your food or mix it together. You are also expected to be reasonably well dressed. Unless you are in a beach environment, wearing beachwear or other skimpy clothing won't be well received – casual but neat clothing is the norm. Some upmarket hotels require neat dress for guests – for men that usually includes trousers or long pants, and perhaps even a collared shirt. When invited to dine with locals, bring a small gift (maybe some flowers or a bottle of wine).

If you're attending a traditional Indian or Chinese meal or a dinner associated with a religious celebration, follow what the locals do. Generally, your hosts will make you feel comfortable, but if you are unsure, ask about the serving customs and the order of dishes. Definitely attend an Indian or a Chinese wedding if you get the opportunity – these celebrations are true culinary feasts.

Environment

Mauritius packs a lot into quite a small space, and the beauty of its landforms – the coral reefs, the dramatic rocky outcrops – play a key role in so many of the country's attractions, either as a stirring backdrop or as destinations worth exploring. But wildlife is where Mauritius' environmental story gets really interesting, from giant tortoises to critically endangered bird species making a comeback.

The Land

Mauritius is the peak of an enormous volcanic chain that also includes Réunion, though it is much older and therefore less rugged than its neighbour.

The island's highest mountains are found in the southwest, from where the land drops slightly to a central plateau before climbing again to the chain of oddly shaped mountains behind Port Louis and the Montagne Bambous to the east. Beyond these mountains a plain slopes gently down to the north coast.

Unlike Réunion, Mauritius has no active volcanoes, although remnants of volcanic activity abound. Extinct craters and volcanic lakes, such as the Trou aux Cerfs crater in Curepipe and the Grand Bassin holy lake, are good examples. Over the aeons, the volcanoes generated millions of lava boulders, much to the chagrin of indentured farm labourers who had to clear the land for sugar cane. Nonetheless, heaps of boulders still dot the landscape and some that have been piled into tidy pyramids are listed monuments!

Mauritius also includes a number of widely scattered inhabited islands, of which the most important is Rodrigues, 600km to the northeast. Rodrigues is another ancient volcanic peak and is surrounded by a lagoon twice the size of the island itself.

Mauritius stakes territorial claim to the Chagos Archipelago (p132), officially part of the British Indian Ocean Territory and controversially ceded to the US military until 2016, with an extension likely for a further 20 years.

Wildlife

The story of Mauritian wildlife certainly didn't end with the dodo. In fact, the island's reputation for extinction has been transformed in recent years by its dramatic success in saving endangered species.

The best source of information is the Mauritian Wildlife Foundation (MWF; www.mauritian-wildlife.org), which was founded in 1984 to protect and manage the country's many rare species. The MWF vigorously supports the creation of national parks and reserves. It has had significant success in restoring the populations of several endangered bird species and in conserving endemic vegetation. While you're welcome to visit its office to get information it can be difficult to find. In any event, its website is a useful resource and contacting it via email with specific questions usually elicits a response. And, of course, a visit to MWF-run Île aux Aigrettes is a highlight of any visit to the island.

Mammals

Mauritius has only one native mammal: the wonderful fruit bat. They're a common sight at twilight as they come to life and begin their night's foraging.

All other mammals on the island were introduced by colonists, with varying degrees of success. Mongooses are typical of the slapdash ecological management of the past – they were introduced from India in the late 19th century to control plague-carrying rats. The intention was to import only males, but some females slipped through and they bred like, well, mongooses. Soon there were mongooses everywhere. They remain fairly common, as are the bands of macaque monkeys that hang out around Grand Bassin and the Black River Gorges. Java deer, imported by the Dutch for fresh meat, and wild pigs, also introduced, roam the more remote forests.

There are two further bat species – the grimly named Mauritius tomb bat and the Mauritian cave bat – but these are not endemic to Mauritius.

Marine Mammals

Marine mammals are most commonly seen along the west coast of Mauritius. Spinner dolphins are the most common species in the bay off Tamarin, while bottlenose dolphins are also present. Dolphin-watching boat excursions set out from many places along the west coast, but we have serious concerns (p88) about their impact on the local populations.

Numerous shark species inhabit Mauritian waters, although you're only likely to encounter them if you're diving on the outer reaches of the reef; few stray into the shallow waters of the lagoon. Common species include grey reef and bull sharks (east coast), blacktip and leopard sharks (north), and white-tip reef sharks (west).

From July or August through to October or November, humpback whales migrate along the west coast of Mauritius en route between the Antarctic and the warmer waters near the equator where they reproduce and calve. Sperm whales are believed to be resident off west-coast Mauritius and hence are present year-round, although they're generally considered more elusive than humpbacks.

Whale-watching is surprisingly low-key in Mauritius when compared to neighbouring Madagascar. This is for two main reasons: first, the main (but by no means the only) season is considered low season, with far fewer visitors in the country; second, unlike dolphin-watching, watching whales takes place out in the open ocean, beyond the lagoon, and therefore requires full-day excursions.

Reptiles & Tortoises

Mauritius, along with Réunion and the Seychelles, once had the largest number of giant tortoises on the planet, a veritable Galapagos of distinct species, of which Mauritius and Rodrigues had two each. Rodrigues in particular once had the highest density of tortoises on earth. Such abundance didn't last long, and all tortoise species on Mauritius and Rodrigues were driven to extinction during the colonial period, when sailors and settlers favoured them as an easy-to-catch and long-lasting source of meat; tortoises could be kept alive on very little food, ideal for long-distance ocean journeys.

The only surviving species in the region, the Aldabra giant tortoise from the Seychelles, was introduced onto Île aux Aigrettes in 2000 and elsewhere in the years that followed. The number of wild tortoises has since grown dramatically. The best places to see them are Île aux Aigrettes; La Vanille, near Souillac; and Rodrigues' François Leguat Reserve.

Native reptiles include the beautiful turquoise-and-red ornate day gecko and Telfair's skink (a clawed lizard), both of which can be seen on Île aux Aigrettes. You can rest easy if you see a slithering critter – there are no dangerous reptiles in Mauritius.

Birds

The dodo may be Mauritius' most famous former inhabitant (other species that were driven to extinction during the early colonial period include the red rail and the solitaire), but Mauritius should be just as famous for the birds it has saved. In fact, an academic review in 2007 found that Mauritius had pulled more bird species (five) back from the brink of extinction than any other country on earth.

The birds you're most likely to see, however, are the introduced songbirds, such as the little red Madagascar fody, the Indian mynah and the red-whiskered bulbul. Between October and May the Rivulet Terre Rouge Bird Sanctuary estuary north of Port Louis provides an important wintering ground for migratory water birds such as the whimbrel, the grey plover, and the common and curlew sandpipers.

MAURITIUS KESTREL

In 1974, the rather lovely Mauritian kestrel (which once inhabited all corners of the island) was officially the most endangered bird species on the planet, with just four known to survive in the wild, including, crucially, one breeding female. There were a further two of the raptors in captivity. The reasons for its dire situation were all too familiar: pesticide poisoning, habitat destruction and hunting. A captive-breeding program and an intensive project of building predator-proof nesting boxes in the wild has led to an amazing

DEAD AS A DODO

Illustrations from the logbooks of the first ships to reach Mauritius show hundreds of plump flightless birds running down to the beach to investigate the newcomers. Lacking natural predators, these giant relatives of the pigeon were easy prey for hungry sailors, who named the bird *dodo*, meaning 'stupid'. It took just 30 years for passing sailors and their pets and pests (dogs, monkeys, pigs and rats) to drive the dodo to extinction; the last confirmed sighting was in the 1660s.

Just as surprising as the speed of the dodo's demise is how little evidence remains that the bird ever existed. A few relics made it back to Europe during the 18th century – a dried beak ended up at the University of Copenhagen in Denmark, while the University of Oxford in England managed to get hold of a whole head and a foot – but until recently our knowledge of the dodo was mainly based on sketches by 17th-century seamen.

However, in 1865 local schoolteacher George Clark discovered a dodo skeleton in a marshy area on the site of what is now the international airport. The skeleton was reassembled by scientists in Edinburgh, and has formed the basis of all subsequent dodo reconstructions, one of which is on display in the Natural History Museum in Port Louis. There is also an accurate reconstruction of a dodo in bronze in the ebony forest on Île aux Aigrettes.

National Park. In that year all five nesting attempts were unsuccessful due to rats. The species appeared doomed. Again, an intensive program of captive breeding and reintroduction into the wild has seen numbers soar, with around 470 thought to be present throughout Black River Gorges National Park and on Île aux Aigrettes (where there were 43 at last count). The Mauritian Wildlife Foundation is seeking to ensure that captive pink pigeons in European zoos will one day form part of the program as a means of enhancing the species' genetic diversity.

ECHO PARAKEET

The vivid colours of the echo parakeet, too, were almost lost to Mauritius. In 1986, between eight and 12 survived. And to make matters worse, it was the last of six endemic parrot species that once inhabited the island. Once again, captive breeding, reintroduction and intensive conservation management have seen the species recover to around 540, all within Black River Gorges National Park. Note that the echo parakeet closely resembles the introduced ringed parakeet, which is far more common and widespread throughout the island.

Once again, captive breeding, reintroduction and intensive conservation management have seen the species recover to around 540, all within Black River Gorges National Park. Your best chance to see them is along Parakeet Trail and Macchabée Trail, and around Mare Longue Reservoir. Note that the echo parakeet closely resembles the introduced ringed parakeet, which is far more common and widespread throughout the island.

OTHER SPECIES

The olive white eye, a small Mauritian songbird, now numbers no more than 150 pairs in the wild, with 35 birds on Île aux Aigrettes. The Mauritian fody has also found a refuge on Île aux Aigrettes, which will serve as a base for future reintroduction programs.

Over on Rodrigues, the recovery of the Rodrigues warbler (from 30 in the 1970s to over 4000 today) and that of the Rodrigues fody (six pairs in 1968; 8000 individuals today) are almost unparalleled in the annals of wildlife conservation.

Offshore islands such as Île Plate and Îlot Gabriel, and off Coin de Mire, Île Ronde and Île aux Serpents, are good places to see seabirds. Note that boats may not land at the latter three islands.

recovery, with numbers now around 400, split between a population in the southeast (250) and one in the southwest (150).

Your best chance to see them is during their breeding season (August to February in the southeast; September to February in the southwest). The likeliest spots are Vallée de Ferney, Lion Mountain and Kestrel Valley; Black River Gorges National Park is also a possibility, though a more remote one.

PINK PIGEON

The pretty pink pigeon has also been pulled back from the brink. In 1986, this once-widespread bird was down to just 12 individuals in the wild, living close to Bassin Blanc in the southern reaches of Black River Gorges

Plants

Almost one-third of the 900 plant species found in Mauritius are unique to these islands. Many of these endemic plants have fared poorly in competition with introduced plants such as guava and privet, and have been depleted by introduced deer, pigs and monkeys. General forest clearance and the establishment of crop monocultures have exacerbated the problem, so that less than 1% of Mauritius' original forest is intact.

For a tropical island, Mauritius isn't big on coconut palms. Instead, casuarinas (also known as *filaos*) fringe most of the beaches. These tall, wispy trees act as useful windbreaks and grow well in sandy soil. The government planted them along the shores to help stop erosion; eucalyptus trees have been widely planted for the same reason.

Other impressive and highly visible trees are the giant Indian banyan and the brilliant red flowering flamboyant (royal poinciana).

Staying with shades of red, one flower you will see in abundance is anthurium, with its single, glossy petal and protruding yellow spadix. The plant originated in South America and was introduced to Mauritius in the late 19th century. The flower, which at first sight you'd swear was plastic, can last up to three weeks after being cut and is therefore a popular display plant. Now grown in commercial quantities for export, it is used to spruce up hotels and public meeting places.

The easiest place to find these and other rare plant species is in the botanical gardens at Pamplemousses.

Mangroves are enjoying a renaissance in Mauritius today. Originally cut down to reduce swamp areas where malarial mosquitoes could breed, they've been discovered to be an important part of the food chain for tropical fish, and thus large projects to develop mangrove areas have been undertaken, particularly on the east coast.

National Parks

Since 1988, several international organisations have been working with the government to set up conservation areas in Mauritius. About 3.5% of the land area is now protected either as national parks, managed mainly for ecosystem preservation and for recreation, or as nature reserves.

The largest park is the Black River Gorges National Park, established in 1994 in the southwest of the island. It covers some 68 sq km and preserves a wide variety of environments, from pine forest to tropical scrub, and includes the country's largest area of native forest.

Two of the most important nature reserves are Île aux Aigrettes and Île Ronde (the latter is closed to the public), both of which are being restored to their natural state by replacing introduced plants and animals with native species.

In 1997, marine parks were proclaimed at Blue Bay (near Mahébourg on the southeast coast) and Balaclava (on the west coast), but the number of visitors to the area makes it difficult to establish rigorous controls and there is a need to encourage local fishers to use less destructive techniques.

IMPORTANT NATIONAL PARKS & RESERVES

PARK	FEATURES	ACTIVITIES	BEST TIME TO VISIT
Balaclava Marine Park	lagoon, coral reef, turtle breeding grounds	snorkelling, diving, glass-bottomed boat tours	all year
Black River Gorges National Park	forested mountains, Mauritian kestrel, echo parakeet, pink pigeon, black ebony trees	hiking, birdwatching	Sep-Jan for flowers
Blue Bay Marine Park	lagoon, corals, fish life	snorkelling, diving, glass-bottomed boat tours	all year
Île aux Aigrettes Nature Reserve	coral island, ebony forests, pink pigeon, olive white eye, Aldabra giant tortoise, Telfairs skink	ecotours, birdwatching	all year

There is also the new and tiny national park of Bras d'Eau, close to Poste Lafayette on Mauritius' east coast.

Environmental Issues

The natural environment of Mauritius has paid a heavy price for the country's rapid development. And despite recent economic setbacks, the government seems keener than ever to encourage more tourists to continue plugging the gap left by a declining sugar industry and a waning textile industry. However, the expansion of tourist facilities is straining the island's infrastructure and causing problems such as environmental degradation and excessive demand on services such as electricity, water and transport.

One area of particular concern is construction along the coast – almost every beach has been developed, and most of the development is tourist related. However, Mauritians are very keen to put environmental concerns first: a proposal for a hotel on Île des Deux Cocos in Blue Bay, for example, met with such fierce resistance that it was abandoned. Conservationists also fervently (and successfully) combated plans to construct a highway through the old forests in the southeast.

The government now requires an environmental-impact assessment for all new building projects, including coastal hotels, marinas and golf courses, and even for activities such as undersea walks. Planning regulations for hotel developments on Rodrigues are particularly strict: they must be small, single storey, built in traditional style and stand at least 30m back from the high-tide mark. Since water shortages are a problem on Rodrigues, new hotels must also recycle their water.

To combat littering and other forms of environmental degradation, the government has established a special environmental police force charged with enforcing legislation and educating the local population. To report wrongdoers, there is even a hotline (☑210 5151).

If anything, the marine environment is suffering even more from overexploitation. The coast off Grand Baie is particularly affected by too many divers and boats concentrated in a few specific locations. In addition, silting and chemical pollution are resulting in extensive coral damage and falling fish populations. Unregulated dolphin-watching (p88) off the west coast is also causing concern for its impact upon the population.

SURVIVAL GUIDE

ⓘ Directory A–Z

ACCOMMODATION

By sheer volume alone, Mauritius offers the greatest range of sleeping options among the islands in the area. There are three main types of accommodation: fully equipped vacation rentals, locally run guesthouses, and larger hotels and resorts.

Seasons

In general, high season runs from around October to March, with a focus on the European winter months. Prices soar at the end of December and the beginning of January. Travellers can expect prices to dip during the low-season months (May to September), often called 'green season'.

Apartments & Villas

Renting a holiday apartment or villa is by far the most economical option in Mauritius, especially if there are several people in your travelling party. There are hundreds of rental options, ranging from small studios in factory-sized complexes to lavish seaside mansions fit for a movie star. If you're travelling with family or friends, a large high-end property can cost as little as €25 per person, which more than rivals the island's hostel-esque relics from an earlier era of travel. But remember, even though rentals represent a better price-to-value ratio on the whole, you always get what you pay for and meals are never included.

Most of the accommodation in this category is privately owned and managed by an umbrella agency that markets a large pool of crash pads. While choices can vary greatly, you should expect, in all but the cheapest places, that your home-away-from-home comes with daily maid service, a fully equipped kitchen, air-con, and concierge service provided by the property manager (make sure to double-check).

Some of the larger agencies:

➡ Idyllic Villas (p128)

➡ CG Villas (p129)

➡ Jet-7 (p89)

➡ EasyRent (p128)

Guesthouses & Chambres d'Hôtes

If you're looking for an island experience that doesn't involve the term 'all-inclusive', Mauritius' guesthouses and *chambres d'hôtes* (B&Bs) are well worth considering. This category of accommodation is managed by locals – often families – who as a rule dote on their guests with genuine hospitality. It's a fantastic way to learn about the *real* Mauritius. In fact, you'll sometimes have the chance to dine with your accommodation's proprietors at their *tables d'hôtes*, which can be equally rewarding experiences.

SLEEPING PRICE RANGES

The following price ranges refer to a double room with bathroom. Unless otherwise stated, breakfast is not included in the price.

€ less than €75 (around Rs 3000)

€€ €75-150 (Rs 3000-6000)

€€€ more than €150 (Rs 6000)

Over the last few years the government has begun increasing regulations for all tourism-related properties. Panic buttons and 24-hour security have, for example, become a compulsory expense for owners, forcing guesthouses to jack up their prices beyond the budget range to pay the bills. As a result, the island's *chambres d'hôtes* are starting to be under threat, especially since all-inclusive resorts have been known to offer bargain-basement prices to stay competitive during the economic downturn. Nonetheless, there's still a scatter of charming spots sprinkled around the island that are, now more than ever, promoting a 'local experience'. You'll find a cluster in Pointe d'Esny, and *chambres d'hôtes* are particularly popular in Rodrigues.

Hotels & Resorts

Rounding out the sleeping circuit is Mauritius' best-known brand of accommodation: the dreamy resorts found on the pages of magazines and in TV commercials for credit cards. And, despite the global economic recession, dozens of these opulent properties continue to spring up each year.

There are, however, two distinct categories of hotel in Mauritius: the luxury resorts that stretch along the coast, and the old-school midrangers that need some serious TLC. It's best to avoid the latter, as many of the top-end properties offer vacation incentives that rival the has-beens, and the guesthouses (which are often cheaper) are generally in better shape.

Upscale properties come in various tiers of luxury – there are three-, four- and five-star resorts. You'll do perfectly well with a three-star charmer, and while the five-star price tags may be high, it is well worth checking with travel agents about hotel-and-flight vacation packages. In fact, no upmarket sleeps should be booked with the public rates – agency rates are always cheaper. If you have your sights set on a luxury vacation, expect to pay €150 per person per night (including half board) at the very minimum. Prices quickly climb all the way up to €1000 per person per night.

ACTIVITIES

You may think that Mauritius is all about the beach, but out on the water there's everything from diving, snorkelling and kitesurfing to kayaking, deep-sea fishing to stand-up paddling. Away from the water's edge there's terrific hiking, excellent horse riding and world-class golfing to be enjoyed.

Catamarans & Yacht Cruises

A catamaran day trip is one of the most popular activities in Mauritius and the excursions on offer get better with each passing year. Hundreds of tourists each day board boats to cruise around the azure lagoon and wavy seas or stop at offshore islets and shallow reefs. Many such excursions include barbecue lunches and/or time for snorkelling.

The most romantic option is the sunset cruise offered by most operators. If you're looking for something a bit more traditional, you'll find myriad fishers in Mahébourg and the surrounding beaches who have transformed their vessels into mini leisure crafts. Most operators include small buffet lunches, alcohol and snorkelling. Make sure to shop around before choosing your cruise – some catamarans are not licensed to land on any islands. Most cruises can be booked through tour agents and hotels. Check out www.catamarancruisesmauritius.com for more information.

Some of the more popular excursions:

➡ Île aux Cerfs (p126) A stunning island off Trou d'Eau Douce on the east coast. Departures are also possible from Mahébourg and elsewhere. Île aux Cerfs is a good option for those who suffer from motion sickness as the boat never leaves the calm lagoon waters.

➡ Îlot Gabriel and Île Plate (p74) Grand Baie is another major hub of cruise activity, with dozens of vessels heading for the wee islands in the north. These are probably our pick of the cruising options as the reefs are pristine and the beaches quiet, and competition keeps prices less inflated.

➡ Île aux Bénitiers (p104) On the western side of the island, this popular cruising option is a half- or full-day trip with the possibility of dolphin-watching.

BOOK YOUR STAY ONLINE

For more accommodation reviews by Lonely Planet authors, check out hotels.lonelyplanet.com. You'll find independent reviews, as well as recommendations on the best places to stay. Best of all, you can book online.

Golf

No island paradise would be complete without a handful of world-class golf courses, and Mauritius has some fine examples of the genre, many of which are situated on five-star resorts.

Our favourite fairways:

➡ Four Seasons Resort at Anahita (p125), near Trou d'Eau Douce – course designed by Ernie Els.

➡ Île aux Cerfs Golf Club (p126), Trou d'Eau Douce – on idyllic Île aux Cerfs; course designed by Bernhard Langer.

➡ Le Saint Géran (p128), Pointe de Flacq – on the east coast.

➡ Tamarina (p92), Tamarin Bay – magnificent complex on the west coast.

➡ Domaine de Bel Ombre (p119), Bel Ombre – perfectly maintained course along the south coast.

➡ Mauritius Gymkhana Club (p61), Vacoas – the fourth-oldest course on earth, and the oldest in the Indian Ocean.

Hiking

For those interested in more than the usual beach activities, Mauritius offers some attractive hikes, with the best selection in the west and the Central Plateau.

Where to Hike

Although we haven't made the trek, locals assured us that it's possible to hike along the entire southern coast, beginning with the stretch from Blue Bay to Souillac.

Most trails are in the areas where the Central Plateau meets the coastal plains. Many of the *domaines* (estates) in the southeastern part of the island offer beautiful trails through the island's oldest forests.

Otherwise, our favourite hikes in Mauritius are the following:

➡ Macchabée Trail (p100), Black River Gorges National Park

➡ Parakeet Trail (p100), Black River Gorges National Park

➡ Le Morne (p103), Le Morne Peninsula

➡ Le Pouce and Corps de Garde (p60), Central Plateau

➡ Lion Mountain (p116), southeastern Mauritius

Resources

A fabulous resource for independent hikers, **Fitsy** (www.fitsy.com) is an outstanding website with detailed GPS and satellite imagery that maps out the course of each trail. We recommend, however, hiring a guide for any of the island's major hikes. Apart from making sure you stay on the right trail, a knowledgeable guide provides invaluable insight into the region's flora and fauna.

Hiking Operators

There are four main outdoor outfits on the island. Otherwise, ask at your hotel for local hiking guides.

➡ Yemaya (p96) Hikes through Black River Gorges National Park.

➡ Yanature (p103) The only company that has permission to ascend Le Morne.

➡ Vertical World (p100) Black River Gorges and elsewhere in the west.

➡ Otélair (p100) Black River Gorges National Park.

Horse Riding

Mauritius has some lovely rambling countryside that's perfect for riding excursions. There are heaps of equestrian outfits throughout the island – you'll find a couple of ranches in the west, an interesting farm in the south, and several outfits in the north. Our pick of the possibilities:

➡ La Vieille Cheminée (p96), Chamarel

➡ Les Écuries du Domaine (p59), Pailles

➡ Horse Riding Delights (p66), Mont Choisy

➡ Domaine de l'Étoile (p117), southeastern Mauritius

➡ Haras du Morne (p104), Le Morne Peninsula

Kitesurfing & Windsurfing

The kitesurfing and windsurfing movements have grown in leaps and bounds over the last decade – you'll find hundreds of wave hunters gathered along the southwest coast, off Le Morne, while Rodrigues is another spot increasingly beloved by kitesurfers in the know; the island hosts the Rodrigues International Kitesurfing Festival in late June or early July.

Our pick of the kitesurfing and windsurfing locations:

➡ Le Morne (p104) South of the headland for experts, west at Kite Lagoon for beginners; good kitesurfing schools.

➡ Rodrigues (p175) Two good kitesurfing schools and its very own festival.

➡ Cap Malheureux (p80) In the north; has a highly regarded kitesurfing school.

Surfing

A small scene led by Australian and South African surfers built up in the 1970s around Tamarin on the west coast (the surf movie *The Forgotten Island of Santosha* was made here), but the wave crashed during the 1980s.

These days, the scene around Tamarin comprises a small community of local and Réunionnais surfers. You can plug into what's happening and rent boards from one of the old-school establishments in Tamarin, such as the Tamarin Hotel (p93).

Le Morne (p104) is the pick of the surf spots these days, with the season beginning in July. One Eye, so named because, so the legend goes, surfers will see a small hole (or 'eye') appear in Le Morne's rockface when they are at the exact spot in the sea to catch the perfect wave, is considered to be the ultimate surfing spot in all of Mauritius.

CHILDREN

Travelling with children in Mauritius presents no particular problems. To put their holiday in context, there's a wonderful series of English-language cartoon books by Henry Koombes (published locally by Editions Vizavi Ltd), including *In Dodoland*, *SOS Shark* and *Meli-Melo in the Molasses*.

For more information, see Lonely Planet's *Travel with Children*.

Practicalities

Most of the high-end hotels have dedicated facilities (like 'kids clubs') for children, and those that don't sometimes have a small playground. Most top-end hotels also include babysitting services. The proliferation of villa leases has made it easy to bring the entire family on vacation, while many hotels and even some *chambres d'hôtes* offer family rooms. Most hotels have cots, although usually only a limited number, so always request one when making your reservation and send a reminder some weeks in advance of your arrival.

Remember that some top-end resorts market themselves as 'adults only'. This is less an indication of risqué behaviour than an attempt by hotels and resorts to appeal to the honeymoon or romantic-getaway market. In other words, kids are not welcome. If you're making a reservation online and there's no option of adding kids to your booking, chances are that's why.

Disposable nappies are widely available in supermarkets, and most car-hire companies have a limited number and range of child safety seats available (the smaller the company, the fewer options you'll have). Baby-changing facilities in restaurants and other public areas are almost nonexistent. Breastfeeding in public is not really the done thing (although it's usually fine within

> ### TOP ATTRACTIONS FOR CHILDREN
>
> Besides the seaside, Mauritius has numerous attractions that make for excellent day excursions for families. Remember, however, that some activities may be subject to minimum-age requirements – phone ahead or check the relevant website before getting the kids all excited. Our favourite attractions for children:
>
> ➡ La Vanille (p120), Rivière des Anguilles
>
> ➡ Île aux Aigrettes (p112), Pointe d'Esny
>
> ➡ Snorkelling, anywhere...
>
> ➡ Casela World of Adventures (p85), Flic en Flac
>
> ➡ Mauritius Aquarium (p63), Pointe aux Piments

hotel or resort grounds), but you're unlikely to feel uncomfortable as long as you're discreet.

CUSTOMS REGULATIONS

In Mauritius, visitors aged 16 years and over may import 200 cigarettes or 250g of tobacco; 1L of spirits; 2L of wine, ale or beer; 250mL of *eau de toilette;* and up to 100mL of perfume.

There are restrictions on importing food, plants and animals, for which permits are required. Other prohibited and restricted articles include spear guns and items made from ivory, shell, turtleshell or other materials banned under the Convention on International Trade in Endangered Species (CITES); it is also illegal to take such items out when you leave.

EMBASSIES & CONSULATES

Many countries do not have representatives in Mauritius and usually refer their citizens to embassies in Pretoria (South Africa). However, Australia, Canada, France, the UK and the US all have embassies in Port Louis. Italy, the Seychelles and Sweden have honorary consulates in Port Louis.

Australian High Commission (☎ 202 0160; www.mauritius.embassy.gov.au; 2nd fl, Rogers House, 5 President John Kennedy St, Port Louis; ☉ 8.30am-3.30pm Mon-Fri)

Canadian Consulate (☎ 212 5500; canada@intnet.mu; 18 Jules Koenig St, Port Louis; ☉ 9am-noon Mon-Fri)

French Embassy (☎ 202 0100; www.ambafrance-mu.org; 14 St Georges St, Port Louis; ☉ 8am-noon Mon-Fri)

Italian Honorary Consulate (☑ 207 7844; 2nd fl, Air Mauritius Bldg, President John Kennedy St, Port Louis; ☺ 8.30am-noon Mon-Fri)

Seychelles Honorary Consulate (☑ 211 1688; gfok@intnet.mu; 616 St James Ct, St Denis St, Port Louis)

Swedish Consulate (☑ 206 3203; Aqualia Bldg, Old Quay D Rd, Port Louis; ☺ 8.30am-4.30pm Mon-Fri)

UK High Commission (☑ 202 9400; bhc@intnet.mu; 7th fl, Les Cascades Bldg, Edith Cavell St, Port Louis; ☺ 7.45am-3.45pm Mon-Thu, to 1.30pm Fri)

US Embassy (☑ 202 4400; mauritius.usembassy.gov; 4th fl, Rogers House, President John Kennedy St, Port Louis; ☺ 7.30am-4.45pm Mon-Thu, to 12.30pm Fri)

INSURANCE

A travel-insurance policy to cover theft, loss and medical problems is a good idea. Some policies specifically exclude dangerous activities, which can include scuba diving, motorcycling and even hiking. Always check the small print and make sure that the policy covers ambulances or an emergency flight home. If you plan on diving, we strongly recommend purchasing dive-specific insurance with DAN (www.diversalert network.org).

Worldwide travel insurance is available at www.lonelyplanet.com/travel-insurance. You can buy, extend and claim online anytime – even if you're already on the road.

INTERNET ACCESS

Most towns have at least one internet cafe and access can be found at most resorts, hotels and guesthouses. Wi-fi connections are increasingly the norm in hotels – most often wi-fi access is restricted to public areas, although it may extend to some rooms.

LEGAL MATTERS

Foreigners are subject to the laws of the country in which they are travelling and will receive no special consideration because they are tourists. If you find yourself in a sticky legal predicament, contact your embassy.

In general, travellers have nothing to fear from the police, who rarely harass foreigners and are very polite if you do need to stop them. Talking on your mobile phone while driving will definitely get you pulled over, but if you're in any sort of minor trouble you'll most likely be let off the hook if it's obvious that you're a tourist (speaking in English helps even more).

LGBT TRAVELLERS

Mauritius has a paradoxical relationship to homosexuality. On one hand, much of the population is young and progressive, gays and lesbians are legally protected from discrimination and individuals have a constitutionally guaranteed right to privacy, and Mauritius has signed the UN Declaration on Sexual Orientation and Gender Identity. At the same time, 'sodomy' is illegal and there remains a rigidly conservative streak to the Mauritian character.

As a result of the latter, gay life remains fairly secretive, mainly existing on the internet, in private and at the occasional party. While there were no gay or lesbian bars or clubs on the island at the time of writing, there are monthly underground club nights organised by text message. La Mariposa (p93), close to Tamarin, is the only place we found that openly advertises itself as gay-friendly.

PRACTICALITIES

→ **Electricity** The supply is 220V, 50Hz; both British-style three-pin sockets and the Continental two-pin variety are commonly used, sometimes in the same room – bring both.

→ **Newspapers** French-language *L'Express* (www.lexpress.mu) and *Le Mauricien* (www.lemauricien.com); English-language weeklies *News on Sunday* and the *Mauritius Times* (www.mauritiustimes.com).

→ **Radio** There's a huge number of local commercial stations broadcasting in Creole and Hindi, and the BBC World Service and Voice of America are readily available. The most popular stations include Kool FM 89.3 Mhz and Taal FM 94.0 Mhz.

→ **Smoking** Prohibited in indoor public places and on public transport; allowed in outdoor restaurants, on beaches, in some hotel rooms and at some workplaces. The trend is towards prohibition, so expect restrictions to increase over time.

→ **Television** Three free TV channels – MBC1, MBC2 and MBC3 – are run by the state Mauritius Broadcasting Corporation (MBC), and there are numerous pay channels. Programming is mainly in Creole, but there are foreign imports in French, English and Indian languages.

→ **Weights & Measures** Mauritius uses the metric system.

For gay and lesbian travellers there's little to worry about. We've never heard of any problems arising from same-sex couples sharing rooms during their holidays. You're still best to avoid public displays of affection outside your hotel and generally to be aware that what might be entirely standard at home may not be viewed in the same light here.

MAPS

Although Mauritius markets itself heavily as a major tourism destination, the island has a frustrating lack of decent maps.

The best map of the island is the satellite imagery on Google Earth. If you don't have printing facilities on hand, try the map produced by the **Institut Géographique Nationale** (IGN; www.ign.fr). The Globetrotter travel map is also a good choice. Both should be available from local bookstores and supermarkets.

Otherwise, see if you can pick up the reasonable *Tourist Map of Mauritius & Rodrigues* by ELP Publications – we found it at Le Village Boutik (p83) in Pamplemousses (Rs 230).

MONEY

The Mauritian unit of currency is the rupee (Rs), which is divided into 100 cents (¢). There are coins of 5¢, 20¢ and 50¢, and Rs 1, Rs 5 and Rs 10. The banknote denominations are Rs 25, Rs 50, Rs 100, Rs 200, Rs 500, Rs 1000 and Rs 2000. While the Mauritian rupee is the island's currency, almost all villas, guesthouses and hotels (and several high-end restaurants usually affiliated with hotels) tether their prices to the euro to counterbalance the rupee's unstable fluctuations and it is possible (and sometimes required) to pay in euros at such places.

ATMs

It's perfectly possible to travel on plastic in Mauritius since ATMs are widespread. Even Rodrigues has a smattering of them. They're mostly located outside banks, though you'll also find them at the airports, at larger supermarkets and in some shopping malls. The majority of machines accept Visa and MasterCard, or any similar cards in the Cirrus and Plus networks, while Amex has a tie-in with Mauritius Commercial Bank (MCB).

Remember, however, that bank fees, sometimes significant ones, can apply – check with your home bank before setting out for Mauritius.

Credit Cards

Visa and MasterCard are the most commonly accepted cards, though Amex is catching up quickly. Nearly all tourist shops, restaurants and accommodation accept payment by credit card, as do car-hire companies, tour agents and so forth. Any establishment well outside the tourist bubble will still expect payment in cash.

A few places add on an extra fee, typically 3%, to the bill to cover 'bank charges'. The cheaper car-hire companies are the worst offenders. To be on the safe side, always ask. Cash advances on credit cards are available from most major banks, including MCB, Barclays, the State Bank and HSBC. Just remember to take your passport.

Exchange Rates

For current exchange rates, see www.xe.com.

Australia	A$1	Rs 26.6
Canada	C$1	Rs 26.9
Euro Zone	€1	Rs 38.9
Japan	¥100	Rs 33.7
NZ	NZ$1	Rs 24.9
UK	UK£1	Rs 46.5
USA	US$1	Rs 35.4

Money Changers

Major currencies and travellers cheques can be changed at the main banks, exchange bureaux and the larger hotels. Bureaux de change sometimes offer slightly better rates than banks and the queues are shorter, but there's usually little difference, and many seem to close without warning when reserves run dry. Hotels tend to have the worst rates and may add an additional service commission. There is no black market in Mauritius.

As a general rule, travellers cheques bring a better rate than cash. Banks don't charge commission on changing cash. As for travellers cheques, the system varies. Some banks, such as HSBC, charge 1% of the total, with a minimum of Rs 200, while MCB and the State Bank levy Rs 50 for up to 10 cheques. Don't forget to take along your passport when changing money. And make sure you hang on to the encashment form, which may have to be presented if you want to change Mauritian rupees back into foreign currency at the end of your stay (although not all airport bureaux de change ask for it).

Tipping

Tipping is not generally practised in Mauritius and is never an obligation. Top-end hotels and restaurants sometimes add a service charge of about 10% to 15% to the bill.

In most resort hotels, tips are always welcome, but most prefer that you contribute to an overall tips box, usually at reception, rather than tipping individual staff.

OPENING HOURS

Hours below are the general rule. Shops in larger seaside resort towns are usually open longer, while on Rodrigues shops and offices generally close earlier than stated below.

Banks 9am to 3.15pm Monday to Friday (extended hours in tourist hubs like Grand Baie and Flic en Flac)

Government offices 9am to 4pm Monday to Friday, 9am to noon Saturday (closed during religious and public holidays)

Post offices 8.15am to 4pm Monday to Friday, 8.15am to 11.45am Saturday (the last 45 minutes are for stamp sales only; many offices close for lunch from 11.15am to noon on weekdays)

Restaurants noon to 3pm and 7 to 10pm; many restaurants close on Sunday

Shops 9am to 5pm Monday to Friday, 8am to noon Saturday; many close around 1pm Thursday

POST

The postal service in Mauritius is generally quick and reliable. In general, mailing services end about 45 minutes before closing and the bureau becomes a retail shop for stamps and envelopes but nothing else.

PUBLIC HOLIDAYS

New Year 1 and 2 January

Thaipoosam Cavadee January/February

Chinese Spring Festival January/February

Abolition of Slavery 1 February

Maha Shivaratri February/March

Ougadi March/April

National Day 12 March

Labour Day 1 May

Assumption of the Blessed Virgin Mary 15 August

Ganesh Chaturti August/September

Divali (Dipavali) October/November

Arrival of Indentured Labourers 2 November

Eid al-Fitr November/December

Christmas Day 25 December

SAFE TRAVEL

Take care when undertaking any kind of adventure sports and make sure your insurance policy covers you in the case of accident. Otherwise, your biggest annoyances here are likely to be environmental (mosquitoes, sunburn and the occasional upset stomach).

The Indian Ocean is a warm tropical ocean, so there are several aquatic nasties to watch out for. Fortunately, few travellers encounter anything more serious than the odd (and often quite painful) coral cut.

Coconuts

Lying under a coconut palm may seem like a tropical idyll, but, as silly as it may sound, there have been some tragic accidents. Take care when walking under coconut trees and don't lie (or park your car) beneath them.

Cyclones

Mauritius lies within the cyclone belt. Most cyclones occur between December (or more commonly, January) and March, although they are not unheard-of as late as April. While direct hits are relatively uncommon, storms kilometres away can bring very strong winds. Most hotels and other accommodation have systems in place (such as lock-downs and flexible eating plans) to deal with such threats.

As soon as a cyclone is detected, a system of alerts is used to inform the public of the level of danger. In Mauritius there are four levels of alert. The alerts and then regular bulletins are broadcast on radio and TV. For current warnings, consult metservice.intnet.mu.

Theft

The risk of theft in Mauritius is small, but nonetheless it's worth being prepared.

Petty theft and break-ins are fairly common outside the resorts. Favourite haunts for thieves are the beaches; Île aux Cerfs is a particular hot spot. The best strategy is not to take any valuables to the beach – and never tempt a passing thief by leaving your belongings unattended.

Be extra careful in crowded places such as markets and avoid walking around with your valuables casually slung over your shoulder. When travelling on public transport, keep your gear near you.

If you hire a car, it's best not to leave anything valuable in it at all. If you must do so, hide everything well out of sight. Wherever possible, park in a secure car park or at least somewhere busy – never park in an isolated spot, especially at night.

Don't leave vital documents, money or valuables lying about in your room. Many hotels provide room safes, which are well worth using. Otherwise, leave your valuables in the safe at reception and ask for a receipt. While most hotels are reliable, to be extra sure, pack everything in a small, double-zippered bag that can be padlocked, or use a large envelope with a signed seal that will reveal any tampering. Count money and travellers cheques before and after retrieving them from the safe.

If you do have something stolen, report it to the police. The chances of their recovering anything are remote, but you'll need a statement proving you have reported the crime if you want to claim insurance.

TELEPHONE

The island's telephone services are generally reliable. In fact, Mauritius offers some of the cheapest mobile-phone services in the world.

The state-controlled **Mauritius Telecom** (www.mauritiustelecom.com) has a virtual monopoly on landlines, although there's an open market for mobile services.

The rate for a call to Australia, Europe or the USA is about Rs 25 per minute. These rates fall by around 25% during off-peak hours (10pm to 6am Monday to Friday and noon on Saturday to 6am the following Monday).

When phoning Mauritius from abroad, you'll need to dial the international code for Mauritius (🖉 230), followed by the seven-digit local number (unless it's a mobile phone, which has eight digits and begins with '5'). There are no area codes in Mauritius.

Mobile Phones

Coverage on Mauritius and Rodrigues is generally excellent and mobile phones are a cheap way to communicate with others. In fact, many Mauritians have more than one mobile phone.

If you have a GSM phone and it has been unlocked, you can keep costs down by buying a local SIM card from either **Orange** (🖉 203 7649; www.orange.mu; Mauritius Telecom Tower, Edith Cavell St, Port Louis) or **Emtel** (🖉 572 95400; www.emtel.com). A starter pack costs around Rs 100, including Rs 86 worth of calls and 20MB of data. To top up your credit you can buy prepaid cards almost anywhere. When buying a SIM card you may need to bring along your passport and a sponsor's signature.

Local calls are charged at between Rs 1.20 and Rs 3.60 per minute, depending on whether you're calling someone on the same network or not. International calls cost a couple of rupees per minute on top of the standard Mauritius Telecom rates.

Purchasing a SIM card package – even for one call home – is much less costly than buying a local phonecard.

TIME

Mauritius is on GMT plus four hours, both on the mainland and on Rodrigues. When it's noon in Port Louis, it's 8am in London, 9am in Paris, 3am in New York and 6pm in Sydney. Mauritius does not operate a system of daylight saving; being equatorial, its sunset and sunrise times vary only slightly throughout the year.

TOILETS

The overwhelming majority of toilets in Mauritius (or at least among those you're likely to use) are of the sit-down, rather than squat, variety.

You'll find free public toilets close to many beaches; most are regularly cleaned and are fine if you find yourself caught short.

TOURIST INFORMATION

Although independent travellers are definitely in the minority, two corporate entities are dedicated to those who don't fall into the package-getaway category. Both have desks in the airport's arrivals hall, and they can assist with hotel bookings (although this is increasingly rare as few travellers arrive in the country without a booking), basic tourist maps and quite general island information.

Also useful is Mauritius Telecom's 24-hour phone service, **Tourist Info** (🖉 152). At any time of day or night you can speak to someone (in English) who will at least try to answer your questions.

Mauritius Tourism Promotion Authority (MTPA; 🖉 208 6397; www.tourism-mauritius.mu) The Mauritius Tourism Promotion Authority is a government-run body essentially responsible for promoting the island and its virtues to foreign markets. MTPA has a constellation of kiosks across the island – although, to be perfectly frank, many were empty during prime business hours, and when we did find someone staffing a booth they tossed us an outdated island map and offered very limited information. You're better off asking tour operators, hotel staff or anyone else accustomed to dealing with travellers' queries.

Association des Hôteliers et Restaurateurs de l'Île Maurice (AHRIM; 🖉 637 3782; www.mauritiustourism.org) The recommended AHRIM is an association of high-quality hotels, guesthouses and restaurants. It is starting to offer guesthouse-plus-airfare packages – an attempt to empower tourists to have a local experience while also benefiting from discounted airfares. Check out its website for details.

TRAVELLERS WITH DISABILITIES

Mauritius makes relatively decent provision for those with mobility problems. Modern buildings conform to international standards for disabled access, although public toilets, pavements and lifts tend not to be as good. Most top-end hotels have wheelchair access, lifts and a handful of rooms with specially equipped bathrooms. In big hotels, there are always plenty of staff around to help and it is often possible to hire an assistant if you want to go on an excursion or a boat trip. With a bit of extra notice, some riding stables, dive centres and other sports operators can cater for people with disabilities.

None of the public-transport systems offer wheelchair access. Anyone using a wheelchair will be reliant on private vehicles.

VISAS

You don't need a visa to enter Mauritius if you are a citizen of the EU, the USA, Australia, Canada, Japan, New Zealand or a number of other countries. You can find more information on the government website (www.passport.gov.mu). Initial entry is granted for a maximum of three months and proof of a planned and paid-for departure is required (though rarely asked for).

Visa Extensions

Extensions for a further three months as a tourist are available from the **Passport & Immigration Office** (210 9312; fax 210 9322; Sterling House, Lislet Geoffrey St, Port Louis). Applications must be submitted with one form, two passport-size photos, your passport, an onward ticket and proof of finances. Two letters may also be necessary – one from you explaining why you want to stay longer, and one from a local 'sponsor' (it can be someone providing accommodation). Providing you can satisfy these demands there should be no problems, but because quite a few visitors overstay their entry permits, there are 'get tough' periods.

VOLUNTEERING

There aren't that many volunteering opportunities in Mauritius, but there are some possibilities in the area of wildlife or marine conservation. Six-month placements on Île aux Aigrettes are possible through the **Mauritian Wildlife Foundation** (MWF; Map p58; 697 6117; www.mauritian-wildlife.org; Grannum Rd, Vacoas; 9am-5pm Mon-Fri), while volunteering at coral reef conservation projects for one week to six months can be arranged through **Working Abroad** (www.workingabroad.com) and others.

WOMEN TRAVELLERS

There are no particular dangers for women in Mauritius, and you won't feel out of place travelling solo. It's still sensible to avoid walking alone along heavily forested trails and roaming around late at night outside of resorts, particularly as most places have very poor or nonexistent street lighting. Port Louis is one place where it really would be foolish for anyone to walk alone after dark, especially near the Jardins de Compagnie (a favoured hang-out of pimps and drug addicts); Le Caudan Waterfront is, as always, something of an exception to this rule, with plenty of people around at most times.

WORK

There are few work opportunities in Mauritius for travellers. Possible exceptions include jobs for experienced divers at one of the country's dive centres, and work (usually unpaid) on board a yacht – for the latter ask at the marina at Le Caudan Waterfront in Port Louis or La Balise Marina (p92) in Black River.

ℹ Getting There & Away

ENTERING THE COUNTRY

Entering Mauritius is usually hassle-free, with no visas required for many nationalities. Customs searches are generally quick and easy if they occur at all.

AIR

Direct flights connect Mauritius with Australia, Asia, the Middle East, Africa and Europe. For further afield, you may need to take a connecting flight from South Africa, the Middle East or Europe.

Airports & Airlines

Mainland Mauritius' only airport is Sir Seewoosagur Ramgoolam International Airport (p57).

Air Mauritius (www.airmauritius.com) is the national carrier. It has a good safety record and a decent international network.

SEA

The **Mauritius Shipping Corporation** (Map p170; 831 0640; www.mauritiusshipping.net; Rue François Leguat; 8.15am-3pm Mon-Fri, to 11am Sat) operates long-haul ferry services between Réunion and Mauritius at least once a week. The journey takes about 11 hours. We're yet to meet a traveller who arrived in or left Mauritius in this way, but the option does exist.

ℹ Getting Around

Mauritius is an easy destination to get around, but to make the most of your time, renting a car will allow you to get from most corners of the island to any other in less than 90 minutes. If you're only having the odd excursion, consider renting a taxi for the day. Catamarans are perfect for getting to the offshore islands. Otherwise, there's a slow but reliable bus network that connects most towns.

AIR

The only regular domestic air connections are those between Sir Seewoosagur Ramgoolam International Airport (p57) on mainland Mauritius and **Sir Gaetan Duval Airport** (Plaine Corail Airport; Map p168; 832 7888; www.airportofrodrigues.com) on Rodrigues. There are at least two daily flights on this route, operated by Air Mauritius, and flying time is around 1½ hours. This is an extremely popular route, so always book ahead as early as you can.

Air Mauritius offers helicopter tours and charters from SSR International Airport to a number of major hotels. A hotel transfer anywhere on the island costs Rs 23,000, while a full one-hour island tour costs Rs 37,000 for up to two passengers; a quick 15-minute jaunt will set you back Rs 15,000. For information and reservations, contact **Air Mauritius Helicopter Services** (603

ARRIVING IN MAURITIUS

Semi-regular buses between Port Louis or Curepipe and Mahébourg go via Sir Seewoosagur Ramgoolam International Airport (p57) and pick up passengers from outside the arrivals hall; if nothing turns up, you may need to head upstairs to departures. For all other destinations, you'll need to change in one of these three cities. Most travellers get where they're going by hiring a taxi – there's a taxi desk with set prices in the arrivals hall. Sample fares are Rs 1500 to Port Louis, Rs 500 to Mahébourg and Rs 2000 to Grand Baie.

3754; www.airmauritius.com/helicopter.htm) or ask your hotel to organise a transfer or trip.

BICYCLE

Cycling isn't really a practical means of long-distance transport in Mauritius – there is simply too much traffic and drivers rarely take cyclists into consideration – but bikes are fine for short hops along the coast. Given that the coast is pleasantly flat, it's amazing how much ground you can cover in a day. The coast roads are also generally (though not always) quieter than those in the interior.

In general, the roads are well maintained, but look out for potholes along country lanes, especially in the western part of the island. Avoid cycling anywhere at night, as most roads are poorly lit.

Most hotels and guesthouses can help you arrange bike rentals (usually mountain bikes). Although many offer this as a complimentary service for guests, expect to pay around Rs 250 per day for a quality bike at those places that don't. You'll usually be asked for a deposit of Rs 5000, either in cash or by taking an imprint of your credit card. Most bikes are in reasonable condition, but be sure to check the brakes, gears and saddle (some are mighty uncomfortable) before riding off into the blue beyond. The bike should have a lock; use it, especially if you leave your bike at the beach and outside shops.

BOAT

Various private operators offer cruises to offshore islands, or snorkelling and fishing excursions. Most commonly this is aboard a catamaran, but speedboat excursions are also possible. For the former, check out www.catamarancruises mauritius.com.

Otherwise, two boats, the M/V *Anna* and the M/S *Mauritius Trochetia*, have two to four monthly passenger services in both directions between Port Louis (Mauritius) and Port Mathurin (Rod-

rigues). The journey takes close to 36 hours. On board you'll find four classes ranging from 2nd class up to deluxe cabins. Services are operated by the Mauritius Shipping Corporation (p153).

BUS

Bus travel is cheap and fun – you'll usually find yourself chatting to gregarious locals – and although you won't set any land-speed records, it's generally a fairly easy and reliable way to get around. There is no countrywide bus service. Instead there are several large regional bus companies and scores of individual operators.

The buses are almost always packed, especially on the main routes, but turnover is quick at all the stops. If you start the trip standing, you're likely to end up sitting.

Be warned that you could have problems taking large bags or backpacks on a bus. If it takes up a seat, you will probably have to pay for that extra seat. A few travellers have even been refused entry to a full bus if they have a large bag, although this is rare.

It's best to stick to express buses whenever possible, as standard buses seem to stop every few metres and can take up to twice as long to reach the same destination. It takes approximately an hour by standard services from Mahébourg to Curepipe, an hour from Curepipe to Port Louis, and an hour from Port Louis to Grand Baie.

The buses are single-deck vehicles bearing dynamic names such as 'Road Warrior', 'Bad Boys' and 'The Street Ruler'. Thus encouraged, it's perhaps not surprising that some drivers harbour Formula 1 racing fantasies; fortunately, the frequent stops slow things down a touch. Though the buses are in varying states of disrepair, the fleet is gradually being upgraded.

Schedules

There are no published timetables. Locals are the best source of information and can help you work out the best way to get from A to B.

Long-distance buses run from around 6am to 6.30pm, though there is a late service between Port Louis and Curepipe until 11pm. Generally there are buses every 15 minutes or so on the major routes, with less frequent express services. Buses in country areas can be few and far between.

Fares & Tickets

Fares range from Rs 15 for a short trip to a maximum of Rs 38 for the run from Port Louis to Mahébourg. Air-conditioned express buses may cost a couple of rupees extra. Tickets are available from the conductor or porter (the conductor's 'assistant'); keep some small change handy. Retain your tickets, as inspectors often board to check them, and press the buzzer when you want to get off. Reservations are not possible.

CAR & MOTORCYCLE

By far the easiest and quickest way to get around Mauritius and Rodrigues is to hire a car. Prices aren't as low as they could be, considering the numbers of visitors who rent vehicles, but you should be able to negotiate a discount if you're renting for a week or more.

Car Hire

To rent a car, drivers must usually be more than 23 years of age (some companies only require a minimum age of 21) and have held a driving licence for at least one year. Payment is generally made in advance. You can pay by credit card (Visa and MasterCard are the most widely accepted), though small companies might add a 3% 'processing fee' for this service. All foreigners are technically required to have an International Driving Licence. Few rental agencies enforce this, but it's safest to carry one as the police can demand to see it.

Rates for the smallest hatchback start at around Rs 1000 a day (including insurance and unlimited mileage) with one of the local operators. Expect rates to start at Rs 1200 and beyond when using an international chain, although daily prices can even start as high as Rs 1600. On top of that you will be required to pay a refundable deposit, usually Rs 15,000; most companies will take an imprint of your credit card to cover this. Policies usually specify that drivers are liable for the first Rs 15,000 of damage in the event of an accident, but more comprehensive insurance is sometimes available for an extra cost.

Although there are dozens of operators on the island, it's best to book ahead during the high-season months (the European winter holidays). The following car-hire companies have airport desks or can deliver to the airport.

ABC (☑ 216 8889; www.abc-carrental.com; 3B, SSR International Airport)

Avis (☑ 405 5200; www.avismauritius.com; 4B, SSR International Airport)

Budget (☑ 467 9700; www.budget.com.mu; 1A, SSR International Airport)

Claire & Sailesh Ltd (☑ 631 4625, 5754 6451; www.clairesaileshltd.com)

Europcar (☑ 637 3240; www.europcar.com; 3A, SSR International Airport)

Hertz (☑ 604 3021, 670 4301; www.hertz.com; 17A, SSR International Airport)

Kevtrav Ltd (☑ 465 4458; www.kevtrav.com; St Jean Rd, Quatre Bornes)

Ropsen (☑ 451 5763; www.ropsen.net; Royal Rd)

Sixt (☑ 427 1111; www.sixt.com; 7B, SSR International Airport)

Motorcycle Hire

There are only a few places where you can hire motorbikes, which is a shame as this is a great way to explore the quiet coastal roads – especially in traffic-free Rodrigues. While you'll occasionally find a 125cc bike, most are 100cc or under; the smaller models are referred to as scooters.

Towns offering motorcycle hire include Grand Baie, Flic en Flac, Mahébourg and Port Mathurin. Your best bet is to ask around your hotel. You should be aware that most motorcycle hire is 'unofficial', so you may not be covered by insurance in case of a collision.

Parking

Parking is free and not a problem in most of Mauritius, although it's best not to leave your car in an isolated spot.

City parking, however, requires payment. There are supervised car parks in Port Louis, but elsewhere you'll have to park on the street, which in a handful of towns involves buying parking coupons – ask a local if you're not sure. Coupons are available from petrol stations and cost from Rs 50 for 10, with each coupon valid for 30 minutes. The same coupons can be used all over the island. Street parking is generally free at night and on weekends; the exact hours, which vary from one town to another, are indicated on signposts.

Road Conditions & Hazards

Most roads are in reasonable condition, although be wary of potholes and poorly signed speed humps on minor or residential roads. The main concern for first-time drivers is that, apart from the motorway that links the airport with Grand Baie (albeit with roundabouts), many roads can be quite narrow – fine under normal conditions,

---

CLIMATE CHANGE & TRAVEL

Every form of transport that relies on carbon-based fuel generates CO_2, the main cause of human-induced climate change. Modern travel is dependent on aeroplanes, which might use less fuel per kilometre per person than most cars but travel much greater distances. The altitude at which aircraft emit gases (including CO_2) and particles also contributes to their climate change impact. Many websites offer 'carbon calculators' that allow people to estimate the carbon emissions generated by their journey and, for those who wish to do so, to offset the impact of the greenhouse gases emitted with contributions to portfolios of climate-friendly initiatives throughout the world. Lonely Planet offsets the carbon footprint of all staff and author travel.

but slightly trickier when buses, trucks and meandering cyclists are factored in. The only solution is to err on the side of caution and remain vigilant. Also watch out for other vehicles overtaking when it's not entirely safe to do so.

Even on the motorway you'll find people wandering across the roads and a generally relaxed attitude. As in most places, the greatest danger comes from other drivers, not the roads. Mauritian drivers tend to have little consideration for each other, let alone for motorbikes. Buses are notorious for overtaking and then pulling in immediately ahead of other vehicles to pick up or drop off passengers; always use extra caution when a bus comes in sight. At night be aware that you'll face an assault course of ill-lit oncoming vehicles, totally unlit bikes and weaving pedestrians. If you sense that you've hit something while driving at night, proceed to the nearest police station. Motorcyclists should also be prepared for the elements, as sudden showers can come out of skies that were clear a second earlier.

Road Rules

Local motorists seem to think they'll save electricity by not switching on their headlights, and the police are better at people control than traffic control. Traffic congestion can be heavy in Port Louis and, to a lesser extent, Grand Baie.

There are many pedestrian zebra crossings, but cross with care. If you cross expecting courtesy or that drivers will be worried about insurance, you'll get knocked over.

Driving is on the left and the speed limit varies from 30km/h in town centres to 110km/h on the motorway – speed limits are usually marked. Even so, not many people stick to these limits and the island has its fair share of accidents. Remember also that the motorway has a series of roundabouts – bearing down on them at 110km/h is a dangerous pastime best avoided.

Drivers and passengers are required to wear seat belts. For lack of sufficient breathalysers, the alcohol limit (legally 0.5g/L) is defined by the police as one glass of beer.

HITCHING

Hitching is never entirely safe in any country in the world, and we don't recommend it. Travellers who decide to hitch should understand that they are taking a small but potentially serious risk. People who choose to hitch will be safer if they travel in pairs and let someone know where they are planning to go.

TAXI

It's sometimes possible to imagine that every adult male in Mauritius is a taxi driver. Drivers will often shout out at travellers they see wandering around Port Louis or Grand Baie, while ranks outside hotels are usually overflowing. Negotiation is key: meters are rarely used and you'll usually be ripped off if you get into a taxi without agreeing on a price first. During the journey most drivers will tout for future business; if you aren't careful, you may find that you've agreed to an all-day island tour. If you aren't interested, make this very clear, as many drivers won't take no for an answer.

Many guesthouse managers/owners have attempted to mitigate their guests' frustration with rip-offs by arranging prices with local taxi drivers. The quotes given under such arrangements, particularly those from small guesthouses, are often acceptable; they can usually arrange competitively priced airport pick-ups as well. Once you've got a feel for the rates, you can venture into independent bargaining. You'll find that prices are fairly standard – you may be able to knock off Rs 100 or Rs 200 here and there, though don't be crestfallen if you can't whittle the driver down to the exact price you're expecting (after all, they've had more practice at this taxi game than you!).

Taxis charge slightly more at night and the cheeky drivers may ask for an extra fee if you want the comfort of air-con. It's also worth remembering that some taxis charge around Rs 1 per minute waiting time. It seems minimal, but it adds up if you stop for lunch or do some sightseeing on foot. Your best bet is to negotiate a set fare with the driver that includes waiting time.

There's a taxi desk at the airport with set prices to just about anywhere on the island.

Taxi Hire

For around Rs 2000 you can hire a taxi for a full-day tour along one or two coasts of the island. You can cut costs by forming a group – the price should *not* be calculated per person. Once you've agreed on a price and itinerary, it helps to get the details down in writing. Although most drivers can speak both French and English, double-check before setting off to ensure you won't face a day-long communication barrier. If you're lucky, you'll get an excellent and informative guide, but note that most drivers work on a commission basis with particular restaurants, shops and sights. If you want to go to the restaurant of your choice, you may have to insist on it. Again, small guesthouses can usually recommend a reliable driver.

Share Taxi

When individual fares are hard to come by, some taxis will cruise around their area supplementing the bus service. For quick, short-haul trips they pick up passengers waiting at the bus stops and charge just a little more than the bus. Their services are called 'share taxis' or 'taxi trains'. Mind you, if you flag down a share taxi, you'll only be swapping a big sardine can for a small one, and if you flag down an empty taxi, you may have to pay the full fare.

DAVID C TOMLINSON / GETTY IMAGES ©

A Glimpse of Paradise

Beaches that defy all superlatives, wild landscapes that will forever be etched into your memory, loads of adventure options, captivating festivals and a glimpse of history – it's impossible to be bored in Mauritius, Réunion and the Seychelles. Paradise found? You be the judge.

Contents
➡ **Outdoor Adventures**
➡ **History & Culture**
➡ **Idyllic Beaches**
➡ **The Ultimate Honeymoon**

Above Praslin (p308), Seychelles

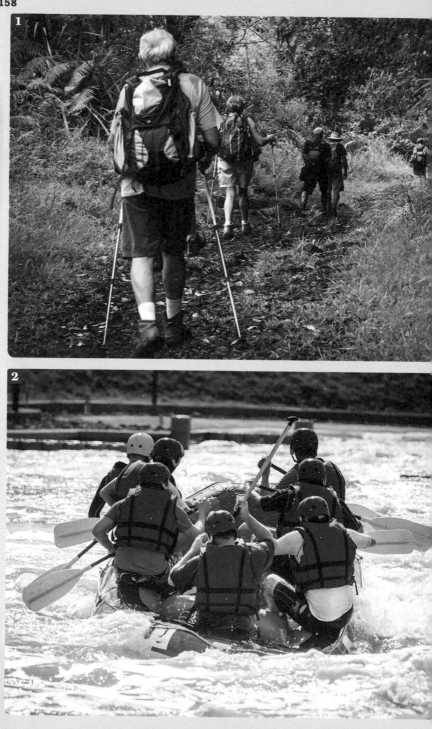

Hiking in Parc National des Hauts de la Réunion (p277) **2.** White-water rafting, Réunion (p265) **3.** Colourful coral reef, Seychelles

Outdoor Adventures

Sure, these divine islands strewn across the peacock-blue Indian Ocean were designed for lounging on a beach or luxuriating in sensuous nature. But when you've finished sipping your cocktail, you may want to get the blood flowing a little more. Plenty of adventure options are readily available.

Underwater Activities

Mauritius, Réunion and the Seychelles are a divers' mecca thanks to a combination of unique features. Healthy reefs, canyon-like terrain, shallow shelves, exciting shipwrecks, seamounts and quick shoreline drop-offs give snorkellers and divers almost instant access to a variety of environments. The water is warm and clear, and teeming with life from the tiniest juvenile tropical fish to the largest pelagic creature.

Canyoning

There's no better way to immerse yourself in grandiose scenery than by exploring the atmospheric canyons in the Cirque de Cilaos or Cirque de Salazie in Réunion; expect various jumps, leaps in crystal-clear natural pools and rappelling. In Mauritius, adventurers abseil down the seven chutes at Tamarin.

Hiking

Criss-crossed with a network of paths ranging from simple nature trails to more challenging itineraries, Réunion has all the flavours of superlative hiking. Mauritius and Rodrigues also boast excellent walking options. The biggest surprise? The Seychelles. On top of world-renowned beaches, this archipelago offers divine coastal ambles and lovely jungle walks.

White-Water Rafting

The wealth of scenic rivers that decorates eastern Réunion make it a water lover's dream destination. Rivière des Marsouins, Rivière des Roches and Rivière Langevin offer top-class runs to get the blood racing.

1. Hindu temple, Port Louis (p48), Mauritius **2.** Indian dancers, Mauritius **3.** Notre Dame Auxiliatrice (p80), Mauritius **4.** Fire-walking ceremony, Mauritius

CULTURA RM EXCLUSIVE / PHILIP LEE HARVEY / GETTY IMAGES ©

History & Culture

Although many come to Réunion, Mauritius and the Seychelles for the incredible beaches and nature, these islands have rich and diverse cultures, influenced by the waves of migrants who gradually populated the islands. Culture buffs with a penchant for architecture and festivals will be in seventh heaven.

Multiculturalism

You'll see almost every shade of skin and hair imaginable, arising from a mixture of African, Indian, Chinese, Arab and French genes. So don't be surprised to see a cathedral, a Tamil temple, a mosque and a pagoda lying almost side by side in larger cities.

Creole Architecture

Some wonderfully preserved colonial buildings can be found in Réunion, Mauritius and the Seychelles. From splendid plantation houses and captivating mansions to humble *cases créoles* and grand colonial buildings harking back to the French East India Company, you're sure to be awed.

Cultural & Religious Festivals

Fabulous festivals provide visitors with a peek into local culture. Divali, the Festival of Lights, is celebrated in the three countries in October or November. In Mauritius and Réunion, impressive fire-walking ceremonies take place in December or January. The Seychelles prides itself on its exuberant carnival.

Music & Dance

In this region of the Indian Ocean, music and dance are part of daily life, from the smallest village to the largest cities. In June, top-name *maloya*, *séga*, salsa, reggae and electro performers from throughout the Indian Ocean and beyond gather in St-Pierre during the three-day Sakifo festival.

WESTEND61 / GETTY IMAGES ©

se Georgette (p309), Praslin, Seychelles **2.** Anse Cocos
l), La Digue, Seychelles **3.** Anse Source d'Argent (p320), La
, Seychelles

Idyllic Beaches

Believe the hype: the Seychelles and
Mauritius have some of the most dreamy
and dramatic beaches you'll find this side
of Bora Bora. Take your pick!

Anse Cocos (La Digue)

Anse Cocos (p321) is a died-and-gone-to-
heaven vision of a beach – a frost-white
strip of sand fringed by turquoise waters.
It can only be reached by foot, meaning
that it always feels secluded.

Anse Georgette (Praslin)

It's like an apparition: the water is so
scintillating and the sand so dazzlingly
white that you'll rub your eyes. Despite
having been engulfed by a resort, Anse
Georgette (p309) is public property, so
you are entitled to plop your towel down
on the sand.

Anse Source d'Argent (La Digue)

OK, we thought the brochure spiel about
Anse Source d'Argent (p320) being
the most photogenic beach in the world
was hype until we clapped eyes on its
crystalline emerald waters and powder-
soft sands. It's even more astounding
when seen from the summit of the granite
hills that loom above the coast.

Pointe d'Esny (Mauritius)

This is it – the celebrity of all of the
beaches of southern Mauritius is Pointe
d'Esny (p112). Immense, crystalline and
glossy, it doesn't disappoint the bevy of
swimmers and snorkellers who dabble in
its gorgeous, lucent depths.

Rodrigues' East Coast

Between Graviers and St François (p175)
in the island's east, the jagged coastline is
regularly punctuated by appealing coves
and stretches of gorgeous beach. The
beauty of these stunning swaths of sand
lies in the fact that they're totally secluded
and there's no road here.

Luxury hotel, Seych[el]

The Ultimate Honeymoon

White-sand beaches. Secluded coves. Coral-coloured sunsets. Swish hotels. Hushed spas. It's not surprising that honeymooners and those seeking a glamorous tropical getaway have long had the Seychelles and Mauritius at the top of their wish lists.

Le Saint Géran (Mauritius)

Le Saint Géran (p128) is a sumptuous, impressive place that manages to get it right on so many levels – it's classy and stylish without being too formal, it's romantic without being too quiet and it's welcoming to families without allowing kids to run riot.

Desroches Island (Seychelles)

For couples in search of an intimate paradise, Château de Feuilles (p314) on Praslin is an extraordinary place to stay. Perched on a beautiful headland with stupendous vistas, this sweet hideaway has nine stone-walled villas dotted around manicured tropical gardens. The uber-romantic poolside restaurant and hilltop Jacuzzi add to the experience.

Silhouette (Seychelles)

If you want to combine romance, outdoors and affordable luxury, Silhouette (p327) is your answer. Here, stylish bungalows complement an already stunning island. Diving, snorkelling, fishing and walking are available.

Frégate (Seychelles)

If you want to live out that stranded-on-a-deserted-island fantasy, you've come to the right place. The 16 opulent villas at Frégate (p329) are so delicious you might not want to leave, except for a beauty treatment in the serene spa.

Frégate Island (p329)

Rodrigues

Best Places to Eat

→ La Belle Rodriguaise (p178)

→ Chez Robert et Solange (p177)

→ Le Marlin Bleu (p171)

→ Mazavaroo (p177)

→ Cases à Gardenias (p178)

Best Places to Sleep

→ Tekoma (p177)

→ Bakwa Lodge (p177)

→ Cases à Gardenias (p176)

→ La Belle Rodriguaise (p176)

→ Chez Bernard & Claudine (p176)

Why Go?

Blissfully isolated over 600km northeast of the mainland, this tiny volcanic outcrop surrounded by a massive turquoise lagoon is a stunning mountainous gem that barely feels connected to its big sister, Mauritius, let alone the wider world.

Often billed as the 'Mauritius of 25 years ago', Rodrigues actually bears little resemblance to its neighbour beyond the scenic strips of peach-tinged sand. The island's population of around 40,000 is predominantly African and Creole – a far cry from the ethnic melting pot on Mauritius' main island – and you won't find a stalk of sugar cane anywhere on Rodrigues' hilly landscape. The pace of life, too, is undeniably slow, which gives the island its time-warped vibe. Great food, some fine natural sites and a host of activities round out an experience that lives long in the memory as one of those beautiful forgotten worlds in some remote corner of the globe.

When to Go

→ November to February means high season and high prices; cyclones are possible from January. Accommodation and air tickets can be hard to come by, so book well in advance if travelling at this time.

→ October, March and April are still considered high season in places, but there are generally fewer crowds. Underwater visibility is especially good for diving and snorkelling at this time. All in all, it's a nice time to be on the island.

→ Lower prices and milder temperatures arrive from May to September, when there's little chance of cyclones.

Port Mathurin

POP 6000

This tiny port is the island's hub, its largest town and, for want of a better word, its capital. The word 'soporific' may come to mind, but during the day the town has a friendly vibe, especially around the buzzing market stalls. Apart from its banks, supermarket and handful of restaurants, there's not much to do here.

◎ Sights

★ Saturday Market   MARKET
(Map p170; ◷ 4.30-10am) The Saturday market is as busy as Rodrigues gets and it's the best place on the island to shop for fresh produce and souvenirs. It's open the rest of the week but really gears up on Saturday, when much of the island turns out. It's next to the bridge near the post office. Turn up later than 10am and you'll wonder what all the fuss is about.

La Résidence   ARCHITECTURE
(Map p170; Rue de la Solidarité) One of the oldest buildings still standing in Port Mathurin, La Résidence dates from 1897, when it provided a fairly modest home for the British chief commissioner. Its facilities are now used as function rooms for the new Regional Assembly. As such, it is closed to the public, although it is possible to get an idea of the structure from the veranda of the tourist office across the road.

⌐ Sleeping

Port Mathurin makes a convenient base if you're travelling by bus, but frankly the options in town lack the quality you'll find outside it and taxis rarely cost much. The main concentration of hotels and guesthouses is found 2km east of town at Anse aux Anglais.

La Cabane d'Ete   APARTMENT €
(Map p168; ☎ 831 0747; www.lacabanedete.com; Baie Malagache; s/d incl breakfast €35/50) Adorable studio accommodation in Baie Malagache,

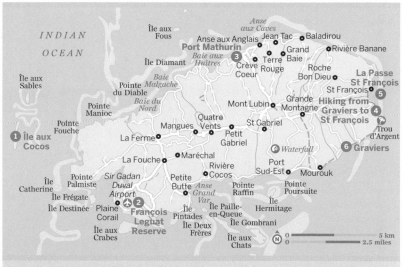

Rodrigues Highlights

1 Île aux Cocos (p173) Taking a boat ride out to the seabird colonies of this small, uninhabited slice of paradise.

2 François Leguat Reserve (p172) Cavorting with hundreds of curious giant tortoises in a lovely setting.

3 Port Mathurin (p167) Getting up early and immersing yourself in the island's busiest market.

4 Graviers to St François (p175) Hiking past Rodrigues' best beaches along the island's northeast coast.

5 La Passe St François (p174) Diving the pristine waters off the east coast.

6 Graviers (p176) Eating the best in local cooking then sleeping by the sea at La Belle Rodriguaise.

Rodrigues

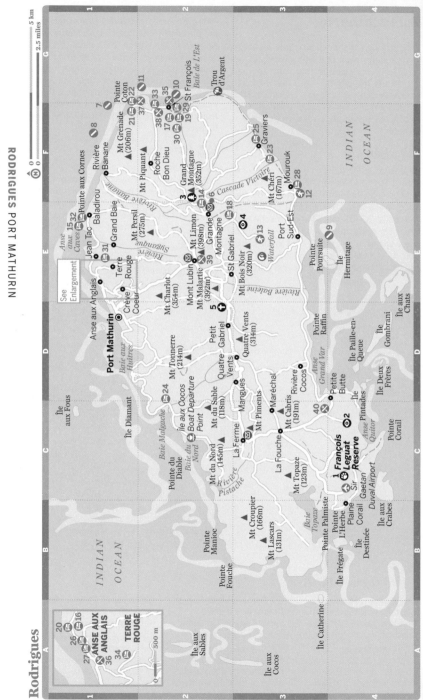

Rodrigues

southwest of Port Mathurin, is what's on offer here. The rooms have a hint of whitewash and bamboo about them, and the location is as far from tourist Rodrigues, such as it is, as you can get. Bookings can be made through Rotourco (p172) in Port Mathurin.

La Varangues GUESTHOUSE €
(Map p170; ☎832 1882; lavarangues@gmail.com; per person incl half board Rs 1000-1500; P ✳ 🛜) The location is either fantastic (great views from the balconies) or in the middle of nowhere (you'll need a car to get anywhere), but this place shares premises with a good restaurant of the same name (p171) and the rooms are clean and well looked after. The lack of a swimming pool will deter some, but the price represents excellent value.

Hébergement Fatehmamode APARTMENT €
(Map p170; ☎5499 2020; www.hebergement-fatehmamode.com; Rue Max Lucchesi; per person without/with half board from Rs 500/800; ✳) Right in the centre of town, these no-frills rooms are about as cheap as things get on the island.

Ti Pavillon GUESTHOUSE €
(Map p168; ☎875 0707; www.tipavillon.com; Anse aux Anglais; s/d Rs 1200/1700; ✳ @ 🛜) This

friendly spot, run by the same people that brought you Auberge du Lagon, welcomes guests with wallet-pleasing prices and simple digs painted in bright primary colours. The common spaces are cluttered with wonderful bits and bobs.

Residence Foulsafat GUESTHOUSE €
(Map p168; ☎831 1760; www.residencefoulsafat. com; Jean Tac; d incl half board €60) High up in the hills with memorable views of the infinite blue, this friendly option has five houses, each with a unique design and theme. Our favourite is the adorable honeymooners' cottage with stone walls and attached gazebo covered with gingerbread trim.

Auberge du Lagon GUESTHOUSE €€
(Map p168; ☎831 2825, 5875 0707; www.tipavillon. com; Jean Tac; s/d incl breakfast €46/63, incl half board €60/87) Down a gravel track in Jean Tac, east of Anse aux Anglais, this fine guesthouse has big-horizon views and a sense of having left the world behind. The garden needs time to grow, but the rooms have a smart-casual look that blends simplicity with carefully chosen ochre and burnt-orange hues. There are also a breezy bar and an infinity pool.

Port Mathurin

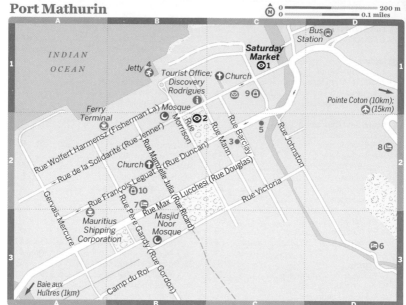

Port Mathurin

◎ Top Sights
1 Saturday Market C1

◎ Sights
2 La Résidence B2

⊕ Activities, Courses & Tours
3 JP Excursions C2
4 Rod Fishing Club B1
5 Rotourco C2

⊜ Sleeping
6 Escale Vacances D3
7 Hébergement Fatehmamode B2
8 La Varangues D2

⊗ Eating
Aux Deux Frères .... (see 5)
La Varangues .... (see 8)

⊛ Shopping
9 Care-Co C1
10 Island Books & Clothing Spot B2

If you prefer mountains over sea, ask about the owners' other guesthouse, Ti Pavillon, up in the hills.

Residence Kono Kono　　　BUNGALOW €€
(Map p168; ☑ 831 0759; www.lekonokono.com; Jean Tac; s/d €50/80) The furnishings couldn't be simpler, but there's something that we like about this place, out in Jean Tac, east of Anse aux Anglais. There's a relaxed vibe, there are big-sky panoramas and the brick-walled, tiled-floored bungalows with pastel shades are tidy.

Le Récif　　　GUESTHOUSE €€
(Map p168; ☑ 831 1804; www.lerecifhotel.com; Caverne Provert; s/d incl half board Rs 2600/3800; ❊) Perched on the cliff just east of Anse aux Anglais, Le Récif has fabulous views from its balcony out over the emerald lagoon. We reckon it's a touch overpriced and it can have a vaguely abandoned air when things are quiet, but the rooms are large and the sunset views are hard to beat anywhere on the island.

Escale Vacances　　　GUESTHOUSE €€
(Map p170; ☑ 831 2555; www.escale-vacances. com; Rue Johnston, Fond La Digue; s/d incl breakfast €61/94, incl half board €70/112; ❊ ☀) Located just outside the town centre, Port Mathurin's most upmarket option occupies a converted colonial mansion that feels somewhat like an old schoolhouse. Rooms are quiet and well appointed.

Coco Villas
GUESTHOUSE €€

(Map p168; ☎831 0449; www.rodrigues-cocovilla.com; Caverne Provert; per person incl half board Rs 1400-2000; ❄🛜) Simple rooms at this family-run place make a quieter alternative to Anse aux Anglais just down the road. Rooms are nothing special, but the price is about right.

Les Cocotiers
HOTEL €€€

(Map p168; ☎831 1058; www.lescocotiersbeachresort.com; Anse aux Anglais; s/d with half board from €131/186; ❄🛜🏊) A great choice at the end of the coastal road, this friendly resort comes with an airy restaurant, an inviting swimming pool and a popular dive centre. Vaco paintings adorn the walls in the rooms, and the beds have colourful duvets to match. Service can be patchy at reception.

🍴 Eating

Port Mathurin has a handful of restaurants, but most options are east of town in the Anse aux Anglais district.

Self-caterers will find several small grocery stores on Rue de la Solidarité and Rue Mamzelle Julia. You can buy fresh fruit from stalls near the post office (mornings only from Monday to Saturday). For quick eats, outlets on Rue de la Solidarité sell *pain fouré* (filled rolls) and noodles for a handful of rupees.

Le Marlin Bleu
SEAFOOD €

(Map p168; ☎832 0701; Anse aux Anglais; mains Rs 225-350; ⊗9.30am-3pm & 5-10pm Wed-Mon) The most sociable spot in Anse aux Anglais, this restaurant gets the thumbs up from expats and is dominated by larger-than-life Mega, the friendly owner who makes sure that everyone's having a good time. The food is excellent with a good mix of seafood, pizza and local dishes. Live football on the miraculously appearing big screen (or any excuse really) means the bar often stays open long after the kitchen closes.

La Varangues
MAURITIAN €

(Map p170; ☎832 1882; mains Rs 275-395; ⊗9am-3pm & 6-10pm) Fresh local cooking at reasonable prices, veranda tables to catch the view out over Port Mathurin and the lagoon, and friendly owners who've recently taken over this prime patch of real estate make this an excellent choice. It's on the road that runs down to Port Mathurin from Mont Lubin, a little over halfway down the hill.

RODRIGUES CUISINE

The highlight of any visit to Rodrigues is sampling the unique local cuisine at one of the island's many *tables d'hôtes* (privately hosted meals). Rodriguans cook a variety of recipes that are quite different from those of their Mauritian neighbours – less emphasis is placed on spiciness and most meals are cooked with minimal amounts of oil. And while octopus dishes have colonised the mainland, the passion for (and most of the actual) *poulpe* or *ourite* comes from Rodrigues.

Meals at the island's best and most well-known *tables d'hôtes* range from Rs 400 to Rs 700. You should always call at least a day ahead to make a reservation.

Here is a list of Rodrigues' must-eats, according to Françoise Baptiste, author, hostess and chef extraordinaire.

➡ *Ourite* – octopus salad with lemon juice, olive oil, pepper, onions and salt. The dried variety has a rather pungent taste and admittedly isn't for everyone.

➡ *Vindaye d'ourite* – boiled tender octopus flavoured with grated curcuma (such as ginger or turmeric), garlic, vinegar, lemon juice and a sprinkle of local spices.

➡ *Saucisses créole* – a variety of meats that are dried and cured locally.

➡ *La torte Rodriguaise* – a small cake of papaya, pineapple or coconut mixed with a cream made from a local root called *corn-floeur.*

Aux Deux Frères
MAURITIAN, INTERNATIONAL €

(Map p170; ☎831 0541; 1st fl, Patriko Bldg, Rue François Leguat; pizza from Rs 215, mains Rs 295-425; ⊗8.30am-2.30pm Mon-Sat, 6.30-10pm Fri & Sat) Perched above a plaza of tour operators, Port Mathurin's slickest haunt serves local and international dishes in swish surrounds. The *marlin fumé avec gingembre* (smoked marlin with ginger) as a starter is small and simple but filled with taste. The restaurant also does pizza, pork brochettes and Creole sausages (the latter when available).

🛍 Shopping

Rue de la Solidarité and Rue Mamzelle Julia are the main shopping streets, but even there you're unlikely to find more than a handful of threadbare shops. Watch for baskets and hats made from dried *vacoa* (pandanus) leaves, items made from coconut fibres and coconut-shell jewellery. Local foodstuffs include preserved lemons, chillies and honey.

Care-Co   HANDICRAFTS
(Map p170; Rue de la Solidarité; ⊘8am-4pm Mon-Fri, to noon Sat) Care-Co sells coconut-shell items, honey and model boats made by people (mostly beekeepers) with disabilities.

Island Books & Clothing Spot   BOOKS
(Map p170; ☑440 0040, 832 1564; Rue François Leguat; ⊘8.30am-4pm Mon-Fri, to 2pm Sat) This small bookshop has a handful of books about Rodrigues and Mauritius, including (while stocks last) the French-language flora and fauna guide to Île aux Cocos. There's another shop at the airport that is supposed to open just before and after flights arrive and depart, but staff aren't always there.

ℹ Information

Discovery Rodrigues (Map p170; ☑832 0867; discoveryrodrigues@intnet.mu; Rue de la Solidarité; ⊘8am-4pm Mon-Fri, to noon Sat, to 10am Sun) Sharing an office and staff with the tourist office, this body oversees visits to Île aux Cocos. Although it organises tours there, it does not organise boat trips over to the island.

Port Mathurin Pharmacy (☑831 2279; Rue de la Solidarité; ⊘7.30am-4.30pm Mon-Fri, to 3pm Sat, to 11am Sun) The only pharmacy on the island.

ISLAND TOURS

JP Excursions (Map p170; ☑5875 0730, 831 1162; www.jpexcursion-rodrigues. com; Rue Barclay) Professional outfit offering the full range of boat excursions, car rental, diving, fishing and kitesurfing.

2000 Tours (Map p168; ☑5765 2100, 831 4703; www.rodrigues-2000tours.com; Rue Max Lucchesi, Grande Montagne) Local operator offering tours to île aux Cocos, car rental, diving and kitesurfing.

Rotourco (Map p170; ☑831 0747; www. rotourco.com; Rue François Leguat) Offers boat tours to Île aux Cocos, as well as car rental.

Rodrigues Regional Library (⊘9am-4.30pm Mon-Fri) Free, slow and password-free wi-fi can be accessed outside the Rodrigues Regional Library – it's a rare commodity on the island.

Tourist Office (Map p170; ☑832 0867; www. tourism-rodrigues.mu; Rue de la Solidarité; ⊘8am-4pm Mon-Fri) Small but helpful tourist office opposite La Résidence (p167).

ℹ Getting There & Away

Regular, old-school Ashok Leyland buses connect Port Mathurin with the rest of the island, but you may have to change buses in Mont Lubin, the island's high point, where all its roads meet.

Around Rodrigues

Most of Rodrigues' more appealing corners lie beyond Port Mathurin, particularly around the southern and eastern coasts and the rugged interior.

◉ Sights

Besides Rodrigues' golden beaches – the best of which flank the island's eastern ridges – there are several interesting sights to take in, including a couple of caves and several noteworthy architectural contributions.

★**François Leguat Reserve**   WILDLIFE RESERVE
(Map p168; ☑832 8141; www.tortoisescavereserve-rodrigues.com; Anse Quitor; adult/child incl tortoises & cave Rs 320/160, tortoises only Rs 200/100; ⊘9am-5pm, tours 9.30am, 10.30am, 12.30pm & 2.30pm) In 1691, François Leguat wrote that there were so many tortoises on Rodrigues that 'one can take more than a hundred steps on their shell without touching the ground'. Sadly, the Rodrigues version of the giant tortoise became extinct, but this reserve is recreating the Eden described by the island's early explorers. Hundreds of tortoises (the outcome of a breeding program) roam the grounds, and 100,000 indigenous trees have been planted over the last four years. Cave visits are also possible.

In the caves, spirited tour leaders point out quirky rock shapes and discuss the island's interesting geological history. Keep an eye out for the tibia bone of a solitaire bird that juts from the cavern's stone ceiling.

There's also a small enclosure with several giant fruit bats (the island's only endemic mammal) and a handful of recently arrived, critically endangered ploughshare tortoises from Madagascar. The on-site museum recounts the history and settlement of the

BOAT EXCURSION 1: ÎLE AUX COCOS

There are 17 small islands sprinkled around Rodrigues' lagoon and perhaps the most interesting of these is Île aux Cocos. Around 1.5km long, and 150m wide at its broadest point, Île aux Cocos is a nature reserve and the only island in the Indian Ocean on which four seabirds – the lesser noddy, brown noddy, fairy tern and sooty tern – all breed. The southern quarter of the island is fenced off as a restricted zone. Elsewhere, there is a virgin quality to the place – the lesser noddies and fairy terns are remarkably tame, just as all wildlife (including the ill-fated dodo) was when the first sailors arrived on Mauritius and Rodrigues.

The reserve is overseen by Discovery Rodrigues (p172) – staff meet all boat arrivals and give a brief (and mostly French) overview of the island's more interesting features. The outfit does not, however, organise the boat trips. To do that you will need to make arrangements through your hotel, a tour operator or directly with boat owners.

Most trips depart from Pointe du Diable, although check with the boat owner when making the booking. If you don't have your own wheels, the owners may be able to arrange a pick-up from your hotel. The departure time could be anywhere from 7am to 10am depending on the tides, and the trip takes an hour each way. You'll probably end up spending around three hours on the island – bring your swimmers.

A trip to Île aux Cocos will cost around Rs 1500 per person if you organise it through your hotel, but it will cost significantly less (Rs 1000 to Rs 1200) if you go directly to the boat owner. This price includes the boat trip, park admission and a picnic lunch.

Boat owners we recommend include:

Rico François (☑875 5270) Departs from Pointe du Diable.

Tonio Jolicouer (☑5875 5720) Departs from Pointe du Diable.

Berraca Tours (☑875 3726) Departs from Pointe du Diable.

Joe 'Cool' (☑5876 2826) Departs from Pointe du Diable.

Christophe Meunier (☑5875 4442, 429 5045) Departs from Anse aux Anglais. Christophe also uses a sailing boat (rather than one with an outboard motor) and sometimes factors in extra time for snorkelling.

island, with detailed information about the extinct solitaire, cousin of the dodo.

The reserve is in the island's southwest and is poorly signposted off the main road around 1.5km northeast of the airport.

Caverne Patate   CAVE
(Map p168; tours Rs 120; ⊙tours 9am, 11am, 1pm & 3pm) Caverne Patate, in the southwestern corner of the island, is an impressive cave system with a few stalagmite and stalactite formations. Visit is by guided tour, during which a guide points out formations with uncanny resemblances to a dodo, Buckingham Palace and even Winston Churchill! The 700m tunnel is an easy walk but gets slippery in wet weather; wear shoes with a good grip and take a light jacket. Watch for the spectacular white-tailed tropicbirds soaring overhead before you go underground.

The track to the caves is signposted off the road from La Ferme (on the main road into Rodrigues from the airport) to Petite Butte. Buses en route to La Fourche can drop you at the turn-off.

Grande Montagne Nature Reserve   NATURE RESERVE
(Map p168; ☑832 5137; www.mauritian-wildlife.org; Grande Montagne; ⊙8am-3pm Mon-Fri) One of the last remaining stands of forest on Rodrigues, this nature reserve crowns the island's summit. The Mauritian Wildlife Foundation (MWF; p112) has overseen the planting of over 150,000 native plant species, and the restoration of this ecosystem has ensured the survival of the Rodrigues fody and the Rodrigues warbler bird species. Trails pass through the forest – although they're not especially well marked, it's difficult to get too lost.

Pick up the useful (and free) *Grande Montagne Nature Reserve Field Guide* at the entrance to help with plant and bird identification. The MWF was due to take over management of the reserve and interpretation centre not long after we were there.

Jardin des 5 Sens   GARDENS
(Map p168; ☑831 5860; Montagne Bois Noir; admission incl tour & small tasting session Rs 250; ⊙tours 10am, 11am, 1pm, 2pm & 3pm) This pretty

WORTH A TRIP

BOAT EXCURSION 2: ÎLE AUX CHATS & ÎLE HERMITAGE

A terrific way to see the eastern coast of Rodrigues is to take a half-day boat excursion out into the lagoon. Numerous operators in Port Sud-Est, Mourouk and Graviers, and all hotels, can make the arrangements, which usually include an hour or two's snorkelling (in an area of surprisingly strong currents), a barbecue lunch on Île aux Chats – one of the larger islands of the eastern lagoon – and then a visit to Île Hermitage, a tiny island renowned for its beauty (and possible hidden treasure). Expect to pay around Rs 1000 per person.

little botanical garden of indigenous Rodriguan plants is an interesting way to spend an hour, not to mention a good initiative. Time your visit to coincide with lunch at the attached Chez Jeanette (p178).

St Gabriel Church   CHURCH
(Map p168) This surprisingly grand church in the middle of Rodrigues has one of the largest congregations in the Port Louis diocese. Constructed between 1936 and 1939, it was built by local volunteers who arduously lugged stone, sand and coral from all corners of the island. Christianity is an integral part of life on the island – hundreds upon hundreds of Rodriguans gather here every Sunday.

🏃 Activities

Birdwatching
Rodrigues is surprisingly well known among bird-watchers, primarily for the continued presence of two species: the Rodrigues warbler (there are now more than 4000 warblers, having recovered from a low of 30 in the 1970s) and the Rodrigues fody (six pairs in 1968, 8000 individuals today). They can be seen across the island, but your best chance to see them is while hiking in the Grande Montagne Nature Reserve (p173).

Diving
Rodrigues' marine environment is remarkably well preserved. The best sites for divers lie off the eastern and southern coasts.

The main dive centres are all based in hotels, but nonguests are always welcome – just ring ahead. Figure on around Rs 1800 for a dive, including equipment.

The best season for diving coincides with high season on the island. From October to December, expect clear visibility, smooth seas, the possibility of whales, and water temperatures above 28°C. January and February are similar but with the danger of cyclones. From March to September, winds are generally stronger and water temperatures fall as low as 23°C.

The pick of the dive sites on Rodrigues:

La Passe St François (Map p168) A kilometre-long channel down to 30m, offering the full gamut of reef species.

La Basilique (Map p168) Tunnels, caves and some fabulous underwater topography.

Le Canyon (Map p168) A truly atmospheric site: a canyon that runs under the reef.

CAFÉ MARRON: THE RAREST PLANT ON EARTH

In 1980 a teacher asked his students to bring in a local plant as part of a school project. One student brought in a plant that baffled everyone. Finally, the experts at the UK's Kew Gardens identified the plant as café marron (*Ramosmania rodriguesii*), which was long thought extinct. Locals had for centuries used the plant as an aphrodisiac and as a treatment for sexually transmitted diseases, and news of its discovery leaked out. The plant was fenced off, but locals kept finding a way through. In 1986 an international operation was mounted: a cutting of the plant was flown from Rodrigues to London, where, within 24 hours, it was in Kew Gardens.

Cuttings were taken and it is from these that the Mauritian Wildlife Foundation has been able to grow more in its plant nursery. The plant is not yet out of danger – one of the plants in the Grande Montagne Nature Reserve (p173) was stolen (a younger, yet-to-flower replacement is labelled and can be seen alongside the main trail), as was another from the foundation's nursery. Even so, more than 50 have been successfully planted in the reserve. No other wild plants have ever been found, but – for the first time in living memory – the original plant recently began to grow fruit.

Bouba Diving
DIVING

(Map p168; ☑ 5920 0413, 5875 0573; www.bouba diving.com; 1/3 dives incl equipment Rs 1850/5270) Professionally run dive centre at Mourouk Ebony Hotel.

Cotton Dive Centre
DIVING, KITESURFING

(Map p168; ☑ 831 8001, 831 8208; www.cotton bayhotel.biz/diving; ⊘ closed Aug) At the Cotton Bay Hotel.

Fishing

Rod Fishing Club
FISHING

(Map p170; ☑ 875 0616; www.rodfishingclub.com; Terre Rouge) The island's leading deep-sea fishing experts make up the Rod Fishing Club, run by Yann Colas. Yann is skipper of the *Black Marlin*, which makes frequent jigging sorties from Port Mathurin. Book via the website and meet at the pier.

Hiking

Hiking is the best way to uncover the island's natural treasures – most notably, its wild, undeveloped beaches. The difficult-to-find *Carte Verte de Rodrigues*, published by the Association Rodrigues Entreprendre Au Féminin, charts the island's eight most popular hikes and provides detailed information on how to access each trailhead using public transportation.

The *Carte Verte* is available for purchase (Rs 100) at a kiosk in central Port Mathurin outside the Alfred Northcoombes Building. If you find it closed (which is often) or it's run out of stock (ditto), call ☑ 876 9170 and staff should be able to find you a copy of the map. Some hotels might also have one.

Kitesurfing

All the pros agree: Rodrigues is one of the best places in the world to kitesurf. **Club Osmosis** (Map p168; ☑ 5875 4961; www.kitesurf-rodrigues. com) and **Nest Kitesurfing School** (Map p168; ☑ 5724 1773, 832 3180; www.thenestkite surfing.com; Anse Mourouk) are the pick of the island's places.

Some of the world's best kitesurfers descend on Rodrigues in late June or early July for the Rodrigues International Kitesurfing Festival, which has been running since 2013.

Ziplining

Tyrodrig
ADVENTURE SPORTS

(Map p168; ☑ 499 6970; www.facebook.com/ tyrodrig.ilerodrigues; Montagne Bois Noir; per person Rs 1000; ⊘ 9am-noon & 1-5pm) If your idea of fun is zipping down a rope suspended over a canyon, then Tyrodrig is all yours. Five cables

---

THE NORTHEASTERN COASTAL WALK

· ·

The island's most famous walk (No 4 on the *Carte Verte*) is the classic, roughly two-hour coastal trail from **Graviers to St François** in the island's east. On the way you'll pass the island's most stunning stretches of sand, including **Trou d'Argent**, one of the Indian Ocean's prettiest cove beaches, almost completely enclosed by low cliffs, and the supposed location of a pirate's hidden booty.

If you're relying on public transport, we recommend beginning in Graviers – buses run to Graviers in the morning but are extremely scarce in the afternoon, when you're likely to have far better luck in St François.

---

hang across the void, ranging from 420m to 110m, with a drop beneath you of between 50m and 100m. The longest zipline in the Indian Ocean region, it's signposted off the main road between Mont Lubin and Grande Montagne.

✯✯ Festivals & Events

Fête du Poisson
CULTURAL

(⊘ 1st week Mar) Rodrigues lives and breathes fish, and the Fête du Poisson marks the opening of the fishing season. It is celebrated with all sorts of festivities, including fishing expeditions – and lots of eating.

Festival Kréol
CULTURAL

(⊘ late Oct) The three-day Festival Kréol entails traditional Creole ceremonies across Rodrigues.

Rodrigues International Kitesurfing Festival
SPORTS

(⊘ Jun or Jul) Some of the world's best kitesurfers descend on Rodrigues in late June or early July for the RIKF, which has been running since 2013.

🛏 Sleeping

The main concentration of hotels and guesthouses is found 2km east of Port Mathurin at Anse aux Anglais, at St François on the eastern coast and along the southern coast. Elsewhere, the guesthouses in the quieter parts of the island offer the get-away-from-it-all experience *par excellence*.

★**Chez Bernard & Claudine**　GUESTHOUSE €

(Map p168; ☑ 831 8242; cbmoneret@intnet.mu; St François; per person incl half board Rs 1300) When St François was known for its end-of-the-world seclusion, this charming Tudor-style lodge was the only place to hang your hat. The well-maintained rooms have moved into a newer building out the back and are large, light and airy. Meals here are delicious, the owners are friendly and you're well placed for walks along the east coast.

La Paillote Creole　GUESTHOUSE €

(Map p168; ☑ 5701 0448; www.lapaillotecreole. chezvotrehote.fr; Graviers; per person incl breakfast/half board Rs 800/1000) Simple but excellent thatched rondavels with tiled floors set in well-maintained grounds win universal acclaim from budget travellers. The garden needs time to mature, but the owners are friendly and there's a wonderfully end-of-the-road feel here.

Chez Jeannette　GUESTHOUSE €

(Le Tropical; Map p168; ☑ 831 5860; www.gite-letropical.com; Montagne Bois Noir; per person incl half board Rs 1400; ☎) Set high on a hill, this fine house, built partly of stone, has eight large, simple rooms that are blissfully quiet. The kitchen serves up fine food and there's even an on-site botanical garden (p173). The perfect mountain retreat.

Piment Guesthouse　GUESTHOUSE €

(Map p168; ☑ 831 8260; www.ilerodriguesgite piment.com; St François; per person incl half board Rs 1000; ❋☎) The rooms here are clean and large, if a little uninspiring, but some come with a kitchen, the family who owns the place is friendly, you're a five-minute walk from the beach and the whole establishment is quiet.

Auberge St François　GUESTHOUSE €

(Map p168; ☑ 831 8752, 5254 8655; www. auberge-rodrigues.com; St François; r/studios from €40/60; ❋) This pleasant seaside option has a long, two-storey row of comfortable rooms and less appealing apartments.

Auberge de la Montagne　GUESTHOUSE €

(Map p168; ☑ 5875 0556, 831 4607; villa@intnet. mu; Grande Montagne; per person Rs 600, incl breakfast/half board Rs 800/1500; ❋) Right at the island's mountainous heart, this guesthouse is run by the charming Baptiste family and set overlooking a wonderful orchard. Twisting hallways – the byproduct of several expansions – lead to three upstairs bedrooms that feel cosy, if a bit dated.

Auberge Lagon Bleu　GUESTHOUSE €

(Map p168; ☑ 831 0075; www.aubergelagonbleu. com; Caverne Provert; s/d/tr Rs 600/800/1000; ❋) Wicker baskets and vibrant artwork abound at this very casual guesthouse on the road towards Jean Tac. Guests congregate in the sociable eating area tucked under tin roofing and drooping laundry lines. Colourful paintings on the walls spruce up the otherwise spartan bedrooms. It's an additional Rs 600 per person for half board.

★**La Belle Rodriguaise**　GUESTHOUSE €€

(Map p168; ☑ 832 4040; www.labellerodriguaise. com; Graviers; incl half board s Rs 2450-3350, d Rs 3800-5600; ❋🏊) Laval and Françoise Baptiste's inviting seaside retreat has sundrenched rooms in charming *case*-style abodes, all with wonderfully unobstructed sea views. Up the hill, guests will find an amoeba-shaped pool and a breezy dining room set on a sweeping veranda. There's a real warmth to the welcome here, the food (p178) is outstanding and the whole place has a wonderfully remote feel. The guesthouse is near the quaint township of Graviers.

★**Cases à Gardenias**　GUESTHOUSE €€

(Map p168; ☑ 832 5751; www.casesagardenias-rodrigues.com; Montagne Bois Noir; per person incl half board from €60; @☎) The most stylish guesthouse on the island, Cases à Gardenias is the pride and joy of the delightful owners, a Belgian-Mauritian couple, who have built up their property from scratch. The beautiful plantation-inspired bedrooms have lovely stonewashed furniture (made by hand), and guests can wander the orchards or help the beekeeper tease out the sticky honey from the apiary.

It's not signposted – take the turn-off towards Chez Jeannette off the main road between Mont Lubin and Grande Montagne and it's the peach-coloured complex around 1km from the turn-off. Meals (p178) are also available here to nonguests.

Kafe Marron　GUESTHOUSE €€

(Map p168; ☑ 5706 0195; www.kafemarron.com; Pointe Coton; r Rs 2200-3200; ℗❋☎) A block from the quiet beach at Pointe Coton, Kafe Marron is a stylish little guesthouse that blends the traditional idea of a *chambre d'hôte* with the modern comforts of a quietly sophisticated B&B. Rooms have tiled floors, ample space and subtle designer touches. Run by Dorothy Lavendhomme, it's a terrific choice.

Lagon Sud   GUESTHOUSE €€
(Map p168; ☑ 5927 0976; monagravier@gmail.com; Graviers; s/d incl half board Rs 2400/3400) A soporific air hangs over this place, but therein lies its charm. The rooms in the main building are really rather nice – throw open the windows and let the sea breeze waft in – and the only things separating you from the beach are a few trees and a barely used sandy track.

★**Bakwa Lodge**   HOTEL €€€
(Map p168; ☑ 686 7662; www.bakwalodge.com; Var Brulé, Mourouk; s/d from €112/192; P ❄ 🌐) One of the most beautiful places to stay on the island, this all-white oasis where the road ends in Mourouk is classy, understated luxury. Large and flooded with natural light, the rooms are decorated with offcuts from old wooden pirogues, and most have both indoor and outdoor showers. The lovely beach helps make up for the lack of a swimming pool.

★**Tekoma**   HOTEL €€€
(Map p168; ☑ 265 5244; www.tekoma-hotel.com; St François; d incl half board €243-375; ❄ @ 🌐 🌊) 🍃 Arguably the finest address on Rodrigues, this stunning place opened in late 2012. Supremely comfortable, free-standing cabins are arrayed around a rocky headland that slopes down to a good beach, and there's a blissful sense of isolation. It also has the aim of being powered entirely by renewable energy, and the food is superb.

Mourouk Ebony Hotel   HOTEL €€€
(Map p168; ☑ 832 3351; www.mouroukebonyhotel.com; Mourouk; s/d incl half board from €130/200; ❄ 🌊) The Mourouk Ebony waits at the end of a wiggling mountain road, and is easily recognised from afar by its bright-orange roofing. The grounds feature gorgeous gardens full of orchids and wildflowers that abut the out-of-this-world beach. Gentle Creole beats waft over the lobby's hand-dyed wicker lounge chairs. The rooms are comfortable, if unspectacular.

Cotton Bay Hotel   HOTEL €€€
(Map p168; ☑ 831 8001; www.cottonbayhotel.biz; Pointe Coton; incl half board s €175-278, d €225-350, ste €275-450; P ❄ 🌐 🌊) Still going strong after more than 20 years in the business, charming Cotton Bay is the island's oldest hotel. The design scheme has an appealing Creole motif: floral trim, bamboo screens and tropically inspired prints adorn the rooms. Perks include a lovely pirogue-themed restaurant, outings on a private catamaran and endless streams of honey-tinged sand.

Pirate Lodge   HOTEL €€€
(Map p168; ☑ 831 8775; www.piratelodge.com; St François; ste incl breakfast from €150; 🌊) These attractive four- to six-bed apartments are set in a scenic palm grove visited by chirping birds. The outside design incorporates colourful Creole-inspired details, while the interiors are much more modern – IKEA-esque knick-knacks dot the living rooms and fully equipped kitchens.

🍴 Eating

Beyond Port Mathurin, most eating establishments operate from locals' homes; there are, however, a couple of full-fledged eateries. The Mourouk Ebony Hotel and Cotton Bay Hotel restaurants are also open to the public. Self-caterers will find small *superettes* (small self-service grocery stores) dotting each fishing village, but supplies are very limited in such places.

★**Chez Robert et Solange**   SEAFOOD €
(Map p168; ☑ 5733 1968; St François; mains Rs 150-500; ⊗ 8am-3pm Tue-Sun) There's an emerging trend on Mauritius and Rodrigues that we like very much: fisherfolk cooking their catch at simple open-air tables by the sea. This is the best such place in Rodrigues, with a fine setting 100m through the trees from the beach and expertly cooked food. If you're going to splurge on lobster, do it here (Rs 1500 per kilogram).

Madame Larose   MAURITIAN €
(Map p168; ☑ 876 1350; Pointe Coton; mains from Rs 350; ⊗ noon-3pm & 6-10pm) On the road down to the beach in Pointe Coton, Madame Larose is a little local gem, with no-frills service and surrounds but good, honest cooking. Fresh fish, an above-average *salade d'ourite* (octopus salad), a mean chicken curry and good salads are among the dishes on offer.

Mazavaroo   MAURITIAN €
(Map p168; ☑ 5724 2282; St François; mains around Rs 275-395; ⊗ 10am-3pm Sun-Fri) Hikers tackling a scenic east-coast jaunt can take a break at this casual, lunch-only affair. Savour the home-cooked seafood (smoked marlin, grilled fish, prawns and lobster) or house speciality *ceviché de thon jaune* (like a yellowfin-tuna tartare).

Mengoz Snack FAST FOOD €

(Map p168; Rte de l'Autonomie, Mont Lubin; mains Rs 50-150; ☺8am-4pm Mon-Sat) It doesn't get much simpler than this, but that's why we like it. In Mont Lubin, next to where the main road through the island branches to Grande Montagne, Port Mathurin and the southwest, this fine little snack bar serves up fried rice or noodles, often with a main dish such as chop suey.

Resto La Caverne MAURITIAN €

(Map p168; Petite Butte; mains from Rs 250; ☺11am-2pm & 6-9pm) If you're visiting Caverne Patate (p173) or the François Leguat Reserve (p172), you could do worse than stop by this quiet little local place above a small grocery store. The octopus dishes are particularly memorable. It's opposite the turn-off to Caverne Patate.

★ **La Belle Rodriguaise** RODRIGUAN €€

(Map p168; ☎832 4040, 832 4359; Graviers; 3-course meal Rs 650; ☺noon-2.30pm) Perfected recipes by Françoise, author of a respected Rodriguan cookbook, are served on a breezy veranda with never-ending ocean views. Meals are mostly for guests of the hotel, but ring ahead if you'd like to crash the party.

Chez Jeanette RODRIGUAN €€

(Le Tropical; Map p168; ☎831 5860; www.gite-le-tropical.com; Montagne Bois Noir; meals Rs 400-500; ☺11am-2pm & 7-9pm) Traditional Rodriguan flavours are what you'll get at this friendly guesthouse (p176) hidden in the hills. Dishes always feature an assortment of vegetables grown in the property's gardens.

Cases à Gardenias RODRIGUAN €€

(Map p168; ☎832 5751; Montagne Bois Noir; meals from Rs 500) Friendly guesthouse (p176) hosts serve a range of homemade goodies: wine, honey, fresh fruit, preserves and cured meats.

❶ Getting Around

BUS

The main bus station (Map p170) is in Port Mathurin. In addition to the airport bus, the most useful routes are those to Grand Baie and Pointe Coton in the east of the island, and to Gravier, Port Sud-Est and Rivière Cocos on the south coast. All apart from the Grand Baie buses pass through Mont Lubin in the centre of the island. Most buses operate every 30 to 60 minutes from about 7am to 4pm Monday to Saturday on most routes. The Sunday service is fairly sporadic. Expect to pay Rs 15 to Rs 40 depending on your destination.

RENTING IN RODRIGUES

Although there are some formal car-rental options in Rodrigues, if you arrange a vehicle through your guesthouse it will likely be a more informal process. That can mean that someone turns up at the airport when you arrive and hands you the keys to a large pick-up. Then away you go, dropping the person off at a spot of their choosing somewhere along the way. While this may be an endearingly Rodriguan way of doing things, it's worth remembering that you may not be insured in the case of an accident – insist on insurance or go with someone else who will provide it.

CAR

The road system in Rodrigues has improved enormously in recent years and sealed roads now lead to most parts of the island. Though 4WD vehicles are no longer strictly necessary, most hire cars are still sturdy pick-ups.

Car rental can be arranged through most hotels and guesthouses and local tour operators, who will deliver all over the island. Expect to pay at least Rs 1200 per day; the price is usually the same whether you have a sedan or a pick-up. Most importantly, make sure you have sufficient petrol before setting off for the day – there are only three petrol stations on the island (in Port Mathurin, Mont Lubin and near the airport, although distances are small).

Three recommended rental agencies to contact in advance are:

➡ JP Excursions (p172)

➡ 2000 Tours (p172)

➡ Rotourco (p172)

BICYCLE & MOTORCYCLE

If your hotel or guesthouse doesn't offer bike or motorcycle rental, contact Rotourco or one of the other travel agencies in Port Mathurin. The going rate is around Rs 200 per day for a bike and Rs 600 to Rs 650 for a scooter. It costs Rs 350 to fill a scooter's petrol tank. Note that unless you're in it for the exercise, we recommend a scooter over a bicycle, as many of the interior roads can be discouragingly hilly.

TAXI

Most taxis on Rodrigues are 4WD pick-ups. Expect to pay between Rs 500 and Rs 1000 depending on location. You can also hire taxis by the day for an island tour; expect to pay Rs 2000 to Rs 3000.

Understand Rodrigues

Rodrigues Today

Despite moves towards greater autonomy, Rodrigues still feels itself ignored by policy-makers on the main island of Mauritius and some are looking to take the next step. As such, complete independence remains a fervent desire for some and, in April 2010, the Muvman Independantis Rodriguais (MIR) was launched when two candidates ran for government positions as 'Rodriguans' rather than 'Mauritians'. Although they were rebuffed, the issue won't go away any time soon.

In the meantime, Rodrigues' Regional Assembly is trying to tackle the overriding problems of population growth, poverty and critical water shortages. This third problem is a grave one, and there is year-round rationing. New hotels and many existing ones are being forced to look towards sustainable water options (including desalination), and it's an issue of long-term concern for the island.

History

Rodrigues is named after the Portuguese navigator Don Diégo Rodriguez, who was the first European to discover the uninhabited island in 1528. Dutch sailors were the next to pay a call, albeit very briefly, in 1601, followed a few years later by the French.

At first Rodrigues was simply a place where ships could take refuge from storms and replenish their supplies of fresh water and meat. Giant tortoises were especially prized because they could be kept alive on board for months. Over the years thousands were taken or killed until they completely died out. Rodrigues also had a big flightless bird, the solitaire, which went the same sorry way as its distant cousin, the dodo.

The first serious attempt at colonisation occurred in 1691 when Frenchman François Leguat and a band of seven Huguenot companions fled religious persecution at home in search of a 'promised land'. Crops grew well and the island's fauna and flora were a source of wonder. Even so, after two years, life on a paradise island began to pall, not least due to the lack of female company. With no boat of their own (the ship they arrived on failed to return as promised), Leguat and his friends built a craft out of driftwood and eventually made it to Mauritius.

In 1735, the French founded a permanent colony on Rodrigues with a small settlement at Port Mathurin, but the colony never really prospered. When the British – who wanted a base from which to attack French-ruled Mauritius – invaded in 1809, they were met with little resistance.

In 1967, Rodriguans distinguished themselves by voting against independence from Britain by a whopping 90% (the rest of Mauritius voted strongly in favour). It was a dramatic illustration of the difference in outlook between the two islands. Following independence, Rodriguans continued to argue that their needs were significantly different from those of the rest of the country and that, in any case, they were being neglected by the central government.

The campaign was led by Serge Clair and his Organisation du Peuple de Rodrigues (OPR), founded in 1976. His patience and political skill eventually paid off. In 2001 it was announced that Rodrigues would be allowed a degree of autonomy, notably in socio-economic affairs and in the management of its natural resources. The following year 18 councillors were elected; the Regional Assembly was formally inaugurated in 2002 with Serge Clair as chief commissioner.

Réunion

POP 845,000 / ☎262

Best Places to Eat

➜ Les Letchis (p266)

➜ L'Eveil des Sens – Le Blue Margouillat (p210)

➜ Auberge Paysanne Le Palmier (p257)

➜ Le QG (p236)

➜ Le Saint-Michel (p201)

Best Places to Sleep

➜ Senteur Vanille (p200)

➜ Rougail Mangue (p254)

➜ Villa Belle (p244)

➜ Diana Dea Lodge & Spa (p267)

➜ Dan'n Tan Lontan (p257)

Why Go?

Réunion is one of the Indian Ocean's last great island adventures. The diversity of landscapes is truly astonishing for such a small pocket. Jutting out of the ocean like a basaltic shield cloaked in green, this scenically magical island is a mini-Hawaii. What to expect? Emerald forests, tumbling waterfalls, awesome mountainscapes, twisting roads, soul-stirring panoramas, energetic coastal cities and a sprinkling of white- or black-sand beaches. The formidable Piton de la Fournaise, one of the world's most accessible active volcanoes, adds to the thrill. Small wonder that Réunion is a dream destination for nature and outdoor lovers. Hiking is the number-one activity, but canyoning, paragliding, rafting, horseback riding, diving, whale-watching and climbing are also available.

There's also plenty to compel culture aficionados. Réunion has a fascinating Creole, African, Indian, Chinese and French heritage, with a wealth of architectural treasures and vibrant festivals that are a great occasion to immerse yourself in local culture.

When to Go

➜ Réunion's climate experiences only two distinct seasons: the hot, rainy summer from December to April and the cool, dry winter from late April to November. Temperatures on the coast average 22°C in winter and 27°C in summer. In the mountains they drop to 11°C and 18°C, respectively.

➜ Peak tourist season is during the French school holidays from July to early September. From October through to the New Year holidays is also busy, but after this everything eases down during cyclone-prone February and March.

➜ The drier winter months are the most favourable for hiking, as some of the trails are simply impassable when it's wet. The east coast is considerably wetter than the west.

➜ Whale-watching season runs from June to October.

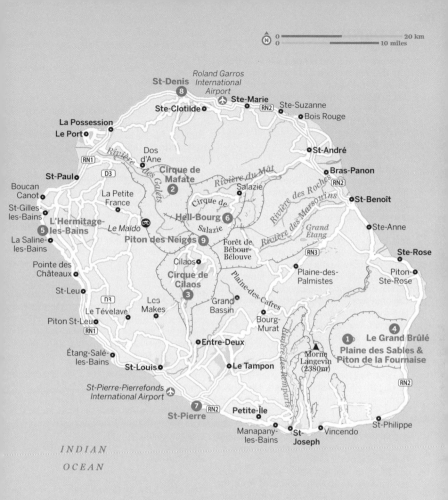

Réunion Highlights

1 Plaine des Sables & Piton de la Fournaise (p236)
Gorging your senses on the Martian landscapes.

2 Cirque de Mafate (p231)
Exploring the topography of these fabulous landforms.

3 Cirque de Cilaos (p217)
Canyoning in this weird-and-wonderful vertical world.

4 Le Grand Brûlé (p258)
Looking out over the barren moonscape of this solidified, pure black lava field.

5 L'Hermitage-les-Bains (p202) Immersing yourself in the island's steamy nightlife.

6 Hell-Bourg (p227)
Checking out this picturesque town and its appealing Creole houses.

7 St-Pierre (p239)
Discovering the colonial heritage and great nightlife.

8 St-Denis (p182) Going heritage-hunting among the Creole buildings.

9 Piton des Neiges (p217)
Huffing to the top of for sensational views.

ST-DENIS

POP 145,300

Francophiles will feel comfortable in St-Denis (san-de-*nee*), the capital of Réunion. Except for the palms and flamboyant trees to remind you that you're somewhere sunnier (and hotter), St-Denis could be easily mistaken for a French provincial enclave, with a flurry of trendy shops, brasseries, bistros and *boulangeries* (bakeries).

With most of Réunion's tourist attractions located elsewhere on the island, most visitors only stay long enough to rent a car before dashing off to more magnetic locations. But St-Denis warrants more than a fleeting glance. Scratch beneath the French polish and you'll soon realise that the city also boasts an undeniably Creole soul, with some delightful colonial and religious buildings and a casual multi-ethnic atmosphere.

If that's not enough, there are always epicurean indulgences. Sip a coffee at a chic cafe listening to a *séga* (traditional African music and dance) or *maloya* (traditional dance music of Réunion) soundtrack or indulge in fine dining at a gourmet restaurant.

History

St-Denis was founded in 1668 by the governor Regnault, who named the settlement after a ship that ran aground here. But St-Denis didn't really start to develop until the governor Mahé de Labourdonnais moved the capital here from St-Paul in 1738; the harbour was in general more sheltered and easier to defend, and water more abundant.

The 19th century ushered in St-Denis' golden age. As money poured in from the sugar plantations, the town's worthies built themselves fine mansions, some of which can still be seen along Rue de Paris and in the surrounding streets. But in the late 1800s the bottom dropped out of the sugar market and the good times came to a stuttering end. St-Denis' fortunes only began to revive when it became the new departmental capital in 1946. To cope with the influx of civil servants, financiers and office workers, the city expanded rapidly eastwards along the coast and up the mountains behind. Even today the cranes are much in evidence as St-Denis struggles to house its ever-growing population.

◉ Sights

St-Denis is devoid of beach, but it boasts a gaggle of well-preserved colonial buildings harking back to the city's heyday in the 19th century. The larger colonial piles are mainly strung out along Rue de Paris, Ave de la Victoire, Rue Pasteur and Rue Jean Chatel. It's also home to a smattering of impressive religious buildings.

Maison Kichenin   HISTORIC BUILDING
(Map p184; 42 Rue Labourdonnais) This perfectly preserved Creole mansion was built in the 1790s and is considered one of the oldest of its kind in St-Denis. The well-proportioned fountain in the garden is a highlight.

**Conseil Général de la Réunion –
Direction de la Culture**   HISTORIC BUILDING
(Villa du Département; Map p184; 18 Rue de Paris) You can't miss this villa – it's one of the most elegant of St-Denis' Creole buildings, with a superb *varangue* (veranda), finely crafted *lambrequins* (filigree-style decoration), and a manicured garden with a fountain. It was built in 1804.

Préfecture   HISTORIC BUILDING
(Map p184; Place de la Préfecture) One of the grandest buildings in St-Denis, the Préfecture began life as a coffee warehouse in 1734 and later served as the headquarters of the French East India Company.

Former Hôtel de Ville   HISTORIC BUILDING
(Town Hall; Map p184; Rue de Paris) Many consider the neoclassical Former Hôtel de Ville, at the north end of Rue de Paris, to be the city's most beautiful building; it's certainly very imposing, with its regimented columns, balustrades, bright-yellow façade and jaunty clock tower.

Palais Rontaunay   HISTORIC BUILDING
(Map p184; 5 Rue Rontaunay) Built in 1854, the Palais Rontaunay is a bourgeois villa which has preserved the elegant style of the 19th century.

Maison Deramond-Barre   HISTORIC BUILDING
(Map p184; 15 Rue de Paris) This colonial structure dating from the 1830s was the family home of former French prime minister Raymond Barre and the birthplace of the poet and painter Léon Dierx. It's well worth a peek for its well-preserved architecture and harmonious proportions.

Mosquée Noor E Islam   MOSQUE
(Map p184; 121 Rue Maréchal Leclerc; ⊘9am-noon & 2-4pm except prayer times) One of St-Denis' most iconic buildings, the Grande Mosquée dominates the centre with its tall minaret. Its cool white-and-green interior is a haven of

peace. The Islamic community in St-Denis is very traditional, so if you wish to visit, dress and behave with respect.

Cathédrale de St-Denis   CHURCH
(Map p184; Place de la Cathédrale) Ambling down Ave de la Victoire, you'll come across the Tuscan-style Cathédrale de St-Denis, which was constructed between 1829 and 1832. As a cathedral this is a disappointment, since it looks more like a small New England mission church with its single, cream-plastered spire.

Pagode Guan Di   BUDDHIST
(Map p184; Rue Sainte-Anne; ⊘8.30-11am Mon, Wed & Sun) Blink and you'll miss this pagoda, which is used by the Chinese community.

Tamil Temple   HINDU TEMPLE
(Kovil Kalikambal Temple; Map p184; 259 Rue Maréchal Leclerc) St-Denis' small but wildly colourful Hindu temple stands out among a row of shops on a busy road. Visitors are not allowed inside the temple.

Musée Léon Dierx   MUSEUM
(Map p184; ☑0262 20 24 82; 28 Rue de Paris; adult/child €2/free; ⊘9.30am-5pm Tue-Sun) Housed in the former bishop's palace, built in 1845, this museum hosts Réunion's most important collection of modern art. The more high-profile works may include paintings, sculptures and ceramics by Rousseau, Gauguin and Bernard (the works exhibited change every three months). You can also see a few paintings by the Réunionnais poet and painter Léon Dierx (1838–1912).

L'Artothèque   GALLERY
(Map p184; ☑0262 41 75 50; 26 Rue de Paris; ⊘9.30am-5.30pm Tue-Sun) FREE This contemporary art gallery hosts changing exhibitions of works by local artists and those from neighbouring countries. It's housed in a handsome pale-yellow villa.

Maison Carrère   MUSEUM
(Map p184; ☑0262 41 83 00; 14 Rue de Paris; €3; ⊘9am-5pm Mon-Sat) This meticulously restored mansion dating from the 1820s is a beautiful example of Creole architecture, with its elaborate veranda and intricate *lambrequins* (filigree-style decoration) on the front of the eaves. The museum does an excellent job of explaining the city's colonial past. It also houses the tourist office.

Musée d'Histoire Naturelle   MUSEUM
(Map p184; ☑0262 20 02 19; Jardin de l'État; €2; ⊘9.30am-5.30pm Tue-Sun) Go eye to eye with lemurs and other stuffed specimens in this museum located in the Jardin de l'État. Besides impressive lemurs, you'll see a good insect and bird collection on the 1st floor.

Jardin de l'État   GARDENS
(Botanical Gardens; Map p184; Rue Général de Gaulle; ⊘7am-6pm) FREE Created in 1763, the attractive Jardin de l'État, at the southern end of Rue de Paris, is a good place to recharge the batteries and be introduced to a variety of tropical plants and trees. The Musée d'Histoire Naturelle stands at the far end of the gardens.

Le Barachois   WATERFRONT
(Map p184) This seafront park, lined by cannons facing out to sea, is a good place to catch the sea breeze in St-Denis. It has an area set aside for *pétanque* (a game similar to bowls), cafes and a monument (Map p184; Place Sarda Garriga) to the Réunion-born aviator Roland Garros, leaning nonchalantly on a propeller.

Notre-Dame de la Délivrance   CHURCH
(Map p184; ⊘8am-6pm) Notre-Dame de la Délivrance (1893), which sits on the hillside across the usually dry Rivière St-Denis, is noteworthy for the statue of St Expédit just inside the door, dressed as a young Roman soldier.

🛏 Sleeping

Most hotels tend to be dull multistorey blocks that are designed with business travellers in mind. Budget beds are an endangered species and the choice of upmarket accommodation is surprisingly limited. There is high demand throughout the year for accommodation, so advance booking is highly recommended.

Chez Nicole Maillot   B&B €
(☑0262 53 81 64; http://chambresdhotesnicolemaillot.jimdo.com; 54 Rue Nono Robert, La Confiance-les-Bas, Ste-Marie; d/tr incl breakfast €55/67; P 🛜 ❄) From this B&B hidden in the hills above the airport, you can easily reach St-Denis (10km), the airport (5km) and the east coast, making it an ideal base. The three rooms are nothing too out of the ordinary, but it's the hush, the sea views, the tropical garden and the small pool that make this place special.

No meals (except breakfast) are served but there's a communal kitchen. There's a two-night minimum stay.

St-Denis

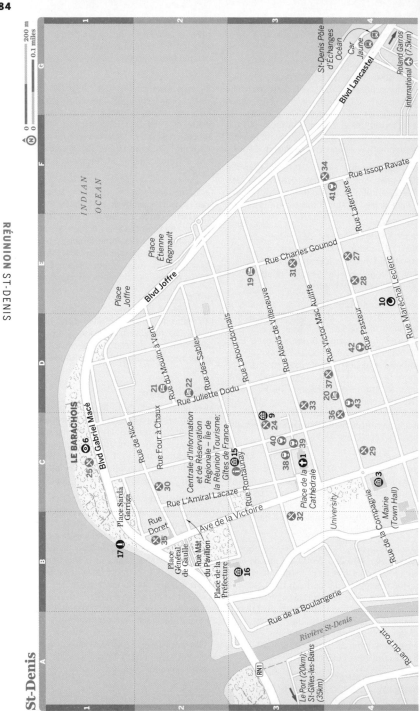

185

RÉUNION ST-DENIS

Rue Maréchal Leclerc
Blvd de l'Océan

18

Rue Roland Garros

Rue Sainte-Marie

Rue de Montreuil

Rue Saint Bernard

14 Rue des Limites

Rue Jules Olivier

Rue Jules Auber

Rue Morseigneur de Beaumont

Rue Général de Gaulle

Rue de Caen

Rue Monthyon

Rue Mazagran

Rue Ruisseau des Noirs

Rue Juliette

Rue Sainte-Anne

Rue Roland Garros

Rue Sainte-Marie

Rue Jean Chatel

Rue Malartic

Rue Poivre

Mercure Créolia
(3km)

11

46

4

Jardin
de l'Etat

Rue de la Source

23

Office du
Tourisme

7 Rue Félix-Guyon

5 12

Rue de Paris

2

8

44

Rue Maréchal Leclerc

26

45

Rue Lucien Gasparin

Rue Général de Gaulle

Rue Fénelon

Rue Bertin

Rue Milius

Rue Philibert

Rue Tourette

Rue de la République

Quai Est

Quai Ouest

Rampes
Ozoux

Rue de la Digue

CD41

Hôtel Bellepierre
(1.2km)

13

St-Denis

Hôtel Phoenix   HOTEL €
(Map p184; ☑0262 41 51 81; http://phoenix-hotel.e-monsite.com; 1 Rue du Moulin à Vent; s €48, d €51-56, incl breakfast; ❄ 🖧) This little number is in a tranquil street within stumbling distance of the centre. The rooms got a lick of paint in 2016, and there are plans to modernise the bathrooms. On the whole, the place is clean and fair value, especially if you consider that rates include breakfast, there's air-con (from 7pm to 7am only) and free wi-fi.

Some rooms face a concrete wall; try for room 5, 6 or 7, with a balcony.

★ La Maison d'Edith   B&B €€
(☑0692 69 66 05; www.maisondedith.com; 59 Chemin Commins, La Montagne; d incl breakfast €100-110; 🅿 🖧 ❄) The owners are passionate about Creole culture and have renovated this mansion with a happy respect for the spirit of the place. Curl up with your sweetie in one of the three rooms complete with period furniture, Creole ceilings and rich fabrics. Best asset is the vast garden, with top ocean views and a superb swimming pool. A great place to decompress.

One minus: bathrooms are not en suite. It's in La Montagne, about 10km from St-Denis (10 to 15 minutes by car) – you'll need a vehicle.

La Villa des Cannes   B&B €€
(Map p260; ☑0692 06 45 22, 0262 37 32 13; www.lavilladescannes.com; 17 Lotissement Lisa, Chiendent, Route du Paradis, Ste-Marie; d/q incl breakfast €150/230; 🅿 ❄ 🖧 ❄) Run by a widely travelled French couple, this boutique-style B&B perched in the hills above Ste-Marie shelters three superb rooms that are individually decorated with a contemporary twist. The Sarkova room may not be to everybody's taste, though; the bathroom is not separated from the bedroom. The glistening pool is the perfect remedy to a day spent on twisty roads.

It's a bit tricky to find; see the website for directions.

Central Hôtel   HOTEL €€
(Map p184; ☑0262 94 18 08; www.centralhotel. re; 37 Rue de la Compagnie; s €56-96, d €76-108, incl breakfast; 🅿 ❄ 🖧) The Central gets by on its handy location, a waddle away from restaurants, bars and shops. It offers bland, fairly

identical-looking hotel rooms without much island flavour, but has private parking (12 spaces only) and all bathrooms were upgraded in 2016. Some rooms come with a balcony. Ask for a 1st-floor room if your suitcase is heavy – there's no lift.

Austral Hôtel HOTEL €€
(Map p184; ✉ 0262 94 45 67; www.hotel-austral. fr; 20 Rue Charles Gounod; s €81-91, d €95-105; P ❄ @ 🛜 ☲) This venerable establishment is not quite the three-star heavyweight it thinks it is, but the rooms have the requisite comforts, location is tip-top, bathrooms were modernised in 2015, facilities are good and there's a small pool. There's limited private parking (arrive early to secure a space).

If you plan to stay here, aim high – the rooms and views get better the higher you go. Rooms 301, 302, 306, 307 and 308 have the best sea views.

Hôtel Bellepierre HOTEL €€€
(✉ 0262 51 51 51; www.hotel-bellepierre.com; 91bis Allée des Topazes; s €187-207, d €200-224, ste from €254, incl breakfast; P ❄ 🛜 ☲) Life feels less hurried in this oasis of calm, about 3km south of the centre. As you'd expect from a four-star establishment, rooms are spacious, well fitted out and comfortable. The pièce de résistance is the medium-sized pool, which seems to melt into the sea on the horizon.

The rooms in the more recent building are the quietest and offer jaw-dropping views over the coast. Lovers of fine food will enjoy the cooking here – the on-site restaurant gets great reviews.

Villa Angélique BOUTIQUE HOTEL €€€
(Map p184; ✉ 0262 48 41 48; www.villa-angelique. fr; 39 Rue de Paris; s €145-185, d €165-195, incl breakfast; ❄ 🛜) The closest thing St-Denis has to a boutique hotel, the Villa Angélique occupies a nicely renovated historic building and is just oozing with atmosphere. It's a modern twist on colonial decor: there are polished wood floors, beautiful wooden furniture, sparkling bathrooms and heavenly beds. There's a reputable on-site restaurant (open to all comers). One downside: there's no private parking.

Mercure Créolia HOTEL €€€
(✉ 0262 94 26 26; www.mercure.com; 14 Rue du Stade, Montgaillard; d €110-215; P ❄ @ 🛜 ☲) Mercure Créolia is located some 4km south of the city centre in a tranquil neighbourhood; your efforts in getting here are rewarded with splendid views over the coast. Rooms are functional and unflashy, and the decor

is nothing special, but the setting and the relaxed-yet-professional feel more than make up for the slightly dated sense of style.

Amenities include a bar, a restaurant and a gym. Note that the cheaper rooms overlook the parking lot. The best asset is the pool, one of the biggest in Réunion. Booking online gets you the best deals.

Le Juliette Dodu HOTEL €€€
(Map p184; ✉ 0262 20 91 20; www.hotel-jdodu. com; 31 Rue Juliette Dodu; s €110-165, d €160-190, ste €215-250, incl breakfast; P ❄ @ 🛜 ☲) Live like a colonial administrator in this stylish 19th-century Creole building. Although the cheaper rooms feel claustrophobic and are unextraordinary, there are still enough vintage touches in the reception area – period furnishings, plump armchairs and old-fashioned tiles – to satisfy the snob within, with the added lure of a pool and a cosy restaurant. Bonus: there's (limited) private parking. It's a two-minute strut south of the Barachois.

🍴 Eating

Thanks to the French passion for gastronomy, St-Denis is heaven for food lovers, with a smorgasbord of eateries to suit all palates and budgets. Note that many bars also serve food.

Perlin Pain Pain BAKERY €
(Map p184; ✉ 0262 23 01 21; www.perlinpainpain. re; 43 Rue de la Compagnie; sandwiches & snacks €3.50-10.50; ⊙ 5.30am-7.30pm Mon-Sat, to noon Sun; 🛜) Hands down the best bakery-deli in St-Denis, with a tantalising array of brioches, croissants, *macatias* (a variety of bun), sandwiches, burgers and bagels. It's also ideal for a refreshing cup of coffee or a quick and affordable sit-down lunch as you explore the city. Excellent breakfasts too. There's a luminous, appealing dining room at the back.

Le Caudan INDIAN €
(Map p184; ✉ 0262 94 39 00; 38 Rue Charles Gounod; mains €8-13; ⊙ 10am-10pm Tue-Sat, to 2pm Sun-Mon) Tasty Indo-Mauritian snacks and ready-made meals are the order of the day at this under-the-radar neighbourhood venture set in a small Creole house. The homemade biryani is the speciality here. A glass of *alouda* (sweet, milky drink) or a cardamom tea will round things off nicely. Takeaways available.

L'Igloo ICE CREAM €
(Map p184; ✉ 0262 21 34 69; www.liglooleffetglace. re; 67 Rue Jean Chatel; ice creams €2-13, mains €10-21; ⊙ 11.30am-midnight Mon-Thu, 3-11.30pm Sun; 🛜) Generous scoops and about 30 flavours

are the trademarks of this drool-inducing ice-cream parlour in the heart of St-Denis. Take your mind off the somewhat tacky white-and-blue Antarctica murals by trying the Banana Split, with its deep, rich flavour; chocoholics will opt for the 'Palette aux 6 Chocolats', with six different chocolate flavours. Snacks and light meals (salads, omelettes) are available at lunchtime.

Le Massalé DESSERTS €

(Map p184; ☑ 0262 21 75 06; 30 Rue Alexis de Ville-neuve; sweets from €0.50; ⏱ 11.30am-7pm Mon-Thu, Sat & Sun & 3-7pm Fri) This teeny outlet tempts you with its colourful array of Indian snacks and sweets to eat in or take away. Perennial favourites include samosas, candy-pink or apple-green *barfi* (a milk-based sweet) as well as *gulab* (fritters flavoured with carda-mom). Wash it down with a glass of *alouda*.

Camions Bars du Barachois FAST FOOD €

(Map p184; Blvd Gabriel Macé; mains €3-7; ⏱ 11am-2pm & 6pm-midnight) If money matters, these cheap and cheerful food vans on the seafront are the ideal pit stop. Get generous sandwiches or everything and anything else from curries to salads. The food's nothing to write home about but they stay open late, even on Sunday.

★ Le 144 INTERNATIONAL €€

(Map p184; ☑ 0262 11 24 07; www.le-144.com; 12 Rue de Nice; mains €12-23, menu €16; ⏱ noon-2.30pm & 7-10pm Tue-Sat; 🐾) A surprisingly hip restaurant inside a Creole house complete with trendy, colourful interior, this cool culi-nary outpost is one of the most atmospheric spots in St-Denis and serves European-inspired dishes with a twist. Local gour-mands rave about the risotto and the 'Burger 144', with *raclette* cheese.

★ Le Reflet des Îles CREOLE €€

(Map p184; ☑ 0262 21 73 82; www.lerefletdesiles. com; 114 Rue Pasteur; mains €14-25; ⏱ noon-2pm & 7-9.30pm Mon-Sat) This much-lauded eatery is the best place in St-Denis to try authentic Creole food by dipping into one of 15 cracking *carris* (curries) and *civets* (stews). There are also Western-style fish and meat dishes on of-fer if your tummy and palate are timid. The menu is translated into English – a rarity in Réunion.

Le Comptoir du Potager MODERN FRENCH €€

(Map p184; ☑ 0692 85 59 31; www.facebook. com/AuComptoirDuPotager; 8bis Rue Labour-donnais; menus €20-23; ⏱ noon-1.45pm Mon-Fri, 7.30-9.30pm Fri & Sat) For contemporary bistro cuisine, this boho-flavoured den is a winner. Pick from creative concoctions chalked on the board, and whatever you do, don't miss out on the exquisite homemade desserts. The concise menu changes every three weeks. It fills up in the blink of an eye at lunchtime, so book a table or show up early.

La Calade MEDITERRANEAN €€

(Map p184; ☑ 0262 20 32 32; www.facebook.com/LaCaladeRestaurant; 88 Rue Pasteur; mains €15-24; ⏱ noon-2pm & 7-10pm Tue-Sat; 🐾) The street en-trance is rather discreet, but the French chef has received much attention since he opened his restaurant. Whether in the flowery garden or inside the elegant dining room, the food here is everything you'd want Mediterranean cuisine to be: super-fresh, packed with fla-vours, and good value.

Snack-Bar Chez Jean-Marc CREOLE €€

(Map p184; ☑ 0262 21 46 70; Rue du Maréchal Leclerc; mains €12-16; ⏱ 11.45am-2.30pm Mon-Sat) The food is simple but fresh and tasty at this low-key eatery hidden within the market (at the back). It's a good place to catch the street vibe and enjoy plenty of local colour.

Bistrot de la Porte des Lilas FRENCH €€

(Map p184; ☑ 0262 41 40 69; www.bistrotdeslilas. fr; 38bis Rue Labourdonnais; mains €12-24, lunch menus €19-24; ⏱ noon-2pm & 7.30-10pm Mon-Sat) This intimate restaurant serves up refined versions of French classics with an exotic twist. At €19, the lunchtime menu is a steal. There's outdoor seating at the back.

Kim Son VIETNAMESE €€

(Map p184; ☑ 0262 21 75 00; 13 Rue du Maréchal Leclerc; mains €9-16; ⏱ noon-2pm Mon-Fri, 7-9.30pm Wed-Sat) A St-Denis classic, Kim Son has been dishing up wholesome Vietnamese cuisine for more than 20 years. Musts include Vietnam-ese salad and spring rolls.

L'Arto Carpe FRENCH €€

(Map p184; ☑ 0262 21 55 48; 9 Ruelle Edouard; mains €14-23; ⏱ noon-2pm & 7-10pm Tue-Sat, bar 10am-midnight Tue-Sat; 🐾) Tucked in a pedes-trianised alley behind the cathedral, this zinging restaurant built in a restored stone structure is a good choice if you're tired of heavy Creole classics. The concise menu in-volves seasonal, fresh ingredients, and dishes are imaginatively prepared and beautifully presented. Tapas (€5 to €11) are served from 6pm. It also doubles as a bar.

Le Roland Garros
BRASSERIE €€

(Map p184; ☑0262 41 44 37; 2 Place du 20 Décembre 1848; mains €16-22, lunch menu €15; ☺noon-midnight; ☎) This St-Denis institution has the feel of a true Parisian bistro – packed and full of attitude. It offers brasserie food that's decent, but the menu covers enough territory to suit most palates. Its tartares and daily specials are well worth a try. Oh, and it's open on Sunday (a rarity in St-Denis).

★La Fabrique
FUSION €€€

(Map p184; ☑0262 19 80 60; www.lafabrique restaurant.re; 76 Rue Pasteur; mains €24-27, lunch menus €25-28, dinner menu €45; ☺noon-2pm Tue-Sat, 7.45-10pm Fri & Sat; ☎) Innovative cuisine reigns supreme under the stewardship of young chef Jehan Colson. With its intimate dining room, small terrace, industrial-chic decor and delicious cuisine, La Fabrique has honed the art of dining out to perfection. Expect succulent concoctions prepared with top-of-the-line ingredients. The wine list is another hit, with well-chosen French tipples.

L'Atelier de Ben
FUSION €€€

(Map p184; ☑0262 41 85 73; www.atelier-de-ben. com; 12 Rue de la Compagnie; mains €24-30, lunch menus €23-27; ☺noon-1.15pm & 7.30-9.15pm Tue-Sat) A true alchemist, the French chef Benoît Vantaux has got the magic formula right, fusing French with Creole and Asian to create stunning cuisine, perfectly matched with French tipples. Exquisite executions extend to the small dessert selection.

🍸 Drinking & Nightlife

Most of Réunion's action is down the coast at L'Hermitage-les-Bains and St-Pierre, but there are a handful of OK nightspots to keep you entertained in St-Denis. The most happening area is beside the cathedral, where more than half-a-dozen bars are concentrated in the span of only one or two blocks.

Le Passage du Chat Blanc
BAR

(Map p184; ☑0692 97 00 05; www.facebook.com/ passage974; 26 Rue Jean Chatel; ☺5pm-midnight Wed-Sun) A trendy crowd flocks to this hugely popular bar. Besides featuring great cocktails, there's live music – house music, afro beat, rock, electro – most nights of the week.

Café Edouard
BAR

(Map p184; ☑0262 28 45 02; 13 Ruelle Edouard; ☺10am-11.30pm Mon-Sat; ☎) The place to hang out, this buzzy bar with outdoor tables has a great selection of beers and spirits. There's also well-priced bar food for lunch and dinner.

KT Dral
BAR

(Map p184; ☑0692 95 92 00; www.facebook. com/ktdral; 5 Ruelle Saint-Paul; ☺10am-11.30pm Mon-Sat; ☎) Tucked in an alley behind the cathedral, this congenial bar is packed to the rafters on weekends and you come here as much for a cocktail as for the lively atmosphere. Don't miss the *concert* (live band) on Thursday or Friday evening. Skip the food.

O'Bar
BAR

(Map p184; ☑0262 52 57 88; 32 Rue de la Compagnie; ☺10am-1am Mon-Thu, 10am-2am Fri-Sat; ☎) A funky drinking spot right in the centre. The streetside terrace allows for a dash of people-watching. Food is only so-so. Tapas are served from 6.30pm.

Le Zanzibar
BAR

(Map p184; ☑0262 20 01 18; 41 Rue Pasteur; ☺bar 5pm-midnight, restaurant noon-2pm & 7-10pm Mon-Sat, 7-10pm Sun) Part bar, part restaurant, this 'tropical bistro' is the hang-out of well-connected locals and serves devilishly good tropical potions. Feeling peckish? Keep up your strength with a tuna tartare or a homemade burger.

Le Prince Club
GAY

(Map p184; ☑0692 38 28 28; 108 Rue Pasteur; ☺10.30pm-4am Fri-Sat) A gay-friendly bar and club.

🛍 Shopping

The main shopping streets are the semi-pedestrianised Rue Maréchal Leclerc and Rue Juliette Dodu.

L'Effet Péi
CLOTHING

(Map p184; ☑0262 29 25 60; www.leffetpei.re; 54 Rue du Maréchal Leclerc; ☺9am-6.30pm Mon-Sat) Fill your suitcase with island-made T-shirts, swimsuits, skirts, shorts, dresses and accessories. For men, women and kids.

Boutique Pardon
CLOTHING

(Map p184; ☑0262 41 15 62; www.shop-pardon.net; cnr Rue Maréchal Leclerc & Rue Jean Chatel; ☺9am-6.30pm Mon-Sat) Get glammed up at this trend-setting boutique stocking island-made shirts, T-shirts, dresses and accessories.

Grand Marché
MARKET

(Map p184; 2 Rue Maréchal Leclerc; ☺8am-6pm Mon-Sat) This market has a mishmash of items for sale, including Malagasy wooden handicrafts, fragrant spices, woven baskets, embroidery, T-shirts, furniture and a jumble of knick-knacks.

ⓘ Information

MEDICAL SERVICES

Cabinet Médical de Garde Saint-Vincent (☑ 0262 477 210; cnr Rue de Paris & Rue Maréchal Leclerc; ⊙ 7pm-midnight Mon-Fri, 2pm-midnight Sat, 8am-midnight Sun) A small clinic (two doctors) that's open outside regular business hours.

Centre Hospitalier Félix Guyon (☑ 0262 90 50 50; Allées des Topazes, Bellepierre) Réunion's main hospital has 24-hour medical and dental treatment and English-speaking staff.

TOURIST INFORMATION

Centrale d'Information et de Réservation Régionale – Île de la Réunion Tourisme (Map p184; ☑ 0810 1600 00; www.reunion.fr) Provides information and does bookings for activities, B&Bs, hotels and *gîtes de montagne*. It also offers hiking information.

Gîtes de France (Map p184; ☑ 0262 72 97 81; www.gites-de-france-reunion.com) Information on *chambres d'hôtes* (family-run B&Bs).

Office du Tourisme (Map p184; ☑ 0262 41 83 00; www.lebeaupays.com; Maison Carrère, 14 Rue de Paris; ⊙ 9am-6pm Mon-Sat; 🛜) Housed in a historic building, the St-Denis tourist office has English-speaking staff and can provide plenty of information, maps and brochures. It also runs excellent cultural tours focusing on St-Denis' rich architectural heritage (minimum two people, €10). Bookings for *gîtes de montagne* (basic mountain cabins or lodges) can also be made here. There's internet and wi-fi access (one hour free).

ⓘ Getting There & Away

AIR

Unless noted otherwise, the following airlines have offices in St-Denis. All airlines also have an office at the airport, which is usually open every day.

Air Austral (☑ 0825 01 30 12; www.airaustral. com; 4 Rue de Nice; ⊙ 8.30am-5.30pm Mon-Fri)

Air France (☑ 3654; www.airfrance.com; 7 Ave de la Victoire; ⊙ 9am-5pm Mon-Fri, 8.30am-noon Sat)

Air Madagascar (☑ 0892 68 00 14; www. airmadagascar.com; 31 Rue Jules Auber; ⊙ 8.15am-12.15pm & 1.30-5pm Mon-Thu, to 4pm Fri)

Air Mauritius (☑ 0262 94 83 83; www.air mauritius.com; 13 Rue Charles Gounod; ⊙ 8.30am-5.30pm Mon-Fri)

Corsair (☑ 3917; www.corsair.fr; 2 Rue Maréchal Leclerc; ⊙ 9am-5.30pm Mon-Fri)

XL Airways (☑ 0892 69 21 23, in France +33 360 04 01 03; www.xl.com) Doesn't have an office in St-Denis.

BUS

St-Denis Pôle d'Échanges Océan (Gare Routière; Map p184; ☑ 0810 12 39 74; www. carjaune.re; Blvd Joffre), the main long-distance bus station, is on the seafront. From here **Car Jaune** (Map p184; ☑ 0810 12 39 74; www.carjaune.re) operates various services. Information for Car Jaune, including all its routes and *horaires* (timetables) around the island and the airport bus service, is available from the information counter at the bus terminal. Some of the more useful routes include the following:

Line O2 West to St-Pierre via Le Port, St-Paul, St-Gilles-les-Bains, St-Leu, Étang-Salé-les-Bains and St-Louis (two hours, about 10 daily, less on Sunday).

Lines E1 or E2 East to St-Benoît via Ste-Suzanne, St-André and Bras-Panon (€2.80, one hour, about 15 daily, less on Sunday).

ZO (express) West to St-Pierre, direct (€5, one hour, about 18 daily, five on Sunday).

ZE (express) East to St-Benoît via St-André (€5, one hour, about 15 daily, three on Sunday).

CAR & MOTORCYCLE

There's not much point in having a car in St-Denis unless you're using the city as a base to explore the rest of the island. If that's the case, you can either pick a car up at the airport or avoid paying the airport surcharge (around €29) by having it delivered to your hotel. There are numerous independent and international agencies (p283).

ⓘ Getting Around

St-Denis is relatively small and getting around the centre on foot is a breeze.

TAXI

Taxis around town are generally expensive. A trip across town will set you back at least €8.

During the day you should have no problem finding a taxi. It gets more difficult at night, when you might have to phone for one. A reliable company offering a 24-hour service is **Taxis Paille-en-Queue** (☑ 0262 29 20 29).

THE WEST

Welcome to Réunion's Sunshine Coast, or Réunion's Riviera, or the leeward coast. However you label it, say hello to this 45km-long string of seaside resorts and suburbs running from St-Paul to St-Louis. It has a wealth of developed tourist facilities and attractions, including the best of the island's beaches.

Sea, sand and sun are not the only raison d'être on the west coast. There's also a superfluity of activities on land and sea, including

DOS D'ANE

After braving St-Denis' busy streets and before tackling the seaside resorts further south, a drive up to the isolated village of Dos d'Ane, way up in the hills above Le Port (take the D1), will give you a breath of fresh air.

Dos d'Ane is an excellent base for hikes in the interior. From Dos d'Ane you can walk into the Cirque de Mafate via the Rivière des Galets route. For a shorter ramble, there are superb views to be had from the **Cap Noir** kiosk, about 20 minutes from the Cap Noir car park above Dos d'Ane (it's signposted), or from the **Roche Verre Bouteille** lookout, less than an hour's walk from the car park. It's possible to do a loop combining the two lookouts (about 1½ hours).

If you like peace and quiet, you'll have few quibbles with the welcoming **Les Acacias – Chez Axel et Patricia Nativel** (☑0262 32 01 47; 34 Rue Germain Elisabeth; dm €20, dm half board €38, d incl breakfast €50; P). It's very simple but clean and the atmosphere is very relaxed. Digs are in two ordinary *chambres d'hôtes* (family-run guesthouses) and four spick-and-span six-bed dorms. The hearty evening meals (dinner €22) go down well after a day's tramping and the views over the northern coast from the terrace are stupendous.

Another option, **Auberge du Cap Noir – Chez Raymonde** (☑0262 32 00 82, 0262 32 07 66; 3 Allée Pignolet, Dos d'Ane; d/q incl breakfast €47/92; P) is ideally sited on a hillside with swoony ocean views. This mellow, down-to-earth B&B offers four well swept rooms at a price that won't make you flinch. Madame Pignolet knows her stuff when it comes to cooking lip-smacking Reunionnais specialities – her *mousse de patate au coulis de chocolat* (sweet potato mousse with chocolate sauce) is simply divine.

Kar'Ouest (www.karouest.re) runs a bus service (line 8A) between Rivière des Galets and Dos d'Ane (about 15km). By car, follow the D1 from Rivière des Galets.

RÉUNION ST-PAUL

diving, whale-watching, paragliding and mountain biking.

Despite the fact that tourist development has got a little out of hand to the south of St-Paul, it's easy to leave the Route des Tamarins that zips along the flanks of the mountains and explore the glorious hinterland and its bucolic offerings – think sugar-cane fields and cryptomeria forests swathing the slopes of the mountains, studded with character-filled villages.

St-Paul

POP 24,000

Try to visit St-Paul on a Friday or Saturday morning, when the local market is in full swing. This lively city also has a handful of architectural treats, including a few well-preserved colonial buildings along the seafront. The long black-sand beach is alluring but swimming is forbidden. For a dip in safer waters, head to nearby Boucan Canot.

⊙ Sights

Cimetière Marin   CEMETERY
(Rue de la Baie) Most tourists who come to St-Paul visit the bright and well-kept Cimetière Marin, the cemetery at the southern end of town. It contains the remains of various famous Réunionnais, including the poet Leconte de Lisle (1818–94) and the pirate Olivier 'La Buse' Levasseur (The Buzzard), who was the scourge of the Indian Ocean from about 1720 to 1730.

Hindu Temple   HINDU TEMPLE
(Rue St-Louis) Find this strikingly colourful temple dating from 1871 on a street running parallel to the seafront.

🛏 Sleeping & Eating

St-Paul has limited accommodation, which is why most visitors choose to stay in St-Denis, a mere 20-minute drive away (if there's no traffic jam), or in the resort towns of Boucan Canot or St-Gilles-les-Bains, a few kilometres to the south.

While St-Paul is short on accommodation options, it has a surprisingly dynamic eating scene, with a good choice of restaurants, ranging from European gourmet dining to *camions-snacks* (snack vans). Make sure you save energy for the animated market on the seafront promenade. It's held all day on Friday and on Saturday morning. With heaps of local vegetables, fruits, spices and savoury snacks, it makes for a colourful experience.

Western Réunion

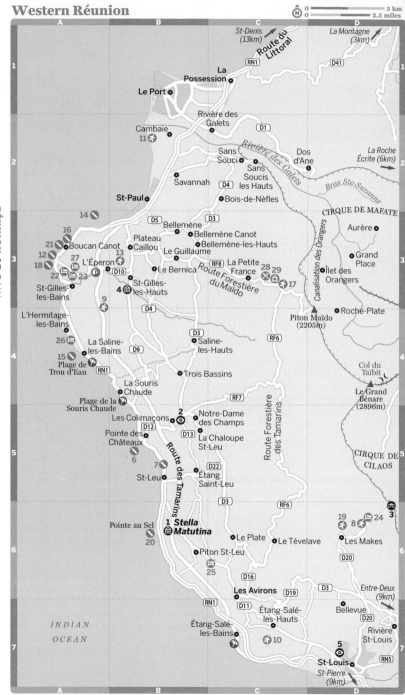

St-Denis
(13km)

La Montagne
(3km)

Route du Littoral

RN1

D41

La Possession

Le Port

Rivière des Galets

D1

Rivière des Galets

Cambaie
11

Sans Souci

Dos d'Ane

La Roche Écrite (6km)

Savannah

Sans Soucis les Hauts

D4

Bras Ste-Suzanne

St-Paul

Bois-de-Nèfles

CIRQUE DE MAFATE

14

D5

Bellemène

D3

Aurère

16

Bellemène Canot

Bellemène-les-Hauts

21 Boucan Canot

Plateau Caillou

13

Grand Place

12

Le Guillaume

27 L'Éperon

18

Le Bernica

RF8 La Petite France

28 29

Îlet des Orangers

22   23

D10

St-Gilles-les-Hauts

Route Forestière du Maïdo

17

St-Gilles-les-Bains

4

Roche-Plate

9

Piton Maïdo
(2205m)

Canalisation des Orangers

L'Hermitage-les-Bains

D4

Col du Taïbit

26

La Saline-les-Bains

D3

Saline-les-Hauts

RF6

Le Grand Bénare
(2896m)

15

D9

Plage de Trou d'Eau

RN1

Trois Bassins

La Souris Chaude

RF7

CIRQUE DE CILAOS

Plage de la Souris Chaude

Les Colimaçons

2

Notre-Dame des Champs

D12

D13

La Chaloupe St-Leu

Route Forestière des Tamarins

Pointe des Châteaux

6   7

D22

St-Leu

Étang Saint-Leu

D3

RF6

Pointe au Sel

1 **Stella Matutina**

19 8 24 3

20

Le Plate

Le Tévelave

Les Makes

25

Piton St-Leu

D16

D20

Les Avirons

D19

D3

Entre-Deux
(9km)

RN1

D11

Bellevue

D20

INDIAN OCEAN

Étang-Salé-les-Bains

Étang-Salé-les-Hauts

10

Rivière St-Louis

Route des Tamarins

5 St-Louis

RN5

St-Pierre
(9km)

Western Réunion

RÉUNION ST-PAUL

Kia Ora
B&B €€

(📞 0262 25 31 68; www.kiaorarun.com; 204 Rue St-Louis; d €90, with shared bathroom €68, incl breakfast; ❄ 🤖 🏊) Your well-travelled hosts keep their three *chambre d'hôte* rooms spick and span and serve delicious breakfasts on a terrace overlooking the pool. One room comes with private facilities, but note that the bathrooms don't have doors.

⭐ La Magie des Glaces
ICE CREAM €

(📞 0262 45 25 48; 1 Rue Edmond Albius; ice creams & crêpes €1.80-7; ⏰ 10am-12.30pm & 2-7pm Tue & Fri-Sun, 2-7pm Wed & Thu) St-Paul's prime ice-cream parlour will leave you a drooling mess. It serves up an excellent array of classic and exotic flavours, all prepared with high-quality ingredients. The tangor and vanilla are outstanding. It also whips up crêpes, pastries, chocolate mousse and macaroons. If only it had sea views, life would be perfect.

Nature
CREOLE, BUFFET €€

(📞 0262 71 45 89; 228 Rue Saint-Louis; mains €13-20, lunch buffet €15; ⏰ noon-2pm Mon-Sat, 7.15-9.30pm Thu-Sat; 🛜) Nature is that easy-to-miss 'secret spot' that locals like to recommend. It serves up a brilliant-value lunch buffet, consisting of about 10 Creole dishes prepared from fresh simple ingredients. The setting is inviting, with a dining room embellished with colourful touches and a few outdoor tables. It also has a takeaway counter (€5 to €8.50).

Le Jardin
EUROPEAN €€

(📞 0262 45 05 82; 456 Rue St-Louis; mains €15-25; ⏰ 11.30am-2pm & 6.30-9pm Mon, Tue & Thu-Sat) This surprisingly atmospheric restaurant at the northern end of town features an open-air dining room, a lounge area and a swimming pool, which will help you switch to 'relax' mode. Food-wise, it concocts French specialities as well as pizzas. Warm and attentive service and a good place for a drink as well.

Le Bout' Chandelle
FRENCH €€

(📞 0262 27 47 18; 192 Rue Marius et Ary Leblond; mains €17-24, lunch menus €17-35; ⏰ noon-1.30pm & 7-9pm Tue-Sat) In a welcoming house back from the bustle on the seafront, this is an agreeable place to dine on French specialities with a Creole twist.

Le Grand Baie
FRENCH, CREOLE €€

(📞 0262 22 50 03; www.facebook.com/restaurant legrandbaie; 14 Rue des Filaos; mains €12-21; ⏰ 11.45am-2pm & 7-10pm Tue-Sun) You're sure to find something to fill a gap at this haven of peace next to the Cimetière Marin, where the menu covers lots of salads as well as *métro* (French) and Creole dishes. With its vast decking terrace and first-class views of the bay, dining really does not get better than this.

La Bas Ter La
FUSION €€€

(☑ 0262 57 10 51; 4 Rue Eugène Dayot; lunch mains €12-16, dinner mains €19-25; ⊙ noon-1.30pm & 7.15-9.30pm Tue-Fri, 7.15-9.30pm Sat; ☎) One of St-Paul's top tables, La Bas Ter La is tucked down a quiet street not far from the seafront. It offers excellent French cuisine with a refined twist, savoured in a stylishly modern dining room. The menu changes regularly – if it's available, how about the exquisite tarte Tatin (upside-down apple tart) flavoured with papaya and ylang ylang?

ℹ Getting There & Away

St-Paul lies on Car Jaune's bus route between St-Denis and St-Pierre. There are express buses every one to two hours in either direction (fewer on Sunday) and much more frequent nonexpress services. More information at www.carjaune.re.

The local bus company **Kar'Ouest** (☑ 0810 45 65 20; www.karouest.re) operates fairly infrequent services from the central bus station to villages up in the hills such as Le Bernica, La Petite France (and further up towards Le Maïdo), Villèle and Le Guillaume, among others.

Les Hauts de St-Paul

A world away from the hurly-burly of the coast, the verdant Hauts de St-Paul is wonderful country for exploring off the beaten track. From St-Paul, use the D5 as a launch pad, then follow your nose (but bring a good map). You'll come across hamlets with such charming names as Sans Soucis les Hauts, Bois-de-Nèfles, Bellemène-les-Hauts, Le Guillaume, Le Bernica... It's as cute as it sounds! Start early morning to get the best views of the coast.

🛏 Sleeping & Eating

Accommodation options are thin on the ground in the area. Frankly said, your best bet is to bunk down in a hotel or apartment in Boucan Canot or St-Gilles-les-Bains and explore the area on a day trip. There are a few modest eating options in most villages.

La Caz des Orangers
GUESTHOUSE €

(☑ 0692 08 23 12, 0262 44 50 32; www.lacazdes orangers.com; 24 Impasse Cernot, Sans Soucis les Hauts; d €54, s/d with shared bathroom €30/36, incl breakfast; P☎) The main reason to stay at this no-frills yet welcoming establishment hidden in Sans Souci les Hauts, about 10km northeast of St-Paul, is if you're hiking to/ from the Cirque de Mafate via the Canalisation des Orangers – the trailhead is just

200m uphill. The guesthouse has a large sitting room, plain bedrooms with minimalist decor and three more comfortable doubles in a separate building.

Add another €15 for dinner. Note that guests can leave their car and luggage for free during their Mafate hiking trip. It costs €2 per day or €10 for overnight parking for nonguests.

ℹ Getting There & Away

Unless you have a lot of time, you need a vehicle. Buses serve most places from St-Paul, but they aren't really convenient for the Hauts.

Le Maïdo & Around

Be prepared for a visual shock: far above St-Paul and St-Gilles-les-Bains on the rim of the Cirque de Mafate, Le Maïdo is one of the most impressive viewpoints in Réunion. The lookout is perched atop the mountain peak at 2205m and offers stunning views down into the Cirque and back to the coast. You should arrive early in the day – by 7am if possible – if you want to see anything other than cloud.

Getting there is half the fun. The sealed Route Forestière du Maïdo winds all the way up to the viewpoint from **Le Guillaume** (14km) in the hills above St-Gilles-les-Bains, offering a scenic drive through cryptomeria forests. You'll find a smattering of attractions along the way to keep you entertained.

A word of warning: expect traffic snarls on Sunday when hundreds of picnicking families set up base in the shade of trees along the road.

🏃 Activities

Le Relais du Maïdo
OUTDOORS

(Map p192; ☑ 0262 32 40 32; Route du Maïdo, PK6.5; ⊙ 9am-5pm Wed-Sun) At an altitude of 1500m, the Relais du Maïdo is a kind of theme park, with a smattering of attractions, mostly geared to children, including pony rides (€6), quad bikes (€5 to €10) and archery (€6).

La Forêt de L'Aventure
OUTDOORS

(☑ 0692 30 01 54; Route Forestière des Cryptoméri-as, La Petite France; adult/child €20/15; ⊙ Wed, Fri, Sat & Sun by reservation) For Tarzan types, La Forêt de L'Aventure has set up two wonderful adventure circuits in a 3-hectare perimeter, with a variety of fixtures, including Tyrolean slides. There's a 'Mini Forêt' for the kiddies (over five). It's signposted, about 500m to the north of La Petite France, after L'Alambic Bègue distillery.

THRILLING DOWNHILLS

The spectacular flanks of Le Maïdo will prove a sort of nirvana for mountain bikers who prefer sitting back and letting gravity do the work. The 35km, 2205m descent follows trails that wind through tamarind and cryptomeria forests and sugar-cane fields. Throughout the ride you're presented with astounding views of the lagoon and the coast.

Rando Réunion Passion (p199) is a professional set-up that offers a range of mountain-bike trips for riders of all levels. The most popular ride is the 'Classique du Maïdo' descent, from the lookout to the coast. If you're a beginner, fear not! You won't ride at breakneck speed, and various stops are organised along the way, where the guide will give you the lowdown on flora and fauna. Half-day packages including bike hire, transport to the start (by minivan) and a guide cost around €60 per person (minimum four). Children over 12 are welcome.

If you want to open up the throttle a little more, opt for the 'Maxi Cap Ouest' (€80) descent.

Hiking

Hiking options abound near Le Maïdo. The peak is the starting point for the tough walk along the Cirque rim to the summit of **Le Grand Bénare** (2896m), another impressive lookout. Plan on six hours return. Hikers can also descend from Le Maïdo into the Cirque de Mafate via the Sentier de Roche-Plate.

🛏 Sleeping & Eating

The village of La Petite France makes a convenient base for an early-morning start up to Le Maïdo.

Both Au Petit Gourmet and Chez Doudou are full to bursting at weekends – dining reservations are advised.

Chez Rose Magdeleine B&B €

(📞 0262 32 53 50; 13 Chemin de l'École, La Petite France; d incl breakfast €45) Run by an affable Creole family, this good-value B&B is a real home away from home. It has few frills but the four rooms are clean as a whistle, and the location, just off the main road in La Petite France, makes a convenient base for an early-morning start up to Le Maïdo. Evening meals are available on request (€22).

Au Petit Gourmet CREOLE €€

(Map p192; 📞 0693 92 46 34; 430 Route du Maïdo; mains €11-15; ⊙ noon-2pm) This unpretentious little joint is a great find on your way to Le Maïdo. The super fresh dishes made from local ingredients all sing in the mouth. Make a beeline for the curry of the day or the chicken curry. A tasty crêpe will finish the meal off sweetly.

Chez Doudou et Alexandra CREOLE €€

(📞 0262 32 55 87; 394 Route du Maïdo, La Petite France; buffet €23; ⊙ noon-2pm Thu-Sun) With its barnlike surrounds, Chez Doudou boasts a kind of ramshackle charm but has no views to speak of. The onus is on earthy regional food, so roll up for comforting Creole *carris* served with all the traditional accompaniments. It's full to bursting at weekends – reservations are advised.

🛍 Shopping

La Petite France is famous for its traditional distilleries producing essential oils from geranium, cryptomeria and vetiver leaves (nice smell!). The distilleries also run small shops where you can stock up on perfumes, soaps and other natural health products. Stop off at some of the places scattered along the main road in La Petite France.

L'Alambic Bègue DISTILLERY

(📞 0692 64 58 25; www.alambicbegue.jimdo.com; 403 Route du Maïdo, La Petite France; ⊙ 8.30am-6pm) A long-standing distillery with an excellent reputation. It features a range of essential oils and health products.

Distillerie du Maïdo – Chez Nanou Le Savoyard DISTILLERY

(Map p192; 📞 0692 61 75 43; www.ladistillerie dumaido.com; 700 La Petite Savoie, La Petite France; ⊙ 8.30am-5.30pm) Here you can stock up on essential oils, perfumes, soaps and other natural health products. Also sells *rhum arrangé* (flavoured rum), honey and jam.

ℹ Getting There & Away

From the central bus station in St-Paul, **Kar'Ouest** (p194) runs three buses a day (Monday to Saturday) to the start of the Sentier de Roche Plate, the footpath into the Cirque de Mafate, which strikes off the road about 3km below the summit. The first bus up the hill leaves at 6am and the last one down is at 5.20pm (line 2, €1.80, one hour).

Boucan Canot

POP 3400

The 'Boucan' checklist: skimpy bikini, designer glasses (imitations may be sniggered at), and sunscreen. This attitude-fuelled little resort town isn't dubbed the Réunionnais St-Tropez for nothing.

◉ Sights

Plage de Boucan Canot   BEACH

Boucan Canot's main beach has been listed as one of Réunion's best, and once you get a glimpse of the gentle curve of the bright white sand, lined with palms and casuarina trees and framed with basalt rocks and cliffs, you'll see why. It gets packed on weekends. A 610m shark net, protecting a large bathing area of 84,000 sq metres, was installed off the beach in December 2015. Stick to the protected area.

Plage de Petit Boucan   BEACH

At the southern end of Boucan Canot's main beach, you'll find this smaller, much quieter beach, but swimming is forbidden and there's no lifeguard.

🛏 Sleeping

If you want to do Boucan Canot in style, you'll find a couple of great options overlooking the beach.

Résidence Les Boucaniers   APARTMENT €€

(☎0262 24 23 89; www.les-boucaniers.com; 29 Route de Boucan Canot; d €82; P✳🛜) These self-catering studios and apartments show some signs of wear and tear but the location, across the road from the beach, is hard to beat. Be sure to book a unit with a sea view. Prices drop to €76 if you stay two nights or more.

Le Boucan Canot   RESORT €€€

(☎0262 33 44 44; www.boucancanot.com; 32 Route de Boucan Canot; s €185-250, d €220-295, ste from €280, incl breakfast; P✳🛜♨) Boucan Canot's iconic hotel stretches over a rocky promontory at the northern end of the beach. Though nothing glam, the rooms are bright and well-appointed and come with a sea view. Due to its position, this four-star establishment gets plenty of sunshine, even in the late afternoon. Another highlight is the food; Le Cap restaurant offers fine à la carte dining.

Le Saint-Alexis Hotel & Spa   RESORT €€€

(☎0262 24 42 04; www.hotelsaintalexis.com; 44 Route de Boucan Canot; d €160-290, ste from €300; P✳@🛜♨) Le Saint-Alexis is a quirkily laid-out four-star resort at the southern tip of the main beach. The rooms are all arrayed around a central patio, which means that none of them have sea views. They're attractively decorated, although the ones in the angles lack natural light. Facilities include a small spa and a large, U-shaped pool that girdles the building.

You may want to book a *rez-de-piscine* room, with direct access to the pool. Breakfast (€25) is served on a terrace with stunning sea views. Frequent online promotional deals provide real value.

✖ Eating

There's a string of snack stands and laidback cafe-restaurants along the seafront promenade.

La Case Bambou   CREPERIE €

(☎0262 59 20 84; 35 Route de Boucan Canot; mains €3-15; ⏱noon-2.30pm & 7-10pm Wed-Sun) Head here for finger-licking crêpes, ice creams, waffles and sandwiches. Wildly popular on weekends.

Le Bambou Bar   BRASSERIE €€

(☎0262 24 59 29; 35 Route de Boucan Canot; mains €10-24; ⏱noon-2.30pm Tue-Sun, 7-10pm daily) A long-standing favourite, the Bambou Bar distinguishes itself with its atmospheric decor – think a thatched roof and plenty of wood and greenery. Order anything from coffee and cocktails to pizzas, Creole staples, seafood, burgers, salads and meat dishes.

La Boucantine   FRENCH, CREOLE €€

(☎0262 33 62 10; 29 Route de Boucan Canot; mains €13-23; ⏱noon-2pm & 6-9.30pm Thu-Tue) One of the better (and slightly quieter) restaurants on this seaside strip, with an inviting terrace that affords lovely sea views. High marks go to the *tajine de poulet aux citrons confits et olives* (chicken stew with preserved lemon and olives) and the catch of the day. Mouthwatering desserts too, including crêpes and chocolate cake.

Le Ti Boucan   INTERNATIONAL €€

(☎0262 24 85 08; 32 Route de Boucan Canot; mains €14-22; ⏱8.30am-10pm; 🛜) On the main strip, this cheerful spot is no place to escape the crowds, but the menu is eclectic. Fish lovers can opt for one of the various tartares (try the tuna tartare), while meat-eaters will plump for the beef fillet or the sirloin steak. Copious salads provide a tempting alternative. The service is friendly and the outside terrace is a delight.

Le Bistrot de Pépé Gentil
BISTRO €€€

(☑ 0262 22 12 78; 15 Place des Coquillages; mains €22-30; ☺ 7-9.30pm Mon-Sat) This much-lauded venture with a vintage feel serves a range of culinary delights that deliciously represent French bistro cooking. The *ris de veau* (veal sweetbreads) and *sole meunière* (sole sautéed in butter and garnished with lemon and parsley) are two specialities to look for, though the menu is in constant flux according to markets and seasons.

Its location on a nondescript square is nothing to write home about; the real clinchers are the food and the civilised atmosphere.

Le Beau Rivage
MODERN FRENCH €€€

(☑ 0262 43 69 43; www.lebeaurivage.re; 58 Rue de Boucan Canot; mains €27-38, lunch menus €25-30, menus €50-72; ☺ noon-1.45pm & 7-9.30pm Tue-Fri, 7-9.30pm Sat) This highly rated eatery offers excellent French cuisine with a refined twist, savoured on a vast and stylish terrace overlooking the beach. Come evening, the atmosphere is romantic to boot – perfect for an intimate meal. The lunch menus are good value by Boucan Canot standards.

❶ Getting There & Away

Car Jaune's line 02 between St-Denis and St-Pierre runs through the centre of Boucan Canot. The St-Denis–Boucan Canot trip (€2) takes about 50 minutes. More information at www.carjaune.re.

St-Gilles-les-Bains

POP 6500

The tourism machine shifts into overdrive in the large resort complex of St-Gilles-les-Bains, with its white sands, restaurants, nightclubs and a boisterous atmosphere on weekends. During the week, however, the atmosphere is much more relaxed and you shouldn't have to fight for a space to lay your towel. There are numerous water activities on offer, from diving to deep-sea fishing.

◉ Sights

Plage des Roches Noires
BEACH

(Map p198) Plage des Roches Noires, in the heart of town, is crowded and neatly striped with sunbeds and parasols, but, beneath all this, it remains an attractive stretch of beach

---

> **SHARK ATTACK PREVENTION**
>
> Shark attacks on surfers and swimmers have been a major issue in Réunion in recent years, especially off St-Leu, Boucan-Canot, St-Gilles-les-Bains, Trois-Bassins and Étang-Salé-les-Bains. Shark nets have been installed along Boucan-Canot and St-Gilles-les-Bains' beaches. Always swim in designated and supervised areas, and watch for the warning signs. Check the website of Prevention Requin Réunion (www.prr.re) and its Facebook page for up-to-date information.

---

excellent for families, with shallow waters and plenty of restaurants. A shark net was installed off the beach in 2016 to increase safety. Watch for the warnings signs, though, and swim only in the supervised area. On the northern side of the Port de Plaisance.

Plage des Brisants
BEACH

(Map p198) Plage des Brisants is a superb stretch of white sand on the southern side of the Port de Plaisance. That said, swimming is forbidden (yes, sharks). It's great for sunbathing.

Aquarium de la Réunion
AQUARIUM

(Map p198; ☑ 0262 33 44 00; www.aquariumdelareunion.com; Îlot du Port; adult/child €9.50/6.50; ☺ 10am-5.30pm) In the modern Port de Plaisance complex, the quite engaging Aquarium de la Réunion houses a series of excellent underwater displays, including tanks with lobsters, barracudas, groupers and small sharks.

🏃 Activities

Boat Excursions

The best way to discover St-Gilles' iridescent lagoon is by joining a boat excursion. Various operators offer *promenades en mer* (boat excursions) and *observation sous-marine* (glass-bottomed tours) along the coast towards St-Leu or St-Paul. *Safaris dauphin* (dolphin encounters), whale-watching trips (from June or July to September or October), sunset cruises and day long catamaran cruises are also available. Tours go every day but are weather-dependent.

Le Grand Bleu
BOATING

(Map p198; ☑ 0262 33 28 32; www.grandbleu.re; Îlot du Port; adult €10-90, child €5-45; ☺ daily) This reputable operator has the largest range

St-Gilles-les-Bains

of tours, from sunset cruises to whale- and dolphin-watching trips. Prices vary according to the duration of the cruise (the shortest tours last 45 minutes) and the type of boat.

Sealife – Visiobul · BOATING
(Map p198; ☏0262 24 49 57; www.facebook.com/visiobulreunion; Îlot du Port; adult/child €13/8; ⊙by reservation) Specialises in glass-bottomed boat tours. Also runs whale- and dolphin-watching trips as well as sunset cruises.

Lady La Fée · BOATING
(Map p198; ☏0692 69 12 99; www.ladylafee.com; Port de Plaisance; half-day trip €50; ⊙by reservation) This small outfit offers half- and full-day trips aboard a catamaran along the west coast. The itinerary is flexible. Sunset cocktail cruises cost €35.

Diving
The waters off St-Gilles offer plenty of scope for diving (including the chance to explore a few wrecks), whatever your level.

Bleu Marine Réunion · DIVING
(Map p198; ☏0262 24 22 00; www.bleu-marine-reunion.com; Port de Plaisance; introductory/single dive €60/50; ⊙8am-5pm Tue-Sun) A fully fledged, well-organised dive shop offering a comprehensive menu of underwater adventures, including diving trips, snorkelling

excursions (€30) and certification courses. Three-/six-dive packages go for €144/280.

Corail Plongée · DIVING
(Map p198; ☏0262 24 37 25; www.corail-plongee.com; Port de Plaisance; introductory/single dive €60/48; ⊙8am-5pm Mon-Sat, to noon Sun) A reputable dive operator, Corail Plongée runs the full gamut of courses for beginners as well as diving trips and snorkelling excursions (€25). Four-/six-dive packages cost €184/268. Add an extra €5 per dive for Nitrox dives.

Ô Sea Bleu · DIVING
(Map p198; ☏0262 24 33 30; www.reunion-plongee.com; Port de Plaisance; introductory/single dive €60/50; ⊙8am-5pm) Professional dive shop that offers the full range of scuba activities. Four-/six-dive packages are €190/280.

Snorkelling trips (€35), certification courses and dolphin-watching trips are also available.

Mountain Biking

Rando Réunion Passion   MOUNTAIN BIKING
(Map p198; ☑ 0262 45 18 67, 0692 21 11 11; www.
descente-vtt.com; 3 Rue du Général de Gaulle; outing €59-90; ☺ by reservation) This professional set-up offers a range of mountain-bike trips for riders of all levels. The most popular ride is the Classique du Maïdo descent, from the Maïdo lookout to the coast. Experienced riders can opt for the Maxi Cap Ouest or La Méga. Prices include transfers.

Sport Fishing

St-Gilles is a good base for fans of Ernest Hemingway. The waters off the west coast are a pelagic playpen for schools of marlin, swordfish, sailfish, shark and tuna. A fishing trip (four to six people) costs from €400/800 per half-/full day. Three recommended outfits:

Réunion Fishing Club (Map p198; ☑ 0262 24 36 10; www.reunionfishingclub.com; Port de Plaisance; half-day outing €100; ☺ 7am-5pm) Leads well-organised fishing trips.

Maevasion (Map p198; ☑ 0262 33 38 04; www.maevasion.com; Port de Plaisance; half-day outing €100; ☺ 8am-5pm) Has good credentials.

Blue Marlin (Map p198; ☑ 0692 65 22 35; www.bluemarlin.fr; Port de Plaisance; ☺ 7am-5pm) A well-established operator. Prices vary according to the size of the party.

🛏 Sleeping

There's plenty of accommodation in the area, but almost everything is booked out during holiday periods and on weekends. The more appealing hotels and *chambres d'hôtes* are in the countryside just north of town or to the south in L'Hermitage-les-Bains.

Hôtel de la Plage   HOTEL €
(Map p198; ☑ 0692 80 07 57, 0262 24 06 37; www.hoteldelaplage.re; 20 Rue de la Poste; s with shared bathroom €30, d €70, with shared bathroom €45-60; ✳ 🛜) The highlights of this long-established and well-run, hostel-like venture are its ultra-central (but noisy) location and colourful communal areas. The eight rooms vary in size, light and noisiness, so ask to see a couple before you settle on one. Rooms 114, 115 and 116 are the best. Breakfast costs €6. Prices drop after three nights. Book ahead.

During the day, finding a parking space might be a problem. The reception is open from 7am to noon.

WORTH A TRIP

MUSÉE DE VILLÈLE

The **Musée de Villèle** (Map p192; ☑ 0262 55 64 10; St-Gilles-les-Hauts; €2; ☺ 9.30am-12.30pm & 1.30-5pm Tue-Sun) is set in the former home of the wealthy and very powerful Madame Panon-Desbassayns, a coffee and sugar baroness who, among other things, owned 300 slaves. The house, which is only accessible on a guided tour, was built in 1787 and is full of elegant period furniture. After the tour, wander the outbuildings and the 10-hectare park.

Legend has it that she was a cruel woman and that her tormented screams can still be heard from the hellish fires whenever Piton de la Fournaise is erupting. Exhibits include a clock presented to the Desbassayns by Napoleon; a set of china featuring Paul et Virginie, the love story by Bernardin de St-Pierre; and, last but not least, a portrait of Madame Panon-Desbassayns in a red turban looking surprisingly impish. Signs are in French and in English.

Thimloc   MOTEL €
(Map p198; ☑ 0262 24 23 24; www.thimloc.fr; 165 Rue du Général de Gaulle; d €60-65; ✳ 🛜) Seven adjoining rooms in a shady garden off the main street. They're unexciting and lack natural light but they're clean, come equipped with a handy outside kitchenette and are located within spitting distance from the beach, shops and restaurants, and there's a fine bakery just across the road.

Hôtel des Palmes   HOTEL €
(Map p198; ☑ 0262 24 47 12; www.hoteldespalmes.fr; 205 Rue du Général de Gaulle; d €75; 🅿 ✳ 🛜) Between St-Gilles and L'Hermitage, this two-star hotel offers a clutch of colourful, good-sized villas, but its location ain't so great – it's sandwiched between the highway and the main road to L'Hermitage – and the pool is no great shakes. A good plan B, especially if you can score room 22, 24, 26, 32, 34 or 36, which are in the middle of the property and are less noisy.

★ La Villa Chriss   B&B €€
(Map p192; ☑ 0692 82 41 00; http://chambre-hote-luxe-reunion.com; Rue d'Anjou; d incl breakfast €120-140; 🅿 ✳ 🛜) Run by Christine and Christine (hence the name), this boutique-style *maison d'hôte* (guesthouse) perched on

the side of a hill rejuvenates the weariest of travellers. It shelters three superb rooms that are decorated with a contemporary twist. A delicious gourmet breakfast is served by the pool, with mind-boggling views of the coast. Not a suitable children.

★ Senteur Vanille
VILLA €€

(Map p192; ☑ 0262 24 04 88, 0692 78 13 05; www. senteurvanille.com; Route du Théâtre; bungalow d €75-100, villa q €160-200; P ✳ ⑨) A true find for peace seekers, Senteur Vanille makes you feel like you've stepped into a Garden of Eden, with mango, lychee and papaya trees all over the grounds. Curl up in a vast, well-equipped villa (ideal for families) or in a cute-as-can-be Creole bungalow. No swimming pool, but Boucan Canot beach is a 20-minute walk down a path.

The wonderful setting makes it easy to meet the three-night minimum stay. It's a few kilometres east of the centre, in the direction of St-Gilles-les-Hauts, signed down a lane beside the Total petrol station. No credit cards.

Le Saint-Michel
HOTEL €€

(Map p192; ☑ 0262 33 13 33; www.hotelsaint-michel.fr; 196 Chemin Summer; s €76, d €96-110, incl breakfast; P ✳ ⑨ ☎) This great little number amid a tropical garden on the outskirts of town has been renovated and looks refreshed. It features 29 rooms (some with sea views). The more spacious ones are in the newer wing. The on-site restaurant offers really superb French cuisine with a Creole twist. It's a two-minute drive to the centre and the beach.

✗ Eating

St-Gilles has plenty of eating options, though standards tend to be more variable than elsewhere on the island.

As well as restaurants, you'll find several *camions-pizzas* (mobile pizza vans) on the main street; they're a good bargain and operate in the evening.

Le Natur'Elle
ICE CREAM, CAFETERIA €

(Map p198; ☑ 0262 33 21 09; www.facebook.com/ restaurant.lenaturelle; 2 Place Paul Julius Bénard; 1-/2-scoop cones €1.50/3, mains €9-16; ⏲ 8.30am-6.30pm Tue-Sat; ⑨) Dither too long over the 20-plus flavours of ice cream and sorbet at this great *glacier* (ice-cream shop) and you'll never make it to the front of the queue. Eschew predictable favourites and indulge in a new taste sensation: ylang ylang, kulfi (a mix of saffron and cardamom), rose or violet. Other treats include heavenly macaroons.

Also serves breakfast and daily specials at lunchtime.

Take it away on your town ventures or enjoy on the shady terrace.

La Frite Une Fois
FAST FOOD €

(Map p198; ☑ 0262 77 89 52; www.facebook.com/ lafriteunefois974; 14 Rue de la Poste; mains €3-8; ⏲ 11am-3pm & 6-8.30pm Tue-Sun) Opened in 2016, this Belgian-run den tucked in a side street close to the beach is famous for its delicious homemade *frites* (French fries). It also serves burgers and *mitraillettes* (sandwiches). And since you're just a couple of blocks from the seafront, La Frite Une Fois is the perfect takeaway for lunch on the beach.

Le Glacier de Marie B
ICE CREAM €

(Map p198; ☑ 0262 24 53 06; 13 Rue de la Poste; ice creams & snacks €2.30-10; ⏲ 1-7pm Tue, 11am-7pm Wed-Fri, to 7.30pm Sat & Sun) You'll lose all self-control at this drool-inducing ice-cream parlour. Amid a mind-boggling array of flavours, the electric-purple *pitaya* screams 'try me'. The vanilla and geranium is also well worth a try. Other treats include pancakes, waffles and smoothies.

La Case à Pains
BAKERY €

(Map p198; ☑ 0262 96 33 01; www.lacaseapains. com; 29 Rue du Général de Gaulle; sandwiches from €4, lunch menu €4.50-8; ⏲ 6.30am-7pm) If you're toying with the idea of doing a beach picnic à la gourmet, it's worth stopping in here for some salads, pastries and well-prepared sandwiches. The signature offering is the *pain frotté à la vanille* (a variety of bread flavoured with vanilla). Also serves breakfast. Has outdoor tables.

Chez Loulou
FAST FOOD €

(Map p198; ☑ 0262 24 40 41; 86 Rue du Général de Gaulle; mains €5-7; ⏲ 7am-1pm & 3-7pm Mon-Sat, 7am-1pm Sun) The most iconic Creole *case* (house) for kilometres around, with a distinctive turquoise facade on the main drag. It's famous for its belt-bustingly good samosas, *macatias*, cakes, croissants, banana cakes and tarts. Good sandwiches and takeaway meals at lunchtime, too.

Need to get online? There's a computer for internet access.

★ Bistrot Case Créole
BISTRO €€

(Map p198; ☑ 0262 24 28 84; www.bistrotcase creole.re; 57 Rue du Général de Gaulle; mains €10-19; ⏲ noon-2pm Tue-Fri, 7.30-9.30pm Tue-Sat) On the main drag, the BCC is known for its consistently delicious and well-priced cuisine, which has a modern edge but is firmly based in the classic Réunionnais and French tradition. On weekdays it lays on an excellent buffet dinner featuring an assortment of curries for just €19 (€21 on Friday and Saturday). If only it had sea views!

Chez Marie FRENCH, CREOLE €€
(Map p198; ☑0262 24 98 87; Port de Plaisance; mains €10-17, menu €14.50; ⊙12.30-2.30pm) With its tiny terrace overlooking the harbour and simple yet well-prepared cuisine, this sweet lil' den is ideal for a quick and affordable sit-down lunch. The trademark here is freshness and great value for money. The octopus salad gets great reviews, but any of the dishes featuring on the menu (salads, tuna tartare, beefsteak etc) will see you right. Save space for the excellent homemade desserts.

Le Joyau des Roches CREOLE €€
(Map p198; www.facebook.com/Le.Joyau.des.Roches; 3 Rue de la Poste; mains €12-19, menu €15; ⊙11.30am-2pm & 7.30-10.30pm Wed-Mon) A thong's throw from the beach, this venue has a tantalising menu showcasing the classics of Creole cuisine, served in snug surrounds complete with elegant furnishings and tropical plants. A few savoury house specials include a scrumptious palm-heart salad, *saucisse baba figues* (sausage served with banana flowers) and papaya gratin. Also does takeaway (€5 to €10).

Chez Les Filles INTERNATIONAL €€
(Map p198; Plage des Brisants; mains €9-19; ⊙noon-3pm Tue-Sun, 7-10pm Thu-Sun) This beachside kiosk is run by a dynamic crew who serve simple fish and meat dishes as well as salads and generous sandwiches (from €3). Servings are large and the ramshackle tables right on Plage des Brisants could well be our favourites along this stretch of coast. It doubles as a bar.

Le DCP SEAFOOD €€
(Map p198; ☑0262 33 02 96; www.restaurant-dcp.fr; 2 Place Paul Julius Bénard; mains €12-25; ⊙noon-2pm & 7-10pm) Fish lovers will find nirvana here: this known-far-and-wide restaurant has a broad assortment of fish delivered daily from the harbour. Order it grilled, steamed, baked or raw. The tartares are reputedly the best on the island. It's near the tourist office.

★**Le Saint-Michel** FRENCH, CREOLE €€€
(Map p192; ☑0262 33 13 33; 196 Chemin Summer; mains €24-28, lunch menus €20-25, dinner

menu €40; ⊙noon-2pm & 7.30-9.30pm) Part of the eponymous hotel, this is the gourmet choice in St-Gilles. With its enticing dining deck by the pool, charming welcome and delicious cuisine, Le Saint-Michel won't disappoint. The menu is a great combination of high-brow, creative gastronomy and timeless classics such as beef fillet. And there's always a great wine to match.

Bookings are essential to guarantee one of the prized tables near the pool.

Chez Nous INTERNATIONAL €€€
(Map p198; ☑0262 24 08 08; www.cheznous974.com; 122 Rue du Général de Gaulle; mains €19-25; ⊙noon-2pm Mon-Fri, 7-11pm daily) This bold bistro is beloved by all who come here. The blackboard menu features flavourful meat and fish dishes, some with an exotic twist. The service may see you twiddling your thumbs when it's crowded. It also has a bar area, with a loungey vibe.

Chez Bobonne FUSION €€€
(Map p198; ☑0262 39 27 96; 3 Rue St-Alexis; mains €22-32; ⊙7.30-10.30pm Mon-Sat) Indulge in delicious French-inspired dishes at this fine-dining restaurant with contemporary decor and mood lighting. The small menu is chalked on the board and changes weekly. There's also a thoughtful wine list. It's tucked away from the main drag.

🍸 Drinking & Nightlife

St-Gilles is one of the top places in Réunion (on an equal footing with St-Pierre) for bar-hopping. The atmosphere is very Zoreilles (mainland French) – you could be mistaken for thinking you're in the French Côte d'Azur. Most places are scattered along Rue du Général de Gaulle and the chichi seafront. As the bars fade from about midnight on, the centre of pleasurable gravity shifts to L'Hermitage. Most bars also serve food.

L'Acacia BAR
(Map p198; ☑0262 27 36 43; 1 Rue de la Poste; ⊙11am-midnight Tue-Sun) A fashionable open-air bar and restaurant on the seafront. Order a mojito and enjoy the top sea views from the upstairs terrace. The food is hit-and-miss.

Cubana Club CLUB
(Map p198; ☑0262 33 24 91; 122 Rue du Général de Gaulle; ⊙7pm-5am Tue-Sat) Kick off the night with a few shots at this salsa-inspired venue featuring bordello-red curtains.

RÉUNION ST-GILLES-LES-BAINS

Esko Bar BAR

(Map p198; ☑0262 33 19 33; www.facebook.com/eskobar.reunion; 131 Rue du Général de Gaulle; ☺7pm-1am Mon-Sat) This chic venue has excellent cocktails, good tapas (from €6) and themed nights – check the Facebook page.

ℹ Information

Office du Tourisme (Map p198; ☑0810 79 77 97; www.ouest-lareunion.com; 1 Place Paul Julius Bénard; ☺10am-1pm & 2-6pm; ☏) Has helpful English-speaking staff. Free wi-fi. Does bookings for *gîtes de montagne*.

ℹ Getting There & Away

Car Jaune's nonexpress buses between St-Denis and St-Pierre (line 01) run through the centre of St-Gilles down Rue du Général de Gaulle. The trip to St-Denis (€2) takes at least one hour. More infomation at www.carjaune.re.

L'Hermitage-les-Bains

POP 6200

L'Hermitage has the bulk of the island's major resorts, a good selection of restaurant and entertainment options, and what is possibly Réunion's most scenic beach. Here, the island has the feel of a vacation destination.

◎ Sights

L'Hermitage is short on specific sights. The long, sandy beach is the main draw.

Plage de L'Hermitage BEACH

(Map p203) Further south of St-Gilles' Plage des Brisants, lined with casuarina trees, is Plage de L'Hermitage, which is an alluring place to fry in the sun. It is safe for swimming – it's protected by a barrier reef and is supervised by lifeguards – and extremely popular on weekends. Snorkelling is OK.

Le Jardin d'Eden GARDENS

(Map p203; ☑0262 33 83 16; www.jardindeden.re; 155 RN1; adult/child €8/4; ☺10am-6pm) Appealing to a wider audience than just plant lovers and gardeners, Le Jardin d'Eden, across the main road from L'Hermitage, is definitely worth an hour or so for anyone interested in tropical flora. Sections of the gardens are dedicated to interesting concepts such as the sacred plants of the Hindus, medicinal plants, edible tropical plants, spices and aphrodisiac plants.

⌊ Sleeping

The sandy beach of L'Hermitage-les-Bains provides sea frontage for a number of resorts. There's also a cache of seaside B&Bs and mid-range hotels.

Camping Ermitage Lagon CAMPGROUND €

(Map p203; ☑0262 96 36 70; www.campingermitage.re; 60 Ave de Bourbon; camping per site 1-6 people €19-35; P☏) This camping ground has modern, functional facilities, but is located near L'Hermitage's clubs, so it may not be quiet on weekends. Shade is in short supply but you're within spitting distance of the beach. You can rent out a whole 'safari tent' for €40 to €52 – quite a good deal by L'Hermitage standards.

Résidence Coco Island GUESTHOUSE €

(Map p203; ☑0262 33 82 41, 0692 37 71 12; www.cocoisland-reunion.com; 21 Ave de la Mer; s €41-70, d €49-79; ❋☏☲) This is a popular budget option, with 23 unimaginative rooms of varying size, shape and appeal – have a look before committing. Cheaper rooms share toilets but have cubicle showers plonked in the corner. All rooms have air-con. Guests can use the communal kitchen and the small pool in the garden beside the reception. Prices drop for stays longer than five nights.

There's free wi-fi access for up to 30 minutes per day.

Les Bougainvilliers GUESTHOUSE €

(Map p203; ☑0262 33 82 48; www.bougainvillier.com; 27 Ruelle des Bougainvilliers; d €58-68; P❋☏☲) For something personal, try this jolly, hospitably run little bolt-hole with 15 rooms. Firm mattresses, colourful walls, a pool, plus a communal kitchen and a flower-filled garden, all just a five-minute stroll from the beach. And free bikes. The catch? It's a wee compact – the pool almost licks the terrace of the downstairs room.

Les Créoles HOTEL €€

(Map p203; ☑0262 26 52 65; www.hotellescreoles.com; 43 Ave de Bourbon; d €110-120; P❋☏☲) On an island where affordable-but-beautiful hotels are a rarity, this small-scale venture is a no-brainer. The comfortable, modern rooms are arrayed around the swimming pool. It feels a bit compact, but it provides a very agreeable stay. Facilities include a bar and a restaurant (open at lunchtime). One quibble: it's not directly on the beach. Check out the website for off-season discounts.

L'Hermitage-les-Bains

at the very south end of the beach at L'Hermitage. Facilities include three restaurants, a huge pool, a bar and direct beach access. For the price, we'd expect a spa.

🍴 Eating

Most hotels have restaurants and happily accept nonguests dropping in for a meal. There's also a handful of attractive beach restaurants, and it's only a short drive north to St-Gilles-les-Bains for an even greater selection of places to eat.

Snack Chez Racine
Jessica CREOLE, SANDWICHES €
(Map p203; ☎ 0692 98 91 35; 42 Blvd Leconte de Lisle; mains €3-8; ⊗ 11am-5.30pm Thu-Mon, to 3pm Tue) Tasty, filling, cheap Creole food and voluminous sandwiches. No surprise, it's popular. For a true local (if lowbrow) experience, try this modest eatery strategically positioned on a street running parallel to the beach. Takeaway is available.

Snack Chez Herbert CREOLE, SANDWICHES €
(Map p203; ☎ 0262 32 42 96; 40 Blvd Leconte de Lisle; mains €3-7; ⊗ 11.30am-5.30pm Tue-Sun) This popular joint is worth visiting for its cheap and wholesome Creole staples. Snacks, salads, sandwiches and other nibbles

Le Récif RESORT €€€
(Map p203; ☎ 0262 70 05 00; www.hotellerecif. com; 50 Ave de Bourbon; d incl breakfast €210-390; P ❄ 🛜 🏊) While not luxurious, this sprawling three-star resort consisting of various pavilions is a reliable base, especially if you can score promotional rates. Furnishings and communal areas are a bit tired, so don't come expecting cutting-edge design. Its main selling points are its location, a coconut's throw from the beach, and its numerous amenities, including two pools, a restaurant and a tennis court.

It's popular with families looking for a safe, quiet spot near the beach. There's a kids club during school holidays.

Lux RESORT €€€
(Map p192; ☎ 0262 70 05 00; www.luxresorts. com; 28 Rue du Lagon; d €185-250; P ❄ 🛜 🏊) Lux pays elegant homage to luxurious colonial architecture, with a gaggle of Creole-style villas scattered amid a sprawling property

are also available. Take your plunder to the beach or grab a (plastic) table on the shaded pavement and watch the *pétanque* players in action just across the road.

★ Le Manta
SEAFOOD €€

(Map p203; ☑ 0262 33 82 44; www.le-manta.re; 18 Blvd Leconte de Lisle; mains €14-17; ⊙ noon-2pm & 7-9.30pm; 🐾) Concealed in a wonderfully overgrown garden, this well-respected restaurant has a great selection of fish and meat dishes, as well as a few Creole classics and salads. Toothsome specialities include *salade Manta,* comprising smoked marlin and tuna, and *sauté de veau aux cèpes* (sautéed veal cooked with mushrooms). No, it's not right on the beach – it's just across the road.

L'Epicurien
CREOLE, FRENCH €€

(Map p203; ☑ 0692 86 49 47; 3 Rue des Îles Éparses; mains €15-23; ⊙ noon-2.30pm & 7-9.30pm) Tasty, filling, affordable Creole and French staples, including beef kebabs, curries, salads and grilled fish. No surprise, it's a hit. It completely lacks glamour but has charm to spare and a gregarious atmosphere. It's slightly set back from the beach.

La Marmite
CREOLE, BUFFET €€

(Map p203; ☑ 0262 33 31 37; 34 Blvd Leconte de Lisle; lunch buffet €18-35, dinner buffet €20-47; ⊙ noon-2pm & 7-10pm Mon-Sat, noon-2pm Sun; 🐾) This longstanding favourite is the best place on the west coast to try out authentic Creole food. You'll need to fast the day before – lunch and dinner at La Marmite are buffet-style, with a wide selection of wood-fired *carris* and salads on offer.

Au K'Banon
FRENCH, SEAFOOD €€

(Map p203; ☑ 0262 33 84 94; www.kbanon.net; Plage de L'Hermitage; mains €16-23; ⊙ 9-11am, noon-2.30pm & 7-10pm Fri & Sat, bar 11am-6pm Mon-Thu & Sun, to 11pm Fri & Sat; 🐾) Sweet! Au K'Banon is right on the beach, and it serves good, fresh food at competitive prices given the five-star location. The menu has something for all: fish dishes, grilled meats, salads and desserts. If it's just the setting you want to absorb, try one of the cocktails (from €6.50). Also serves breakfast.

Coco Beach
FRENCH, CREOLE €€

(Map p203; ☑ 0262 33 81 43; www.facebook.com/coco.beach.hacienda; Plage de L'Hermitage; mains €12-20; ⊙ noon-2pm & 7-10pm, bar 11am-11pm; 🐾) This perennial fave overlooking the beach serves fish and meat grills, salads and tapas (from 5.30pm). It's also a good place to hang

out and just enjoy the tropical atmosphere and fashionable buzz with a fresh Dodo beer in hand. There's live music on Fridays, Saturdays and Sundays.

Big appetite? Make a beeline for the all-you-can-eat buffet dinner (€20) on Fridays, Saturdays and Sundays. The Sunday Creole brunch (€20) is another hit.

La Bobine
EUROPEAN €€

(Map p203; ☑ 0262 33 94 36; www.la-bobine.com; Plage de L'Hermitage; mains €17-25; ⊙ 11am-11pm; 🐾) This sprightly restaurant with an exotic feel enjoys a perfect location, slap bang on the beach – if the terrace was any nearer to the water you'd have to swim to dinner. The wide-ranging menu features salads, fish and meat dishes as well as homemade desserts. There's also a snack section (until 5pm), with a choice of sandwiches, salads and light meals (€8 to €13).

It's also a fantastic place to sip a cocktail (from €7). There's live music on Thursday evenings.

🍷 Drinking & Nightlife

Party, party, party! L'Hermitage rocks on weekends. The unchallenged capital of Réunion's club scene, it has the greatest density of discos on the island. The fun starts late – after midnight – and places typically close around 5am. You don't need to be completely dolled up but if you're wearing shorts and flip-flops you'll be turned away.

All beach restaurants have bars and stay open well after the kitchen has closed.

L'Arena
CLUB

(Map p203; ☑ 0262 38 12 05; www.facebook.com/arena.ermitage; 1 Rue des Îles Éparses; ⊙ 10pm-5am Wed, Fri & Sat) A long-standing hot spot, L'Arena continues to draw good-looking and well-dressed hordes looking to get down to salsa, *kizomba* (a type of dance from Angola) and Latin rock music (among others).

La Villa Club
CLUB

(Map p203; ☑ 0692 60 19 00; www.lavilla-club.com; 71 Ave de Bourbon; ⊙ 11pm-5am Fri & Sat) L'Hermitage's top nightspot positively sizzles on a Friday and Saturday night when the dance floors are packed. Tropical, electro and dance music dominate the play list.

Le Loft
CLUB

(Map p203; ☑ 0692 67 44 54; www.facebook.com/leloftsaintgilles; 1 Rue des Îles Éparses; ⊙ 10pm-5am Thu-Sat) A pulsating club playing a little bit of this and a little bit of that. Also has karaoke.

Moulin du Tango
CLUB

(Map p203; 📞 0262 24 53 90; www.moulin-du-tango.re; 9 Ave de Bourbon; ⊙ 10pm-5am Wed, Fri & Sat) Bump your hips with a mature crowd in this dance club famous for its themed nights.

La Gueule de Bois
BAR

(Map p203; 📞 0262 22 90 06; www.facebook.com/lagueuledebois974; 5 Rue des Îles Éparses; ⊙ 7pm-midnight Wed-Sun) The name of this cheerful den is a French expression meaning 'hangover', which is pretty appropriate given the incendiary cocktails (€9) on offer. It hosts live bands on Sunday evening. Food is also served.

ℹ️ Getting There & Away

Car Jaune's nonexpress buses (line 02) between St-Denis (€2, one hour) and St-Pierre run through L'Hermitage. More information at www.carjaune.re.

La Saline-les-Bains

POP 2900

If you find the scene in nearby St-Gilles and L'Hermitage a little too much, head to La Saline-les-Bains. Though immediately to the south of L'Hermitage along the coast, it has a distinct atmosphere. Here it's more mellow, more alternative, more nonconformist.

◎ Sights

The main beach is a stellar stretch of white sand and is usually less crowded than its northern counterparts at St-Gilles or L'Hermitage. It has shallow, calm waters, making it an ideal location for families.

Plage de la Souris Chaude
BEACH

(La Souris Chaude, La Saline-les-Bains) Not a fan of tan lines? Head due south and lay your towel on Plage de la Souris Chaude, which is a favourite among nudists (only just tolerated) and gay men (head to the northern tip of the beach). It remains largely off the tourist radar, not least because it's a bit hard to find.

Plage de Trou d'Eau
BEACH

At the southern end of the main beach, Plage de Trou d'Eau is a nice place to relax and have a swim.

🏃 Activities

Stand-up paddle boarding is a great way to explore the lagoon at a gentle pace. **Ecole de Stand Up Paddle du Lagon** (📞 0692 86 00 59, 0262 24 63 28; La-Saline-les-Bains; courses from €25; ⊙ 10am-5pm) offers one- or two-hour courses

run by a qualified instructor. The beachfront restaurant Planch'Alizé (p206) rents canoes, kayaks and paddleboats (from €6 per hour).

🛌 Sleeping

L'Amarina
GUESTHOUSE €

(📞 0693 97 02 81, 0262 33 81 60; www.facebook.com/Amarinareunion; 30 Rue des Ormeaux; d with shared bathroom €40-45, studio €55-60; 🖥️🛜❄️) Under new management since 2014, this well-run guesthouse has been upgraded and makes a great base for budgeteers. It is nicely small scale, with just five fan-cooled rooms and two studios that share well-scrubbed bathrooms. All units are neat and tidy, but without air-con they feel a bit airless during the hottest months.

The Mafate room enjoys a large terrace with good sea views, while the Cilaos studio offers ample space and also comes equipped with a private terrace. Common areas include a sitting room, kitchen and swimming pool (from 8am to 7pm). The guesthouse is in a residential area, a 10-minute stroll from the beach. There's also a pizzeria and a bakery nearby. Cash only.

Le Vacoa
HOTEL €

(📞 0262 24 12 48; www.levacoa.com; 54 Rue Antoine de Bertin; d €59-65; ❄️🛜❄️) A five-minute stroll from the beach, this little two-storey *résidence hôtelière* (mini-resort) won't knock your socks off but it contains 15 modern, well-appointed (albeit hanky-sized) rooms arranged around a central courtyard. Expect a bit of road noise during the day. Precious perks include a kitchen for guests' use and a pocket-sized pool.

⭐ La Closerie du Lagon
APARTMENT €€

(📞 0692 86 32 47, 0262 24 12 56; www.closerie-du-lagon.fr; 78ter Rue Lacaussade; d €110; 🅿️❄️🛜) Alain and Charles are your kindly hosts at this ravishing abode, which consists of a splendid apartment with all mod cons in a peaceful property by the beach (but no sea views from the apartment). It's fully equipped. Intimate, chic and gay friendly. There's a two-night minimum stay. Bonus: free bikes. Cash only.

Le Dalon Plage
BUNGALOW €€

(📞 0692 04 94 26, 0262 34 29 77; www.ledalon.jimdo.com; 6 Allée des Tuits Tuits, La Souris Chaude; studio d €75-85, s/d incl breakfast €55/60; 🅿️❄️🛜❄️) It's just a short amble from the Plage de la Souris Chaude to this hedonistic, gay-friendly place. Guests are allowed (if not incited) to swim naked in the gleaming pool.

Too prudish? Slumber in one of the two fully equipped studios; the cheaper one is slightly darker than the other. There's also a small, plain room with shared bathroom in the owners' house.

The flowery garden is a feast for the eyes – it helps that François, one of the two owners, is a gardener.

La Maison du Lagon HOTEL €€
(☑ 0262 24 30 14; www.lamaisondulagon.com; 72 Rue Auguste Lacaussade; s €78-123, d €98-133, ste €190, incl breakfast; P ❋ 🛜 🌊) This villa has a compact but respectable collection of various-sized rooms and apartments, but only four units have direct sea views. They all feel a little past their prime on the inside, but they are clean, and the location, right by the beach, is tip-top. There's a small pool at the entrance of the property as well as a kitchenette.

Tip for couples: book the stand-alone Zen chalet (€115), which is a sweet spot. There's limited private parking (four spaces only).

Akoya Hotel & Spa LUXURY HOTEL €€€
(☑ 0262 61 61 62; www.akoya-hotel.com; 6 Impasse des Goélands; d €220-350, ste €360-400; P ❋ 🛜 🌊) By far the fanciest hotel on the west coast, this venture that opened in late 2015 features a cluster of three-storey buildings amid beautifully landscaped grounds and offers plenty of amenities, including two reputable restaurants, a bar, a vast spa and, best of all, a top-notch infinity pool with sweeping ocean views. One proviso: you'll need to cross the road to get to the beach.

The 104 rooms are all equipped to a very high standard, but only half of them enjoy sea views.

Hôtel Swalibo HOTEL €€€
(☑ 0262 24 10 97; www.swalibo.com; 9 Rue des Salines; s €110-150, d €140-190, incl breakfast; P ❋ 🛜 🌊) This small (some would say 'cramped') two-storey hotel is a good deal if you can get online specials. The rooms, which sport colourful walls and are arranged around a gleaming pool, are well appointed but some rooms on the ground floor lack natural light and the furnishings need a freshen-up. There's an on-site restaurant. It's 200m away from the beach.

🍴 Eating

⭐ Planch'Alizé EUROPEAN, SANDWICHES €€
(☑ 0262 24 62 61; www.planchalize.net; 25 Rue des Mouettes; mains €12-25; ⊙ noon-2.30pm daily, 7-9pm Wed-Sun, bar 9am-late; 🛜) Visitors and locals flock to this bustling little *paillotte* (beach restaurant) for reliable seafood as well as meat dishes, lavish salads and tempting desserts, including crêpes and a stunning *crème brûlée au géranium* (crème brûlée flavoured with geranium). All at very honest prices. It's also a fantastic spot for a drink any time of the day.

Arrive early to secure a table overlooking the beach. For a snack, call by the adjacent takeaway outlet, which turns out tasty sandwiches, salads and homemade desserts (from €3). Live bands sometimes play here on Friday from 6.30pm. Sun lounges, snorkelling gear and paddle boards are available for hire.

La Bodega EUROPEAN €€
(☑ 0262 35 66 69; Plage de Trou d'Eau; mains €15-22; ⊙ noon-3pm & 6.30-9.30pm, bar 9am-10pm) Worth a mention for its breezy deck overlooking the lagoon, memorable sea views and jovial atmosphere, La Bodega serves a wide range of dishes, including tapas and seafood, and there's a snack section if you prefer a sandwich or a waffle (from €3). More than the food, though, it's the beachside location that's the real draw. There's live music on Friday and Sunday evenings.

La Bonne Marmite CREOLE €€
(☑ 0262 39 82 49; Route du Trou d'Eau; mains €12-16, dinner buffet €19; ⊙ 7-9.30pm Mon-Sat) Pounce on The Good Cooking Pot's excellent-value dinner buffet, which features 12 wholesome *carris*, and you'll leave perfectly sated. It's a coconut's throw from the beach (with the sea just out of sight, alas).

Le Copacabana FRENCH €€€
(☑ 0262 24 16 31; www.copacabana-plage.com; 20 Rue des Mouettes; mains €18-27; ⊙ 9-10.30am & noon-3pm daily, 7-10pm Fri & Sat, bar 9am-7pm; 🛜) This trendy bar-restaurant has a peerless position right on the beach. Enjoy well-prepared fish and meat dishes as well as excellent homemade desserts. Le Copa is also the most fashionable spot for a night-time tipple or a refreshing fruit juice any time of the day. The catch? It's pretty expensive. It also rents out sun lounges.

ℹ️ Getting There & Away

Car Jaune's nonexpress buses between St-Denis and St-Pierre (line O2) run through La Saline-les-Bains (from St-Denis, €2, 1¼ hours). More at www.carjaune.re.

St-Leu

POP 33,600

Since the good old days of the sugar industry ended, forward-looking St-Leu has transformed itself into a mecca for outdoor enthusiasts. This is the place to get high – legally: no doubt you'll be tempted to join the paragliders who wheel down from the Hauts to the lagoon. Scuba divers also swear that the drop-offs here are the best on the island.

St-Leu has a smattering of handsome stone buildings dating from the French colonial era, such as the *mairie* (town hall) and the church opposite. Other attractions are the shady park along the seafront and a protected beach that is popular with families.

St-Leu is also optimally placed for explorations of the coast and forays into the Hauts.

⊙ Sights

Notre-Dame de la Salette   CHURCH
(Map p207; Sente la Salette) The little white chapel of Notre-Dame de la Salette, perched on the side of the hill to the east of town, was built in 1859 as a plea for protection against the cholera epidemic sweeping the entire island. Whether by luck or divine intervention, St-Leu was spared from the epidemic, and thousands of pilgrims come here each year on 19 September to offer their thanks.

Kelonia   MUSEUM
(☑ 0262 34 81 10; www.museesreunion.re/kelonia; 46 Rue du Général de Gaulle, Pointe des Châteaux; adult/child €7/5; ⊙ 9am-5pm) Don't miss this ecologically conscious marine and research centre dedicated to sea turtles, about 2km north of St-Leu. It features exhibits, interactive displays and big tanks where you can get a close-up look at the five different varieties of turtle found in the waters around Réunion, especially the green turtle *(Chelonia mydas)*. Guided tours are available.

Kids love the place but adults will also be blown away by this well-organised venture.

🏃 Activities

Diving

The dive spots off Pointe au Sel to the south of St-Leu offer some of the best underwater landscapes in Réunion, while the lagoon closer to St-Leu is good for coral.

B'leu Océan   DIVING
(Map p192; ☑ 0262 34 97 49; www.bleuocean.fr; 25 Rue du Général Lambert; introductory/single dive €60/53; ⊙ 8am-5pm) A professional centre that

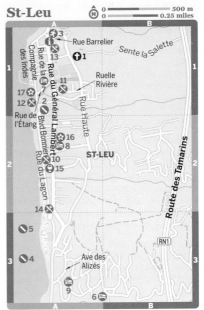

St-Leu

caters just as well to beginners as it does to advanced divers. Five- and 10-dive packages are €240/440. Prices include equipment rental.

Excelsus
DIVING

(☑0262 34 73 65; www.excelsus-plongee.com; Impasse des Plongeurs, Pointe des Châteaux; introductory/single dive €62/52; ☺8am-5pm) This efficient operation offers a full range of dives for all levels. Three-/six-dive packages cost €150/288. Prices include equipment rental.

Abyss Plongée
DIVING

(Map p207; ☑0262 34 79 79; www.abyss-plongee. com; 17 Blvd Bonnier; introductory/single dive €62/47; ☺8am-5pm Mon-Sat, to noon Sun) This reputable outfit has a full menu of reef and wreck dives and runs certification courses. Three- and six-dive packages go for €135/260. Prices include equipment rental.

Réunion Plongée
DIVING

(☑0262 34 77 77, 0692 85 66 37; www.reunion plongee.com; 13 Ave des Artisans; introductory/ single dive €65/52; ☺8.30am-4.30pm) A small outfit with good credentials. Four-/six-dive dive packages cost €192/282.

Paragliding

St-Leu is one of the world's top spots for paragliding, with excellent uplifting thermals year-round. If you're new to dangling yourself in the air, you can tandem paraglide with one of the many operators offering flights. The most popular launch pad is at an altitude of 800m, high above the town. There's another launch pad at 1500m. The descent from the mountain is amazing, with heart-stopping views over the lagoon and the coast. Children over six are welcome.

Azurtech
PARAGLIDING

(☑0692 85 04 00; www.azurtech.com; Pointe des Châteaux; tandem flight €75-110; ☺8am-5pm) A long-standing favourite. It has a range of tandem flights, including a 40-minute 'Must' flight, which comes recommended. Kids over five are welcome.

Parapente Réunion
PARAGLIDING

(☑0262 24 87 84, 0692 82 92 92; www.parapente-reunion.fr; 1 & 103 Rue Georges Pompidou, Route des Colimaçons, Pointe des Châteaux; tandem flight €75-110; ☺8am-5pm) A well-established operator. Offers a range of tandem flights, including a fantastic 'Sunset Flight' above the lagoon.

Bourbon Parapente
PARAGLIDING

(Map p207; ☑0692 87 58 74; www.bourbon parapente.com; 4 Rue Haute; tandem flight €80-

---

DIVING ST-LEU

St-Leu features splendid wall diving and good coral fields, but fish life is said to be less abundant than off St-Gilles-les-Bains. Here walls tumble steeply to several dozen metres.

Tombant de la Pointe au Sel (Map p192) South of St-Leu, this is widely regarded as Réunion's best all-round dive site. In addition to great scenery, this stunning drop-off offers a fabulous array of fish life and seldom fails to produce good sightings of pelagics, especially tuna, barracudas and jacks. Suitable for experienced divers.

Le Jardin des Kiosques (Map p207) With a depth ranging from 3m to 18m, it's very secure yet atmospheric for beginners. It's all about little canyons and grooves.

La Maison Verte (Map p207) A relaxing site, blessed with good coral formations in less than 6m.

Antonio Lorenzo (Map p192) Wreck enthusiasts will make a beeline for this well-preserved vessel that rests in about 38m on a sandy bottom off Pointe des Chateaux. Fish life is dynamic, and penetration in the hull is possible.

110; ☺8am-5pm) An experienced outfit. It has a range of tandem flights lasting from 20 minutes to 40 minutes. Kids over five are welcome.

Surfing

The surfing scene is no longer what it used to be, following several shark attacks that occurred off Boucan Canot, Pointe des Trois Bassins and St-Gilles-les-Bains. It's wise to seek local advice before hitting the waves.

🎭 Festivals & Events

Leu Tempo Festival
THEATRE

(www.lesechoir.com; ☺May) A very popular theatre festival at Le Séchoir – Le K venue in St-Leu. Also features dance, circus and music. Early May.

Fête de Notre-Dame de la Salette
RELIGIOUS

(Festival of Notre Dame de la Salette; ☺Sep) Pilgrimage to the miracle-working Madonna at the chapel of Notre-Dame de la Salette (p207). Fair and street events over 10 days in September.

🛏 Sleeping

There aren't any resorts in St-Leu. Most accommodation here consists of a few little hotels in the backstreets or on the outskirts of town. You'll need your own wheels to get to the beach.

Résidence Les Pêcheurs　　BUNGALOW €
(Map p207; ☑ 0262 34 91 25, 0692 85 39 84; http://les.pecheurs.pagesperso-orange.fr; 27 Ave des Alizés; d/q €52/82; ᴘ 🛰 ❄) Find this clean, friendly and well-run venture in a quiet neighbourhood on the southern edge of town. It consists of six bungalows with partial sea views. They're spacious, practical and well kitted out, but there's no air-con (only fans). There's no beach nearby, but guests can chill by the small pool. Three nights minimum. Brilliant value.

Palais d'Asie　　APARTMENT €
(Map p207; ☑ 0262 34 80 41, 0692 86 48 80; lepalaisdasie974@wanadoo.fr; 5 Rue de l'Étang; d €40-45; ᴘ 🛰 ❄ ☀) One of St-Leu's best bargains, though the 'Palais' bit is a gross misnomer. It's comfortably central, with minimally furnished but functional rooms. And yes, it does have its own (tiny) swimming pool. Prices drop to €35 to €40 for stays longer than two nights.

Repos Laleu　　APARTMENT €€
(Map p207; ☑ 0262 34 93 84; 249 Rue du Général Lambert; d/q €60/75; ᴘ 🛰 ❄) Offers eight fully equipped studios as well as two large apartments, smack-dab in the centre. Note that one-week stays are preferred.

Iloha Seaview Hotel　　HOTEL €€
(☑ 0262 34 89 89; www.iloha.fr; 44 Rue Georges Pompidou, Route des Colimaçons, Pointe des Châteaux; s €75-85, d €90-170, bungalows €130-190; ᴘ 🛰 ❄ ☀) The Iloha is a very good all-round hotel-cum-resort set in a sprawling property on Route des Colimaçons, north of town. Its tidy rooms and simply designed bungalows offer a great choice for everyone from couples to families. Precious perks include two pools, two restaurants, a spa and well-tended gardens. Views take in the lagoon. Check the website for special offers.

★ **Le Blue Margouillat**　　BOUTIQUE HOTEL €€€
(Map p207; ☑ 0262 34 64 00; www.bluemargouillat.com; Impasse Jean Albany; d €175-240; ᴘ 🛰 ❄ ☀) This delightful hotel on the southern outskirts of St-Leu adds a welcoming touch of glam to the local hotel scene, with just 14 artfully designed and sensitively furnished rooms, an award-winning restaurant, an inviting pool and smashing views. That said, the odd layout of the bathrooms – no doors and no walls, only a thick curtain – may not be to everybody's taste.

For the best sea views, angle for one of the upstairs rooms.

🍴 Eating

L'Orange Givrée　　CAFETERIA €
(Map p207; ☑ 0692 48 94 39; 2 Rue Barrelier; mains €4-10; ⏱ 11.30am-3.30pm Mon-Sat) Blink and you'll miss the tiny entrance of this funky little den next to the tourist office. It whips up appetising salads, *plats du jour* (daily specials), wraps, sandwiches, fruit juices and other treats at wallet-friendly prices. Make sure you save room for the criminally addictive banana cake.

★ **Au Bout La Bas**　　EUROPEAN €€
(Map p207; ☑ 0262 55 98 72; 37 Rue du Lagon; mains €10-20; ⏱ noon-2pm & 7-10pm Tue-Sat) Brimming with good cheer, this tropical cocoon in a street running parallel to the seafront serves excellent value-for-money food. A sampling of choices might include a burger with homemade fries, a copious salad or a toothsome *tartine* (a slice of bread with toppings). The homemade desserts are every bit as devastatingly delicious as they sound. Mmm, the chocolate cake.

Sarah Beach　　INTERNATIONAL €€
(Map p192; ☑ 0262 10 23 37; www.facebook.com/restosb; 44 Rue du Général Lambert; mains €17-22; ⏱ noon-1.45pm & 7-9.30pm Thu-Mon) At the northern entrance of town, this restaurant has a great position overlooking the lagoon. With such appealing surroundings, many alfrescoholics would go back to this breezy veranda by the sea for the location alone, but the well-priced eclectic fare is delightful too, especially the *pierrades* (a hot stone surface on which you cook thin strips of meat or fish), the house speciality.

Villa Vanille　　EUROPEAN €€
(Map p207; ☑ 0262 34 03 15; www.restaurant-lavillavanille.fr; 69 Rue du Lagon; mains €11-22; ⏱ 11.45am-2.15pm & 7-10pm) No plastic chairs at this zinging spot, but teak furnishings and an agreeable terrace. Villa Vanille has the most eclectic menu in town. Choose from frondy salads, excellent tuna tartares, meat dishes and ice creams. Lounge on the beach across the road once you've finished your meal – this is the life!

Le Zat CREOLE, SEAFOOD €€
(Map p207; ☑0262 42 20 92; 14 Rue de la Compagnie des Indes; mains €14-18; ☺12.30-3.30pm; 🛜) Near the harbour, this unpretentious open-air joint majors in fish and meat dishes as well as salads. Good homemade desserts too. The menu changes daily, as displayed on a handwritten blackboard. It's also a supremely chilled place to sip a tropical potion and nibble on tapas.

★**L'Eveil des Sens –
Le Blue Margouillat** MODERN FRENCH €€€
(Map p207; ☑0262 34 64 00; www.blue-margouillat. com; Impasse Jean Albany; mains €26-38, menus €69-109; ☺7.30-9pm daily, noon-1pm Sun) This elegant restaurant inside Le Blue Margouillat hotel is the top-end darling of the west coast. Marc Chappot's creative dishes are artfully prepared and presented, and all provide a burst of flavour. Another draw is the romantic setting: tables are set around the pool or on the colonial-style terrace. Prices have escalated over the last few years, but dining here is a memorable experience.

Il Etait Une Fois FRENCH €€€
(Map p207; ☑0692 68 96 19; 1 Ruelle Rivière; mains €24-29; ☺7-9pm Tue-Sat) Tucked away on a side street running perpendicular to the main road, 'Once Upon a Time' offers something different. There's no menu, just a selection of the day's dishes depending on seasonal produce and the chef's mood. Its rustic, plant-filled terrace is also a welcoming place to eat.

🍷 Drinking & Nightlife

Although St-Leu can't rival L'Hermitage-les-Bains or St-Pierre, it does have a few great places for a night out.

Le Zinc BAR
(Map p207; ☑0262 22 29 11; 228 Rue du Général Lambert; ☺5pm-midnight Thu-Sun) Le Zinc is St-Leu's liveliest spot (an easy distinction, given the lack of competitors). Come for the good fun, great mix of people, wicked cocktails and great music, with DJs or live bands every evening.

☆ Entertainment

Le Séchoir – Le K CONCERT VENUE
(Map p207; ☑0262 34 31 38; www.lesechoir.com; 209 Rue du Général Lambert) One of Réunion's venues for contemporary theatre, dance and music, as well as puppet shows, circus acts and other cultural activities. The organisers

also put on open-air concerts and film shows in the area. Contact the tourist office to find out about the latest shows.

**Rondavelle Les Filaos –
Chez Jean-Paul** CONCERT VENUE
(Map p207; ☑0692 58 58 38; www.lesfilaos-chezjeanpaul.re; 17 Rue de la Compagnie des Indes; ☺7.30am-8.30pm) Like bees to honey, St-Leusiens swarm on this modest, open-air bar close to the beach when live bands perform on Sunday evenings. Good blend of electro, *maloya* (traditional dance music), rock and jazz. During the day the 'Ronda' is esteemed for its cheap sandwiches, freshly squeezed fruit juices and cold beers.

ℹ Information

Office du Tourisme (Map p207; ☑0262 34 63 30; www.saintleu.re; 1 Rue Barrelier; ☺1.30-5.30pm Mon, 9am-noon & 1.30-5.30pm Tue-Fri, 9am-noon & 2-5pm Sat; 🛜) At the north end of the main road passing through the centre of town. It has brochures galore and helpful, English-speaking staff. *Gîtes de montagne* can also be booked here. Free wi-fi.

ℹ Getting There & Away

Car Jaune's buses between St-Denis (€2, 1¼ hours) and St-Pierre (€2, 1¼ hours) run through the centre of St-Leu. The bus station is near the town hall. More information at www.carjaune.re.

Around St-Leu

After getting active in St-Leu, there's no better way to wind down than by exploring the villages that cling to the sloping hills high above the town. The zigzagging roads are scenic to boot and the atmosphere wonderfully laid-back.

◎ Sights

To the north of St-Leu, take the D12, known as Route des Colimaçons – a series of intestine-like S-curves – then veer due south on the D3 to **La Chaloupe St-Leu** before plunging back to the coast via **Piton St-Leu**, where the brightly painted **Hindu temple** is worth a gander. If you really want to get away from it all, you could continue to drive uphill from the village of **Les Colimaçons** until you reach the Route Forestière des Tamarins, which threads for 38km across the slopes from Le Tévelave to Le Maïdo – sensational. Whatever your itinerary, a good road map or a GPS unit is essential as it's easy to get disoriented.

★Stella Matutina MUSEUM
(Map p192; ☑0692 33 32 03; www.museesreunion.
re/musee/stella-matutina; 6 Allée des Flamboy-
ants; ☉1-5.30pm Mon, 9.30am-4.45pm Tue-Sun)
Réunion's most beloved museum reopened
its doors in 2015 after a massive renovation.
About 4km south of St-Leu on the D11 to
Piton St-Leu and Les Avirons, it's dedicated
primarily to the sugar industry, but also provides fascinating insights into the history of
the island, especially slavery and the colonial
cra. It includes a state-of-the-art 4D cinema.
There's a shop and a cafeteria.

**Conservatoire Botanique
National de Mascarin** GARDENS
(Map p192; ☑0262 24 92 27; www.cbnm.org; 2
Rue du Père Georges, Les Colimaçons; adult/child
€7/5; ☉9am-5pm Tue-Sun) On the Route des
Colimaçons, on the slopes north of St-Leu,
this attractive garden is in the grounds of a
19th-century Creole mansion and contains
an impressive collection of native plant species, all neatly labelled, as well as many from
around the Indian Ocean. Spitting distance
from the Conservatoire is the **Église du
Sacré-Coeur**. This majestic church was built
in 1875, using lava stones.

🛏 Sleeping & Eating

There are several peaceful villages within
10km of St-Leu that offer accommodation
in a relaxed, rural setting. Many places boast
bird's-eye views down to the coast.

Grocery stores and a few snack bars can be
found in most villages. B&Bs can also prepare
meals on request. For more eating options,
your best bet is to drive down to St-Leu.

**Le Balcon Créole – Chez François
et Michèle Huet** B&B €
(Map p192; ☑0692 67 62 54, 0262 54 76 70; www.
balcon-creole.fr; 202 Chemin Potier, Les Colimaçons;
d incl breakfast €50-60; P🅿🛜) The four rooms
here are sparkling, fresh and colourful, and
provide a very cushy landing after a hard
day's driving. The two more expensive ones
come with splendid sea views. When it comes
to preparing fish dishes, the Huets know
their stuff (dinner €26). It's signposted, uphill
from the botanical garden.

Ask for the spacious Creole-style *gîte*
(lodge/self-catering accommodation) in the
flower-filled garden if you intend to stay
more than four nights.

★Les Lataniers APARTMENT €€
(Map p192; ☑0262 34 74 45, 0692 25 13 38; www.
les-lataniers.com; 136ter Rue Adrien Lagourgue, Piton
St-Leu; d €85-140, q €120-140; P🅿🛜🏊) An excellent surprise, with tasteful decor, a fantastic
garden with panoramic views and a stunning
pool looking straight out to the sea. The four
apartments are huge, well appointed and
sun-filled. It's an ideal base for hikers as the
owner is a keen walker with lots of route
information on the island. On the southern
fringes of Piton St-Leu, towards Les Avirons.

There's a three-night minimum stay, and
one-week stays are preferred.

Caz' Océane B&B €€
(☑0692 74 63 94, 0262 54 89 40; www.chambred
hoteslareunioncazoceane.com; 28 Chemin Mutel,
Notre-Dame des Champs; s €55, d €65-85, incl
breakfast; P🅿🛜) Run by a Belgian couple, this
snug B&B in the hamlet of Notre-Dame des
Champs is a reliable base. No one would ac-
cuse the four rooms and the apartment of
being over decorated but they are kept ship-
shape. The owners can cook some reputedly
good evening meals (€25) and rates include
an ample breakfast. English and German are
spoken.

The icing on the cake? A Jacuzzi with
million-dollar views – great for post-hike
unwinding.

❶ Getting There & Away

You'll need your own wheels to explore the Hauts
(hills) above St-Leu.

Le Tévelave

POP 1600

Le Tévelave, about 10km up an impossibly
twisty road in the hills above Les Avirons, is a
gem of a village. It offers a real taste of rural
life and is a great base for walkers. You can
really feel a sense of wilderness and seclusion
here, light years away from the bling and
bustle of the coast. At the top of the village is
the starting point for the Route Forestière des
Tamarins, which leads through a cryptomeria
forest and emerges 36km later below Le Maïdo. Picnic sites abound along the road.

🛏 Sleeping & Eating

L'Écorce Blanc INN €€
(☑0692 02 16 30; www.lecorce-blanc.com; 46 Rue
Francis Rivière, Le Tévelave; d incl breakfast €65-90;
P🅿🛜) Perched at a height of 1040m, this

friendly *ferme auberge* (farm inn) is beloved by locals for its authentic home cooking (meals €25, by reservation). Pity about the dull indoor dining room, though. There are also four snug, wood-panelled rooms in the same building as the dining room (noisy at meal times); they feature good bedding and sparkling bathrooms.

Be warned, though: driving up the 600m-long access road to the farm inn calls for solid driving skills.

ⓘ Getting There & Away

You'll need your own wheels to get to Le Tévelave as bus services are infrequent.

Étang-Salé-les-Bains

POP 14,000

Kilometres away from the hullabaloo around St-Gilles, Étang-Salé-les-Bains is a low-key resort more for locals than foreign tourists, though its superb black-sand beach is no longer a secret for in-the-know sunbathers and swimmers.

◉ Sights & Activities

Very few visitors know that diving is available at Étang-Salé-les-Bains. The sites are almost untouched.

Plage de L'Étang-Salé-les-Bains   BEACH
The generous stretch of ash-coloured beach on the northern outskirts of town is great for sunbathing and swimming, and offers excellent sunset vistas. Most of the beach has a shallow bottom with a gradual slope. Swimming is forbidden outside the supervised area, which is marked by buoys.

Croc Parc   ZOO
(Map p192; ✆0262 91 40 41; www.crocparc.re; 1 Route Forestière; adult/child €10/8; ⊙10am-5pm) Wanna keep the kids happy? Take a small detour to this zoo, near Étang-Salé-les-Hauts (it's signposted). There are about 100 crocodiles at the complex, as well as iguanas and tortoises. Feeding demonstrations are held at 4pm on Wednesday and Sunday.

Plongée Salée   DIVING
(✆0262 91 71 23; www.plongeesalee.com; 5 Rue Mottet de Narbonne; introductory/single dive €66/55; ⊙by reservation) The owners of this reputable outfit take only small diving groups, with a selection of around 15 dive sites for all levels; see the schedule on the website.

🛏 Sleeping & Eating

You'll find a few *camions-snacks* along the beach as well as several popular eateries in the street running parallel to the beach.

Les Sables Noirs   HOSTEL €
(✆0262 38 04 89, 0692 08 06 28; 88B Ave Raymond Barre, Étang-Salé-les-Hauts; dm €15, d with shared bathroom €40; ❉🅿🛜) If being near the beach isn't a must, this hostel-like venture efficiently run by Evelyne is manna from heaven for thrifty travellers. It shelters one seven-bed dorm (with air-con), one 11-bed dorm (with fan) and a few doubles, which are all clean and functional. Facilities include a communal kitchen and a large terrace at the back.

It's in Étang-Salé-les-Hauts, about 4km away from Étang-Salé-les-Bains, near the church. It's easy to get to the beach by bus.

Camping Municipal de l'Étang-Salé-les-Bains   CAMPGROUND €
(✆0262 91 75 86; www.camping-reunion.com; Rue Guy Hoarau; camping per site €22-28) There are 70 shady sites at this trim camping ground a short walk back from the beach. The ablution blocks have been upgraded and are in good nick.

Zot Case en Natte   BUNGALOW €€
(✆0262 26 57 73, 0692 82 33 26; 3 Impasse Alamanda, Route des Canots; bungalows for 2-3 nights €268; 🅿❉🛜) This place is a bit tricky to find, tucked away in a side street in Étang-Salé-les-Hauts, but it's well worth the detour if you're after something quirky. Picture this: a lovely Creole house sheltering three atmospheric rooms with parquet flooring. Longer stays are preferred.

Framissima Floralys & Roseaux des Sables   HOTEL €€
(✆0262 91 79 79; www.floralys.re; 2 Ave de l'Océan; d €70-115, q €95-180; ❉🛜🏊) This well-run three-star abode is set in an attractive 3-hectare garden beside the roundabout in the middle of town and a two-minute walk from the beach. It comprises two sections: the Floralys, with modern yet impersonal rooms set in a cluster of cottages, and the Roseaux des Sables, with upscale, fully equipped villas, at the far end of the property.

Le Bambou   FRENCH, CREOLE €€
(✆0262 91 70 28; 56 Rue Octave Bénard; mains €9-24; ⊙11.30am-9.30pm Thu-Tue; 🛜) This well-oiled machine near the main roundabout is known for its kilometre-long menu featuring lots of salads, pizzas, pasta dishes, crêpes,

Creole classics, grilled meats and fish. The food ain't gourmet and doesn't claim to be, but if you need to fill a gap any time of the day, this is your baby. On weekdays, the €11 lunch menu is brilliant value.

ℹ Information

Office du Tourisme (☑ 0820 203 220; www.sud.reunion.fr; 74 Rue Octave Bénard; ☺ 9am-noon & 1-4.30pm Mon-Sat; ☎) It's housed in the old train station on the roundabout that marks the town centre. *Gîtes de montagnes* can be booked here. Also sells books, maps and crafts. Free wi-fi.

ℹ Getting There & Away

Car Jaune's nonexpress buses between St-Denis and St-Pierre (line SO2) run through Étang-Salé-les-Bains. The town also lies on Car Jaune's coastal bus route (line S3) between St-Joseph and St-Paul. More information at www.carjaune.re.

St-Louis

POP 52.600

If St-Gilles and L'Hermitage are very Westernised and touristy, St-Louis, by contrast, falls below many travellers' radars. This is the heart of Tamil culture on the west coast, and it won't take long to feel that the city exudes an undeniably exotic atmosphere. The town doesn't have anything fantastic to offer, but it is certainly worth a quick stop to admire a handful of religious buildings, including a Tamil temple, a splendid mosque and the biggest church on the island.

Most travellers travel to St-Louis to catch the bus to Cilaos or to visit the Sucrerie du Gol, a sugar refinery that lies about 1.5km west of of the centre.

◉ Sights

Sucrerie du Gol　　　DISTILLERY
(Map p192; ☑ 0262 91 05 47; www.tereos-ocean-indien.com; Rond-Point du Gol, St-Louis; adult/child €8/5; ☺ 9am-7pm Tue-Sat, tours by reservation Jul-Dec) A highlight (and a major landmark, with its big chimneys) near St-Louis is this old sugar refinery, about 1.5km west of the centre. You can tour the refinery, one of only two on the island still functioning, during the cane harvest (July to December).

🛏 Sleeping & Eating

There's nowhere to stay in central St-Louis, and we can't think of a good reason to do so anyway. You're less than 10 minutes by car from St-Pierre.

You'll find a few snack bars and simple eateries along the main road. For more options, head to nearby St-Pierre.

ℹ Getting There & Away

Car Jaune buses between St-Denis and St-Pierre run through St-Louis. Buses to Cilaos (€1.80, 1½ hours) run from the bus station. More details at www.carjaune.re.

Entre-Deux & Le Dimitile

POP 6260

The sweet little village of Entre-Deux, high in the hills 18km north of St-Pierre, got its name (which means 'between two') because it is situated on a ridge between two valleys: the Bras de Cilaos and the Bras de la Plaine. Entre-Deux is a delightful place to stay and get a taste of rural life.

◉ Sights

Entre-Deux boasts a wealth of *cases créoles*, traditional country cottages surrounded by well-tended and fertile gardens, many of which are being restored. There's also a strong tradition of local crafts, including natty slippers made from the leaves of an aloe-like plant called *choca*.

Espace Culturel Muséographique du Dimitile – Camp Marron　　MUSEUM
(ECM; Map p216; ☑ 0692 39 73 26; Le Dimitile; admission €2, with an audio guide €5; ☺ by reservation) Just before the summit of Le Dimitile, this modest yet well-organised museum does a good job of explaining *marronage* (the act of escaping plantation life) and tracing the history of slavery in Réunion. Sadly, its opening hours are unreliable; contact the tourist office in Entre-Deux or call ahead.

🏃 Activities

Le Dimitile　　HIKING
(Map p216) The hike up the slopes of iconic Le Dimitile (1837m) is tough but you'll be rewarded with a sensational view over the Cirque de Cilaos. There are several options to reach the viewpoint. The tourist office can provide information and sketch maps detailing the various routes.

The shortest route, called **Sentier de la Chapelle**, starts from the end of the D26 (there's a small parking area), about 10km from Entre-Deux, at an altitude of 1100m. Count on a five-hour return slog.

LES MAKES & LA FENÊTRE

One of Réunion's best-kept secrets, Les Makes boasts a wonderful bucolic atmosphere and a lovely setting. Snuggled into the seams of the Hauts, it's accessible via a tortuous secondary road from St-Louis (12km). At almost 1200m, breathing in the fresh alpine air here is enough therapy for a lifetime.

It would be a sin to visit Les Makes and not take the forest road that leads to **La Fenêtre** (The Window; Map p192) viewpoint, another 10km further uphill. The view over the entire Cirque de Cilaos and the surrounding craggy summits that jab the skyline will be etched in your memory forever. La Fenêtre is also a wonderful picnic spot. Hint: arrive early, before it gets cloudy.

Les Makes area is also ideal for stargazing. The **Observatoire Astronomique** (Map p192; ☑ 0262 37 86 83; www.ilereunion.com/observatoire-makes; 18 Rue Georges Bizet, Les Makes; adult €4-10, child €2.50-5; ☉ by reservation) offers stargazing programs from 9pm to midnight. It's best to call ahead to confirm the program is on. **Centre Équestre de la Fenêtre** (Map p192; ☑ 0692 19 25 65; 31 Rue Montplaisir, Les Makes; per hour €16; ☉ Tue-Sat by reservation) can arrange guided horse-riding trips in the forests around Les Makes. It's a great way to soak up the scenery.

Should you fall under the spell of charming Les Makes (no doubt you will), you can bunk down at the adorable **Le Vieil Alambic – Chez Jean-Luc d'Eurveilher** (Map p192; ☑ 0262 37 82 77; www.levieilalambic.com; 55 Rue Montplaisir, Les Makes; d incl breakfast €55; P ☎) on the road to La Fenêtre, at an altitude of about 1000m. It features four uninspiring but tidy rooms (no views) and highly respected traditional meals (from €25). Prices drop by €5 if you stay three nights or more.

Getting to Les Makes by public transport is not really an option. You'll need a car.

To soak up the atmosphere, it's not a bad idea to overnight at one of the *gîtes* near the summit. Le Dimitile is also endowed with a strong historical significance; *marrons* (runaway slaves) took refuge in the area in the late 19th century.

Just before the viewpoint is Espace Culturel Muséographique du Dimitile (p213).

Kreolie 4x4 TOUR
(☑ 0692 86 52 26; www.kreolie4x4.com; day trip incl lunch €100; ☉ by reservation) This well-regarded outfit organises excellent 4WD tours and specialises in day trips that include Entre-Deux and the viewpoint at Le Dimitile (1837m). Guides are informative, providing interesting titbits on the area's flora and fauna (in French).

★ Festivals & Events

Fête du Choca FAIR
(Festival of Choca; ☉ Jul) This festival celebrates crafts made from *choca* leaves; held in Entre-Deux.

🛏 Sleeping

Gîte Valmyr – Le Boucan des Cabris Marrons GÎTE €
(Map p216; ☑ 0692 98 34 73; Le Dimitile; dm incl half board €37; ☉ Wed-Sat) Not far from the lookout that affords splendid views down into the Cirque de Cilaos, this is a great find for walkers and nature lovers. Digs are in basic six- to 10-bed dorms. Run by Valmyr Talbot, who is a local character, this *gîte* is famous for its feisty atmosphere. Book ahead.

Gîte Émile GÎTE €
(Map p216; ☑ 0692 67 24 54; Le Dimitile; dm incl half board €37) Up on Le Dimitile. Has basic accommodation in five- to 12-person dorms. From the *gîte* to the viewpoint, it's a 30- to 45-minute walk.

Villa Oté B&B €€
(☑ 0692 41 60 38, 0262 39 03 43; www.villaote. com; 29 Rue Maurice Berrichon; d incl breakfast €95; P ☎ ☀) A beautifully manicured haven, with delightful gardens and a great pool enclosed by charming guest quarters. The three rooms are individually designed and each one has its own entrance. One quibble: no air-con and no fans. The pool is accessible between 9.30am and 7pm. Some English is spoken. Dinner costs €27.

L'Échappée Belle B&B €€
(☑ 0692 55 55 37, 0262 22 91 31; www.lechappee-belle.com; 13 Impasse du Palmier; d incl breakfast €105; P @ ☎ ☀) Concealed behind high walls down a cul-de-sac near the *mairie* (town

hall), this bright, contemporary four-room B&B has a number of points in its favour, not least its vast tropical garden and its pool – lovely for unwinding after a day's explorations. There's also a communal kitchen, a Jacuzzi and a dining room in the garden. One downside: there's no air-con.

✕ Eating

Le Régal des Hauts
PIZZA, CREOLE €
(☑ 0692 72 81 45; 3 Rue Jean Lauret; mains €6-12; ◷ 11.30am-1.30pm Mon-Sat, 6.30-9.30pm daily) Wood-fired pizzas go down a treat at this lively joint near the town hall. They come either red or white (with or without tomato base), and are thin and relatively crispy. For something local, try the Victoria, with pineapple and chicken, or the Creole, with smoked sausage and spices. It's strong on Creole staples, too.

L'Estanco
FAST FOOD €
(☑ 0262 44 14 28; 1 Rue Payet; mains €7-13; ◷ 11.30am-1.45pm Tue-Sun, 6.45-7.45pm Tue-Fri) The food here is unmemorable but it's super-central and it's open for dinner – a rarity in Entre-Deux.

Le Royal Palmiste
CREOLE, BUFFET €€
(☑ 0262 42 09 90; 12 Rue de l'Eglise; buffet €15; ◷ 11.30am-1.45pm Tue-Sun) Nothing extraordinary in this simple but sweet place in a cute *case*, just wholesome Creole cuisine that hits the spot every time. It lays on a great-value buffet lunch featuring about eight offerings, including *choca* (a quirky-tasting vegetable). Takeaways (€6 to €8) available.

L'Arbre à Palabres
CREOLE, INTERNATIONAL €€
(☑ 0262 44 47 23; 29 Rue Césaire; mains €11-16; ◷ noon-1.30pm Tue-Sun) For a menu that strays a little off the familiar 'sausage *rougail*' (sausages cooked in tomato sauce) and chicken curry' path, try this cute eatery in a Creole house, near the tourist office. The menu changes daily, according to what's available at the market. You can also dine in the cool shade of a massive lychee tree on the terrace at the rear.

Le Longanis
CREOLE €€
(☑ 0262 39 70 56; www.le-longanis.com; 9bis Rue du Commerce; mains €12-15; ◷ 11.30am-1.45pm Thu-Tue, 7-9pm Mon & Thu-Sat) This typically Creole venue, right in the centre, whips up lip-smacking, dirt-cheap meals. Grab a dish from the daily specials, add a salad and you're sorted. Takeaway is available (€6).

❶ Information

Tourist Office (☑ 0262 39 69 80; www.ot-entredeux.com; 9 Rue Fortuné Hoareau; ◷ 8am-noon & 1.30-5pm Mon-Sat) Occupies a pretty *case créole* on the road into the village. Staff can arrange guided visits (usually in French) of the village (adult/child €10/5) and can provide leaflets on walks in the region (including climbing Le Dimitile) and on local artisans.

❶ Getting There & Away

Car Jaune's line S5 operates a bus service (€2, 40 minutes) between Entre-Deux and the bus station in St-Pierre. There are five to seven buses a day from Monday to Saturday and two on a Sunday.

THE CIRQUES

Simply magical. Knitted together like a three-leaf clover, the Cirques of Cilaos, Salazie and Mafate are Réunion's heart and soul. They're different in spirit from the rest of the island – more inward-looking, more secretive, more traditional. The fast-paced and hedonistic coastal life seems light years away.

This rugged region is a fantastic playground for the stimulus-needy, with staggering mountain scenery, a mesh of well-marked trails and impressive canyons that beg to be

---

GO GREEN IN THE CIRQUE DE CILAOS

You can get a better understanding of the environment and traditional life of the Cirque de Cilaos by visiting **Îlet Chicot** (Map p216; ☑ 0692 08 08 21, 0692 72 27 17; Îlet Chicot; hut per person with half board €40; ◷ 10am-3pm Mon-Sun), which can be reached by foot only. The Hoarau family aims to give you a sensitive introduction to the *vie lontan* (traditional life of yore). Their property is reached after an easy 10-minute walk from the D242, about 6km from Cilaos (look for the sign on the right). It features an organic garden with fruit-bearing trees, medicinal herbs and aromatic plants. Wanna go bush? Stay in one of the three *ti cases* (huts), which are constructed using vetiver straw. They're simple, but it's wonderful to be able to linger amid the beauty of the natural surroundings and enjoy the views over Cilaos. The lack of electric lights makes for great stargazing.

The Cirques & Les Hautes Plaines

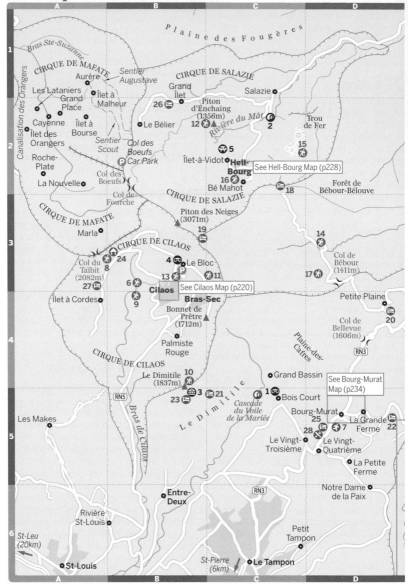

explored. Even if you don't fancy outdoor adventures, it's worth visiting these awesomely photogenic amphitheatres just for the views.

The Cirques first began to be settled by *marrons* (runaway slaves) in the 18th century, and their descendants still inhabit some of the villages of the Cirques. The people residing here are adamantly tied to their traditional lifestyle.

Each Cirque has its own personality – try to include all three of them when planning your trip.

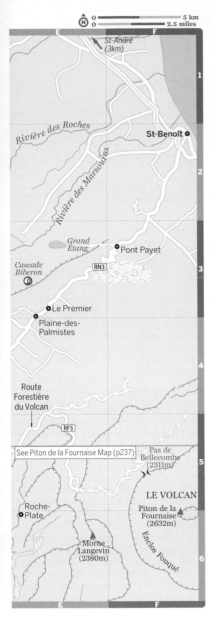

banks of cloud add a touch of the bizarre. A sweet sprinkling of secluded hamlets top off this area's indisputable allure. For outdoorsy types, the Cirque de Cilaos is hard to beat.

To get here, clunk in your seatbelt and take a deep breath: the RN5, which connects St-Louis with Cilaos, 37km to the north, is Réunion's premier drive (and that is saying a lot). Snaking steeply around more than 400 twists and turns along the way up into the amphitheatre, it provides an endless stream of stunning vista-points. *Bon voyage!*

ℹ️ Getting There & Away

To get to the Cirque de Cilaos by public transport, there's only one option: by bus from St-Louis (37km). From St-Louis bus station, there are regular bus services to Cilaos. From Cilaos, you'll find bus services to Bras-Sec and Îlet-à-Cordes.

Cilaos

POP 5500

Cilaos is ensnared by scenery so mind-blowingly dramatic it's practically Alpine. One name says it all: **Piton des Neiges** (3071m). The iconic peak towers over the town of Cilaos, acting like a magnet to hiking fiends. But there's no obligation to overdo it: a smattering of museums and plenty of short walks mean this incredible dose of natural magnificence can also be appreciated at a more relaxed pace.

The largest settlement in any of the Cirques, Cilaos sits 1200m above sea level. Developed as a spa resort at the end of the 19th century, the town's fortunes still rest on tourism, particularly hiking and canyoning, backed up by agriculture and the bottled mineral-water industry. The area is known for the production of lentils, embroidery and wine.

Cilaos fills up quickly on weekends. But despite its popularity there are no massive hotels or blaring discos, only low-key, small-scale operations.

◎ Sights

La Roche Merveilleuse   VIEWPOINT
(Marvellous Rock; Map p216) Head to the Marvellous Rock for an eagle-eye panorama of Cilaos. It's accessible on foot or by road. From Cilaos, take the road to Bras-Sec. The turn-off to La Roche Merveilleuse is signposted on the left, after about 2km. Bring a picnic – the setting is enchanting and there are a few kiosques to protect picnickers from any rain.

RÉUNION CIRQUE DE CILAOS

Cirque de Cilaos

The setting couldn't be more grandiose. Think snaggle-toothed volcanic peaks, deep ravines and forests that are straight out of a Brothers Grimm fairy tale. At times, swirling

The Cirques & Les Hautes Plaines

Maison de la Broderie   MUSEUM

(Map p220; ☑ 0262 31 77 48; Rue des Écoles; adult/child €2/1; ⊙ 9.30am-noon & 2-5pm Mon-Sat, to noon Sun) Entirely modernised in 2014, this museum is home to an association of 30 or so local women dedicated to keeping Cilaos' embroidery tradition alive. They embroider and sell children's clothes, serviettes, place settings and tablecloths. It's laborious work: a single placemat takes between 12 and 15 days to complete. You can watch the women at work in the workshop upstairs.

The originator of Cilaos' embroidery tradition was Angèle Mac-Auliffe, the daughter of the town's first doctor of thermal medicine. Looking for a pastime to fill the long, damp days in the Cirque, Angèle established the first embroidery workshop with 20 women producing what later evolved into a distinctive Cilaos style of embroidery.

Maison des Vins du
Chai de Cilaos   MUSEUM

(Map p220; ☑ 0262 31 79 69; 34 Rue des Glycines; ⊙ 9am-noon & 2-5.30pm Mon-Sat) FREE You can learn more about Cilaos wine at the Maison des Vins du Chai de Cilaos. A short film (in French) is followed by a wine-tasting session. Take home a bottle from about €12.

Philippe Turpin's Studio   GALLERY

(Map p220; ☑ 0262 31 73 64, 0692 28 03 03; www.facebook.com/philippeturpinartiste; 2 Route des Sources; ⊙ 9am-6pm Sat & Sun, by reservation weekdays) The sculptor, painter and printmaker Philippe Turpin, who etches on copper and then rolls the prints off the inky plates, has a studio that is open to the public. Turpin captures the wonder of Réunion in a fantastical, almost medieval way; his renditions of the Cirques resemble illustrations of fairy kingdoms.

🏃 Activities

Cilaos is a superb playground for outdoorsy types, with a superfluity of activities on offer, including canyoning, hiking and rock climbing.

Canyoning

Of the stellar spots for canyoning in Réunion, the Cilaos area tops the list, with three major canyons that draw action-seekers like bees to a honeypot: Canyons de Gobert, Fleurs Jaunes and Bras Rouge. All are very atmospheric; you can expect various jumps, leaps into natural pools and jaw-dropping rappelling. Access to the canyons involves a preliminary five- to 45-minute hike (and back). The time spent in the canyon is about three to five hours. The most suitable canyons for beginners and families are Canyon de Gobert and Mini Fleurs Jaunes (which is a section of Fleurs Jaunes). Fleurs Jaunes is a more aerial circuit, with seven rappels, including a 55m (yes!) rappel.

All canyoning outings are led by a qualified instructor. Some of the major operators don't have offices but can be reached by phone.

Run Évasion
ADVENTURE SPORTS

(Map p220; ☎ 0262 31 83 57; www.canyon-reunion.fr; 23 Rue du Père Boiteau; canyoning outings €55-85; ☺8am-noon & 2-6pm Mon-Sat, to 5pm Sun) This well-established operator has canyoning tours for all levels. Prices vary depending on the number of people and the duration of the outing. It can also organise hiking trips.

Bouisset Fabrice
ADVENTURE SPORTS

(☎ 0692 66 22 73; bouisset.fabrice@wanadoo.fr; canyoning outings €55-65; ☺ by reservation) Fabrice Bouisset is a qualified canyoning instructor and leads excellent canyoning outings around Cilaos, including Fleurs Jaunes.

Canyon Ric a Ric
ADVENTURE SPORTS

(☎ 0692 86 54 85; www.canyonreunion.com; ☺ canyoning outings per person €55-85 by reservation) Canyon Ric a Ric is one of the major canyoning operators in the area. Prices depend on the duration of the outing.

Cilaos Aventure
ADVENTURE SPORTS

(☎ 0692 66 73 42; www.cilaosaventure.com; canyoning outings €55-80; ☺ by reservation) This reliable outlet can arrange all kinds of canyoning trips in the area, including Fleurs Jaunes, Gobert and Bras Rouge. See the website for schedules.

Aparksa Montagne
OUTDOORS

(☎ 0692 66 50 09; www.aparksa-montagne.com; Cilaos; ☺ by reservation) For canyoning trips (from €55) or guided walks, this outfit has good credentials. The owner, Thomas Percheron, has lived in South Africa and is fluent in English.

Cycling & Mountain Biking

The Cirque de Cilaos, with its dramatic topography and great scenic roads, is superb cycling terrain for experienced cyclists. Novices can ride to La Roche Merveilleuse (p217). The road to Bras-Sec is another stunner.

Tof Bike
MOUNTAIN BIKING

(Map p220; ☎ 0692 25 61 61; 29 Rue du Père Boiteau; half-/full day €14/19; ☺8.30am-noon & 2.30-6pm Mon-Sat, to noon Sun) This outfit rents out mountain bikes in tip-top condition and gives advice on various circuits. A map is provided.

Hiking

There are fabulous hiking options in the vicinity of Cilaos, with well-marked trails suitable for all levels of fitness. The tourist office produces a small leaflet that gives an overview of the walks in the Cirque.

Col du Taïbit
HIKING

(Map p216) An iconic climb to the pass that separates the Cirque de Cilaos from the Cirque de Mafate. From the pass you can walk down to Marla in the Cirque de Mafate in about 45 minutes. The starting point is signposted on the D242 (the road to Îlet à Cordes), 5km from Cilaos. About 4½ hours return, with 830m of altitude gain.

Le Kervéguen
HIKING

(Map p216) This hike offers splendid views of the Cirque. The starting point is signposted on the D241 (the road to Bras-Sec), 5km from Cilaos. About five hours return.

THE CIRQUES & THE VOLCANO FROM ABOVE

The helicopter dilemma: you're loath to add to noise and air pollution. But your heart is set on a bird's-eye view of the magnificent Cirques and the volcano. While the trips aren't cheap (between €85 and €320, depending on the duration of the tour), most travellers rate them as a highlight of their visit to Réunion. Contact **Helilagon** (Map p192; ☎ 0262 55 55 55; www.helilagon.com; Altiport de L'Éperon, 190 Chemin Summer, St-Paul; tours €95-319; ☺by reservation) or **Corail Hélicoptères** (Map p192; ☎ 0262 22 22 66; www.corail-helicopteres.com; Route Cannière, St-Gilles-les-Bains; tours €95-320; ☺ by reservation).

If you really want to feel the wind in your hair, several outfits offer tandem microlight flights with a qualified instructor. They run about 10 different tours around the island, starting at €45 for a gentle tour above the lagoon. Needless to say, all flights are dependent on the prevailing weather conditions. For more information, contact the following:

Felix ULM (Map p192; ☎ 0692 87 32 32; www.felixulm.com; 68 Rue Marthe Bacquet, Cambaie; tours €75-250; ☺ by reservation)

Ô Passagers du Vent (Map p192; ☎ 0262 42 95 95; www.ulm-reunion.com; 1 Rue Henri Cornu, Cambaie, St-Paul; tours €45-190; ☺ by reservation)

Papangue ULM (☎ 0692 08 85 86; www.papangue-ulm.fr; Route de Maperine, Ste-Marie; tours €80-170)

Cilaos

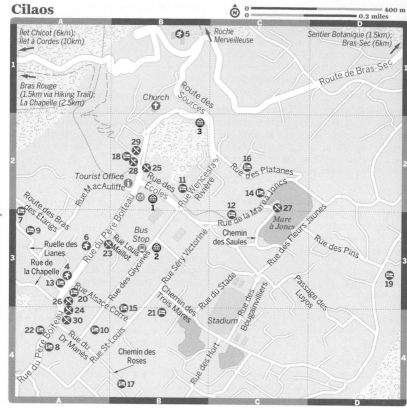

Cilaos

Sentier Botanique
WALKING

(Map p216) An easy 90-minute loop with a focus on local flora (most species are labelled). Perfectly suitable for families. It starts at La Roche Merveilleuse.

Bras Rouge
WALKING

(Map p216) An easy walk to the top of a waterfall. Plan on 2½ hours return.

La Chapelle
HIKING

(Map p216) This path connects Cilaos to a cave near a river (about five hours return).

La Roche Merveilleuse
HIKING

(Map p216) The gentle ramble (about two hours return) to this lookout is rewarded with lofty views over Cilaos. Also accessible by car (p217).

Rock Climbing

Rock climbing is becoming increasingly popular in Cilaos, where there is no shortage of awesome cliffs and gorges, particularly the stunning Fleurs Jaunes area, which is home to dozens of mind-boggling ascents, graded 4 to 8 (easy to difficult). For novices, there are also *falaise-écoles* (training cliffs that are specially equipped for beginners). Run Évasion (p219) and Cilaos Aventure (p219) employ qualified instructors. Plan on €50 per person.

🎊 Festivals & Events

Fête de la Vigne
WINE

(Wine Harvest Festival; ⊙ Jan) A popular wine fair, where local winemakers promote their wines.

Cross du Piton des Neiges
SPORTS

(⊙ May) Running race to the Piton des Neiges.

Fête des Lentilles
FOOD

(Festival of Lentils; ⊙ Oct) This agricultural fair held in Cilaos celebrates lentils through various exhibitions, conferences, tastings and recipe contests.

🛏 Sleeping

Cilaos has ample choice of accommodation options, but it can become crowded at weekends and during the tourist season – book ahead.

★ Au Cœur du Cirque
RENTAL HOUSE €

(Map p220; ☑ 0692 44 68 94; www.aucoeur ducirque.com; 3A Route du Bras des Étangs; d from €48, 3-6 people €120; ⓟ 🞩) This hidden treasure is one of Cilaos' best retreats. Au Cœur du Cirque is a cute-as-a-button cottage in a

CLIMBING PITON DES NEIGES

The mind-boggling ascent to Réunion's highest point (3071m) is vigorous, but the 360-degree panorama at the summit is worth the effort. It's usually done in two days, with an overnight stay in **Gîte de la Caverne Dufour** (Map p216; ☑ 0692 67 74 26, 0262 51 15 26; dm €17-19, breakfast/dinner €6/19), reached after three hours from the start of the path at Le Bloc, between Cilaos and Bras-Sec (it's signposted).

From the *gîte* (self-catering accommodation), the summit is reached after about 1½ hours amid lunar landscapes. Hard-core hikers may want to complete the round trip in one day (about 10 hours).

well-tended property blessed with sweeping Cirque views. Cocooned in a wonderfully private setting, it consists of a kitchen, sitting room, bathroom, terrace and two bedrooms – perfect for families, friends or a loved-up couple looking for an escape.

Note that the €48 rate (for two) applies from Sunday to Thursday. On Friday and Saturday, there's a flat rate of €120 (for up to six people) – plan your stay accordingly.

★ La Case Bleue
GÎTE €

(Map p220; ☑ 0692 65 74 96; www.gitecase bleu.e-monsite.com; 15 Rue Alsace Corré; dm/d €16/40) An excellent deal, this *gîte* occupies an attractive Creole house painted in blue. Top marks go to the light-filled dorm, the back-friendly mattresses, the salubrious bathrooms and the practical communal kitchen. There's also a modest double with its own entrance and bathrooms – ideal for couples, although it opens onto the dorm's terrace, which may be noisy if the *gîte* is full.

Breakfast costs €6. There are only 11 beds, so book ahead.

La Carte Postale
BUNGALOW €

(Map p220; ☑ 0693 50 10 33; http://colonia location.free.fr; 9 Rue de la Mare à Joncs; s/d incl breakfast €50/70; ⓟ) Two spick-and-span, self-contained Creole-style bungalows enjoy a spiffing location above Mare à Joncs (a small pond) with a picture-postcard view of the Cirque. Guests are entitled to a discount at the restaurant below, which is run by the same owners.

RÉUNION CIRQUE DE CILAOS

THERMES DE CILAOS

Cilaos' *sources thermales* (thermal springs), which are heated by volcanic chambers far below the surface, are said to relieve rheumatic pain, among other bone and muscular ailments. For visitors to **Thermes de Cilaos** (Map p144; ☑0262 31 72 27; www.cg974.fr/thermes; Route de Bras-Sec; ⊙8.30am-12.30pm & 1.30-5pm Mon-Tue & Thu-Fri, to 12.30pm Wed, 9am-5pm Sun), several health treatments are offered, including a 20-minute hydromassage (€15) – bliss after a long day's hiking in the Cirque.

The springs were first brought to the attention of the outside world in 1815 by a goat hunter from St-Louis. A track into the Cirque was constructed in 1842, paving the way for the development of Cilaos as a health spa for rich colonials. The thermal station was opened in 1896 and the tradition continues today.

Chez Anne   B&B €
(Map p220; ☑0692 43 68 04; chezanne413@ orange.fr; 4 Rue des Glycines; s/d €35/60; ⊛) This well-presented B&B has sparsely furnished but spacious and light rooms (opt for one upstairs). Add an extra €2.50 per person for breakfast.

Casa Celina   GUESTHOUSE €
(Map p220; ☑0692 15 47 47; www.casacelina 974.com; 12 Rue du Père Boiteau; d €52-67; ⊛) This well-run place occupies a skilfully refurbished house. The five rooms border on diminutive but the architect has maximised limited space. Add €10 per person for breakfast. There's a restaurant downstairs.

Le Bois de Senteur   B&B €
(Map p220; ☑0692 29 81 20, 0262 31 91 03; www. leboisdesenteur.com; 4 Chemin des Roses; d/q incl breakfast €60/80; ⓟ⊛) This trim place in a peaceful cul-de-sac is brought to life with lashings of colourful paint on the facade. Inside, the 10 rooms are modestly furnished and feel a tad compact; if available, ask for one of the upstairs rooms, which have balconies and afford dashing views of the Piton des Neiges (especially rooms 6, 7 and 10).

Le Calbanon   GÎTE €
(Map p220; ☑0692 09 27 30; www.lecalbanon.fr; 1 Rue des Thermes; dm/d €16/35; ⊛) This modest *gîte d'étape* (walkers lodge) boasts a con-

venient location in the centre of town and offers simple accommodation in dorms. A few doubles are also available. There's a communal kitchen, too. Dinners are available on request (€20).

Clair de Lune   GÎTE €
(Map p220; ☑0692 82 47 13, 0692 00 57 54; 10 Rue Wenceslas Rivière; dm/d with shared bathroom, incl breakfast €20/40; ⓟ) Run by Alex, who knows a thing or 50 about Cilaos, this congenial spot has rooms of varying size and shape, with three- to seven-bed dorms and one double. Bathrooms are shared. The living area is a good place to swap tales with like-minded travellers.

La Roche Merveilleuse   GÎTE €
(Map p220; ☑0262 31 82 42; 1 Rue des Platanes; dm €16-18, d €42-45, with shared bathroom €40-42; ⓟ⊛) This all-wood *gîte* looks like a Canadian chalet transplanted to Cilaos. Opt for one of the four snug doubles, which feel like cosy birds' nests, but the real appeal is the panoramic view from the terrace.

Otroiza   HOTEL €€
(Map p220; ☑0692 05 25 93, 0262 31 50 12; www. otroiza.com; 3A Rue du Père Boiteau; d €80-90; ⓟ⊛) This newish hotel offers reasonably priced rooms with a clean modern design; pick of the bunch are the rooms at the back, with plenty of natural light and splendid mountain views. All come with attractive tiled bathrooms, crisp linen and excellent bedding. There are only 10 rooms, which ensures intimacy.

Hôtel des Neiges   HOTEL €€
(Map p220; ☑0262 31 72 33; www.hoteldesneiges. reunion.fr; 1 Rue de la Mare à Joncs; d €82-92; ⓟ⊛≋) One of Cilaos' few mid-price accommodation options, this abode has a range of well-maintained rooms in a two-storey, motel-like building. The decor is nothing special, but the relaxed feel and great amenities – two heated pools, a neat garden, a restaurant and a sauna – more than make up for the slightly dated sense of style. Frequent online promotional deals provide real value. It's well worth springing for one of the 'Confort Plus' rooms, which have a more modern feel.

Le Platane   INN €€
(Map p220; ☑0262 31 77 23; www.hotel-restaurant-cilaos.re; 46 Rue du Père Boiteau; s/d incl breakfast €65/85; ⊛) No rustic decor here but clean lines, muted tones, good bedding and sparkling bathrooms. It's also supercentral. Of

the four rooms, the Piton des Neiges has the best views. One quibble: it's above the eponymous restaurant (where the reception is), which means it might be a bit noisy at times.

Note that bathrooms are open in the Piton des Neiges and Kerveguen rooms.

Le Cilaos
HOTEL €€

(Map p220; ☎0262 31 85 85; www.leschenets-lecilaos.re; 40E Chemin des Trois Mares; s €97-117, d €129-149, ste €149-169, incl breakfast; P@☎☲) Under new management since 2015, Cilaos' biggest hotel is in a transition period. The public areas have been spruced up, and most rooms should have been renovated by the time you read this. Facilities include a small heated pool, a sauna, a *hammam* (Turkish bath), three Jacuzzis, a bar and a restaurant with great mountain views.

Le Bois Rouge
B&B €€

(Map p220; ☎0262 47 57 57, 0692 69 94 30; http://leboisrouge.com; 2 Route des Sources; s/d incl breakfast €90/109; P☎) Somewhere between a boutique hotel and B&B, the Bois Rouge has five immaculate rooms that boast parquet flooring made of precious wood as well as cosy terraces. Angle for the Bois Noir, Ti Natte or Tamarin rooms, which offer the best views. Bonus: free transfers to the start of most hiking trails near Cilaos. Generous breakfasts, too. Discounts are available in low season.

Le Vieux Cep
HOTEL €€

(Map p220; ☎0262 31 71 89; www.levieuxcep-reunion.com; 2 Rue des Trois Mares; d incl breakfast €104-149; P☎☲) One of Cilaos' largest establishments, Le Vieux Cep has its pros and cons: on the plus side it's welcoming and well located; it enjoys great views of Piton des Neiges; it has solid amenities, including a restaurant, a small sauna and a heated pool; and the Superior rooms have been modernised. Downside: most rooms are cramped and lack character.

Case Nyala
B&B €€

(Map p220; ☎0692 87 70 14, 0262 31 89 57; www.case-nyala.com; 8 Ruelle des Lianes; s/d €65/80, bungalow d/tr €90/105, incl breakfast; ☎) On a quiet backstreet near the centre, this little Creole place with lemon-yellow walls and green shutters harbours four diminutive yet cosy rooms. They lack natural light but are kept tidy, and there's a communal kitchen. The complimentary rum in the glass flasks on the shelves will help you forget that this place is a tad overpriced (by Cilaos standards).

Hôtel Tsilaosa
HOTEL €€

(Map p220; ☎0262 37 39 39; www.tsilaosa.com; Rue du Père Boiteau; s/d incl breakfast €111/135; P@☎) This well-run four-star abode in a restored Creole home offers a smooth stay, with 15 rooms that are imaginatively decked out in local style; those upstairs boast mountain views (rooms 15 and 16 are the best). The owner has set up a wine cellar in the basement and offers tastings of Cilaos tipples (€8) when he's in town.

✗ Eating

Despite the choice of eateries on offer, don't expect gastronomic thrills in Cilaos. Most places tend to rest on their laurels, with rather stodgy fare served in generic surrounds. On the bright side, Cilaos holds a few surprises up its sleeve. It's noted for its lentils, grown mainly around Îlet à Cordes, and its wines.

Self-caterers will find grocery stores along the main street.

★ L'Instant Plaisirs
CREPERIE €

(Map p220; ☎0692 45 71 99; 28 Rue du Père Boiteau; mains €3.50-14, menus €13-15; ☺noon-8pm Wed-Thu, 11.30am-8pm Fri-Sun) If you're growing weary of heavy regional dishes, this cute crêperie is a godsend. It's renowned for its gourmet crêpes and galettes made from quality ingredients. The grey-and-white decor gives it a fresh, modern feel, and the handmade crêpes are really first class. Where else could you savour a galette stuffed with Bleu d'Auvergne cheese?

Boulangerie du Cirque
BAKERY €

(Map p220; ☎0262 31 85 12; 32 Rue du Père Boiteau; sandwiches €2-3.50; ☺6am-7pm Mon-Sat, to noon Sun) Has a good assortment of sandwiches and pastry treats, including appetising chocolate éclairs.

Salon de Thé de l'Hôtel Tsilaosa
TEAHOUSE €

(Map p220; ☎0262 37 39 39; Rue du Père Boiteau; pastries €4; ☺3-6pm; ☎) This delightfully peaceful venue in the Hôtel Tsilaosa's tearoom will torment the sweet-toothed with homemade cakes and pies and about 15 varieties of tea. Try the *tarte à la confiture de pêche* (peach jam pie), the house's signature offering.

Boulangerie Dambreville
BAKERY €

(Map p220; 64 Rue du Père Boiteau; pastries & sandwiches from €0.90; ☺6.30am-6.30pm Mon-Sat, to noon Sun) Ask a local where they go for the best *macatias* and croissants and they

A TOAST IS IN ORDER

After an unusual gustatory experience? Sample a glass of *vin de Cilaos* (Cilaos wine), served in most restaurants in town. Not to be deprived of their wine, the French brought vines with them to Réunion in the 17th century. They were originally grown along the west coast, but in the late 19th century settlers introduced vines into the Cirques, cultivating them on trellises outside their houses or on tiny terraces hacked out of the hillside. For years, the wines they produced were sugary sweet whites, reminiscent of sherry and tawny port. In the late 1970s, however, a few enterprising growers in Cilaos upgraded their vine stock and began producing something far more palatable. In addition to sweet and dry whites, growers now produce rosés. They are not necessarily the most distinguished of wines but they're improving in quality, especially the rosés. The harvest season takes place in January.

point to this delectable little bakery. It has a wide variety of cavity-inducing goodies, as well as excellent sandwiches made with baguettes (from €2).

La Perle du Lac
CREOLE, BUFFET €€

(Map p220; ☑ 0262 52 84 29; 9 Rue de la Mare à Joncs; buffet €18-20; ⊙ 11.30am-2.30pm & 7-9.30pm Wed & Fri-Mon, 11.30am-2.30pm Thu; 🛜) Bring an empty tum: there's no à la carte dining here, but a mean buffet featuring all the Creole classics. It's more honest than refined, but at these prices you're unlikely to have much to complain about. There's a small terrace overlooking the Mare à Joncs pond.

Chez Luçay
CREOLE, CHINESE €€

(Map p220; ☑ 0692 09 18 70; Rue du Père Boiteau; mains €12-20, menus €20-25; ⊙ 11.30am-2.30pm & 6.30-9pm) This outfit gets kudos for its expansive menu that will satisfy even the pickiest eater. Choosing the main course is a real nail-biter – should it be deer stew, lamb shank or pork in oyster sauce? Save a cranny for one of the homemade desserts (chocolate mousse, anyone?).

Les Sentiers
CREOLE €€

(Map p220; ☑ 0262 31 71 54; 63 Rue du Père Boiteau; mains €12-20; ⊙ noon-2.30pm & 7-9pm Thu-Mon; 🛜) Come lunch and dinner, this

cute *case créole* is alive with action. Tables spill from inside out onto a breezy terrace. Food-wise, the menu features all the Creole classics, with an emphasis on Cilaos lentils as an accompaniment. The rustic decor is easy on the eye, with exposed beams and laminate floors. At €14, the eight-course *buffet créole* is a steal.

Chez Noë
CREOLE €€

(Map p220; ☑ 0262 31 79 93; 40 Rue du Père Boiteau; mains €11-22, menus €28-35; ⊙ 11.30am-2pm & 6.30-9pm Tue-Sat, to 2pm Sun) A long-standing institution, Chez Noë is almost a rite of passage in Cilaos. It churns out invigorating Creole favourites such as sausage with lentils and *gratin de chouchou* (choko; a green squash-like vegetable that is served baked with cheese) as well as salads. Bonus: there's an enticing, shady terrace in warm weather. Shame that tables are not well spaced.

Le Cottage
CREOLE €€

(Map p220; ☑ 0262 31 04 61; 2 Chemin des Saules; mains €13-20, menus €18-26; ⊙ noon-2pm & 6.30-9pm Tue-Sun) The all-wood surrounds boast a kind of rustic charm and the dining room overlooks the Mare à Joncs (reserve a table near the windows). In addition to a good selection of palate-pleasing Creole dishes, it serves meat and seafood grills. Downside: there's no terrace.

Le Petit Randonneur
CREOLE €€

(Map p220; ☑ 0262 31 79 55; 61 Rue du Père Boiteau; mains €10-19; ⊙ noon-2pm Sat-Thu, 6.30-9pm Sat) A favourite haunt of hungry walkers, this family-run restaurant serves up hearty local dishes such as smoked sausages and curries, as well as moderately priced *plats du jour* (daily specials) and crêpes, best enjoyed on the terrace.

Le Platane
CREOLE, PIZZERIA €€

(Map p220; ☑ 0262 31 77 23; 46 Rue du Père Boiteau; mains €9-23; ⊙ 9am-10pm Thu-Tue) The most eclectic menu in town. Here you can wrap your mandibles around salads, pasta, meat and fish dishes as well as *carris*, but skip the unexceptional pizzas.

❶ Information

There aren't any banks in Cilaos, but you'll find two ATMs, one at the post office and another **ATM** (Rue du Marché) in the street leading to the small covered market.

Tourist Office (Map p220; ☑ 0820 203 220; www.sud.reunion.fr; 2bis Rue Mac Auliffe; ⊙ 8.30am-12.30pm & 1.30-5pm Mon-Sat,

9am-noon Sun; 🕿) The tourist office is particularly helpful, with multilingual staff who provide reliable information about local and long-distance walks and dispense lists of accommodation, restaurants and activities. The office has pamphlets on bus schedules in the Cirque and sells walking maps. You can also book *gîtes de montagne* here. Also has free wi-fi and sells handicrafts.

❶ Getting There & Away

Cilaos is located 112km from St-Denis by road and 37km from the nearest coastal town, St-Louis.

Buses to Cilaos' bus stop (Map p220) depart from St-Louis. There are about 12 buses daily, and eight on Sunday (€1.80, 1½ hours). The last service up to Cilaos leaves St-Louis at 6.30pm (5.30pm on Sunday); going down again, the last bus leaves Cilaos at 6.05pm (5.20pm on Sunday).

There are nine buses a day (four on Sunday) from Cilaos to Bras-Sec (€1.80) between 6am and 7pm. For Îlet à Cordes (€1.80) there are about nine buses daily (four on Sunday) from 5.50am to 7pm, with the last bus back at 6pm. The tourist office in Cilaos has timetables.

Another option is the minibus service offered by the **Société Cilaosienne de Transport** (SCT; ☑ 0262 31 85 87, 0692 66 13 30), which costs €30 for two people for Îlet à Cordes. The same outfit provides transport from Cilaos to Le Bloc (for the Piton des Neiges and Hell-Bourg; €10 for two people) and to the trailhead for the Col du Taïbit (for Mafate; €15 for two people), saving you at least an hour's walking time in each case.

Îlet à Cordes

POP 490

Îlet à Cordes is a marvellous stop-the-world-and-get-off place and you'll leave with reluctance. The setting is truly photogenic: wherever you look, this tiny *écart* (settlement) is cradled by soaring mountains, with major peaks looming on the horizon. Vineyards and fields where lentils are grown complete the picture.

🛏 Sleeping & Eating

Apart from a modest cafe-bar, you won't find any restaurant in Îlet à Cordes. Most visitors opt for a hearty Creole dinner at their B&B.

**Au P'tit Coin Charmant –
Chez Hélène Payet**   B&B €

(☑ 0262 35 18 13, 0692 68 49 68; 13 Chemin Terre-Fine; d incl breakfast €45) Set in an alluring tropical garden, this well-run B&B offers few frills, just a genuine Creole welcome and hearty meals (dinner €25) that get rave reviews from travellers.

Le Gîte de l'Îlet   B&B €

(☑ 0262 25 38 57, 0692 64 74 48; www.gitedelilet.re; 27 Chemin Terre-Fine; s €50, d €50-58; ⌨) This is a real find, provided you opt for the slightly dearer upstairs rooms. They're super spacious, light-filled and come with a balcony and great mountain views. The downstairs rooms, which can sleep two to six, are a tad sombre and cramped, and lack views. The heated pool is an added bonus.

Solange Grondin, your amenable hostess, prides herself on her farm cooking, which usually means chicken, *brèdes chouchou* (a mix of local vegetables) and homemade cakes. Dinners cost €25.

Le Tapacala   B&B €€

(Map p216; ☑ 0692 69 57 50; www.facebook.com/LeTapacala; 2C Chemin Les Orangers; d incl breakfast €139) Not your average B&B, this upscale venture is the pride and joy of Mickael Gonthier and his spouse, your hosts, who can speak English and German and are well clued-up about the island. The three rooms are huge and tastefully designed, with clean lines, dark tiles and elegant furnishings, and open onto a well-tended tropical garden. Dinner costs €30.

Overall, it's a very pleasant place to stay but, despite the initial 'wow' factor, it's a bit overpriced by Cilaos standards. It's at the entrance to Îlet à Cordes (coming from Cilaos).

Le Reposoir   CAFE €

(☑ 0692 70 08 15; 20 Chemin Terre-Fine; ☺ 7am-7pm Mon-Sat, to 1pm Sun) This modest cafe-bar serves snacks and sandwiches, and has a limited selection of goods if you're fixing your own food.

❶ Getting There & Away

There are nine buses a day (four on Sunday) between Cilaos and Îlet à Cordes. The tourist office in Cilaos has timetables. Another option is the minibus service offered by the Société Cilaosienne de Transport, which costs €30 for two people from Cilaos.

Bras-Sec

POP 640

You've reached *le bout du monde* (the end of the earth) in Bras-Sec, about 6km from Cilaos. This is a place to just kick back and enjoy the get-away-from-it-all atmosphere. If you've got itchy feet, a recommended hike is the Tour du Bonnet de Prêtre, a 4½-hour loop that skirts around the bizarrely shaped peak that lies south of the village.

RÉUNION CIRQUE DE CILAOS

🛏 Sleeping & Eating

You might find the odd place selling snacks along the main road. Otherwise, Cilaos isn't far away at all.

Gîte Courtois　　　　　　　BUNGALOW €
(☑ 0262 25 59 44, 0692 23 31 96; 7ter Chemin Saül; per person €18) Four self-contained bungalows on the main street. Nothing fancy, but they get the job done and can sleep up to six (at a pinch).

L'Oiseau de Paradis　　　　　BUNGALOW €
(☑ 0692 16 98 18; 33 Chemin Saül; per person €18) This three-room Creole cottage on the main street is a good deal for self-caterers. It can sleep up to eight.

Les Mimosas　　　　　　　　　B&B €
(☑ 0262 96 72 73, 0692 69 84 93; www.allonsla reunion.com/gite-les-mimosas; 29 Chemin Saül; d/ tr/q incl breakfast €40/50/68; ℗) Everything is ultra-laid-back at this homey venture on the main street, and your affable hosts will treat you like family. Digs are in four doubles that were renovated in 2015 (think a new lick of paint) and a family room that can sleep up to six. The dinner menu (€25) is based on good quality local produce, including poultry and home-grown vegetables.

ℹ Getting There & Away

There are nine buses a day (four on Sunday) from Cilaos to Bras-Sec between 6am and 7pm. The tourist office in Cilaos has timetables.

Cirque de Salazie

If you need a break from beach-bumming and want to cool off in forested mountains, head to the Cirque de Salazie with its soul-stirring array of soaring peaks, sublime vistas, thundering waterfalls, tortuous roads and a spattering of rural hamlets.

The winding mountain road that slithers into the Cirque from St-André offers awesome views and is reason enough to make the trip. Yet the prize at the end of it is golden too: with its Creole colour, Hell-Bourg is the crowning glory of the Cirque.

The Cirque de Salazie is a bit 'flatter' (although 'flat' is not the first word that will spring to mind when you see it!) than the Cirque de Cilaos, but the scenery as you approach is nearly as awesome. The vegetation is incredibly lush and waterfalls tumble down

the mountains, even over the road in places – Salazie is the wettest of the three Cirques.

ℹ Getting There & Away

To get to the Cirque de Salazie by public transport, there's only one option – by bus from St-André (17km). From St-André bus station, there are seven buses a day (three on Sunday) to Salazie. From Salazie, you'll find regular bus services to Hell-Bourg, Grand Îlet and Le Bélier. There's only one petrol station, in Salazie – fill up in St-André.

Salazie

POP 4000

The road alongside the gorge of the Rivière du Mât from St-André to Salazie, which lies at the eastern entrance to the Cirque, winds past superb waterfalls. There's not much to detain you in Salazie, though, and most visitors press on to Hell-Bourg. You'll have to change buses here if you're heading further up into the Cirque.

◉ Sights

Cascade du Voile de la Mariée　　　WATERFALL
(Bridal Veil Falls; Map p216) On the southern outskirts of Salazie, along the road to Hell-Bourg and just north of the turn-off to Grand Îlet, are these spectacular waterfalls on your left. They drop in several stages from the often cloud-obscured heights into the ravine at the roadside. You get an even better view from the Grand Îlet road.

🛏 Sleeping & Eating

Unless your car has broken down, it's hard to imagine why you'd want to stay in Salazie; Hell-Bourg, which is the epicentre of tourism in the Cirque de Salazie, is only 8km further south.

There are a handful of eateries along the main road. You're better off pressing on to Hell-Bourg, which offers a wider choice of eating options.

ℹ Getting There & Away

Salazie is 17km by road from the nearest coastal town, St-André. The road through the Cirque is magnificent, but hair-raising in sections. The road to Grand Îlet turns off the Hell-Bourg road just south of Salazie.

There are seven buses daily from St-André to Salazie (€1.80, 35 minutes). If you're travelling to Hell-Bourg and Grand Îlet by bus, you'll have to change here.

Hell-Bourg

POP 2200

The town of Hell-Bourg emerges like a hamlet in a fairy tale after 9km of tight bends from Salazie. You can't help but be dazzled by the fabulous backdrop – the majestic mountain walls that encase Hell-Bourg like a grandiose amphitheatre. No prize for guessing that this rugged terrain offers fantastic hiking opportunities. It offers plenty of more sedentary opportunities as well. Culture aficionados will get their fill in this quintessential Réunionnais town with its enchanting centre, where old Creole mansions line the streets.

Hell-Bourg takes its curious name from the former governor Amiral de Hell. It served as a thermal resort until a landslide blocked the spring in 1948.

◉ Sights

Architecture and history buffs should take a look at the town's appealing **Creole buildings**, with their typical wrought-iron *lambrequins* (filigree-style decoration). These buildings date back as far as the 1840s, when Hell-Bourg was a famous resort town that attracted a rather well-heeled crowd. You can go on a guided tour organised by the tourist office.

★ Musée des Musiques et Instruments de l'Océan Indien   MUSEUM

(Museum of the Music & Instruments from the Indian Ocean; Map p228; ☑ 0262 46 72 23; www.maisonmorange.fr; 4 Rue de la Cayenne; adult/child €7/5; ☺ 10am-6pm Tue-Sun) After years of anticipation, Réunion's most ballyhooed new music museum has opened its doors in Hell-Bourg. In October 2015, the innovative Musée des Musiques et Instruments de l'Océan Indien welcomed its first visitors, showcasing hundreds of musical instruments from Africa, India, China and Madagascar in a small yet state-of-the-art exhibition space. Don't miss the opportunity to embark on a musical and visual journey.

Thermal Bath   RUINS

(Map p228) FREE Visitors can see the ruins of the old baths, which were in use until 1948. They are found in a ravine a 10-minute walk west of town (walk past Le Relais des Cimes hotel at the western end of Rue Général de Gaulle; it's signposted). It's a quiet and leafy spot.

Rivière du Mât   PICNIC AREA

(Map p216) From Îlet-à-Vidot, the asphalted road continues for about 2km until a small parking lot. From here, a steep footpath leads in about 15 minutes to the Rivière du Mât valley. Cross the footbridge and you'll soon reach a lovely picnic site by the river.

Bé Mahot   VILLAGE

About 3.5km from Hell-Bourg, Bé Mahot is a cute hamlet that's well worth visiting. With its clunky, colourful Creole houses clinging on the hillside and fantastic vistas of the Cirque, it's scenic to boot. There are several picnic sites along the road.

Îlet-à-Vidot   VILLAGE

The landscape surrounding the hamlet of Îlet-à-Vidot, about 2km from Hell-Bourg, is little short of breathtaking. The iconic, flat-topped Piton d'Enchaing, covered with thick vegetation, seems to stand guard over the village.

Maison Folio   HISTORIC BUILDING

(Map p228; ☑ 0262 47 80 98; 20 Rue Amiral Lacaze; admission €4, guided tour €5; ☺ 9-11.30am & 2-5pm) One of the loveliest of Hell-Bourg's Creole houses is this typical 19th-century bourgeois villa almost engulfed by its densely planted garden. You can wander around the property or opt for the guided tour run by the owners. They show you around, pointing out the amazing variety of aromatic, edible, medicinal and decorative plants, and give insights into local culture. If the owners' son is around, he'll be happy to run a tour in English.

☆ Activities

Hiking

Not surprisingly, the Hell-Bourg area is an adventure playground for hiking enthusiasts, with a good selection of day hikes. Hikers doing the Tour des Cirques route will have to pass through Hell-Bourg as they cross the Cirque de Salazie.

➡ **Hell-Bourg–Gîte de Bélouve** – about four hours return, with 570m of altitude gain. From Gîte de Bélouve (p242), you can continue to the Trou de Fer viewpoint (seven hours return from Hell-Bourg).

➡ **Piton d'Enchaing** (Map p216) – this soaring 1356m peak is a popular but challenging five- to six-hour hike (return) from Îlet-à-Vidot, with 670m of altitude gain.

Hell-Bourg

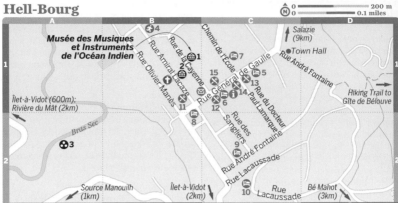

Hell-Bourg

➡ **Source Manouilh** (Map p216) – an exhilarating six-hour loop, with a net altitude gain of about 600m.

➡ **Hell-Bourg–Gîte du Piton des Neiges** – a pleasant alternative to Cilaos if you're planning to hike up to Piton des Neiges. Expect a tough seven-hour climb (one way), with a net altitude gain of 1470m.

Canyoning

The canyoning options available in the Cirque will make your spine tingle. Get wet at Trou Blanc, which is said to be the most 'aquatic' canyon in Réunion, with lots of *toboggans* (plunging down water-polished chutes) and leaps. Some sections are appropriately named 'The Washing Machine', 'The Bath', 'The Aquaplaning'... Another reputable canyon is Voile de la Mariée, near Salazie, which is a more aerial circuit that includes a

50m rappel, but it was closed when we visited. Note that these canyons are not accessible during the rainiest months (from December to March).

Austral Aventure ADVENTURE SPORTS
(Map p228; ☎0692 87 55 50, 0262 32 40 29; www.australaventure.fr; 42 Rue Amiral Lacaze; half-/full-day canyoning outings €55/75; ☺by reservation) This professional outfit has canyoning trips to Trou Blanc and Trou de Fer (from Hell-Bourg), as well as guided hikes to Forêt de Bébour-Bélouve (€50).

Alpanes ADVENTURE SPORTS
(☎0692 77 75 30; www.alpanes.com; canyoning outings €50-95; ☺by reservation) Offers canyoning trips to Trou Blanc (and, if reopened, Voile de la Mariée). Doesn't have an office in Hell-Bourg.

🛏 Sleeping

⭐ La Mandoze
GÎTE €

(Map p228; ☑ 0262 47 89 65, 0692 65 65 28; 14 Chemin de l'École; dm €18, d with shared bathroom incl breakfast €45; P 📶) This *gîte* set in a Creole house has all the hallmarks of a great deal: well-maintained dorms that can sleep six people, recently renovated shared bathrooms, a tranquil location and a tab that won't burn a hole in your pocket. For those wanting more privacy, three adjoining doubles, with wood-panelled walls, are available. They're compact but get the job done.

Breakfast (€6) and dinner (€20) are available. The owner, Patrick Manoro, is a mine of local knowledge and occasionally plays guitar for his guests in the evening.

Le Relais des Gouverneurs
B&B €

(Map p228; ☑ 0262 47 76 21; www.relaisdesgouverneurs.fr; 2bis Rue Amiral Lacaze; d €65-80, q €90, incl breakfast; P 📶) Although the structure is starting to show its age, this B&B is still a reliable option. The two Superieure rooms feature four-poster beds, wooden floors and clean bathrooms. The cheaper Standard rooms are less exciting and lack intimacy, but the densely vegetated grounds add a lot of charm. Dinners (€25) are available if there's a minimum of six people. Families can plump for the large Familiale units.

Gîte du Piton d'Anchaing
GÎTE €

(Map p228; ☑ 0692 33 93 35; www.facebook.com/pitondanchaing; 53bis Rue Général de Gaulle; dm €18; 📶) Occupying a cute Creole house on the main drag, this well-run *gîte* is a secure spot to hang your rucksack, with four salubrious (if a bit boxy) four- to six-bed rooms, well-scrubbed bathrooms and a nice communal kitchen. Breakfast costs €5.

Le Relax
CAMPGROUND €

(☑ 0692 66 58 89; 21 Chemin Bras-Sec, Îlet-à-Vidot; camping €11; P) Head to this homely camping fround in the hamlet of Îlet-à-Vidot, about 2km northwest of Hell-Bourg, if you're after a peaceful setting to pitch your tent within a grassy (and shady) property. The ablution block is in good nick and there's a kitchen for guests' use. No meal service, but there's a (modest) grocery store nearby.

Laurent, the sporty owner (he has run the Grand Raid race), can take you to various scenic spots in the area and provide you with a wealth of information (alas, in French) about local plants and architecture.

Chez Madeleine Parisot
GÎTE €

(Map p228; ☑ 0262 47 83 48; www.gitemadoparisot.sitew.com; 31 Rue Général de Gaulle; dm €16; 📶) This homely *gîte d'étape* on the main drag features two- to five-bed rooms in several Creole-style buildings full of nooks and crannies. Some rooms are better than others, so ask to see a few before committing. Breakfast (€5) and dinner (€18) are available. You can park for free in front of the *gîte*.

⭐ Chambre d'Hôte des Agrumes
B&B €€

(☑ 0692 43 05 70, 0692 65 51 82; www.chambredhotesdesagrumes.com; 7 Chemin Manouilh, Îlet-à-Vidot; d incl breakfast €80; P 📶) If you're after hush and seclusion, these four stand-alone Creole-style bungalows scattered in an Eden-like garden are the answer. They're spacious and impeccably maintained, with spick-and-span bathrooms and a private terrace. Evening meals (€20) garner warm praise. Find this B&B in the hamlet of Îlet-à-Vidot, about 2.5km northwest of Hell Bourg.

Le Relais des Cimes
HOTEL €€

(Map p228; ☑ 0262 47 81 58; www.relaisdescimes.com; 67 Rue Général de Gaulle; s €70-78, d €81-89, incl breakfast; P 📶) The rooms in the motel-like building lack character but they're fresh and tidy. Most upstairs rooms have mountain views. There's a second building across the street, which features four atmospheric rooms that occupy two tastefully refurbished Creole houses; ask for the 'Chambres Case Créole'. Wi-fi is available at the restaurant.

Les Jardins d'Héva
HOTEL €€

(Map p228; ☑ 0262 47 87 87; www.lesjardinsdheva.com; 16 Rue Lacaussade; d incl breakfast €98; P 📶) This relaxing option perched on the southern outskirts of town features five colourful bungalows with a Creole flavour, each with two adjoining rooms; they're all decorated differently. Two glitches: they turn their back on the fantastic views of the Cirque, and lack intimacy (terraces are shared). The real steal is the mini spa featuring a sauna and a Jacuzzi – access is free for guests.

There's an on-site restaurant if you're feeling too lazy to travel elsewhere, and a small gift shop. The owner, Alice Deligey, speaks English.

🍴 Eating

While Cilaos is known for its lentils, Hell-Bourg is synonymous with *chouchou*, a green, pear-shaped vegetable first imported from Brazil in 1834. It comes in salads, gratins and as *chouchou gateau* to finish. You can stock up on basic provisions at the grocers and other food shops along the main road.

Chez Maxime's CREOLE €

(Map p228; ☑ 0693 94 46 76; 18 Rue Amiral Lacaze; mains €9-11; ⊗ noon-2pm Wed-Mon) Wholly unpretentious and bearing not an ounce of belabored design, this easy-to-miss venture at the end of the main drag whips up cheap Creole eats, including a few desserts, that make the perfect lunch on a budget. Takeaway is available.

Patis' Salazes BAKERY €

(Map p228; ☑ 0262 47 85 40; 43 Rue Général de Gaulle; sandwiches €2-4; ⊗ 6am-6pm) This bakery whips up tasty sandwiches made with great ingredients, and bakes mouthwatering pastries, including *macatias*.

Le P'tit Koin Kréol CREOLE €

(Map p228; ☑ 0693 92 62 00; 35 Rue Général de Gaulle; mains €7-9; ⊗ noon-3pm) This postage-stamp-sized eatery in a cute Creole house is a good place to sample authentic Réunion-nais fare prepared mama-style. Tour your taste buds with a *gratin de chouchous* or a tasty curry. For dessert, try the belt-bustingly good banana cake. Sandwiches (from €3) are also available. There are only four tables; if it's full, don't despair – it also does takeaway.

Crêperie Le Gall CREPERIE €

(Map p228; ☑ 0262 47 87 48; 55 Rue Général de Gaulle; mains €3-12; ⊗ noon-2pm Thu-Tue) The only place for kilometres around that serves pancakes. Yes, pancakes! Try the Ti Chou Chou with, you guessed it, *chouchou*. Wash it all down with a *bolée de cidre* (bowl of cider). *Gratins* (baked vegetables with melted cheese) and salads also feature on the menu.

Les Jardins d'Héva CREOLE, BUFFET €€

(Map p228; ☑ 0262 47 87 87; 16 Rue Lacaussade; lunch buffet €15-18, dinner buffet €28; ⊗ noon-1.30pm Thu-Tue, 6.30-8pm daily; ☎) Les Jardins d'Héva rocks a superb setting: central Hell-Bourg at your feet, the jagged peaks of the Cirques in the distance, and a luminous dining room. Settle back and feast on an assortment of well-prepared Creole staples, salads and homemade desserts. The lunch buffet is excellent value.

Le Relais des Cimes CREOLE €€

(Map p228; ☑ 0262 47 81 58; 67 Rue Général de Gaulle; mains €12-17, menus €18-23; ⊗ noon-2pm & 7-8.30pm) At this Hell-Bourg stalwart the food has a temptingly pronounced regional flavour. Among the many winners are the Hell-Bourg trout, the roasted guinea fowl with peach and the *vindaye de thon* (tuna flavoured with grated turmeric), all served at affordable prices in rustic surrounds (think wooden ceilings and red tablecloths).

Ti Chou Chou CREOLE €€

(Map p228; ☑ 0262 47 80 93; 42 Rue Général de Gaulle; mains €12-23, menus €18-26; ⊗ 11.30am-1.45pm & 6.30-7.45pm Sat-Thu) This small restaurant, with its colourful facade on the main drag, is run by a friendly young team. Herbivores will opt for the *assiette ti chouchou*, which offers a combination of *chouchou*, *cresson* and *capucine* (all local vegetables). There's a shady terrace at the back. It's usually closed for dinner in low season.

ⓘ Information

Office du Tourisme (Map p228; ☑ 0262 47 89 89; www.est.reunion.fr; 47 Rue Général de Gaulle; ⊗ 8.30am-noon & 1-5.30pm; ☎) Has pamphlets on hiking options and bus schedules in the Cirque. Can also arrange bookings at *gîtes de montagne* and guided tours in English if given advance notice. Offers free wi-fi.

ⓘ Getting There & Away

Buses from Salazie to Hell-Bourg run about every two hours from 6.45am to 6.20pm (€1.80, about 20 minutes). In the opposite direction, there are services from 6.15am to 5.45pm. There are four buses in each direction on Sunday.

Grand Îlet & Col des Boeufs

This is a sweet, picturesque spot. About 17km west of Salazie, accessed by a scenic white-knuckle road, Grand Îlet really feels like the end of the line. The village sits at the base of the ridge separating the Cirque de Salazie and the Cirque de Mafate. Above the village is the mountain pass of Col des Bœufs, which forms the main pedestrian route between the two Cirques; access is via the village of **Le Bélier**, 3km above Grand Îlet, where you'll find the start of the tarred *route forestière* (forestry road) that leads to Col des Bœufs. The *route forestière* is dotted with a number of *kiosques* (picnic shelters) that are popular at weekends.

🛏 Sleeping & Eating

There's only one independent eatery in Grand Îlet. Most visitors opt for a *table d'hôte* meal (served at a *chambre d'hôte*), or drive down to Hell-Bourg.

EXPLORING CIRQUE DE MAFATE

Despite its remoteness and seclusion, the Cirque de Mafate is populated. In the valleys, plateaus and spurs that slice up the jaw-dropping terrain are scattered discreet little Creole settlements that retain a rough-diamond rural edge. Not much happens in these villages but it's hard not to fall under the spell of their phenomenal setting.

The southern part of the Cirque is called **Haut Mafate** (Higher Mafate) and receives the bulk of visitors. It comprises peaceful **Marla**, the highest hamlet of the Cirque at an altitude of 1621m; **La Nouvelle**, dubbed the 'capital of Mafate' and one of the main gateways to the Cirque, perched on a plateau at an altitude of 1421m; and **Roche-Plate**, at the foot of the grandiose Maïdo.

The northern part of the Cirque is called **Bas Mafate** (Lower Mafate) and is considered even more secretive than Haut Mafate. It comprises Îlet à Bourse, Îlet à **Malheur, Aurère, Grand Place, Cayenne, Les Lataniers** and **Îlet des Orangers**. The two tiny communities of Grand Place and Cayenne lie above the rushing Rivière des Galets near the Cirque's main outlet.

Le Papangue
B&B €

(📋 0692 60 30 67; nelson.boyer@wanadoo.fr; 6 Chemin Camp Pierrot; d incl breakfast €70; P 🅿️) At the end of a long day's driving, it's a joy to snuggle into the freshly pressed bed sheets of this B&B off the road to Le Bélier. There are three good-sized rooms, with parquet flooring and wood panelling on the walls. One quibble: two rooms face a concrete wall.

Le Cimendef – Chez Noeline et Daniel Campton
B&B €

(Map p216; 📋 0262 47 73 59; campton.cimendef@wanadoo.fr; 735 Route du Bélier, Casabois; d/ste incl breakfast €50/85; P 🅿️) All four rooms are very simply laid-out yet pleasing and are graced with views over the Cimendef (2226m). There's also an atmospheric suite featuring timber floor, a luminous bathroom, Creole ceilings, teak furniture, an enticing orange colour scheme and your own terrace; prices drop to €75 if you stay two nights or more. Dinner, available certain evenings, is €24.

A convenient base if you want to arrive early morning at Col des Bœufs.

Chez Liliane Bonnald
B&B €

(📋 0262 47 71 62; liliane.bonnald@wanadoo.fr; 17 Chemin Camp-Pierrot; d incl breakfast €40-60; P 🅿️) In a modernish house on the road to Le Bélier, the three rooms upstairs won't be selected for a *Wallpaper* photo shoot but fit the bill for a night or two. You're better off choosing the more recent units (€60), which stand on a little knoll about 100m away. They're spick and span, luminous and proffer ample mountain views.

Liliane Bonnald, your affable host, is a good cook too. Dinner costs €25.

Snack Le Grand Îlet – Chez Serge
CREOLE €

(📋 0262 47 71 19; 48 Rue du Père Mancel; mains €6-11; ⏱ 11am-2pm & 6.30-8pm Fri-Wed) This economical, neon-lit eatery set in a modern house by the main road is worth stopping at for its short list of flavoursome daily specials, which may include sausage *rougail*, roasted chicken or pork stew. Everything's fresh and homemade. Takeaway meals are available (€6). Brilliant value.

❶ Getting There & Away

There are eight buses a day (four on Sunday) from Salazie to Grand Îlet and Le Bélier between 6.45am (9.15am on Sunday) and 6.20pm. Heading back to Salazie services depart from Le Bélier between around 5.45am and 5pm (7am to 5.20pm on Sunday), calling at Grand Îlet 10 minutes later.

From Le Bélier to Col des Bœufs, there are two buses (line 82C) per day on Monday, Wednesday, Friday and Sunday. The tourist office in Hell-Bourg has timetables.

If you have your own car, you can leave it in the guarded car park (parking one/two days €2/10) at Le Petit Col, 6.5km up the *route forestière* and only 20 minutes' walk below the Col des Bœufs.

Cirque de Mafate

Surrounded by ramparts, criss-crossed with gullies and studded with narrow ridges, Cirque de Mafate is the wildest and the most remote of Réunion's Cirques. Nothing can prepare you for that first glimpse of this geologic wonder, with its shifting colours, blissful serenity (except for the occasional whirring

FORAYS INTO THE CIRQUE DE MAFATE

If you have a day to spare, do not miss the opportunity to hike into the Cirque de Mafate. From the car park just below Col des Bœufs, it takes only two hours to descend to La Nouvelle, dubbed 'the capital of Mafate'; it makes a great half-day hike, and you can have lunch in La Nouvelle. A longer option is to take the **Sentier Scout** which branches off the *route forestière* (forestry road; it's sign-posted, about 2.3km before the car park at Col des Bœufs) and leads to Aurère in Bas Mafate; you can spend the night in Aurère and walk back to the *route forestière* the next day by following the super scenic **Sentier Augustave** – a lovely loop.

of choppers) and unsurpassed grandeur. No cars, no towns, no stress. Just soaring mountains, deep ravines and a sprinkle of tiny hamlets where time seems to have stood still.

Apart from its grandiose topography, what sets the Cirque de Mafate apart is its relative inaccessibility, despite being very close to the coastal fleshpots. There are no roads that lead into the Cirque (although a *route forestière* runs right up to the pass at Col des Bœufs), so the villages that are scattered in this giant extinct volcano are accessible only by foot.

❶ Getting There & Away

Mafate is only accessible on foot via various routes. The most convenient one is from the Col des Bœufs in the Cirque de Salazie. Other routes into Mafate from the Cirque de Salazie are the Sentier Scout and Sentier Augustave. From the Cirque de Cilaos, access is possible via the Col du Taïbit (2082m).

From the west coast, the most straightforward way to get into the Cirque de Mafate is via Rivière des Galets. Other options are from Sans Souci via the Canalisation des Orangers and from Le Maïdo down to Roche-Plate.

Aurère

POP 80

The tiny *îlet* (hamlet) of Aurère is perched Machu Picchu–like above the precipitous canyon of the Bras Bémale in the Cirque de Mafate. It's usually the first port of call for hikers who tackle the Bas Mafate loop. It's nothing more than a few colourful *cases*

(Creole-style houses) but it offers plenty of rural charm in a magical setting.

🛏 Sleeping & Eating

Aurère has one modest grocery store. All meals are provided by the *gîtes*. Call the *gîtes* to book your meals at least a day in advance.

Gîte Narcisse Libelle　　　　　　GÎTE **€**
(☑ 0692 09 18 86, 0262 43 86 38; Mafate; dm with half board €40) A welcoming venture on the outskirts of Aurère, on the way to Îlet à Malheur. Two four-bed dorms.

Gîte Boyer Georget – Le Poinsettia　GÎTE **€**
(☑ 0692 08 92 20; Mafate; dm with half board €39, r per person with half board €42) Beds are in five- to 11-bed dorms. Also has three doubles and a small grocery store.

Auberge Piton Cabris – Charlemagne Libelle　　　　　GÎTE **€**
(☑ 0692 26 33 59, 0262 43 36 83; Mafate; dm €19) Four four-bed dorms. Good views from the terrace. Add €6 for breakfast and €19 for dinner.

❶ Getting There & Away

Aurère can be reached on foot only. Most visitors start from Rivière des Galets, a three-hour hike to the west.

LES HAUTES PLAINES & THE PITON DE LA FOURNAISE

Réunion's only cross-island road passes through the Plaine-des-Cafres and the Plaine-des-Palmistes, collectively known as Les Hautes Plaines. At an altitude of about 1000m, the air is refreshingly crisp and often swathed in misty fog – a blessing if you're coming from the scorching coastal cities.

These relatively large open areas actually form the saddle that separates the massif (comprising the three Cirques) from the volcano, Piton de la Fournaise. And what a volcano! It ranks as one of the most active volcanoes on Earth, playing in the same league as Hawaii. It's also one of the most accessible ones – you can trek up the caldera.

Because there's a road from the Hautes Plaines that approaches within a few kilometres of the summit of the volcano, nearly all visitors approach it from this side.

GRAND BASSIN - THE LOST VALLEY

The utterly picturesque valley of Grand Bassin, known as Mafate en miniature (Mafate in miniature), is one of the few areas in Réunion that is only accessible on foot. Thanks to its splendid isolation, this little morsel of paradise is a dream come true for those seeking to kick off their shoes for a few days and sample authentic rural Réunionnais life.

Grand Bassin is formed by the confluence of three rivers. Near to where they join is a quiet hamlet with a handful of *gîtes* (self-catering accommodation). From the hamlet, follow the river towards the west and you'll soon reach a few rock pools where you can dunk yourself. Further west, you can descend at the base of the impressive **Cascade du Voile de la Mariée** waterfall.

Even if you don't take the path down to the hamlet, you can look down into the valley from the Belvédère (p234) viewpoint.

Grand Bassin has a dozen *gîtes* scattered in the village. Digs are in rustic dorms or in modest doubles, but that's part of the fun. Book at least one day in advance. Day trippers will fork out €18 to €20 for a meal at one of the local *gîtes*, usually a wholesome *carri* (curry) made with locally grown products. Bookings are advised.

Le Randonneur (☑ 0692 78 04 50; www.gitelerandonneur.net; Grand Bassin; per person with half board €40-45) A chalet-like venue with good views. A bit more expensive than other venues in Grand-Bassin, but it feels more intimate, with only three doubles and three quadruples, all tiled.

La Vieille Tonnelle (☑ 0262 27 51 02, 0262 59 20 27; Grand Bassin; per person with half board €40) La Vielle Tonnelle has two snug doubles. Luc, the friendly owner, will treat you to a wicked *rhum bois* (rum flavoured with an endemic wood). Good homemade jams.

Les Orchidées (☑ 0692 17 34 57, 0692 03 90 38; Grand-Bassin; per person with half board €38-45) On the eastern outskirts of the hamlet, Les Orchidées has two quadruples, two eight-bed dorms and two doubles. Good homemade honey.

Le Paille-en-Queue (☑ 0262 59 03 66, 0692 24 31 73; Grand-Bassin; per person with half board €40) Features two doubles and six- to eight-bed dorms.

Auberge de Grand-Bassin (☑ 0262 59 10 34, 0692 26 74 55; Grand Bassin; per person with half board €40) This auberge has two doubles and six- to 16-bed dorms.

Les Mimosas (☑ 0692 16 09 90; www.lesmimosas.re; Grand-Bassin; d with half board €195; 🛜) This B&B has been beautifully built and decorated using local materials. The all-wood bungalow sits in a superb tropical garden and sports two doubles that are as cosy as a bird's nest. Great for couples or families. Vegetarian meals can be arranged.

Plaine-des-Cafres & Around

Velvet-green hills and pastures undulating off into the horizon. Fresh air. Mist. Filled with iconic pastoral landscapes, the Plaine-des-Cafres area bears an unexpected likeness to Bavaria. It is cool, relaxing and oxygenated. Chalk that up to altitude. It sits 1200m above sea level and is regularly massaged by cool breezes. Once a refuge for runaway slaves from the coast, the Plaine-des-Cafres is a vast, gently rolling area that spreads between the Cirques and Piton de la Fournaise.

The most interesting place on the Plaine-des-Cafres from a visitor's perspective is **Bourg-Murat**, which is the obvious launch pad for the volcano. It's in this rural settlement where the Route Forestière du Volcan turns off to Piton de la Fournaise.

◉ Sights

Cité du Volcan   MUSEUM
(Map p234; ☑ 0262 59 00 26; www.maisondu volcan.fr; RN3, Bourg-Murat; adult/child €9/6; ☺ 1-5pm Mon, 9.30am-4.45pm Tue-Sun) Everything you need to know about Piton de la Fournaise and volcanoes in general should become clear at the excellent Cité du Volcan. It was completely refurbished and modernised in 2013, so you can expect state-of-the-art facilities and animations, including a spectacular 4D entertainment attraction, for which an extra €2 is charged.

Bourg-Murat

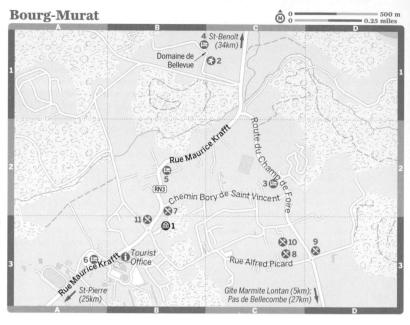

Bourg-Murat

⊙ Sights
1 Cité du Volcan B3

⊕ Activities, Courses & Tours
2 Écuries du Volcan C1

⊜ Sleeping
3 Chez Alicalapa-Tenon C2
4 Gîte de Bellevue B1
5 Gîte de la Fournaise B2
6 Hôtel l'Ecrin A3

⊗ Eating
7 Hôtel-Auberge du Volcan B2
8 Le QG...C3
9 Palais du Fromage D3
10 Relais Commerson C3
11 Ti Resto Lontan B3

Belvédère VIEWPOINT
(Map p216; Bois Court) From this viewpoint near Bois Court, you can look down into the splendid valley of Grand Bassin.

🏃 Activities

Centre Équestre Alti Merens HORSE RIDING
(Map p216; ☎0692 31 47 92; www.alti-merens. re; 120 Rue Maurice Krafft, PK26; 1/2/3hr rides €30/50/75; ⊙by reservation) This equestrian

centre lies on the southern edge of Bourg-Murat.

Écuries du Volcan HORSE RIDING
(Map p234; ☎0692 66 62 90; www.ecuriesduvolcan. e-monsite.com; 9bis Domaine Bellevue, Bourg-Murat; 1/3hr rides €20/60; ⊙9am-noon & 2-5pm) A well-run equestrian centre on the northern edge of Bourg-Murat. The three-hour ride, called 'La Ronde', comes recommended. For beginners and kids, the 'Discovery' tour around Piton Desforges is a great option.

🎉 Festivals & Events

Fête du Miel Vert FOOD
(Festival of Honey; ⊙Jan) A rural fair that celebrates honey, held in Plaine-des-Cafres.

🛏 Sleeping

Bourg-Murat and the surrounding area have a good selection of accommodation choices, including a couple of simple hotels, making it a handy base. Bookings on weekends are essential.

Chez Alicalapa-Tenon B&B €
(Map p234; ☎0262 59 10 41, 0692 08 80 09; c.alicalapatenon@ool.fr; 164 Route du Champ de Foire, Bourg-Murat; s/d incl breakfast €40/50; [P]🐾) This sweet B&B in a modern house makes a

good base for exploring the area, with six simple wood-panelled rooms that are kept spick and span. Ask for a room that opens onto the garden. Dinner costs €20.

La Ferme du Pêcher Gourmand INN €

(Map p216; ☑0262 59 29 79, 0692 66 12 48; www.pechergourmand.re; RN3, PK25; s €60, d €65-75, q €150, bungalow d €100, incl breakfast; ☺closed 2 weeks in Feb & 3 weeks in Sep; P 🛜) This modern *auberge* (farm inn) is run by a friendly couple and is surrounded by a pleasant garden. The five adjoining rooms are a bit of a squeeze and bathrooms are tiny, but the setting more than compensates. There's also a stand-alone bungalow, which offers more privacy, and two larger *cases* (Creole-style houses) that are ideal for families.

Bonus: there's a widely acclaimed on-site restaurant – it's worth opting for half board.

Gîte Marmite Lontan GÎTE €

(Map p216; ☑0692 60 51 38; www.marmitelontan.com; Route Forestière du Volcan; s with shared bathroom incl half board €40; P) Not your average *gîte*, this little cracker radiates a ramshackle air, from the quirky facade, which is entirely covered with thongs, to the dining room, which is a Pandora's box of *objets lontan* (utensils and other knick-knacks from the old days). The five dorms are neat and can sleep two to four people.

The *gîte* is isolated on the Route Forestière du Volcan about 5km from the centre of Bourg-Murat. It's closed two to three months per year (usually February, June and December). No wi-fi.

Gîte de Bellevue GÎTE €

(Map p234; ☑0262 59 15 02, 0692 07 80 83; www.gitedebellevue.re; Domaine de Bellevue, Bourg-Murat; dm €16, bungalow d €45; P) A good find in a bucolic setting, this property has two doubles and two quads, all scrubbed attentively. There's also a smaller bungalow for couples. Bar breakfast (€6) is available; no other meals are provided but there are kitchen facilities.

Gîte de la Fournaise GÎTE €

(Map p234; ☑0692 22 89 88, 0262 59 29 75; www.gitedelafournaise.re; 202 RN3, Bourg-Murat; dm/s/d €16/30/36; P🛜) On the main road, this well-regarded venue harbours a six-bed dorm and two quadruples that are in good nick and come with their own bathroom. The French owner is extra nice and offers to pick up walkers from the nearby walking trails (and drop them off the next morning).

Hôtel l'Ecrin HOTEL €€

(Map p234; ☑0262 59 02 02; www.ecrin-hotel.re; RN3, PK27, Bourg-Murat; s/d/q incl breakfast €60/84/121; P🛜) A cluster of small cottages scattered amid gardens that carpet a knoll. The rooms are a tad frayed around the edges but it's an acceptable plan B.

✗ Eating

★ Palais du Fromage CHEESE €

(Map p234; ☑0262 59 27 15; Rue Alfred Picard, Bourg-Murat; cheese & waffles €2.50-6; ☺9am-5pm Tue-Sun) The aptly named 'Cheese Palace' is famous for its superb range of cheeses, including a delicious *fromage au miel* (cheese flavoured with honey), best enjoyed at a picnic table in the cryptomeria forest nearby. Also concocts waffles, pancakes, yoghurts and fruit juices. Find it on the outskirts of Bourg-Murat, towards the volcano. Cash only.

Ti Resto Lontan INTERNATIONAL €€

(Map p234; ☑0262 43 90 42; RN3, PK27, Bourg-Murat; mains €10-21; ☺11.30am-2.30pm & 6.30-9.30pm Wed-Mon) Don't let the bland building put you off – this jovial venture has won a faithful following for its value-for-money seasonal fare. Tuck into tasty *carris*, copious salads and simply cooked meat and fish dishes. For dessert, try the belt-bustingly good fruit mousse. Service is friendly and the laid-back atmosphere is conducive to a nice, relaxed meal.

La Ferme du Pêcher Gourmand CREOLE, FRENCH €€

(Map p216; ☑0262 59 29 79; www.pechergourmand.re; RN3, PK25; mains €14-19; ☺noon-2pm Sat & Sun, 7-8.30pm Tue-Sat, closed 2 weeks in Feb & 3 weeks in Sep; 🛜) This *ferme-auberge* (farm restaurant) on the main road south of Bourg-Murat offers superb value for money and delicious farmhouse food. Along with duck preparations and seasonal vegetables, signature dishes include pork curry and cassoulet (meat and bean stew). Save a cranny for the vanilla crème brûlée. Well worth reserving ahead, especially on weekends.

Le Vieux Bardeau CREOLE, BUFFET €€

(Map p216; ☑0262 59 09 44; RN3, PK24; mains €12-23, buffet €14-23; ☺11.30am-2pm Mon, Tue & Thu-Sat, noon-2pm Sun, 6.30-8pm Thu-Sat; 🛜) Recapture the atmosphere of the colonial era in this gracefully ageing diva occupying a lemon-yellow Creole mansion beside the main road in Le Vingt-Quatrième. Come here for lunch to make the best of the great-value buffet featuring eight different starters and five curries. You'll also find grills and salads à la carte.

Relais Commerson
CREOLE €€

(Map p234; ☑ 0692 60 05 44; 37 Bois Joly Potier, Bourg-Murat; mains €16-25, menus €18-40; ⊙ noon-2pm Wed-Sun & 7-8pm Fri & Sat) The Relais' rustic dining room plays host to a menu laden with inspired Creole dishes and a tempting selection of desserts. On weekdays it lays on an excellent buffet lunch for just €18.

Hôtel-Auberge du Volcan
CREOLE, FRENCH €€

(Map p234; ☑ 0262 27 50 91; RN3, PK27, Bourg-Murat; mains €12-18, menu €17; ⊙ 11.30am-1.30pm Tue-Sun, 6.30-8.30pm Tue-Sat) You'll find all the usual Creole favourites and a sprinkling of *métro* dishes served in hearty portions in this country inn in the centre of Bourg-Murat. It's not memorable, but it can fill a gap.

★ Le QG
INTERNATIONAL €€€

(Map p234; ☑ 0262 38 28 55, 0692 48 22 80; 60bis Rue Alfred Picard, Bourg-Murat; mains €16-35; ⊙ noon-10pm; 🐾) What do you get if you cross a Réunionnais chef (André), a Senegalese waiter (Abdou) and a snug dining room? The QG! The eclectic menu features exquisitely cooked *rougail zandouille* (chitterlings stew Creole-style) and divine grilled meats as well as a few Senegalese specialities, including *poulet yassa* (grilled chicken marinated in a thick onion and lemon sauce). A winning formula.

Oh, and it's the only place for miles around that offers some entertainment (think: karaoke) on Friday evening. It's sometimes open for breakfast too. Book ahead on weekends.

❶ Information

Tourist Office (Map p234; ☑ 0262 27 40 00; www.tampontourisme.re; 160 Rue Maurice Krafft, Bourg-Murat; ⊙ 9am-5pm; 🐾) Near the Engen petrol station, the tourist office does bookings for *gîtes de montagnes* and has brochures and walking maps. Free wi-fi.

❶ Getting There & Away

There are three buses daily each way between St-Benoît and St-Pierre via Plaine-des-Cafres and Plaine-des-Palmistes (line S2). More information at www.carjaune.re.

Piton de la Fournaise (The Volcano)

The magnum opus of Mother Nature in Réunion, Piton de la Fournaise is the island's most famous natural attraction. Simply dubbed *le volcan* (the volcano) by Réunionnais, Piton de la Fournaise is not a dormant monster, but an active geological wonder that erupts with great regularity; in April 2007 the central, 900m-wide crater collapsed by 300m, and new lava fields were formed on its southeastern flanks, down to the coast. In August 2015 a new eruption occurred, though less powerful.

The good news is that it's one of the world's most accessible active volcanoes, and it's possible to hike up to the crater rim. You can also fly over the volcano or simply enjoy the scenery from a viewpoint right on the crater's outer rim, where the road ends.

◉ Sights

★ Plaine des Sables
NATURAL SITE

(Map p237) You've reached the end of the world! The Plaine des Sables is a wide windswept plain, made of ashes. With its lunar landscape, it could form a perfect backdrop for a new version of *Mad Max*. From the Pas des Sables, the road plunges down to the plain and becomes a dirt road with wicked potholes before continuing uphill to Pas de Bellecombe.

Pas de Bellecombe
VIEWPOINT

(Map p237) From the viewpoint at Pas de Bellecombe (2311m), the 'entrance' to the volcanic area, you'll be rewarded with mesmerising views of the volcano and its outer crater, known as Enclos Fouqué. The very photogenic, small scoria cone with bizarre ochre hues you can see to the east in Enclos Fouqué is Formica Leo. The main crater, the 900m-wide Dolomieu Crater, is active.

Pas des Sables
VIEWPOINT

(Map p237) About 22km from Bourg-Murat, there's a fabulous viewpoint at Pas des Sables (2360m), from where you can gaze at the barren moonscape that is the Plaine des Sables.

Belvédère du Nez-de-Bœuf
VIEWPOINT

(Map p237) On your way to the volcano, be sure to pause at this viewpoint (it's signposted) to enjoy unsurpassable views over the valley gouged by the Rivière des Remparts.

Piton de la Fournaise

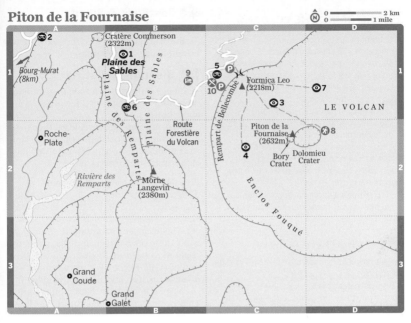

Piton de la Fournaise

🛏 Sleeping & Eating

There's only one accommodation option, at the Gîte du Volcan (p237). Unsurprisingly, it's in high demand, especially during the trekking season, so be sure to reserve well ahead.

Gîte du Volcan GÎTE €
(Map p237; ☑ 0692 85 20 91; Route du Volcan; dm €16-18, bungalow d incl breakfast €60, restaurant lunch mains €14-18, dinner menu €25; ⊗restaurant noon-2pm Thu-Tue; P) If you wish to stop overnight to soak up this grandiose scenery, the 65-bed Gîte du Volcan boasts a stunning location, a 15-minute walk from Pas de Bellecombe. Digs are in basic four- to 12-bed dorms. There's also one cute bungalow that comes with bathroom. Hot water is limited and is token-operated, and there are no sockets in the dorms.

The restaurant is open at lunch for day trippers and serves up five different dishes. The real clinchers are the picture windows with lovely mountain views.

In principle, bookings are to be made through Centrale d'Information et de Réservation Régionale – Île de la Réunion Tourisme (p190) or through any tourist office, but the caretakers usually accept travellers who haven't reserved if the *gîte* is not full (but reservations are essential during the trekking season). Credit cards are accepted.

Le Relais de Bellecombe CAFETERIA €
(Map p237; Pas de Bellecombe; snacks from €1; ⊗8am-4pm) This modest place near the parking lot at Pas de Bellecombe sells snacks, sandwiches (€4) and refreshments.

MONITORING THE VOLCANO

Scientists keep a close watch on the volcano's moods, and are poised to issue warnings if things look to be gathering steam. At the first sign of an eruption, the paths near the volcano and the road up to it will be closed.

A webcam has been positioned on the outer crater rim, due north of Piton de la Fournaise. It allows walkers to check out the weather conditions that prevail near the volcano and curious travellers to simply admire the monster in its full grandeur.

The images update every five minutes. Go to www.fournaise.info/webcam.php.

❶ Getting There & Away

There's no public transport to/from the Piton de la Fournaise.

The main gateway to the volcano is Bourg-Murat. From there, the scenic, zigzagging Route Forestière du Volcan leads to Pas de Bellecombe, about 30km southeast of Bourg-Murat. The gradual change of scenery is mind-boggling. The grassy meadows and cryptomeria forests typical of the Hautes Plaines progressively change to scrubland and Martian landscape.

Plaine-des-Palmistes

POP 5500

There were once large numbers of palm trees on the Plaine-des-Palmistes (hence the name), but as a result of heavy consumption of palm-heart salad, few now remain. The town itself is spread out along the highway and has only one specific sight, the Domaine des Tourelles.

◉ Sights

Domaine des Tourelles HISTORIC BUILDING
(☑0262 51 47 59; www.tourelles.re; 260 Rue de la République; ⊙9am-5pm Mon-Fri, 10am-5pm Sat & Sun) A lovely 1920s Creole building just south of the town centre, Domaine des Tourelles now houses a shop selling local produce and souvenirs. Outside, you'll also find a cluster of crafts shops. The rather motley assortment of crafts on offer include paintings, carvings, and products made of bronze, honey and candles, among others.

✳ Festivals & Events

Fête des Goyaviers FOOD
(Festival of Guava; ⊙Jun) A celebration of guava held in Plaine-des-Palmistes.

🛏 Sleeping & Eating

Plaine-des-Palmistes is a good base for Forêt de Bébour-Bélouve, with a few B&Bs, a *gîte* and a hotel.

There are some fairly standard Creole restaurants and fast-food outlets along the main road through town. The Domaine des Tourelles has a good cafeteria, too.

Gîte du Pic des Sables & Chambre d'Hôte des Agrumes GÎTE, B&B €
(Map p216; ☑0262 51 37 33; 2 Allée des Filaos, Plaine-des-Palmistes; dm/d incl breakfast €25/75; 🅿) This cleanish but cramped *gîte d'étape* is on the road to Forêt de Bébour-Bélouve, about 4km from the highway (in the direction of Petite Plaine). For more comfort and privacy, opt for one of the two adjoining *chambre d'hôte* at the back of the garden. They're airy, spacious and functional. Hearty Creole meals are served at dinner (€25). No wi-fi.

La Ferme du Pommeau HOTEL €€
(☑0262 51 40 70; www.pommeau.fr; 10 Allée des Pois de Senteur; s €63, d €78-87, restaurant mains €15-24, menus €26-38; ⊙restaurant noon-1.30pm & 7-8pm Mon-Sat; 🅿🛜🏊) In a quiet location on the eastern edge of town, this rambling two-star hotel consists of several buildings that shelter clean yet uninspiring rooms. The Superior ones are slightly dearer but offer more privacy. Its standout feature is the heated pool at the back – bliss after a long day's driving. There's a reliable restaurant on-site which strives to use only local ingredients.

The dining room is suitably rustic, with plenty of wood, a hearth and great mountain views. Specialities include chicken curry, lamb cutlet and duck stuffed with mushrooms.

Le Relais des Plaines CREOLE, FRENCH €€
(☑0262 20 00 68; 303 Rue de la République; mains €11-16, menus €15-19; ⊙11.30am-2pm Thu-Tue, 6.30-8.45pm Thu-Mon; ☑) Traditional cuisine is given a modern makeover at this restaurant occupying a tastefully restored Creole house just off the main road. The menu is short but you'll find tempting daily specials as well as a few vegetarian options – a rarity in the area.

HIKING UP PITON DE LA FOURNAISE

Réunion's iconic feature, Piton de la Fournaise is simply a must-do for walkers. From Pas de Bellecombe, it's possible to hike up to **Balcon du Dolomieu** (Map p237), a viewpoint on the northeastern side of the Dolomieu Crater rim, from where you can gaze down upon the bottom of the caldera, some 350m below. Balcon du Dolomieu is a five-hour, 14km out-and-back walk. It's graded moderate and has an altitude gain of about 500m. It can get very busy, but the eerie landscape more than makes up for the crowds of people. Note that since the 2007 eruption it's no longer possible to do a circuit around the Dolomieu Crater and the Bory Crater; ignore all maps showing this circuit, as they're not up to date.

From the car park at Pas de Bellecombe, follow the path to the northeast down to a door (closed when the volcano is active). This is where the path starts in earnest by plunging 527 steps to the floor of the immense Enclos Fouqué, reached after about 15 minutes. You're now walking on a field of solidified lava. The route across the lava plain is marked with white paint spots. At times it can feel like you are walking on Mars, with only the dry crunch of the cinders underfoot for company. You'll first pass the very photogenic **Formica Leo** (a small scoria cone) and, about 45 minutes from the start, a spectacular cavern in the lava known as **Chapelle de Rosemont** (Map p237) comes into view. From here, the path veers to the left and takes a gradual route up the eastern wall of the cone until it reaches the Balcon du Dolomieu viewpoint. Beware! There's no guard rail, just a white line.

While the volcano walk is popular and is not technically demanding, it shouldn't be undertaken lightly. The landscape here is harsh and arid, despite the mist that can drench hikers to the skin. The chilly wind whips away moisture, leaving walkers dehydrated and breathless.

Early morning is the best time to climb the volcano, as you stand a better chance of clear views, but this is when everyone else hits the trail as well.

Since the eruption of April 2007, two new walks in the Enclos Fouqué have been established. They do not lead to Dolomieu Crater, but to **Piton Kapor** (Map p237; about three hours return), a small volcanic cone north of Piton de la Fournaise, and to **Cratère Rivals** (Map p237) (about four hours return), in the southwestern part of the Enclos. Leaflets detailing these routes are available at the tourist office in Bourg-Murat.

Many people get a head start by staying at the Gîte du Volcan (p237) and leaving at the crack of dawn, so be sure to book well in advance.

Les Platanes –
Chez Jean-Paul   CREOLE, CHINESE **€€**
(🖉0262 51 31 69; 291 Rue de la République; mains €13-16; ☺noon-2pm Tue-Sun) One of the best-known eateries in the area, this colourful spot on the main drag is popular with Réunionnais families – a good sign. The atmosphere is laid-back and the food is similarly unpretentious with the emphasis on hearty, home-cooked Creole and Chinese staples as well as homemade desserts. All at very honest prices.

If you happen to be in town on Sunday, don't miss the 10-course buffet (€20).

❶ Getting There & Away

Plaine-des-Palmistes is situated on the cross-island highway between St-Benoît and St-Pierre. There are three buses a day in each direction. More information at www.carjaune.re.

ST-PIERRE

POP 82,400

If you need to let off steam before (or after) heading off into the Cirques, you've come to the right place. St-Pierre pulses with an energy unknown elsewhere on the island, especially at weekends. Havana it ain't, but this vibrant, feisty, good-natured city knows what really counts in life: having a good time.

If St-Denis is Réunion's administrative and business capital, enchanting St-Pierre is its throbbing heart. Basking in the clear light of the southwest, the 'capital of the south' has an entirely different feel from its northern counterparts. It remains unmistakably more Creole than cosmopolitan and rather staid St-Denis.

St-Pierre

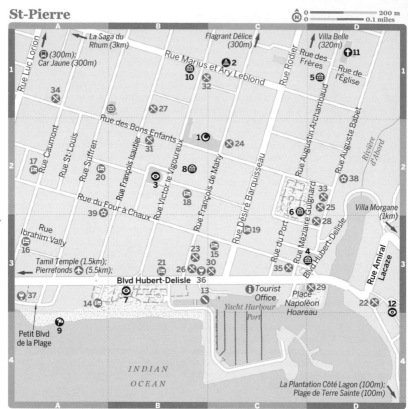

◉ Sights

Compact, colourful St-Pierre is easily seen in a day on foot. You'll find a scattering of colonial and religious buildings in the centre.

Plage de Terre Sainte BEACH
(Terre Sainte) This small, intimate beach in the Terre Sainte neighbourhood is never crowded. It's great for sunbathing.

Plage de St-Pierre BEACH
(Map p240) One of St-Pierre's major draws is its beach, a fine sweep of pale sand massaged by aquamarine waters. It's exposed to the prevailing winds, though. Stick to the protected area.

Main Market MARKET
(Map p240; Blvd Hubert-Delisle; ⊙7am-noon Sat) If you're in St-Pierre on a Saturday morning, be sure to browse around the joyous, thriving main market, which sprawls along the seafront at the west end of Blvd Hubert-

Delisle – a staple of local life. You'll find a busy produce section, tacky bric-a-brac and plenty of food stalls.

**Sœurs de Saint-Joseph
de Cluny** HISTORIC BUILDING
(Map p240; Rue Marius et Ary Leblond) Don't miss this grand Creole mansion that was built in the late 18th century.

Chinese Temple BUDDHIST TEMPLE
(Map p240; Rue Marius et Ary Leblond) If you like temples, this discreet yet vividly colourful building is well worth a peek.

Tamil Temple HINDU TEMPLE
(Shri Mahabadra Karli; Ravine Blanche) West of the centre, this highly colourful Tamil temple is well worth a gander. Visitors are not allowed inside the temple.

Attyaboul Massadjid Mosque MOSQUE
(Map p240; Rue François de Mahy; ⊙9am-noon & 2-4pm) You'll be impressed by the massive

St-Pierre

proportions of St-Pierre's mosque, which extends an entire block. Its slender minaret is particularly striking. Visitors can enter the inner courtyard during opening times (and outside prayer times).

La Saga du Rhum MUSEUM
(Map p248; ☑0262 35 81 90; www.sagadurhum. fr; Chemin Fredeline; adult/child €10/7; ⊙10am-5pm) Those who want to understand how the ambrosia called rum starts in the sugar-cane fields and ends on their palates should really come to the museum called La Saga du Rhum, which is set on the site of the Isautier estate, one of the oldest rum distillers on Réunion. It's about 5km northwest of Saint-Pierre (in the direction of Bois d'Olives).

St-Pierre Church CHURCH
(Map p240; Rue Augustin Archambaud; ⊙8am-5pm) Built in 1765, St-Pierre church is one of St-Pierre's many architectural gems and features an elegant peristyle and two towers.

Hôtel de la Sous-Préfecture HISTORIC BUILDING
(Map p240; Rue Augustin Archambaud) An elegant landmark east of the centre, the neo-classical Hôtel de la Sous-Préfecture begs to be admired.

Médiathèque Raphaël Barquisseau HISTORIC BUILDING
(Map p240; Rue des Bons Enfants) This lovingly restored building dates from the thriving era of the French East India Company.

Entrepôt Kervéguen HISTORIC BUILDING
(Map p240; Rue du Four à Chaux) You can't miss this imposing building at the eastern end of Rue du Four à Chaux. Entrepôt Kervéguen was used as a warehouse by the French East India Company.

Hôtel de Ville HISTORIC BUILDING
(Map p240; Place de la Mairie) The Hôtel de Ville ranks among St-Pierre's most spectacular historic buildings. It started life as a coffee warehouse for the French East India Company during the 18th century.

Terre Sainte AREA
(Map p240) It's well worth exploring this quaint neighbourhood, situated to the east of the centre. Though no longer the traditional fishing village it used to be, this area has its own peculiar appeal, especially along the seashore, where fishers can be seen playing dominoes in the late afternoon.

WORTH A TRIP

FORÊT DE BÉBOUR-BÉLOUVE

An absolute must-see, the majestic Forêt de Bébour-Bélouve could set the stage for a new version of *Jurassic Park*, with a mix of tamarind trees, huge *fanjan* (fern trees) and moss. It lies to the northwest of Plaine-des-Palmistes, and is accessible via a surfaced forest road which begins at Petite Plaine, just southwest of Plaine-des-Palmistes, and finishes 20km further on, near a bluff lording over the Cirque de Salazie.

Activities

Forêt de Bébour-Bélouve is a popular walking area, with a network of footpaths of varying levels of difficulty. The tourist office at Plaine-des-Palmistes has a leaflet on walks in the forest.

Sentier du Trou de Fer (Map p216) A relatively easy 3.5km walk that leads to a lookout from where you can marvel at horseshoe-shaped falls known as the Trou de Fer, hailed as one of the most spectacular natural sights in Réunion: it has graced the covers of many books. The path starts at the Gîte de Bélouve. About four hours return.

Sentier de la Tamarineraie (Map p216) Starting from the Gîte de Bélouve, this 1½-hour loop will take you through a spectacular tamarind forest. Expect great views of the Cirques along the way.

Tour du Piton Bébour (Map p216) This easy 1¼-hour walk makes a loop around a small *piton* (mountain) and winds through cryptomeria forest.

Sentier Botanique de la Petite Plaine (Map p216; Forêt de Bébour-Bélouve) A 45-minute loop with interpretative panels about flora.

Sleeping & Eating

Gîte de Bélouve (Map p216; ☑ 0692 85 93 07; dm €16-18, d with shared bathroom €42-45, breakfast/lunch/meal €6/12/19; ⊘ restaurant 12.30-2pm Thu-Tue, dinner 7pm, closed lunch Feb) At the end of the forest road that crosses the majestic Forêt de Bébour-Bélouve, about 25km away from Plaine-des-Palmistes, this *gîte* (self-catering accommodation) appears like a mirage. Picture this: it's scenically wedged onto a bluff lording over the Cirque de Salazie. Digs are in six- to 12-bed dorms. There are also two snug doubles. Hearty meals are served in the charmingly rustic dining area.

It's an obvious base if you want to explore the forest – there's a good network of footpaths – or walk to the Trou de Fer lookout (about four hours return). If you're driving, take note that cars are not allowed beyond the parking lot that lies about 400m before the *gîte* (there's a gate), which means you'll have to walk the final stretch. Cash only.

Getting There & Away

There's no public transport to the Forêt de Bébour-Bélouve. With your own wheels, take the D55 from Plaine-des-Palmistes until La Petite Plaine, then follow the surfaced forestry road until it stops at a car park, about 400m before Gîte de Bélouve. From Plaine-des-Palmistes, it's a 25-kilometre drive.

Covered Market　　　　　　　　MARKET
(Map p240; Rue Victor le Vigoureux; ⊘ 8am-6pm Mon-Sat) Housed in a metallic structure dating from 1856, the small covered market is a great place to wander if you're after fresh fruit, vegetables, local spices and herbs, bags made from *vacoa* (screw-pine fronds) and the usual assortment of Malagasy crafts.

🏃 Activities

There's excellent diving between St-Pierre and Grand Bois.

Demhotel　　　　　　　　DIVING
(Map p248) A lovely dive off Grand Bois along a contoured plateau with plenty of protruding basaltic formations and arches. Fish life is usually dense.

Les Ancres & Le Tombant aux Ancres　　　　DIVING
(Map p248) A sloping reef festooned by healthy coral formations. You'll also see some old anchors dotted around the reef.

Plongée Australe
DIVING

(Map p240; ☑0692 14 01 76; www.plongeeaustrale.
com; Harbour; introductory/single dive €60/52;
⏱8am-5pm) This low-key diving venture
specialises in small groups and offers an intimate feel to its aquatic adventures. Five-/10-
dive packages cost €235/470.

✯ Festivals & Events

Sakifo
MUSIC

(www.sakifo.com; ⏱Jun) One of the highlights
of Réunion's events calendar, Sakifo is a great
music festival with an eclectic program that
might include styles as diverse as *maloya*,
salsa, blues and African. Held in early June
in St-Pierre.

🛏 Sleeping

St-Pierre has a variety of hotels and B&Bs
that cater for a range of budgets. Most are
concentrated down towards the seafront.
Reservations are essential at weekends. For
longer stays, the tourist office also has a list
of self-catering apartments.

Hôtel Cap Sud
HOTEL €

(Map p240; ☑0262 25 75 64; www.hotel-cap
sud-reunion.com; 6 Rue Caumont; d/tr €50/70;
❄️🛜) You certainly won't fall in love with this
uninspiring building not far from the seafront, but it's better inside than it looks from
the street. The 16 rooms have been freshened
up and some upstairs rooms afford great sea
views. It's well priced and conveniently located. There's on-street parking. No lift.

Chez Papa Daya
HOSTEL €

(Map p240; ☑0692 12 20 12, 0262 25 64 87; www.
chezpapadaya.com; 27 Rue du Four à Chaux; s €30,
with shared bathroom €25, d €40, with shared bathroom €30-35, q €65; 🅿❄️🛜) Run by affable
Roger, this traveller-friendly stalwart shelters
20 simple, scrupulously clean rooms of varying sizes and shapes. What it lacks in style
is made up for by an ace location, a waddle
away from the seafront, shops, eateries, bars
and clubs. Parking is available, but there are
only six spaces. Facilities include a small
kitchen (breakfast only).

L'Escale Touristique
HOSTEL €

(Map p240; ☑0692 60 58 58, 0262 35 20 95;
www.hotelescaletouristique.com; 14 Rue Désiré Barquisseau; s with shared bathroom €30, d €40, with
shared bathroom €30-35; 🅿❄️🛜) The closest
thing to a hostel you'll find in St-Pierre, this
well-run place has spotlessly clean rooms and

RÉUNION FOR CRAZIES

If you want to work off any extra kilos
gained in Réunion's fine restaurants,
here's the solution: take part in the
Grand Raid, one of the world's most
challenging cross-country races. It's
held every October. The route traverses
the island from St-Pierre to St-Denis,
taking in parts of the Mafate and Cilaos
Cirques and the Plaine-des-Cafres.

Covering some 165km, the Grand
Raid would be a challenging race over
level ground, but runners also have
to negotiate a total of some 10,000m
of altitude change, hence the race is
nicknamed La Diagonale des Fous (the
'Cross-Country for Crazies')! The pack
leaders can complete this agonising run
in 22 hours or less, but contestants are
allowed up to 64 hours to finish.

Too difficult for you? Try the 'easier'
Trail de Bourbon, which starts from
Cilaos and covers 93km, or the Mascareignes, which starts from Grand Îlet in
the Cirque de Salazie and covers 67km.

For more information, contact the
Association Grand Raid (www.grand
raid-reunion.com).

an optimal location near the seafront. Air-con
is available in 12 rooms (out of 15); the cheaper ones are fan-cooled. Added perks include
private parking, a communal kitchen and a
laundry area. Prices drop by €5 if you stay
two nights or more.

Ask for room 101, 102 or 103, with balcony.
Towels are provided in the rooms equipped
with private facilities.

La Plantation Côté Lagon
B&B €€

(☑0693 92 53 01, 0262 45 63 28; www.la-plantation.
re; 79 Rue Amiral Lacaze, Terre Sainte; d incl breakfast €98-140; ❄️🛜🏊) La Plantation's main
drawcard? Its sensational position across the
road from the small beach in the Terre Sainte
neighbourhood. The five rooms, which are
done out in grey, taupe and chocolate shades,
have a fresh, modern feel, but don't have sea
views. An added bonus is the postage-stamp-
sized pool.

The included breakfast is one of the best
you'll have in town, and it's served on a
breezy terrace overlooking the beach. One
weak point: there's no private parking.

La Morgabine B&B €€

(Map p240; ☑0692 17 88 00; www.lamorgabine.com; 21 Rue Caumont; d €80-130; ☺closed May-Sep; ❄🌐⊠) West of the centre, this boutique B&B feels like a warm, soft nest. It conceals two supremely comfortable rooms designed with utmost grace and done out in taupe, beige and white shades. The swimming pool sits in a beautiful garden. Other perks include a Jacuzzi and a well-equipped communal kitchen. Breakfast costs from €10. There's on-street parking. Cash only.

Le Saint-Pierre HOTEL €€

(Map p240; ☑0262 61 16 11; www.hotellesaint-pierre.fr; 51 Ave des Indes; d €109-129; P❄🌐⊠) A stone's throw from the covered market and the seafront, Le Saint-Pierre has modern, stylish rooms with masculine hues (all grey and taupe), balconies, super comfy beds and walk-in showers. Hint: room 212 boasts two great terraces. Facilities include a bar-restaurant and a small swimming pool. There are often good deals available on room rates; check the website or call the reception.

Lindsey Hotel HOTEL €€

(Map p240; ☑0262 24 60 11; www.lindsey-hotel-reunion.fr; 21b Rue François Isautier; d €98-120; P❄🌐⊠) Tucked in a side street near the covered market, this pert three-star venture in a large Creole-style building is perfectly poised for all of St-Pierre's attractions. The 18 rooms sport modern furnishings, and feel fresh and comfortable. Rooms 7, 12 and 14 are the best, with a balcony and city views. The small pool is abonus. Breakfast costs €10.

Villa Morgane B&B €€

(☑0262 25 82 77; www.villamorgane.re; 334 Rue Amiral Lacaze, Terre Sainte; d €112-127, ste €178; ❄🌐⊠) You'll go giddy over the ever-so-slightly OTT interior of this *maison d'hôte* in a quiet street in the Terre Sainte neighbourhood. The nine themed rooms and suites are very different in design and colour scheme and are spread out on two floors. There's a small but nicely laid-out tropical garden where guests can chill by the pool. There's on-street parking.

Of all the rooms, the Pompéi suite, complete with frescos and ornate stucco ceilings, is the most impressive, but is a bit sombre. Avoid the Venise and Jacaranda rooms, which feel cramped, and aim for the Botticelli or Alexandra rooms (€127), upstairs, with ample space, lots of natural light and a private terrace. No meals are provided except breakfast (€10 to €12).

Alizé Plage HOTEL €€

(Map p240; ☑0970 35 30 14; www.hotel-restaurant-alize-plage.fr; 17bis Blvd Hubert-Delisle; d €95-110; ❄🌐) Pro: its position right on the beach is peerless. Con: its location off the main boulevard cops the full brunt of the peak-hour traffic noise (and the nearby food vans in the evening). The hotel features 15 rooms, nine of which overlook the beach. There's an on-site restaurant. The weak point? No private parking.

★**Villa Belle** B&B €€€

(☑0692 65 89 99; www.villabelle.e-monsite.com; 45 Rue Rodier; s €160-210, d €170-230, ste €300; P❄🌐⊠) Occupying a converted Creole mansion, this oh-so-chic *maison d'hôte* is the epitome of a refined cocoon, revelling quietly in minimalist lines, soothing colour accents and well-thought-out decorative touches. Like the rest of the place, the communal areas are a sensory interplay of light, wood and stone. After a day of turf pounding, relax in the stress-melting pool. It's gay friendly.

Breakfast (€20 to €40) and dinner (€65) are available by request. Prices drop by 15% if you stay three nights or more.

Villa Delisle Hotel & Spa CASINO HOTEL €€€

(Map p240; ☑0262 70 77 08; www.hotel-villadelisle.com; 42 Blvd Hubert Delisle; s €175-235, d €190-250, ste €300-340, incl breakfast; P❄🌐⊠) Right on the seafront, this modern hotel is full of vibrant colours and character. Rooms aren't lavish but are modestly stylish, and the Superior ones have balconies. Facilities include two restaurants, a small spa and a swimming pool.

🍴 Eating

The excellent Creole, French, Italian and Asian restaurants make this town as pleasing to the belly as it is to the eye; you won't want to be skipping any meals here. Many bars also double up as restaurants.

Les Délicatesses Casta BAKERY €

(Map p240; ☑0262 57 95 14; 65 Rue des Bons Enfants; sandwiches €4; ☺5.45am-7pm Mon-Sat, to noon Sun) A prime spot for morning pastries, midday sandwiches and healthy salads, and afternoon snacks.

Manciet BAKERY €

(Map p240; ☑0262 25 06 73; www.manciet-lucien-saint-pierre.fr; 64 Rue Victor le Vigoureux; pastries from €0.90; ☺6.30am-12.30pm & 2.30-6.30pm Tue-Sat, to 12.30pm Sun) This gourmet emporium is a veritable feast of perfectly presented pastries, cakes, pies and chocolates. And bread. And *macatias*. Simply divine.

Snack Galam Massala   INDIAN €

(Map p240; ☎0692 37 12 98; 5 Rue du Four à Chaux; mains €8-11; ⊙11am-2pm Tue-Sat) You wouldn't guess it from the humble surrounds, but this family-run place is praised for its lip-smacking biryanis and other tasty Indian staples, including beef or chicken curry. The concise menu changes daily, and features at least one vegetarian dish.

Castel Glacier   ICE CREAM, CAFETERIA €

(Map p240; ☎0262 22 96 56; www.facebook. com/castelglacier; 38 Rue François de Mahy; ice creams €2.50-5, mains €13-17; ⊙11.45am-6pm Mon-Fri, noon-7pm Sat, 3.15-9pm Sun; 🔊) Generous scoops and about 20 flavours are the trademarks of this drool-inducing ice-cream parlour opposite the mosque. Also serves up snacks, well-presented salads and light meals at lunchtime, as well as crêpes any time of the day.

Restaurant des Bons Enfants   CREOLE €

(Map p240; ☎0262 25 08 27; 114 Rue des Bons Enfants; mains €6-8; ⊙11am-2pm & 6-9.30pm) Occupying a small Creole house, this simple venture whips up hearty Creole specialities at economical prices. That said, the decor is super dull and boring – it's best to take away.

★Ancre Terre et Mer   MODERN FRENCH €€

(Map p240; ☎0262 27 57 52; www.facebook. com/ancreterreetmer; 31 Rue Amiral Lacaze; mains €13-25; ⊙noon-1.30pm & 7-9.45pm Tue & Thu-Sat) A hop and a skip from the seafront (but no views), this attractive garden restaurant boasts a seductively cosy terrace and serves up delectable burgers, tartares and risottos. Local gourmands swear by the Sud-Ouest burger, filled with duck breast and foie gras (fattened liver). Something sweet to finish? Try the brownie with vanilla ice cream.

★La Kaz à Léa   INTERNATIONAL €€

(Map p240; ☎0262 25 04 25; 34 Rue François Isautier; mains €15-25, lunch menu €15; ⊙noon-2pm & 7-9.30pm Mon-Sat; 🔊) You won't find a more atmospheric place in St-Pierre than this much-loved *case*, with its shady terrace and cosy dining room. It offers beautifully presented Creole, *métro* and Asian-inspired dishes as well as scrumptious homemade burgers. Desserts are delightful, especially the *tarte Tatin* made with papaya. At €15, the three-course lunch menu is a steal. Lovely.

La Lune dans le Caniveau   BISTRO €€

(Map p240; ☎0262 01 73 66; 1bis Rue Auguste Babet; mains €13-19; ⊙7-11pm Mon-Sat; 🍴) Stylishly decorated in a hip bistro style, this local treasure entices with simple yet inventive offerings that spoil your taste buds without spoiling your budget. The intimate dining room is cheerfully decorated, and the kitchen turns out well-prepared fish and meat dishes, as well as a few vegetarian options.

Belo Horizonte   FRENCH €€

(Map p240; ☎0262 22 31 95; 10 Rue François de Mahy; mains €10-13; ⊙noon-2pm Mon-Sat, 7-9.30pm Thu-Sat) Walls saturated in coloured accents and other fancy decorative touches – some walls are covered with flip-flops – set the tone of this zinging joint where you can tuck into salads, hot tarts, pizzas, pasta dishes and daily specials. The sun-dappled patio garden is enticing. You can also take away.

Kaz Nature   CAFETERIA €€

(Map p240; ☎0262 25 30 86; www.facebook. com/kaznature; 6 Rue François de Mahy; mains €8-19, lunch menus €13-15; ⊙noon-2.30pm Mon-Sat; 🔊) This slick modern eatery does a brisk business with office workers – always a sign that you've found a good bargain. It speedily serves tasty wraps, crunchy salads, melt-in-the-mouth tarts and other healthy goodies.

Le Cap Méchant d'Abord   BUFFET €€

(Map p240; ☎0262 91 71 99; 11 Blvd Hubert-Delisle; mains €10-18, buffets €20-25; ⊙11.30am-2.30pm & 7.30-10pm Tue-Sat, 11.30am-3pm Sun) Commanding an enviable location directly on the seafront, this large and busy restaurant is famous for one thing and one thing only: its brilliant-value all-you-can-eat buffets. It also concocts Creole and Chinese dishes, and takeaway is available.

★O'Baya   FUSION €€€

(Map p240; ☎0262 59 66 94; www.facebook. com/Elara.et.Grego; 7 Rue Auguste Babet; mains €18-24; ⊙noon-1.30pm Tue-Fri, 7-9.30pm Tue-Sat) Sick of stodgy *carris*? Then head here for lovable fusion fare served in a strong design-led interior. The menu drips with panache and the chef prepares succulent concoctions prepared with top-of-the-line ingredients. Musts include beef fillet and gingerbread-crusted fish steak. There's also an array of sweet temptations. Prices are surprisingly reasonable for the quality of the fare.

RÉUNION ST-PIERRE

Est Bento
ASIAN €€€

(Map p240; ☑ 0262 02 08 03; 1ter Rue Auguste Babet; mains €19-32; ☺ noon-2pm & 7.30-9.30pm Mon, Tue, Thu & Fri, 7.30-9.30pm Sat) Satisfy those pangs for bento and other Asian treats at this popular restaurant. Here you can tuck into specialities that are hard to find elsewhere – a godsend after too many curries or French-inspired dishes. The Japanese-style decor and brisk service add to the appeal.

Le DCP
SEAFOOD €€€

(Map p240; ☑ 0262 32 21 71; 38bis Blvd Hubert Delisle; mains €16-26; ☺ noon-2pm & 7-10pm) This immutable seafood favourite on the seafront gets the thumbs up for its choice of fish dishes cooked to crispy perfection. There's no outdoor seating, though.

Flagrant Délice
FUSION €€€

(☑ 0692 87 28 03; 115 Rue François de Mahy; mains €15-29, lunch menu €20; ☺ noon-1.30pm Tue-Fri, 7.30-9.30pm Tue-Sat) This inviting eatery housed in a private villa is a gourmand's playpen, with a tempting selection of imaginative dishes. Be good to yourself with pork tenderloin in pineapple sauce, toothfish steak with chorizo cream and luscious wines. The setting is another draw: tables are arranged around a small pool in a tropical garden.

🍷 Drinking & Nightlife

Night owls, rejoice: St-Pierre has a well-established party reputation. It has plenty of drinking options ranging from elegant cafes to lively waterfront bars and hole-in-the-wall cocktail joints. The best buzz can be found on the seafront. Most drinking spots also serve food.

Les Sal' Gosses
BAR

(Map p240; ☑ 0262 96 70 36; 38 Blvd Hubert-Delisle; ☺ 10.30am-midnight) This cool den on the seafront hosts gigs from local bands – usually on Wednesday. Good blend of jazz, soul and funk. Also has a wide-ranging menu (but the food is only so so), tapas and billiards.

Long Board Café
BAR

(Map p240; ☑ 0692 82 09 95; 18 Petit Blvd de la Plage; ☺ 10am-1am Tue-Fri, 5pm-1am Sat & Sun) Spiffing setting, in a Creole house with a terrace opening onto the seafront – a great place for quaffing a sunset beverage. Offers live entertainment and karaoke on selected evenings, usually on Friday and Saturday.

⭐ Entertainment

Ti Coq Misik
LIVE MUSIC

(Map p240; ☑ 0262 01 71 25; 53 Rue du Four à Chaux; ☺ 6pm-1am Tue-Sat) No rock and roll and no R & B here – this popular venture is famed for the quality of its live-music sessions featuring *maloya* (traditional dance music), salsa and African sounds. It also serves food.

Le Toit
LIVE MUSIC

(Map p240; ☑ 0262 35 55 53; 16 Rue Auguste Babet; ☺ 6pm-midnight Tue-Sat) Attracting mostly Zoreilles (mainland French) regulars, this lively bar is packed to the rafters on weekends. It hosts live bands on Thursday, Friday and Saturday evenings. Great-value beers and cocktails are two more reasons to drop by. Skip the food.

ℹ️ Information

Tourist Office (Map p240; ☑ 0820 220 202; www.sud.reunion.fr; Capitainerie, Blvd Hubert-Delisle; ☺ 8am-6pm Mon-Sat, to noon Sun) Has English-speaking staff and can provide useful brochures and a town map. You can book *gîtes de montagne* here and it can also organise guided tours in English.

ℹ️ Getting There & Away

AIR

Air Mauritius and Air Austral operate daily flights between **Saint-Pierre-Pierrefonds International Airport** (Map p248; ☑ 0262 96 77 66; www.pierrefonds.aeroport.fr; St-Pierre), 5km west of St-Pierre, and Mauritius.

Air Austral (☑ 0825 01 30 12; www.air-austral. com; 6 Blvd Hubert-Delisle; ☺ 8.30am-5.30pm Mon-Fri, to 11.45am Sat)

Air Mauritius (☑ 0262 94 83 83; www.air mauritius.com; 7 Rue François de Mahy; ☺ 8.30am-5.30pm Mon-Fri)

BUS

St-Pierre is an important transport hub. **Car Jaune** (☑ 0810 12 39 74; www.carjaune.re) has a long-haul bus stop at the long-distance **bus station** (cnr Rue Presbytère & Luc Lorion) west of town. Buses to/from St-Denis run frequently along the west coast via St-Louis and St-Gilles-les-Bains (1½ hours, €2) or direct via the Route des Tamarins if it's a Z'éclair service (line ZO, one hour, €5). There are also three services a day to St-Benoît via Plaine-des-Palmistes (line S2, two hours, €2) and the same number around the south coast through Manapany-les-Bains, St-Joseph and St-Philippe (line S1, 2½ hours, €2). There are also three daily buses to Entre-Deux (line S5). For Cilaos, change in St-Louis.

THE WILD SOUTH

Aaaah, the Sud Sauvage (Wild South), where the unhurried life is complemented by the splendid scenery of fecund volcanic slopes, occasional beaches, waves crashing on the rocky shoreline and country roads that twist like snakes into the Hauts. In both landscape and character, the south coast is where the real wilderness of Réunion begins to unfold. Once you've left St-Pierre, a gentle splendour and a sense of escapism become tangible. The change of scenery climaxes with the Grand Brûlé, where black lava fields slice through the forest and even reach the ocean at several points.

St-Pierre to St-Joseph

Life – and travel – becomes more sedate as you head west through some of the south coast's delicious scenery. With only a few exceptions, urban life is left behind once the road traverses **Grand Bois** and snakes its way along the coastline via **Grande Anse** and **Manapany-les-Bains**.

If you want to explore the Hauts, take the turn-off for **Petite Île**. From Petite Île, a scenic road wobbles slowly up to some charming villages. Continue uphill until the junction with the D3. If you turn left, you'll reach **Mont-Vert-les-Hauts**, approximately 5km to the west (and from there it's an easy drive downhill to the coast via Mont-Vert-les-Bas); if you turn right, you will cross **Manapany-les-Hauts** before reaching **Les Lianes** for St-Joseph.

◉ Sights & Activities

Plage de Grande Anse BEACH

(Grande Anse) Beach lovers should stop at Plage de Grande Anse, which is framed with basaltic cliffs and features a white-sand beach, a protected tide pool and picnic shelters. On weekends, the beach is often swamped with locals. Note that it's not safe to swim outside the tide pool due to unpredictable currents.

Take the D30 that branches off the RN2 and winds down for about 2km to the beach.

Tide Pool BEACH

(Manapany-les-Bains) Find this lovely swimming spot at Manapany-les-Bains. There's no proper beach here (the shore is rocky) but there's a protected tide pool where you can splash about. It gets crowded on weekends.

L'Écurie du Relais HORSE RIDING

(Map p248; ☑0262 56 78 67, 0692 00 42 98; www.ecuriedurelais.com; 75 Chemin Léopold Lebon, Manapany-les-Hauts; 1hr/day €20/115; ⊗by reservation Tue-Sun) Seeing the area from the saddle of a horse is a fun way to experience the visual appeal of the region, even if you're not an experienced rider. This well-established equestrian centre has guided trips in the Hauts as well as day tours to Grande Anse. The two-hour ride (€36) takes you to rarely visited points in the Hauts with stunning views of Plaine-des-Grègues.

✺ Festivals & Events

Fête de l'Ail FOOD

(Festival of Garlic; ⊗Oct) A rural fair that celebrates garlic in Petite Île; held in October.

🛏 Sleeping

The area between St-Pierre and St-Joseph has a good range of lodging options, including two hotels and a handful of great B&Bs. Despite some signs on the road, many places are not easy to find. Check locations on the website (if there is one) or call ahead. Of course, some words in French for directions always helps.

If you want to pamper yourself, opt for the Palm Hotel & Spa (p250).

★**La Cour Mont Vert** B&B €

(☑0262 31 21 10; www.courmontvert.com; 18ter Chemin Roland Garros, Mont-Vert-les-Bas; d incl breakfast €75; P🕑) Your heart will lift at the dreamy views over the coast; your body will rejuvenate with the Valatchy family's healthy meals (€27); your soul will find peace in the four button-cute Creole bungalows set in rural grounds awash with mangoes and lychees. Simply arrive, absorb and enjoy. Rates drop to €65 if you stay at least five nights.

Gandalf Safari Camp GUESTHOUSE €

(☑0262 58 45 59, 0692 40 78 39; www.gandalfsafari camp.de; 87 Blvd de l'Océan, Manapany-les-Bains; s €55, d €60-65, ste €100, incl breakfast; ❋@🕑) The German owners have long lived in Africa – hence the name. Their B&B features five rooms that are individually designed, with such themes as Kreol, Malagasy, Arab, Chinese and Indian, but feel a tad compact due to the cubicle shower plonked in the corner. Good English is spoken. Air-con is extra (€5). Rates drop by €5 if you stay two nights.

The Malagasy room, complete with wooden masks and other delightful knick-knacks,

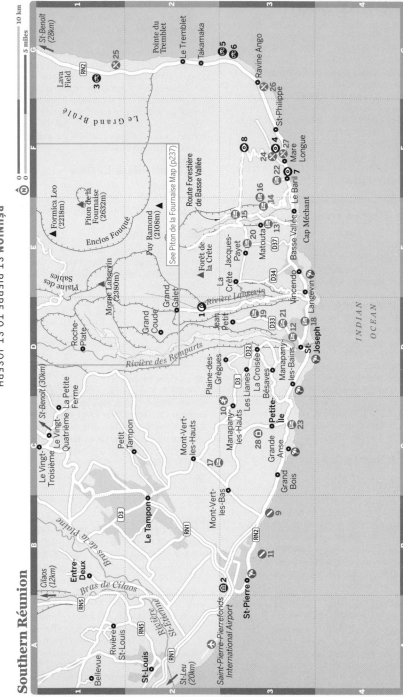

Southern Réunion

St-Pierre to St-Joseph

Southern Réunion

is the best (and the most spacious). The Kreol is the cheapest, but its bathrooms are outside. There's also a larger suite. Perks include a kitchen for guests' use and a relaxing garden, plus 4WD tours can be organised (€60). It's a five-minute stroll from Manapany-les-Bains' tide pool. Cash only.

L'Eau Forte   APARTMENT €
(☎0262 56 32 84; www.eau-forte.fr; 137bis Blvd de L'Océan, Manapany-les-Bains; d €55; ✿☎) Bargain! Perfect for self-caterers, this fully equipped, spick-and-span villa boasts an ace location, on a velvety emerald hillside just above Manapany's tide pool, with sublime views of the rocky coastline. Don't fancy cooking? Find a restaurant a coin's toss down the road. There's no minimum stay, but one-week stays are preferred. Cash only. Book early.

Note that it's exposed to the noise of the surf when the sea is rough.

Vérémer   B&B €
(Map p248; ☎0262 31 65 10, 0692 72 91 95; www. chambre-gite-veremer.com; 40 Chemin Sylvain Vitry, Petite Île; d incl breakfast €50-63, gîte d €60; ℙ✿☎✉) Vérémer houses three few-frills but tidy rooms in two neat Creole buildings nestled in a well-tended tropical garden, with superlative views and a splendid pool that guests can use from breakfast to dinner (except Sunday afternoon). Grande Anse beach is 3.5km away. It's gay friendly.

The slightly dearer Mer room is on the small side but opens onto the garden and the pool and enjoys great sea views, while La

Cour and La Verte rooms offer more privacy. There's also a lovely *gîte* that can be rented for four nights or more.

Chez Maoul   B&B €
(☎0262 56 82 26; www.chemaoul.re; 6 Rue du Piton, Petite Île; d incl breakfast €60; ✿☎✉) The four wood-clad rooms in this homely B&B nestled in a junglelike garden have a cabin-in-the-woods feel but offer a fine sense of originality. The two upstairs rooms get more light, while the Katimini has more character, with Creole ceilings, parquet flooring and colourful paintings. Avoid the Do-Myel room, which feels a bit boxy. The tiny pool is an added bonus.

Creole-inspired *table d'hôte* dinners (€15) can be arranged if there's a minimum of six guests; the food is great and varied, with home-grown vegetables.

★La Bulle Verte   B&B €€
(Map p248; ☎0262 33 58 80, 0692 87 94 90; www. labulleverte.re; 91 Chemin Piton Filaos, Mont-Vert-les-Hauts; d incl breakfast €78; ℙ☎) If you're looking for the perfect compromise between style, atmosphere and seclusion, then look no further than this little slice of heaven immersed in greenery (look at the picture on the website – no photoshopping). The three cosy rooms are individually decorated and have great picture windows. Our favourite is the 'Cabane', sporting colourful touches, wooden beams and a great terrace.

Dinner is available on Thursday, Friday and Saturday (€30). Oh, and there's a Jacuzzi in the garden.

Soleil Couchant   HOTEL €€

(☑ 0262 31 10 10; www.hotel-reunion-soleilcouchant.com; 2 Chemin de L'Araucaria, Mont-Vert-les-Bas; d €68-90; P ✳ ☎ ☲) This small complex features three pavilions shaped like cubic Tetris pieces, which sit on a grassy patch of land. The nine rooms are bright and tidy, but are very simply furnished and lack character. The real draws are the ocean vistas – straight from heaven – and the gleaming (heated) pool. There's an on-site restaurant, but food is only so so.

It's well worth opting for the rooms with panoramic views, especially rooms 1 and 2.

Palm Hotel & Spa   LUXURY HOTEL €€€

(☑ 0262 56 30 30; www.palm.re; Grande Anse, Petite Île; d €240-330, ste €360-410, lodges €510-590, incl breakfast; P ✳ @ ☎ ☲) If you're really looking to push the boat out in the Wild South, then to be honest there's only this five-star resort. Peacefully reposed on a promontory overlooking the cerulean ocean, it sports well-furnished units that are designed with finesse but, frustratingly, only the three lodges face out towards the sea. From the hotel, a steep path leads down to Plage de Grande Anse.

Facilities include two pools, a luxurious spa and two gourmet restaurants (open to nonguests by reservation).

✗ Eating

For lunch, your best bet is to stop at a restaurant or snack bar near Plage de Grande Anse or Manapany-les-Bains. For dinner, order a meal at your B&B or hotel.

★ Les Badamiers   CREOLE €

(☑ 0262 56 97 53; 22 Chemin Neuf, Grande Anse, Petite Île; mains €10-12; ⊙ noon-1.30pm Mon-Sat, 7-8.30pm Mon, Tue, Thu & Fri) Heartily recommended by locals, this family-run eatery in a private house spins tasty *carris* and ace homemade desserts (Mmm, the *tarte Tatin* with papaya and cinnamon...). The menu is concise but everything is fresh, the atmosphere is reliably jovial and the prices incredibly good value for the area. The icing on the cake: a terrace with stupendous sea views.

It's about 100m away from the beginning of the road that descends to Grande Anse. No credit cards.

Chez Jo   INTERNATIONAL €€

(☑ 0262 31 48 83; 143 Blvd de L'Océan, Manapany-les-Bains; mains €10-21; ⊙ 9am-5.30pm Mon, Tue, Thu & Sun, to 9pm Fri & Sat) In this buzzy eatery overlooking the tide pool in Manapany-les-Bains, you're bound to find something on the menu that takes your fancy. Treat yourself to grilled fish and meat dishes, salads or Creole staples, or just pop in for an exquisite fruit juice (€3 to €6). Good sandwiches (€3 to €5) and takeaway meals, too.

🛍 Shopping

Maison de L'Abeille   FOOD

(Map p248; ☑ 0262 56 95 03; 68 Chemin Laguerre, Petite Île; ⊙ 9.30am-noon & 1.30-5pm Wed-Sat, to noon Sun) Not a craft shop but a bee farm, the Maison de L'Abeille sells natural products, including honey and gingerbread. Also has *légumes lontan* (traditional vegetables).

Dekocéan   ARTS & CRAFTS

(☑ 0692 04 05 25; www.dekocean.com; 41 Rue Joseph Suacot, Petite Île; ⊙ 10am-noon & 2-6pm Tue-Sat) Isabelle Biton specialises in porcelain painting. She paints Réunion-inspired designs (Creole *cases,* people, fruits, flowers and chameleons) on plates, cups and bowls.

ℹ Information

Maison du Tourisme du Sud Sauvage (Tourist Office; ☑ 0262 37 37 11; www.sud.reunion.fr; 15 Allée du Four à Chaux, Manapany-les-Bains; ⊙ 9.30am-noon & 1-5.30pm Mon-Fri, 10am-5pm Sat; ☎) Has brochures and maps, and offers free wi-fi access. It also does bookings for *gîtes de montagne*. Off the road that leads to the tide pool.

ℹ Getting There & Away

Car Jaune's buses between St-Pierre and St-Benoît (line S1) run through Grande Anse and Manapany-les-Bains. More information at www.carjaune.re.

St-Joseph

POP 38,100

The Wild South's hub, modernish St-Joseph (say 'St-Jo' if you want to sound local) won't leap to the top of your list of preferred destinations in Réunion but it offers useful services, including supermarkets and banks with ATMs. While it oozes the kind of sunny languor you'd associate with the tropics, the bustling shopping streets at peak hours impart the energy (and stress) of a city.

◉ Sights & Activities

If you can, plan to be in St-Jo on a Friday morning, when the streets spill over with numerous stalls.

For a bird's-eye view of St-Jo and the coast, you can walk up to Piton Babet, the knoll that lies between the main road and the ocean. It shouldn't take more than 10 minutes.

🛏 Sleeping

Accommodation options are thin on the ground in St-Jo; most visitors tend to stay in B&Bs in the Hauts or in nearby Manapany-les-Bains.

L'Arpège Austral   B&B €
(Map p248; 📞 0262 56 36 89, 0692 70 74 12; http://arpegeaustral.minisite.fr; 53 Rue des Prunes; s/d incl breakfast €50/55; P 🛜) It's wonderful to be so near St-Joseph (2.5km), yet in such a serene spot. Sylvie, your hostess, offers two light-flooded rooms with sloping ceilings. They're quite simple but get the job done. For more privacy, the adjoining bungalow, decked out with a small private terrace, fits the bill. It's on the road to Grand Coude (follow the D33).

La Case   APARTMENT €
(Map p248; 📞 0262 56 07 50; www.case.fr; 2 Rue Jean Bart; d with shared bathroom €37, studio d €50-70, q €75; P ❄🛜≋) If it weren't located on the main road, this laid-back venture set in a well-groomed garden would feel like a little oasis. The three rooms in the main house are bright and airy with minimal decor and plain, functional furniture; toilets are shared. At the back of the compound, the five adjoining studios are well maintained and open onto a rectangular pool.

For families, there's also a larger unit. There isn't much atmosphere but it's a good base to explore the area. On the eastern edge of town.

★ A La Maison   B&B €€
(Map p248; 📞 0262 10 29 44, 0692 25 33 20; www.alamaison974.com; 105 Rue des Prunes; d incl breakfast €85; P ❄🛜≋) Relax and feel *à la maison* (at home) in this enchanting modern house on the northern outskirts of St-Jo. The two bedrooms are smallish but light, airy and immaculate, with exquisite bathrooms. The 'Payanke' enjoys an attractive veranda, while the 'Soleil' opens onto a flowering garden. The lovely swimming pool calls for cooling dips.

A perfect hostess, Rosemay makes you feel immediately at ease and helps you plan your day over a generous breakfast. And do have dinner (€25); there's nothing she likes better than to prepare a tasty meal for her guests.

WORTH A TRIP

RIVIÈRE DES REMPARTS

If you really want to get away from it all, check out the Rivière des Remparts, an easily overlooked splendour immediately north of St-Joseph. This valley – one of the wildest in the south – is accessible on foot (or by 4WD). The classic hike is along the river, up to the hamlet of Roche-Plate, and on to Nez de Bœuf on the road that leads to Piton de la Fournaise. Allow about four hours to reach Roche-Plate from St-Joseph, and another four hours to Nez de Bœuf.

You can break up your journey in Roche-Plate. Both the Gîte de la Rivière des Remparts – Morel Jacqueline (p252) and the Gîte Le Mahavel (p252) feature well-scrubbed dorms. Both are closed during the rainy season. Bookings are essential.

Note that 4WD transfers from St-Joseph can be arranged by the *gîtes* (self-catering accommodation; €150 return, up to 12 people), but the best way to get a feel for the valley is to explore it on foot.

🍴 Eating

There's no shortage of places to eat at lunchtime, but if you happen to be in town for dinner, the town feels almost deserted. There are a few snack bars and pizzerias that stay open in the evening, though.

Le Joséphin   BAKERY €
(📞 0262 37 14 20; 6 Rue du Général de Gaulle; sandwiches & salads €3-6; ⏰ 7am-5pm Mon-Sat) If you're planning a picnic, stop at this mouth-watering bakery, which sells tarts, pastries, breads and other treats. You'll also find sandwiches and salads. The streetside terrace allows for people-watching.

Le 4 Epices   CREOLE €
(📞 0262 48 84 66; 12 Rue du Général de Gaulle; mains €5-9; ⏰ 11.30am-1.30pm Mon-Sat) Literally a hole in the wall. There's only room for a few cramped tables, but there's no better lunchtime deal around. You can eat in or take away.

ℹ Getting There & Away

St-Joseph lies on Car Jaune's coastal bus route between St-Pierre and St-Benoit (line S1). More information at www.carjaune.re.

Around St-Joseph

Starting from St-Joseph you can cherry-pick an itinerary in the hinterland that takes in drowsy hamlets where locals all know each other, green-velvet mountains cloaked in layers of wispy cloud, rolling sugar-cane fields, twisting roads and panoramas to make the heart beat faster.

Follow the picturesque D3 that cuts inland before swinging northwestwards to Manapany-Les-Hauts. You'll pass **Bésaves** and **Les Lianes**. You could also drive up to **Plaine-des-Grègues** (follow the D32, which branches off the D3 in La Croisée), the highest village of the area, which crouches in a bowl of mountains. This village is famed for its plantations of curcuma and vetiver, which are both used in perfumery.

◉ Sights

Maison du Curcuma   MUSEUM
(☑ 0262 37 54 66; www.maisonducurcuma.fr; 14 Rue du Rond, Plaine-des-Grègues; ☺ 9am-noon & 1.30-5pm) FREE Learn more about the virtues (and fragrances) of turmeric and vetiver at this small museum in a cute Creole house. It also sells delicious homemade marmalades and jams as well as locally grown spices.

✯ Festivals & Events

Fête du Safran   FOOD
(Festival of Saffron; ☺ Nov) A celebration of saffron held in Plaine-des-Grègues, near St-Joseph, in November.

⬛ Sleeping & Eating

Accommodation options are limited way up in the hills. Most visitors base themselves in St-Joseph, Grande Anse or Petite Île and drive up to Bésaves and Plaine-des-Grègues.

You won't find any restaurants in the area, just small grocery stores. For more options, consider driving to St-Joseph or Petite Île.

Chez Nathalie Hoareau   B&B €
(☑ 0262 37 61 92; www.giterunsud.com; 205 Rue Edmond Albius, Bésaves; s €50, d €55-60, q €85, incl breakfast; P ☏) Get back to basics at this welcoming village address in the gently rolling Hauts de St-Joseph. It features three plain rooms at the back and a manicured garden. Breakfast, which is served by the super hospitable Nathalie, is a feast of delicious homemade jams. Sadly, no dinner is offered, so you'll have to drive down to St-Joseph (7km). No credit cards.

The dearer room has kitchen facilities. Prices drop by €5 if you stay three nights or more.

Gîte Le Mahavel   GÎTE €
(☑ 0692 20 76 52; Roche-Plate; dm with half board €42; ☺ closed mid-Dec–Apr) This well-scrubbed *gîte* has four- to eight-bed dorms as well as a double. Bookings are essential.

**Gîte de la Rivière des Remparts –
Morel Jacqueline**   GÎTE €
(☑ 0692 68 35 32; Roche-Plate; dm with half board €40; ☺ closed Jan-Mar) A well-run *gîte* with 10- to 12-bed dorms. Bookings are essential.

❶ Getting There & Away

There are buses roughly every hour leaving from St-Joseph bus station to Bésaves, Les Lianes and Plaine-des-Grègues.

St-Joseph to Grand Coude

The timeless hamlet of Grand Coude, perched on a plateau at an altitude of 1300m, boasts a marvellous setting, with the soaring **Morne Langevin** (2380m) as the backdrop. Here you'll be smitten by the mellow tranquillity and laid-back lifestyle.

From St-Joseph, take the narrow D33, which passes through **Jean Petit** and twists its way across splendidly rugged scenery of looming peaks and deep gorges. Pull over for a picnic at **Petit Serré**, where a narrow ridge divides two valleys: the valley of the Rivière Langevin on your right and the valley of the Rivière des Remparts on your left. At one point the ridge is little wider than the road itself – you have the feeling of driving on a razor's edge!

At the end of the D33, about 15km north of St-Joseph, Grand Coude appears like a mirage.

◉ Sights

La Maison de Laurina   MUSEUM
(☑ 0692 68 78 72; www.lamaisondulaurina.fr; 24 Chemin de la Croizure, Grand Coude; €12; ☺ by reservation) Caffeine addicts should make a beeline for La Maison de Laurina, the owner of which grows a top-quality variety of coffee, the Bourbon Pointu. The admission price is a bit steep but it includes a visit to the plantation and tastings of various homemade delicacies flavoured with coffee (biscuits, liquor, rum). It's in Grand Coude, in the same location as the B&B L'Eucalyptus.

Le Labyrinthe En Champ Thé   GARDENS
(☑0692 60 18 88; www.enchampthe.com; 18 Rue Étienne Mussard, Grand Coude; adult/child €5.50/4.50, guided tour €8.50/4.50; ⊙9am-noon & 1-5pm Mon-Sat, 9am-5pm Sun) At the entrance of Grand Coude, Le Labyrinthe En Champ Thé is worth an hour or so for anyone interested in tropical flora, with an emphasis on tea and geranium. This botanical garden is the only place in Réunion where tea is cultivated. A 50g bag costs €10. You can also purchase syrups, jellies and essential oils from geranium.

🛏 Sleeping & Eating

Accommodation is limited to a handful of B&Bs along the D33.

There's nowhere to eat along the road to Grand Coude, so bring your own food if you're planning on being here for lunch. If you stay in a B&B, you can order dinner.

L'Eucalyptus – Chez
Marie-Claude Grondin   B&B €
(☑0692 68 78 72; 24 Chemin de la Croizure, Grand Coude; s/d incl breakfast €40/50) Absolute peace and quiet prevail at this unfussy B&B. Choose between the dinky all-wood bungalow or one of the two simple rooms in a charming Creole building. Unwind in the generous garden, where coffee and geranium fill the air. Excellent Creole meals are served at dinner (€25) – you'll be treated to homemade desserts and vegies from the garden.

La Plantation   B&B €€
(Map p248; ☑0693 92 53 01, 0262 45 63 28; www.la-plantation.re; 124 Route de Jean Petit, Jean Petit; d €90-100, ste €115, incl breakfast; 🅿❄🛜🏊) This upmarket B&B nestled amid sugar-cane fields boasts a small pool, an outdoor Jacuzzi and lush tropical garden with staggering views of the coast. There are three individually decorated rooms and one larger suite, all featuring handsomely designed bathrooms. Note that only one room comes with sea views. It's on the road to Grand Coude, about 5km from St-Joseph.

At the end of the day, make sure you treat yourself to a copious *table d'hôte* (€25); the delicious Creole specialities are made using local produce. Owner Sabine speaks English, Italian and German.

Au Lapin d'Or   B&B €€
(☑0692 70 09 18, 0262 56 66 48; rolande.sadehe@hotmail.fr; 55bis Chemin Concession, Jean Petit; s/d incl breakfast €63/75; 🅿🛜) Do you like rabbit? We dare ask because the owners of this pert

little B&B (which translates as 'Golden Rabbit') in Jean Petit raise rabbits, meaning you'll enjoy them prepared Creole-style at dinner (€24). Accommodation-wise, the three rooms are outfitted with cheerful pastels and super clean bathrooms that don't have proper doors, just curtains.

Don't miss out on the homemade *rhum tisane* (aromatic rum), best enjoyed under a gazebo in the garden.

ℹ Getting There & Away

A few daily buses run between St-Joseph and Grand Coude, but it's much more convenient to explore the area with your own wheels.

St-Joseph to St-Philippe

The coastline between St-Joseph and St-Philippe is definitely alluring: a string of rocky coves and dramatic cliffs pounded by crashing waves and backed by steep hills clad with dense forests and undulating sugar-cane fields, with a few black-sand beaches thrown in for good measure.

Inland, it's no less spectacular. Abandon your map and follow the sinuous secondary roads that wiggle up to the Hauts and creep through beguiling settlements, which warrant scenic drives and boast killer views over the ocean and plunging canyons.

Rivière Langevin

About 4km east of St-Joseph, you'll reach the coastal town of Langevin. From the coast, the Rivière Langevin valley slithers into the mountains. Come prepared: this scenic valley is extremely popular with picnicking families on Sunday.

⊙ Sights & Activities

If you need to cool off, there are plenty of natural pools along the river where you can dunk yourself. Our favourites include Trou Noir (it's signposted) and a pool that lies about 300m before the Cascade de la Grande Ravine (you can't miss it).

The Rivière Langevin valley was made for canyoning. Expect lots of slippery dips, exhilarating water jumps, short swims and fun scrambles in a picturesque setting – it's immensely fun!

Cascade de la Grande Ravine   WATERFALL
(Map p248) A narrow road follows the wide stony bed of the Rivière Langevin and leads

to Cascade de la Grande Ravine, a majestic waterfall that drops into a broad pool. Admire it from a lookout by the road, about 9km from the junction with the coastal road.

Aquasens ADVENTURE SPORTS
(☑ 0692 20 09 03; www.aquasens.re; outings €50-70; ⊙ by reservation) This professional adventure centre runs fantastic guided *randonnées aquatiques* (a mix of walking, sliding, swimming and some serious jumping or plunging down water-polished chutes into natural pools) along the Rivière Langevin. Outings last from one hour to four or five hours, depending on the circuit. They can be undertaken by participants of all ages provided they can swim.

🛌 Sleeping

There aren't any sleeping options in the Rivière Langevin valley. The nearest hotels and B&Bs are in St-Joseph, Manapany-les-Bains, Vincendo and Le Baril.

✖ Eating

If you haven't brought a picnic, there's a bevy of cheap and cheerful eateries along the Rivière Langevin at the entrance to the valley. They're pretty much of a muchness and serve up Creole classics, which you can eat inside or take away.

Le Benjoin CREOLE €
(☑ 0262 56 23 90; 114 Route de la Passerelle; mains €6-16; ⊙ 11.30am-2pm Sat-Thu) One of a number of popular eateries along the river, this ramshackle venture has a good terrace for a sandwich, a takeaway curry (from €6) or a beer but we wouldn't recommend eating in as the service is lacklustre and the food is bog-standard Creole fare. It's famed for its *thé dansant* (tea dance) on Sunday (from 9am).

❶ Getting There & Away

You'll need your own wheels to explore the Rivière Langevin valley. Note that it's hard to find a parking space on weekends – come early.

Vincendo & Les Hauts

In Vincendo, few visitors get wind of the black-sand **beach** fringed by *vacoa* trees a few kilometres south of the RN2. Swimming is forbidden because there are some dangerous currents, but it's a great place for a picnic.

Back in the village, follow the D34 that goes uphill to the north and takes you to the hamlet of **La Crête**. From there, the D37

leads due east to another peaceful settlement, **Jacques-Payet**, before zigzagging downhill to the junction with the coastal road.

🛌 Sleeping & Eating

Given the scarcity of eating options in the area, most B&Bs and *gîtes* can prepare meals on request.

★ Rougail Mangue GUESTHOUSE €
(☑ 0262 31 55 09; www.rougailmangue.com; 12 Rue Marcel Pagnol, Vincendo; s/d/tr/q €39/59/75/90, bungalows €70; P ✳ 🛜 ❄) You'd never guess it from the road but this guesthouse is a great find. The ground floor is occupied by a smart lounge area, one six-bed room, two squeaky-clean quads and a cheery double that opens onto a well-tended garden. For a higher degree of privacy, book the smallish bungalow, with stupendous sea views. It's on the main road, between Langevin and Vincendo.

The coup de grâce is the glorious pool, with the ocean as a backdrop, and the outdoor Jacuzzi (€5). Air-con is extra (€5), except in the bungalow. Note that the bathroom in the bungalow is tiny and has no door, just a curtain. Add €3 for breakfast (or €15 for a gargantuan brunch), best enjoyed alfresco under a gazebo. There's also a kitchen. Book ahead.

Ferme-Auberge Desprairies B&B €
(Map p248; ☑ 0692 64 61 70, 0262 37 20 27; www.ferme-auberge-desprairies.com; 44 Route de Matouta, Matouta; d incl breakfast €45; P 🛜) One of the best things about this peaceful inn is the road to it, which travels through sugar-cane fields despite being only a couple of kilometres from the coast. The six rooms are strictly unmemorable but are kept tidy, and in this location for this price, you won't hear anyone complaining. Rooms 1, 2 and 3 have sea views.

The owners also prepare delicious home-cooked meals (€22). Follow the D37 to the east to get here.

La Table des Randonneurs GÎTE €
(Map p248; ☑ 0692 61 73 47; 17 Chemin des Barbadines, Jacques-Payet; dm/d incl breakfast €25/50, bungalows €50) Way up in the hills, the 'Hikers' Table' is a safe bet if you're counting the euros, with two doubles (one of which has private facilities), one quad and one six-bed room in a modern house. They're down to earth, functional and simply furnished. There's also one self-contained bungalow that can sleep four people. No wi-fi. It's about 7km northeast of Vincendo (follow the D37).

The menu (€25 to €30) features local delicacies like smoked duck with *vacoa* and pork with palm hearts.

La Médina du Sud
APARTMENT €€

(☑ 0692 61 07 56; bouali1@hotmail.com; 23 Rue de la Marine, Vincendo; d for 2 nights €150; P ❄ ⊚ ⊠) Despite the name, not much resembles a 'medina' in this modern building by the turn-off for the beach. The three flats are characterless but fully equipped, well proportioned and perfectly serviceable, with the added bonus of a pool.

Les Grands Monts
B&B €€

(☑ 0692 17 53 42; www.facebook.com/Les-Grands-Monts; 2A Impasse Sabine, Vincendo; d incl breakfast €125; P ❄ ⊚ ⊠) Looking for a night at some place extra special? Make a beeline for this lovely *maison d'hôte* in a historic stone building. It shelters three spacious rooms that ingeniously blend volcanic stones and hardwoods. However, the open bathrooms in two rooms may not be to everyone's taste. The pool in the garden is a delight. Evening meals cost €30. It's in a cul-de-sac about 300m north of the RN2.

ⓘ Getting There & Away

Car Jaune's buses between St-Pierre and St-Benoît (line S1) run through Vincendo. More at www.carjaune.re. To get to the Hauts, you'll need your own wheels.

Basse-Vallée & Cap Méchant

The Basse-Vallée area is known for its production of baskets, bags (called *bertels*), hats and other items from *vacoa* fronds. It's also famous for its rugged coastline, particularly Cap Méchant, one of the most extraordinary landscapes on the southern coast.

◉ Sights

Cap Méchant
NATURAL SITE

Cap Méchant is one of the eeriest landscapes in the south, with huge lava fields, windswept black cliffs, rows of *vacoa* trees and the mandatory picnic shelters. From the headland you can follow an excellent coastal path along the sea cliffs (bring sturdy shoes).

🛏 Sleeping

There are a few B&Bs within walking distance of Cap Méchant as well as a B&B and two *gîtes* along the Route Forestière de Basse Vallée, further up in the hills. If you prefer to stay in a hotel, you'll have to head to Grande Anse, Mont-Vert-les-Bas or St-Pierre.

★ Gîte de Yoleine et Théophane
GÎTE €

(Map p248; ☑ 0262 37 13 14, 0692 87 25 43; Route Forestière, Basse-Vallée; dm with half board €48, cabin d with half board €120) One of southern Réunion's best-kept secrets, this rural paradise surrounded by forest and sugar-cane fields is a great place to come down a few gears. Way up in the hills, it shelters several six-bed dorms, each with its own bathroom, and a small cabin. At dinner the super friendly owners will treat you with the freshest island ingredients.

Access is a bit tricky; it can be reached on foot (about 30 minutes), or with a car in dry weather via a scenic 2km dirt track from the Route Forestière (signed at the junction, about 5.5km above the village of Basse-Vallée) – it can't get more Wild South than this.

Ferme-Auberge Le Rond de Basse Vallée
INN €

(Map p248; ☑ 0692 69 65 51; Route Forestière, Basse-Vallée; d incl breakfast €45; P) Head up the Route Forestière to find this *ferme-auberge*, a great place to commune with nature. There are four simple rooms with spick-and-span bathrooms in a Creole-style building in harmony with the environment. The restaurant is across the road and features regional dishes with authentic flavours, including *vacoa*, a local speciality. A full meal will set you back €25.

Gîte de Montagne de Basse Vallée
GÎTE €

(Map p248; ☑ 0262 37 36 25; Route Forestière, Basse-Vallée; dm €16-18) This simple *gîte de montagne* is about 8km north of Basse Vallée, along the Route Forestière. It comprises four- to eight-bed dorms and a communal kitchen. Bookings must be made through the Centrale de Réservation (www.resa.reunion.fr) or any tourist office on the island, but if you arrive without a reservation and there's space, the caretaker will probably let you in. Breakfast costs €6, dinner €19.

Chambre d'Hôte du Cap Méchant
B&B €€

(☑ 0692 36 26 16, 0262 28 57 50; www.chambrecap-mechant.com; 34 Rue Labourdonnais, Basse-Vallée; d incl breakfast €70; P ❄ ⊚ ⊠) A hop from Cap Méchant, this abode features five bungalows arrayed around a tiny pool. They're comfortable but tightly packed together, so don't expect lots of privacy. Each bungalow has its own strong chromatic vibration: electric blue, orange, green. The owner loves colour! Evening meals cost €26.

Coco Vanille
B&B €€

(☑ 0262 93 18 76, 0692 94 51 12; www.coco-vanille.com; 68 Rue Labourdonnais, Basse-Vallée; d incl breakfast €64-70; 🛜🌊) This laid-back B&B is a good deal with cool rooms, small bathrooms, a few fancy touches and a small breakfast terrace. The swimming pool in the tropical garden is a great addition when it's stifling hot. It's within walking distance of Cap Méchant. Dinner costs €20. No credit cards.

✗ Eating

There are three large restaurants at Cap Méchant as well as numerous picnic shelters.

Le Pinpin
CHINESE, CREOLE €€

(☑ 0262 37 04 19; Cap Méchant; mains €11-17; ⊙ 11.30am-2pm Thu-Tue) There's sure to be a dish on the extensive menu that suits your palate. Very popular with families.

L'Étoile de Mer
CHINESE, CREOLE €€

(☑ 0262 37 04 60; Cap Méchant; mains €10-16; ⊙ 11.30am-2pm) The food is a crowd-pleasing mix of Chinese dishes, Creole staples and *métro* classics.

Le Cap Méchant
CHINESE, CREOLE €€

(☑ 0692 85 39 28; Cap Méchant; mains €10-22; ⊙ 11.30am-2pm Tue-Sun) Le Cap Méchant is mobbed at weekends but almost deserted on weekdays. It serves great *carris*, chop sueys and *porc au palmiste* (pork with palm hearts).

❶ Getting There & Away

Cap Méchant lies on Car Jaune's coastal bus route between St-Pierre and St-Benoît. More information at www.carjaune.re.

Le Baril

POP 2200

Le Baril is the last settlement before St-Philippe. Most people stop here for the Puits des Anglais (the Wells of the British), one of the most spectacular attractions along this stretch of coast.

◉ Sights

Puits des Anglais
NATURAL SITE

(Map p248; Le Baril) The main attraction in Le Baril is the Puits des Anglais (Wells of the British), a splendid saltwater pool that has been constructed in the basaltic rock. It's mobbed at weekends but you'll have the whole place to yourself during the week.

🛏 Sleeping

There's no hotel in Le Baril, only a handful of atmospheric B&Bs.

Le Pinpin d'Amour
B&B €

(Map p248; ☑ 0262 37 14 86; www.pinpindamour.com; 56 Chemin Paul Hoareau, Le Baril; d incl breakfast €65-75; 🅿✳@🛜) Spending a night at this original *chambre d'hôte* makes a good story to tell the folks back home. Your hosts have a passion for *vacoa* and *pinpin* (the palm's edible artichoke-like fruit), meaning you'll be guaranteed to taste them at dinner (€27 to €30). Accommodation-wise, the six appealing, if a bit itty-bitty and sombre, rooms sport pastel-coloured walls and honey-boarded floors.

The dearer rooms have a small veranda but no views to speak of. One quibble: the portable air-conditioners are a bit noisy. It's amid the sugar-cane fields above Le Baril, about 2km from the coastal road. There's a 10% discount for stays of two nights and more.

★ Le Four à Pain
B&B €€

(☑ 0692 36 61 55; huet-jean-marc@hotmail.fr; 63C RN2, Le Baril; d incl breakfast €75; 🅿✳🛜🌊) Simplicity, character and a great welcome make Le Four à Pain special. Rooms, in two adorable Creole-style cottages, are light and fresh with contemporary decor, and have their own entrance. You're in a superb setting, with fine mature trees that shade a wonderfully quiet tropical garden. The *coup de grâce* is the lovely pool – pure bliss after a bout of sightseeing.

Don't miss out on the luscious evening meals (€26); you'll be guaranteed to sample palm-heart salad – the owner is a major producer in the south. It's off the main road.

✗ Eating

Apart from Warren Hastings, independent restaurants are scarce in Le Baril. Your best bet is to order a meal at your B&B.

Le Ti Vacoa
CREOLE, SANDWICHES €

(☑ 0692 92 20 24; Le Puits des Anglais, RN2, Le Baril; mains €4-8; ⊙ 10am-9pm Tue-Sat) This unfussy little kiosk could hardly be better situated; it overlooks the saltwater pool at Puits des Anglais. The menu concentrates on simply prepared Creole mains as well as composed salads that always please, not to mention a wide selection of appetising sandwiches (from €2.50). Also does takeaway.

Warren Hastings
CREOLE €€

(Map p248; ☑0692 52 03 82; 103A RN2; mains €12-16; ☺11am-2pm & 6.30-9pm) The food looks as good as it tastes at this surprisingly upbeat cafe-cum-bistro on the main road. It serves winningly fresh dishes prepared with local ingredients as well as delectable tapas.

★ Auberge Paysanne
Le Palmier
CREOLE €€€

(Map p248; ☑0692 69 03 48; 21 Chemin Ceinture, Le Baril; menu €27; ☺11.30am-1pm by reservation Sat-Thu) Plenty of smiles from the owners, recipes plucked straight out of grandma's cookbook, a serene setting in the Hauts and lovely views from the terrace – if you're after an authentic Creole experience, this place is hard to beat. Here you can eat local specialities that are hard to find elsewhere, such as chicken with palm hearts and papaya cake.

Note that it's not a walk-in restaurant – it's a private home that's open by reservation only. It's signposted from the main road.

ⓘ Getting There & Away

Car Jaune's buses between St-Pierre and St-Benoît (line S1) run through Le Baril. More information at www.carjaune.re.

St-Philippe
POP 5100

The only town of consequence in the Wild South (along with St-Joseph), St-Philippe has a wonderfully down-to-earth, unfussy ambience. Although this friendly little town is devoid of overwhelming sights, it has a slew of (good) surprises up its sleeves and is optimally placed for explorations of the coast and forays into the Hauts. Oh, and St-Philippe lies in the shadow of Piton de la Fournaise.

Vegetarians, rejoice: St-Philippe is the self-proclaimed capital of *vacoa* (screw-pine fronds). No joke – no less than 5000 visitors turn up to join St-Philippois townsfolk for the 10-day Fête du Vacoa in August.

◉ Sights

Sentier Botanique de
Mare Longue
GARDENS

(Map p248; Chemin Forestier) This pristine forest has an end-of-the-world feeling that will appeal to those in search of hush. From the car park you can tackle one of the three interpretative trails in the primary forest. It's inland between Le Baril and St-Philippe, a few kilometres north from Le Jardin des Parfums et des Épices.

Le Jardin des Parfums
et des Épices
GARDENS

(Map p248; ☑0692 66 09 01; www.jardin-parfums-epices.com; 7 Chemin Forestier; adult/child €6.10/3.05; ☺tours 10.30am & 2.30pm) Inland between Le Baril and St-Philippe, don't miss the 3-hectare garden, Le Jardin des Parfums et des Épices. It contains over 1500 species in a natural setting in the Mare Longue forest, 3km west of St-Philippe. Knowledgable and enthusiastic guides present the island's history, economy and culture through the plants; tours are in French.

Fishing Harbour
HARBOUR

With its handful of colourful fishing boats, the teensy fishing harbour is worth a peek.

★☆ Festivals & Events

Fête du Vacoa
FAIR

(Festival of Vacoa; ☺Aug) Celebrates crafts made from *vacoa* (screw-pine fronds); held in St-Philippe.

🛏 Sleeping

You can find B&B accommodation and self-catering options in St-Philippe, which is a great base for the south coast and Le Grand Brûlé. A five-star resort should be completed by 2018 – stay tuned.

★ Dan'n Tan Lontan
BUNGALOW €

(☑0262 47 71 06, 0692 65 14 29; www.dantanlontan.com; 19 Allée des Palmiers; d €54-70; P ❋ 🛜 ⛱) Swap stress for bliss at this enticing venue in a splendid property, a five-minute walk from the centre. Handsome, well-thought-out and practical, the three Creole-style, fully equipped cottages are engaging places to stay. Relax in the garden, doze by the superb pool or enjoy a glass of something on your shady terrace. One of the area's best-kept secrets, without a doubt.

Le Palmier
B&B €

(☑0262 37 04 11, 0692 02 85 71; nicolelepalmier @yahoo.fr; 8 Rue de la Pompe; s/d incl breakfast €46/52; P ❋ 🛜 ⛱) Lacking excitement, maybe, but this friendly B&B down a little lane at the east end of St-Philippe is a safe bet. Rooms are ordinary, with immaculate tiles, tiny bathrooms and colourful bedspreads. Avoid the larger one at the back, which has obstructed views. Guests can use the pool in front of the owners' house if they stay at least two nights.

Au Domaine du Vacoa
B&B €€

(☑0262 37 03 12, 0692 64 89 89; www.domaine
duvacoa.fr; 12 Chemin Vacoa; d incl breakfast €70;
P❋🌐🐕) This B&B set in a pert little *case
créole* features two adjoining rooms enhanced with splashes of colour, back-friendly
mattresses and spotless bathrooms. Au
Domaine du Vacoa's ultimate trump card,
though, is its small infinity pool with great
sea views. At dinner (€26 to €28), warm your
insides with duck, *vacoa* and other vegetables from the garden – all organic, of course.

✖ Eating

St-Philippe has only one eatery – small wonder that most visitors end up eating at their
B&B or *gîte*.

Marmite du Pêcheur
SEAFOOD €€

(Map p248; ☑0262 37 01 01; 18A RN2, Ravine
Ango; mains €15-30, Sunday buffet €25; ☉noon-
2pm Thu-Tue) Can't stomach one more morsel
of *carri poulet* (chicken curry)? Then opt for
this eatery where cuisine is predominantly
fishy: crab, shrimps, fish and mussels, climax-
ing with a gargantuan *marmite du pêcheur*
(€30), a kind of seafood stew. Downside: the
dining room doesn't register even a blip on
the charm radar. It's just off the main road,
east of St-Philippe.

La Bicyclette Gourmande
CREOLE, CHINESE €€

(☑0693 93 71 93; 43 Rue Leconte de Lisle; mains
€13-19; ☉11.30am-2pm Wed-Sun, 6.30-8.30pm
Thu-Sun) This laid-back eatery set in a small
Creole house has an agreeable terrace which
overlooks the main road (not so peaceful).
The eclectic menu covers enough territory to
please most palates, from Creole classics to
mainstream Chinese and *métro* dishes.

❶ Getting There & Away

Line S1 buses between St-Benoît (€2, 1¼
hours) and St-Pierre (€2, one hour) stop at
the town hall in St-Philippe. More information at www.carjaune.re.

Le Grand Brûlé

The crowning glory of the Wild South, the
arid, eerie landscape of Le Grand Brûlé is a
6km-wide volcanic plain formed by the main
lava flow from the volcano. This is where the
action goes when the volcano is erupting. The
steep slopes above, known as Les Grandes
Pentes, have funnelled lava down to the coast
for thousands of years.

◉ Sights

Le Grand Brûlé is rife with natural attractions, including spectacular solidified lava
flows.

Le Grand Brûlé Platform
VIEWPOINT

(Map p248; RN2) In April 2007, in one of the
most violent eruptions ever recorded, an impressive lava flow was formed, about 2km
north of Pointe du Tremblet. The road was
cut off for several months. It's a primal experience to drive through the barren moonscape that is this huge expanse of solidified,
pure-black lava field. It's forbidden to walk
across the lava flow, but a viewing platform
has been built just off the RN2.

Pointe de la Table
VIEWPOINT

(Map p248; RN2) In 1986 the lava unusually
flowed south of Le Grand Brûlé to reach the
sea at Pointe de la Table, a headland that lies
a few hundred metres north of Puits Arabe.
This eruption added over 30 hectares to the
island's area, and more than 450 people had
to be evacuated and several homes were lost.
An interpretative trail has been set up and
makes for a lovely hike on the basaltic cliffs
pounded by the ocean.

Puits Arabe
VIEWPOINT

(Map p248) Leaving St-Philippe to the east,
you'll first come across Puits Arabe (Wells of
the Arabs), a manmade hole in the basaltic
rock. It's a popular picnic site, with shelters
scattered amid rows of *vacoa* trees.

🏃 Activities

Visitors to Réunion don't have to confine
themselves to exploring the surface of its
volcanic formations – at Le Grand Brûlé, it's
possible to go caving inside volcanic tubes
(elongated tunnels formed by the cooling and
rapid hardening of lava) and walk *under* the
volcano.

Caving & Canyoning

A number of operators organise guided excursions through the lava tubes at Le Grand
Brûlé. The tunnels are generally quite tall
(and there are some openings in the ceilings,
which allows for superb plays of light), but
be prepared to stoop or squeeze at times.
Another plus is that it's suitable for all ages
– bring the kids (aged 8 and over)! All you
need is good shoes; torches and helmets are
provided.

Prices vary between €50 and €75, depending on the length and duration of the circuit.

Envergure Réunion ADVENTURE SPORTS
(☑0693 43 23 52; www.canyon-speleo.re; outing €50-75; ☺by reservation) A long-standing favourite for canyoning in southern Réunion and guided excursions through the lava tubes at Le Grand Brûlé.

Speleo Canyon ADVENTURE SPORTS
(☑0692 11 50 13; www.speleocanyon.re; outing €50-75; ☺by reservation) Julien Dez is a qualified instructor with lots of experience around Réunion. He can arrange canyoning outings, guided treks as well as guided excursions through the lava tubes of Le Grand Brûlé.

Rougail Rando ADVENTURE SPORTS
(☑0692 92 14 34; 1 RN2, Le Tremblet; outing from €50; ☺by reservation) Juanito specialises in guided excursions through the lava tubes at Le Grand Brûlé. Prices include gear rental.

🍽 Sleeping & Eating

There's only one accommodation option in the Le Grand Brûlé area. You can base yourself in St-Joseph, St-Philippe or Ste-Rose and visit the area on a day trip.

A smattering of so-called 'restaurants' (in fact, private homes turned into casual eateries) are dotted along the RN2 between St-Philippe and Le Grand Brûlé.

Le Crabe Sous la Varangue B&B €€
(☑0262 92 13 56; www.crabevarangue.canalblog.com; 1 RN2, Le Tremblet; s €65, d €75-80, incl breakfast; P☎) This quirky B&B sits in isolated splendour on the main road between St-Philippe and Le Grand Brûlé. The two individually decorated rooms in the main house have pretty painted concrete floors and colourful walls, but are a bit sombre, while the third one occupies a cosy Creole house endowed with polished parquet floors. No air-con, but each room has a fan. Dinner (€28) is only available on Friday and Saturday. The owner runs excursions to the lava tubes in Le Grand Brûlé.

★Chez Moustache CREOLE €€
(☑0692 33 27 03; 9 RN2, Le Tremblet; mains €10-15; ☺11.30am-2.30pm Sat-Mon, Wed & Thu) A welcoming family-run outfit in a picturesque Creole house complete with a courtyard garden, Chez Moustache serves authentic Creole specialities at honest prices. The food is grounded in island tradition, as testified by the wood-fired oven. The menu changes nightly, and includes only four or five mains, but brevity guarantees freshness. It's about 5km south of the 2007 lava flow.

Le Vieux Port CREOLE, SEAFOOD €€
(Map p248; ☑0692 15 79 31; 112 RN2, Le Tremblet; mains €11-19; ☺11.30am-2.30pm) A fine specimen of a restaurant, Le Vieux Port is ideally situated in a tropical garden about 500m south of the 2007 lava flow. It is strictly local cuisine – albeit of a refreshingly creative nature. Locals rave about the *rougail boucané* (smoked pork ribs prepared Creole-style) and the delicious palm-heart salad. Takeaway is available. Reservations are advised on weekends.

It also features a repertoire of fish dishes that you won't find elsewhere, such as *maccabit* (a kind of grouper). Cash only.

🛍 Shopping

Escale Bleue Vanille FOOD
(☑0262 37 03 99; www.escale-bleue.fr; 7 RN2, Le Tremblet; ☺9.30am-12.30pm & 1.30-5.30pm) Learn how vanilla is prepared and purchase a sweet-scented vanilla pod at this small family-run operation.

ⓘ Getting There & Away

Le Grand Brûlé lies on Car Jaune's coastal bus route (line S1) between St-Pierre and St-Benoît. More information at www.carjaune.re.

THE EAST

The east coast is everything the west coast is not: low-key, unpretentious and luxuriant (yes, it *does* get much more rain). While this coast lacks the beaches of the west, the region makes up for it with spectacular waterfalls and fantastic picnic spots. The main produce of the area is sugar cane, but the region is also known for its vanilla plantations and fruit orchards.

This coastal stretch is also considered to be 'other', partially as it's the bastion of Tamil culture in Réunion. Here you'll find a distinctive atmosphere, with numerous temples and colourful religious festivals. For visitors it's an opportunity to discover a Réunion you never imagined.

Tourism in this area remains on a humble scale, with no star attractions. However, it's worth taking a few days to explore the quiet recesses of this less-visited part of the island where you can experience Réunion from a different perspective.

Eastern Réunion

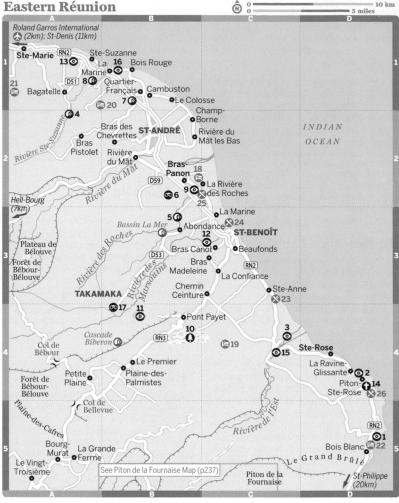

Roland Garros International (2km); St-Denis (11km)

Ste-Marie [RN2]
13
21
Bagatelle
4
Ste-Suzanne
La Marine 16 Bois Rouge
[D51] 8
Quartier-Français
7
20
Cambuston
Le Colosse
Champ-Borne
Bras des Chevrettes
ST-ANDRÉ
Rivière du Mât les Bas
Bras Pistolet
Rivière du Mât
Bras-Panon 18
[D59] 9 6
La Rivière des Roches
25
5 Abondance
La Marine 24
12 **ST-BENOÎT**
Bassin La Mer
Bras Canot
Beaufonds
Hell-Bourg (7km)
Plateau de Bélouve
Forêt de Bébour-Bélouve
TAKAMAKA
17 11
Bras Madeleine
La Confiance [RN2]
Chemin Ceinture
Ste-Anne 23
Pont Payet
10
3
19
15
Ste-Rose
Cascade Biberon
[RN3]
Col de Bébour
Le Premier
Plaine-des-Palmistes
La Ravine-Glissante 2
Piton-Ste-Rose 14 26
Forêt de Bébour-Bélouve
Petite Plaine
Col de Bellevue
Rivière de l'Est
[RN2]
Plaine-des-Cafres
Bourg-Murat
La Grande Ferme
Le Vingt-Troisième
1
Bois Blanc 22
See Piton de la Fournaise Map (p237)
Piton de la Fournaise
Le Grand Brûlé
St-Philippe (20km)

INDIAN OCEAN

0 — 10 km
0 — 5 miles

Ste-Suzanne & Around

POP 20,500

The seaside town of Ste-Suzanne is usually glimpsed in passing by most tourists on the route down the coast, which is a shame because there are charming pockets in the area that beg discovery, including the splendid Rivière Ste-Suzanne, which is both a playground for outdoorsy types and a hot spot for sunbathers and picnickers.

⊙ Sights

Lighthouse   LIGHTHOUSE

(Rue du Phare) Next to the tourist office, the small lighthouse – the only one on the island – is worth a gander. It was built in 1845. It's still in operation.

Cascade Délices   WATERFALL

(Map p260; Quartier-Français) In the Quartier-Français district, Cascade Délices is an easily accessed waterfall. It's only 4m high, but the junglelike setting will appeal to nature lovers, and you can dunk yourself in the cool water. It's signposted.

Eastern Réunion

Cascade Niagara — WATERFALL

(Map p260) Just beyond the church towards the southern end of town is a road signposted inland to Cascade Niagara, a 30m waterfall on the Rivière Ste-Suzanne. At the end of the road, about 2km further on, you wind up at the waterfall. On weekends it's a popular picnic site.

Bassin Boeuf — WATERFALL

(Map p260) If you need to cool off, the Bassin Boeuf waterfall beckons with its enticing natural pools fringed with stone slabs, ideal for picnicking and sunbathing. Well worth the detour.

From Ste-Suzanne, follow the D51 towards Bagatelle for about 7km until the signpost 'Bassin Boeuf'. Leave your car at the small parking area and walk several minutes down a dirt road to the Rivière Ste-Suzanne. To get to the waterfall, cross the river and follow the path on the right for about five minutes.

La Vanilleraie — PLANTATION

(Map p260; ☑0262 23 07 26; www.lavanilleraie. com; Allé Chassagne, Domaine du Grand Hazier; tours adult/child €5/3; ◔8.30am-noon & 1.30-5pm Mon-Sat) At Domaine du Grand Hazier, a superb 18th-century sugar-planter's residence about 3km southwest of Ste-Suzanne, you'll find La Vanilleraie, where you can see vanilla preparation and drying processes and also purchase vanilla pods. Guided tours are available at 9am, 10am, 11am, 2pm, 3pm and 4pm. The manager speaks English.

Chapelle Front de Mer — HINDU TEMPLE

Notable religious buildings in Ste-Suzanne include the Chapelle Front de Mer, an ornate Tamil temple built on a pebbly beach north of town (it's unsigned).

🏃 Activities

Alpanes — ADVENTURE SPORTS

(☑0692 77 75 30; www.alpanes.com; full-day trip €60; ◔by reservation) The top spot for canyoning in the east is the spectacular Rivière Ste-Suzanne. Expect jumps, leaps in natural pools and scrambling over rocks.

Niagara Vertical — ADVENTURE SPORTS

(Map p260; ☑0692 48 55 54; Cascade Niagara; adult €25; ◔Sat & Sun, by reservation) If you want to see Cascade Niagara from a different perspective, this outfit has set up two via ferrata circuits of varying degrees of difficulty. Children over 16 are welcome.

🛏 Sleeping & Eating

Ste-Suzanne doesn't have an abundance of sleeping options. With your own wheels, you may prefer to stay in St-Denis and visit the area on a day trip.

The eating scene in Ste-Suzanne can optimistically be described as 'dull', but you're not far from St-Denis' gourmet restaurants.

La Rond' Dada — BUNGALOW €

(Map p260; ☑0692 87 39 33; www.larondada.com; 13 Chemin Rila Ah-Teng, Commune Carron; d €60; P❄🛜) This well-designed, spacious (41 sq

RÉUNION STE-SUZANNE & AROUND

LITTLE INDIA

If you happen to be around Ste-Suzanne and St-André at certain periods of the year, you'll discover a very exotic side of the island, with lots of colourful festivals organised by the Tamil community. If you're about, be sure to join in the heady hype of these local festivals. In January, don't miss Tamil **fire-walking ceremonies**, when participants enter a meditative state and then walk over red-hot embers as a sign of devotion to various deities. Thousands of goats are slaughtered as offerings and are distributed among the participants. Another must-see is the **Cavadee festival**, which usually takes place in January or February. In October or November, make a beeline for **Divali** (aka Dipavali), the Festival of Light. Dancers and decorated floats parade through the town centre. Visitors are welcome. Contact the tourist office (p263) in St-André for specific dates.

metres) bungalow set in a well-tended tropical garden behind the owner's house feels like a cosy doll's house and proffers ample coastal views. It's a great deal for self-caterers and a handy base for the east. There's a two-night minimum stay.

Le Pharest GUESTHOUSE €
(☑ 0262 98 91 10; www.pharest-reunion.com; 22 Rue Blanchet; s €34-58, d €52-62, q €115, incl breakfast; P❄️🛜🏊) Near the lighthouse, this compact tropical cocoon offers five wooden bungalows that are set in an exuberant garden. They're fairly ramshackle and filled with wholly unpretentious furniture, but are kept in good nick. Precious perks include a small swimming pool and a restaurant (menus €17 to €38). What sets it apart, though, is the congenial atmosphere and the friendly welcome of Nadège and Patrick.

Air-con is extra (€4.50). If you stay three nights or more, it's worth opting for the fully equipped, spacious (51 sq metres) *gîte* across the road (€240 for three nights).

ℹ️ Information

Tourist Office (☑ 0262 52 13 54; www.lebeau pays.com; 5 Rue du Phare; ⊙ 9am-12.30pm & 1.30-5pm Mon-Sat; 🛜) Beside the lighthouse. *Gîtes de montagnes* can be booked here. Has free wif-fi.

ℹ️ Getting There & Away

Ste-Suzanne is served by Car Jaune bus routes running between St-Denis and St-Benoît (lines E1 and E2). Buses between St-André and St-Denis (line E4) also stop at Ste-Suzanne. Buses stop at the town hall and at Quartier Français. More information at www.carjaune.re.

St-André & Around

POP 56,600

St-André is the epicentre of Tamil culture in Réunion, and you'll see more women draped in vividly coloured saris than Zoreilles (mainland French) wearing designer glasses and trendy shirts. Busy streets transport you to a city somewhere in India with curry houses, sari shops and bric-a-brac traders. You'll definitely feel closer to Bombay than Paris.

The mainly Tamil population in the area is descended from indentured labourers who were brought from India to work in the sugar-cane fields and factories after slavery was abolished in 1848.

⊙ Sights

St André's Indian atmosphere is most apparent in the Hindu temples dotted around the town.

Sucrerie de Bois-Rouge DISTILLERY
(Map p260; ☑ 0262 58 59 74; www.distilleriesavanna. com; 2 Chemin Bois Rouge; guided tour adult/child €10/5, distillery €7/3; ⊙ 9am-6.30pm Mon-Fri, to 4.30pm Sat Jul-Dec, 9am-4pm Mon-Sat Jan-Jun) This sugar refinery is on the coast 3km north of St-André. During the cane harvest (July to December) visitors are shown around the huge, high-tech plant, following the process from the delivery of the cut cane to the final glittering crystals. The two-hour tour includes the neighbouring distillery, where the by-products (cane juice and molasses) are made into rum. From January to June, you can only visit the distillery. There's a shop, Tafia et Galabé, where you can sip (and buy) the good stuff.

Children under seven years aren't allowed into the refinery.

Temple of Colosse HINDU TEMPLE
(Route de Champ Borne) Temple of Colosse is, by far, the most striking Tamil temple in Réunion. With its brightly painted decor, it's very photogenic. Since it's not open to the public, you'll have to content yourself with peering through the railings.

Plantation de Vanille Roulof PLANTATION
(📱 0692 10 87 15; www.lavanilledelareunion.com; 470 Chemin Deschanets; guided tours €4; ⊙9am-4pm Mon-Sat, guided tours 11am, 2pm, 3pm & 4pm Mon-Sat) If you're after Réunion's Vanille Bourbon, head to this small family-run operation where you can buy vanilla pods at reasonable prices (€10 for 25g). You can also find out about the technique of 'marrying' the vanilla, a delicate operation in which the flowers are fertilised by hand.

Maison Martin Valliamé HISTORIC BUILDING
(1590 Chemin du Centre; guided tours incl snacks €8.50; ⊙9am-12.30pm & 1.30-5pm Mon-Fri) Worth a look is this handsome colonial villa dating from 1925, northeast of the centre. Guided tours in French are available on the hour from 10am to 4pm.

Temple du Petit Bazar HINDU TEMPLE
(Ave de l'Île de France) This small Tamil temple is not far from the centre.

🛏 Sleeping & Eating

There are no good places to stay in St-André, but you're not more than half an hour from St-Denis, and most travellers visit on a day trip. The nearest accommodation choices are in Ste-Anne, Bras-Panon and Ste-Suzanne.

Le Velli CREOLE €€
(📱0262 46 03 38; www.restaurant-velli.com; 336 Route de Champ Borne; mains €16-25; ⊙11.30am-2.30pm Mon-Sat) Dining at this inviting restaurant near the Temple of Colosse is all about having a good time enjoying the finer pleasures of life. The cuisine is resolutely Creole, well prepared and well priced.

Le Beau Rivage CHINESE, CREOLE €€
(📱0262 46 08 66; 873 Route de Champ Borne; mains €12-16; ⊙noon-1.45pm Tue-Sun, 7-9pm Tue, Wed, Fri & Sat) True to its name (The Beautiful Shore), Le Beau Rivage boasts a fantastic location: it's on the seafront, beside the church ruins in Champ-Borne. That said, the dining room is quite dull; ask for a table near the windows. The cuisine is predominantly Chinese and Creole. Its good-value lunch buffet (€20) served on Sunday is very popular with Réunionnais families.

❶ Information

Tourist Office (📱0262 46 16 16; www.est. reunion.fr; Maison Martin Valliamé, 1590 Chemin du Centre; ⊙9am-12.30pm & 1.30-5pm Mon-Fri; 🛜) Has plenty of brochures. Contact it for specific dates of Tamil festivals.

VANILLA UNVEILED

The vanilla orchid was introduced into Réunion from Mexico around 1820, but early attempts at cultivation failed because of the absence of the Mexican bee that pollinates the flower and triggers the development of the vanilla pod. Fortunately for custard lovers everywhere, a method of hand-pollination was discovered in Réunion in 1841 by a 12-year-old slave, Edmond Albius. Vanilla was highly prized in Europe at the time and Albius' discovery ushered in an economic boom, at least for the French 'vanilla barons'.

The vanilla bubble burst, however, when synthetic vanilla – made from coal – was invented in the late 19th century. Réunion's vanilla industry was almost wiped out, but in recent years the growing demand for natural products has led to something of a revival. You'll now find vanilla 'plantations' hidden in the forests from Ste-Suzanne south to St-Philippe.

The majority of Réunion's crop is exported (Coca-Cola is the world's single biggest buyer), but vanilla is still a firm favourite in local cuisine. It crops up in all sorts of delicacies, from cakes and pastries to coffee, liqueurs, even vanilla duck and chicken. Best of all is the sublime flavour of a vanilla-steeped *rhum arrangé* (a mixture of rum, fruit juice, cane syrup and a blend of herbs and berries).

❶ Getting There & Away

Car Jaune buses from St-Denis to St-Benoît pass through St-André (€2, 50 minutes). If you're travelling to Salazie by bus (€1.80, 35 minutes), you will have to change here; there are seven buses daily in each direction (three on Sunday). More details at www.carjaune.re.

Bras-Panon

POP 12,300

Bras-Panon is Réunion's vanilla capital, and most visitors come here to see (and smell!) the fragrant vanilla-processing plant. The town is also associated with a rare sprat-like delicacy known as *bichiques*. In early summer (around November or December) these are caught at the mouth of the Rivière des Roches as they swim upriver to spawn.

RÉUNION BRAS-PANON

◉ Sights

There aren't many sights in town, but you'll find a couple of great natural attractions in the hinterland.

Bassin La Paix & Bassin La Mer   WATERFALL
(Map p260) A blissful site is Bassin La Paix, in the Rivière des Roches valley, about 2.5km west from Bras-Panon (it's signposted). From the car park, a path quickly leads down to a majestic waterfall tumbling into a large rock pool. It's an ideal picnic spot. For a more off-the-beaten-track experience, you can continue upstream to Bassin La Mer, another cascading delight that can be reached on foot only. The start of the trail is at the end of the car park. It's an enjoyable (though exposed and hot) 40-minute walk. Reward yourself with a dip in the swimming holes at the bottom of the falls.

Coopérative de Vanille Provanille   FACTORY
(Map p260; ☑ 0262 51 70 12; www.provanille.fr; 21 RN2; tours adult/child €5/free; ⏰ 8.30am-noon & 1.30-5pm) This working vanilla-processing plant offers an introduction to the process of producing Réunion's famous Vanille Bourbon via a 45-minute guided tour and a film on the history of vanilla cultivation. You'll find various vanilla products at the factory shop.

✪✪ Festivals & Events

Fête des Bichiques   FOOD
(Festival of Bichiques; ⏰ Oct) This rural fair celebrates the rare sprat-like delicacy known as *bichiques*. In Bras-Panon.

🛏 Sleeping

Chez Éva Annibal   INN €
(Map p260; ☑ 0262 51 53 76; 6 Chemin Rivière du Mât; d with shared bathroom incl breakfast €45; 🅿 ✳ 🛜) Set in a modern house, this inn has three functional but clean rooms with sloping ceilings and communal facilities above the dining room. A good deal for the price.

La Passiflore   B&B €
(Map p260; ☑ 0262 51 74 68; www.lapassiflore. re; 31 Rue des Baies-Roses; d incl breakfast €60; ✳ 🛜 🏊) Run by a well-travelled *métro* couple, this B&B stands in a haven of tropical peace near the main road. The three smallish rooms with their own entrance are embellished with a few exotic bits and bobs; avoid the 'Amis' room (with shared bathrooms) in the owners' house. Float in the scintillating pool or bask in the sunny garden. Air-con is extra (€5). There's on-street parking.

✗ Eating

There aren't many restaurants in Bras-Panon but you'll find a smattering of takeaway outlets offering Creole staples in the centre.

★ Chez Éva Annibal   CREOLE €€
(Map p260; ☑ 0262 51 53 76; 6 Chemin Rivière du Mât; dinner €25; ⏰ noon-1pm & 7-8pm Mon-Sat, noon-1pm Sun) Chez Éva Annibal is something of an institution on the island. Pack a hearty thirst and giant-sized appetite before venturing into this plain but feisty inn. The Full Monty feast comprises rum, *gratin de légumes* (baked vegetables), fish curry, duck with vanilla, and cakes, all clearly emblazoned with a Creole Mama stamp of approval. Pity about the very ordinary dining room.

Le Ti' Piment   FRENCH, CREOLE €€
(Map p260; ☑ 0262 23 46 79; www.facebook. com/letipiment; 1bis Rue Roberto; mains €13-21; ⏰ 11.30am-2pm & 7-9pm Mon-Sat) About 400m southeast of Coopérative de Vanille, Le Ti' Piment is a popular place serving French and Creole dishes in a pleasant, convivial space that combines style with informality. Look for chicken cooked with olives, deer stew and duck breast flambéed in rum. And desserts are satisfyingly sinful. Also does takeaway.

St-Benoît & Around

POP 36,500

Sugar-cane fields, lychee and mango orchards, rice, spices, coffee... Great carpets of deep-green felt seem to have been draped over the lower hills that surround St-Benoît, a major agricultural and fishing centre.

Bar a few impressive religious buildings – a mosque, a church and a Tamil temple on the outskirts of town – St-Benoît is not over-burdened with tourist sights. The area's best features lie elsewhere; turn your attention from the coast and plant it firmly on the cooler recesses of the hills and valleys to the west. The Rivière des Marsouins valley in particular is a delight, with its plunging waterfalls and luxuriant vegetation. Small wonder that Réunion's best white water is found here.

◉ Sights

Grand Étang   LAKE
(Map p260) Around 12km southwest of St-Benoît along the road towards Plaine-des-Palmistes is the 3km road to Grand Étang (Big Pond). This pretty picnic spot lies at the bottom of an almost-vertical ridge separating it from the Rivière des Marsouins valley. Most

BELVÉDÈRE DE L'EDEN

A fabulous place to chill out is **Belvédère de l'Eden** (Map p260), an aptly named viewpoint, in upcountry Bras-Panon. From Bras-Panon, take the road to St-André, then turn left onto the D59 (in the direction of Vincendo, Bellevue) for about 9km (follow the signs) until you reach a car park. From there, follow the meandering trail signed L'Eden. After about 20 minutes, you'll discover a wonderfully secluded picnic spot locals wish you hadn't. The views of the coast are incomparable.

people simply walk around the lake, following a well-defined path. It's muddy in places, but shouldn't take more than three hours from the car park, including a side trip to an impressive waterfall.

Takamaka Viewpoint   VIEWPOINT
(Map p260; D53) North of St-Benoît the D53 strikes southwest, following the Rivière des Marsouins 15km upstream to end beside the Takamaka viewpoint. Be prepared to fall on your knees in awe: despite a small power plant near the viewpoint, the overwhelming impression is of a wild, virtually untouched valley, its vertical walls cloaked with impenetrable forests. Here and there the dense green is broken by a ribbon of cascading water.

Forêt Ste-Marguerite   FOREST
(Map p260; Ste-Marguerite; ⊙9am-4pm Tue-Sun) For a complete change of pace and atmosphere, consider spending some time in the protected 159-hectare Forêt Ste-Marguerite, way up in the hills. Fans of flora will get their kicks here; there are over 150 indigenous species of plant. A network of easy walking trails snakes through the quiet forest.

Take the RN3 in the direction of Plaine-des-Palmistes until you reach a roundabout at Chemin Ceinture; Forêt Ste-Marguerite is signed on the left.

🏃 Activities
White-Water Rafting
The Rivière des Marsouins and Rivière des Roches offer magical white-water experiences for both first-time runners and seasoned enthusiasts.

Oasis Eaux Vives   RAFTING
(Map p260; ☑0692 00 16 23; www.oasisev.com; half-day excursions €45-50; ⊙by reservation) A secure rafting operator with loads of experience. It runs half-day rafting trips on the Rivière des Marsouins and Rivière des Roches.

Run Aventures   RAFTING
(Map p260; ☑0262 64 08 22; www.runaventures.com; half-day trips €50-60) Specialises in rafting trips on the Rivière des Marsouins and Rivière des Roches.

Horse Riding
Horse riding is a low-impact way to soak up the drop-dead gorgeous scenery near St-Benoît.

Ferme Équestre du Grand Étang   HORSE RIDING
(☑0262 50 90 03; riconourry@wanadoo.fr; RN3, Pont Payet; half-/full day €55/130; ⊙by reservation) The Ferme Équestre du Grand Étang, just beyond the turn off to Grand Étang, arranges half-day treks to Grand Étang; the full-day trek includes lunch. It's also possible to arrange longer excursions to Bassin Bœuf or Bras Canot (one or two days). Ask for Fanou, who can speak English.

For experienced riders, one-day excursions in the area of Piton de la Fournaise – most notably in the far west-looking Plaine des Sables – are also on offer (€150; horses are transferred by van).

🛏 Sleeping & Eating
There's nowhere to stay in St-Benoît itself, but you'll find a slew of B&Bs in the nearby coastal towns.

St-Benoît has a couple of eating options, but we suggest driving a few kilometres west to Bras Canot, which has a couple of eateries by the Rivière des Marsouins.

Longanis Lodge   VILLA €€
(☑0692 76 84 52; www.longanilodge.com; 95 Chemin Harmonie, Abondance; lodge d/q €110/150; ⊡� 🛜) The Longanis stuns with its design-led architecture and bucolic setting by a river shaded by majestic *longani* trees. The huge villa can accommodate up to six people, so it's a fantastic deal for friends and families. There's no restaurant nearby, but the owner can prepare meals on request (€25). It's possible to reserve for a night or two, but longer stays are preferred.

It's in Abondance, about 5km from St-Benoît (take the road to Takamaka).

OFF THE BEATEN TRACK

ÎLET BETHLÉEM

Very few visitors have heard about Îlet Bethléem (Map p260), a magical spot by the Rivière des Marsouins that locals would like to keep for themselves. Reached after a 15-minute walk from the car park, it features an old chapel (1858) – still a pilgrimage site – and a smattering of picnic shelters amid lush vegetation. It's also an excellent swimming spot, with lots of natural rock pools. Follow the D53 in the direction of Takamaka, then turn left after about 1km (it's signposted).

Unfortunately, the area is sometimes sprinkled with rubbish.

Le Beauvallon   SEAFOOD, CREOLE €€
(Map p260; ☑0262 50 42 92; Rue du Stade Raymond-Arnoux, Rivière des Roches; mains €12-18; ⊙11.30am-2.30pm daily, 6.30-9pm Tue-Sat) Le Beauvallon is well known to everyone in the area, not least for its location beside the mouth of the Rivière des Roches and its seasonal, scrumptious *carri bichiques* (curry made with a sprat-like delicacy). On the flipside, the vast dining room doesn't contain one whit of soul or character. Also does takeaway (€5 to €7).

Le Régal' Est   FRENCH, SEAFOOD €€
(☑0262 97 04 31; 9 Place Raymond Albius, St-Benoît; mains €13-21, menu €16; ⊙11.30am-1.30pm Mon-Sat, 7-8.30pm Fri & Sat) This attractive venture located upstairs in the covered market serves a modern, creative fish and meat menu. Not all the dishes work, though. The lunchtime menu is good value.

★ Les Letchis   CREOLE €€€
(Map p260; ☑0692 66 55 36; www.lesletchis.com; 42 Îlet Danclas, Bras Canot; mains €20-30, weekend menu €38; ⊙11.30am-1.45pm Wed-Sun) Les Letchis boasts a fantastic location in a luxuriant garden by the Rivière des Marsouins. The menu is an ode to Creole classics and 'riverfood'; standouts include *carri bichiques* and braised duck. If you want to explore new culinary territories, try *carri chevaquines* (a curry made from small freshwater prawns) or *carri anguilles* (eel curry). Reservations are advised.

In early 2016, it opened an annex called La Plantation on the same property; it specialises in light meals and snacks.

ℹ Getting There & Away

From St-Benoît a scenic road (the RN3) cuts across the Plaine-des-Palmistes to St-Pierre and St-Louis on the far side of the island. Alternatively, you can continue south along the coast road, passing through Ste-Anne, Ste-Rose, St-Philippe and St-Joseph to reach St-Pierre.

St-Benoît is a major transport hub. Bus services to and from St-Denis run approximately every half-hour (€2, 1¼ hours). There are also two services linking St-Benoît and St-Pierre: line S2 (€2, two hours) follows the RN3 over the Plaine-des-Palmistes; line S1 (€2, 2½ hours) takes the coast road via St-Philippe, St-Joseph and Manapany-les-Bains. More information at www.carjaune.re.

Ste-Anne
POP 3800

About 5km south along the coast from St-Benoît, Ste-Anne is an unpretentious town that's noted for its visually striking church. There's no beach, but if you're in the mood for a dip, there are some enticing natural pools.

◉ Sights & Activities

Église   CHURCH
(Place de l'Église) You can't help but be dazzled by this surprisingly extravagant church that was erected in 1857. The facade of the building is covered in stucco depictions of fruit, flowers and angels. The overall effect is flamboyant rather than tasteful, and is reminiscent of the mestizo architecture of the Andes in South America.

Pont des Anglais   BRIDGE
(Map p260) Between Ste-Anne and Ste-Rose is the graceful Pont des Anglais suspension bridge over the Rivière de l'Est, now bypassed by the main highway but open to pedestrians. It was claimed to be the longest suspension bridge in the world at the time of its construction in the late 19th century.

Bassin Bleu   SWIMMING
(Map p260) If you need to cool off, there's no better place than Bassin Bleu, appropriately dubbed 'the lagoon of the east', at the mouth of a river, on the southern edge of town. It's a superb swimming spot, with crystal-clear water and big boulders. Take a plunge! Note that it's mobbed at weekends.

🛏 Sleeping & Eating

Accommodation options are scarce in the area. If you want to do the east coast in style, consider staying at the Diana Dea Lodge & Spa, which is ranked as one of the most atmospheric ventures in Réunion.

In the mood for a simple Creole or Chinese meal at a few-frills eatery? Perfect, because this is the only option available in town.

⭐ Diana Dea

Lodge & Spa   BOUTIQUE HOTEL €€€
(Map p260; ☑ 0262 20 02 02; www.diana-dea-lodge.re; 94 Chemin Helvetia, Cambourg, Ste-Anne; s €215-315, d €230-330, incl breakfast; P ❄ 🛜 ☲) What a surprise it is to come upon a boutique hotel in such a remote location – Diana Dea Lodge is set high in the hills above Ste-Anne (it's signposted) and is reached after 12km of numerous twists and turns amid cane fields. It's also set apart by its design, which combines wood and stone. Be forewarned: you may never want to leave.

Precious perks include a heated pool, a spa, a bar and a top-notch restaurant (open to nonguests by reservation) – not to mention astounding views of the coast. This is one of those special places that lingers in the mind for its serenity.

Il Etait Une Fois dans l'Est   CREOLE €
(Map p260; ☑ 0692 64 60 11; 133 RN2; mains €6-11; ⊙ 11.30am-2.30pm Sun-Fri) It's not cutting-edge cuisine at this humble place on the main road, but the daily specials are all flawlessly cooked. Don't be put off by the location on the main road; there's a peaceful dining room with sea views at the back.

L'Auberge Créole   CHINESE, CREOLE €€
(☑ 0262 51 10 10; 1 Chemin Case; mains €9-28, menus €20-36; ⊙ 11.30am-2pm Tue-Sun, 6-8pm Tue-Sat) At this respected venue, the menu roves from Creole dishes and *métro* classics to pizzas (evenings only) and Chinese specialities at prices that are more sweet than sour. Pity about the drab, neon-lit interior; take your order to go and eat under *vacoa* trees at Bassin Bleu.

ℹ Information

Tourist Office (☑ 0262 47 05 09; www.est.reunion.fr; Place de l'Église; ⊙ 9am-12.30pm & 1.30-5pm Mon-Sat; 🛜) Has brochures and does bookings for *gîtes de montagne*. Free wi-fi.

ℹ Getting There & Away

Ste-Anne is a stop on the coastal bus route (line S1) from St-Benoît to St-Pierre. More information at www.carjaune.re

Ste-Rose & Around

POP 6800

South of St-Benoît, the landscape becomes more open and less populated as the road hugs the coast around Piton de la Fournaise, the volcano which regularly spews lava down its flanks. The small fishing community of Ste-Rose has its harbour at the inlet of La Marine.

South of Ste-Rose the first tongues of lava from Piton de la Fournaise start to make their appearance. Beyond Anse des Cascades, the main road continues south along the coast, climbs and then drops down to cross the 6km-wide volcanic plain known as Le Grand Brûlé.

⊙ Sights

At the picturesque **harbour** you'll see a **monument** to the young English commander Corbett, who was killed in 1809 during a naval battle against the French off the coast.

Further south you'll reach **La Cayenne**, which has a superb picnic area scenically perched on a cliff overlooking the ocean – well worth a pause.

Notre Dame des Laves   CHURCH
(Map p260; Piton Ste-Rose) The lava flow from a 1977 eruption went through Piton Ste-Rose, split when it came to the church and reformed again on the other side. Many people see the church's escape as a miracle of divine intervention. A wooden log 'washed up' by the lava now forms the lectern inside the church, while the stained-glass windows depict various stages of the eruption. It's about 4.5km south of Ste-Rose.

Anse des Cascades   BAY
(Map p260) This scenic *anse* (bay) is beside the sea about 3km south of Piton Ste-Rose. The water from the hills drops dramatically into the sea near a traditional little fishing harbour. The coconut grove is splendid and is a hugely popular picnic spot, and there's a well-frequented restaurant close to the shore.

RÉUNION STE-ROSE & AROUND

Bananaland – Domaine d'Aldachris FARM
(Map p260; ☑0262 53 49 74; 371ter RN2, Piton Ste-Rose; €4; ☺9am-4pm Sun-Thu) Just north of Piton Ste-Rose is this family-run operation where you can visit a banana plantation and buy various banana products, including delicious jam, to-die-for cakes and different varieties of exceptionally sweet bananas. Everything is homemade and organic.

🛏 Sleeping

⭐ **Matilona** B&B €
(☑0692 85 86 86; http://matilona.monsite-orange. fr; 84 Chemin du Petit Brûlé, Ste-Rose; d/studio incl breakfast €65/70; Ⓟ❋🛜🏊) You wouldn't guess from outside, but this B&B housed in a converted supermarket (yes!) is a great find. Push the door open and you're in another reality: five simple yet inviting rooms and two studios with modern bathrooms, generously sized communal areas and a seductive garden overflowing with colourful plants. And a killer pool. Dinner (€30) is available three days a week.

Monsieur is a former chef, so you can expect to eat well. There's also a kitchen for guests' use. Prices drop by €5 if you stay two nights or more. Brilliant value.

Le Joyau des Laves INN €
(Map p260; ☑0262 47 34 00; 474ter RN2, Piton Ste-Rose; d €43-53, mains €12-18, menus €15-28; ☺restaurant noon-2pm Wed-Mon; Ⓟ🛜) On a headland 7km south of Ste-Rose, this friendly inn has three plain rooms. The more expensive one is spacious and blessed with great sea views. Even if you're not staying, it's worth phoning ahead to eat in the restaurant and try local specialities such as palm hearts and *baba figues* (banana flowers) from the surrounding gardens. Breakfast is extra (€5).

La Fournaise HOTEL €
(☑0262 47 03 40; www.hotellafournaise.fr; 154 RN2, Ste-Rose; d €64-69; Ⓟ❋🛜🏊) There's a fresh feel in this modernish venture on the main road. Spruce rooms, shiny-clean toilets, an on-site restaurant (*menu* €20) and a pool are the order of the day here. The catch? It's sorely lacking in charm. Go for a room with a sea view; the cheaper ones at the back overlook the parking lot. Note that the restaurant is open for dinner only.

Ferme-Auberge La Cayenne B&B €
(☑0262 47 23 46; www.ferme-auberge-lacayenne. fr; 317 Ravine Glissante; d incl breakfast €57; Ⓟ🛜) This well-established guesthouse scores points for its location: it's perched above the sea, 1.5km south of Ste-Rose. The six rooms are small and utilitarian but the views of the swishing indigo waters from the balcony are nothing short of charming. One quibble: there's no air-con. The owner, Madame Narayanin, cooks beautifully (dinner €27), using mostly home-grown ingredients.

Let the breeze tickle your skin while you eat authentic Indian and Creole cuisine alfresco on the covered terrace.

Cana Suc BUNGALOW €€
(☑0692 77 81 96; www.canasuc.re; 219 RN2, Ste-Rose; d incl breakfast €90, bungalow q Fri & Sat/3 weekday nights €250/240; Ⓟ🛜) This is an adorable nest with a row of three well-designed Creole bungalows opening onto expansive lawns. One unit is a *chambre d'hôtes*, while the two other ones are fully-equipped *gîtes* that are rented for longer stays. Tip: if you book a *gîte* during the week, it will cost you only €240 for three nights (€250 if you stay on Friday and Saturday). Wi-fi is available near the owner's house at breakfast time.

🍴 Eating

As everywhere along Réunion's east coast, the dining scene is pretty tame. You'll find a few eateries serving good Creole staples in the vicinity of Notre-Dame des Laves church. If you stay at a B&B or at the only hotel in town, dinner is available on request.

Le Kedaï CHINESE, CREOLE €
(☑0692 11 60 48; 205 RN2; mains €6-9; ☺10.30am-2pm daily, 6-9pm Wed-Mon) You'll find solid Chinese and Creole fare and heaping portions at this no-frills joint on the main thoroughfare. It doles out sandwiches (from €3), curries, noodles, pork and chicken dishes, prawns and pizzas. Good fruit juices, too. Takeaway is available. Oh, and it's open in the evening – an exception on the east coast!

Le Métis CREOLE €
(Map p260; ☑0692 57 77 33; 378bis RN2, Piton Ste-Rose; mains €9-12; ☺11.30am-2.30pm & 6.30-9pm Wed-Mon) If you're looking for a quick food fix, check out the options at this cheap-and-cheerful eatery opposite Notre Dame des Laves church. It specialises in Creole classics. Takeaway is available (€5 to €7).

Snack Chez Louiso FAST FOOD €
(☑0262 47 26 57; 46 Chemin de la Marine, Ste-Rose; sandwiches €2-3, mains €5-10; ☺11am-3pm Tue-Sun) Chez Louiso is a modest open-air eatery overlooking the harbour. The menu is limited

to sandwiches and a couple of daily specials, but they're well prepared and sizzling-hot value. Grab a (plastic) table and soak up the great ocean views.

Restaurant Le Corail CREOLE €€
(Map p260; ☑0262 23 75 36; RN2, Piton Ste-Rose; mains €12-15; ⊙9.30am-3pm) About 300m south of Notre Dame des Laves church, this colourful Creole house is your spot for Creole curries and stews. There's an inviting terrace but it overlooks the main road – expect some traffic noise during the day. Your best bet is to take away (€6 to €8) – you'll find plenty of atmospheric spots along the coast.

Restaurant des Cascades CREOLE, SEAFOOD €€
(Map p260; ☑0262 47 20 42; Anse des Cascades; mains €12-25, menus €17-25; ⊙noon-3pm Sat-Thu) A local and tourist favourite, this beach restaurant in a lovely coconut grove bursts to the seams on weekends. It serves fresh fish and Creole dishes as well as meat grills and a lovely palm-heart salad. The lunch buffet (€12, starters and mains) served on weekdays is brilliant value.

Nab a seat if it's not too busy, otherwise take your order to go and enjoy it in a quieter spot near the beach.

ℹ Getting There & Away

Buses running from St-Benoît to St-Pierre (line S1) make handy stops near Notre Dame des Laves and Anse des Cascades. More information at www.carjaune.re.

UNDERSTAND RÉUNION

Réunion Today

Réunion is one of the richest islands in the Indian Ocean. The standard of living is fairly high, and it's no surprise. As a French *département* (a French overseas territory), the island receives a lot of financial support from mainland France *(la métropole)*. Despite this assistance, Réunion faces numerous challenges as it grapples with finding housing and job opportunities for its expanding population without compromising what makes the island so special – its extraordinary natural riches.

The New Coastal Road

This is the biggest infrastructure project in Europe (yes, Europe). After much controversy, the construction of the Nouvelle Route du Littoral has begun. This engineering feat involves the building of a new coastal highway between St-Denis and La Grande Chaloupe (north of St-Paul). The masterpiece of these herculean works is a 5400m-long offshore viaduct along the coastline. Currently, the existing Route du Littoral, the key artery connecting the capital to the northwest, is often closed due to landslides, causing mayhem for its estimated 60,000 daily motorists. With an estimated project-completion date of 2020 (and budget of €1.6 billion), these huge civil engineering works are expected to reduce congestion and sustain growth on the island but face strong opposition on fiscal and environmental grounds.

The Shark Crisis

In less than eight years, Réunion has earned the grim distinction of being one of the most active shark-attack zones in the world. Since 2011, there have been 18 shark attacks around the island resulting in seven deaths (five surfers and two swimmers). All attacks occurred along the west coast, between Boucan Canot and L'Étang-Salé-les-Bains. This resulted in a major crisis and lots of tension between the surfing community, local environmentalists and the local government about what measures should be taken. Finally, swimming and surfing have been banned around the island in all but a few places. By early 2016, two beaches devoid of barrier reefs – one in Boucan Canot and one in St-Gilles-les-Bains – were equipped with shark nets. In March 2016, surfers started to return to some of their favourite spots.

Tourism in the Doldrums

Tourism is a major source of income and a key economic sector in Réunion, but the island largely stays under the radar. While elsewhere in the Indian Ocean (especially in Mauritius and the Seychelles) tourism thrives, Réunion's 2014 stats fell to equal those of 2006 (around 405,000), despite the fact that 40% of the island was designated a Natural World Heritage Site in 2010. This prestigious recognition has fostered high hopes but has not been synonymous with a higher influx of foreign tourists. The vast majority of visitors are French. There's a huge potential for growth – experts say that one million tourists per year could be an easy target – but there are a few hurdles: despite some publicity campaigns, Réunion remains underpromoted in Anglophone markets; English is not widely spoken on the island; the cost of flights is still prohibitive; and the lack of direct flights to European cities (bar Paris) is problematic – not to mention the negative publicity following the fatal shark attacks over the last few years. While visitors won't complain about the uncrowded beaches and world-class mountainscapes, boosting tourism remains a key economic hurdle for the island.

Structural Unemployment

Unemployment is Réunion's number-one problem, with the unemployment rate currently hovering around 28% (60% among people aged between 15 and 24), way above the national average (about 10%). It's particularly problematic for women and young people without qualifications. This situation has led to simmering social unrest, peaking in a series of riots in Le Port in February 2012 and February 2013. Strikes – to put pressure on local government and employers and avoid job cuts – are common in the private sector. On an island with a rapidly increasing population and limited resources, the extent and persistence of local unemployment is a major challenge and solutions have yet to be found. Many Réunionnais have to leave their island to find a job in France. Small wonder that the construction of the Nouvelle Route du Littoral, a mammoth infrastructure project, is seen as an effective way to create jobs on the island.

An Ever-Growing Population

Estimates suggest that the population of Réunion will reach one million by 2030. With high levels of unemployment and an ever-growing population, the island is set for some fundamental challenges and housing is emerging as one of them. Already there is tremendous pressure on land available for building. Most of the population is concentrated on the coastal strip, where the towns are gradually beginning to merge into one continuous urban 'ring'. Houses are also spreading slowly up the hillsides and traffic congestion is becoming a major headache. While the behemoth Route du Littoral construction project will ease some pressure off unemployment and congestion (eventually), Réunion needs to find sustainable, long-term solutions to these challenges.

History

Both specks in the Indian Ocean, Réunion and Mauritius share a similar, fascinating history. An uninhabited island, Réunion was colonised by the French after the mid-17th century but later fell briefly under British rule. As in Mauritius, the colonisers introduced plantation crops and African slaves. Later came Indian indentured labourers and Chinese merchants, creating an ethnic diversity which is one of these islands' most distinctive characteristics. While Mauritius gained its independence in 1968, Réunion remains an overseas department of France.

Welcome to Paradise

The first visitors to the uninhabited island were probably Malay, Arab and European mariners, none of whom stayed. Then, in 1642, the French took the decision to settle the island, which at the time was called Mascarin. The first settlers arrived four years later, when the French governor of Fort Dauphin in southern Madagascar banished a dozen mutineers to the island.

On the basis of enthusiastic reports from the mutineers, King Louis XIV of France officially claimed the island in 1649 and renamed it Île Bourbon, after Colbert Bourbon, who had founded the French East India Company.

However appealing it seemed, there was no great rush to populate and develop the island. It was not until the beginning of the 18th century that the French East India Company and the French government took control of the island.

Coffee Anyone?

Coffee was introduced between 1715 and 1730 and soon became the island's main cash crop. The island's economy changed dramatically. As coffee required intensive labour, African and Malagasy slaves were brought by the shipload. During this period, cereals, spices and cotton were also introduced as cash crops.

Like Mauritius, Réunion came of age under the governorship of the visionary Mahé de Labourdonnais, who served from 1735 to 1746. However, Labourdonnais treated Île de France (Mauritius) as a favoured sibling, and after the collapse of the French East India Company and the pressure of ongoing rivalry with Britain the governance of Île Bourbon passed directly to the French crown in 1764.

> ## BLACK HISTORY
>
> The late 18th century saw a number of slave revolts, and many resourceful Malagasy and African slaves, called *marrons*, escaped from their owners and took refuge in the mountainous interior. Some of them established private utopias in inaccessible parts of the Cirques, while others grouped together and formed organised communities with democratically elected leaders. These tribal chieftains were the true pioneers of the settlement of Réunion, but most ultimately fell victim to bounty hunters who were employed to hunt them down. The scars of this period of the island's history are still fresh in the population's psyche; perhaps from a sense of shame, there's surprisingly little record of the island's Creole pioneers except the names of several peaks (Dimitile, Enchaing, Mafate, Cimendef) where they were hunted down and killed.

A Brief British Interlude

The formerly productive coffee plantations were destroyed by cyclones very early in the 19th century, and in 1810, during the Napoleonic Wars, Bonaparte lost the island to the *habits rouges* (redcoats). Under British rule, sugar cane was introduced to Réunion and quickly became the primary crop. The vanilla industry, introduced in 1819, also grew rapidly. They didn't stay long: just five years later, under the Treaty of Paris, the spoil was returned to the French as Île Bourbon. The British, however, retained their grip on Mauritius, Rodrigues and the Seychelles.

The French Return

In 1848 the Second Republic was proclaimed in France, slavery was abolished and Île Bourbon again became La Réunion. At the time, the island had a population of over 100,000 people, mostly freed slaves. Like Mauritius, Réunion immediately experienced a labour crisis and, like the British in Mauritius, the French 'solved' the problem by importing contract labourers from India, most of them Hindus, to work the sugar cane.

Réunion's golden age of trade and development lasted until 1870, with the country flourishing on the trade route between Europe, India and the Far East. Competition from Cuba and the European sugar-beet industry, combined with the opening of the Suez Canal (which short-circuited the journey around the Cape of Good Hope), resulted in an economic slump: shipping decreased, the sugar industry declined, and land and capital were further concentrated in the hands of a small French elite. Some small planters brightened their prospects by turning to geranium oil.

After WWI, in which 14,000 Réunionnais served, the sugar industry regained a bit of momentum, but it again suffered badly through the blockade of the island during WWII.

Réunion Becomes a DOM

Réunion became a Département Français d'Outre-Mer (DOM; French Overseas Department) in 1946 and has representation in the French parliament. Since then there have been feeble independence movements from time to time but, unlike those in France's Pacific territories, these have never amounted to much. While the Réunionnais seemed satisfied to remain totally French, general economic and social discontent surfaced in dramatic anti-government riots in St-Denis in 1991.

The turn of the century marked a new era for Réunion; the local authorities managed to sign a few agreements with the French state, which confirmed the launching of subsidised *grands chantiers* (major infrastructure works), including the expressway called the Route des Tamarins and the Nouvelle Route du Littoral (a new expressway between St-Paul and St-Denis). So far, only the Route des Tamarins has been completed.

Culture

Réunion is often cited as an example of racial and religious harmony, and compared with mainland France it is. While Marine Le Pen's far-right party wins 27% to 30% of national vote, it doesn't exceed 3% in Réunion. Not that it's all hunky-dory. Réunion suffers from the same problems of a disaffected younger generation as in mainland Europe. But on the whole it's a society that lives very easily together, and the Réunionnais are quietly but justifiably proud of what they have achieved.

Daily Life

Contemporary Réunionnais are a thoroughly 21st-century people. The vast majority of children receive a decent standard of education and all islanders have access to the national health system, either in Réunion or in France. There are traffic jams, everyone is on a mobile (cell) phone, and flashy cars are ubiquitous. But beneath this modern veneer, there are many more traditional aspects.

One of the strongest bonds unifying society, after the Creole language, is the importance placed on family life. It's particularly made evident at the *pique-nique du dimanche en famille* (Sunday family picnic). Religious occasions and public holidays are also vigorously celebrated, as are more personal family events, such as baptisms, first communions and weddings.

Though Réunion can't be mistaken for, say, Ibiza, Réunionnais share a zest for the fest. On weekends St-Gilles-les-Bains, L'Hermitage-les-Bains and St-Pierre are a magnet for Réunionnais from all over the island. The towns turn wild on those evenings as flocks of night owls arrive en masse to wiggle their hips and guzzle pints of Dodo beer and glasses of rum.

On a more mundane level, you'll quickly realise that the possession of a brand-new car is a sign of wealth and respect. The 'car culture' is a dominant trait; small wonder that traffic jams are the norm on the coastal roads. Many Réunionnais spend up to two hours daily in their car going to and from work! One favourite topic of conversation is the state of the roads, especially the tricky Route du Littoral between St-Paul and St-Denis, which is sometimes closed due to fallen rocks.

SUNDAY PICNIC: A RÉUNIONNAIS INSTITUTION

At the weekend there's nothing the Réunionnais like better than trundling off to the seaside or the mountains for a huge family picnic – think giant-sized rice cookers replete with hearty *carris* (curries) in the company of *gramounes* (grandparents) and *marmailles* (children). To get the most sought-after picnic shelters, some members of the family sometimes arrive at 4am to reserve them! Visitors are welcome, and are usually invited to share a meal.

Another noticeable (though less immediately so) characteristic is the importance of *la di la fé* (gossip). If you can understand a little bit of French (or Creole), tune in to Radio Free Dom (www.freedom.fr) – you'll soon realise that gossip is a national pastime.

Despite the social problems that blight any culture, on the whole it's a society that lives very easily together.

Population

Cultural diversity forms an integral part of the island's social fabric. Réunion has the same population mix of Africans, Europeans, Indians and Chinese as Mauritius, but in different proportions. Cafres (people of African ancestry) are the largest ethnic group, comprising about 45% of the population. Malbars (Hindu Indians) comprise about 25% of the population, white Creoles (people of French ancestry) 15%, Europeans (also known as Zoreilles) 7%, Chinese 4% and Z'arabes (Muslim Indians) 4%.

The bulk of the island's population lives in coastal zones, with Malbars living predominantly in the east. The rugged interior is sparsely populated. Because the birth rate has remained quite high, a third of the population is under 20 years of age.

Réunion also sees a continual tide of would-be immigrants. With a system of generous welfare payments for the unemployed, the island is seen as a land of milk and honey by those from Mauritius, the Seychelles and some mainland African countries. In recent years there has been significant immigration from the neighbouring Comoros and Mayotte Islands.

Gender Equality

Réunion is refreshingly liberal and equality between the sexes is the widely accepted norm. Divorce, abortion and childbirth outside marriage are all fairly uncontentious issues. However, it's not all rosy: women are poorly represented in local government and politics, and domestic violence is prevalent. This is closely connected to high rates of alcoholism.

Religion

An estimated 70% of the population belongs to the Catholic faith, which dominates the island's religious character. It's evidenced in the many saints' days and holidays, as well as

THE ODD CULT OF ST EXPÉDIT

You can't miss them. Red shrines honouring St Expédit are scattered all over the island, including on roadsides. St Expédit is one of Réunion's most popular saints, though some scholars argue there never was a person called Expédit. Whatever the truth, the idea was brought to Réunion in 1931 when a local woman erected a statue of the 'saint' in St-Denis' Notre-Dame de la Délivrance church in thanks for answering her prayer to return to Réunion. Soon there were shrines all over the island, where people prayed for his help in the speedy resolution of all sorts of tricky problems.

Over the years, however, worship of the saint has taken on the sinister overtones of a voodoo cult: figurines stuck with pins are left at the saint's feet; beheaded statues of him are perhaps the result of unanswered petitions. The saint has also been adopted into the Hindu faith, which accounts for the brilliant, blood-red colour of many shrines. As a result the Catholic Church has tried to distance itself from the cult, but the number of shrines continues to grow.

in the names of towns and cities. Religious rituals and rites of passage play an important part in the lives of the people, and baptisms, first communions and church weddings are an integral part of social culture.

About a quarter of Réunionnais are Hindus, which is the dominant faith in the east. Traditional Hindu rites such as *teemeedee,* which features fire-walking, and *cavadee,* which for pilgrims entails piercing the cheeks with skewers, often take place. Muslims make up roughly 2% of the population; as in Mauritius, Islam tends to be fairly liberal.

Interestingly, a great deal of syncretism between Hinduism, Islam and Catholicism has evolved over the years. In fact, many of the Malbar-Réunionnais participate in both Hindu and Catholic rites and rituals.

Apart from celebrating the Chinese New Year, the Sino-Réunionnais community (making up about 3% of the population) is not very conspicuous in its religious or traditional practices.

Religious tolerance is the norm. Mosques, churches, Hindu temples and pagodas can be found within a stone's throw of each other in most towns.

Arts

One of the greatest pleasures of visiting Réunion is experiencing Creole-flavoured French culture or French-flavoured Creole culture, depending on how you look at it. For news of cultural activities on the island, keep an eye on the local press and visit local tourist offices, where you can pick up flyers, theatre programs and a number of free events guides such as the monthly *Azenda* (www.azenda.re).

Literature

Few Réunionnais novelists are known outside the island and none are translated into English. One of the most widely recognised and prolific contemporary authors is the journalist and historian Daniel Vaxelaire. His *Chasseurs de Noires,* an easily accessible tale of a slave-hunter's life-changing encounter with an escaped slave, is probably the best to start with.

Jean-François Samlong, a novelist and poet who helped relaunch Creole literature in the 1970s, also takes slavery as his theme. *Madame Desbassayns* was inspired by the remarkable life story of a sugar baroness.

Other well-established novelists to look out for are Axel Gauvin, Jules Bénard, Jean Lods and Monique Agénor.

Music & Dance

Réunion's music mixes the African rhythms of reggae, *séga* (traditional slave music) and *maloya* with French, British and American rock and folk sounds. Like *séga, maloya* is derived from the music of the slaves, but it is slower and more reflective, its rhythms and words heavy with history, somewhat like New Orleans blues; fans say it carries the true spirit of Réunion. *Maloya* songs often carry a political message and up until the 1970s the music was banned for being too subversive.

Instruments used to accompany *séga* and *maloya* range from traditional homemade percussion pieces, such as the hide-covered *rouleur* drum and the maraca-like *kayamb,* to the accordion and modern band instruments.

The giants of the local music scene, and increasingly well known in mainland France, are Danyel Waro, Firmin Viry, Granmoun Lélé (deceased), Davy Sicard, Kaf Malbar and the group Ziskakan. More recently, women have also emerged on the musical scene, including Christine Salem and Nathalie Nathiembé. All

KABARS

If you're passionate about Creole music, try to attend a *kabar*. A *kabar* is a kind of impromptu concert or ball that is usually held in a courtyard or on the beach, where musicians play *maloya* (traditional dance music of Réunion). It's usually organised by associations, informal groups or families, but outsiders are welcome. There's no schedule; *kabars* are usually advertised by means of word of mouth, flyers or small ads in the newspapers. You can also enquire at the bigger tourist offices.

are superb practitioners of *maloya*. Favourite subjects for them are slavery, poverty and the search for cultural identity.

As for Creole-flavoured modern grooves, the Réunionnais leave those to their tropical cousins in Martinique and Guadeloupe, although they make for popular listening in Réunion. It's all catchy stuff, and you'll hear it in bars, discos and vehicles throughout the islands of the Indian Ocean.

Architecture

The distinctive 18th-century Creole architecture of Réunion is evident in both the grand villas built by wealthy planters and other *colons* (settlers/colonists) and in the *ti' cases*, the homes of the common folk.

Local authorities are actively striving to preserve the remaining examples of Creole architecture around the island. You can see a number of beautifully restored houses in St-Denis and in the towns of Cilaos, Entre-Deux, Hell-Bourg and St-Pierre, among other places. They all sport *lambrequins* (filigree-style decorations), *varangues* (verandas) and other ornamental features.

Food & Drink

Réunion is a culinary delight: thanks to a mix of influences and prime fresh ingredients (plentiful seafood, succulent meat, spices, aromatic plants, and fruit and vegetables bursting with flavour), you're certain to eat well wherever you go. There's a balanced melange of French cuisine (locally known as *cuisine métro*) and Creole specialities and flavours, not to mention Indian and Chinese influences.

Staples & Specialities

It's impossible to visit Réunion without coming across *carri* (curry), which features on practically every single menu. The sauce comprises tomatoes, onions, garlic, ginger, thyme and saffron (or turmeric) and accompanies various kinds of meat, such as chicken *(carri poulet)*, pork *(carri porc)* and duck *(carri canard)*. Seafood *carris*, such as tuna *(carri thon)*, swordfish *(carri espadon)*, lobster *(carri langouste)* and freshwater prawn *(carri camarons)* are also excellent. Octopus curry, one of the best you'll eat, is called *civet zourite* in Creole. Local vegetables can also be prepared *carri*-style – try *carri baba figue* (banana-flower *carri*) and *carri ti jaque* (jackfruit *carri*) – but they incorporate fish or meat. *Carris* are invariably served with rice, *grains* (lentils or haricot beans), *brèdes* (local spinach) and *rougail*, a spicy chutney that mixes tomato, garlic, ginger and chillies; other preparations of *rougail* may include a mixture of green mango and citrus. *Rougail saucisse* (sausages cooked in tomato sauce), served with rice and vegetables, is a Creole favourite. A common Tamil stew is *cabri massalé* (goat *carri*).

Seafood lovers will be delighted to hear that the warm waters of the Indian Ocean provide an ample net of produce: lobster, prawns, *légine* (toothfish), swordfish, marlin, tuna and shark, among others. Freshwater prawns, usually served in *carri*, are highly prized.

Snacks include samosas, *beignets* (fritters) and *bonbons piments* (chilli fritters).

WHERE TO EAT

Réunion has a fine range of eating options, and it's not necessary to book except on weekends. Dinners served at B&Bs should be booked the day before.

Restaurants The mainstay of Réunionnais dining and you're never far from one.

Tables d'hôte Home-cooked meals served at B&Bs.

Cafes Very popular in St-Denis and St-Pierre.

Takeaway outlets Serve cheap Creole staples.

Markets The best places to stock up on fresh fruits and vegetables.

BREAKFASTS

Breakfast is decidedly French: *pain-beurre-confiture* (baguette, butter and jam) served with coffee, tea or hot chocolate is the most common threesome. Added treats may include croissants, *pain au chocolat* (chocolate-filled pastry), brioches and honey.

DESSERTS

Desserts are equally exciting, with tropical fruit pies and jams, exotic sorbets and ice creams. If you like carb-laden cakes, you'll be happy. Each family has its own recipe for *gâteaux maison* (homemade cakes), which come in various guises. They are usually made from vanilla, banana, sweet potato, maize, carrot, guava... One favourite is *macatia* (a variety of bun), which can also be served at breakfast. You'll also find plenty of patisseries selling croissants and pastries. Baguettes can be bought from every street corner.

FRUITS

Fruits reign supreme in Réunion. Two iconic Réunionnais fruits are *litchis* (lychees) and *ananas Victoria* (pineapple of the Victoria variety). Local mangoes, passionfruit and papaya are also fabulously sweet. The local vanilla is said to be one of the most flavoursome in the world.

Vegetarians & Vegans

Vegetarians won't go hungry. Réunionnais love vegetables, eating them in salads or in gratins (a baked dish). You'll certainly come across *chou chou* (choko; a speciality in the Cirque de Salazie), lentils (a speciality in the Cirque de Cilaos), *bois de songe* (a local vegetable that looks like a leek) and *vacoa* (screw-pine fronds), not to mention *bring-elles* (aubergines) and *baba figue* (banana flower). Salads, rice and fruits are ubiquitous. In Chinese restaurants, menus feature vegetarian dishes, such as chop suey and noodles. Most supermarkets have vegetarian fare too, and *chambre d'hôte* owners will be happy to cook vegetarian dishes if you let them know well in advance.

Drinks

Rum, rum, rum! Up in the hills, almost everyone will have their own family recipe for *rhum arrangé*, a heady mixture of local rum and a secret blend of herbs and spices. In fact, not all are that secret. Popular concoctions include *rhum faham*, a blend of rum, sugar

---

DARE TO TRY

If you're a gastronomic adventurer, start your culinary odyssey with *salade de palmiste*, a delectable salad made from the bud of the palmiste palm tree, known as the 'heart of palm'. The palm dies once the bud is removed, earning this wasteful salad delicacy the title 'millionaire's salad'. For something a bit more unusual, try *carri bichiques* (curry made with a sprat-like delicacy), which is dubbed *le caviar réunionnais* (Réunionnais caviar). You might need to seek out *larves de guêpes* (wasps' larvae), another local delicacy that is available from April to October. Fried and salted, they reputedly increase sexual stamina.

You may also want to learn the terms for *carri pat' cochons* (pig's trotter *carri*) and *carri anguilles* (eel *carri*) so you don't accidentally order them in a restaurant. Réunionnais also drool over *carri tang* (tenrec curry, a small Malagasy hedgehog-like creature), which you're not likely to find served in restaurants.

---

and flowers from the faham orchid; *rhum vanille*, made from rum, sugar and fresh vanilla pods; and *rhum bibasse*, made from rum, sugar and tasty *bibasse* (medlar fruit). The family *rhum arrangé* is a source of pride for most Creoles; if you stay in any of the rural *gîtes* or *chambres d'hôtes* you can expect the proprietor to serve up their version with more than a little ceremony.

Réunion being French territory, wine is unsurprisingly taken seriously. Along with French wines, you'll find a good choice of South African reds and whites. The island also has a small viniculture in Cilaos, where you can do a tasting.

The local brand of beer, Bourbon (known as Dodo), is sold everywhere. It is a fairly light, very drinkable beer. Another local beer is the Picaro, which comes as a pale ale and an amber ale. Foreign beers are also available. For a refresher, nothing beats a fresh fruit juice or a glass of Cilaos, a high-quality sparkling water from Cirque de Cilaos.

The French take their coffee seriously and it's a passion that hasn't disappeared just because they're now in the Indian Ocean. A cup of coffee can take various forms but the most common is a small, black espresso called simply *un café*.

Environment

Réunion lies about 220km southwest of Mauritius, at the southernmost end of the great Mascareignes volcanic chain. Réunion's volcano, Piton de la Fournaise, erupts with great regularity, spewing lava down its southern and eastern flanks. The last major eruption occurred in 2015, with almost 2½ months of continuous volcanic activity.

The Land

There are two major mountainous areas on Réunion. The older of the two covers most of the western half of the island. The highest mountain is Piton des Neiges (3071m), an alpine-class peak. Surrounding it are three immense and splendid amphitheatres: the Cirques of Cilaos, Mafate and Salazie. These long, wide, deep hollows are sheer-walled canyons filled with convoluted peaks and valleys, the eroded remnants of the ancient volcanic shield that surrounded Piton des Neiges.

The smaller of the two mountainous regions lies in the southeast and continues to evolve. It comprises several extinct volcanic cones and one that is still very much alive, Piton de la Fournaise (2632m). This rumbling peak still pops its cork relatively frequently in spectacular fashion. In 2007 lava flows reached the sea and added another few square metres to the island. Since 1998 there have been spectacular eruptions almost every second year – attractions in their own right. No one lives in the shadow of the volcano, where lava flowing down to the shore has left a remarkable jumbled slope of cooled black volcanic rock, known as Le Grand Brûlé.

These two mountainous areas are separated by a region of high plains, while the coast is defined by a gently sloping plain which varies in width. Numerous rivers wind their way down from the Piton des Neiges range, through the Cirques, cutting deeply into the coastal plains to form spectacular ravines.

Wildlife

ANIMALS

The mammals which you are likely to see are introduced hares, deer, geckoes, rats and, if you're lucky, chameleons. Tenrecs (called *tang* in Creole), which resemble hedgehogs, are a species introduced from Madagascar.

The most interesting creepy crawlies are the giant millipedes – some as long as a human foot – which loll around beneath

THE SEOR

You'll find information on local birds and where to spot them on the website of the Société d'Études Ornithologiques de la Réunion (SEOR; www.seor.fr), an organisation working to save some of the island's rarest species.

rocks in more humid areas. Other oversized creatures are the yellow-and-black *Nephila* spiders whose massive webs are a common sight. You'll also find the *Heteropoda venatoria* or huntsman spider, called *babouk* in Creole.

As far as bird life is concerned, of the original 30 species endemic to the island, only nine remain. The island's rarest birds are the *merle blanc* (cuckoo shrike) – locals call it the *tuit tuit*, for obvious reasons – and the black petrel. Probably the best chance of seeing – or, more likely, hearing – the *tuit tuit* is directly south of St-Denis, near the foot of La Roche Écrite.

Bulbuls, which resemble blackbirds (with yellow beaks and legs but grey feathers) and are locally known as *merles,* are also common. Birds native to the highlands include the *tec-tec* or Réunion stonechat, which inhabits the tamarind forests. There's also the *papangue* (Maillardi buzzard), a protected hawk-like bird which begins life as a little brown bird and turns black and white as it grows older. It is Réunion's only surviving bird of prey and may be spotted soaring over the ravines.

The best-known seabird is the white *paille-en-queue* (white-tailed tropicbird), which sports two long tail plumes.

Mynahs, introduced at the end of the 18th century to keep the grasshoppers under control, are common all over the island, as are the small, red cardinal-like birds known as fodies.

The best spots to see bird life are the Forêt de Bébour-Bélouve above Hell-Bourg, and the wilderness region of Le Grand Brûlé at the southern tip of the island.

PLANTS

Thanks to an abundant rainfall and marked differences in altitude, Réunion boasts some of the most varied plant life in the world. Parts of the island are like a grand botanical garden. Between the coast and the alpine peaks you'll find palms, screw pines (also known as pandanus or *vacoa*), casuarinas *(fi-laos)*, vanilla, spices, other tropical fruit and vegetable crops, rainforest and alpine flora.

Réunion has no less than 700 indigenous plant species, 150 of which are trees. Unlike Mauritius, large areas of natural forest still remain. It's estimated that 30% of the island is covered by native forest.

Gnarled and twisted and sporting yellow, mimosa-like flowers, the *tamarin des Hauts* (mountain tamarind tree) is a type of acacia and is endemic to Réunion. One of the best places to see these ancient trees is in the Forêt de Bébour-Bélouve, east of the Cirque de Salazie.

At the other extreme, the lava fields around the volcano exhibit a barren, moon-like surface. Here the various stages of vegetation growth, from a bare new lava base, are evident. The first plant to appear on lava is the heather-like plant the French call *branle vert (Philippia montana)*. Much later in the growth cycle come tamarind and other acacia trees.

Afforestation has been carried out mainly with the Japanese cryptomeria, *tamarin des Hauts,* casuarina and various palms.

Like any tropical island, Réunion has a wealth of flowering species, including orchid, hibiscus, bougainvillea, vetiver, geranium, frangipani and jacaranda.

National Parks

It is estimated that nearly a third of the 25km-long lagoon along the west coast from Boucan Canot south to Trois Bassins has already suffered damage from a variety of causes: sedimentation, agricultural and domestic pollution, cyclones, fishing and swimmers. To prevent the situation deteriorating further, a marine park was set up in 1997. In addition to educating local people on the need to keep the beaches and the water clean, marine biologists have been working with local fishers and various water-sports operators to establish protection zones. A fully fledged nature reserve – the Réserve Naturelle Marine de la Réunion (www.reservemarinereunion.fr) – was created in 2007.

Part of the interior of the island is protected too. The Parc National des Hauts de la Réunion (www.reunion-parcnational.fr) was established in early 2007, resulting in half of Réunion's total land area now being under protection. There's a tightly regulated core area of 1000 sq km, including the volcano,

the mountain peaks and the areas around Mafate and Grand Bassin, surrounded by a buffer zone of some 700 sq km to encompass most of the ravines.

Environmental Issues

The central problem confronting Réunion is how to reconcile environmental preservation with a fast-growing population in need of additional housing, roads, jobs, electricity, water and recreational space.

Despite the establishment of the Parc National des Hauts de la Réunion and the Réserve Naturelle Marine de la Réunion, the island is facing major issues, all related to two massive engineering works. The 'smaller' is the Route des Tamarins, which was completed in 2009. This 34km expressway that slices across the hills above St-Gilles-les-Bains required numerous bridges over the ravines. According to local environmentalists, the road cut across the only remaining savannah habitat on the island.

The second major engineering project is the Nouvelle Route du Littoral (new coastal highway). Taking seven years to complete, this expressway will link capital Saint-Denis to La Possession and will be built on columns rising out of the ocean. The scheme has been met with anger by environmentalists, who claim that such major infrastructure works will have a negative impact on marine life. They have started to file lawsuits to derail the project. However, local authorities claim this project is vital for the economy and development of the island.

RÉUNION ENVIRONMENT

SURVIVAL GUIDE

ℹ Directory A–Z

ACCOMMODATION

It's wise to book well in advance, particularly in high season (the mainland France and local school holidays, particularly July, August and from mid-December to mid-January). If you're planning a hiking trip in September, October or November, it's also imperative to book *gîtes de montagne* as early as possible.

Hotels Range from two-star ventures to a few luxury resorts.

Gîtes Range from basic mountain lodges to more comfortable options.

B&Bs These small, family-run houses provide good value. More luxurious versions are more like a boutique hotel.

Meublés de Tourisme A great choice for self-caterers.

Camping

Bad news for those who want to spend their holiday under canvas: there are only two official camping grounds, on the southwest coast at Étang-Salé-les-Bains and L'Hermitage-les-Bains. You'll also find a couple of *camping chez l'habitant* (informal, privately run camping grounds) in Îlet-à-Vidot and Bébour-Bélouve. The Cirque de Mafate also features a few simple camping spots.

You can camp for free in some designated areas in the Cirques, but only for one night at a time. Setting up camp on Piton de la Fournaise (the volcano) is forbidden for obvious reasons.

Chambres d'Hôtes

Chambres d'hôtes are the French equivalent of B&Bs. They are normally tucked away in the hills or in scenic locations and offer a window into a more traditional way of life. Options include everything from restored Creole houses or modern buildings to rooms in family houses. On the whole standards are high, and rooms are generally good value. B&B rates are from around €45 for a double room. Upmarket versions are more like boutique hotels. Breakfast is always included.

Many *chambres d'hôtes* also offer *tables d'hôtes* (hearty evening meals) at around €18 to €30 per person (set menu), but this must be reserved in advance (usually the day before). This is a fantastic way to meet locals and sample the local cuisine.

Chambres d'hôtes can be booked by phoning the owners directly.

Gîtes de Montagnes

Gîtes de montagne are basic mountain cabins or lodges, operated by the local authorities through the **Centrale d'Information et de Réservation Régionale – Île de la Réunion Tourisme** (p190). It is possible to organise a walking holiday using the *gîtes de montagne* only.

The *gîtes de montagne* in Réunion are generally in pretty good condition. Thanks to solar power, they all have electricity, although not all get as cushy as providing warm showers.

Gîtes de montagne must be booked and paid for in advance, and charges are not refundable unless a cyclone or a cyclone alert prevents your arrival. In practice, you won't be denied access if you just turn up without your voucher, but you may not have a bed if it's full. Last-minute reservations may be accepted, as there are often last-minute cancellations.

You can book through the Centrale d'Information et de Réservation Régionale – Île de la Réunion Tourisme or through any tourist office on the island, including those in St-Denis, Cilaos, Salazie, Hell-Bourg, St-Gilles-les-Bains, St-Pierre, St-Leu, St-André, Ste-Anne, and Bourg-Murat. It's highly recommended that you book well in advance, especially during the busy tourist seasons, as there's only a limited number of places available. One night's accommodation without food costs €16 or €18 per person depending on season.

When staying in a *gîte de montagne*, you have to call the *gîte* at least one day ahead to book your meals (or you can ask for this to be done for you when you make the original booking). Dinner costs from €15 to €19, and usually consists of hearty *carris*. Breakfast costs around €6 and normally consists of coffee, bread and jam. Payment is made directly to the caretaker, in cash.

Sleeping arrangements usually consist of bunk beds in shared rooms, so be prepared for the communal living that this entails, although the more recent *gîtes* usually have a few private rooms. Sheets and blankets are provided, though you might want to bring a sheet sleeping bag (a sleep sheet).

It's not a bad idea to also bring along toilet paper and a torch. It can get quite chilly at night, so warm clothing will be in order. Some places will let you cook, but many kitchens are so basic – and sometimes grimy – that you probably won't bother.

On arrival and departure you must 'book' in and out with the manager, who will collect your voucher and payment for meals. In theory, you're not meant to occupy a *gîte* before 3pm or remain past 10am.

BOOK YOUR STAY ONLINE

For more accommodation reviews by Lonely Planet authors, check out hotels. lonelyplanet.com. You'll find independent reviews, as well as recommendations on the best places to stay. Best of all, you can book online.

Gîtes d'Étape

Gîtes d'étapes, sometimes simply called *gîtes*, are privately owned and work in roughly the same way as the *gîtes de montagne*, offering dorm beds and meals. Some places even have doubles. One main difference is that you can book these places directly with the owners. There are numerous *gîtes d'étapes* in the Cirque de Mafate, and others dotted around the island; most are in the vicinity of walking trails. The host will often offer meals or cooking facilities.

Meublés de Tourisme & Apartments

Meublés de tourisme and apartments are private houses and lodges that families and groups can rent for self-catering holidays, normally by the week or weekend. There are dozens of *meublés de tourisme* and apartments scattered all over the island.

Most offer lodging for four or more people, with facilities of varying standards. Costs vary from around €350 to €700 per week and from €120 to €280 for a weekend (note that not all offer bookings for just a weekend). If you average out the per-person, per-week price and factor in cooking several meals in the house, *gîte* stays can actually be quite economical. Plus, the *gîte* owner often lives nearby and can be a mine of local information.

Apartments and *meublés de tourisme* can be booked by phoning the owners directly. A deposit of some sort is usually required in advance.

Hotels

If you're after serious cosseting and ultraposh digs, you might be looking at the wrong place. Most hotels on the island are rated as one-, two- or three-star, and lots are unclassified. There is only a sprinkling of four- and five-star hotels.

Hotels are found in St-Denis and around the beach resorts of the west coast, though you'll also find some in the attractive mountain towns of Cilaos and Hell-Bourg.

CHILDREN

→ Réunion is an eminently suitable destination if you're travelling with the kids in tow. With its abundance of beaches, picnic spots and outdoor activities, plus its healthy food, it offers plenty to do for travellers of all ages in a generally hazard-free setting.

→ Most locals have a number of children themselves and will not be troubled by a screaming child at the next table.

→ There are excellent medical facilities in the main cities.

→ For more information, see Lonely Planet's *Travel with Children*.

Practicalities

→ A few hotels offer kids clubs and many places provide cots for free and additional beds for children at a small extra cost. Most *chambres d'hôtes* welcome children.

→ Many restaurants have children's menus with significantly lower prices.

→ Nappies (diapers) are readily available.

→ Breastfeeding in public is not a problem.

→ The main car-hire companies can supply safety seats at additional cost.

CONSULATES

Since Réunion isn't independent, only a few countries have diplomatic representation.

Belgium Consulate (☑ 0262 97 99 10; chatel@ groupechatel.com; 80 Rue Adolphe Pegoud, Ste-Marie)

German Consulate (☑ 0692 73 68 98; st-denis@hk-diplo.de; 64 Ave Eudoxie Nonge, Ste-Clotilde)

Madagascar Consulate (☑ 0262 72 07 30; consulat-madrun@wanadoo.fr; 29 Rue St Joseph Ouvrier, St-Denis)

Seychelles Consulate (☑ 0262 57 26 38; hrop@wanadoo.fr; 67 Chemin Kerveguen, Le Tampon)

Swiss Consulate (☑ 0262 52 56 41; reunion@ honrep.ch; 3bis Impasse Tapioca, Bois Rouge)

CUSTOMS REGULATIONS

→ The following items can be brought into Réunion duty-free: 200 cigarettes, 50 cigars, 1L of strong liquor or 2L of liquor that is less than 22% alcohol by volume, 2L of wine, 50mL of perfume and 250mL of *eau de toilette*. Anything over the limit must be declared on arrival.

→ There are restrictions on importing plants and animals, for which import permits are required.

→ With regards to currency, anyone entering or leaving the island must declare sums in excess of €10,000.

ELECTRICITY

220V, 50Hz AC, using European-style two-round pins.

RÉUNION DIRECTORY A–Z

EATING PRICE RANGES

The following price ranges refer to a main course. The service charge is included in the bill.

€ less than €10

€€ €10 to €20

€€€ more than €20

INTERNET ACCESS

Many midrange and all top-end hotels offer wi-fi access, as do B&Bs, many cafes, restaurants and most tourist offices, usually without charge. In hotels, coverage may be restricted to public areas. The connection is generally good. The wi-fi icon indicates which venues have wi-fi access.

LEGAL MATTERS

➺ French police have wide powers of search and seizure and can ask you to prove your identity at any time.

➺ Foreigners must be able to prove their legal status in France (eg passport, visa, residency permit) without delay.

➺ If the police stop you for any reason, be polite and remain calm. Verbally (and of course physically) abusing a police officer can lead to a hefty fine.

➺ People who are arrested are considered innocent until proven guilty, but can be held in custody until trial.

➺ Possession and use of drugs is strictly illegal and penalties are severe.

LGBT TRAVELLERS

French laws concerning homosexuality prevail in Réunion, which means there is no legal discrimination against homosexual activity and homophobia is relatively uncommon. People are fairly tolerant, though by no means as liberal as in mainland France; open displays of affection may be regarded with disdain, especially outside St-Denis.

Throughout the island, but particularly on the west coast, there are restaurants, bars, operators and accommodation places that make a point of welcoming gays and lesbians. Certain areas are the focus of the gay and lesbian communities, among them St-Denis, St-Pierre and La Saline-les-Bains.

MAPS

➺ For most purposes the IGN (Institut Géographique National; www.ign.fr) *Carte Touristique La Réunion* map, at a scale of 1:100,000 (1cm = 1km), which covers the island in one sheet, is perfectly adequate.

➺ The most detailed and accurate maps for hiking are the six 1:25,000 scale maps published by IGN.

➺ Maps can be purchased at most bookshops in St-Denis and in St-Pierre. The larger tourist offices also sell them.

MONEY

As in France, the unit of currency is the euro (€), which is divided into 100 cents. Euro coins come in denominations of 1¢, 2¢, 5¢, 10¢, 20¢ and €1 and €2. Banknotes are issued in denominations of €5, €10, €20, €50 and €100.

ATMs

➺ ATMs are the easiest way to access funds while in Réunion, but banks charge foreign-transaction fees plus a per-use ATM charge.

➺ Most banks and post offices have an ATM (known as a *guichet automatique de banque* or *gabier*).

➺ Visa and MasterCard are the most widely accepted.

➺ Check with your bank before you leave home to ensure that the card you plan to use to withdraw cash doesn't have a low daily or weekly limit.

➺ If you're heading off into the Cirques, it's wise to stock up with euros beforehand – Cilaos has two ATMs and Hell-Bourg has only one. Mafate doesn't have an ATM.

Credit Cards

Credit cards will prove the cheapest and easiest way to pay for major purchases in Réunion. Visa (Carte Bleue) and MasterCard (Eurocard) are the cards most widely accepted by hotels, restaurants, supermarkets, adventure centres, petrol stations and stores. Credit cards are mandatory if you want to rent a car, as they'll be used as a form of *caution* (deposit). Smaller places, however, sometimes refuse cards for small amounts (typically under €15) and it's rare for *chambres d'hôtes* and *gîtes d'étapes* to take credit cards.

It's a good idea to check with your credit-card company before leaving home about charges on international transactions.

Exchange Rates

For current exchange rates, see www.xe.com.

Australia	A$1	€0.67
Canada	C$1	€0.68
Japan	¥100	€0.88
NZ	NZ$1	€0.64
UK	UK£1	€1.18
USA	US$1	€0.89

Money Changers

→ All banks in Réunion have dropped their foreign-exchange facilities in favour of ATMs.

→ There's only one *bureau de change* on the island; it's outside Roland Garros International Airport.

→ As a general strategy, it's sensible to bring a fair supply of euros with you and to top up from the ATMs.

Tipping

Tipping is not expected in Réunion.

OPENING HOURS

Banks 8am–4pm, Monday to Friday or Tuesday to Saturday.

Bars 10am–midnight (or when the last customer leaves).

Clubs 10pm–4am Friday and Saturday.

Government offices 8.30am–noon and 2pm–5pm Monday to Thursday, to 3pm Friday.

Restaurants 11.30am or noon–2pm and 6.30pm or 7pm–9.30pm; often closed on one or two days of the week.

Shops and businesses 8.30am–5pm or 6pm Monday to Saturday, often with a break from noon–1pm or 2pm. Some shops close on Monday.

PUBLIC HOLIDAYS

Most of Réunion's offices, museums and shops are closed during *jours fériés* (public holidays).

New Year's Day 1 January
Easter Monday March/April
Labour Day 1 May
Victory Day 1945 8 May
Ascension Day late May or June
Bastille Day (National day) 14 July
Assumption Day 15 August
All Saints' Day 1 November
Armistice Day 1918 11 November
Abolition of Slavery Day 20 December
Christmas Day 25 December

SAFE TRAVEL

Overall, Réunion is relatively safe compared with most Western countries, but occasional robberies do occur.

→ Don't leave anything of value in a rental car or on the beach and ensure that your room or bungalow is securely locked.

→ Violence is rarely a problem, and muggings are almost unheard of. Intoxicated people are the most likely troublemakers.

→ Unfortunately Réunion has a bad record when it comes to road safety, which means that you must drive defensively at all times. Potential dangers include drunk drivers, excessive speed, twisting roads and blind bends.

PRACTICALITIES

→ **Newspapers & Magazines** Daily regional newspapers include French-language Journal de *l'Île de la Réunion* (www.clicanoo.re) and *Le Quotidien* (www.lequotidien.re), both good for features and events listings.

→ **Radio** Tune in to Réunion 1re, Kreol FM or Radio Free Dom for local news (in French and Creole).

→ **Smoking** Prohibited in indoor public places and on public transport but is allowed in outdoor restaurants and on beaches. As with elsewhere, the trend is towards prohibition, so expect restrictions to increase over time.

→ **TV** One government channel, Réunion 1re, as well as the independent Antenne Réunion and Canal + Réunion; most programming comes from mainland France.

→ **Weights & Measures** Réunion uses the metric system.

Swimming

→ Swimmers should always be aware of currents and riptides. Seek advice before entering the water.

→ Shark attacks on surfers or swimmers have been a problem over the last few years. Always heed any advice, such as shark warning signs, that you might come across, and stick to the lifeguard-patrolled beaches in St-Gilles-les-Bains, St-Leu, L'Hermitage-les-Bains, La Saline-les-Bains, Étang-Salé-les-Bains and St-Pierre. Swim only inside lagoons and protected areas. In a effort to improve the safety of swimmers and surfers, shark nets were installed off Les Roches Noires beach in St-Gilles-les-Bains and Boucan Canot beach in early 2016.

TELEPHONE

→ All telephone numbers throughout Réunion consist of 10 digits; landline numbers start with ☐ 0262, and mobile-phone numbers start with ☐ 0692 or ☐ 0693.

→ If calling a Réunion landline or mobile number from abroad (bar France), you'll need to dial your country's international-access code, Réunion's country code (☐ 262), then the local number minus the initial 0. Calling abroad from Réunion, dial 00 for international access, then the country code, then the area code and local number.

→ There are no area codes in Réunion.

Mobile Phones

➡ For mobile phones, Réunion uses the GSM 900/1800 system, which is compatible with Europe and Australia, but incompatible with North American GSM 1900.

➡ The network covers most towns and villages throughout the island, including the Cirque de Mafate.

➡ If your GSM phone has been 'unlocked', it is also possible to buy a SIM card with either of the two local network operators: Orange (www. orange.re) and SFR (www.sfr.re). A starter pack costs around €15 including €5 worth of calls. Recharge cards are readily available, or you can top up your credit by phone or online. When buying a SIM card, you'll need to bring along your passport.

TOURIST INFORMATION

There are generally *offices du tourisme* (tourist offices) in most main towns across the island. Most of them have at least one staff member who speaks English. Tourist-office staff provide maps, brochures and the magazines *Ileenile* (www.ile-en-ile.com) and *Guide Run*, which are useful directories of hotels, restaurants and other places of interest to visitors.

Île de la Réunion Tourisme (IRT; www.reunion. fr) Réunion's regional tourist office has a website with easy-to-browse information on activities, attractions and places to stay, among others.

TRAVELLERS WITH DISABILITIES

Independent travel is difficult for anyone who has mobility problems in Réunion. Only upmarket hotels have features specifically suited to wheelchair use.

Negotiating the streets of most towns in a wheelchair is frustrating given the lack of adequate equipment, and most outdoor attractions and historic places don't have trails suited to wheelchair use. Some notable exceptions are Kelonia (p207) in St-Leu, the renovated Cité du Volcan (p233) in Bourg-Murat and Stella Matutina (p211) museum near St-Leu. With a bit of extra warning, some riding stables, dive centres and other sports operators can cater for people with disabilities.

Download Lonely Planet's free Accessible Travel guide from http://lptravel.to/AccessibleTravel.

VISAS

Though Réunion is a French department, it's not part of the Schengen treaty. The visa requirements for entry to Réunion are almost the same as for France, bar a few exceptions. For EU nationals, a national ID or a passport suffices. Citizens of a number of other Western countries, including Australia, the USA, Canada and New Zealand, do not need visas to visit Réunion as tourists for up to three months; they need only a passport.

Other nationals should check with the French embassy or consulate nearest your home address to find out if you need a visa. For example, South African citizens need a visa to enter mainland France but don't require a visa for Réunion. For up-to-date information on visa requirements see www.diplomatie.gouv.fr.

WOMEN TRAVELLERS

➡ The sight of women travelling, be it in a group or alone, is not met with too much surprise or curiosity, and women travelling by themselves should encounter no difficulties, as long as sensible precautions observed in most Western countries are adhered to.

➡ Women can enter most bars alone, but there are still a few places where this may attract unwanted attention – you'll get a pretty good idea when you enter.

➡ It's not advisable to walk alone on the trails in the interior.

❶ Getting There & Away

Although it's just a tiny speck in the Indian Ocean, Réunion is fairly straightforward to get to, though access is limited to flights only. Flights and tours can be booked online at lonelyplanet. com/bookings.

AIR

Direct flights connect Réunion with Comoros, France, India, Mauritius, Mayotte, Thailand, the Seychelles and South Africa. For further afield, you'll need to take a connecting flight from South Africa, Mauritius, Asia or France.

CLIMATE CHANGE & TRAVEL

Every form of transport that relies on carbon-based fuel generates CO_2, the main cause of human-induced climate change. Modern travel is dependent on aeroplanes, which might use less fuel per kilometre per person than most cars but travel much greater distances. The altitude at which aircraft emit gases (including CO_2) and particles also contributes to their climate change impact. Many websites offer 'carbon calculators' that allow people to estimate the carbon emissions generated by their journey and, for those who wish to do so, to offset the impact of the greenhouse gases emitted with contributions to portfolios of climate-friendly initiatives throughout the world. Lonely Planet offsets the carbon footprint of all staff and author travel.

Airports & Airlines

Réunion has two international airports. The vast majority of flights come into **Roland Garros International Airport** (☑ 0262 28 16 16; www.reunion.aeroport.fr; Ste-Marie) about 10km east of St-Denis. Coming from Mauritius, you have the option of landing at Saint-Pierre-Pierrefonds International Airport (p246), in the south of the island near St-Pierre.

Air Austral (p190) is the national carrier. It has a good safety record and a decent international network.

ℹ Getting Around

BICYCLE

The haste of most motorists and the steep and precarious nature of the mountain roads means that those considering cycling as a form of transport in Réunion should be prepared for some hair-raising and potentially dangerous situations.

BUS

Réunion's major towns and many of the little ones in between are linked by bus. The island's bus service is known as **Car Jaune** (www.carjaune.re) and has distinctive yellow buses. The main bus station is on Blvd Lancastel on the St-Denis seafront.

Car Jaune provides regional minibus services for several areas on the island; they run from St-Benoît, St-Joseph, Ste-Rose, St-Leu and St-Paul. These convoluted local routes can be fairly confusing, particularly if you don't speak much French. Of most use to travellers are the buses from St-André to Salazie, Salazie to Hell-Bourg, Grand Îlet and Le Bélier, and the buses from St-Louis to Cilaos, Îlet à Cordes and Bras-Sec.

CAR & MOTORCYCLE

Travelling by car is by far the most convenient way to get around the island.

Hire

Car hire is extremely popular in Réunion, and rates are very reasonable. Rates start at €35 per day (including third-party liability insurance and unlimited kilometres) and can drop as low as €25 per day if you rent for several weeks. Most companies require a credit card, primarily so that you can leave a deposit.

Most companies stipulate that the driver must be at least 21 (sometimes 23) years of age, have held a driving licence for at least a year, and have a passport or some other form of identification. EU citizens can drive on their national driving licence; from elsewhere, you'll need an international driving licence.

Collision-damage waivers (CDW, or *assurance tous risques*) are not included and vary greatly from company to company. The *franchise* (excess) for a small car is usually around €800. You

can reduce it to zero (or at least to half) by paying a daily insurance supplement.

All major firms have a desk at the airports. There are also plenty of independent operators around the island. They are cheaper than international companies but their rental cars are usually older. Most offer delivery to the airport for a surcharge. Reputable ones include the following:

Auto-Europe (www.autoeurope.com)

Cool Location (www.cool-location.fr; 43 Rue Jules Auber, St-Denis)

Degrif' Loc – Bonne Route (☑ 0262 26 29 44, 0692 05 18 32; www.degrifloc.re; St-Louis)

Europcar (☑ 0262 93 14 15; www.europcar-reunion.com; Roland Garros International Airport)

ITC Tropicar (☑ 0262 24 01 01; www.itctropicar.re) Has offices in St-Denis, St-Pierre, St-Gilles-les-Bains and at the airport.

Mik Location (☑ 0262 35 30 66; www.mik-location.re) Offices in St-Denis and St-Pierre.

Multi Auto (☑ 0692 70 37 03, 0262 29 01 66; www.multiauto.re) In Ste-Clotilde and St-André.

Petrol stations are very easy to come by. A litre of unleaded costs €1.27. Most stations accept credit cards.

Road Conditions

The road system on the island is excellent and well signposted. Inaugurated in June 2009, the Route des Tamarins is a four-lane expressway that connects Saint-Paul to Étang-Salé – 34km – and branches onto the existing RN1. It creates a direct route between the two biggest cities, St-Denis in the north and St-Pierre in the south.

Routes départementales, the names of which begin with the letter D (or RD), are tertiary local roads, many of them very tortuous.

Road Rules

Like mainland France, Réunion keeps to the right side of the road. Speed limits are clearly indicated and vary from 50km/h in towns to 110km/h on dual carriageways. Drivers and passengers are required to wear seatbelts. The blood-alcohol content limit is 0.5g/L.

Seychelles

POP 91,500 / 📞 248

Best Places to Eat

➡ La Grande Maison (p303)

➡ Loutier Coco (p326)

➡ Café des Arts (p317)

➡ Les Lauriers (p316)

➡ Anse Soleil Café (p307)

Best Places to Sleep

➡ Château de Feuilles (p314)

➡ Bird Island Lodge (p329)

➡ Maia Luxury Resort & Spa (p306)

➡ Chalets d'Anse Forban (p301)

➡ Anse Takamaka View (p305)

Why Go?

Close your eyes. And just imagine. You're lazing on a talcum-powder beach lapped by topaz waters and backed by lush hills and big glacis boulders. Brochure material? No, just routine in the Seychelles. With such a dreamlike setting, the Seychelles is unsurprisingly a choice place for newlyweds. But for those looking for more than a suntan or romance, this archipelago offers a number of high-energy distractions. There are jungle and coastal walks, boat excursions, and diving and snorkelling to keep you buzzing. Ecotourism is big – there are marine parks and natural reserves filled with endemic species that are easy to approach. The Seychelles is more affordable than you think. On top of ultra-luxurious options, the country has plenty of self-catering facilities and family-run guesthouses that offer local colour. So if you are suffering from visions of tropical paradise, here is your medicine.

When to Go

➡ From December to March, the trade winds bring warmer, wetter air streams from the northwest. From June to September the southeast trades usher in cooler, drier weather but the winds whip up the waves and you'll want to find protected beaches. The turnaround periods (April to May and October to November), which are normally calm and windless, are ideal. Temperatures range between 24°C and 32°C throughout the year.

➡ Rainfall varies considerably from island to island and from year to year. Mahé and Silhouette, the most mountainous islands, get the highest rainfall.

➡ Accommodation can be hard to find during the peak seasons from December to January and July to August. The Seychelles lies outside the cyclone zone.

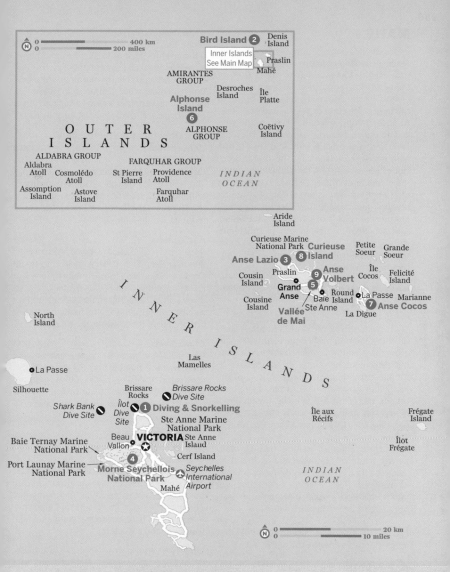

Seychelles Highlights

1 Mahé (p286) Diving and snorkelling among the north coast's dense marine life.

2 Bird Island (p329) Living out that stranded-on-a-desert-island fantasy on this secluded outcrop.

3 Anse Lazio (p308) Splashing around in the gin-clear waters of this beautiful beach.

4 Morne Seychellois National Park (p300) Looking for the smallest frog on earth while exploring forested mountains.

5 Vallée de Mai (p308) Hearing yourself say 'Oh, these coconuts are so sexy!'.

6 Alphonse Island (p329) Living out your deserted island fantasy on this coral islet.

7 Anse Cocos (p321) Spending hours lazing on the near-perfect beach.

8 Curieuse Island (p316) Scratching the leathery neck of a giant tortoise.

9 Anse Volbert (p308) Enjoying the stretch of white sand and turquoise waters.

MAHÉ

By far the largest and most developed of the Seychelles islands, Mahé is home to the country's capital, Victoria, and to about 90% of the Seychelles' population. As such it's both as busy as the Seychelles gets, and home to the largest selection of resorts and activities, from the hiking possibilities across the rugged interior of Morne Seychellois National Park to diving pristine sites and snorkelling with whale sharks in or just beyond the glorious bays caressed by the gorgeously multi-hued waters of Mahé. The west coast, from top to bottom, is one long string of stunning beaches and outstanding accommodation, but there are plenty of secret gems elsewhere. And wherever you're based, paradise lies close at hand – a bus or car ride of no more than 20 minutes will bring you to fabulous natural attractions.

Victoria

POP 26,450

Welcome to one of the world's smallest capital cities. Victoria may be the country's main economic, political and commercial hub, but peak hour here lasts an unbearable 15 minutes! It is home to about a third of the Seychelles' population, but even so Victoria retains the air of a provincial town. While it may not fulfil all fantasies about tropical paradise, the city still has a little charm and a little promise when you scratch beneath the surface. There's a bustling market, manicured botanical gardens and a fistful of attractive old colonial buildings sidling up alongside modern structures and shopping plazas. It's also a good place to grab last-minute gifts before heading home.

Oh, and there's the setting. Victoria is set against an impressive backdrop of hills that seem to tumble into the turquoise sea.

◉ Sights

The rather dilapidated old courthouse beside the clock tower is an appealing example of Creole architecture. Other architectural highlights include the colonial buildings that are scattered along Francis Rachel and Albert Sts.

★ Market   MARKET
(Map p292; Market St; ☺5.30am-5pm Mon-Fri, to noon Sat) No trip to Victoria would be complete without a wander through the covered market. It's small by African standards, but

it's a bustling, colourful place nonetheless. Alongside fresh fruit and vegetables, stalls sell souvenirs such as local spices and herbs, as well as the usual assortment of *pareos* (sarongs) and shirts. Early morning is the best time to come, when fishmongers display an astonishing variety of seafood, from parrotfish to barracuda. It's at its liveliest on Saturday.

★ Cathedral of the Immaculate Conception   CHURCH
(Map p292; Olivier Marandan St) This imposing cathedral is noteworthy for its elegant portal and colonnaded facade. The extraordinary building immediately west of the cathedral is the **Domus** – it's the priest's residence and a national monument.

Kaz Zanana   GALLERY
(Map p292; ☑4324150; www.georgecamille.sc; Revolution Ave) This gallery, in a traditional Creole wooden structure, exhibits the work of George Camille, one of the Seychelles' best-loved painters. There's an on-site cafe and it's a short uphill walk from the main downtown area. Some of the artworks are for sale.

Clock Tower   MONUMENT
(Map p292; cnr Francis Rachel St & Independence Ave) The focal point of the city centre is this downsized replica of the clock tower on London's Vauxhall Bridge. It was brought to Victoria in 1903 when the Seychelles became a crown colony.

Botanical Gardens   GARDENS
(Map p292; ☑4670500; Rs 100; ☺8am-5pm) The manicured botanical gardens, full of streams and birdsong, are about a 10-minute walk south of the centre. Star attractions are the *coco de mer* palms lining the main alley. There's also a spice grove, a pen of giant tortoises, a patch of rainforest complete with fruit bats, and a cafeteria.

Liberty Monument   MONUMENT
(Map p292; 5th June Ave) Unveiled in 2014 to mark 38 years of independence, this eye-catching bronze sculpture is the work of British-born Seychellois artists Tom Bowers.

Sri Navasakthi Vinyagar Temple   HINDU SITE
(Map p292; Quincy St) With its brightly painted decor, Victoria's small but eye-catching Hindu temple stands out among a row of nondescript buildings. It's used by the city's small Indian community.

Mahé

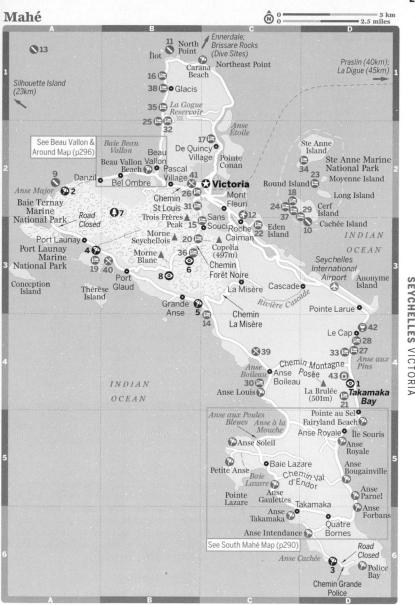

SEYCHELLES VICTORIA

Natural History Museum MUSEUM
(Map p292; ☑ 4321333; Independence Ave; Rs 15;
☉ 8.30am-4.30pm Mon-Thu, to noon Fri & Sat) The
rather ramshackle Natural History Museum
is worth a quick visit to learn about the islands' geology, fauna and flora.

Old Courthouse HISTORIC BUILDING
(Map p292; Francis Rachel St, Supreme Court)
The rather dilapidated old courthouse beside
the clock tower is an appealing example of
Creole architecture.

Mahé

Sheikh Mohamed bin Khalifa Mosque   MOSQUE

(Map p292; off Francis Rachel St) Tucked away from the main drag is this modern mosque, which serves Victoria's small Muslim community. It's at its busiest for Friday noon prayers.

Anglican Church   CHURCH

(St Paul's Cathedral; Map p292; Albert St) Taking pride of place in the centre of town is the Anglican church, with its renovated facade and elegant tower.

🏃 Activities

Victoria can be a good place to organise boat trips or excursions, with a few reputable travel agencies dotted around the town centre.

Marine Charter Association   BOATING

(MCA; Map p292; ☑4322126; mca@seychelles.net; 5th June Ave, Victoria) Marine Charter Association runs glass-bottomed boat tours to Ste Anne Marine National Park for €80/45 per adult/child.

Mason's Travel   TOURS

(Map p292; ☑4288888; www.masonstravel.com; Revolution Ave; ⊙8am-4.30pm Mon-Fri, to noon Sat) A well-established travel agency. Offers a wide array of tours around Mahé and to other islands.

Creole Travel Services   TOUR

(Map p292; ☑2297000; www.creoletravelservices.com; Albert St; ⊙8am-4.40pm Mon-Fri, to noon Sat) This reputable travel agency offers the full range of services, including ticketing, car hire and tours around Mahé and to other islands. Also shelters a bureau de change and sells ferry tickets to Praslin.

🛏 Sleeping

We can't think of a single reason to make Victoria your Mahé base – most visitors visit the capital on a day trip and then return to sleep by the sea or high in the mountains. In any event, Victoria's range of accommodation is slim, with one of the best choices on nearby Eden Island.

Calypha Guesthouse
GUESTHOUSE €

(Map p287; ☑ 4241157; www.seychelles.sc/calypha; Ma Constance; s/d incl breakfast €42/65; ❋ ☎) This family-run guesthouse, about 3km north of Victoria in a not-so-attractive area, won't be the most memorable stay of your trip but is OK for a night's kip. The six rooms are in sore need of TLC but are otherwise in reasonable condition. Note that air-con is extra (€10 per day). Creole-style dinners are available on request (€15). Cash only.

★ Beau Séjour
GUESTHOUSE €€

(Map p287; ☑ 4226144; www.beausejourhotel.sc; Curio Rd, Bel Air; r incl breakfast €91; P ❋ ☎) A guesthouse with style, this is a lovely place to dawdle in and soak up the tranquil charm from the foot of the Trois Frères – the location is one of the best in northern Mahé. It's sparkling clean and has character in abundance. Only rooms 1 and 5 have a view (other rooms are at the back). Meals on request.

Mountain Rise
HOTEL €€

(Map p287; ☑ 4225308, 2716717; mountainrise@seychelles.net; Sans Souci Rd; s/d incl breakfast €95/120; P ☎ ☎) Up on the road to Sans Souci (but an easy bus ride from the centre), Mountain Rise is in an atmospheric, airy heritage home that offers five unadorned yet spacious rooms. There's also a good Creole restaurant and a swimming pool. No air-con, but the location benefits from cooling breezes.

Hotel Bel Air
HOTEL €€€

(Map p287; ☑ 4224416; www.seychelles.net/belair; Bel Air Rd; r incl breakfast €165) If you really want to be in Victoria, the closest hotel to the centre is Hotel Bel Air, on the road to Sans Souci. A 2013 renovation has improved things but we'd expect more than decent rooms for this price.

✗ Eating

Victoria isn't known for its restaurants – it's better for quick snacks and fast food than sit-down restaurants. Marie-Antoinette and not-far-away Eden Island are notable exceptions.

★ La Pause
INTERNATIONAL €

(Map p292; ☑ 2537881; www.lapause-seychelles.com; Revolution Ave; mains from Rs 100; ☺ 9.30am-4.30pm Mon-Fri) This is a popular spot for a weekday bite in the heart of town. Friendly Malaika and Olivier do juices, smoothies, sweet and savoury crêpes, salads, sandwiches and pastries, with a wickedly delicious chocolate fondant for dessert. There are just four

tables at the window, but here it's all about the food, wherever you decide to eat it.

Lai Lam Food Shop
FAST FOOD €

(Map p292; Benezet St; mains Rs 30-60; ☺ noon-4pm Mon-Fri) Order roast chicken, smoked fish with rice or other wholesome Creole staples at this crazily popular takeaway outlet smack-dab in the centre. Perfect to fill up on the cheap and take in the vibe from Victoria's working crowd.

Double Click
CAFETERIA €

(Map p292; ☑ 4224796; Palm St; mains Rs 50-110; ☺ 8am-9pm Mon-Sat, 9am-8pm Sun) This buzzy eatery, popular with students, rustles up light meals including salads, soups and sandwiches. It's nothing special but prices are competitive and there's internet access.

★ Marie-Antoinette
CREOLE €€

(Map p287; ☑ 4266222; Serret Rd; menu Rs 275; ☺ noon-3pm & 6.30-9pm Mon-Sat) Marie-Antoinette isn't just a restaurant, it's an experience, especially at dinner. It occupies a beautiful, if somewhat dated, wood-and-iron colonial Seychellois mansion. Bring an empty stomach – the *menu* (set menu of the day) includes fish and aubergine fritters, grilled fish, chicken curry, fish stew, rice and salad, and it hasn't changed since the 1970s.

Restaurant du Marché
SEAFOOD €€

(Map p292; ☑ 4225451; Market St; mains Rs 125-255; ☺ 7am-3pm Mon-Sat) The food is fresh and tasty at this unpretentious yet appealing eatery within the market (upstairs). Typical dishes include smoked-fish salad, tuna steak and fish fillet in coconut milk. It's a good place to catch local vibes and enjoy plenty of local colour.

Sam's Pizzeria
PIZZA €€

(Map p292; ☑ 4323495; Francis Rachel St; mains Rs 160-275; ☺ 11am-3pm & 6-11pm) Walls here are adorned with paintings by local artist George Camille, which gives the place a splash of style. Get things going with pizza cooked in a wood-fired oven, salad, pasta or grilled fish and meat. And yes, it's open on Sunday – a rarity in Victoria. Takeaway is available.

News Café
CAFETERIA €€

(Map p292; ☑ 4322999; Albert St, Trinity House; mains Rs 150-210; ☺ 8.30am-5pm Mon-Fri, to 3pm Sat) This cheerful cafe-bar overlooking the main drag is an excellent venue to devour a comforting breakfast (muesli!) and read the daily newspapers, or to take a lunchtime break from town.

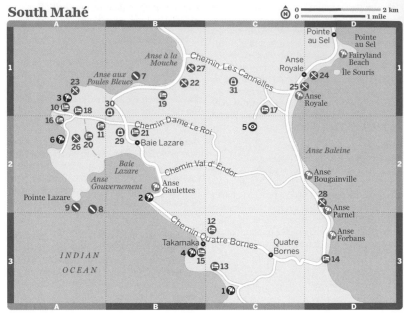

South Mahé

Pirates Arms INTERNATIONAL €€

(Map p292; ☑ 4225001; Independence Ave; mains Rs 110-260; ☺ 9am-11pm Mon-Sat, noon-11pm Sun) Once *the* meeting point in Victoria, the Pirates Arms has closed for major renovations. There are plans for a new bar, restaurant and even hotel on the site.

Le Cafe de l'Horloge INTERNATIONAL €€€
(Map p292; ☑4323556; Francis Rachel St; mains Rs 225-485; ☉9am-10pm Mon-Sat) The Balinese-meets-Amazonian decor of this 1st-floor eatery overlooking the clock tower is easy on the eye, with dark-wood furnishings, tropical plants and candlelit tables. The extensive menu takes in fish, meat, salad, pizza and ice cream. The quality of the food is nothing to write home about, but at least the surroundings are a nice place to do so.

Drinking & Nightlife

There's nowhere in downtown Victoria that we recommend for an evening drink – like port cities the world over, its bars are rough-and-ready places where you need to keep your wits about you. Either visit Level Three Bar (take a taxi) or, better still, head for Eden Island or Beau Vallon instead.

Level Three Bar BAR
(Map p292; Latanier Rd; ☉5pm-late Mon-Fri) Despite the odd location in a nondescript building near the harbour, Level Three Bar is worth considering for its affordable cocktails (Rs 150) and its cool atmosphere.

Shopping

★Sunstroke ART
(Map p292; ☑4224767; www.georgecamille.sc; Market St; ☉9am-5pm Mon-Fri, 9.30am-1pm Sat) George Camille's lovely paintings can be found at this art gallery, with original paintings, prints, postcards and T-shirts all for sale.

Seychelles Island Foundation GIFTS & SOUVENIRS
(SIF; Map p292; ☑4321735; www.sif.sc; Mont Fleuri Rd, Victoria; ☉9am-4pm Mon-Fri) If you want to buy a *coco fesse* (the fruit of the coco de mer palm), head to the Seychelles Island Foundation, which has some stock and will issue you the required export permit. Be prepared to fork out about €200.

Camion Hall ARTS & CRAFTS
(Map p292; Albert St; ☉9am-5pm Mon-Sat) Head to this small shopping mall right in the centre for creative and interesting locally made arts and crafts.

Information

You'll have no trouble finding banks with ATMs and exchange facilities as well as bureaux de change in the centre.

Barclays Bank (Albert St; ☉8.30am-2.30pm Mon-Fri, to 11.30am Sat)

Barclays Bank (Independence Ave; ☉8.30am-2.30pm Mon-Fri, to 11am Sat) Changes cash and has two ATMs.

Behram's Pharmacy (☑4225559; Francis Rachel St, Victoria House; ☉8.30am-4.45pm Mon-Fri, 8.15am-12.30pm Sat)

Victoria Hospital (☑4388000; Mont Fleuri) The country's main hospital.

Tourist Office (Map p292; ☑4671300; www.seychelles.travel; Independence Ave; ☉8am-4pm Mon-Fri) Has a few brochures and decent maps of Mahé, Praslin and La Digue.

Getting There & Around

Victoria is the main transport hub for buses around Mahé and for boats to Praslin and La Digue.

Coming from the airport, a taxi into town costs around Rs 400. Alternatively, cross the road and pick up any bus heading north. From the boat jetty, it's a 10- to 15-minute walk into the city centre, from where onward buses and taxis are frequent.

Victoria has a compact city centre that can be easily covered on foot. For nearby Eden Island, there's no public transport, but a taxi shouldn't cost more than Rs 150.

Eden Island

Opened for business in 2012 and fast becoming one of the coolest places on Mahé, Eden Island has a luxury hotel, yacht marina, some fine bars and restaurants and a modern shopping mall. With waterside villas on sale – it's the only place in the Seychelles where foreigners are permitted to buy land – it's already becoming a smart alternative to Victoria.

Sleeping & Eating

Eden Island has just one hotel, the Eden Bleu, but it's easily the most comfortable choice this close to Victoria.

Eden Island's waterside restaurants are gathering a reputation for both quality, sophistication and atmosphere – everything that most of Victoria's restaurants lack. There are also a handful of ice-cream parlours scattered around the shopping mall.

★Eden Bleu Hotel HOTEL €€€
(Map p287; ☑4399100; www.edenbleu.com; s/d from €295/325) The closest hotel to the airport, the Eden Bleu overlooks the marina on Eden Island. Its stylish rooms have Nespresso machines and in-room Apple TV. The high levels of comfort compensate a little for the lack of a beach – it's more business hotel than beach resort but it does fill an important niche and does exceptionally well.

Victoria

0 — 200 m
0 — 0.1 miles

Cathedral of the Immaculate Conception

Bus Terminal & SPTC Office

Cat Cocos Catamaran to Praslin

Freedom Square

Tourist Office

Île Hodoul

Stadium

Inner Harbour

Hotel Bel Air (100m);
Mountain Rise (2km);
Beau Séjour (3.5km)

Jardin des Enfants

Latanier Rd

Nature Seychelles (1.7km); (8km)

Riviere Trois Frères

Botanical Gardens

Mont Fleuri Rd

Canal

Marie-Antoinette (350m)

Oliver Marandan St

Quincy St

Market St

Benezet St

Albert St

Revolution Ave

Huteau La

Manglier St

5th June Ave

Flamboyant Ave

Long Pier Rd

Independence Ave

State House Ave

Francis Rachel St

Liberation Ave

Bois de Rose Ave

Palm St

Bravo   INTERNATIONAL €€

(Map p287; ☎4346020; mains Rs 180-575; ⊙noon-late Mon-Sat) This open-air restaurant overlooking the marina at Eden Island provides an agreeable dining experience with mostly Italian food. Everything's pretty good, but if you want a recommendation, go for the Mega Burger or the seared tuna salad.

🍷 Drinking & Nightlife

Eden Island's main restaurant precinct along the waterfront has an excellent bar, the Boardwalk, and a number of restaurants that become bars after the kitchen closes.

The Boardwalk   LOUNGE

(Map p287; ☎4346622; Eden Island; ⊙8am-midnight Mon-Thu, to 1am or later Fri & Sat) As good for a morning coffee as a late-night cocktail, this slice of sophistication could be the coolest place on the island. With wicker sofas on a pontoon out on the water and downbeat tunes keeping things mellow, it's our pick for the best bar in the country.

🛍 Shopping

The Eden Plaza, on the right as you cross the bridge from the mainland, may be small by standards elsewhere, but it's easily the

Victoria

largest and most modern in the Seychelles. It has a few brand names such as Billabong and Quiksilver, a pharmacy, ice-cream parlours, and bars and restaurants.

Eden Art Gallery   ART
(Map p287; ☑ 2514707; Shop 103, Eden Plaza; ◎10am-6pm Mon-Fri, to 2pm Sat) This large showroom sells local artworks and photography, framed and unframed, with mostly prints and the occasional original work.

❶ Information

Eden Pharmacy (☑ 2501500; Eden Plaza; ◎9am-7pm Mon-Fri, 10am-3pm Sat)

❶ Getting There & Away

Eden Island is connected to the main Mahé Island via a bridge, around 4km south of Victoria.

There's no public transport to Eden Island, but a taxi to/from downtown Victoria should cost no more than Rs 150.

Ste Anne Marine National Park

Ste Anne Marine National Park, off Victoria, consists of six islands, two of which rank among the most accessible of the Seychelles 115 islands – day trippers are permitted to land on **Cerf Island** and Moyenne Island (p294). There's good snorkelling and each island has its own personality.

The largest of the six islands, and only 4km east of Victoria, is **Ste Anne Island**, which boasts ravishing beaches. **Round Island** was once home to a leper colony, but these days it's better known for the offshore snorkelling and seriously alluring beaches. For almost a decade there have been plans for a luxury resort on **Long Island** – Pelangi Resorts took up the lease in 2015 so perhaps those plans will finally come to fruition. The smallest island of the lot, **Cachée**, lies southeast of Cerf. It's uninhabited.

🏃 Activities

The park is fantastic for **swimming** and **snorkelling**, although the coral is no longer as awesome as it was. Silting from construction works in the bay has led to significant coral damage, compounded by several episodes of coral 'bleaching'. There are superb **beaches** lapped by emerald waters, but expect some algae. Note that the park authorities charge a fee of €10 per person (free for children under 12 years) to enter the marine park. Tour operators usually include this in their prices.

Cerf Island Explorer   DIVING
(Map p287; ☑ 2570043; palblanchard@hotmail.com; Cerf Island; ◎Mon-Sat by reservation) For diving inside Ste Anne Marine National Park, contact Cerf Island Explorer, an outfit run by Marseillais Philippe Blanchard, who provides personalised service at affordable prices (€65/80 for a single/introductory dive). Dedicated snorkelling trips cost €40 (two people minimum). If you're not staying in the park, he can arrange pick-ups from Eden Island.

TREASURE ISLAND?

Moyenne Island has a rather unusual backstory. The island was uninhabited for most of the first half of the 20th century, but was purchased for £8000 by former UK newspaper editor Brendon Grimshaw. Grimshaw, the island's only full-time inhabitant, spent 50 years transforming the island, hacking back the jungle but replanting more than 16,000 trees in a bid to create his very own tropical paradise. He also set up a breeding program for Aldabra tortoises and transformed the island into a nature reserve, charging day visitors for the privilege of visiting. Local legend asserts that pirate treasure lies buried on the island – Grimshaw excavated two sites and found evidence of human-made hiding places but no loot – and two graves found on the island are believed to be those of pirates. When Grimshaw died in 2012, his dream was realised when the Seychelles' government incorporated Moyenne into Ste Anne Marine National Park.

🛏 Sleeping

Although most visitors arrive on day trips by boat, there are a handful of luxury resorts on the islands (and a couple of upper-midrange options) within the national park itself. These make fabulous escapist alternatives to staying on the mainland.

⭐ Fairy Tern Chalet   APARTMENT €€

(Map p287; ☑ 4321733; www.fairyternchalet. sc; Cerf Island; d €147; ❄🤗) Run by an affable South African couple, this is a great place to get away from it all; it's the most reasonable option within Ste Anne Marine National Park. Digs are in two squeaky-clean, spacious bungalows overlooking the beach. If you don't fancy cooking, the restaurant at L'Habitation Cerf Island is a five-minute walk away. Free canoes.

Villa de Cerf   BUNGALOW €€

(Map p287; ☑ 2523161; www.villadecerf.com; Cerf Island; r with half board from €185; ❄🤗🏊) This establishment occupies an elegant Creole mansion with an unparalleled location on the beach. Stay four nights and you get the third free.

Enchanted Island Resort   RESORT €€€

(Map p287; ☑ 4672727; www.enchantedseychelles. com; Round Island; villa incl breakfast €800-1900; ❄@🤗🏊) The epitome of a luxurious island retreat, this Round Island resort, within Ste Anne Marine National Park, has stunning, spacious villas, all turned out in a classical style. The balcony bath-tub in one has our pick for the best bath-tub-with-a-view anywhere in the Seychelles. Private pools, a first-rate restaurant and a sense of utter exclusivity round out a rather impressive package.

Cerf Island Resort   RESORT €€€

(Map p287; ☑ 4294500; www.cerf-resort.com; Cerf Island; s/d with half board from €250/280; ❄🤗🏊) This venture strikes a perfect balance between luxury, seclusion and privacy (there are only 24 villas), on a hillside. This is a romantic resort, extremely quiet and popular with honeymooners, and the rooms have a lovely wood-and-bamboo design scheme. Facilities include a small pool and a spa. One grumble: the beach lacks the wow factor.

Sainte Anne Island   RESORT €€€

(Map p287; ☑ 4292000; www.beachcomber-hotels.com; Ste Anne Island; d with half board from €394; ❄🤗🏊) Spread over 220 hectares of private land, this sprawling resort features an infinity pool, five restaurants, a handful of bars, a well-respected spa, gym, water-sports centre, kids club, tennis courts and gift shops. It comprises 87 villas (some with their own pool) scattered amid well-tended gardens and coconut palms. The icing on the cake: three beaches, all with different orientations.

L'Habitation Cerf Island   HOTEL €€€

(Map p287; ☑ 4323111, 2781311; www.lhabitation cerf.net76.net; Cerf Island; d/ste with half board from €191/248; ❄🤗🏊) This comfortable little colonial-style hotel is right on the beach, and just a 10-minute boat ride from Victoria. It has a tranquil, convivial and homey atmosphere with 12 sunny rooms, two villas and lovely gardens (but not much shade). The restaurant serves superfresh seafood. Prices drop for stays longer than three nights.

ℹ Getting There & Away

Unless you're staying in one of the luxury resorts and can therefore arrange a boat transfer to the island in question, the only way to get to the park and its islands is on an organised boat tour.

Beau Vallon & the North Coast

Beau Vallon, 3km from Victoria on Mahé's northwest coast, has the island's longest and, some would say, best beach. While it may be overbuilt by Seychellois standards, you'll find it remarkably low-key and quiet if you've experienced other tropical destinations. The seaside ambience, with fishers selling fresh fish late in the afternoon in the shade of *takamaka* trees, adds a dash of real life.

North of Beau Vallon, there's some great scenery up the coast to **Glacis** and **North Point**. With your own wheels, it's a scenic drive on a narrow road that hugs the coastline, with intermittent, lovely views over secluded coves at the foot of the cliffs.

West of Beau Vallon, the coastal road passes **Bel Ombre**, which has some good accommodation options and a little fishing harbour, and ends at **Danzil**, where La Scala restaurant lies. From there, you can walk to Anse Major (p304). Ah, Anse Major...

◎ Sights

A long, brilliant-white arc of sand laced by palms and *takamaka* trees, **Beau Vallon beach** is the most popular in Mahé. Here the water is deep enough for swimming, but watch out for swells between June and November. There's usually a lifeguard on duty.

If you're after a more intimate and secluded strip of sand, head to the lovely **beach** that's just beside the Sunset Beach Hotel – no, it's not private. Going north, drive past the hotel and after 150m look for a little cement path on the left, amid the vegetation.

🏃 Activities

As with elsewhere in the Seychelles, diving and snorkelling are the main activities; the latter can often be combined with a trip on a glass-bottom boat.

Diving

There's plenty of great diving within the bay of Beau Vallon, including a few wrecks, as well as some top-notch dive sites well outside the bay.

Blue Sea Divers　　　　　DIVING
(Map p296; ☑2526051; www.blueseadivers.com; Beau Vallon; ⊙daily) This French-run operation offers the full slate of diving adventures, including introductory dives (from €97), single dives (from €55), certification courses and

CARANA BEACH

Here's a secret, only known to locals (whisper it softly): Carana Beach. This tiny, dreamlike cove lapped by lapis lazuli waters offers a small patch of sand framed by big boulders, with a couple of palm trees leaning over the shore. It's at Northeast Point; look for a cement road on the left, in a high-gradient descent of the road, or ask locals.

various dive and snorkelling packages. It also runs cruises around the Seychelles aboard the splendid live-aboard dive boat *Galatea* (www.diving-cruises.com), which started operating in June 2013.

Underwater Centre/ Dive Seychelles　　　　　DIVING
(Map p296; ☑4345445, 4247165; www.diveseychelles.com.sc; Beau Vallon; ⊙daily) This English-run, well-oiled Professional Association of Diving Instructors (PADI) five-star dive centre is in the Berjaya Resort. Walk-in prices are from €60 per dive with full gear. Certification courses and dive packages are available.

Big Blue Divers　　　　　DIVING
(Map p296; ☑4261106; www.bigbluedivers.net; Beau Vallon; ⊙Mon-Sat) North of Beau Vallon, this small PADI outfit has introductory dives (€95), single dives (from €50), dive packages and certification courses.

Snorkelling & Boat Tours

The bay of Beau Vallon hosts a few good snorkelling spots, especially along the rocky shore up the coast to North Point. It's also the main launching pad for boat excursions and snorkelling trips to Baie Ternay at the northwestern tip of the island, where the reefs are healthy and marine life plentiful. Full-day excursions include entry fees to the park, barbecue lunch and snorkelling gear. The best season is from April to October. A group of four to six persons is required. Contact a recommended operator (or ask your hotel or guesthouse to do it for you).

At the Berjaya Resort, Underwater Centre/ Dive Seychelles (p295) fits snorkelling (€20 to €30) in during its dive outings to L'Îlot, Baie Ternay Marine National Park and the lighthouse. It also rents snorkelling gear (€10 per day).

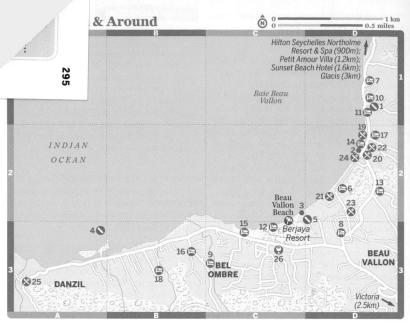

Beau Vallon & Around

Teddy's Glass Bottom Boat BOATING
(☎ 2511125, 2511198; teddysgbb@yahoo.com; half-/
full-day trip €60/90; ⊙ by reservation) Good credentials. Runs glass-bottom trips to Baie Ternay and Ste Anne Marine National Park that
include swimming and snorkelling stops.

Blue Marlin BOATING
(Map p296; ☎ 2510269, 2516067; Beau Vallon; full-
day trip €90) Full-day boat trips, which include

a barbecue lunch on Thérese Island and snorkelling at Baie Ternay Marine National Park.

**Dolphin Nemo Glass
Bottom Boat** BOATING
(Map p296; ☎ 2596922, 4261068; dolphin.nemo@
yahoo.com; Beau Vallon; full-day trip €90; ⊙ by res-
ervation) Does the standard tours to Ste Anne
Marine National Park and Baie Ternay. It has
a small kiosk on the beach, just in front of the
Berjaya Resort.

🛏 Sleeping

Beau Vallon and Bel Ombre offer the widest range of accommodation in north Mahé, with a good mix of luxury resorts and self-catering villas set on or just back from the lovely beach.

Casadani   APARTMENT €
(Map p296; ☎2511081, 4248481; www.casadani.sc; Bel Ombre; s/d incl breakfast €75/90; P❄🖥) Soothingly positioned on a velvety emerald hillside just above the coastal road, this popular venture is a good deal if you can score a room with a sea view. The 25 rooms are well-appointed yet utilitarian, but you'll be too busy soaking up the fabulous views from the vast shared terrace to mind. Car and boat hire are also possible.

Beau Vallon Residence   APARTMENT €
(Map p296; ☎2516067; www.beauvallonresidence.sc; Beau Vallon; s/d/q €50/60/80; P❄🖥) This has one self-contained apartment that can sleep four people, and it's very well kept and priced. It's not on the beach and there's no view, but you're in a quiet property, close to shops and banks. And Beau Vallon beach is just a five- to 10-minute stroll down the road. Excellent value. Book early.

Romance Bungalows   APARTMENT €€
(Map p296; ☎4247732; www.romance-bungalows.com; Beau Vallon; r Rs1084-1817; P❄🖥) Attractive bungalows right across the road from the beach, loads of repeat visitors, spacious, well-appointed rooms with a spotless kitchen; Romance Bungalows ticks many of the right boxes for a comfortable stay. The beach is only steps away and all amenities are within easy reach.

Ocean View Guesthouse   APARTMENT €€
(Map p296; ☎2522010; www.choiceseychelles.com; Bel Ombre; s/d incl breakfast from €65/80; P❄) A great-value port of call. Above the road in Bel Ombre, this jolly good villa shelters four immaculate rooms with balcony. The upstairs ones proffer splendid views of the bay. The cheaper Vakwa room, at the back, has no view. It's a 20-minute walk to Beau Vallon beach.

Villa Rousseau   VILLA €€
(Map p296; ☎2520646; www.villarousseau.com; Bel Ombre; d/q €80/180; ❄) A three-bedroom villa with all mod cons, in a quiet property above Ocean View Guesthouse. Prices are for the whole villa – a bargain for couples.

WHALE-SHARK-SPOTTING

Between August and October it's common to see whale sharks offshore from Mahé's north and west coasts. Underwater Centre/Dive Seychelles (p295) runs dedicated snorkelling trips focusing on whale sharks in September and October (€135 to €150). It also runs whale-shark monitoring programs.

Yarrabee   APARTMENT €€
(Map p287; ☎4261248; www.seychelles-yarrabee.com; Glacis; studios €80-160; ❄🖥) Two fully equipped studios and a three-bedroom unit with heavenly views of the bay. It's near a tiny beach and a small supermarket.

Diver's Lodge Guesthouse   GUESTHOUSE €€
(Map p296; ☎4261222; www.diverslodge.sc; Glacis; d incl breakfast €90-130; P❄🖥) Just above the main coast road, next to a dive centre, these four rooms in a modern villa are large, pathologically clean and equipped to a high standard. The ones upstairs are significantly dearer but offer fleeting glimpses of the ocean through the foliage of exotic trees. Dinner can be arranged on request.

The owner's husband runs Teddy's Glass Bottom Boat – convenient if you plan to arrange a boat trip.

Beach House   APARTMENT €€
(Map p296; ☎2522010; www.choicevilla.sc; Beau Vallon; s/d incl breakfast from €90/110; ❄🖥) In an area where economical options are on the verge of extinction, the Beach House represents reasonable value. The four functional and spacious rooms ensure a decent night's sleep for guests keen to roll out of bed and onto Beau Vallon beach, just across the road.

Georgina's Cottage   GUESTHOUSE €€
(Map p296; ☎4247016; www.georginascottage.sc; Beau Vallon; r incl breakfast €75-120; ❄🖥) This friendly operation has catered to budget travellers for years. After a serious makeover in 2012, it now features dearer but more comfortable rooms in an attractive Creole building. Its location is hard to beat: it's a 20m frisbee throw from the beach, and it's also close to dive centres, restaurants and shops. Eddy, the manager, is full of local info.

★**Hilton Seychelles Northolme Resort & Spa** VILLAS €€€
(Map p287; ☑4299000; www.hilton.com; Glacis; villas €300-1300; P✴@⎙☎) This gorgeous villa-only property is the smallest Hilton in the world and we love it all the more for it. There's a quiet sophistication and intimacy about the place, and the villas are exceptional – we'd move in and stay forever at their new Grand Ocean Pool Villas with big-sky views, private swimming pools and stunning design if we could.

★**H Resort Beau Vallon** RESORT €€€
(Map p296; ☑4387000; www.seychelles.h-hotel. com; Beau Vallon; ste/villa from €475/1015; P✴@⎙☎) One of the most attractive properties to open in Beau Vallon in recent years, H Resort has supremely comfortable suites and villas which make appealing use of wood, wicker and linen. The site is draped along the southern end of beautiful Beau Vallon beach, but sheltered by the trees. Good restaurants, excellent service and stylish public areas round out a terrific package.

★**Le Méridien Fisherman's Cove** RESORT €€€
(Map p296; ☑4677000; www.lemeridienfishermans cove.com; Bel Ombre; d incl breakfast from €300; P✴⎙☎) A reliable resort with a staggering bow-shaped lobby and 70 stylish rooms with modern design – bathrooms are not separate from bedrooms. Rooms are tightly packed together but face the sea and are buffered by lush gardens. The atmosphere is more convivial than intimate. Facilities include two restaurants, a bar, a spa and a pool. One minus: the beach is disappointingly thin.

Petit Amour Villa VILLA €€€
(Map p287; ☑2578039; www.petitamourvilla. com; Glacis; d/ste incl breakfast from €203/280; P✴@⎙☎) Consistently positive reviews are hardly surprising given what's on offer here – simply magnificent rooms, fabulous views and rooms that range from classic luxury to a refined combination of dark wood and contrasting colours. Meals are excellent. There's a minimum three-night stay.

Apartments Sables d'Or APARTMENT €€€
(Map p296; ☑4247404; www.sables-dor.sc; 1-/2-bedroom apt €350/495) Lovely, modern, self-catering apartments right on Beau Vallon's lovely beach make this one of the best choices on this corner of Mahé. The owners

are a mine of information about the island and there are numerous restaurants a short walk away. There's a six-night minimum stay.

Sunset Beach Hotel HOTEL €€€
(Map p287; ☑4261111; www.thesunsethotelgroup. com; Glacis; s/d incl breakfast from €252/310; P✴@⎙☎) This sunset-friendly seducer boasts an ace location on a little headland. The 28 units, divided into three categories, hide coolly among rocks and trees. The slightly dated rooms vary in shape, size and quality (the best ones are the Junior suites) and there's a lovely bar overlooking the ocean. There's direct beach access and excellent snorkelling options just offshore. There's a minimum stay of four nights.

Bliss BOUTIQUE HOTEL €€€
(Map p287; ☑2711187, 4261369; www.bliss-hotel. net; Glacis; d/ste with half board from €250/400; P✴⎙☎) The Bliss Seaside building shelters eight rooms decorated with natural materials and ocean views that will leave you speechless. The Hillside rooms, which are in a building across the road, are much less inspiring, despite the tropical garden. Amenities include a pool, a little spa and a great wooden sundeck with direct access to a small (rocky) beach.

Hanneman Holiday Residence APARTMENT €€€
(Map p296; ☑4425000; www.hanneman-seychelles.com; Beau Vallon; studio €105-126, apt €126-234; ✴⎙☎) This muscular villa was certainly not conceived by the most inspired architect on the island but inside it's much more welcoming, with six impeccable apartments equipped to a very high standard. There's also a cheaper, smaller studio for two people (€105). Bathrooms are so meticulous you could eat off the floor. There's a nifty pool too. Discounts are available when it's slack. It's a five-minute jog to the beach.

La Clef des Îles BOUTIQUE HOTEL €€€
(Map p296; ☑537100; www.clefdesiles.com; Beau Vallon; d/tr/q €250/310/370; ✴⎙) Pro: it's right on Beau Vallon beach, sandwiched between a pizzeria and a dive centre – the location is irresistible and right in the thick of things. Con: it's right on Beau Vallon beach, sandwiched between a pizzeria and a dive centre – it lacks privacy. Four creatively designed, generously sized, fully equipped apartments have a terrace or a balcony that look onto the beach.

✕ Eating

Beau Vallon and the surrounding area have some excellent restaurants, some of which combine excellent food with waterside views.

If you're self-catering, you'll find convenience stores supplying basic foodstuffs and other necessities on the beach road and around the junction with the Bel Ombre road.

On weekends, the beachside footpath and car park immediately south of La Plage Restaurant fills with vendors grilling and barbecuing local sausages, fish and other cheap eats.

Baobab Pizzeria   PIZZA €
(Map p296; ☑4247167; Beau Vallon; mains Rs 115-175; ⊙noon-3.30pm & 6.30-9.30pm) Madame Michel presides over this unpretentious, sand-floored eatery right on the beach. After a morning spent in the waves, reenergise with a piping-hot pizza, a plate of spag or fish and chips.

★ Boat House   BUFFET, SEAFOOD €€
(Map p296; ☑4247898; www.boathouse.sc; Beau Vallon; lunch mains Rs 250-500, buffet dinner adult/child Rs 425/250; ⊙noon-4.30pm & 7.30-9.30pm) This long-standing venture is a great place for a slap-up meal. Its Creole-themed buffet dinner should satisfy all but the hungriest visitors, with about 20 different dishes on offer, including Creole curries, salads and barbecued fish (usually tuna and, if you're lucky, red snapper). It also has a limited but tasty selection of fish dishes at lunchtime.

Coral Asia   SUSHI €€
(Map p296; ☑4291000; Coral Strand Hotel, Beau Vallon; nigiri from Rs 20, set menus from Rs 240; ⊙noon-10pm) On an open-sided elevated platform above the beach at the Coral Strand Hotel, Coral Asia does excellent sushi that expats and locals rave about. We especially love the 'Corner Menu' which includes four sashimi and *nigiri*, eight maki rolls, a salad, a hot main and a papaya sashimi for dessert, all for a very reasonable Rs 350.

La Fontaine   EUROPEAN, SEAFOOD €€
(Map p296; ☑4422288; Beau Vallon; pizzas from Rs 145, mains Rs 225-575; ⊙noon-10pm Mon-Sat) You're sure to find something to fill a gap at this unpretentious eatery across the road from the beach (no sea views). The menu is a mixture of French, Italian and island influences, with seafood at the fore.

La Perle Noire   ITALIAN, SEAFOOD €€€
(Map p296; ☑4620220; Bel Ombre; mains Rs 310-620; ⊙6.30-9.30pm Mon-Sat) The 'Black Pearl' scores high on atmosphere, with an eye-catching nautical theme and seafaring paraphernalia liberally scattered around the dining rooms. The food – mostly fish and meat dishes with an Italian twist – gets good reviews from the many repeat visitors.

La Scala   ITALIAN, SEAFOOD €€€
(Map p296; ☑4247535; www.lascala.sc; Danzil; mains Rs 200-450; ⊙7.15-10pm Mon-Sat) An old favourite of visitors and locals alike, this restaurant specialises in quality Italian homemade pasta (the *gnocchi della casa* tastes particularly good, despite the dated decor) and good seafood amid the low-lit ambience on the breezy terrace overlooking the sea. The tiramisu will finish you off sweetly. It's at the end of the coast road near Danzil.

La Plage   INTERNATIONAL €€€
(Map p296; ☑4620240; Beau Vallon; mains Rs 290-575; ⊙noon-10pm Thu-Tue) With waterside tables overlooking the northern end of Beau Vallon, La Plage lives up to its name. Presentation is impeccable, decor is enticing, with large, well-spaced tables and high ceilings, and the place fills up reliably. Dishes include seafood linguine and an excellent mixed seafood platter.

🍸 Drinking & Nightlife

Beau Vallon is the most 'happening' (by Seychellois standards, which isn't saying much) area on Mahé. The bars at Le Méridien Fisherman's Cove, Hilton Seychelles Northolme and Sunset Beach Hotel are great for a sunset cocktail.

Tequila Boom   CLUB
(Map p296; Bel Ombre; ⊙9pm-late Fri & Sat) The pick of the predominantly local nightclubs, this place along the main road in Bel Ombre, close to Beau Vallon, plays local music that'll have you up and dancing in no time.

ℹ Getting There & Away

Buses leave regularly from Victoria for Beau Vallon (Rs 7, 15 to 30 minutes), either straight over the hill via St Louis, or the long way round via Glacis. The last bus to Victoria leaves at around 7.30pm; it's a Rs 200 taxi ride if you miss it.

MAHÉ'S BEST DIVE SITES

Shark Bank (Map p287) Mahé's signature dive, for experienced divers only. The name is misleading, because there are very few sharks around this 30m-tall granite plateau 9km off Beau Vallon (Mahé). Instead, you'll encounter brissant rays the size of Mini Mokes, eagle rays, barracuda, batfish, and teeming yellow snapper and bigeyes. There is nearly always a strong current at this site.

Îlot (Map p287) This granite outcrop, just off north Mahé, consists of several large boulders topped by a tuft of palm trees. The current in the channel can be quite strong, but the cluster of boulders yields one of the highest densities of fish life in the Seychelles. Golden-cup coral festoons the canyons and gullies, and gorgonians and other soft corals abound. Îlot is about a 15-minute boat ride from Beau Vallon.

Brissare Rocks (Map p285) About 5km north of Mahé, this granite pinnacle is accessed from Beau Vallon. The site features abundant fire coral and great concentrations of yellow snapper, wrasse, parrotfish and fusiliers, as well as groupers and eagle rays. It's covered with bright-orange sponges and white gorgonians.

Twin Barges (Map p296) If you need a break from offshore dives, these two adjoining shipwrecks will keep you happy. They sit upright on the seabed in about 20m in Beau Vallon bay.

Aldebaran (Map p287) This boat was scuttled in 2010 off Anse Major; the maximum depth is 40m. It shelters moray eels, groupers and rays.

Alice in Wonderland (Map p290) Famous for its healthy coral formations. Off Anse à la Mouche.

Jailhouse Rock (Map p290) A high-voltage drift dive for experienced divers with prolific fish life. Off Pointe Lazare.

Shark Point (Map p290) Whitetips, nurse sharks and grey reef sharks are commonly sighted here. Off Pointe Lazare.

Morne Seychellois National Park

While the dazzling coastline of Mahé is undoubtedly the main attraction, it's crucial that you take the time to explore the island's mountainous interior. The splendid Morne Seychellois National Park encompasses an impressive 20% of the land area of Mahé and contains a wide variety of habitats, from coastal mangrove forests up to the country's highest peak, the Morne Seychellois (905m). Choked in thick forest, the enigmatic central part of the park is virtually deserted and can only be reached by walking trails; you don't have to go very far before the outside world starts to feel a long, long way away.

⊙ Sights & Activities

If you can't take one of the hiking trails through the park, a scenic, sinuous road cuts a swath through the heart of the park with some splendid views opening up en route. Both Mission Lodge and the Tea Factory are accessible along the road.

Mission Lodge   HISTORIC SITE

(Map p287) Close to the highest point you can reach on Mahé by road, Mission Lodge has a superb lookout with spectacular views of central Mahé and the west coast, and some low-slung stone ruins slowly returning to the forest (a school was built here by the London Missionary Society in the 19th century to care for slave children who had been dumped on the island after the abolition of slavery). Queen Elizabeth II took tea in the small pavilion in 1972.

SeyTé Tea Factory   FARM

(Map p287; ☑ 4378221; Sans Souci Rd; Rs 25; ☺ 7am-4pm Mon-Fri) At the working tea factory, about 3km above Port Glaud, free 20-minute tours take you through the tea-making process. It's best to visit before noon, when you can see the whole process from drying to packing. There's also a gift shop where you can sample and purchase the fragrant SeyTé and citronnelle. There are fine west-coast views from the car park and you can watch the spectacular white-tailed tropicbirds take flight from here.

🛏 Sleeping

A couple of appealing options hide among the trees high in the mountains. Otherwise, you'll need a vehicle to visit on a day trip or to reach the trailheads.

★ Copolia Lodge   B&B €€
(Map p287; 📞 2761498; www.copolialodge.com; Bel Air, Sans Souci; d incl breakfast €195-275; P ❄ 🤖 🐕) Copolia Lodge is magical, if you don't mind the sense of isolation – it's a 15-minute drive uphill from Victoria. Poised on a greencry-shrouded promontory, this very well-run villa proffers cracking views of the coastal plain and Ste Anne Marine National Park. It sports six bright, immaculate rooms with clean lines, ample space and lots of amenities, including a superb pool.

The Station   GUESTHOUSE €€€
(Map p287; 📞 4225709; www.thestationseychelles. com; Sans Souci; r from €200) High on the hill, this wellbeing spa and hotel is utterly different to anywhere else on the island. White-washed rooms, lovely views from the public areas and free yoga classes are the hallmarks here. There's an on-site restaurant and lovely little shop selling essential oils and the like.

🍴 Eating

There are no restaurants to speak of in the park so bring your own sustenance, especially if you're here to hike. At Mission Lodge at the lookout, a small stall sells local snacks and tea.

ℹ Getting There & Away

A few buses per day connect Port Glaud and Port Launay with Victoria.

The road over the mountains from Victoria to Port Glaud (take the Bel Air Rd, which branches off Liberation Ave, and continue on Sans Souci Rd), which cuts through the Morne Seychellois National Park, is a stunning scenic drive.

East Coast

Let's face it: much of the east coast is given over to housing, so there are only a few spots that fit the picture-postcard ideal. And swimming is not *that* tempting, with very shallow waters and a profusion of algae – hard-core beach lovers may be disappointed. This is not to say the east coast isn't a worthwhile place to visit. South of the airport are a number of small enclaves and undeveloped areas where travellers looking for peace and isolation will find both in no short supply.

👁 Sights & Activities

The oft-overlooked, little-known **Fairyland Beach** offers shimmering waters and great snorkelling around tiny **Île Souris**, just off-shore. Other good strips of sand are found at **Anse Royale, Anse Bougainville, Anse Parnel** and **Anse Forbans**, further south.

★ Takamaka Bay   DISTILLERY
(Map p287; 📞 4372010; www.takamaka.sc; Le Cap; guided tours Rs 150; ⊙ 8.30am-4pm Mon-Fri, tours 10am-3pm) On this popular tour you learn the story behind the island's main distillery and about the rum-making procedure. The tour runs for between 30 and 45 minutes and concludes with a tasting and an opportunity to purchase bottles of rum. There is also a forest walk and a small stand of sugar cane. It features a well-regarded bar-restaurant.

Le Jardin du Roi   GARDENS
(Map p290; 📞 4371313; Enfoncement, Anse Royale; adult/child Rs 110/free; ⊙ 10am-5pm) Located 2km up in the hills above Anse Royale, this spice garden owes its existence to Pierre Poivre, the French spice entrepreneur. There is a self-guided walk around the 35-hectare orchard-crossed-with-forest. The planter's house contains a one-room **museum** and there's a cafe-restaurant with smashing views down to the coast. Homemade jams, marmalade and spices are available at the gift shop.

🛏 Sleeping

The east coast may not be the sexiest part of the island, but we've unearthed a smattering of excellent-value (by Seychellois standards), family-run ventures from where you can easily reach the western coast, by bus or by car.

★ Chalets d'Anse Forban   BUNGALOW €€
(Map p290; 📞 4366111; www.forbans.com; Anse Forbans; d €145-168, q €235-336; P ❄ 🤖) Tranquillity: this family-friendly place has 12 sparkling-clean, fully equipped bungalows that are well spaced out; recent furniture and mattresses; expansive lawns; a lovely beach with good swimming; and fisherfolk selling their catch on the beach in the afternoon. Add a few sun loungers and the proximity of a store, and you have a great deal. There's a minimum stay of three nights.

★ Devon Residence   APARTMENT €€
(Map p287; 📞 2512721; www.devon.sc; Pointe au Sel; villas €100-150; P ❄ 🤖) No, you're not hallucinating, the view is real. Poised on a greenery-shrouded hillside, the five villas

TOP NATURE WALKS IN THE MORNE SEYCHELLOIS NATIONAL PARK

If you have itchy feet, there are excellent walks in the Morne Seychellois National Park, with a number of hiking trails through the jungle-clad hills. These are detailed in a series of leaflets that are available at the botanical gardens in Victoria (p286). The trails are poorly signed, though, so it's not a bad idea to hire a guide, who will also provide natural and cultural insights. **Jacques Barreau** (☏4242386, 2579191) and **Basile Beaudoin** (☏2514972) lead hiking and birdwatching trips into the park and charge between €60 and €90 for an informative day's walk with picnic and transport (between €40 and €65 for a half-day). You can also contact **Terence Belle** (☏2722492), who charges between €35 and €50 for a half-day, but he only works on Saturday and Sunday. Bring plenty of water.

Danzil to Anse Major

The walk to this secluded beach takes you along a coast fringed by impressive glacis rock formations. The path starts at the end of the road at Danzil, heading west from Beau Vallon, a few hundred metres further up from La Scala restaurant. It's a fairly easy one-hour romp, but most of the path is exposed to the sun. Before descending to the beach, the path goes past a lookout that affords fantastic vistas of Anse Major. The beach is blissfully quiet, and good for swimming, though there can be strong currents. Return by the same route.

Tea Factory to Morne Blanc

The imposing white bulk of Morne Blanc (667m) and its almost-sheer 500m face make a great hiking destination. Although the track is only 600m long, it is quite steep – climbing 270m from start to finish. Plan on roughly an hour for the ascent. The reward is a tremendous view over the west coast. The path starts 250m up the road from the tea factory (p300) on the cross-island road from Victoria to Port Glaud, and passes through the old tea plantation. Along the trail watch for the pendulous jackfruit plant and endemic bird species such as the Seychelles sunbird, Seychelles bulbul and the undeniably lovely blue pigeon; white-tailed tropicbirds soar high above the summit. You have to descend the same way.

Copolia

This is the most popular walk on Mahé, and one of the easiest high-country walks. It also has a pleasant Indiana Jones feel – you walk almost all the way amid a thick jungle, with lots of interesting fauna and flora. Now is your chance to spot leaf insects and the *Sooglossus gardineri*, the smallest frog on earth. Watch also for the distinctive (and carnivorous) pitcher plants close to the trail's highest point. The trail starts on the cross-island Chemin Forêt Noire about 5km above Victoria. It's only just over 1km to the granite platform of Copolia (497m), but the final section is quite steep; allow roughly two hours there and back. The views of Victoria and Ste Anne Marine National Park are sensational.

Trois Frères

Trois Frères (Three Brothers) refers to the three cliffs that tower over Victoria. The path is signed from the Sans Souci forest station on the Chemin Forêt Noire, about 4km from Victoria. The first part of the walk, up to a kiosk from where you get ample views, is fairly easy and can be covered in about one hour. The second leg, to the cross on the summit (699m), is tricky to follow and involves some scrambling – take a guide. Still game? Allow an extra two hours to reach the summit. You have to descend the same way.

Mare aux Cochons

This moderately difficult hike begins at Danzil. It diverts from the main route down to Anse Major to climb past the ruins of an old cinnamon factory, then through abundant groves of fruit and pandanus palms to the upland valley of Mare aux Cochons, with its high-altitude marsh. Return the way you came, or continue down to Port Glaud. Count on three to four hours. The trails can be difficult to follow so take a guide.

overlook Anse Royale. They're extremely well appointed, spacious, bright and immaculate. A flotilla of perks, including free transfers to/ from the airport, daily cleaning, free wi-fi, TV and washing machine make this one of the best-value stays you'll have.

Koko Grove Chalets
BUNGALOW €€

(Map p290; ☑ 2585986; www.kokogrove.nl; Anse Royale; chalets €100-155; P ❄ ☂) If you're after hush and seclusion, then these three timbered chalets, outstandingly positioned in the velvety emerald hills above Anse Royale, are the answer. The three units are self-contained, with cosy living areas and private verandas overlooking the tiny swimming pool, with the ocean as a backdrop. It's 400m before Le Jardin du Roi.

Jamelah Apartments
APARTMENT €€

(Map p287; ☑ 2523923, 4410819; jamelah@in telvision.net; Le Cap; d €70, apt €80-110, incl breakfast; P ❄ ☞) This reliable option is run by Florie, who has a great insight into the needs of the budget traveller. The two serviceable rooms (each with balcony and sea views) are a cast-iron bargain. If you're travelling with kids, opt for one of the four self-contained apartments in a separate building. They face a small 'beach', adequate for a waist-high dip at high tide.

Résidence Charlette
APARTMENT €€

(Map p287; ☑ 2715746; www.residencecharlette. com; Le Cap; 1-/2-bedroom apt from €40/70; P ❄ ☞) An unfussy abode with an unpretentious appeal. The dual attractions are the affordable rates and the spotlessness of the two self-catering apartments, set on grassy garden areas. Bonuses: free transfers to/from the airport, free laundry service and a Creole dinner for stays of one week or more. No meals, but there are a few stores nearby.

Lalla Panzi Beach Guesthouse
GUESTHOUSE €€

(Map p287; ☑ 4376411; www.lalla-panzi-beach. com; Le Cap; r incl breakfast €60; ❄) Lalla Panzi is not the beachfront paradise you were dreaming of, but it's a neat property leading down to the sea. This friendly guesthouse offers four scrupulously clean rooms arranged around a cosy lounge; rooms 2 and 3 have sea views. Furnishings are slightly dated and the decor is a tad kitsch but that's part of the charm.

✖ Eating

East-coast Mahé has a handful of OK beach restaurants but La Grande Maison, at the Takamaka Distillery, could just be the best restaurant anywhere in the Seychelles.

Les Dauphins Heureux Café-Restaurant
CREOLE, CAFE €€

(Map p290; ☑ 4430100; www.lesdauphinsheureux. com; Anse Royale; mains Rs 225-450; ◷ 8-10am, noon-3.30pm & 7-9.30pm Mon-Sat, 8-10am & 1-4pm Sun) A classic beachfront setting with a shady terrace and a tropical garden characterises this classy eatery with a modernish feel. Choose between subtly flavoured fish, seafood, curries and meat from an elaborate menu – we enjoyed the ginger crab. Head here on Sundays for the excellent Creole buffet (Rs 400) served at lunchtime.

Surfers Beach Restaurant
CREOLE €€

(Map p290; ☑ 2783703; www.surfersbeach.sc; Anse Parnel; pizzas from Rs 110, mains Rs 140-330; ◷ noon-9.30pm) In a sublime location overlooking the seductive beach at Anse Parnel, Surfers Beach is a heart-stealing, open-air joint. Linger over salads, grilled fish or octopus curry while enjoying the caress of the breeze on your face.

Le Jardin du Roi
SEAFOOD €€

(Map p290; ☑ 4371313; Anse Royale; mains Rs 110-275; ◷ 10am-4.30pm) The setting is wonderful at this cafe-restaurant way up the hills at the spice garden (p301), and it puts you in the mood for a fruit juice or a crunchy salad as soon as you sit down. Seafood and sandwiches also feature on the menu. Save room for ice creams: they're confected fresh on the premises with fruits from the garden.

Kaz Kreol
SEAFOOD, PIZZA €€

(Map p290; ☑ 4371680; Anse Royale; mains Rs 150-415; ◷ noon-9.30pm Tue-Sun, 4-9.30pm Mon) Right on the beach at Anse Royale, this venue with a casual atmosphere and ramshackle charm strikes a good balance between seafood, wood-fired pizzas and meat, not to mention a wide choice of Chinese specialities. It's all fairly uninspired; don't expect swift service.

★ La Grande Maison
CONTEMPORARY CREOLE €€€

(Map p287; ☑ 2522112; Takamaka Distillery, Le Cap; lunch tapas Rs 60-120, dinner mains Rs 350-500; ◷ noon-3pm & 7-9.30pm Tue-Sat) At Takamaka Bay (p301), La Grande Maison is the home kitchen of Christelle Verheyden, one of the country's most talented chefs. The atmosphere, in a wonderfully restored and airy colonial home, is a fine backdrop for Verheyden's exquisite tastes built around the best local (and often organic) ingredients. Verheyden is also a sommelier – the wines are as excellent as the cooking.

🍷 Drinking & Nightlife

Katiolo   CLUB
(Map p287; ☑ 4375453; Anse Faure; men/women Rs 100/50; ☺ 9pm-late Wed, Fri & Sat) The east coast is home to one of Mahé's most popular nightclubs. It's a fairly hip venue, so dress up rather than down.

🔒 Shopping

Domaine de Val des Prés   ARTS & CRAFTS
(Map p287; Anse aux Pins; ☺ 9.30am-5pm) The Domaine de Val des Prés at Anse aux Pins consists of a cluster of craft shops grouped around an old plantation house with a few bits of memorabilia. The rather motley assortment of crafts on offer includes model boats, pottery, paintings, clothing and products fashioned from the hugely versatile coconut tree.

ℹ Getting There & Away

Buses leave regularly from Victoria for the east coast. The last bus to Victoria leaves Anse Royale around 7.30pm.

West Coast

The west coast is exquisite on the eyes. There are one or two sights to aim for, but it's the beaches and coastal scenery that are the star attractions. Wilder than the east, this is the part of Mahé where green hills tumble past coconut-strewn jungles before sliding gently into translucent waters.

There's only a handful of settlements, including the fishing villages of **Anse Boileau**, **Grande Anse** and **Port Glaud**. If it really is isolation you're after, continue north on the narrow coastal road to **Baie Ternay**, which is as far as you can go at present.

The west coast is easily accessed from the east coast via several scenic roads that cut through the mountainous interior.

◉ Sights

Beautiful beaches are something of a west-coast speciality, from Anse Petit Police in the south to Anse Port Launey in the north.

Anse Major   BEACH
(Map p287) One of the most beautiful beaches on Mahé, Anse Major is only accessible on foot from Danzil. The setting is a match for any beach in the Seychelles, although swimming can be dangerous.

Anse Port Launay   BEACH
(Map p287) Close to the Constance Ephelia (p306), just 50m beyond Port Launay Bus Terminal, this gorgeous circle of sand can feel like paradise with its overhanging trees, turquoise waters and lovely views.

Petite Anse   BEACH
(Map p290) This pristine curve of white sand is accessible via the Four Seasons Resort (p306); wait at the gate and a buggy will take you down to the beach. Come late afternoon: as the sun lowers, the sky deepens to orange. This beach just might be heaven, despite the fact that it has been partly privatised by the hotel. Visitors can use the hotel's beach-restaurant for food and drink.

Grande Anse   BEACH
(Map p287) Grande Anse is an immense swath of sand that glimmers with a fierce but utterly enchanting beauty. No other beach provides the same opportunities for long, solitary walks. It's not suitable for swimming, though, due to strong currents.

Anse Soleil   BEACH
(Map p290) The idyllic little beach of Anse Soleil is a pocket-sized paradise. You can pause here for lunch – there's a beach restaurant (p307) – but beware, you may never want to leave. It's accessible via a secondary road (it's signposted).

Anse Takamaka   BEACH
(Map p290) The gently curving Anse Takamaka is a gorgeous strand for walking unfettered on white sand and gaping at sunsets. Facilities include Batista's bar-restaurant (p307).

Anse Louis   BEACH
(Map p290) To the north of Anse à la Mouche the coast is a bit less glam but appealing nonetheless. If you can find access to Anse Louis, where the superswish Maia Luxury Resort (p306) lies, you'll be rewarded with a superlative beach you never knew existed.

Anse Intendance   BEACH
(Map p290) A top-end resort lines the northern portion of this high-profile beach. The southern end is almost deserted and offers

good swimming and snorkelling. The sunset views are some of the best in the Seychelles. From the police station at Quatre Bornes, take the 1.7km concrete road that leads down to Anse Intendance.

Anse Petite Police & Police Bay   BEACH
(Map p287) From the village of Quatre Bornes, a road leads to Police Bay, a splendid, blissfully isolated spot at the southern tip of the island. Sadly, the currents are too dangerous for swimming, but the beaches are great places to watch the surf (bring a picnic).

🏃 Activities

Underwater Centre/
Dive Seychelles   DIVING
(☑ 4345445, 4247165; www.diveseychelles.com.sc; Beau Vallon) In conjunction with MCSS (www.mcss.sc), this dive outfit based in Beau Vallon organises whale-shark-spotting off Mahé's west coast in September and October.

Dive Resort Seychelles   DIVING
(Map p290; ☑ 4372057, 2717272; www.scubadiveseychelles.com; Anse à la Mouche; ◷ Mon-Sat) This well-esteemed venture takes beginners and experienced divers to some truly impressive dive sites off the southwestern coast. An introductory/single dive costs €90/55.

🛏 Sleeping

Accommodation in west Mahé ranges from self-catering apartments offering various levels of comfort to some of Mahé's swankiest hotels with everything laid on.

La Rocaille   BUNGALOW €
(Map p290; ☑ 2524238; lelarocaille@gmail.com; Anse Gouvernement Rd, Anse Soleil; d €70; P) This is a pleasant find, but there's only one unit, on the hill that separates Anse Gouvernement from Anse Soleil. It's simple but well-kept, and the grounds are nice enough, with lots of vegetation and birdsong. You'll need a car if you're staying here. There's no air-con.

The friendly owners, who live next door, offer fruits to guests and are happy to drive them to the nearest village to stock up on food supplies (it's self-catering). The nearest beach is at Anse Gouvernement, about 400m down the hill.

★ Anse Takamaka View   APARTMENT €€
(Map p290; ☑ 2510007; www.atv.sc; Takamaka; d/q €130/170; P ❋ 🛜 ☒) No photo retouching on the website – we guarantee that the views from the terrace are *that* terrific, the pool

(complete with a pool bar) *that* scintillating, and the three villas *that* roomy and comfortable. Run by a Seychellois–German couple, this wonderfully peaceful property is a winner. Meals (€18) are available twice a week. The minimum stay is three nights.

It's secluded and not on the beach, so you'll need your own wheels to stay here. Free pick-up at the airport.

★ La Maison Soleil   APARTMENT €€
(Map p290; ☑ 2712677, 2516523; www.maisonsoleil.info; Anse Soleil Rd; s €90-110, d €110-210; P ❋ 🛜) Seeking a relaxing cocoon with homey qualities without the exorbitant price tag? Run by artist Andrew Gee, whose gallery is just next door, this champ of a self-catering option has all the key ingredients, with three tasteful apartments, prim bathrooms and a colourful garden. Anse Soleil is within walking distance. There's a minimum stay of three nights.

Anse Soleil Beachcomber   HOTEL €€
(Map p290; ☑ 4361461; www.beachcomber.sc; Anse Soleil; s/d incl breakfast €104/120; P ❋ 🛜) This family-run hotel, among rocks on the idyllic cove of Anse Soleil, has location sorted. The clean and simple rooms with private terraces are less exciting than the location, but the flowery grounds add charm. Rooms 6, 7 and 8 open onto the sea, but the more recent Premier rooms, slightly set back from the shore, are much larger.

Half board is available, but Anse Soleil Café (p307) is next door.

Blue Lagoon Chalets   APARTMENT €€
(Map p290; ☑ 4371197; www.seychelles.net/blagoon; Anse à la Mouche; d €140; P ❋ 🛜) The friendly owner here offers four well-cared-for holiday units that are peppered across a well-tended park, a hop from the seashore. They sleep up to four people and are fully equipped.

Chez Batista's   BUNGALOW €€
(Map p290; ☑ 4366300; www.chezbatista.com; Anse Takamaka; d €82-106, ste from €165, incl breakfast; P ❋ 🛜) Your only concern here: whether to frolic on the beach *now* or first sip a cocktail at the restaurant. This long-standing venue on Takamaka beach features 11 bland but acceptable rooms (no sea views) and two villas right on the beach. The property feels a bit crowded and service can be irregular but it's the idyllic location that's the pull.

La Residence
APARTMENT €€

(Map p290; ☑4371733; www.laresidence.sc; Anse à la Mouche; studios/apt/bungalows €81/95/175; P❄🌐) Perched on a hillside, the five fully equipped studios and three villas are roomy, straightforward and tidy, if a touch old-fashioned. The buildings are functional rather than whimsical but there are good views from the terrace (despite the odd power line).

Anse Soleil Resort
APARTMENT €€

(Map p290; ☑4361090; www.ansesoleil.sc; Anse Soleil; 1-/2-bedroom villas incl breakfast €92/150; P❄🌐) Run by a hospitable family, this discreet number has just four self-catering apartments; the Kitouz is the best, but all are well-equipped, nicely laid out, spacious, and come with a large terrace from where you can soak up the view over Anse à la Mouche (if you can ignore the power lines). Meals (€15) are available on request.

★Maia Luxury Resort & Spa
RESORT €€€

(Map p287; ☑4390000; www.maia.com.sc; Anse Louis; d incl breakfast from €1955; P❄@🌐🌊) One of Mahé's most exclusive hotels, this place will render you speechless – you'll never want to leave. Overlooking glorious Anse Louis, it's truly beautiful, with great expanses of white beach, palm-shaded landscaped grounds, a splendid infinity pool and 30 gorgeous villas – each with its own pool. Nothing is too much trouble for the obliging staff.

★Banyan Tree
RESORT €€€

(Map p290; ☑4383500; www.banyantree.com; Anse Intendance; d incl breakfast from €702; P❄🌐🌊) The Banyan Tree is a gorgeous property. Three highlights: the spa, possibly the most attractive on Mahé (and that's saying a lot); a fabulous location on a greenery-shrouded hillside with heavenly views of the sea; and 54 wonderfully roomy and stylish villas that get plenty of sunshine, even in late afternoon.

★Four Seasons Resort
RESORT €€€

(Map p290; ☑4393000; www.fourseasons.com/seychelles; Petite Anse; d incl breakfast from €965; P❄🌐🌊) With its stadium-sized villas perched on a hillside, swoony ocean views, sense of privacy and lovely spa, this five-star bigwig, opened in 2009, is a fab place for honeymooners and loved-up couples. The bedrooms and bathrooms are massive, and both masterpieces of understatement despite luxuries such as works of art adorning the walls, teak furnishings, high-quality linen and king-size beds.

Constance Ephelia
RESORT €€€

(Map p287; ☑4395000; www.epheliaresort.com; Port Launay; d with half board from €370; P❄🌐🌊) High on ambition, but low on atmosphere, this sprawling resort is not bad if you can get online promos. Its public facilities are its strength: two beaches with free water sports, tennis courts, two pools, a fitness centre, five restaurants, a kids club... Due to its position on the island's northwest corner, it gets plenty of natural light from sunrise to sunset.

Valmer Resort
BUNGALOW €€€

(Map p290; ☑4381555; www.valmerresort.com; Baie Lazare; d from €200; P❄🌐🌊) A cluster of well-organised villas cascades down a hillside cloaked in green, each enjoying stupendous ocean views. Apart from the four ordinary 'garden studios', which are just off the main road, the 17 units are sun-filled, capacious and tasteful. A real hit is the pool, built at the foot of a big granite boulder. There's an on-site restaurant (by the pool).

AVANI Barbarons
RESORT €€€

(Map p287; ☑4673000; www.avanihotels.com; Barbarons; d incl breakfast from €415; P❄🌐🌊) The '80s-style exterior could use a facelift, but it's one of the least expensive resorts you'll find for a beachfront stay on Mahé. While there is nothing remarkable about the flimsy motel-like structure, the 124 rooms are OK and amenities include a small spa, a pool and tennis courts, as well as B-level restaurants and grounds.

✖ Eating

Most luxury hotels welcome outside guests at their restaurants (by reservation), but there are also some fabulous places to eat along the west coast, with seaside perches something of a speciality.

★Maria's Rock Cafeteria
CAFETERIA €€

(Map p290; ☑4361812; Anse Gouvernement Rd, Anse Soleil; mains Rs 215-295; ⊙10am-9pm Wed-Mon) Now here's something different. Maria, the Seychellois spouse of artist Antonio Filippin, runs this quirky restaurant beside her husband's studio. The cavernous interior is discombobulating, with granite tabletops and concrete walls sprayed with paint. Food-wise, it majors on fish and meat dishes, grilled at your table on a stone plate. Skip the pancakes.

Chez Plume
FRENCH, SEAFOOD €€

(Map p287; ☑4355050; www.aubergeanseboileau.com; Anse Boileau; mains Rs 210-660; ⊙7.15-10pm Mon-Sat) The granddaddy of west-coast dining, Chez Plume can still cut it. It serves local specialities such as Creole black pudding and fish dishes such as the intriguing *capitaine blanc* with passionfruit sauce. The decor is romantic, in an old-fashioned way, and the service generally good.

Anchor Café – Islander Restaurant
INTERNATIONAL €€

(Map p290; ☑4371289; Anse à la Mouche; lunch mains Rs 150-295, dinner mains Rs 180-750; ⊙noon-9pm Mon-Sat; ☎⚲) This family-run restaurant takes its cooking seriously. Its champion dishes include blackened fish, a range of Creole curries (including lobster curry), grilled red snapper, plus the obligatory catch of the day. A few vegetarian options also grace the menu.

★Anse Soleil Café
SEAFOOD €€€

(Map p290; ☑4361700; Anse Soleil; mains Rs 250-400; ⊙noon-3pm) Don't miss this unpretentious little eatery ideally positioned right on the beach. The menu has simply prepared seafood (such as grilled crab or seafood curry) and various chop sueys. It doesn't take reservations and there are only a few tables – come at noon sharp or after 1.30pm. The gruff, sometimes rude, service is, some would say, part of the charm.

★Del Place
CREOLE, EUROPEAN €€€

(Map p287; ☑2814111; Port Glaud; mains Rs 210-545; ⊙11am-10pm) This delightful spot weds cafe-cool to excellent cooking. The centrepiece is local seafood: octopus straight from the lagoon, baked red snapper in banana leaf, seafood platters and Creole curries, including the rarely seen crab curry. Throw in great salads, local tapas, wickedly cool cocktails and beautiful beach views and it adds up to our favourite west-coast venue.

Chez Batista's
SEAFOOD €€€

(Map p290; ☑4366300; Anse Takamaka; mains Rs 180-450; ⊙noon-3.30pm & 6.30-9pm Mon-Sat, noon-3.30pm Sun) The impressive thatched canopy, the sand floor and the endless turquoise bay that spreads out in front of you help you switch to 'relax' mode. And it's the location that outshines the food which is sometimes good, sometimes average. The eclectic lunch buffet (Rs 405) is a good option on Sunday. It's wise to book on weekends.

Opera
SEAFOOD €€€

(Map p290; ☑4371943; www.opera-mahe.com; Anse à la Mouche; mains Rs 130-600; ⊙noon-midnight Tue-Sun) Across the road from the beach (but no views to speak of), this modern eatery is an acceptable plan B with pasta, pizza, panini and some passable seafood grills. There's a Sunday buffet with live music, but service at any time can be sloooow.

Shopping

The glorious southwest seems to be an endless source of inspiration for a number of artists, and you'll find small galleries signposted all the way along the coast road.

Michael Adams' Studio
ART

(Map p290; ☑4361006; www.michaeladamsart.com; Anse à la Mouche; ⊙by appointment) Visit Michael Adams' studio, where silkscreen prints burst with the vivid life of the forests. They are irresistible and highly collectable, so bring plenty of rupees if you're thinking of buying. Even if you don't ring ahead and you're driving by, stop in at his studio – it could be open, though don't count on it.

Lazare Gallery
ANTIQUES

(Map p290; ☑2516577; Baie Lazare; ⊙9am-6pm Tue-Sat) This eclectic place is part antique showroom, part museum, and it's worth picking through the treasure on offer – when we visited it included local driftwood, a framed photo of a youthful Duke of Edinburgh and all manner of local bric-a-brac. It's just south of the Anse Soleil turn-off, or immediately north of the petrol station.

Gerard Devoud's Studio
ART

(Map p290; ☑4381515; Baie Lazare; ⊙10am-7pm) Gerard Devoud's eye-goggling paintings are sure to enliven your bedroom. His studio is at Valmer Resort, but opening hours can vary.

Art Arc
ARTS & CRAFTS

(Map p290; ☑2510977; Baie Lazare; ⊙10am-8pm Wed-Sat & Mon) Antonio Filippin's somewhat risqué woodcarvings and quirky studio, Art Arc, are perched on a hill between Anse Gouvernement and Anse Soleil.

Tom Bowers
ART

(Map p290; ☑4371518; artworks@seychelles.net; Chemin Les Cannelles; ⊙by reservation) This British-born artist creates some truly amazing bronze sculptures and his works are increasingly being commissioned for public places, such as the Liberty Monument (p286) in Victoria.

Getting There & Away

Buses leave regularly from Victoria for the west coast. The last bus to Victoria leaves Quatre Bornes around 7.30pm.

SEYCHELLES WEST COAST

PRASLIN

A wicked seductress, Praslin has lots of temptations: stylish lodgings, tangled velvet jungle that's ripe for exploration, curving hills dropping down to gin-clear seas, gorgeous stretches of silky sand edged with palm trees and a slow-motion ambience. No, you're not dreaming, but this is the Seychelles you dreamed of when you first imagined this tropical archipelago.

Lying about 45km northeast of Mahé, the second-largest island in the Seychelles is closer to the sleepiness of La Digue than the relative hustle and bustle of Mahé. Like Mahé, Praslin is a granite island, with a ridge of small mountains running east–west along the centre, and the svelt interior, especially the Vallée de Mai, is fascinating for its flora and bird life. Its combination of manageable size (you're never more than 90 minutes from anywhere else on the island) and stellar attractions makes Praslin a fine choice for your Seychelles holiday.

⊙ Sights

Praslin's most appealing sights are its beaches, with Anse Lazio the highlight, but Anse La Blague, Anse Consolation and Anse Volbert are all world-class by anyone's standards.

★ Anse Lazio   BEACH

Anse Lazio, on the northwest tip of the island, is picture-perfect everywhere you look and it often turns up in lists of the world's most beautiful beaches. The long beach has lapis lazuli waters, a thick fringe of palm

and *takamaka* trees, and granite boulders at each extremity. There's some good snorkelling among the rocks along the arms of the bay and there's a beachside restaurant. Despite its popularity, it never feels crowded, but watch your valuables here.

★ Anse Volbert   BEACH

This long, gently arching beach is the most popular strand on the island. It's great for safe swimming and sunbathing, and it's also good for water sports. There are plenty of facilities, including restaurants and hotels. A small islet – Chauve-Souris – floats offshore. You can swim to it for snorkelling.

★ Vallée de Mai   NATIONAL PARK

(Map p310; www.sif.sc; adult/child under 12 Rs 305/free; ⊗8.30am-5.30pm) Gorgeous World Heritage–listed Vallée de Mai is one of only two places in the world where the rare coco de mer palm (see box, p314) grows in its natural state (the other being nearby Curieuse Island). It's also a birding hot spot: watch for the endemic Seychelles bulbul, the lovely blue pigeon, the Seychelles warbler and the endangered black parrot, of which there are between 500 and 900 left in the wild. It's a real slice of Eden. Last tickets sold at 4.30pm.

Three hiking trails (plus a number of connecting minor subtrails) lead through this primeval, emerald-tinged forest, which remained totally untouched until the 1930s. The shortest is about 1km and the longest is 2km and all are clearly marked and easy going – perfect for families. As you walk amid the forest, the atmosphere is eerie, with the monstrous

---

DIVING PRASLIN & LA DIGUE

Aride Bank Off Aride Island, this pristine site can be accessed from Praslin if you don't mind the tedious 30-minute boat trip to get to the site. A hot fave among local divemasters, it features rays, snappers, nurse sharks, jacks, barracudas and Napoleon wrasses as well as magnificent seafans.

Booby Islet (Map p310) Approximately halfway between Aride and Praslin, this exposed seamount consistently sizzles with fish action. In less than 20m of water, you'll come across parrotfish, Napoleon wrasses, moray eels, turtles, eagle rays and nurse sharks.

Anse Sévère (Map p318) An easy site, close to the shore of La Digue.

Cousin (Map p310) An easy site in the waters off Cousin Island.

Marianne Island An islet east of La Digue, famous for its dense fish life (including grey sharks, stingrays, barracudas, eagle rays and nurse sharks) and contoured seascape.

White Bank Stunning seascape (tunnels, arches) and prolific fish life, including shoals of jacks and the occasional guitar shark.

Ave Maria Rocks A seamount northwest of La Digue. Noted for its shark sightings and prolific marine life.

leaves of the coco de mer soaring 30m to a sombre canopy of huge fronds. Signs indicate some of the other endemic trees to look out for (there are more than 50 other indigenous plants and trees), including several varieties of pandanus (screw pines) and latanier palms.

There are free guided visits at 9am and 2pm, but we recommend taking a private guide for a 1½- to two-hour guided walk through the forest – you'll miss so much if you go it alone.

There's an informative visitor centre, cafe and excellent shop on-site.

Anse La Blague   BEACH
Head to Anse La Blague on the east coast if you're after a secluded picnic spot. Very few tourists make it to this isolated beach, which feels like the world's end. It has no facilities, other than shady *takamaka* trees. You might come across a few fishers with their catch of *cordonnier* (jobfish).

Anse Consolation   BEACH
Draped along a corner of the island that sees few visitors, Anse Consolation is a fine stretch of sand to spend an afternoon.

Anse Marie-Louise   BEACH
At the island's southern tip, Anse Marie-Louise is a pretty spot. There are no facilities and no parking lot; just pull over at the side of the road and voila – you're at the beach. Continuing along the coastal road to the west, you'll find numerous coves and other beaches.

Grand Anse   BEACH
(Map p310) Grand Anse has a long, typically beautiful beach, but swimming is only average, with shallow waters and a profusion of algae.

Praslin National Park   FOREST
(Map p310) This national park is spread across the hills of Praslin's interior. At its core is the Unesco World Heritage–listed Vallée de Mai, one of the most beautiful stands of forest anywhere in the Seychelles.

🏃 Activities

Praslin's natural attractions provide the basis for so many memorable experiences on the island, from the weird-and-wonderful forest of Vallée de Mai to offshore islands and underwater reefs.

ANSE GEORGETTE

Bad news: Anse Georgette, which is an indescribably lovely stretch of white sand at the northwestern tip of the island, has been engulfed by the sprawling Constance Lémuria resort (p313). Good news: it remains a public beach that is accessible to anybody. In order not to be turned back at the gate of the Lémuria, call reception beforehand – they will inform the guards. Once inside the property, you can get to Anse Georgette on foot or take the hourly 'shuttle' (a buggy) operated by the resort – isn't it cute? You can also get there by taxi boat from Anse Volbert; **Sagittarius Taxi Boat** (Map p310; ☑ 2512137, 4232234; Anse Volbert; ⊙ 9am-5pm) can arrange drop-offs and pick-ups (€40 per person).

Anse Georgette could hardly be more tranquil. The seas here are fairly calm, the bay is safe and the vista of the surrounding green hills is dramatic. There are no amenities but you'll find everything you need at the resort, which lies in the adjacent bay to the south.

Diving & Snorkelling
Whether you're an experienced diver or a novice slapping on fins for the first time, you'll find superb dive sites off Praslin.

The best snorkelling spots can be found at Anse Lazio, around St Pierre Islet and off Baie Laraie on Curieuse.

White Tip Dive Centre   DIVING
(Map p310; ☑ 2514282, 4232282; www.whitetip divers.com; Anse Volbert) At the eastern end of Paradise Sun Hotel (p315), this small, professional outfit has years of experience diving the sites around Praslin and La Digue. It charges reasonable rates (by Seychellois standards); an introductory dive is €75 while single dives cost from €50. Packages, certification courses and snorkelling trips are also available.

Octopus Dive Centre   DIVING
(Map p310; ☑ 2512350, 4232350; www.octopus diver.com; Anse Volbert) This dive school is very experienced after more than a decade running dives around the island. An introductory dive is only €70. A standard dive runs upwards of €50. Also offers dive packages, certification courses and snorkelling trips.

Praslin

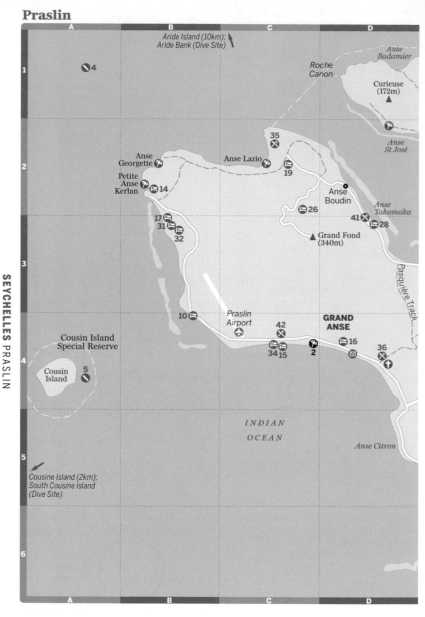

Aride Island (10km);
Aride Bank (Dive Site)

Anse
Badamier

Roche
Canon

Curieuse
(172m)

Anse
St José

35

Anse Lazio

Anse
Georgette

19

Petite
Anse
Kerlan

14

Anse
Boudin

26

Anse
Takamaka

41

28

17

31

32

Grand Fond
(340m)

Pasquière Track

Cousin Island
Special Reserve

10

Praslin
Airport

GRAND
ANSE

42

Cousin
Island

5

34 15

2

16

36

INDIAN

OCEAN

Anse Citron

Cousine Island (2km);
South Cousine Island
(Dive Site)

SEYCHELLES PRASLIN

Lémuria Dive Centre DIVING
(Map p310; ☑4281281; www.constancehotels.
com/en/experiences/diving; Anse Kerlan) This
luxurious diving school is inside the Constance Lémuria resort (p313) but is open
to nonguests (by reservation). It runs the full
gamut of courses for beginners as well as diving trips. An introductory dive costs a whopping €150. Single dives are €90.

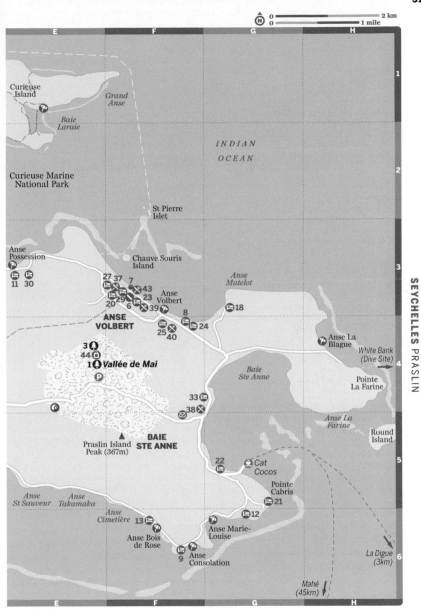

Kayaking

It's not a bad idea to rent a kayak and explore Anse Volbert at your leisure and paddle round Chauve Souris Island. Sagittarius Taxi Boat (p309) handles rentals.

🛏 Sleeping

Demand for accommodation is high in Praslin. To avoid disappointment, particularly in high season, book your accommodation well in advance.

Praslin

Anse Volbert, with its restaurants and other tourist facilities, makes a good base. Grand Anse is busier and less attractive, but also less touristy, and there are some decent options within walking distance of the Baie Ste Anne jetty.

Approximately halfway between Anse Lazio and Anse Volbert, Anse Possession is convenient to both. It's also a good, quiet base. There's a thin strip of sand but it can't rival the beaches at Anse Lazio or Anse Volbert.

Grand Anse & Anse Kerlan

Sunset Cove Villa   APARTMENT €€
(Map p310; ☑2513048; www.sunset-cove-villa. com; Anse Kerlan; r €75-150; P ❈) Pinch yourself – you're just steps from the sea. OK, there's no proper beach here because of erosion, but the setting is truly appealing. Digs are in two comfortable, well-equipped and light-filled houses. No meal service, but there's a small supermarket nearby.

Seashell Self Catering   APARTMENT €€
(Map p310; ☑2513764; csetheve@hotmail.com; Anse Kerlan; d €70; P ❈ ☎) This sturdy house built from granite stones scores goals with a combination of affordable rates and a handy position – the sea is just 100m away, though the beach is not that great because of erosion and seaweed. The two large, spotless studios are pleasantly furnished, with tiled floors, sparkling bathrooms, good bedding and a terrace. Both have a kitchenette.

There's a supermarket close by.

Islander Guesthouse   APARTMENT €€
(Map p310; ☑2781224, 4233224; www.islander-seychelles.com; Anse Kerlan; d €112-218, 2-bedroom apt from €177, villas from €253; P ❈ ☎) The good people at the Islander are not setting out to win any 'best in its class' awards with their establishment but its virtue is its good shape and you'll be made to feel at home. The four bungalows (eight rooms in total) are unpretentious but clean and the property opens onto Anse Kerlan. Air-con is extra (€8).

There's an on-site restaurant.

Villas de Mer
HOTEL €€

(Map p310; ☑4233972; Grand Anse; d incl breakfast from €138; ⊞✳☎☲) Villas de Mer is a great midrange option with good accommodation for its price following a full refit. Here the 10 rooms occupy two rows of low-slung buildings facing each other. A highlight is the restaurant, which has a fabulous beach frontage and serves fresh seafood. The atmosphere is relaxed and friendly.

★Constance Lémuria
RESORT €€€

(Map p310; ☑4281281; www.constancehotels.com; Anse Kerlan; d incl breakfast from €580; ⊞✳☎☲) Praslin's top-drawer establishment occupies the island's whole northwest tip. If you're not bowled over by the voluminous foyer and marvellous spa, you will be by the three-tiered infinity pool, three gorgeous beaches and expansive grounds where the villas blend in among the rocks and water features. Facilities include three restaurants, a kids club and a magnificent 18-hole golf course (open to nonguests).

Dhevatara Beach Hotel
BOUTIQUE HOTEL €€€

(Map p310; ☑4237333; http://hermesretreats.com/en/dhevatara.aspx; Grand Anse; d from €356; ⊞✳☎☲) Dhevatara is a boutique-like luxury venture loaded with more cool than any other on the island. With only 10 rooms divided in two categories (garden views and ocean views), it's a great choice for couples. Rooms are not huge but are individually designed; the ones upstairs get more natural light. Facilities include a spa.

Indian Ocean Lodge
RESORT €€€

(Map p310; ☑4283838; www.indianoceanlodge.com; Grand Anse; s/d incl breakfast from €211/242; ⊞✳☎☲) Indian Ocean Lodge has gone upmarket since a freshen-up in 2011, but has retained its reasonable prices; it's a great place to enjoy a midrange-style resort without breaking the bank. The rooms combine classical luxury and elegant simplicity, and have balconies that afford good sea views. Amenities include a pool and a restaurant. It's appropriate for couples and families alike.

Castello Beach Hotel
HOTEL €€€

(Map p310; ☑4298900; www.castellobeachhotel.com; Anse Kerlan; s/d €266/330; ⊞✳@☎☲) This four-star, suites-only hotel has large rooms, an above-average restaurant and a lovely sunset-facing location on a small stretch of sand. Wood floors and wicker furnishings give it a nicely casual feel, although not many of the suites have beach views.

🛏 Anse Consolation Area

Bonnen Kare Beach Villa
APARTMENT €€

(Map p310; ☑4322457; www.bonnenkare.com; Anse Consolation; d/q €140/250) A lovely option for a group of friends or a family, this secluded four-room villa opening onto an idyllic sandy cove really fulfils the dreams of a private beach getaway. Don't fancy cooking? The maid can prepare meals on request. No air-con.

Coco de Mer Hotel & Black Parrot Suites
RESORT €€€

(Map p310; ☑4290555; www.cocodemer.com; Anse Bois de Rose; d incl breakfast from €288; ⊞✳☎☲) The exclusive Black Parrot Suites, perched on a headland with fantastic ocean views, afford serious cosseting and a hideaway: the 12 stylish suites and adjoining spa appeal to couples after a low-key, tranquil honeymoon (no children under 14). Along the shore, resort-like Coco de Mer has 40 refurbished rooms, a gym, tennis court, two restaurants, shops and a bar.

🛏 Baie Ste Anne & Pointe Cabris

Susan Self-Catering
GUESTHOUSE €

(Map p310; ☑2595569, 4232124; Baie Ste-Anne; s/d incl breakfast €35/70; ⊞✳) Run by an elderly woman, this homey pick, on the northern fringes of Baie Ste Anne, has a laid-back vibe. The one room is small and its furnishings are a bit dated, but do the job. Although the setting is nothing special, it's clean, the welcome is warm, the garden is blossoming with colour and the food (dinner €15) has a good reputation.

Le Port Guest House
GUESTHOUSE €

(Map p310; ☑4232262; mapool.leport@gmail.com; Baie Ste-Anne; d/q €60/100; ✳) Not far from the jetty, this friendly guesthouse has three comfortable, fuss-free rooms, two of which enjoy partial sea views. The area doesn't scream 'vacation' but Anse Volbert is easy to reach by bus. Good value.

Le Grand Bleu
APARTMENT €

(Map p310; ☑4232437; gbleu@seychelles.net; Pointe Cabris; d €65; ⊞✳☎) Bargain! Le Grand Bleu features two well-appointed villas nestled in a flowery garden. Each unit has two rooms with bathrooms, a terrace with gorgeous sea views (it's on a hillside), and its own kitchenette. No meal service, but you can head to Chalets Côté Mer & Le Colibri, on the same property (same family).

SEXY COCONUTS

This must be the sexiest fruit on earth. The *coco fesse* (the fruit of the coco de mer palm) looks like, ahem, buttocks with a female sex. It has been the source of many legends and erotic lore, given its peculiar shape. This rare palm grows naturally only in the Seychelles.

Only female trees produce the erotically shaped nuts, which can weigh over 30kg. The male tree possesses a decidedly phallic flower stem of 1m or longer, adding to the coco de mer's steamy reputation.

Harvesting the nuts is strictly controlled by the Seychelles Island Foundation (p291), an NGO that manages the Vallée de Mai on behalf of the government.

★ **Château de Feuilles** HOTEL €€€
(Map p310; ✆ 4290000; www.chateaudefeuilles. com; Pointe Cabris; d incl breakfast from €580; P❋🗇🐾) Paradise awaits in this bijou hideaway sitting on an unfathomably beautiful headland near Baie Ste Anne. Nine luxurious, stone-walled villas are ingeniously deployed over several acres of tropical gardens. A serene symphony of earth tones and natural textures, elegant furnishings, sensational views, high-class amenities (including complimentary car), an uber-romantic poolside restaurant and a hilltop – every detail is spot on. Three-night minimum stay.

**Chalets Côté Mer &
Le Colibri** BUNGALOW €€€
(Map p310; ✆ 4294200; www.chaletcotemer.com; Pointe Cabris; d incl breakfast €150-193; P❋🗇🐾) A good deal close to Baie Ste Anne. Features a clutch of A-framed bungalows and villas on a verdant hillside with glorious views over La Digue. The Colibri bungalows are slightly hipper than the no-frills Chalets Côté Mer. Aim for the Colibri, Magpie, Fairytern, Katiti or Kato, which are the best laid out. The cheaper units are fan-cooled. Minimum three nights.

🛏 Anse Volbert Area

L'Hirondelle APARTMENT €€
(Map p310; ✆ 4232243; www.seychelles.net/ hirondelle; Anse Volbert; apt from €145; P🗇) The four rooms won't knock your socks off but they're comfortable and fully equipped, and each has a balcony or a terrace that commands a blue-green lagoon vista. Downsides: it's not shielded from the noise of the coast road and there's no air-con. Breakfast is €10.

Rosemary's Guest House GUESTHOUSE €€
(Map p310; ✆ 4232176; www.ile-tropicale.com/ rosemary; Anse Volbert; r incl breakfast from €80; ❋🗇) Yes, you read those prices right (we asked twice). Relaxed and friendly, this homey place features two types of rooms. The four fan-cooled rooms in the two older buildings feel a bit tired but are tidy, while the four with air-con occupy a modern building overlooking the beach. Though the property feels a tad compact, the location is ace. Meals available on request.

★ **Le Duc de Praslin** HOTEL €€€
(Map p310; ✆ 4232252; www.leduc-seychelles. com; Anse Volbert; s/d incl breakfast from €255/330; P❋🗇🐾) This little island of subdued glamour, a *coco fesse*'s throw from the beach, is one of the most appealing options on Praslin. The generous-sized, sensitively furnished rooms have all mod cons and orbit around an alluring pool and a nicely laid-out tropical garden. Another plus is the excellent on-site restaurant, Café des Arts (p317). If only it had ocean views, life would be perfect.

Acajou Beach Resort RESORT €€€
(Map p310; ✆ 4385300; www.acajouseychelles. com; Côte D'Or; s/d from €289/335; P❋@🗇🐾) 🌿 Beautiful rooms decked in wood and white linen and set in a lush tropical garden are the highlights of this excellent resort close to Anse Volbert. It all fronts onto a gorgeous beach, plus there's a good spa and three restaurants. Half the resort's electricity needs come from solar power and it has a range of eco initiatives.

Raffles Praslin RESORT €€€
(Map p310; ✆ 4296000; www.raffles.com/ praslin; Anse Takamaka; d incl breakfast from €568; P❋@🗇🐾) Luxurious villas, each with its own private plunge pool and many with uninterrupted views of paradise, make this one of the premier properties on Praslin. You can count on a two-tiered infinity pool, seven excellent restaurants, a luxury spa and service that rarely misses a beat. The beach here is excellent, but you're also close to Anse Lazio.

★ **Les Villas D'Or** VILLA €€€
(Map p310; ✆ 4232777; www.lesvillasdorseychelles. com; Côte D'Or; d/q from €252/495; P❋@🗇🐾) Beautifully appointed, self-catering villas

separated from the sea only by a lush garden strewn with palms are the hallmarks of this excellent property. There are 10 villas, two of which are suitable for families. It's close to Anse Volbert.

Paradise Sun Hotel RESORT €€€
(Map p310; ☑4293293; www.paradise-sun. seychelleshotel24.com; Anse Volbert; d with half board from €380; P❋@≋) If you're looking for the classic Seychelles setting, complete with shady palms, lagoon views and a splendid china-white stretch of sand just steps from your door, then this resort-style operation won't disappoint. It offers 80 comfy rooms with dark-wood fixtures and granite bricks, ample space and heaps of amenities, including a dive centre and a water sports centre.

L'Archipel RESORT €€€
(Map p310; ☑4284700; www.larchipel.com; Anse Gouvernement; d incl breakfast from €335; P❋@≋) This resort occupies a large, nicely landscaped plot by the beach at Anse Gouvernement (the eastern tip of Anse Volbert). Squeezed between the spacious, stand-alone, split-level units are a swimming pool and restaurant. The walk up to the highest bungalows may leave unfit guests panting. You'll find all the usual resort facilities on-site.

Les Lauriers BUNGALOW €€€
(Map p310; ☑4232241; www.laurier-seychelles. com; Anse Volbert; s €100-140, d €125-175, incl breakfast; P❋@) A pleasant oasis, despite the lack of sea views and the odd landscaping of the compound. Run by friendly Edwin and Sybille, it features six uncomplicated and smallish but neat rooms as well as eight spacious bungalows. The carved-wood posts on the terrace are a nice touch. It's well worth opting for half board (from €175 for two), given the attached high-quality restaurant.

🛏 Anse Possession

Chalets Anse Possession APARTMENT €€
(Map p310; ☑4232180; www.chalets-anse-possesion.com; Anse Possession; d €60-100, q €100-130, incl breakfast; P❋@) Four two-bedroom villas are set in lush greenery off the coast road. Although not the height of luxury, they're clean, comfy, roomy and serviceable – perfect for the traveller who's not fussy. Meals (from €10) can be served on request. The owners can pick you up at the jetty. Excellent value.

Sea View Lodge APARTMENT €€
(Map p310; ☑2711965; www.seaviewlodge-praslin.com; Anse Possession; d €130-200; P❋@) This place has four units, including two villas perched on a hillside. The verandas have stunning views over the bay and Curieuse Island. The smaller 'Banana' bungalows feel like cosy bird's nests and will appeal to couples on a tighter budget, while the larger house closer to the coastal road is great for families. All are fully equipped and superclean.

🛏 Zimbabwe

★**Maison du Soleil** BUNGALOW €
(Map p310; ☑2576315, 2562780; jeanlouis@ seychelles.net; Zimbabwe; d €50-85) Almost too good to be true. A location scout's dream, this self-catering villa perched on a hilltop offers million-dollar views of Curieuse and Praslin's northern coastline. There's a second villa, a bit further down the hill. OK, both are very modestly furnished, there's no air-con (and no wi-fi) and you need wheels to stay here, but those are the only gripes.

🛏 Anse Lazio

Le Chevalier APARTMENT €€
(Map p310; ☑4232322; www.lechevalierbay.com; Anse Lazio; d incl breakfast from €145; P❋) Finally, Anse Lazio has produced a place to stay. The owners of the eponymous restaurant rent eight rooms in two separate buildings; the best rooms occupy the modern house at the back. They're a bit sterile, but the location is fantastic – you're a stone's throw from one of the most famous beaches in the world.

🍴 Eating

Since most people eat in their hotels or guesthouses, there are relatively few independent restaurants on Praslin. Most hotels have excellent restaurants that are open to all comers (by reservation).

🍴 Grand Anse & Anse Kerlan

Restaurant Paradisier SEAFOOD, PIZZA €€
(Map p310; ☑4237537; Grand Anse; mains Rs 150-425; ☉noon-9pm) Considered one of the best restaurants in Grand Anse, this place concocts Creole classics, copious sandwiches and tasty pizzas that you can enjoy in an atmospheric garden terrace complete with wrought-iron furnishings. Also does takeaway. If only it had beach frontage, life would be perfect.

WORTH A TRIP

CURIEUSE ISLAND

Curieuse Island is a granite island 1.5km off Praslin's north coast. A leper colony from 1833 until 1965, Curieuse is today used as a breeding centre for giant Aldabra tortoises. The wardens at the **giant tortoise farm** show visitors round the pens, after which you're free to explore the rest of the island. Nearby Baie Laraie is a fantastic place for swimming and snorkelling. From Baie Laraie, a path leads to **Anse José**, where you can visit the **doctor's house**; it contains a small historical museum. If you fancy a dip after your picnic, the **beach** is lovely: a stretch of pristine pale golden sand fringed with lofty palm trees and framed by massive granite boulders.

Most visitors to Curieuse Island arrive on an organised tour, usually in combination with Cousin and St Pierre Islet. Tours are arranged through Praslin's hotels or any touroperator. Day trips cost around €125/60 for an adult/child including lunch, landing fees and the marine-park entry fee. The alternative is to charter your own boat from Anse Volbert. Sagittarius Taxi Boat (p309), on the beach beside the Paradise Sun Hotel,charges €35 for Curieuse, including fees; Curieuse with St Pierre costs €40. You'll also find taxi boats at Anse Possession, or you could contact Edwin at Les Lauriers (p315), whose tours get rave reviews from travellers.

Breeze Garden   CAFE €€
(Map p310; 4237000; Grand Anse; mains Rs 205-350; 1-9.30pm) In a verdant property near the west coast's main church, Breeze Garden has agreeably green surroundings and offers salads, curries, pasta dishes, pizzas and wok dishes; try the tempura prawns or Creole fish curry. Takeaway is also available.

Capricorn   SEAFOOD €€€
(Map p310; 4233224; Anse Kerlan; mains Rs 250-425; lunch & dinner Mon-Sat) At Anse Kerlan, Capricorn is the good on-site restaurant at Islander's (p312). It's famous for its 'octopus Patrick-style' (octopus in a saffron sauce) and homemade desserts.

Baie St Anne

Coco Rouge   CREOLE €€
(Map p310; 2581014; Baie Ste-Anne; mains Rs 140-320; 9am-2.30pm & 6.30-10pm) Tasty Creole cooking is the simple secret to the success of this agreeable roadside restaurant in Baie Ste Anne. It features fresh fish and unusual local specialities such as breadfruit. The setting is less than exciting, but the restaurant does takeaway, so why not make a picnic of it at the beach of your choice. Cash only.

Anse Volbert Area

★**Les Lauriers**   BUFFET €€
(Map p310; 4232241; Anse Volbert; buffet Rs 450; 7.30-10pm Thu-Tue) Charismatic Edwin and his Belgian spouse prepare a spectacular Creole buffet at dinner. It begins with fine hors d'oeuvre displayed on a boat-shaped table (the avocado salad is to die for), followed by sizzling meat and expertly grilled fish (usually red snapper, jack and job).

★**PK's @ Pasquière & Gastropub**   INTERNATIONAL €€
(Map p310; 4236242; Anse Boudin; mains Rs 225-495; 11am-8.30pm Mon-Sat, 9am-4pm Sun) You can see this place from the coastal road thanks to its distinctive position in a secluded hillside property with pretty coastal views. Tables are widely spaced and the menu has a lightness of touch missing from many of its peers. The meat or seafood dishes are all heartily recommended, but we especially like the seafood platter. Great value.

Gelateria de Luca   ICE CREAM, PIZZERIA €€
(Map p310; 4232706; Anse Volbert; mains Rs 160-375; 9am-9.30pm) Praslin's prime ice-cream parlour will leave you a drooling mess. Order a *coppa tropicale*, and you'll see why. It also whips up pasta, pizza and various snacks at lunchtime, while dinner is a more formal affair, with dishes such as grilled lamb chop, pork spare ribs and fish fillet.

Village du Pecheur   SEAFOOD, INTERNATIONAL €€
(Map p310; 2611111; www.thesunsethotelgroup.com; Anse Volbert; mains Rs 180-330; 11am-9pm) Classy decor, a sandy floor that segues effortlessly onto lovely Anse Volbert, and dishes such as seafood curry flavoured with cinnamon leaf and served with Creole chutney and rice make this an excellent choice for those keen to eat by the sea.

La Goulue   EUROPEAN €€

(Map p310; ☑ 4232223; Anse Volbert; mains Rs 150-295; ⊙ noon-9.30pm Tue-Sun) This little eatery doesn't have beach frontage but the terrace catches some breeze. The menu features Creole staples and various filling snacks.

★ Café des Arts   INTERNATIONAL €€€

(Map p310; ☑ 4232170; www.cafe.sc; Anse Volbert; mains Rs 450-800; ⊙ noon-2.30pm & 6-9.30pm Tue-Sun) Praslin's most stylish restaurant is in the Le Duc de Praslin hotel (p314). Flickering candles, colourful paintings, swaying palms, a breezy terrace and the sound of waves washing the beach will rekindle the faintest romantic flame. The food is suitably refined; flavourful Seychellois favourites are whipped into eye-pleasing concoctions.

La Pirogue   INTERNATIONAL €€€

(Map p310; ☑ 4236677; Anse Volbert; mains Rs 160-680; ⊙ noon-9.30pm; ☑) This cheerful cafe-restaurant serves simple but well-prepared meals, including salads you can tuck into without hesitation. There's a good selection of fish and meat dishes, as well as vegetarian options and sandwiches.

✗ Anse Lazio

Bonbon Plume   SEAFOOD €€€

(Map p310; ☑ 4232136; Anse Lazio; mains Rs 285-485; ⊙ noon-3pm) Tourist trap or front-row seat to paradise? Both perhaps. With such a location – the palm-thatched canopy is right on the beach at gorgeous Anse Lazio – tables are in high demand: ring ahead if you want your feet in the sand.

Le Chevalier   INTERNATIONAL, SEAFOOD €€€

(Map p310; ☑ 4232322; www.lechevalierbay.com; Anse Lazio; mains Rs 200-375, menus Rs 400-850; ⊙ 8am-3.30pm, dinner by reservation) OK, Le Chevalier is not right on the beach and the setting is frustratingly bland (think a vast, tiled, open-air room on the ground floor of a modern villa), but the menu offers lots of variety and includes salads, burgers and fish dishes. Breakfast is served until 10.30am.

🛍 Shopping

Kreolor   ARTS & CRAFTS

(Map p310; Vallée de Mai; ⊙ 9am-4.30pm) Perhaps the best boutique on Praslin, Kreolor at the entrance to Vallée de Mai sells artfully designed wooden crafts (many in the shape of the coco de mer), jewellery and other tasteful souvenirs.

ⓘ Information

You'll find several banks and bureaux de change in Grand Anse, Baie Ste Anne and Anse Volbert. All banks have ATMs and exchange facilities.

Vallée de Mer Visitor Centre (☑ 4236220; www.sif.sc; Vallée de Mer; ⊙ 9am-5pm) The informative visitor centre at the trailhead to the walks through Vallée de Mer has information panels on major bird and plant species and (usually) staff on hand to answer questions.

ⓘ Getting There & Away

Praslin airport is 3km from Grand Anse and has up to 25 daily flights to/from Mahé.

Regular ferry services connect Praslin with Mahé and La Digue. The port is in Baie Ste Anne.

ⓘ Getting Around

You can hire bikes through your accommodation or from **Maki Shop** (☑ 4277711; Anse Volbert; ⊙ 9am-6pm) for Rs 150 per day.

Hopping around the small islands off Praslin is done by chartered boat; trips are usually organised through the hotels or tour operators.

Praslin has a decent bus service (Rs 7) as well as the usual taxis. A taxi ride from the Baie Ste Anne jetty to Anse Volbert or Grand Anse will set you back Rs 300.

A car is a great way to see the island. For car hire, you can negotiate directly with car-rental companies; the tourist office has a list or make arrangements through your accommodation. Expect to pay about €50 per day for the smallest car.

LA DIGUE

Remember that tropical paradise that appears in countless adverts and glossy travel brochures? Here it's the real thing, with jade-green waters, bewitching bays studded with heart-palpitatingly gorgeous beaches, and green hills cloaked with tangled jungle and tall trees. As if that weren't enough, La Digue is ideally situated as a springboard to surrounding islands, including Félicité, Grande Soeur and the fairy-tale Île Cocos.

Despite its lush beauty, La Digue has managed to escape the somewhat rampant tourist development that affects Mahé and Praslin. Sure, it's certainly not undiscovered, but La Digue has a more laid-back feel than the other main islands, with only a few surfaced roads and virtually no motorised cars (bar a few taxis). It is definitely more of a back-to-nature place than a jet-set-tourist haven, making it possible to find that deserted *anse* (bay) where you really feel like you've been stranded in paradise.

La Digue

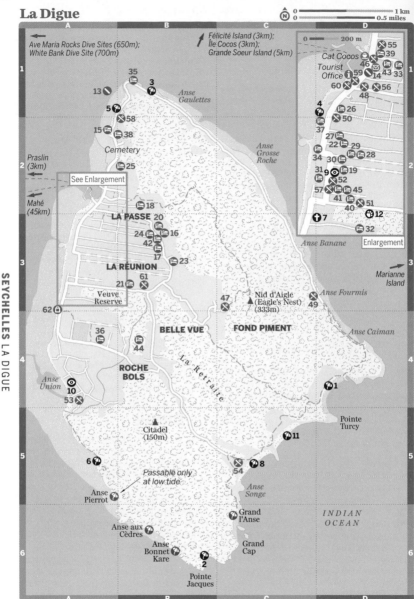

Ave Maria Rocks Dive Sites (650m);
White Bank Dive Site (700m)

Félicité Island (3km);
Île Cocos (3km);
Grande Soeur Island (5km)

Anse Gaulettes

Anse Grosse Roche

Praslin (3km)

Mahé (45km)

See Enlargement

Cemetery

LA PASSE

LA RÉUNION

Veuve Reserve

BELLE VUE

FOND PIMENT

ROCHE BOLS

La Retraite

Anse Union

Citadel (150m)

Passable only at low tide

Anse Pierrot

Anse aux Cèdres

Anse Bonnet Kare

Pointe Jacques

Nid d'Aigle (Eagle's Nest) (333m)

Anse Fourmis

Anse Caiman

Anse Banane

Marianne Island

Pointe Turcy

Anse Songe

Grand l'Anse

Grand Cap

INDIAN OCEAN

Cat Cocos
Tourist Office

Enlargement

SEYCHELLES LA DIGUE

Sights

La Passe VILLAGE
(Map p318) A visit to tiny La Passe almost feels like stepping back in time, so perfectly does it capture the image of a sleepy tropical port. Apart from a few trucks and taxis, very

few motorised vehicles clog the streets. Men and women talk shop on the jetty while waiting for the ferry to arrive. Children ride bicycles on the tree-lined roads. Come Saturday night, most islanders head to the seafront for some serious dancing and drinking.

La Digue

Veuve Reserve
WILDLIFE RESERVE
(Map p318; ☐ 2783114; La Passe; ⊙information centre 8am-noon & 1-4pm Mon-Fri) **FREE** La Digue is the last refuge of the black paradise flycatcher, which locals call the *veuve* (widow). This small forest reserve, which has been set aside to protect its natural habitat, is thought to shelter about 15 pairs of the bird. The male has long black tail feathers. There are several walking trails punctuated with interpretive panels about flora.

L'Union Estate & Copra Factory
HISTORIC SITE
(Map p318; Rs 100; ⊙8am-5pm) At one time, the main industry on La Digue was coconut farming, centred on L'Union Estate coconut plantation south of La Passe. These days L'Union Estate is run as an informal 'theme park', which harbours the Old Plantation House, a colonial-era graveyard, a boatyard and the obligatory pen of giant tortoises.

Church
CHURCH
(Map p318; La Passe) With its striking yellow and white facade, this Catholic church is well worth a gander and also makes a colorful scene on Sunday morning when it is bursting with a devout congregation dressed in white and belting out rousing hymns.

HIKING LA DIGUE

If your muscles are starting to shrivel after one too many days of beach-basking, take the time to explore the island's recesses that can only be reached by walking paths – you'll discover plenty of secret spots only known to locals. Tracks are not well defined and are difficult to find and to follow; it's advisable to go with a guide. Walking guides include Robert Agnes, whose company, **Sunny Trail Guide** (☎ 2525357; www.sunnytrailguide.net; La Passe; ☺ by reservation), has good credentials; Henry Bibi, who runs **Paradise Tours** (☺ by reservation); and Gerard Niole, who runs **Coco Trail** (☎ 2502396, 2535447; www.cocotrailguide.com; ☺ by reservation). Reckon on €30 to €40 per person, depending on the walk. Fruits and snacks are included.

Nid d'Aigle

Ready to huff and puff? Tackle Nid d'Aigle (Eagle's Nest), the highest point on La Digue (333m), which commands sensational views. From La Passe, follow the inland concrete road that leads up to Snack Bellevue (it's signposted), then take the narrow path that starts behind the Snack. After about 15 minutes, you'll reach an intersection on a ridge; turn right and follow the path until you reach Nid d'Aigle (no sign) after another 10 minutes. From Nid d'Aigle, it's possible to descend to Anse Cocos (add another 90 minutes), but a guide is mandatory as the path is overgrown.

Grand Anse to Anse Cocos

If you have time for only one walk, choose this option, because it's the most scenic. The coastline between Grand Anse and Anse Marron is extremely alluring: a string of hard-to-reach inlets lapped by azure waters, with the mandatory idyllic beach fringing the shore, and vast expanses of chaotic granite boulders. From Loutier Coco, it takes roughly 1¼ hours to reach Anse Marron (p321), a gem of solitude. It's poorly marked; you'll definitely need a guide. From Anse Marron, you can continue as far as Anse Source d'Argent at low tide, but there's a short section where you'll have to walk knee-deep in the water. If you do continue until Anse Source d'Argent, you may be asked to pay Rs 100 when you exit L'Union Estate coconut plantation.

Around Anse Source d'Argent

From Anse Source d'Argent, a memorable adventure consists of climbing up the granite hills that loom above the southwest coast before getting down to **Anse Pierrot**, from where you can continue along the shore to **Anse aux Cèdres** and **Anse Bonnet Kare** (and back to Anse Source d'Argent along the shore). The beauty of these stunning swaths of sand lies in the fact that they're totally secluded and there's no road here. It's an arduous climb to reach the top of the granite hills but the panoramic views will be etched in your memory forever. It's a half-day excursion. It's also possible to continue as far as Anse Marron and up to Grand Anse.

◉ Beaches

Anse Source d'Argent   BEACH
(Map p318; Rs 100; ☺ 8am-5pm) Most new arrivals head straight for the beach at Anse Source d'Argent, and it's easy to see why. Picture this: a dazzling white-sand beach backed by naturally sculpted granite boulders and lapped by emerald waters. It's not perfect, though; Anse Source d'Argent can get pretty crowded, especially at high tide when the beach virtually disappears. Another downside: Anse Source d'Argent is scenic, but not

that great for swimming due to the shallow water (and, occasionally, seaweed).

Make sure you come for longer than a day; once the day trippers have left you can walk around or curl up under the shade of the trees and feel like you have this uninhabited piece of paradise all to yourself. For the best photo ops, come in the late afternoon (keep your entrance ticket with you) when the colours are most intense. This beach is one of the few facing west, so you can watch some fabulous sunsets.

If you're feeling peckish, a couple of shacks sell fruits and refreshments.

Take note that the path down to Anse Source d'Argent runs through the old L'Union Estate coconut plantation. In other words, you'll have to pay Rs 100 (valid for a day) to access the beach.

Anse Marron   BEACH
(Map p318) At the southern tip of the island, the tiny inlet of Anse Marron is a hidden morsel of tranquillity. The fact that this fantastically wild beach can only be reached on foot adds to its wonderful sense of remoteness. It's also superscenic: the white crescent of sand is backed by a chaotic jumble of gigantic granite blocks, where you'll find some protected natural pools.

Anse Cocos   BEACH
(Map p318) From Petite Anse, you can take your beach towel further north to the wonderfully scenic Anse Cocos, which is reached by a rather vague track that starts at the southern end of Petite Anse. The bay here is dazzling to behold: a salt-white strip of sand lapped by turquoise waters, and backed by casuarina trees and craning palms – it's a gorgeous place to sun yourself. Because of rip currents, Anse Cocos isn't good for swimming; for a dip, head to the northern tip of the beach, which has protected pools.

Grand Anse   BEACH
(Map p318) On the southeast coast, Grand Anse is a stunning beach to sun yourself on, and it sees fewer visitors than Anse Source d'Argent because of the effort required to get there (though you can easily walk or cycle the 4km or so from La Passe). It's La Digue's longest beach. One caveat: swimming may be dangerous because of the strong offshore currents during the southeast monsoon, from April to October. Apart from a massive casuarina tree, there's not much shade.

Petite Anse   BEACH
(Map p318) North of Grand Anse, the wonderfully dramatic crescent of Petite Anse is accessible on foot only. Strong riptides make it dangerous for swimming but it's a lovely place to kick back and sunbathe. From Grand Anse, it's an easy 15-minute walk along a well-defined path.

Anse Réunion   BEACH
(Map p318) True, Anse Réunion, south of La Passe, hardly compares to La Digue's other beaches – there is usually algae drifting along the shore – but it's an easy walk from town and a pretty place to watch the sun set.

Anse Sévère   BEACH
(Map p318) On the northern outskirts of La Passe, Anse Sévère is not the most photogenic beach on La Digue but the peace you find sitting here under a *takamaka* tree may be as good as it gets on the island. It's lapped by jade waters that just beg to be swum in, with Praslin, Félicité and Île Coco in the background. The fact that it's protected by a barrier reef makes it safe for children, and there's good snorkelling at the southern end.

Depending on tides, it may be strewn with seaweed.

Anse Patates   BEACH
(Map p318) At the northern tip of the island, this beach framed by big glacis boulders is alluring, but a bit too petite to be called perfect. It offers some good snorkelling, though.

🏃 Activities
There's more to La Digue than sexy beaches. When you have finished recharging the batteries, there's a startling variety (for such a small island) of adventure options available.

Boat Excursions
Taking a boat excursion to nearby **Île Cocos**, **Félicité** and **Grande Soeur** will be one of the main highlights of your visit to the Seychelles and it's well worth the expense. Full-day tours typically stop to snorkel off Île Cocos and Félicité and picnic on Grande Soeur. The best snorkelling spots can be found off the iconic Île Cocos.

Most lodgings and travel agencies on La Digue can arrange such trips. Prices are about €115, including a barbecued fish lunch. Half-day tours can also be organised (€55 to €65).

Diving & Snorkelling
La Digue features a range of excellent dive sites, including the iconic White Bank. Snorkelling is also top-notch. Sweet spots around the island include Anse Sévère and Anse Patates. Île Cocos and Félicité seem to be tailored to the expectations of avid snorkellers, with glassy turquoise waters and a smattering of healthy coral gardens around. All boat tours include snorkelling stops.

Azzurra Pro-Dive   DIVING
(Map p318; ☎4292525; www.ladigue.sc; Anse Réunion; introductory/single dive €95/66; ⊙8am-5pm) This PADI-certified dive centre organises a variety of dive trips and certification courses. Six- and 10-dive packages cost €310/495 and include gear hire. Based at La Digue Island Lodge (p324).

Trek Divers DIVING
(Map p318; ☑2513066; www.trekdivers.com; La Passe; introductory dive €90, 2-tank dive €120-135; ⊙ by reservation) This small dive outfit is run by Christophe, who has plenty of experience. Half- and full-day dive trips are offered aboard a comfortable catamaran.

🛏 Sleeping

Noticeably devoid of large resorts, La Digue prefers self-catering apartments, quiet villas and family guesthouses tucked down narrow lanes. Most of the accommodation is in the midrange bracket but you'll also find a couple of smart hotels. All accommodation options are located in or around La Passe. Discounts are usually offered for longer stays. Credit cards may not be accepted by guesthouses or some smaller lodgings; check when booking.

Zegret BUNGALOW €
(Map p318; ☑2602599; riciapat@hotmail.com; La Passe; d €60) This low-key venture is one of the sweetest accommodation deals on La Digue. It features one large bungalow with three rooms, a sitting room and a fully equipped kitchen. It's in a verdant property, a short amble from the centre of town.

Oceane's Self Catering APARTMENT €
(Map p318; ☑4234553, 2511818; www.oceane. sc; La Passe; s/d €65/100; ❋🛜) Yes, the four apartments in this modern villa are a bit cramped and have no views, but they're tidy, well equipped and serviceable. The place offers little extras such as gazebos and a Jacuzzi in the garden, which turns an average place into a great place to stay. It's family-run and friendly. Each room has a kitchenette.

La Passe Guest House – Chez Marie-Anne GUESTHOUSE €
(Map p318; ☑4234391; lapasseguesthouse@ gmail.com; La Passe; s €40, d €65-75, incl breakfast, bungalow d/q €90/110; ❋) Unfussy, low-key and priced a hair lower than the competition – a bonanza for budget-conscious visitors. The four rooms won't have you writing 'wish you were here' postcards, but you can save the postage for sampling the good Creole dinners (€15) prepared by Marie-Anne, the friendly owner. For families or couples in search of more privacy, a stand-alone, fully equipped bungalow is also available. The more expensive rooms and the bungalow have air-con.

★ Cabanes des Anges APARTMENT €€
(Map p318; ☑4234112, 2529115; www.cabanes desanges.sc; La Passe; incl breakfast d/apt €140/160; ❋🛜🏊) This well-regarded establishment comprises three adjoining rooms and six apartments. They're slightly set back from the main road, so peace and quiet are assured. Everything has been designed with a cool contemporary crispness. Bedrooms are big and flooded with light, with tiled floors and shiny-clean bathrooms.

★ Chalets d'Anse Réunion BUNGALOW €€
(Map p318; ☑2564611, 4235165; www.chalets dansereunion.com; La Passe; d €125; ❋🛜) The three bungalows, with their tiled floors, sunset-friendly balconies, sparkling bathrooms and generously sized rooms with mezzanine, are light and well-equipped. Add the lovely natural surroundings, warm welcome and spectacular rates and you have a real winner. The food is local and quite delicious (breakfast/dinner €13/25). Brilliant value.

★ Anse Sévère Bungalow BUNGALOW €€
(Map p318; ☑4247354; clemco@seychelles.net; Anse Sévère; d/q €115/120) This self-catering, fuss-free two-bedroom house with a fab sea frontage at the southern end of Anse Sévère is a great deal for families. Your biggest quandary here: a bout of snorkelling (or swimming) or a snooze on the white-sand beach? There's no air-con, but the location benefits from cooling sea breezes. Book early.

★ Pension Hibiscus APARTMENT €€
(Map p318; ☑4234029, 2575896; www.hibiscus ladigue.com; La Passe; s/d €70/100; ❋🛜) Pension Hibiscus shines under the care of its owner, friendly Jennita. Set back from the main road in a quiet area, it features five rooms that occupy two modern houses. It all feels very proper and immaculate, in a chilled-out setting. A hedge of tropical plants between the two houses ensures privacy. Free wi-fi near reception.

O Soleil APARTMENT €€
(Map p318; ☑2734890, 2735311; www.osoleil chalets.com; Anse Sévère; d €135-150; ❋🛜) This American-run venture comprises six spacious bungalows spitting distance from Anse Sévère. They're fully equipped and come with top-quality furniture, comfy beds and spick-and-span bathrooms. A good deal.

Pension Michel BUNGALOW €€
(Map p318; ☑4234003; www.pensionmichel.sc; La Passe; s/d incl breakfast €100/120; ❋🛜) If a beachfront location isn't a priority, then this small property down a dirt road is a nice place to ensconce yourself. A handful of

SEYCHELLES LA DIGUE

colourful bungalow-style studio apartments with small terraces and renovated bathrooms surround a quiet garden. There's a reputable on-site restaurant (dinner Rs 300). Wi-fi access is free for the first 24 hours.

Villa Veuve BUNGALOW €€
(Map p318; ☑2516608; www.villaveuve.com; La Passe; d incl breakfast €100-120, d with half board €135-150; ❄🛜) Down a dirt road on the southern outskirts of La Passe is this small complex of virginal white bungalows. They're quite soulless but functional, well-equipped and good value, and are scattered around a flower-filled property. Bonus: the on-site restaurant serves buffet-style dinners – it's worth opting for half board.

Maison Charme de L'Île APARTMENT €€
(Map p318; ☑2512542; www.maisoncharmedelile. com; L'Union, La Passe; d €120; ❄🛜🍴) Maison Charme de L'île offers homestyle comfort and a superquiet location for an affordable price. A two-minute bike ride from the waterfront, the four roomy, light-drenched, lovingly kept apartments have been styled with flair, and there's a tiny pool should you wish to cool off. Each unit has a front veranda and small backyard. Breakfast is €10.

Marie France Beachfront Apartments APARTMENT €€
(Map p318; ☑4234018; www.ladigueapartments. com; La Passe; d incl breakfast €135; ❄🛜) Yes, the three apartments above the owners' house don't have much island flavour (the white colour scheme is a bit too clinical), but they open onto the seashore (no beach) and offer fab sea views – a rarity in this price bracket on La Digue. They all come with a balcony and a kitchenette equipped with a fridge and microwave. Dinner (€25) can be arranged on request.

Kaz Digwa Self Catering BUNGALOW €€
(Map p318; ☑2513684, 2575457; kazdigwa@gmail. com; La Passe; d €100, q €125-150; ❄) Serviceable and cosy are the watchwords at this welcoming abode that comprises two wooden chalet-like bungalows in a beautifully manicured garden. They're well-appointed, relaxing and spacious – the larger one has two bedrooms – and the kitchens are brilliantly equipped. Meals, too, if you're too lazy to cook.

JML Holiday Apartment GUESTHOUSE €€
(Map p318; ☑2524415; http://jml-apartments. com; La Passe; d incl breakfast €90, with half board €110; ❄) Simple, good-value rooms are on

offer at this welcoming guesthouse in a quiet location. The superfriendly owners live next door and offer lots of local information. Substantial breakfasts and dinners (on request) are other pluses.

Buisson Guesthouse GUESTHOUSE €€
(Map p318; ☑2592959; www.buissonladigue.jimdo. com; La Passe; s/d incl breakfast €60/90; ❄🛜) Down a dirt road, south of the harbour-front, is this cute house in a proudly maintained and flowered little property. It shelters two simple, neat rooms; opt for the larger one, which has a lounge (same price).

Domaine Les Rochers APARTMENT €€
(Map p318; ☑4235334; www.domainelesrochers. com; La Passe; d €130-170; ❄🛜) Run by a pleasant Greek-Seychellois couple, this place offers six large, well-thought-out apartments with separate bedrooms, immaculate en suites and well-equipped kitchens, but what really makes this place special are the verdant gardens and sense of privacy. The owner has plenty of tips on exploring La Digue. Breakfast costs a whopping €16. Free wi-fi.

Veronic Guesthouse GUESTHOUSE €€
(Map p318; ☑4234743, 2592463; seyladigue@ yahoo.com; La Passe; s/d/q €40/80/140; ❄) Embedded in a manicured tropical garden, this venture is a good option for budget-conscious travellers, with three comfortable, fully equipped bungalows. Brilliant value.

Cocotier du Rocher BUNGALOW €€
(Map p318; ☑4234489, 2514889; www.cocotier durocher.com; La Passe; d €110-135; ❄🛜) This charming venture has four bungalows (eight rooms in total) that are embedded in blooming tropical gardens. They're fully equipped, prettily decorated and kept scrupulously clean. The more recent units are the most expensive. Verena and her son Stéphane, your courteous hosts, go above and beyond to ensure you enjoy your stay. Breakfast (€15) and dinner (€25) are available on request.

Casa de Leela BUNGALOW €€
(Map p318; ☑4234193, 2512223; www.casa-de-leela.bplaced.net; La Passe; d €120-160, q 220-250, incl breakfast; ❄🛜🍴) A few hundred metres inland from the coastal road, this reliable venture is a great option, with four well-designed and very spacious bungalows with all mod cons. They blend perfectly into the landscaped gardens. Another draw is the small swimming pool – a rarity on La Digue.

Bois d'Amour
BUNGALOW €€

(Map p318; ☎4234490, 2529290; www.boisd amour.de; La Passe; d €110) Three all-wood, fully equipped chalets (six rooms in total) in an Eden-like garden replete with tropical flowers and exotic fruit trees. They're amply sized and well spaced out, and may remind you of the little house on a Swiss cuckoo clock. Add an extra €30 per person for half board (breakfast and dinner). Minuses: no air-con and no wi-fi access.

Calou Guest House
BUNGALOW €€

(Map p318; ☎4234083, 2781327; www.calou guesthouse.com; La Passe; d with half board €130; ❄🛜) As we speak, the people behind this well-established venture are jackhammering away for what promises to be a pretty serious makeover. The whole process is expected to be completed by 2017. The new Calou will feature a clutch of spacious bungalows in a leafy plot.

Birgo Guest House
GUESTHOUSE €€

(Map p318; ☎234518; www.birgo.sc; La Passe; s/d incl breakfast €55/110; ❄🖾) A commendable guesthouse in a balmy garden setting. All eight rooms are clean, well organised (air-con, a private terrace, daily cleaning) and serviceable. There's a tiny pool, too.

Fleur de Lys
BUNGALOW €€

(Map p318; ☎4234459; www.fleurdelysey.com; La Passe; d €120; ❄🛜) A chilled universe is created here by a lazy-day garden and a clutch of trim, functional Creole-style bungalows with spotless bathrooms and kitchenettes. Breakfast is extra (€12).

Sitronnelle Guest House
GUESTHOUSE €€

(Map p318; ☎4234230; La Passe; s/d incl breakfast €40/80; ❄) Quite a good deal for solo travellers, but less so for couples (although rates are negotiable for longer stays), this guesthouse on the inland road in La Passe offers five unadorned but acceptable rooms arranged around a courtyard. Ambience is not this place's forte. Dinner costs €15.

★La Digue Holiday Villa
COTTAGE €€€

(Map p318; ☎2514047, 4235265; www.ladigue holidayvilla.com; La Passe; d €165; ❄🛜🖾) These six stylish apartments nestled in a landscaped plot are decorated with the design-conscious in mind: a cheerful mix of wood and stone, sparkling kitchens, quality fixtures, and a soothing yellow and green palette. To top it off, there's a pool in the flowering garden.

Evening meals can be arranged for about Rs 200. Free wi-fi. A place of easy bliss.

★Domaine de L'Orangeraie Resort & Spa
HOTEL €€€

(Map p318; ☎4299999; www.orangeraie.sc; Anse Sévère; d incl breakfast from €300; ❄🛜🖾) Tropical luxury at its best. Dramatically deployed on hilly grounds in a sea of spruce greenery, this place feels like heaven. No expense has been spared in dousing guests in sassy swank: creative landscaping, natural materials and high-class amenities (including a superb spa and two restaurants). Villas are furnished in muted earth tones with subtle Asian accents. Step inside and let the Zen-like tranquillity envelop you.

One weak point: the artificial beach next to the restaurant is nothing special.

Le Repaire
BOUTIQUE HOTEL €€€

(Map p318; ☎2530594, 4234332; www.lerepaire seychelles.com; La Passe; d incl breakfast €190-230; ❄🛜🖾) This nearly-but-not-quite boutique hotel will appeal to design-savvy travellers, with stylish furniture, soothing tones, walk-in showers, a lovely garden, tiny pool and spiffing seaside location (but the shore is no good for swimming). It's worth paying the extra for a sea-facing superior room, as the standard rooms are darker and have no views to speak of. Free wi-fi and kayaks.

La Diguoise
B&B €€€

(Map p318; ☎4234713, 2510332; diguoise@ seychelles.net; La Passe; s €105-180, d €180-210, incl breakfast; ❄🛜🖾) An expansive, lushly fabulous garden and lovely pool are the highlights of this well-run venture located in a quiet area. The rooms in the two main houses are scrupulously clean and a healthy size, but the furnishings feel slightly dated. There are also two smaller, less exciting rooms in a low-rise building at the back of the garden. Dinner costs €20. Credit cards are accepted, but there's a 5% surcharge. Free wi-fi.

La Digue Island Lodge
RESORT €€€

(Map p318; ☎4292525; www.ladigue.sc; Anse Réunion; s €95-261, d €111-365, incl breakfast; ❄🛜🖾) This hodgepodge of a resort comprises A-frame chalets packed rather close together, plus an atmospheric plantation house and standard rooms, some with sea views. The public areas are getting tired but the beachfront location and exotic gardens are hard to beat. Amenities are solid, with two restaurants, two bars, a dive centre and a pool.

L'Océan Hotel
HOTEL €€€

(Map p318; ☑4234180; www.hotelocean.info; Anse Patates; s/d incl breakfast €165/200; ❄️🛜) A safe bet, with an oceanfront location. The hotel's total capacity is eight, making it wonderfully intimate. Every bedroom boasts stupendous views of the sea and is decorated with driftwood, shells and paintings by local artist George Camille. Hint: aim for the Petite Soeur and Grande Soeur rooms. There's no beach but snorkelling is excellent just offshore. There's an on-site restaurant.

Château St Cloud
HOTEL €€€

(Map p318; ☑4234346; www.chateaustcloud.sc; La Passe; s €145-250, d €200-350, incl breakfast; ❄️🛜🏊) One of the most reliable bases on the island, Château St Cloud has three categories of room, with prices varying by size and location, as well as a restaurant and a lovely pool surrounded by a tropical Garden of Eden.

Pick of the bunch are the superior rooms, which are dotted on a forest-clad hillside, while the four deluxe rooms, set in a former colonial building, are superspacious and marry modern and Creole design influences. If you opt for a standard room, take an upstairs one (numbers 12 to 16) as these get more natural light.

🍴 Eating

La Passe has a smattering of fully fledged eateries. Other options worthy of interest include the hotel restaurants, which are also open to the public, and a clutch of very affordable takeaway outlets. Self caterers will find small grocery stores and one supermarket in La Passe.

Mi Mum Takeaway
CREOLE €

(Map p318; La Passe; mains Rs 50-75; ⏱11.30am-2pm Mon-Sat) Hidden next to a nondescript building off the main road, this lively joint is off the radar for most visitors but comes recommended by savvy locals. It's a good-value stomach filler for those in need of some honestly prepared stews, curries, sandwiches, and fish and chips at low prices. You can eat alfresco or take away. Look for the small sign almost opposite the petrol station.

Gregoire's Pizzeria
PIZZA €

(Map p318; ☑4292557; La Passe; mains Rs 90-180; ⏱11am-2.30pm & 6-9.30pm) Delicious pizzas on La Digue? Yes, it's possible. Gregoire's serves bubbling thin-crust pizza baked in a brick oven, all decorated with a simple line-up of choice toppings such as smoked

fish and cheese. There are also some well-rendered pastas. Despite the colourful walls, decor is a bit dull and there's no view to speak of. Takeaway is available.

Takamaka Café
CREOLE, SANDWICHES €

(Map p318; Anse Sévère; mains Rs 50-180; ⏱9am-3.30pm) Recharge the batteries with a fresh fruit platter or a generous sandwich at this shack nudging pleasingly up Anse Sévère. Also serves salads, fish and chips, chicken and tuna.

Gala Takeaway
CREOLE €

(Map p318; ☑2525951; La Passe; mains Rs 50-80; ⏱10am-8.30pm Mon-Sat) If you're looking for a quick food fix at unbeatable prices, check out the tempting options at this lively spot near Veuve Reserve. Dig into budget savouries such as stir-fried fish, pork curry, burgers and salads. Save a cranny for the delicious banana pie. It has indoor and outdoor seating.

Bor Lanmer Takeaway
FAST FOOD €

(Map p318; La Passe; mains Rs 50-60; ⏱11.30am-3pm & 6-9pm) Off the main intersection, this friendly, hole-in-the-wall place dishes up excellent *barquettes* (cartons) of fried rice, chicken or pork with vegetables, fish and other Creole staples at puny prices. It has a few outdoor tables.

Tarosa Takeaway
CREOLE €

(Map p318; La Passe; mains Rs 50-60; ⏱11.30am-2pm & 6.30-8pm) Fill your grumbling tummy without battering the wallet in this buzzing bolthole on the main drag. It has a range of daily specials, such as pork curry, grilled fish and spaghetti.

Bakery
BAKERY €

(Map p318; La Passe; ⏱9am-7pm Mon-Sat, 4-7pm Sun) This tiny bakery and grocery store near the pier sells fresh bread and cakes. Come early; by 10am the cakes are sold out.

STC
SUPERMARKET €

(Map p318; ☑4234024; La Passe; ⏱8.30am-6pm Mon-Fri, to 2pm Sat, to 1pm Sun) STC is the best-stocked supermarket on the island. It sells almost everything self-caterers could want.

⭐The Fish Trap Bar & Restaurant
INTERNATIONAL €€

(Map p318; La Passe; mains Rs 150-290; ⏱noon-3pm & 7.45-9pm, bar 7.30am-10pm; 🛜) In a great location on the water's edge, this snazzy restaurant is one of the most atmospheric places to eat around La Passe. The menu runs the gamut from seafood to meat dishes and salads to Creole staples. It's also a great place to linger over a fruity cocktail (from Rs 150) as the sun sinks low on the horizon.

★ **Chez Jules Restaurant** CREOLE, SEAFOOD €€
(Map p318; ☑ 4244287; Anse Banane; mains Rs 180-210; ☉ 10am-4pm) You really need to know this place is here at Anse Banane on the east coast, but luckily now you do. You'll be surprised such good stuff can come from a place so secluded. Excellent grilled fish fillet and tasty octopus salad are just some of the few specialities on offer. The cherry on top: lovely sea views.

★ **Lanbousir** SEAFOOD €€
(Map p318; Anse Union; mains Rs 180-220; ☉ 12.30-3pm) This ramshackle eatery run by a gang of affable ladies is an ideal spot for a filling lunch after (or before) working your tan at nearby Anse Source d'Argent. Start things off with smoked-fish salad, move on to a meltingly tender fish fillet, then finish with a rich banana or vanilla cake. Wash it all down with a chilled coconut. It's within L'Union Estate & Copra Factory (p319).

Zerof CREOLE, BUFFET €€
(Map p318; ☑ 4234439; La Passe; mains Rs 200-250, dinner buffet Rs 420; ☉ noon-3pm & 6.30-8.30pm) Zerof is a great spot to savour traditional Creole meals before (or after) hitting the powdery sand for the day. On Wednesday and Sunday evenings, it lays on an excellent buffet featuring about 10 Creole offerings.

Refle de Zil INTERNATIONAL €€
(Map p318; La Passe; mains Rs 160-275; ☉ 11.30am-9.30pm; ☞) The hardest thing about eating at this local favourite is deciding between the delectable meat or fish dishes, salads and pizzas. Good desserts, too. Oh, and there's free wi-fi.

Bellevue CAFETERIA €€
(Map p318; ☑ 2527856; Belle Vue; mains Rs 150-200, dinner Rs 500; ☉ noon-3pm, sunset dinner 5.30pm, bar 10am-6pm) It's a hell of a hike or ride to get to this eagle's eyrie, but you'll be amply rewarded with cardiac-arresting views from the terrace. At lunchtime, it serves up the usual suspects at very reasonable prices. Dinner is a more romantic affair; prices include transfers to La Passe. A good deal.

Chez Marston INTERNATIONAL €€
(Map p318; ☑ 4234023; La Passe; mains Rs 120-250; ☉ 11.30am-9.30pm) To be totally honest the food here isn't all that great, but the at-

mosphere is relaxed and the menu covers most tastes with salads, sandwiches, prawns, fish or crab curries, pizzas, pastas, omelettes and burgers as well as a couple of vegetarian options. Desserts include pancakes and ice creams.

★ **Domaine de L'Orangeraie Resort & Spa – Le Combava** INTERNATIONAL €€€
(Map p318; ☑ 4299999; Anse Sévère; mains lunch Rs 300-420, dinner Rs 450-580; ☉ noon-3pm & 7-9.15pm) This elegant restaurant within the Domaine de L'Orangeraie Resort & Spa (p324) offers the intoxicating mix of fine dining, romantic atmosphere, cool setting and attentive service. The sleek dining room by the hotel's swimming pool is particularly magical in the evening. If nothing else, come for the suave desserts (from Rs 190) – the chocolate brownie with coconut ice cream is unforgettable.

★ **Loutier Coco** BUFFET €€€
(Map p318; ☑ 2514762; Grand Anse; buffet Rs 350; ☉ 12.30-3pm, bar 9am-4.30pm) A complete overhaul in early 2016 transformed this casual beach shack on Grand Anse beach into a fully fledged restaurant, complete with cold tiled floors, concrete walls and a proper roof. What has not changed, though, is the lavish buffet served at lunchtime (come early). The spread includes grilled fish, traditional Creole curries and salads, fruit and coffee.

Le Repaire ITALIAN €€€
(Map p318; ☑ 4234332; www.lerepaireseychelles.com; La Passe; mains Rs 200-400; ☉ 12.30-2.30pm Wed-Mon, 7-9.30pm daily) Le Repaire stands apart by cooking Italian classics that will rock your world. Chef Remo is Italian and imports some key ingredients from Italy, so you can expect well-executed pasta dishes, risottos, pizzas as well as fish and meat mains. They are served in a sophisticated yet casual room that opens onto a flourishing tropical garden.

There's a range of exemplary desserts, including an addictive tiramisu.

🍸 Drinking & Nightlife

The cafeteria-bar Tarosa is the most 'happening' spot in town and transforms itself into an open-air club on Saturday evening.

If it's just the setting you want to absorb, check out the bars at the largest hotels.

Tarosa CLUB
(Map p318; La Passe; ☉ 10pm-2am Fri & Sat) This open-air bar-cum-club is a good place to rub shoulders with locals.

🛍 Shopping

You'll find various souvenir shops in La Passe, near the jetty, as well as a couple of art galleries.

Barbara Jenson Studio ART
(Map p318; ☑ 4234406; www.barbarajensonstudio.com; Anse Réunion; ☺ 9.30am-6pm Mon-Sat) Barbara's work reflects the unique landscape and ethnically diverse people of the Seychelles.

ℹ Information

Hospital (☑ 4234255; La Passe) Has basic health-care services.
Tourist Office (Map p318; ☑ 4234393; www.seychellesladigue.com; La Passe; ☺ 8am-noon & 1-4.30pm Mon-Fri, 9am-noon Sat) Provides basic information and helps organise tours.

ℹ Getting There & Away

The island is easily reached by boat from both Mahé and Praslin. Praslin is only about 5km from Praslin.

The **Inter-Island Ferry Pty** (☑ 4232329, 4232394; www.cat-cocos-seychelles.com; one-way adult/child €15/7.50) operates a catamaran service between Praslin and La Digue. There are about seven departures daily (five on Sunday) between 7am (9am on Sunday) and 5.15pm (5.45pm on Friday, Saturday and Sunday) from Praslin and between 7.30am (9.30am on Sunday) and 5.45pm (6.15pm on Friday, Saturday and Sunday) from La Digue. The crossing takes less than 20 minutes.

Cat Cocos (Map p318; ☑ 4324843; www.cat-cocos-seychelles.com; La Passe; ☺ 6.30am-5pm) runs a once- or twice-daily service to La Digue from Mahé (€75); it makes a brief stop in Praslin before continuing to La Digue.

ℹ Getting Around

BICYCLE

There are a few surfaced roads on the island. Given that it is less than 5km from north to south, by far the best – and most enjoyable – way to get around is on foot or bicycle. There are loads of bikes to rent. Operators have outlets near the pier, or you can book through your hotel or guesthouse. Most places charge between Rs 100 and Rs 150 per day.

TAXI

There are only a handful of taxis on La Digue, as most people get around on bicycle or on foot. A one-way ride from the pier to Grand Anse costs around Rs 250.

OTHER INNER ISLANDS

Apart from Mahé, Praslin and La Digue, the other main islands making up the Inner Islands group include Bird, North, Silhouette, Frégate and Denis Islands. These widely scattered islands are all run as exclusive island retreats.

Apart from the sense of exclusivity, what makes these hideaways so special is their green ethos. They're all involved in pioneering conservation projects and are sanctuaries for various rare species.

Silhouette

Silhouette is the pyramid-shaped island you see looming on the horizon from Beau Vallon on Mahé. With steep forested mountain peaks rising from the ocean above stunning palm-shaded beaches, Silhouette is a truly magnificent island hideaway, though only 20km north of Mahé. The highest point is Mt Dauban (740m), and there are some truly wild stretches of beach at Anse Mondon, Anse Lascar, Anse Patate and Grand Barbe. Silhouette is famed for its biological diversity and it's home to a variety of unique habitats and ecosystems. There's a small research station based in the village of **La Passe** that focuses on the conservation of giant tortoises and the monitoring of sea turtles and bats.

🛏 Sleeping & Eating

La Belle Tortue VILLA €€€
(☑ 2569708; www.labelletortue.com; Silhouette; s €260-400, d €320-600, with half board; ❄ ❢) This upscale venture is a more intimate alternative to a resort, with six rooms in three modern villas cocooned in exotic gardens. They are roomy, light-filled and beautifully attired, with elegant furnishings and solid amenities, and overlook a lovely sandy bay. The nearby beach is not the best on the island, but there's good swimming and snorkelling.

Hilton Seychelles Labriz Resort & Spa RESORT €€€
(☑ 4293949; www.hiltonseychelleslabriz.com; Silhouette; d incl breakfast from €350; ❄ ❢ ❆) Possibly the most affordable private-island resort in the Seychelles, the five-star Hilton Seychelles Labriz comprises 111 villas spread along a narrow sandy area east of the island. The list of facilities is prolific, with seven restaurants, a wonderful spa and a state-of-the-art diving centre. Nature walks are available.

Silhouette

ℹ Getting There & Away

Most guests come to Silhouette by boat from Beau Vallon on Mahé. Transport is handled directly by your place of lodging and is arranged in conjunction with accommodation.

North Island

About 6km north of Silhouette, North Island is the last word in exclusivity and its hotel is generally lauded as a milestone in the 'couture castaway' Indian Ocean experience. The arrival by helicopter says it all: laid-back indulgence and James Bond glamour.

🛏 Sleeping

North is a private island. All visitors coming here stay at the resort.

North Island   RESORT €€€
(☏ 4293100; www.north-island.com; d with full board €6100; ✳@🛜🏊) 🌿 Welcome to one of the most luxurious hotels in the world. It ticks all the right boxes, with dazzling-white beaches, an award-winning spa, a gourmet restaurant, a top-notch dive centre and, of course, your own butler to attend to your every whim. The 11 ultraluxurious suites, which blend wood, glass and stone, define the term 'barefoot chic'.

There's a green ethos; natural habitats are being restored for the reintroduction of critically endangered species, and the resident ecologist takes guests on guided walks where they can witness sea turtles nesting on the beach. It's the kind of place where you expect to see corporate moguls and movie stars chilling out.

ℹ Getting There & Away

All guests come to North Island by helicopter from Mahé. Transport is handled directly by the resort and is arranged in conjunction with accommodation.

Denis Island

You land on a strip of coral by the sea. There's a white-sand beach lapped by luxuriously warm waters, a shimmering lagoon with every hue from lapis lazuli to turquoise, plus palm and casuarina trees leaning over the shore. Welcome to Denis, a coral island that lies about 95km northeast of Mahé.

If working your suntan ceases to do it for you, there are nature walks along scenic pathways as well as fishing, snorkelling and diving trips that will keep you active. Wildlife lovers will enjoy it here too; although Denis is small – barely 1.3km in length and 1.75km at its widest point – it's a sanctuary for a variety of species, including giant tortoises, magpie robins, paradise flycatchers and Seychelles warblers. From July to December you may see turtles laying eggs on the beach.

🛏 Sleeping

Denis Private Island   RESORT €€€
(☏ 4295999, 4288963; www.denisisland.com; d incl breakfast from €890; ✳@🛜) 🌿 Impressive Denis Private Island is essentially *Swiss Family Robinson* meets stylish travel magazine. The 25 villas are just steps from the dazzling white beach. They have a gorgeous feel, with lots of wood, quality furnishings and elegant showers – not to mention the outdoor bathroom. Diving and fishing are catered for amply, and the entire place feels eerily empty even at full capacity.

Food is organic and prepared from produce grown on the island farm. The international clientele is mainly made up of couples, but families are also welcome. All guests get around by bicycle or on foot. There's no pool, but who needs one when there's such an unbelievable beach on your doorstep?

ℹ Getting There & Away

Denis Island is serviced by charter flights from Mahé. Transport is handled directly by the resort and is arranged in conjunction with accommodation.

Bird Island

Bird is the ultimate in ecotourism and birdlife-viewing. Hundreds of thousands of sooty terns, fairy terns and common noddies descend en masse between April and October to nest on this coral island that lies 95km north of Mahé. You just have to sit on your veranda and birds will come to land on your head. Hawksbill turtles breed on the island's beaches between November and March, while their land-bound relatives lumber around the interior. Green turtles also use the sandy shores for their nests.

🛏 Sleeping

★ **Bird Island Lodge**   LODGE €€€
(☑ 4224925, 4323322; www.birdislandseychelles. com; s/d with full board from €323/411; ☎) 🍴 No TV. No air-con. No phones (but there's wi-fi). Just you, masses of birds, 18 giant turtles, the inky-blue ocean and sensational beaches. Enjoy this slice of untouched paradise in one of the 24 simple yet genuinely ecofriendly and agreeably designed chalets.

ⓘ Getting There & Away

Bird Island is approximately 100km north of Mahé and is serviced by daily flights from Mahé. Transport is handled directly by the resort and is arranged in conjunction with accommodation.

Frégate Island

A 20 minute helicopter flight from Mahé brings you to fairy-tale Frégate, which is both a wildlife sanctuary and a hideaway for celebs and millionaires who find serenity in the exclusive Fregate Island Private. The island has no less than seven beaches, including awesome Anse Victorin and Anse Maquereau, which are regularly voted the world's best.

🛏 Sleeping

Fregate Island Private   RESORT €€€
(☑ in Germany +49 (0) 7221 900 8071; www.fregate. com; Frégate Island; d incl full board from €4500; ✳ @ 🏊 🏊) 🍴 Part of the Oetker group, this exclusive retreat takes barefoot luxury into another realm. Perched on a hillside, the 16 sea-facing villas – featuring a private pool and an open-air Jacuzzi – are reached by alleys that wind through the lush vegetation. Villas 3 to 8 have direct beach access.

You won't get bored on Frégate. Swim in the jewelled waters of Anse Macquereau, enjoy breakfast on a dinky platform perched in the canopy, take a fishing, diving or snorkelling trip. Don't leave without taking a guided walk with the resident conservationist, who'll show you the organic farm and the hatchery for giant tortoises. If you're lucky, you may see hawksbill turtles nesting on Grande Anse.

ⓘ Getting There & Away

Most guests come to Frégate Island by helicopter from Mahé. Transport is handled directly by the resort and is arranged in conjunction with accommodation.

ALPHONSE ISLAND

Alphonse Island, about 400km southwest of Mahé, is a world-famous flyfishing destination. The gin-clear waters of the sandbanks that shelve the perimeters of the lagoon are made for battles with the bonefish, the giant trevally, the triggerfish and other species. Alphonse is also increasingly promoting its diving potential, which is unrivalled in the country (if not in the Indian Ocean). The best thing is that it also appeals to romantics and families.

Alphonse is a small, thickly vegetated island that's surrounded by a vast lagoon and healthy reef gardens. From the air, it looks like a giant shark's tooth. It does have some great beaches, although they're not the main drawcard.

OUTER ISLANDS

The **Amirantes Group** lies about 250km southwest of Mahé. Its main island is **Desroches**. Another 200km further south, the **Alphonse Group** is another cluster of coral islands that provides some of the best saltwater fly-fishing in the world. The largest of the group is the 1.2km-wide **Alphonse Island**, which offers tourist infrastructure.

The **Aldabra Group** is the most remote of the Outer Island groups. It includes **Aldabra Atoll**, which is a Unesco World Heritage Site and nature reserve and lies more than 1000km from Mahé. Aldabra Atoll is home to about 150,000 giant tortoises, and flocks of migratory birds fly in and out in their thousands. Until now the islands have only really been accessible to scientists, volunteers and a very small number of tourists. Unfortunately, the Aldabra Group is currently off limits to foreigners, due to the risk of piracy in the area. Check with the Seychelles Island Foundation (p291) for the latest information.

🛏 Sleeping

Currently Alphonse Island Resort on Alphonse Island is the only accommodation option in the Outer Islands. The resort on Desroches Island has closed for renovation.

★Alphonse Island Resort   RESORT €€€
(✉ in South Africa +27 21 556 5763; www.alphonse-island.com; Alphonse Island; r per person with half board US$675-875; ☺Nov-Apr; ❄ ⚡ ❄) 🖋 This laid-back establishment seduces those who stay here with a row of cosy A-framed chalets and villas that open onto a garden with direct access to the lagoon. With wooden furnishings and modern amenities, they represent a nicely judged balance between comfort, rustic charm and tropical atmosphere. Various fishing and diving packages are available, and snorkelling trips can be arranged.

The on-site dive centre and fishing centre both have a great reputation for service and professionalism. Nature walks around the island can also be organised. There's wi-fi access at the restaurant.

Desroches Island Resort   RESORT €€€
Under new management, this private island resort has closed for major renovations. It should reopen by 2017.

❶ Getting There & Away

The only accessible island is Alphonse Island, which is serviced once or twice weekly by charter flights from Mahé. The duration of the flight is about one hour.

UNDERSTAND SEYCHELLES

Seychelles Today

The Seychelles has come a long way since independence, and it prides itself on having attained stability and a certain prosperity. Standards of health, education and housing have steadily improved, and the country enjoys the highest annual per-capita income in Africa. After years of communist rule, the Seychelles is gradually evolving towards a free-market economy in order to attract foreign investors. Other good news: piracy has declined significantly as a threat off the coast.

Economic Progress

Economically, the Seychelles is in pretty good shape. In a climate of global stagnation, the 4.30% growth of the country's economy in 2015 (after a whopping 6.20% in 2014) is a respectable figure. Tourism, which is the mainstay of the economy, has been picking up in recent years and the number of arrivals to the Seychelles is on the increase, with more than 275,000 visitors in 2015 (160,000 in 2009 and 208,000 in 2012). Most airlines based in the Gulf, including Emirates, Qatar Airways (which should soon restart its flights to the Seychelles) and Etihad, have launched frequent, well-priced services to the Seychelles from their respective hubs, and offer excellent connections with all major capitals in the world. Air Seychelles, the national carrier, also resumed direct flights to Paris in July 2015 (after four years of interruption).

The other pillar of the economy is industrial fishing, which is one of the country's biggest foreign-exchange earners. Tuna is a very big export.

In April 2015, two decades after first applying, the country finally became a member of the World Trade Organization (WTO).

Nevertheless, the economy remains vulnerable to external events. Despite attempts to strengthen its agricultural base and use more locally manufactured products, the Seychelles continues to import the vast majority of its needs. As a result, even a slight dip in export earnings causes major ructions in the economy.

Political Stagnation?

Politically, the situation has barely evolved in 40 years. The ruling party, the Seychelles People's Progressive Front (SPPF), led by President James Michel, has been governing the country since 1977. After campaigning for a third term, President James Michel was reelected in December 2015 after gaining 50.2% of the vote – a margin of a mere 193 votes. His political opponent Wavel Ramkalawan cried foul over irregularities and claimed that the government bought votes.

While René has been much criticised over the years, there's no denying that he has helped improve the economy. But with the same faces in power for almost four decades, many Seychellois now aspire to *sanzman* (change), more democracy and more freedom of press. The next presidential elections are due in 2020.

Drugs in Paradise

One major problem has tarnished the paradisaical image of the Seychelles over the last few years: drug trafficking (and drug use). Although it has not reached the level of drug smuggling in, say, the Caribbeans, it's now considered as a big issue in the country. According to the United Nations Office on Drugs and Crime (UNODC), the delivery by sea of heroin and other drugs to Africa, Europe and Asia has seen a dramatic shift towards the southern route in recent years, and the Seychelles has become a major transit point for drug smugglers. Given the Seychelles is an archipelago that's so isolated in the Indian Ocean, with porous borders and limited resources and infrastructure to monitor them, it's hard to curtail drug trafficking, despite increased controls and seizures carried out by the National Drug Enforcement Agency (NDEA). It's believed that drugs enter the country by air and by boat.

The Seychelles is not only used as a hub; drugs, particularly heroin, are increasingly being consumed within the Seychelles. According to estimates by the Seychelles Ministry of Health, there are more than 1000 heroin users in the country, which has a devastating impact on the social fabric and causes significant health challenges.

Crackdown on Piracy

With the increase in acts of piracy in the entire Western Indian Ocean in the late 2000s, the Seychelles found itself exposed to attacks led by Somali pirates. The government called on the international community for assistance and signed an agreement with the US and other Western nations to combat piracy in the Seychellois territorial waters. And it worked. Given its strategic position, the country has become the centre of a crackdown on attacks at sea by Somali pirates. In 2013, the Regional Anti-Piracy, Prosecution and Intelligence Coordination Centre (RAPPICC) was established in partnership with the UK. It aims to boost the fight against piracy-related, transnational organised crime in the region by bringing together policing skills and fostering better coordination between intelligence services. The result? Thanks largely to multinational naval patrols and the presence of heavily armed guards on cargo ships, the number of attacks has fallen dramatically over the last few years.

History

Like Mauritius and Réunion, the Seychelles had no indigenous population predating the European colonisers, and until the 18th century it was uninhabited. The islands were first spotted by Portuguese explorers, but the first recorded landing was by a British East India Company ship in 1609. Pirates and privateers used the Seychelles as a temporary base during lulls in their marauding.

The Colonial Period

In 1742 Mahé de Labourdonnais, the governor of what is now Mauritius, sent Captain Lazare Picault to investigate the islands. Picault named the main island after his employer (and the bay where he landed after himself) and laid the way for the French to claim possession of the islands 12 years later.

It took a while for the French to do anything with their possession. It wasn't until 1770 that the first batch of 21 settlers and seven slaves arrived on Ste Anne Island. After a few false starts, the settlers began growing spices, cassava, sugar cane and maize.

In the 18th century the British began taking an interest in the Seychelles. The French were not willing to die for their colony and didn't resist British attacks, and the Seychelles became a British dependency in 1814. The British did little to develop the islands except increase the number of slaves. After abolition in 1835, freed slaves from around the region were also brought here. Because few British settled, however, the French language and culture remained dominant.

In 1903 the Seychelles became a crown colony administered from London. It promptly went into the political and economic doldrums until 1964, when two political parties were formed. France Albert René, a young lawyer, founded the Seychelles People's United Party (SPUP). A fellow lawyer, James Mancham, led the new Seychelles Democratic Party (SDP).

Independence

Mancham's SDP, made up of business people and planters, won the elections in 1966 and 1970. René's SPUP fought on a socialist and independence ticket. In June 1975 a coalition of the two parties gave the appearance of unity in the lead-up to independence, which was granted a year later. Mancham became the first president of the Republic of Seychelles and René the prime minister.

The flamboyant Sir Jim (as James Mancham was known) – poet and playboy – placed all his eggs in one basket: tourism. He became a jet-setter, flying around the world with a beautiful socialite on each arm, and he put the Seychelles on the map.

The rich and famous poured in for holidays and to party, party, party. Adnan Khashoggi and other Arab millionaires bought large tracts of land, while film stars and celebrities came to enhance their glamorous images.

According to René and the SPUP, however, the wealth was not being spread evenly and the country was no more than a rich person's playground. René stated that poor Creoles were little better off than slaves.

The René Era

In June 1977, barely a year after independence, René and a team of Tanzanian-trained rebels carried out an almost bloodless coup while Mancham was in London attending a Commonwealth Conference. In the following years, René consolidated his position by deporting many supporters of the outlawed SDP. Opposed to René's one-party socialist state, these *grands blancs* (white landowners) set up 'resistance movements' in Britain, South Africa and Australia.

The country fell into disarray as the tourist trade dried to a trickle. The 1980s saw a campaign of civil disruption by supporters of the SDP, two army mutinies and more foiled coup attempts.

Finally, facing growing international criticism and the threatened withdrawal of foreign aid, René pulled a political about-face in the early 1990s; he abandoned one-party rule and announced the return to a multiparty democracy.

Elections were held in 1992 under the watchful eye of Commonwealth observers. René and his renamed Seychelles People's Progressive Front won 58.4% of the votes; Mancham, who had returned to the Seychelles, fielded 33.7% for his SDP and claimed the results were rigged.

René maintained his grip on power, while the SDP's star continued to wane. Even Mancham himself abandoned the SDP in favour of the centrist Seychelles National Party (SNP) in 1999. In the 2002 elections, the SNP, led by Wavel Ramkalawan, an Anglican priest, confirmed its stand as the main opposition party by winning more than 42% of the vote.

The Long Road to Democracy

In April 2004 René finally relinquished the presidency to the former vice president, James Michel, who had stood by René through thick and thin. After a close race with Wavel Ramkalawan, the opposition leader, Michel won the 2006 presidential election, gaining 53.5% of the vote.

Michel has not seemed willing to cede his power to any of his opponents; he prematurely dissolved the National Assembly in March 2007, following the boycott of assembly proceedings by the opposition party. The ensuing general elections in May 2007 returned 18 SPPF members against seven members of the SNP opposition party led by Wavel Ramkalawan (exactly the same numbers as before the dissolution). Though these elections were held democratically, the opposition claimed that the government bought votes.

On the economic front, in 2008 the highly indebted country was forced to turn to the IMF for assistance. A package of reforms was passed, including the free floating of the rupee, the abolition of all exchange restrictions and massive cuts in public spending. Debt was frozen and the economy quickly rebounded.

Culture

Like its neighbours Mauritius and Réunion, the Seychelles is often cited as an example of racial and religious harmony, and compared with most countries it is. The vast majority of Seychellois people are welcoming and helpful. There's not much anticolonial feeling evident – it has long been replaced with a sense of national pride that developed after independence. There's even a lingering fondness for such British institutions as afternoon tea, while French cultural influence has waned somewhat, mainly because it is regarded as rather elitist.

Lifestyle

Thanks to the islands' close links with Europe, the contemporary face of the Seychelles is surprisingly modern. The main island of Mahé is a rather sophisticated place, characterised as much by Western-style clothing, brand-new cars, mobile phones and modern houses as by any overt signs of traditional Creole culture. But beneath this strongly Westernised veneer, many aspects of traditional Creole culture survive. They live on in dance, music, hospitality, ancient beliefs, the language, the carefree attitude and in many other day-to-day ways of doing things.

The society continues to be largely male-dominated. Fortunately for women, the tourism industry is regarded as an equal-opportunity employer.

Most Seychellois are Catholic, but marriage is an unpopular institution. The reasons cited are that not marrying is a relic of slavery, when marriages simply didn't take place, and that marriage is expensive. As a result an estimated 75% of children are born out of wedlock. There's no taboo about illegitimacy.

For visitors, there are few rules and regulations to be followed, beyond respecting local attitudes towards nudity and visiting places of religious worship.

People of Seychelles

The population of the Seychelles is more strongly African than in Mauritius or Réunion, but even so you'll see almost every shade of skin and hair imaginable, arising from a mixture of largely French and African genes, together with infusions of Indian, Chinese and Arab blood. Distinct Indian and Chinese communities make up only a tiny proportion of the ethnic mix, however, the rest being Creole. As for the *grands blancs,* most were dispossessed in the wake of the 1977 coup.

As in Mauritius and Réunion, it is the Creole language, cuisine and culture that helps bind the Seychelles' society. More than 90% of the population speaks Creole as their first language, though most also speak English – the language of government and business – and French.

Religion

Nearly 90% of Seychellois are Roman Catholic, 7% are Anglican and 2.5% belong to the rapidly expanding evangelical churches. The remainder belong to the tiny Hindu, Muslim and Chinese communities largely based in Victoria.

Most people are avid churchgoers. On a Sunday, Victoria's Catholic and Anglican cathedrals, as well as the smaller churches scattered around the main islands, are full.

There is also a widespread belief in the supernatural and in the old magic of spirits known as *gris gris.* Sorcery was outlawed in 1958, but a few *bonhommes* and *bonnefemmes di bois* (medicine men and women) still practise their cures and curses and concoct potions for love, luck and revenge.

Arts

Since these islands were originally uninhabited, the Creoles are the closest the country has to an indigenous population. Many aspects of their African origins survive, including the *séga* and *moutia* dances.

Literature

Among the most important local authors writing in Creole are the poet-playwright Christian Sevina, short-story author and playwright Marie-Thérèse Choppy, poet Antoine Abel and mystery writer Jean-Joseph Madeleine. Unfortunately their works are not yet available in English.

In fact, there is surprisingly little English-language fiction about these islands. Most authors go in for travelogues and autobiographies. The one exception is long-time resident Glynn Burridge, who mixes fact and fiction in his short stories. They are published locally in two volumes under the title *Voices: Seychelles Short Stories,* and are available in bookshops in Victoria.

Music & Dance

The Indian, European, Chinese and Arabic backgrounds of the Seychellois are reflected in their music. Patrick Victor and Jean-Marc Volcy are two of the Seychelles' best-known musicians, playing Creole pop and folk music. Other local stars are Emmanuel Marie and the late Raymond Lebon, whose daughter Sheila Paul made it into the local charts with an updated rendering of her father's romantic ballads.

Visual Arts

Over recent decades, more and more artists have settled in the Seychelles and spawned a local industry catering to souvenir-hungry tourists. While shops are full of stereotypical scenes of palm trees and sunsets, there are also some talented artists around.

Michael Adams is the best-known and most distinctive contemporary artist. George Camille is another highly regarded artist who takes his inspiration from nature. Other notable artists are Barbara Jenson, who has a studio on La Digue, Gerard Devoud at Baie Lazare and Nigel Henry at Beau Vallon.

Look out, too, for works by Leon Radegonde, who produces innovative abstract collages; Andrew Gee, who specialises in silk paintings and watercolours of fish; and the sun-drenched paintings of Christine Harter. The painter and sculptor Egbert Marday produces powerful sketches of fisherfolk and plantation workers, but is perhaps best known for the statue of a man with a walking cane, situated outside the courthouse on Victoria's Independence Ave. Lorenzo Appiani produced the sculptures on the roundabouts at each end of 5th June Ave in Victoria.

Food & Drink

The real beauty of Seychellois cuisine is its freshness and simplicity. Meat lovers, come prepared: it is heavily influenced by the surrounding ocean, with fish appearing as the main ingredient in many dishes. Cultural influences are also distinctive, with a blend of European (mostly French and Italian) and African gastronomic delights.

Staples & Specialities

Fish, fish, FISH! And rice. This is the most common combination (*pwason ek diri* in Creole patois) in the Seychelles, and we won't complain – fish is guaranteed to be served ultrafresh and literally melts in your mouth. You'll devour bourgeois, capitaine, shark, job, parrotfish, caranx, grouper and tuna, among others. To bring variety, they are cooked in innumerable guises: grilled, steamed, minced, smoked, stewed, salted, baked, wrapped in a banana leaf; the list goes on and on.

Seafood lovers will have found their spiritual home in the Seychelles; lobster, crab, shellfish (especially *trouloulou* and *teck teck*, two local varieties of shells) and octopus are widely available.

The Seychelles is dripping with tropical fruit, including mango, banana, breadfruit, papaya, coconut, grapefruit, pineapple and carambola. Mixed with spices, they make wonderful accompaniments. Vanilla, cinnamon and nutmeg are used to flavour stews and other preparations.

You'll also find meat, mostly beef and chicken, but it's imported.

Vegetarians & Vegans

Restaurant menus in the Seychelles are dominated by fish, seafood and meat dishes, though there are actually a few salad and pasta dishes that are meat-free. If you're self-catering, you'll have much more choice, with a good selection of fruits and vegetables.

Where to Eat

There's a full gamut of restaurant types, from funky shacks and fast-food outlets to ritzy restaurants. Larger hotels have a choice of restaurants, with one always serving buffets (usually Creole or seafood). There is not a vast selection of street snacks to choose from in the Seychelles, but street vendors sell fresh fruit and fish – a good option if you're self-catering. Grocery stores are also widely available. The Victoria market is another good place to stock up on fresh food.

Many visitors to the Seychelles opt for packages that include breakfast and dinner at their hotel. If you'd prefer to sample local specialities, enjoy the Seychelles' many fine eateries, feast on views and share a beach picnic with the locals, you'll find that a bed and breakfast will allow you more flexibility.

Drinks

Freshly squeezed juices and coconut water are the most natural and thirst-quenching drinks around. If you want to put some wobble in your step, Seybrew, the local brand of beer, is sold everywhere. Eku, another locally produced beer, is a bit harder to find. Wine is available at most restaurants.

Environment

The Seychelles is an archipelago that lies about 1600km off the east coast of Africa and just south of the equator. For such a small country it supports a large variety of flora and fauna. Because of the islands' isolation and the comparatively late arrival of humans, many species are endemic to the Seychelles. The country is a haven for wildlife, particularly birds and tropical fish.

The Land

The Seychelles is made up of 115 islands, of which the central islands (including Mahé, Praslin and La Digue) are granite and the outlying islands are coral atolls. The granite islands, which do not share the volcanic nature of Réunion and Mauritius, appear to be peaks of a huge submerged plateau that was torn away from Africa when the continental plates shifted about 65 million years ago.

Wildlife

ANIMALS

Common mammals and reptiles include the fruit bat or flying fox, the gecko, the skink and the tenrec (a hedgehog-like mammal imported from Madagascar). There are also some small snakes, but they are not dangerous.

More noteworthy is the fact that giant tortoises, which feature on the Seychelles coat of arms, are now found only in the Seychelles and the Galápagos Islands, off Ecuador. The French and English wiped out the giant tortoises from all the Seychelles islands except Aldabra, where happily more than 100,000 still survive. Many have been brought to the central islands, where they munch their way around hotel gardens, and there is a free-roaming colony on Curieuse Island.

Almost every island seems to have some rare species of bird: on Frégate, Cousin, Cousine and Aride there are magpie robins (known as *pie chanteuse* in Creole); on Cousin, Cousine and Aride you'll find the Seychelles warbler; La Digue and Denis have the *veuve* (paradise flycatcher); and Praslin has the black parrot. The bare-legged scops owl and the Seychelles kestrel live on Mahé, and Bird Island is home to millions of sooty terns.

PLANTS

The coconut palm and the casuarina are the Seychelles' most common trees. There are a few banyans and you're also likely to see screw pines, bamboo and tortoise trees (so named because the fruit looks like the tortoises that eat it).

There are about 80 endemic plant species. Virgin forest now exists only on the higher parts of Silhouette Island and Mahé, and in the Vallée de Mai on Praslin, which is one of only two places in the world where the giant coco de mer palm grows wild. The other is nearby Curieuse Island.

National Parks

The Seychelles currently boasts two national parks and seven marine national parks, as well as several other protected areas under government and NGO management. In all, about 46% of the country's total land mass is now protected as well as some 45 sq km of ocean.

Environmental Issues

Overall the Seychelles has a pretty good record for protecting its natural environment. As early as 1968, Birdlife International set the ball rolling when it bought Cousin Island and began studying some of the country's critically endangered species. This was followed in the 1970s with legislation to establish national parks and marine reserves.

Not that the government's record is entirely unblemished. In 1998 it authorised a vast land-reclamation project on Mahé's northeast coast to provide much-needed space for housing. More recently, the construction of Eden Island, an artificial island with luxury properties off Mahé's east coast, has also raised concerns. Both projects have caused widespread silting, marring the natural beauty of this coast indefinitely, though the alternative was to clear large tracts of forest.

Tourism has had a similarly mixed effect. Every year, more resort hotels and lodges pop up, most notably on formerly pristine beaches or secluded islands. On the other hand, tourist dollars provide much-needed revenue for funding conservation projects. Local attitudes have also changed as people have learned to value their environment.

Further impetus for change is coming from NGOs operating at both community and government levels. They have notched up some spectacular successes, such as the Magpie Robin Recovery Program, funded by the Royal Society for the Protection of Birds and Birdlife International. From just 23 magpie robins languishing on Frégate Island in 1990, there are now nearly 250 living on Frégate, Cousin, Denis and Cousine Islands. Similar results have been achieved with the Seychelles warbler on Cousin, Cousine and Aride Islands.

As part of these projects, a number of islands have been painstakingly restored to their original habitat by replacing alien plant and animal species with native varieties. Several islands have also been developed for eco-tourism, notably Frégate, Bird, Denis, North, Silhouette and Alphonse Islands. The visitors not only help fund conservation work, but it is also easier to protect the islands from poachers and predators if they are inhabited. With any luck, this marriage of conservation and tourism will point the way to the future.

SEYCHELLES ENVIRONMENT

SURVIVAL GUIDE

ℹ️ Directory A–Z

ACCOMMODATION

Accommodation should always be booked in advance, particularly during peak periods (Christmas to New Year and Easter).

Guesthouses & Self-Catering Accommodation

No, you don't need to remortgage the house to visit the Seychelles if you stay in one of the cheaper guesthouses or self-catering establishments that are burgeoning on Mahé, Praslin and La Digue. Self-catering options are private homes, villas, residences, studios or apartments that are fully equipped and can be rented by the night. The distinction between self-catering options and guesthouses is slim. Typically, rooms in guesthouses don't come equipped with a kitchen, and breakfast is usually offered. That said, at most self-catering ventures, breakfast and dinner are available on request. Standards are high: even in the cheapest guesthouse you can expect to get a room with a private bathroom and air-con, as well as a daily cleaning service. Both options are generally excellent value, especially for families or a group of friends. Most cost between €80 and €190. Many offer discounts for extended stays.

They also offer good opportunities for cultural immersion; they're mostly family-run operations and provide much more personal, idiosyncratic experiences than hotels.

Resorts & Hotels

For those whose wallets overfloweth, there's no shortage of ultraswish options. They're straight from the pages of a glossy, designer magazine, with luxurious villas oozing style and class, and fabulously lavish spas in gorgeous settings.

For those whose budget won't stretch quite this far, there are also a few good-value, moderate-range affairs around Mahé, Praslin and La Digue, with prices around €250 for a double.

Note that hotels commonly offer internet specials well below the advertised 'rack rates'. It is also well worth checking with travel agents about hotel-and-flight holiday packages, which usually come cheaper.

BOOK YOUR STAY ONLINE

For more accommodation reviews by Lonely Planet authors, check out hotels.lonelyplanet.com. You'll find independent reviews, as well as recommendations on the best places to stay. Best of all, you can book online.

SLEEPING PRICE RANGES

The following price ranges refer to a double room with bathroom. Unless otherwise stated, breakfast is not included in the price.

€ less than €75

€€ €75–€150

€€€ more than €150

Expect to pay €180 per person per night (including half board) at the very minimum. Prices quickly climb all the way up to €1000 per person per night.

Virtually all the hotels charge higher rates during peak periods.

All-inclusive, full-blown resorts featuring a wide range of recreational facilities and entertainment programs are quite rare in the Seychelles.

Private Island Resorts

If you want to combine escapism with luxury, the Seychelles offers a clutch of ultraexclusive hideaways that almost defy description. They include Alphonse, Bird, Desroches, Félicité, Silhouette, North, Frégate and Denis Islands. This is where you really are buying into the dream. They offer every modern convenience but still preserve that perfect tropical-island ambience – the Robinson Crusoe factor – and feature an atmosphere of romance, rejuvenation and exotic sensuality. Each private-island resort has its own personality and devotees. There's minimal contact with the local people, though. Expect to pay between a cool €450 to a whopping €4500 a night, full board.

CHILDREN

➡ The Seychelles is a very child- and family-friendly place.

➡ Most hotels cater for all age groups, offering babysitting services, kids' clubs and activities especially for teenagers.

➡ While children will happily spend all day splashing around in the lagoon, boat trips around the islands should also appeal.

➡ Communing with giant tortoises is a sure-fire hit and visiting some of the nature reserves can be fun.

➡ Finding special foods and other baby products can be difficult, especially outside Victoria, so you might want to bring your favourite items with you.

CUSTOMS REGULATIONS

➡ The following items can be brought into the Seychelles duty-free: 400 cigarettes, 2L of strong liquor, 2L of wine and 200mL of eau de toilette.

→ Anything over the limit must be declared on arrival. There are restrictions on importing plants and animals, for which import permits are required.

→ A special permit is required to export coco de mer, and a certificate must be obtained from the seller.

ELECTRICITY

The Seychelles uses 220V, 50Hz AC; plugs in general use have square pins and three points.

EMBASSIES & CONSULATES

Countries with diplomatic representation in the Seychelles include the following:

British High Commission (✆ 4283666; bhcvictoria@fco.gov.uk

French Embassy (✆ 4382500; www. ambafrance-sc.org

German Honorary Consulate (✆ 4601100; victoria@hk-diplo.de

LGBT TRAVELLERS

The Seychellois are generally tolerant of gay and lesbian relationships as long as couples don't flaunt their sexuality, but there is no open gay or lesbian scene in the Seychelles.

For gay and lesbian travellers, there's little to worry about. We've never heard of any problems arising from same-sex couples sharing rooms during their holidays. That said, open displays of affection could raise eyebrows.

INTERNET ACCESS

→ There are a couple of internet cafes in Victoria. Outside the capital, internet cafes are harder to find.

→ Many midrange and all top-end hotels offer wi-fi, as do self-catering establishments and some restaurants and cafes; in many cases wi-fi access is restricted to public areas and is not free of charge.

→ In our listings, establishments with wireless are identified with a 🛜 icon.

→ If you will be in the Seychelles for a while, consider buying a USB stick (dongle) from local mobile provider **Cable & Wireless** (www. cwseychelles.com), which you can then load with airtime and plug into your laptop.

→ Connection is still fairly slow by Western standards.

LEGAL MATTERS

Foreigners are subject to the laws of the country in which they are travelling and will receive no special consideration because they are tourists. If you find yourself in a sticky legal predicament, contact your embassy.

All towns and most villages have their own police station. In general, travellers have nothing to fear from the police, who rarely harass foreigners and are very polite if you do need to stop them.

> **BOOKING SERVICES**
>
> **Seychelles Travel** (www.seychelles. travel) Has a list of accommodation options.
>
> **Seyvillas** (www.seyvillas.com) Hotels and self-catering villas, placing the accent on originality and authentic hospitality.
>
> **Seychelles Bons Plans** (www.seychelles bonsplans.com) A selection of well-run and well-priced establishments.
>
> **Seychelles Resa** (www.seychelles-resa. com) Look for special offers.
>
> **Holidays Direct Seychelles** (www. holidays-direct-seychelles.com) Specialises in small hotels and villas, and has last-minute deals.

Possession and use of drugs is strictly illegal and penalties are severe.

MAPS

There's a frustrating lack of decent maps of the archipelago. The best map of the island is the satellite imagery on Google Earth. You can also pick up the *Map of Seychelles*, a tourist map of the three main islands that's available at the tourist offices on Mahé, Praslin and La Digue.

MONEY

→ The unit of currency is the Seychelles rupee (Rs), which is divided into 100 cents (¢). Bank notes come in denominations of Rs 10, Rs 25, Rs 50, Rs 100 and Rs 500; there are coins of Rs 1, Rs 5, 1¢, 5¢, 10¢ and 25¢.

→ Euros are the best currency to carry. Prices for most tourist services, including accommodation, excursions, diving, car hire and transport, are quoted in euros and can be paid in euros (and less frequently in US dollars), either in cash or by credit card. But you can also pay in rupees. In restaurants, prices are quoted in rupees but you can also pay in euros.

→ The four main banks are Barclays Bank, Seychelles Savings Bank, Nouvobanq and Mauritius Commercial Bank (MCB). They have branches on Mahé, Praslin and La Digue. You'll also find numerous money changers. There's no commission for changing cash.

→ ATMs, which accept major international cards, are at the airport and at all the major banks in Victoria. You'll also find ATMs at Beau Vallon and Anse Royale on Mahé and on Praslin and La Digue. Remember, however, that bank fees, sometimes significant ones, can apply; check with your home bank before setting out for the Seychelles.

→ Major credit cards, including Visa and MasterCard, are accepted in most hotels, restaurants and tourist shops. Many guesthouses will still expect payment in cash. A few places add on an extra fee, typically 3%, to the bill to cover 'bank charges'.

Exchange Rates

For current exchange rates, see www.xe.com.

Australia	A$1	Rs 10.1
Canada	C$1	Rs 10.1
Euro Zone	€1	Rs 14.8
Japan	¥100	Rs 13.7
NZ	NZ$1	Rs 9.5
UK	UK£1	Rs 17.6
USA	US$1	Rs 13.2

Tipping

Tipping is not generally practised in the Seychelles and is never an obligation. Top-end hotels and restaurants sometimes add a service charge of about 10% to 15% to the bill.

OPENING HOURS

Banks Usually 8.30am–2pm Monday to Friday, and to 11am Saturday.

Government offices 8am–4pm or 5pm Monday to Friday.

Restaurants 11am–2pm or 3pm and 6pm–9pm daily.

Shops and businesses Typically 8am–5pm Monday to Friday, and to noon Saturday.

PUBLIC HOLIDAYS

New Year 1 and 2 January
Good Friday March/April
Easter Day March/April
Labour Day 1 May
Liberation Day 5 June
Corpus Christi 10 June
National Day 18 June
Independence Day 29 June
Assumption 15 August
All Saints' Day 1 November
Immaculate Conception 8 December
Christmas Day 25 December

TELEPHONE

→ The telephone system is efficient and reliable.

→ Telephone cards are available from **Cable & Wireless** (www.cwseychelles.com)). Local calls within and between the main islands, as well as international calls, cost around Rs 4 per minute.

→ When phoning the Seychelles from abroad, you'll need to dial the international code for the Seychelles (☑ 248), followed by the seven-digit local number.

EATING PRICE RANGES

The following price ranges refer to a main course. The service charge is included in the bill.

€ under Rs 150

€€ Rs 150–300

€€€ over Rs 300

→ There are no area codes.

→ Calling abroad from the Seychelles, dial 00 for international access, then the country code, area code and local number.

Mobile Phones

→ Many foreign mobile services have coverage in the Seychelles, but roaming fees are high.

→ There is mobile reception on Mahé, Praslin, La Digue, North Island, Frégate Island and Silhouette Island.

→ If you have a GSM phone and it has been 'unlocked', you can use a local SIM card (Rs 50) purchased from either **Cable & Wireless** (www.cwseychelles.com)) or **Airtel** (☑ 4610615; Huteau Lane, Victoria; ⊗ 8.30am-4pm Mon-Fri, to noon Sat). When buying a SIM card you'll need to bring along your passport.

→ Recharge cards are widely available, or you can top up your credit by phone or online.

→ For an idea of international rates, calls to North America, Australia and the UK with Cable & Wireless cost roughly Rs 10 per minute.

TIME

The Seychelles is on GMT plus four hours. When it's noon in Victoria, it's 8am in London, 9am in Paris, 3am in New York and 6pm in Sydney. The Seychelles does not operate a system of daylight saving; being equatorial, its sunset and sunrise times vary only slightly throughout the year.

TOURIST INFORMATION

The very well-organised Seychelles Tourism Bureau (www.seychelles.travel) is the only tourist information body in the Seychelles. The head office (p291) is in Victoria. It has two offices on Praslin and one office on La Digue.

TRAVELLERS WITH DISABILITIES

Most luxury hotels conform to international standards for disabled access, and it's usually possible to hire an assistant if you want to take an excursion. Apart from that, special facilities for travellers with disabilities are few and far between in the Seychelles, and no beach is equipped with wheelchair access.

VISAS

➡ Nationals of most Western countries don't need a visa to enter the Seychelles, just a valid passport.

➡ Initial entry is granted for the period of visit (with a maximum of three months) and proof of a planned and paid-for departure is required. Immigration officers will also require that you mention the name, address and phone number of the place where you are staying in the Seychelles; they may even ask for proof of a hotel (or other accommodation) booking.

VOLUNTEERING

Want to get involved in turtle tagging, whale-shark monitoring or researching certain animal species? **Nature Seychelles** (Map p287; ☑ 4601100; www.natureseychelles.org; Roche Caiman), Seychelles Island Foundation (p291) and **Marine Conservation Society Seychelles** (MCSS; www.mcss.sc) all have volunteer programs.

WOMEN TRAVELLERS

Generally speaking, women travellers should have few problems getting around solo in the Seychelles. As in any country, women should use their common sense when going to isolated stretches of beach and inland areas alone.

ⓘ Getting There & Away

Most visitors arrive by air. A few come with their own yachts or sailing boats.

Flights, cars and tours can be booked online at lonelyplanet.com/bookings.

AIR

Direct flights connect the Seychelles with China, France, Germany, Kenya, India, Madagascar, Mauritius, Réunion, South Africa, Sri Lanka and the UAE. For further afield, you'll need to take a connecting flight from South Africa, Europe or the Middle East.

Airports & Airlines

The **Seychelles International Airport** (Map p287; ☑ 4384400; www.seychellesairports. travel), about 8km south of Victoria, is the only international airport in the Seychelles.

Air Seychelles (☑ 4391000; www.air seychelles.com; Independence Ave, Victoria; ⊗8am-4pm Mon-Fri, to noon Sat) is the national carrier. It has a good safety record and a fairly limited international network, but has a code-share agreement with Etihad Airways.

SEA

There aren't any boat services between the Seychelles and other destinations in the Indian Ocean.

ⓘ Getting Around

AIR

Air Seychelles takes care of all interisland flights, whether scheduled or chartered. The only scheduled services are between Mahé and Praslin, with around 25 flights per day in each direction. The fare for the 15-minute hop costs about €132 return. The luggage limit is only 20kg. Air Seychelles also flies to Bird, Denis, Frégate and Desroches Islands, but on a charter basis; these flights are handled directly by the hotels on the island.

La Digue and Silhouette Island (and all other islands) can be reached by helicopter.

Note that Mahé is the only hub for flights within the Seychelles.

BICYCLE

Bicycles are the principal form of transport on La Digue. On Praslin you can rent bikes at Anse Volbert or through your accommodation. Mahé is a bit hilly for casual cyclists and most visitors rent cars, so bike rental is hard to find there.

BOAT

Travel by boat is very easy between Mahé, Praslin and La Digue, with regular and efficient ferry services. For all other islands you have to charter a boat or take a tour.

Mahé to Praslin

The **Cat Cocos** (☑ 4324842, 4324844; www. cat-cocos-seychelles.com) catamaran makes three return trips daily between Mahé and Praslin. Departing from Victoria, the journey takes

---

CLIMATE CHANGE & TRAVEL

Every form of transport that relies on carbon-based fuel generates CO_2, the main cause of human-induced climate change. Modern travel is dependent on aeroplanes, which might use less fuel per kilometre per person than most cars but travel much greater distances. The altitude at which aircraft emit gases (including CO_2) and particles also contributes to their climate change impact. Many websites offer 'carbon calculators' that allow people to estimate the carbon emissions generated by their journey and, for those who wish to do so, to offset the impact of the greenhouse gases emitted with contributions to portfolios of climate-friendly initiatives throughout the world. Lonely Planet offsets the carbon footprint of all staff and author travel.

PRACTICALITIES

⇒ **Newspapers & Magazines** Key newspapers include the government-controlled daily *Seychelles Nation* (www.nation.sc) and the daily *Today in Seychelles* (www.today.sc).

⇒ **Radio** Seychelles Broadcasting Corporation (www.sbc.com)runs the main radio station and 24-hour music station, Paradise FM. BBC World Service and Radio France International (RFI) are available in Mahé.

⇒ **Smoking** Prohibited in indoor public places, at workplaces and on public transport; allowed in outdoor restaurants, on beaches and in some hotel rooms.

⇒ **TV** SBC broadcasts in English, French and Creole. BBC World, France 24 and CNN are available on satellite.

⇒ **Weights & Measures** The Seychelles uses the metric system.

about one hour (not that much longer than the plane, if you include check-in time) and the fare is €60 one way; children under 12 pay half fare. In high season it's advisable to book your ticket at least a day in advance with the ferry company or through a travel agent.

Mahé to La Digue

The Cat Cocos runs a once- or twice-daily service to La Digue from Mahé (€75); it makes a brief stop in Praslin before continuing to La Digue.

Praslin to La Digue

Inter-Island Ferry Pty (p327) operates a catamaran service between Praslin and La Digue. There are about seven departures daily (five on Sunday) between 7am (9am on Sunday) and 5.15pm (5.45pm on Friday, Saturday and Sunday) from Praslin and between 7.30am (9.30am on Sunday) and 5.45pm (6.15pm on Friday, Saturday and Sunday) from La Digue. The crossing takes less than 20 minutes.

BUS

Good news: if you have time, you don't really need to rent a car to visit the islands.

Mahé

An extensive bus service operates throughout Mahé. Destinations and routes are usually marked on the front of the buses. There is a flat rate of Rs 5 whatever the length of journey; pay the driver as you board. Bus stops have signs and shelters and there are also markings on the road.

Timetables and maps of each route are posted at the terminus in Victoria, where you can also pick up photocopied timetables (Rs 5) at the SPTC office (Map p292). All parts of the island are serviced, but for many trips, you'll have to change buses in the capital.

Praslin

Praslin boasts a relatively efficient bus service. The basic route is from Anse Boudin to Mont Plaisir (for Anse Kerlan) via Anse Volbert, Baie Ste Anne, Vallée de Mai, Grand Anse and the airport. Buses run in each direction every hour (every half-hour between Baie St Anne and Mont Plaisir) from 6am to 6pm. Anse Consolation and Anse La Blague are also serviced. For Anse Lazio, get off at Anse Boudin and walk to the beach (about 20 minutes; 1km). Timetables are available at the two tourist offices. There is a flat fare of Rs 7.

CAR & MOTORCYCLE

If you want to be controller of your own destiny, your best bet is to rent a car. Most of the road network on Mahé and Praslin is sealed and in good shape. More of a worry are the narrow bends and the speed at which some drivers, especially bus drivers, take them.

Drive on the left, and beware of drivers with fast cars and drowsy brains – especially late on Friday and Saturday nights. The speed limit is supposed to be 40km/h in built-up areas, 65km/h outside towns, and 80km/h on the dual carriageway between Victoria and the airport. On Praslin the limit is 40km/h throughout the island.

On La Digue and all other islands there aren't any car-rental companies – all tourists get around on foot or by bike.

Car Hire

There are any number of car-rental companies on Mahé and quite a few on Praslin. Due to healthy competition, the cheapest you're likely to get on Mahé is about €40 to €45 a day for a small hatchback. Rates on Praslin are about €5 to €10 more expensive. You can book through your hotel or guesthouse. Most apartment and guesthouse owners have negotiated discounts with car-rental outlets for their clients. A number of companies also have offices at the airport.

Drivers must be over 23 years old and have held a driving licence for at least a year. Most companies accept a national licence.

TAXI

Taxis operate on Mahé and Praslin and there are even a handful on La Digue. They are not metered. Agree on a fare before departure.

Survival Guide

Health

As long as you stay up to date with your vaccinations and take some basic preventive measures, you'd have to be pretty unlucky to succumb to most of the health hazards covered here. Réunion has a fair selection of tropical diseases on offer, but you're much more likely to get a bout of diarrhoea or a sprained ankle than an exotic disease.

Chikungunya epidemics have been an issue in Réunion and in Mauritius in the past, so check the latest before travelling.

BEFORE YOU GO

A little planning before departure, particularly for preexisting illnesses, will save you a lot of trouble later. Before a long trip, get a check-up from your dentist and your doctor if you require regular medication or have a chronic illness, eg high blood pressure or asthma. You should also organise spare contact lenses and glasses (and take your optical prescription with you); get a first-aid and medical kit together; and arrange necessary vaccinations.

Travellers can register with the **International Association for Medical Assistance to Travellers** (www.iamat. org). Its website can help travellers find a doctor who has recognised training. You might also consider doing a first-aid course (contact the Red Cross or St John Ambulance) or attending a remote medicine first-aid course, such as that offered by the **Royal Geographical Society** (www.wildernessmedicaltraining. co.uk).

If you are bringing medications with you, carry them in their original containers, clearly labelled. A signed and dated letter from your physician describing all medical conditions and medications, including generic names, is also a good idea. If carrying syringes or needles, be sure to have a physician's letter documenting their medical necessity.

Insurance

Find out in advance whether your insurance plan will make payments directly to providers or will reimburse you later for health expenditures (in many countries doctors expect payment in cash). It is vital to ensure that your travel insurance will cover outdoor activities, including paragliding, diving and canyoning, as well as the emergency transport required to get you to a good hospital, or all the way home, by air and with a medical attendant if necessary. Not all insurance policies cover this, so be sure to check the contract carefully. If you need medical care, your insurance company may be able to help locate the nearest hospital or clinic, or ask at your hotel. In an emergency, contact your embassy or consulate.

Medical Checklist

It is a very good idea to carry a medical and first-aid kit with you, to help yourself in the case of minor illness or injury. Following is a list of items you should consider packing.

➡ antidiarrhoeal drugs (eg loperamide)

➡ acetaminophen (paracetamol) or aspirin

➡ anti-inflammatory drugs (eg ibuprofen)

RECOMMENDED VACCINATIONS

The **World Health Organization** (www.who.int/en) recommends that all travellers be adequately covered for diphtheria, tetanus, measles, mumps, rubella and polio, as well as for hepatitis B, regardless of their travel destination.

Although no vaccinations are officially required, many doctors recommend hepatitis A and B immunisations just to be sure; a yellow-fever certificate is an entry requirement if travelling from an infected region.

→ antihistamines (for hay fever and allergic reactions)

→ antibacterial ointment (eg Bactroban) for cuts and abrasions (prescription only)

→ steroid cream or hydrocortisone cream (for allergic rashes)

→ bandages, gauze, gauze rolls

→ adhesive or paper tape

→ scissors, safety pins, tweezers

→ thermometer

→ pocket knife

→ DEET-containing insect repellent for the skin

→ sunblock

→ oral rehydration salts

→ iodine tablets (for water purification)

→ syringes and sterile needles (if travelling to remote areas)

Websites

There is a wealth of travel-health advice available on the internet – www.lonelyplanet. com is a good place to start. The World Health Organization publishes a superb book called *International Travel and Health*, which is revised annually and is available online for free at www.who.int/ ith. The following are other health-related websites of general interest:

Centers for Disease Control and Prevention (www.cdc.gov)

Fit for Travel (www.fitfortravel. scot.nhs.uk)

MD Travel Health (www.md travelhealth.com)

You may also like to consult your government's travel-health website, if one is available:

Australia (www.smartraveller. gov.au)

Canada (www.phac-aspc.gc.ca)

UK (www.doh.gov.uk)

USA (www.cdc.gov/travel)

IN MAURITIUS, RÉUNION & SEYCHELLES

Availability & Cost of Health Care

Health care in Mauritius and Réunion is generally excellent; the Seychelles is pretty good by African standards, but some travellers have been critical of the standard of the public health system. Generally, public hospitals offer the cheapest service, but may not have the most up-to-date equipment and medications; private hospitals and clinics are more expensive but tend to have more advanced drugs and equipment and better trained medical staff.

Infectious Diseases

It's a formidable list but, as we say, a few precautions go a long way.

Chikungunya

This viral infection transmitted by certain mosquito bites was traditionally rare in the Indian Ocean until 2005 when an epidemic hit Réunion, Mauritius and the Seychelles. The unusual name means 'that which bends up' in the East African language of Makonde, a reference to the joint pain and physical distortions it creates in sufferers. Chikungunya is rarely fatal, but it can be, and it's always unpleasant. Symptoms are often flu-like, with joint pain, high fever and body rashes being the most common.

It's important not to confuse it with dengue fever, but if you're diagnosed with Chikungunya expect to be down for at least a week, possibly longer. The joint pain can be horrendous and there is no treatment; those infected need simply to rest inside (preferably under a mosquito net to prevent reinfection), taking gentle exercise to avoid joints stiffening unbearably. The best way to avoid it is to avoid mosquito bites, so bring plenty of repellent, use the anti-mosquito plug-ins wherever you can and bring a mosquito net if you're really thorough.

Hepatitis A

Hepatitis A is spread through contaminated food (particularly shellfish) and water. It causes jaundice and, although it is rarely fatal, it can cause prolonged lethargy and delayed recovery. If you've had hepatitis A, you shouldn't drink alcohol for up to six months afterwards, but once you've recovered, there won't be any long-term problems. The first symptoms include dark urine and a yellow colour to the whites of the eyes. Sometimes a fever and abdominal pain might be present. Hepatitis A vaccine (Avaxim, VAQTA, Havrix) is given as an injection: a single dose will give protection for up to a year, and a booster after a year gives 10-year protection. Hepatitis A and typhoid vaccines can also be given as a single-dose vaccine (Hepatyrix or Viatim).

Hepatitis B

Hepatitis B is spread through infected blood, contaminated needles and sexual intercourse. It can also be passed from an infected mother to the baby during childbirth. It affects the liver, causing jaundice and occasionally liver failure. Most people recover completely, but some people might be chronic carriers of the virus, which could lead eventually to cirrhosis or liver cancer. Those visiting high-risk areas for extended periods or those with increased social or occupational risk should be immunised. Many countries now routinely include hepatitis B as part of routine childhood vaccinations. It is given singly or can be given at the same time as hepatitis A (Hepatyrix).

A course will give protection for at least five years. It can be given over four weeks or six months.

HIV

Human immunodeficiency virus (HIV), the virus that causes acquired immune deficiency syndrome (AIDS), is an enormous problem throughout Africa, but is most acutely felt in sub-Saharan Africa. The virus is spread through infected blood and blood products, by sexual intercourse with an infected partner, and from an infected mother to her baby during childbirth and breastfeeding. It can be spread through 'blood to blood' contacts, such as with contaminated instruments during medical, dental, acupuncture and other body-piercing procedures, and through sharing used intravenous needles.

At present there is no cure; medication that might keep the disease under control is available, but these drugs are too expensive for the overwhelming majority of Africans, and are not readily available for travellers either. If you think you might have been infected with HIV, a blood test is necessary; a three-month gap after exposure and before testing is required to allow antibodies to appear in the blood.

Leptospirosis

Cases of leptospirosis have been reported in Réunion. It spreads through the excreta of infected rodents, especially rats. It can cause hepatitis and renal failure, which might be fatal. Symptoms include flu-like fever, headaches, muscle aches and red eyes, among others. Avoid swimming or walking in stagnant waters.

Malaria

The risk of malaria in Mauritius and Réunion is extremely low; there is no risk in the Seychelles.

Rabies

Rabies is spread by receiving the bites or licks of an infected animal on broken skin. In Mauritius, Réunion and the Seychelles the risk is mainly from dogs. It is always fatal once the clinical symptoms start (which might be up to several months after an infected bite), so post-bite vaccination should be given as soon as possible. Post-bite vaccination (whether or not you've been vaccinated before the bite) prevents the virus from spreading to the central nervous system. Three preventive injections are needed over a month. If you have not been vaccinated, you will need a course of five injections starting 24 hours after being bitten or as soon as possible after the injury. If you have been vaccinated, you will need fewer post-bite injections, and have more time to seek medical help.

Traveller's Diarrhoea

Although it's not inevitable that you will get diarrhoea while travelling in the region, it's certainly possible. Sometimes dietary changes, such as increased spices or oils, are the cause. To avoid diarrhoea, only eat fresh fruits or vegetables if cooked or peeled, and be wary of dairy products that might contain unpasteurised milk. Although freshly cooked food can often be a safe option, plates or serving utensils might be dirty, so you should be highly selective when eating food from street vendors (make sure that cooked food is piping hot all the way through).

If you develop diarrhoea, be sure to drink plenty of fluids, preferably an oral rehydration solution containing water (lots), and some salt and sugar. A few loose stools don't require treatment, but if you start having more than four or five stools a day, you should start taking an antibiotic (usually a quinoline drug, such as ciprofloxacin or nor-

floxacin) and an antidiarrhoeal agent (such as loperamide) if you are not within easy reach of a toilet. However, if diarrhoea is bloody, persists for more than 72 hours or is accompanied by fever, shaking chills or severe abdominal pain, you should seek medical attention.

Yellow Fever

Although yellow fever is not a problem in Mauritius, Réunion or the Seychelles, travellers should still carry a certificate as evidence of vaccination if they have recently been in an infected country. For a list of these countries, visit the websites of the **World Health Organization** (www.who.int/ith) or the **Centers for Disease Control and Prevention** (www.cdc.gov). A traveller without a legally required, up-to-date certificate may be vaccinated and detained in isolation at the place of entry for up to 10 days or possibly repatriated.

Diving Health & Safety

Health Requirements

Officially, a doctor should check you over before you do a course, and fill out a form full of diving health questions. In practice, most dive schools will let you dive or do a course if you complete a medical questionnaire, but the checkup is still a good idea. This is especially so if you have any problem at all with your breathing, ears or sinuses. If you are an asthmatic, have any other chronic breathing difficulties or any inner-ear problems, you shouldn't do any scuba diving.

A simple medical certificate is compulsory for diving in Réunion (but not for introductory dives). You can get one from your doctor in your home country or have it emailed to the dive centre. Otherwise, you can get one from any doctor in Réunion.

Decompression Sickness

This is a very serious condition – usually, though not always, associated with diver error. The most common symptoms are unusual fatigue or weakness; skin itch; pain in the arms, legs (joints or mid-limbs) or torso; dizziness and vertigo; local numbness, tingling or paralysis; and shortness of breath.

The most common causes of decompression sickness (or the 'bends' as it is commonly known) are diving too deep, staying at depth for too long or ascending too quickly. This results in nitrogen coming out of solution in the blood and forming bubbles, most commonly in the bones and particularly in the joints or in weak spots such as healed fractured sites.

Note that your last dive should be completed 24 hours before flying in order to minimise the risk of residual nitrogen in the blood that can cause decompression injury.

The only treatment for decompression sickness is to put the patient into a recompression chamber. There are recompression chambers in Mauritius, Réunion and the Seychelles.

Insurance

In addition to normal travel insurance, it's a very good idea to take out specific diving cover, which will pay for evacuation to a recompression facility and the cost of hyperbaric treatment in a chamber. **Divers Alert Network** (www. diversalertnetwork.org) is a nonprofit diving-safety organisation. It provides a policy that covers evacuation and recompression.

Environmental Hazards

Heat Exhaustion

This condition occurs following heavy sweating and excessive fluid loss with inadequate replacement of fluids and salt, and is particularly common in hot climates when taking unaccustomed exercise before full acclimatisation. Symptoms include headache, dizziness and tiredness. Dehydration is already happening by the time you feel thirsty – aim to drink sufficient water to produce pale, diluted urine. Self-treatment is by fluid replacement with water and/or fruit juice, and cooling by cold water and fans. The treatment of the salt-loss component consists of consuming salty fluids as in soup, and adding a little more table salt to foods than usual.

Heatstroke

Heat exhaustion is a precursor to the much more serious condition of heatstroke. In this case there is damage to the sweating mechanism, with an excessive rise in body temperature; irrational and hyperactive behaviour; and eventually loss of consciousness and death. Rapid cooling by spraying the body with water and fanning is ideal. Emergency fluid and electrolyte replacement is usually also required by intravenous drip.

Insect Bites & Stings

Mosquitoes in the region rarely carry Chikungunya and dengue fever, but they (and other insects) can cause irritation and infected bites. To avoid these, take the same precautions as you would for avoiding malaria, including wearing long pants and long-sleeved shirts, using mosquito repellents, avoiding highly scented perfumes or aftershaves etc. Bee and wasp stings cause major problems only to those who have a severe allergy to the stings (anaphylaxis), in which case carry an adrenaline (epinephrine) injection.

Leeches may be present in damp rainforest conditions; they attach themselves to your skin to suck your blood. Salt or a lighted cigarette end will make them fall off. Ticks can cause skin infections and other more serious diseases. If a tick is found attached, press down around the tick's head with tweezers, grab the head and gently pull upwards.

Marine Life

A number of Indian Ocean species are poisonous or may sting or bite. Watch out above all for sea urchins. Other far rarer creatures to look out for include the gaudy lionfish with its poisonous spined fins, and the cleverly camouflaged – and exceptionally poisonous – stonefish, which lives camouflaged amid coral formations. Some shells, such as the cone shell, can fire out a deadly poisonous barb. The species of fire coral, which looks like yellowish brush-like coral growths, packs a powerful sting if touched.

Shark attacks on surfers have been a major issue in Réunion in recent years, especially off Boucan Canot, St-Gilles-les-Bains, Trois Bassins and Étang-Salé-les-Bains. Stick to supervised and protected beaches. In the Seychelles, two fatal shark attacks on swimmers were reported in 2011; both occurred at Anse Lazio.

TAP WATER

It's not safe to drink the tap water in Rodrigues; stick with bottled water if you visit the island. As a general rule, the tap water in Réunion, the Seychelles and the rest of Mauritius is safe to drink, but always take care immediately after a cyclone or cyclonic storm as mains water supplies can become contaminated by dead animals and other debris washed into the system. Never drink from streams as this might put you at risk of waterborne diseases.

Language

Along with the local Creoles, French is spoken (and official) in all three destinations included in this book. You'll find that menus on the islands are mostly in French, with English variations in some cases.

CREOLES

The Cre46oles spoken in Mauritius, Réunion and Seychelles are a blend of French and an assortment of African languages, with some regional variations. Seychelles Creole is similar to that of Mauritius, but differs significantly from the Creole spoken in Réunion. Note also that the Creole spoken in Mauritius and Seychelles is more comprehensible to French people than that of Réunion, even though Réunion itself is thoroughly French.

Mauritius

The official languages of Mauritius are English and French. English is used mainly in government and business. French is the spoken language in educated and cultural circles, and is used in newspapers and magazines. You'll probably find that most people will first speak to you in French and only switch to English once they realise you're an English speaker. Most Indo-Mauritians speak Bhojpuri, derived from a Bihari dialect of Hindi.

There are major differences between the pronunciation and usage of Creole and standard French. Here are some basic phrases you may find handy.

WANT MORE?

For in-depth language information and handy phrases, check out Lonely Planet's *French Phrasebook*. You'll find it at **shop.lonelyplanet.com**, or you can buy Lonely Planet's iPhone phrasebooks at the Apple App Store.

How are you?	Ki manière?
Fine, thanks.	Mon byen, mersi.
I don't understand.	Mo pas comprend.
OK.	Correc.
Not OK.	Pas correc.
he/she/it	li
Do you have ...?	Ou éna ...?
I'd like ...	Mo oulé ...
I'm thirsty.	Mo soif.
Cheers!	Tapeta!
Great!	Formidabe!

Réunion

French is the official language of Réunion, but Creole is the most widely spoken language. Few people speak English.

Keep in mind that a word that means one thing in French can mean something completely different in Creole, and where a word does have the same meaning, it's usually pronounced differently in Creole. Creole also has a number of *bons mots* and charming idioms, which are often the result of Hindi, Arab and Malagasy influences or misinterpretations of the original French word. For example, *bonbon la fesse* (bum toffee) is a suppository, *conserves* (preserves) are sunglasses, and *cœur d'amant* (lover's heart) is a cardamom seed. *Coco* is your head, *caze* is your house, *marmaille* is your child, *baba* is your baby, *band* means 'family', *le fait noir* means 'night', and *mi aime jou* means 'I love you'.

There are two basic rules of Creole pronunciation: r is generally not pronounced (when it is, it's pronounced lightly), and the soft j and ch sounds of French are pronounced as 'z' and 's' respectively. For example, *manzay* is the Creole equivalent of French 'manger' (to eat), *zamais* is used for 'jamais' (never), and you'll hear *sontay* instead of 'chanter' (to sing).

Seychelles

English and French are the official languages of the Seychelles. Most people speak both, although French Creole (known as Kreol Seselwa) is the lingua franca. Kreol Seselwa was 'rehabilitated' and made semi-official in 1981, and is increasingly used in newspapers and literature. These days, most Seychellois will use English when speaking to tourists, French when conducting business, and Creole in the home.

Seychelles Creole is similar to that of Mauritius and Martinique, but differs remarkably from that of Réunion. The soft pronunciation of certain French consonants is hardened and some syllables are dropped completely. The soft j becomes 'z', for example. The following Creole phrases can get you started:

Good morning./ Good afternoon.	*Bonzour.*
How are you?	*Comman sava?*
Fine, thanks.	*Mon byen, mersi.*
What's your name?	*Ki mannyer ou appel?*
My name is ...	*Mon appel ...*
Where do you live?	*Koté ou resté?*
I don't understand.	*Mon pas konpran.*
I like it.	*Mon kontan.*
Where is ...?	*Ol i ...?*
How much is that?	*Kombyen sa?*
I'm thirsty.	*Mon soif.*
Can I have a beer, please?	*Mon kapa ganny en labyer silvouplé?*

FRENCH

The pronunciation of French is pretty straightforward for English speakers as the sounds used in spoken French can almost all be found in English. There are just a couple of exceptions: nasal vowels (represented in our pronunciation guides by o or u followed by an almost inaudible nasal consonant sound m, n or ng), the 'funny' *u* (ew in our guides) and the deep-in-the-throat *r*. Bearing these few points in mind and reading our pronunciation guides as if they were English, you'll be understood just fine.

In the following phrases we have included masculine and femine forms where necessary, separated by a slash and indicated with the abbreviations 'm/f'.

Basics

Hello.	*Bonjour.*	bon·zhoor
Goodbye.	*Au revoir.*	o·rer·vwa
Excuse me.	*Excusez-moi.*	ek·skew·zay·mwa
Sorry.	*Pardon.*	par·don
Yes./No.	*Oui./Non.*	wee/non
Please.	*S'il vous plaît.*	seel voo play
Thank you.	*Merci.*	mair·see
You're welcome.	*De rien.*	der ree·en

How are you?	
Comment allez-vous?	ko·mon ta·lay·voo
Fine, and you?	
Bien, merci. Et vous?	byun mair·see ay voo
My name is ...	
Je m'appelle ...	zher ma·pel ...
What's your name?	
Comment vous appelez-vous?	ko·mon voo· za·play voo
Do you speak English?	
Parlez-vous anglais?	par·lay·voo ong·glay
I don't understand.	
Je ne comprends pas.	zher ner kom·pron pa

Accommodation

Do you have any rooms available?	
Est-ce que vous avez des chambres libres?	es·ker voo za·vay day shom·brer lee·brer
How much is it per night/person?	
Quel est le prix par nuit/personne?	kel ay ler pree par nwee/per·son
Is breakfast included?	
Est-ce que le petit déjeuner est inclus?	es·ker ler per·tee day·zher·nay ayt en·klew

campsite	*camping*	kom·peeng
dorm	*dortoir*	dor·twar
guesthouse	*pension*	pon·syon
hotel	*hôtel*	o·tel
youth hostel	*auberge de jeunesse*	o·berzh der zher·nes
a ... room	*une chambre ...*	ewn shom·brer ...
single	*à un lit*	a un lee
double	*avec un grand lit*	a·vek un gron lee
twin	*avec des lits jumeaux*	a·vek day lee zhew·mo
with (a) ...	*avec ...*	a·vek ...
air-con	*climatiseur*	klee·ma·tee·zer
bathroom	*une salle de bains*	ewn sal der bun
window	*fenêtre*	fer·nay·trer

Directions

Where's ...?
Où est ...?   oo ay ...

What's the address?
Quelle est l'adresse?   kel ay la·dres

Could you write the address, please?
Est-ce que vous pourriez es·ker voo poo·ryay
écrire l'adresse, ay·kreer la·dres
s'il vous plaît? seel voo play

Can you show me (on the map)?
Pouvez-vous m'indiquer poo·vay·voo mun·dee·kay
(sur la carte)? (sewr la kart)

at the corner	au coin	o kwun
at the traffic lights	aux feux	o fer
behind	derrière	dair·ryair
in front of	devant	der·von
far (from)	loin (de)	lwun (der)
left	gauche	gosh
near (to)	près (de)	pray (der)
opposite ...	en face de ...	on fas der ...
right	droite	drwat
straight ahead	tout droit	too drwa

Eating & Drinking

What would you recommend?
Qu'est-ce que vous kes·ker voo
conseillez? kon·say·yay

What's in that dish?
Quels sont les kel son lay
ingrédients? zun·gray·dyon

I'm a vegetarian.
Je suis zher swee
végétarien/ vay·zhay·ta·ryun/
végétarienne. vay·zhay·ta·ryen (m/f)

I don't eat ...
Je ne mange pas ... zher ner monzh pa ...

Cheers!
Santé! son·tay

That was delicious.
C'était délicieux! say·tay day·lee·syer

Please bring the bill.
Apportez-moi a·por·tay·mwa
l'addition, s'il vous plaît. la·dee·syon seel voo play

I'd like to reserve a table for ...	Je voudrais réserver une table pour ...	zher voo·dray ray·zair·vay ewn ta·bler poor ...
(eight) o'clock	(vingt) heures	(vungt) er
(two) people	(deux) personnes	(der) pair·son

Key Words

appetiser	entrée	on·tray
bottle	bouteille	boo·tay
breakfast	petit déjeuner	per·tee day·zher·nay
children's menu	menu pour enfants	mer·new poor on·fon
cold	froid	frwa
delicatessen	traiteur	tray·ter
dinner	dîner	dee·nay
dish	plat	pla
food	nourriture	noo·ree·tewr
fork	fourchette	foor·shet
glass	verre	vair
grocery store	épicerie	ay·pees·ree
highchair	chaise haute	shay zot
hot	chaud	sho
knife	couteau	koo·to
local speciality	spécialité locale	spay·sya·lee·tay lo·kal
lunch	déjeuner	day·zher·nay
main course	plat principal	pla prun·see·pal
market	marché	mar·shay
menu (in English)	carte (en anglais)	kart (on ong·glay)
plate	assiette	a·syet
spoon	cuillère	kwee·yair
wine list	carte des vins	kart day vun
with/without	avec/sans	a·vek/son

Meat & Fish

beef	bœuf	berf
chicken	poulet	poo·lay
crab	crabe	krab
lamb	agneau	a·nyo
oyster	huître	wee·trer
pork	porc	por
snail	escargot	es·kar·go
squid	calmar	kal·mar
turkey	dinde	dund
veal	veau	vo

Fruit & Vegetables

apple	pomme	pom
apricot	abricot	ab·ree·ko
asparagus	asperge	a·spairzh
beans	haricots	a·ree·ko
beetroot	betterave	be·trav
cabbage	chou	shoo
cherry	cerise	ser·reez

corn	maïs	ma·ees
cucumber	concombre	kong·kom·brer
grape	raisin	ray·zun
lemon	citron	see·tron
lettuce	laitue	lay·tew
mushroom	champignon	shom·pee·nyon
peach	pêche	pesh
peas	petit pois	per·tee pwa
(red/green) pepper	poivron (rouge/vert)	pwa·vron (roozh/vair)
pineapple	ananas	a·na·nas
plum	prune	prewn
potato	pomme de terre	pom der tair
pumpkin	citrouille	see·troo·yer
shallot	échalote	eh·sha·lot
spinach	épinards	eh·pee·nar
strawberry	fraise	frez
tomato	tomate	to·mat
vegetable	légume	lay·gewm

Other

bread	pain	pun
butter	beurre	ber
cheese	fromage	fro·mazh
egg	œuf	erf
honey	miel	myel
jam	confiture	kon·fee·tewr
pasta/noodles	pâtes	pat
pepper	poivre	pwa·vrer
rice	riz	ree
salt	sel	sel
sugar	sucre	sew·krer
vinegar	vinaigre	vee·nay·grer

Drinks

beer	bière	bee·yair
coffee	café	ka·fay
(orange) juice	jus (d'orange)	zhew (do·ronzh)
milk	lait	lay
red wine	vin rouge	vun roozh
tea	thé	tay
(mineral) water	eau (minérale)	o (mee·nay·ral)
white wine	vin blanc	vun blong

Emergencies

Help!
Au secours! — o skoor

Leave me alone!
Fichez-moi la paix! — fee·shay·mwa la pay

I'm lost.
Je suis perdu/perdue. — zhe swee·pair·dew (m/f)

Call a doctor.
Appelez un médecin. — a·play un mayd·sun

Call the police.
Appelez la police. — a·play la po·lees

I'm ill.
Je suis malade. — zher swee ma·lad

It hurts here.
J'ai une douleur ici. — zhay ewn doo·ler ee·see

I'm allergic to ...
Je suis allergique ... — zher swee za·lair·zheek ...

Where are the toilets?
Où sont les toilettes? — oo son ley twa·let

Shopping & Services

I'd like to buy ...
Je voudrais acheter ... — zher voo·dray ash·tay ...

Can I look at it?
Est-ce que je peux le voir? — es·ker zher per ler vwar

I'm just looking.
Je regarde. — zher rer·gard

I don't like it.
Cela ne me plaît pas. — ser·la ner mer play pa

How much is it?
C'est combien? — say kom·byun

It's too expensive.
C'est trop cher. — say tro shair

Can you lower the price?
Vous pouvez baisser le prix? — voo poo·vay bay·say ler pree

There's a mistake in the bill.
Il y a une erreur dans la note. — eel ya ewn ay·rer don la not

ATM	guichet automatique de banque	gee·shay o·to·ma·teek der bonk
credit card	carte de crédit	kart der kray·dee
internet cafe	cybercafé	see·bair·ka·fay
post office	bureau de poste	bew·ro der post
tourist office	office de tourisme	o·fees der too·rees·mer

Time & Dates

What time is it?
Quelle heure est-il? — kel er ay til

It's (eight) o'clock.
Il est (huit) heures. — il ay (weet) er

It's half past (10).
Il est (dix) heures et demie. — il ay (deez) er ay day·mee

morning	*matin*	ma·tun
afternoon	*après-midi*	a·pray·mee·dee
evening	*soir*	swar
yesterday	*hier*	yair
today	*aujourd'hui*	o·zhoor·dwee
tomorrow	*demain*	der·mun
Monday	*lundi*	lun·dee
Tuesday	*mardi*	mar·dee
Wednesday	*mercredi*	mair·krer·dee
Thursday	*jeudi*	zher·dee
Friday	*vendredi*	von·drer·dee
Saturday	*samedi*	sam·dee
Sunday	*dimanche*	dee·monsh
January	*janvier*	zhon·vyay
February	*février*	fayv·ryay
March	*mars*	mars
April	*avril*	a·vreel
May	*mai*	may
June	*juin*	zhwun
July	*juillet*	zhwee·yay
August	*août*	oot
September	*septembre*	sep·tom·brer
October	*octobre*	ok·to·brer
November	*novembre*	no·vom·brer
December	*décembre*	day·som·brer

Transport

boat	*bateau*	ba·to
bus	*bus*	bews
plane	*avion*	a·vyon
train	*train*	trun
first	*premier*	prer·myay
last	*dernier*	dair·nyay
next	*prochain*	pro·shun

I want to go to ...
Je voudrais aller à ...   zher voo·dray a·lay a ...

Does it stop at ...?
Est-ce qu'il s'arrête à ...?   es·kil sa·ret a ...

At what time does it leave/arrive?
À quelle heure est-ce   a kel er es
qu'il part/arrive?   kil par/a·reev

Can you tell me when we get to ...?
Pouvez-vous me   poo·vay·voo mer
dire quand   deer kon
nous arrivons à ...?   noo za·ree·von a ...

I want to get off here.
Je veux descendre   zher ver day·son·drer
ici.   ee·see

a ... ticket	*un billet ...*	un bee·yay ...
1st-class	*de première classe*	der prem·yair klas
2nd-class	*de deuxième classe*	der der·zyem las
one-way	*simple*	sum·pler
return	*aller et retour*	a·lay ay rer·toor
aisle seat	*côté couloir*	ko·tay kool·war
delayed	*en retard*	on rer·tar
cancelled	*annulé*	a·new·lay
platform	*quai*	kay
ticket office	*guichet*	gee·shay
timetable	*horaire*	o·rair
train station	*gare*	gar
window seat	*côté fenêtre*	ko·tay fe·ne·trer

I'd like to hire a ...	*Je voudrais louer ...*	zher voo·dray loo·way ...
4WD	*un quatre-quatre*	un kat·kat
car	*une voiture*	ewn vwa·tewr
bicycle	*un vélo*	un vay·lo
motorcycle	*une moto*	ewn mo·to

child seat	*siège-enfant*	syezh·on·fon
diesel	*diesel*	dyay·zel
helmet	*casque*	kask
mechanic	*mécanicien*	may·ka·nee·syun
petrol/gas	*essence*	ay·sons
service station	*station-service*	sta·syon·ser·vees

Is this the road to ...?
C'est la route pour ...?   say la root poor ...

(How long) Can I park here?
(Combien de temps)   (kom·byun der tom)
Est-ce que je peux   es·ker zher per
stationner ici?   sta·syo·nay ee·see

The car/motorbike has broken down (at ...).
La voiture/moto est   la vwa·tewr/mo·to ay
tombée en panne (à ...).   tom·bay on pan (a ...)

I have a flat tyre.
Mon pneu est à plat.   mom pner ay ta pla

I've run out of petrol.
Je suis en panne   zher swee zon pan
d'essence.   day·sons

I've lost my car keys.
J'ai perdu les clés de   zhay per·dew lay klay der
ma voiture.   ma vwa·tewr

Behind the Scenes

SEND US YOUR FEEDBACK

We love to hear from travellers – your comments keep us on our toes and help make our books better. Our well-travelled team reads every word on what you loved or loathed about this book. Although we cannot reply individually to your submissions, we always guarantee that your feedback goes straight to the appropriate authors, in time for the next edition. Each person who sends us information is thanked in the next edition – the most useful submissions are rewarded with a selection of digital PDF chapters.

Visit **lonelyplanet.com/contact** to submit your updates and suggestions or to ask for help. Our award-winning website also features inspirational travel stories, news and discussions.

Note: We may edit, reproduce and incorporate your comments in Lonely Planet products such as guidebooks, websites and digital products, so let us know if you don't want your comments reproduced or your name acknowledged. For a copy of our privacy policy visit lonelyplanet.com/privacy.

OUR READERS

Many thanks to the travellers who used the last edition and wrote to us with helpful hints, useful advice and interesting anecdotes:

Sarah Almond, Michel Bal, Barbara Calvi, Jennifer Cartaino, Howard Chan, Mark Darter, Joseph Funk, Claire Gilmore, Lucie Lacombe, Audun Lem, Samira Lindner, Alexander McLarren, Pertti Metiainen, Jakub Nalepa, Carina Ek Petrini, Will Rogers, Peter Sharrock, Björn Suttka, Eva Torkar, Caroline Vassarotti

WRITER THANKS

Anthony Ham

Sincere and undying thanks to Matt Phillips who keeps sending me to places like this and for years of shared passions. In Mauritius, special thanks to Deon in Trou aux Biches, Laval and Françoise Baptiste in Rodrigues, Teddy and Shekti in Rodrigues, and Dr Vikash Tatayah of the Mauritian Wildlife Foundation. To Jan, for keeping the home fires burning and for a lifetime of sacrifice. And to Marina, Carlota and Valentina, my companions on the road – *os adoro*.

Jean-Bernard Carillet

Big thanks to all the people I met while on the road for their tips and recommendations, including Jean-Paul and Axelle, Cosimo, Isabelle Dupuis and Elsie. At LP, thanks to Matt Phillips for his trust and all the editors and cartos for their commitment. A heartfelt *merci beaucoup* to fellow author Anthony, who is a pleasure to work with. Last but not least, a *gros bisou* to my daughter Eva, who's also in love with Réunion.

ACKNOWLEDGEMENTS

Climate map data adapted from Peel MC, Finlayson BL & McMahon TA (2007) 'Updated World Map of the Köppen-Geiger Climate Classification', Hydrology and Earth System Sciences, 11, 163344.

Cover photograph: Grand Anse, Praslin, Seychelles; Davide Erbetta/4Corners ©

THIS BOOK

This 9th edition of Lonely Planet's *Mauritius, Réunion & Seychelles* guidebook was researched and written by Jean-Bernard Carillet and Anthony Ham, who also wrote the previous edition. This guidebook was produced by the following:

Destination Editor Matt Phillips

Product Editor Jenna Myers

Senior Cartographer Corey Hutchison

Book Designer Wibowo Rusli

Assisting Editors Sarah Bailey, Nigel Chin, Charlie Claxton, Melanie Dankel, Kellie Langdon, Anne Mulvaney, Rosie Nicholson, Charlotte Orr

Cover Researcher Naomi Parker

Thanks to Jennifer Carey, Gemma Graham, Liz Heynes, Alexander Howard, Lauren Keith, Claire Naylor, Karyn Noble, Kirsten Rawlings, Kathryn Rowan, Ellie Simpson, Vicky Smith, Angela Tinson, Anna Tyler, Brana Vladisavljevic

Index

Map Legend

Sights
- Beach
- Bird Sanctuary
- Buddhist
- Castle/Palace
- Christian
- Confucian
- Hindu
- Islamic
- Jain
- Jewish
- Monument
- Museum/Gallery/Historic Building
- Ruin
- Shinto
- Sikh
- Taoist
- Winery/Vineyard
- Zoo/Wildlife Sanctuary
- Other Sight

Activities, Courses & Tours
- Bodysurfing
- Diving
- Canoeing/Kayaking
- Course/Tour
- Sento Hot Baths/Onsen
- Skiing
- Snorkelling
- Surfing
- Swimming/Pool
- Walking
- Windsurfing
- Other Activity

Sleeping
- Sleeping
- Camping

Eating
- Eating

Drinking & Nightlife
- Drinking & Nightlife
- Cafe

Entertainment
- Entertainment

Shopping
- Shopping

Information
- Bank
- Embassy/Consulate
- Hospital/Medical
- Internet
- Police
- Post Office
- Telephone
- Toilet
- Tourist Information
- Other Information

Geographic
- Beach
- Gate
- Hut/Shelter
- Lighthouse
- Lookout
- Mountain/Volcano
- Oasis
- Park
- Pass
- Picnic Area
- Waterfall

Population
- Capital (National)
- Capital (State/Province)
- City/Large Town
- Town/Village

Transport
- Airport
- Border crossing
- Bus
- Cable car/Funicular
- Cycling
- Ferry
- Metro station
- Monorail
- Parking
- Petrol station
- Subway station
- Taxi
- Train station/Railway
- Tram
- Underground station
- Other Transport

Note: Not all symbols displayed above appear on the maps in this book

Routes
- Tollway
- Freeway
- Primary
- Secondary
- Tertiary
- Lane
- Unsealed road
- Road under construction
- Plaza/Mall
- Steps
- Tunnel
- Pedestrian overpass
- Walking Tour
- Walking Tour detour
- Path/Walking Trail

Boundaries
- International
- State/Province
- Disputed
- Regional/Suburb
- Marine Park
- Cliff
- Wall

Hydrography
- River, Creek
- Intermittent River
- Canal
- Water
- Dry/Salt/Intermittent Lake
- Reef

Areas
- Airport/Runway
- Beach/Desert
- Cemetery (Christian)
- Cemetery (Other)
- Glacier
- Mudflat
- Park/Forest
- Sight (Building)
- Sportsground
- Swamp/Mangrove

OUR STORY

A beat-up old car, a few dollars in the pocket and a sense of adventure. In 1972 that's all Tony and Maureen Wheeler needed for the trip of a lifetime – across Europe and Asia overland to Australia. It took several months, and at the end – broke but inspired – they sat at their kitchen table writing and stapling together their first travel guide, *Across Asia on the Cheap*. Within a week they'd sold 1500 copies. Lonely Planet was born.

Today, Lonely Planet has offices in Franklin, London, Melbourne, Oakland, Dublin, Beijing and Delhi, with more than 600 staff and writers. We share Tony's belief that 'a great guidebook should do three things: inform, educate and amuse'.

OUR WRITERS

Anthony Ham

Mauritius, Rodrigues, Seychelles Anthony is an experienced travel and nature writer who has written or contributed to more than 100 Lonely Planet guidebooks, including *Madagascar*, and *Mauritius, Réunion & Seychelles* and almost two dozen African countries. When he's not writing for Lonely Planet, Anthony writes about Africa, the Middle East, Spain and Scandinavia for newspapers and magazines around the world. His particular passions are wildlife, wild places and searching for remote corners of the earth. Find out more about him at www.anthonyham.com.

Jean-Bernard Carillet

Réunion, Seychelles Paris-based journalist and photographer Jean-Bernard has clocked up numerous trips to the Indian Ocean and written extensively about Réunion and the Seychelles. Being a diving instructor, he was all too happy to check out the best dive sites in the region for this guide, before putting on his hiking shoes to explore the rugged Cirques in Réunion. In the Seychelles, he searched for the perfect beach, the best grilled fish, the most romantic spot and the best-value hotels. Jean-Bernard has contributed to many Lonely Planet titles, both in French and in English.

Published by Lonely Planet Global Limited
CRN 554153
9th edition – Dec 2016
ISBN 978 1 78657 215 8
© Lonely Planet 2016   Photographs © as indicated 2016
10 9 8 7 6 5 4 3 2 1
Printed in China